MODERN
Real Estate Practice

SIXTEENTH EDITION

Fillmore W. Galaty

Wellington J. Allaway

Robert C. Kyle

Dearborn™
Real Estate Education

This publication is designed to provide accurate and authoritative information in regard to the subject matter covered. It is sold with the understanding that the publisher is not engaged in rendering legal, accounting, or other professional service. If legal advice or other expert assistance is required, the services of a competent professional person should be sought.

Senior Vice President and General Manager: Roy Lipner
Publisher and Director of Distance Learning: Evan M. Butterfield
Editorial Project Manager: Louise Benzer
Development Editor: Amanda Rahn
Content Consultant: Judith A. Nolde, J.D.
Editorial Production Manager: Bryan Samolinski
Typesetting: Ellen Gurak
Creative Director: Lucy Jenkins

Published by Dearborn™ Real Estate Education
a Division of Dearborn Financial Publishing, Inc.®
a Kaplan Professional Company®
30 South Wacker Drive
Chicago, IL 60606-7481
www.dearbornRE.com

Printed in the United States of America.

05   10   9   8   7

Library of Congress Cataloging-in-Publication Data

Galaty, Fillmore W.
  Modern real estate practice / Fillmore W. Galaty, Wellington J. Allaway, Robert C. Kyle.—16th ed.
    p. cm.
  Includes index.
  ISBN 0-7931-4428-0
    1. Real estate business—Law and legislation—United States. 2. Vendors and
purchasers—United States. 3. Real property—United States. I. Allaway, Wellington J. II.
Kyle, Robert C. III. Title.

KF2042.R4 G34 2002
346.7304'37—dc21   2002031384

CONTENTS

PREFACE

Since it first appeared in 1959, *Modern Real Estate Practice* has set the industry standard for real estate education. This book has helped provide more than three million readers with a critical edge as they enter the world of real estate. Whether you are preparing for a state licensing examination, fulfilling a college or university requirement, looking for specific guidance about buying a home or an investment property, or simply expanding your understanding of this fascinating field, you can rely on *Modern Real Estate Practice,* the recognized authority for accurate and comprehensive information in a format that is easy to use.

Just as today's real estate market is challenging and complex, today's real estate students are increasingly sophisticated and demand a high level of expertise and efficiency. This 16th Edition of *Modern Real Estate Practice* meets those expectations. In response to expanding state licensing requirements and the growing body of laws that govern the practice of real estate, this edition contains revisions and new features designed to make it an even more effective tool, no matter what your goal.

■ NEW FEATURES

New Look—The first thing readers may notice about this edition is that we've changed the way it looks. A new, more readable page design, featuring color highlights and redesigned illustrations, makes the student's experience with this book both more pleasant *and* more educationally effective. And for the first time in 43 years we've included photographs to powerfully drive home the "real world" impact of real estate principles.

New Media—Bundled in the back of this edition is a *Modern Real Estate Practice test-building* CD-ROM that lets students mix and match the hundreds of questions in *Modern Real Estate Practice* into their own custom quizzes. The software tracks performance on each self-built test, and provides helpful rationales explaining the "why" behind the answers.

New Math Section—The popular *MathFAQs* feature, introduced in the 15th edition, has been thoroughly updated and expanded. In addition to the useful T-bar method for problem-solving, traditional equations are also included.

New Links—New and updated WWWeb.Links direct students to their state's real estate regulatory agencies, where they can often find state statutes, real estate regulations, and other useful information online.

A note about the WWWeb.Links: While we've provided the most current and accurate site addresses available, things are always changing on the Internet. So you may have to use the Web link provided as a starting point to find what you need. We've provided a key to both the Uniform Resource Locator (URL) and the site name to make your search easier.

This edition of *Modern Real Estate Practice* also retains the successful features developed for previous editions, including the following:

WWWeb.Link

- *Modern Real Estate Practice* connects you to the Internet with *WWWeb.Links*—margin features that point to the Web addresses of relevant government and professional association Internet sites, essentially bringing a whole world of information to you! Just look for the WWWeb.Link icon.
- Each chapter opens with four *Learning Objectives* that tell you what concepts and information you should be able to identify, describe, explain, and distinguish when you've finished.
- *Key terms* appear at the beginning of each chapter. This feature not only lets you know what important vocabulary words you should look for as you read but helps you to study and review as well.
- *Chapter Review* and *Sample Examination* questions have been thoroughly reviewed by a testing expert with experience in actual real estate licensing exam design. Questions have been revised and replaced where necessary with more demanding fact-pattern problems that encourage students to understand and apply information rather than just memorize, an important test-taking and exam preparation skill. The questions have been carefully designed to follow the style and content of the most widely used testing services and to demonstrate the types of questions students will likely encounter on their state licensing exams. The *Answer Key* includes specific page references to the text.
- *Margin Notes* help direct readers' attention to important vocabulary terms, concepts, and study tips. The margin notes help readers move more easily through the text, locate issues for review, and serve as memory prompts for more efficient and effective studying.

One thing, however, has stayed the same. As in previous editions, the fundamental goal of *Modern Real Estate Practice,* 16th Edition, is to help students understand the dynamics of the real estate industry and pass their licensing exams. In this edition, we've met that challenge, providing you with the critical information you need to pass the real estate examination, buy or sell property, or establish a real estate career.

■ A FINAL NOTE

We like to hear from our readers. Like the hundreds of instructors who have helped us develop each edition, like the real estate professionals who have been willing to share their expertise, you are a partner in the *Modern Real Estate Practice* series. The only way we can be sure we've succeeded—and know what we need to improve—is if you tell us.

Your comments are invaluable because they help us evaluate the current edition and continue to improve future ones. Please let us know what you thought of this edition of *Modern Real Estate Practice.*

Did it help you? Has your understanding of the real estate industry increased? How did you do in your course or on your license exam? What additional or different information would improve the book?

Thank you for your help and for joining the ranks of successful *Modern Real Estate Practice* users!

The Publisher

ACKNOWLEDGMENTS

Like a real estate transaction, this book is the product of teamwork and cooperation among professionals. The authors express their gratitude and appreciation to the instructors and other real estate professionals whose invaluable suggestions and advice help *Modern Real Estate Practice* remain the industry's leading real estate principles text. Whether they responded to instructor surveys, provided reviews and suggestions for improving the previous edition, or reviewed the manuscript for this edition, the participation of these professionals—and their willingness to share their expertise—is greatly appreciated.

■ REVIEWERS—16TH EDITION

Doris S. Barrell, Northern Virginia Association of REALTORS®
Douglas R. Barry, Grempler Real Estate Institute
James Berg, Currey Management Institute
Lyn Broad, Weichert Real Estate School
Chuck Byers, GRI, CRB, Pioneer Real Estate School
Donald A. Campbell, Jr., Don Campbell Realty
Linda A. Doherty, Champion Institute of Real Estate
Richard Gendreau, Bemidji State University
Don Harlan, Harlan, Lyons, & Associates, LLC
Kay Hedge, Long & Foster Institute of Real Estate
Edith Lank, Real Estate Educators Association
David M. Maull, CRS, GRI, Long & Foster School of Real Estate
Roy L. Ponthier, Jr., Ph.D., First Professional Real Estate School, Inc.
Jane Rosen, Environmental Engineer, Assessment & Compliance Services
Marcia Russell, DREI, Marcia Russell Seminars
Deborah Schwark, Currey Management Institute
Dave Sirota, Consultant
Marie S. Spodek, DREI, Professional Real Estate Services
Steven Weiser, Hondros College

The authors would also like to thank the following people for their contributions to recent editions:

Robert H. Allen, National Real Estate Institute
Penny Alston, Wardley Real Estate School
Jean Anglin, Chattanooga State Community College
Jim Anselmi, Academy Real Estate School
Christopher O. Ashe, Learning Unlimited
Donald R. Bates, Mountain Empire Community College
Thomas E. Battle, Center for Real Estate Education and Research
E. E. Bayliss III, Ford Fairfax Community College
Tom Bowen, Professional School of Real Estate
Paul Boyter, CRS, GRI, McColly School of Real Estate
Dianna Brouthers, Homefinders of America
Thomas Bull, McColly School of Real Estate

Virgil V. Bullis, Sr., Delaware Tech
Leona Busby, Long & Foster Institute of Real Estate
Marie Callas, Iowa Association of REALTORS®
Alice W. Cater, Lamar University Institute of Technology
Peter J. Certo, Gabelli School of Business
Charles Civer, Scottsdale Community College
Richard J. Clemmer, D&D School of Real Estate
Ginny Commins, Windermere Education
Kay Knox Crawford, Continual Learning Institute
David Dean, Litchfield County Real Estate School
Gregory Dunn, U.S. Books, Inc.
John Eaton, Ocean School of Real Estate
Dr. Kenneth W. Edwards, GRI, Linn-Benton Community College
William B. Frost, Weichert Real Estate School
Katherine J. Gandy, Spokane Falls Community College and American Business
and Professions Institute
Richard Garnitz, Kelley Academy of Real Estate
Michael Craig Glazer, Ivy Tech State College
Helen L. Grant, Moseley-Flint Schools of Real Estate, Inc.
Edward A. Guinane, Real Estate School of Siouxland
Terry Hastings, Ridgefield Adult Education
Terry Hayes, Real Estate Brokerage Education
Arthur W. Heinbuch, Allied Institutes of Real Estate
Ray Henry, Arizona Institute of Real Estate
Mary Hibbler-Kee, Bess Technical College/UAB Options
Russell S. Hicks, The Real Estate School
Carl R. Hurst, Hurst Education Center
Diana T. Jacob-Rouhoff, Northwestern State University of Louisiana and
Lincoln Graduate Center
F. Jeffrey Keil, J. Sargeant Reynolds Community College
John H. Kilroy, Jefferson County Board of Education
Rick Knowles, Capital Real Estate Training
Dr. Corbet J. Lamkin, Southern Arkansas University
Allen Lamont, Lamont School of Real Estate
Craig Larabee, Larabee School of Real Estate
Jerome D. Levine, Tunxis Community-Technical College
Richard S. Linkemer, American School of Real Estate, Ltd.
Joyce Magee, Genesee Community College
Denise M. Mancini, J.W. Riker
Charline Mason, Charline Mason Seminars Unlimited
Peggy Ann McConnochie, Alaska Coastal Homes, Inc.
Paul McLaughlin, Esquire
Thomas L. Meyer, Cape Girardeau School of Real Estate
Coad Miller, Central Nebraska Community College
J. Leo Milotte, CRB, CRS, GRI, Milotte Associates Real Estate School
John R. Morgan, Morgan Testing Services
Monte Needler, Ivy Tech State College
Edward Neeley, Russell & Jeffcoat Real Estate Institute of Training & Education
Robert Neuwoehner, Heartland School of Real Estate
Jessie L. Newman, Grempler Real Estate Institute
Mary M. Otis, Northern Virigina Association of REALTORS®

Andrew G. Pappas, Capital Community Technical College/Manchester Community Technical College
Joyce D. Remsburg, Trident Technical College
Walter L. Rice, Quality Workshops
John D. Rinehart, CRB, CRS, GRI, The Real Estate Institute of York County, Inc.
Robbie Robison, Allegany College
Kathy Roosa, Kathy Roosa School of Real Estate
Jay Rose, Esq., Tucker School of Real Estate
Phyllis Rudnick, CRS, GRI, Annex Real Estate School
Susann Shadley, Eastern Idaho Technical College
Don Shrum, The Real Estate School, Houston
Bill Standiford, Ed Smith School of Real Estate
Allan R. Stevenson, GRI, CRB, Frostburg State University
Rita Stuckart, Jack White Real Estate School
Wayne A. Tarter, Greenville Tech
Ruth A. Vella, Omega Real Estate School
Howard E. Walker, Nashville School of Real Estate
Cynthia L. Weber, ABC Real Estate School
Donald Dwight Wells, Troy State University
Brenda S. White, Brenda White School of Real Estate
John P. Wiedemer, Houston Community College
Don W. Williams, Alabama Courses in Real Estate—ACRE
Judith B. Wolk, Charleston Trident Association of REALTORS®
Jerry L. Wooten, Tucker School of Real Estate
John Wright, Iowa Real Estate School of Cedar Rapids

The authors would also like to extend a special thanks to Donald A. White, DREI, of Prince George's Community College for his careful review and revision of the chapter questions and practice exams and to Joyce Bea Sterling, DREI, of Northern Kentucky Real Estate School, for her revision of the *MathFAQs* portion of the text.

The originators of the real estate forms contained in this publication make no representations or warranties relating to compliance with applicable state law in any other jurisdiction. The forms are provided here for illustrative purposes only and are protected by copyright laws.

Each new edition of *Modern Real Estate Practice* builds on earlier editions. The authors gratefully acknowledge the many real estate professionals and others who have contributed to prior editions of this book.

Finally, the authors would like to recognize the entire staff of Dearborn Real Estate Education. In particular, the authors thank Judith A. Nolde, Content Consultant; Evan Butterfield, Publisher and Director of Distance Learning; Louise Benzer, Editorial Project Manager; Amanda Rahn, Development Editor; Bryan Samolinski, Editorial Production Manager; Lucy Jenkins, Creative Director; Ellen Gurak, Typesetter; and Ronald Liszkowski, copy editor, for their excellent work on this new edition.

Fillmore W. Galaty
Wellington J. Allaway
Robert C. Kyle

PART

I

PRINCIPLES

CHAPTER ONE

INTRODUCTION TO THE REAL ESTATE BUSINESS

■ **LEARNING OBJECTIVES** *When you've finished reading this Chapter, you should be able to:*

■ **identify** the various *careers* available in real estate and the *professional organizations* that support them.

■ **describe** the five categories of real property.

■ **explain** the operation of *supply and demand* in the *real estate market*.

■ **distinguish** the *economic, political*, and *social factors* that influence supply and demand.

■ **define** the following *key terms:*

broker	salesperson
market	supply and demand

■ **WHY LEARN ABOUT...** THE REAL ESTATE BUSINESS?

When people think of "real estate"—even people who are considering a real estate career—they tend to think about brokers and salespersons. While partly accurate, that's the small view. The fact is, *real estate* is a very big business encompassing the following and more:

■ It is composed of a wide variety of professionals (and professional opportunities).
■ It involves many different kinds of properties, each with its own special characteristics and issues.
■ It defines a huge segment of the American economy, with its own market forces. ■

The successful real estate professional understands the big picture. He or she knows that each individual transaction, no matter how big or how small, has an economic effect that ripples far beyond the parties gathered around the table.

■ A VERY BIG BUSINESS

Real estate transactions are taking place all around you, all the time. When a commercial leasing company rents space in a mall or the owner of a building rents an apartment to a retired couple, it's a real estate transaction. If an appraiser gives an expert opinion of the value of farmland or a bank lends money to a professional corporation to purchase an office building, it's a real estate transaction. Most common of all, when an American family sells its old home and buys a new one, the family takes part in the real estate industry. Consumers of real estate services include buyers and sellers of homes, tenants and landlords, investors and developers. Nearly everyone, at some time, is involved in a real estate transaction.

All this adds up to big business—complex transactions that involve billions of dollars every year in the United States alone. The services of millions of highly trained individuals are required: attorneys, bankers, trust company representatives, abstract and title insurance company agents, architects, surveyors, accountants, tax experts, and many others, in addition to buyers and sellers. All these people depend on the skills and knowledge of licensed real estate professionals.

■ REAL ESTATE: A BUSINESS OF MANY SPECIALIZATIONS

Despite the size and complexity of the real estate business, many people think of it as being made up of only brokers and salespersons. Actually, the real estate industry is much bigger than that. Appraisal, property management, financing, subdivision and development, counseling, and education are all separate businesses within the real estate field. To succeed in a complex industry, every real estate professional must have a basic knowledge of these specialties.

Brokerage—*Brokerage* is the business of bringing people together in a real estate transaction. A **broker** acts as a point of contact between two or more people in negotiating the sale, purchase, or rental of property. A broker is defined as a person or company licensed to buy, sell, exchange, or lease real property for others and to charge a fee for these services. A broker may be the agent of the buyer or the seller or of both, or the broker may not be anyone's agent. The property may be residential, commercial, or industrial. A salesperson is a licensee employed by or associated with the broker. The **salesperson** conducts brokerage activities on behalf of the broker. The broker, however, is ultimately responsible for the salesperson's acts. Brokerage is discussed in detail in Chapter 5.

Appraisal—*Appraisal* is the process of estimating a property's market value, based on established methods and the appraiser's professional judgment. Although their training will give brokers some understanding of the valuation process, lenders generally require a professional appraisal, and property sold by court order requires an appraiser's expertise. Appraisers must have detailed knowledge of the methods of valuation. In many states, appraisers must be licensed or certified to carry out local transactions. Appraisers must be licensed or certified for many federally related transactions. Appraisal is covered in Chapter 18.

Property management—A *property manager* is a person or company hired to maintain and manage property on behalf of its owner. By hiring a property manager, the owner is relieved of such day-to-day management tasks as finding new tenants, collecting rents, altering or constructing new space for tenants, ordering repairs, and generally maintaining the property. The scope of the manager's work depends on the terms of the individual employment contract, known as a *management agreement.* Whatever tasks are specified, the basic responsibility of the property manager is to protect the owner's investment and maximize the owner's return on his or her investment. Property management is discussed in Chapter 17.

Financing—*Financing* is the business of providing the funds that make real estate transactions possible. Most transactions are financed by means of mortgage loans or trust deed loans secured by the property. Individuals involved in financing real estate may work in commercial banks, savings associations, and mortgage banking and mortgage brokerage companies. A growing number of real estate brokerage firms affiliate with mortgage brokers to provide consumers with "one-stop-shopping" real estate services. Financing issues are examined in Chapter 14 and Chapter 15.

Subdivision and development—*Subdivision* is the splitting of a single property into smaller parcels. *Development* involves the construction of *improvements* on the land. These improvements may be either on site or off site. Off-site improvements, such as water lines and storm sewers, are made on public lands to serve the new development. On-site improvements, such as new homes or swimming pools, are made on individual parcels. While subdivision and development normally are related, they are independent processes that can occur separately. Subdivision and development are discussed further in Chapter 19.

Home Inspection—*Home inspection* is a profession that allows practitioners to combine their interest in real estate with their professional skills and training in the construction trades or in engineering. Professional *home inspectors* conduct a thorough visual survey of a property's structure, systems, and site conditions and prepare an analytical report that is valuable to both purchasers and homeowners. Increasingly wary consumers are relying on the inspector's report to help them make purchase decisions. Frequently, a real estate sales contract will be contingent upon the inspector's report. While professional home inspectors are usually prohibited from practicing real estate, many of them are also licensed as real estate agents. Some of the things inspectors typically look for in a property are discussed in Chapter 21.

Counseling—*Counseling* involves providing clients with competent independent advice based on sound professional judgment. A real estate counselor helps clients choose among the various alternatives involved in purchasing, using, or investing in property. A counselor's role is to furnish clients with the information needed to make informed decisions. Professional real estate counselors must have a high degree of industry expertise.

Education—*Real estate education* is available to both practitioners and consumers. Colleges and universities, private schools, and trade organizations all conduct real estate courses and seminars, from the principles of a prelicensing program to the technical aspects of tax and exchange law. State licensing laws establish the minimum educational requirements for obtaining—and keeping—a real estate license. Continuing education helps ensure that licensees keep their skills and knowledge current.

Other areas—Many other real estate career options are available. Practitioners will find that real estate specialists are needed in a variety of business settings. Lawyers who specialize in real estate are always in demand. Large corporations with extensive land holdings often have their own real estate and property tax departments. Local governments must staff both zoning boards and assessment offices.

■ PROFESSIONAL ORGANIZATIONS

Many trade organizations serve the real estate business. The largest is the National Association of REALTORS® (NAR), whose Web site is www.realtor.com. NAR is composed of state, regional, and local associations. NAR also sponsors various affiliated organizations that offer professional designations to brokers, salespersons, appraisers, and others who complete required courses in areas of special interest. Members subscribe to a Code of Ethics and, if eligible, are entitled to be known as REALTORS® or REALTOR-ASSOCIATES®

WWWeb.Link

www.ashi.com	www.naifa.com
www.boma.org	www.nareb.com
www.ccim.com	www.realtor.com
www.cre.org	www.rebac.net
www.irem.org/index2.html	www.reea.org
www.naeba.org	

The National Association of Real Estate Brokers (NAREB), whose members are known as *Realtists*, also adheres to a Code of Ethics. NAREB arose out of the early days of the civil rights movement as an association of racial minority real estate brokers in response to the conditions and abuses that eventually gave rise to fair housing laws. Today, NAREB remains dedicated to equal housing opportunity.

> **Five Categories of Real Property**
>
> 1. Residential
> 2. Commercial
> 3. Industrial
> 4. Agricultural
> 5. Special-Purpose

Other professional associations include the Appraisal Institute, the American Society of Appraisers (ASA), the National Association of Independent Fee Appraisers (NAIFA), and the Real Estate Educators Association (REEA). The growth in buyer brokerage, discussed in Chapter 5, led to the formation of organizations such as the Real Estate Buyer's Agent Council (REBAC), now associated with NAR, and the National Association of Exclusive Buyer's Agents (NAEBA). Other organizations include the Building Owners and Managers Association (BOMA), the Institute of Real Estate Management (IREM), the Commercial Investment Real Estate Institute (CIREI), and the American Society of Real Estate Counselors (ASREC). Home inspectors may be members of the American Society of Home Inspectors® (ASHI), a national professional organization. Members of ASHI are expected to comply with its Standards of Practice and Code of Ethics.

■ TYPES OF REAL PROPERTY

Just as there are areas of specialization within the real estate industry, there are different types of property in which to specialize. Real estate can be classified as

- *residential*—all property used for single-family or multifamily housing, whether in urban, suburban or rural areas;
- *commercial*—business property, including office space, shopping centers, stores, theaters, hotels and parking facilities;
- *industrial*—warehouses, factories, land in industrial districts, and power plants;
- *agricultural*—farms, timberland, ranches, and orchards; or
- *special-purpose*—churches, schools, cemeteries, and government-held lands.

The market for each of these types of property can be subdivided into the *sales market*, which involves the transfer of title and ownership rights, and the *rental market*, in which space is used temporarily by lease.

IN PRACTICE   Although it is possible for a single real estate firm or an individual real estate professional to perform all the services and handle all classes of property discussed in this Chapter (unless restricted by a state's license law), this is rarely done. While such general services may be available in small towns, most firms and professionals specialize to some degree, especially in urban areas. Some licensees perform only one service for one type of property, such as residential sales or commercial leasing.

■ THE REAL ESTATE MARKET

A **market** is a place where goods can be bought and sold. A market may be a specific place, such as the village square. It also may be a vast, complex, worldwide economic system for moving goods and services around the globe. In either case, the function of a market is to provide a setting in which supply and demand can establish market value, making it advantageous for buyers and sellers to trade.

Supply and Demand

> When supply increases and demand remains stable, prices go down. When demand increases and supply remains stable, prices go up.

Prices for goods and services in the market are established by the operation of **supply and demand**. Essentially, *when supply increases and demand remains stable, prices go down; when demand increases and supply remains stable, prices go up.* Greater supply means producers need to attract more buyers, so they lower prices. Greater demand means producers can raise their prices because buyers compete for the product.

■ **FOR EXAMPLE** Here's how one broker describes market forces: "In my 17 years in real estate, I've seen supply and demand in action many times. When a car maker relocated its factory to my region a few years back, hundreds of people wanted to buy the few higher-bracket houses for sale at the time. Those sellers were able to ask ridiculously high prices for their properties, and two houses actually sold for more than the asking prices! On the other hand, when the naval base closed and 2,000 civilian jobs were transferred to other parts of the country, it seemed like every other house in town was for sale. We were practically giving houses away to the few people who were buying."

> *Uniqueness* and *immobility* are the two characteristics of land that have the most impact on market value.

Supply and demand in the real estate market. Two characteristics of real estate govern the way the market reacts to the pressures of supply and demand: *uniqueness* and *immobility* (see Chapter 2). *Uniqueness* means that, no matter how identical they may appear, no two parcels of real estate are ever exactly alike; each occupies its own unique geographic location. *Immobility* refers to the fact that property cannot be relocated to satisfy demand where supply is low. Nor can buyers always relocate to areas with greater supply. For these reasons, real estate markets are local markets. Each geographic area has different types of real estate and different conditions that drive prices. In these small, well-defined areas, real estate offices can keep track of both what type of property is in demand and what parcels are available.

IN PRACTICE

Technological advances and market changes have widened the real estate professional's local market. No longer limited to a single small area, brokers and salespersons must track trends and conditions in a variety of different and sometimes distant local markets. Technology—office computers, information networks, and laptop personal computers (PCs), cellular phones, fax machines and a growing arsenal of other devices—helps real estate practitioners stay on top of their wide-ranging markets.

Because of real estate's uniqueness and immobility, the market generally adjusts slowly to the forces of supply and demand. Though a home offered for sale can be withdrawn in response to low demand and high supply, it is much more likely that oversupply will result in lower prices. When supply is low, on the other hand, a high demand may not be met immediately because development and construction are lengthy processes. As a result, development tends to occur in uneven spurts of activity.

Even when supply and demand can be forecast with some accuracy, natural disasters such as hurricanes and earthquakes can disrupt market trends. Similarly, sudden changes in financial markets or local events such as plant relocations or environmental factors can dramatically disrupt a seemingly stable market.

Factors Affecting Supply

Factors that tend to affect the supply side of the real estate market's supply and demand balance include labor force availability, construction and material costs, and government controls and financial policies.

Labor force and construction and material costs. A shortage of skilled labor or building materials or an increase in the cost of materials can decrease the amount of new construction. High transfer costs, such as taxes, and construction permit fees can also discourage development. Increased construction costs may be passed along to buyers and tenants in the form of higher prices and increased rents which, can further slow the market.

WWWeb.Link

www.fanniemae.com   www.ginniemae.gov
www.federalreserve.gov   www.hud.gov/fha/fhahome.html
www.freddiemac.com

Factors that affect the supply of real estate are

■ labor force,
■ construction costs,
■ government controls, and
■ government financial policies.

Government controls and financial policies. The government's monetary policy can have a substantial impact on the real estate market. The Federal Reserve Board establishes a *discount rate* of interest for the money it lends to commercial banks. That rate has a direct impact on the *interest rates* the banks in turn charge to borrowers. These interest rates play a significant part in people's ability to buy homes. Such government agencies as the Federal Housing Administration (FHA) and Ginnie Mae (Government National Mortgage Association) can affect the amount of money available to lenders for mortgage loans. See Chapter 15. Fannie Mae and Freddie Mac (Federal Home Loan Mortgage Corporation) are private companies under congressional charter that provide financial services and products that make it possible for low-income, moderate-income, and middle-income families to buy homes.

Virtually any government action has some effect on the real estate market. For instance, federal environmental regulations may increase or decrease the supply and value of land in a local market. Real estate taxation is one of the primary sources of revenue for local governments. Policies on taxation of real estate can have either positive or negative effects. High taxes may deter investors. On the other hand, tax incentives can attract new businesses and industries. And, of course, along with these enterprises come increased employment and expanded residential real estate markets.

Local governments also can influence supply. Land-use controls, building codes, and zoning ordinances help shape the character of a community and control the use of land. Careful planning helps stabilize and even increase real estate values. The dedication of land to such amenities as forest preserves, schools, and parks also helps shape the market. Zoning and land-use controls are discussed in Chapter 19.

Factors Affecting Demand

Factors that tend to affect the demand side of the real estate market include population, demographics, and employment and wage levels.

Population. Because shelter is a basic human need, the demand for housing grows with the population. Although the total population of the country continues to rise, the demand for real estate increases faster in some areas than in others. In some locations, however, growth has ceased altogether or the population has declined. This may be due to economic changes (such as plant closings), social concerns (such as the quality of schools or a desire for more open space), or population changes (such as population shifts from colder to warmer climates). The result can be a drop in demand for real estate in one area, matched by an increased demand elsewhere.

Factors that affect the demand for real estate are

■ population,
■ demographics, and
■ employment and wage levels.

Demographics. *Demographics* is the study and description of a population. The population of a community is a major factor in determining the quantity and type of housing in that community. Family size, the ratio of adults to children, the ages of children, the number of retirees, family income, lifestyle, and the growing number of single-parent and empty-nester households are all demographic factors that contribute to the amount and type of housing needed.

IN PRACTICE

Niche marketing is the phrase used to refer to the targeted marketing of specific demographic populations. For example, as baby boomers age and look for retirement housing, their need or demand is considered a niche market.

Employment and wage levels. Decisions about whether to buy or rent and how much to spend on housing are closely related to income. When job opportunities are scarce or wage levels low, demand for real estate usually drops. The market might, in fact, be affected drastically by a single major employer moving in or shutting down. Licensees must be aware of the business plans of local employers.

As we've seen, the real estate market depends on a variety of economic forces, such as interest rates and employment levels. To be successful, licensees must follow economic trends and anticipate where they will lead. How people use their income depends on consumer confidence. Consumer confidence is based not only on perceived job security but also on the availability of credit and the impact of inflation. General trends in the economy, such as the availability of mortgage money and the rate of inflation, will influence an individual's decision as to how to spend his or her income.

■ SUMMARY

Although brokerage is the most widely recognized real estate activity, the industry provides many other services. These include appraisal, property management, property development, home inspection, counseling, property financing, and education. Most real estate firms specialize in only one or two of these areas; however, the highly complex and competitive nature of our society requires that a real estate person be knowledgeable in a number of fields.

Real property can be classified by its general use as residential, commercial, industrial, agricultural, or special-purpose. Although many brokers deal with more than one type of real property, they usually specialize to some degree.

A market is a place where goods and services can be bought and sold and where price levels can be established based on supply and demand. Because of its unique characteristics, real estate is relatively slow to adjust to the forces of supply and demand.

The supply of and demand for real estate are affected by many factors, including changes in population and demographics, wage and employment levels, construction costs, availability of labor, and governmental monetary policy and controls.

QUESTIONS

1. A professional estimate of a property's market value, based on established methods and using trained, professional judgment, is performed by a(n)
   a. real estate broker.
   b. real estate appraiser.
   c. real estate counselor.
   d. home inspector.

2. In general, when the supply of a certain commodity increases,
   a. price tends to rise.
   b. price tends to drop.
   c. demand for it tends to rise.
   d. demand for it tends to drop.

3. Which of the following factors primarily affects supply in the real estate market?
   a. Population
   b. Demographics
   c. Employment
   d. Government financial policies

4. Which of the following factors is most likely to influence demand for real estate?
   a. The number of real estate brokers in the area
   b. The number of full-time real estate salespersons in the area
   c. The wage levels and employment opportunities
   d. The price of new homes being built in the area

5. Property management, appraisal, financing, and development are all examples of
   a. factors affecting demand.
   b. specializations within the real estate industry.
   c. non–real estate professions.
   d. activities requiring broker management and supervision.

6. A REALTOR® is best described as an individual who is
   a. a specially licensed real estate professional who acts as a point of contact between two or more people in negotiating the sale, purchase, or rental of property.
   b. any real estate broker or salesperson who assists buyers, sellers, landlords, or tenants in any real estate transaction.
   c. a member of the National Association of Real Estate Brokers who specializes in residential properties.
   d. a member of the National Association of REALTORS®.

7. A major manufacturer of automobiles announces that it will relocate one of its factories, along with 2,000 employees, to Smallville. What effect will this announcement likely have on Smallville's housing market?
   a. Houses will be likely to become less expensive as a result of the announcement.
   b. Houses will likely become more expensive as a result of the announcement.
   c. Because the announcement involves an issue of demographics, not of supply and demand, housing prices will stay the same.
   d. The announcement involves an industrial property; residential housing will not be affected.

8. A licensee who has several years of experience in the industry decided to retire from actively marketing properties. Now she helps clients choose among the various alternatives involved in purchasing, using, or investing in property. What is her profession?
   a. Real estate counselor
   b. Real estate appraiser
   c. Real estate educator
   d. REALTORS®

9. The words broker and REALTOR® are
   a. interchangeable.
   b. different categories of membership in NAR.
   c. different titles offered by separate professional organizations.
   d. unrelated: A broker is a real estate licensee and a REALTOR® is a member of NAR.

10. The two characteristics that have the most impact on the market value of land are
    a. uniqueness and immobility.
    b. improvement and indestructibility.
    c. demographics and construction costs.
    d. scarcity and permanence of investment.

CHAPTER TWO

REAL PROPERTY AND THE LAW

■ **LEARNING OBJECTIVES** *When you've finished reading this Chapter, you should be able to:*

■ **identify** the rights that convey with ownership of real property and the characteristics of real estate.

■ **describe** the difference between real and personal property, and the various types of personalty.

■ **explain** the types of laws that affect real estate.

■ **distinguish** among the concepts of land, real estate, and real property.

■ **define** the following *key terms:*

accession	fixture	severance
air rights	heterogeneity	situs
annexation	improvement	subsurface rights
area preference	land	surface right
appurtenance	nonhomogeneity	trade fixture
bundle of legal rights	personal property	water rights
chattel	real estate	
emblements	real property	

■ WHY LEARN ABOUT... REAL PROPERTY AND THE LAW?

Real estate is a market like any other one. Real property is a product, and the licensee is the salesperson. As any successful salesperson will tell you, product knowledge is the key to success. You need to know enough about your product to be able to educate and guide your clients and customers, whether they are buyers, sellers, renters, or investors. Also, you are dealing with a product that has very specific and often very complicated legal issues involved. This Chapter will help you understand the most basic, fundamental principles of the product you will be handling for the rest of your career. ■

■ LAND, REAL ESTATE, AND REAL PROPERTY

The words *land*, *real estate*, and *real property* are often used interchangeably. To most people, they mean the same thing. Strictly speaking, however, the terms refer to different aspects of the same idea. To fully understand the nature of real estate and the laws that affect it, licensees must be aware of the subtle yet important differences in meaning of these words.

Land

Land is defined as *the earth's surface extending downward to the center of the earth and upward to infinity, including permanent natural objects such as trees and water.* (See Figure 2.1.)

Land, then, means not only the surface of the earth but also the underlying soil. It refers to things that are *naturally* attached to the land, such as boulders and plants. It includes the minerals and substances that lie far below the earth's surface. Land even includes the air above the earth, all the way up into space. These are known respectively as the *subsurface* and the *airspace*. Most of the surface of the earth, of course, is not land at all, but water. Special state and local laws govern the ownership of the wetter part of the earth, including lakes and rivers, as discussed in Chapter 7.

Real Estate

Real estate is defined as land *at, above, and below the earth's surface, plus all things permanently attached to it, whether natural or artificial.* (See Figure 2.1.)

The term *real estate* is similar to the term *land*, but it means much more. *Real estate* includes not only the natural components of the land but also all manmade improvements. An **improvement** is any artificial thing attached to the land, such as a building or a fence. The term *improvement*, as used in the real estate industry, refers to *any* addition to the land. The word is neutral. It doesn't matter whether the artificial attachment makes the property better looking or more useful; the land is still said to be *improved*. Land also may be improved by streets, utilities, sewers, and other additions that make it suitable for building.

Land, Real Estate, and Real Property

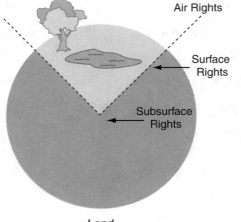

Air Rights

Surface Rights

Subsurface Rights

Land
Earth's surface to the center of the earth and the airspace above the land, including the trees and water

Real Estate
Land plus permanent human-made additions

The Bundle of Rights

Real Property
Real estate plus bundle of legal rights

Real Property

The term *real property* is the broadest of all. It includes both land and real estate. Real property is defined as *the interests, benefits, and rights that are automatically included in the ownership of land and real estate*. (See Figure 2.1.)

Real property includes the surface, subsurface, and airspace, any improvements, and the legal rights of ownership that attach to ownership of a parcel of real estate.

Traditionally, ownership of real property is described as a bundle of legal rights. In other words, a purchaser of real estate actually buys the rights of ownership held by the seller. These rights include the

- right of *possession;*
- right to *control* the property within the framework of the law;
- right of *enjoyment* (that is, to use the property in any legal manner);
- right of *exclusion* (to keep others from entering or using the property); and
- right of *disposition* (to sell, will, transfer, or otherwise dispose of or encumber the property).

The concept of a bundle of rights comes from old English law. In the Middle ages, a seller transferred property by giving the purchaser a handful of earth or a bundle of bound sticks from a tree on the property. The purchaser, who accepted the bundle, then owned the tree from which the sticks came and the land to which the tree was attached. Because the rights of ownership (like the sticks) can be separated and individually transferred, the sticks became symbolic of those rights. (See Figure 2.2.)

The word *title* to real property has two meanings: (1) the right to or ownership of the land as represented by the owner's bundle of rights and (2) evidence of

FIGURE 2.2

**The Bundle of
Legal Rights**

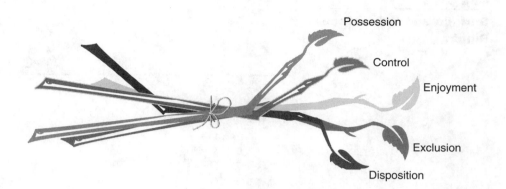

Possession

Control

Enjoyment

Exclusion

Disposition

that ownership by a deed. *Title* refers to ownership of real property, not to a printed document. The document by which the owner transfers title to the real property is the *deed.*

Real property is often coupled with the word *appurtenance*. An **appurtenance is a right or privilege** associated with the property, although not necessarily a part of it. Typical appurtenances include parking spaces in multiunit buildings, easements, water rights, and other improvements. An appurtenance is connected to the property, and ownership of the appurtenance normally conveys to the new owner when the property is sold.

IN PRACTICE

When people talk about buying or selling homes, office buildings, and land, they usually call these things real estate. For all practical purposes, the term is synonymous with *real property* as defined here. Thus, in everyday usage, *real estate* includes the legal rights of ownership specified in the definition of real property. Sometimes people use the term *realty* instead.

Subsurface, air, and water rights. The right to use the surface of the earth is referred to as a **surface right.** However, real property ownership can also include **subsurface rights,** which are the rights to the natural resources lying below the earth's surface. Although it may be difficult to imagine, the two rights are distinct. An owner may transfer his or her surface rights without transferring the subsurface rights.

■ **FOR EXAMPLE** Anne sells the rights to any oil and gas found beneath her farm to an oil company. Later, Anne sells the remaining interests (the surface, air, and limited subsurface rights) to Bob, reserving the rights to any coal that may be found in the land. Bob sells the remaining land to Charles, but Bob retains the farmhouse, stable, and pasture. After these sales, four parties have ownership interests in the same real estate: (1) the oil company owns all the oil and gas; (2) Anne owns all the coal; (3) Bob owns the farmhouse, stable, and pasture; and (4) Charles owns the rights to the remaining real estate. (See Figure 2.3.)

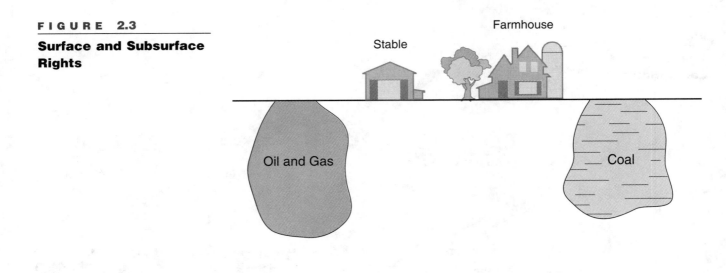

FIGURE 2.3

Surface and Subsurface Rights

WWWeb.Link   www2.law.cornell.edu

The rights to use the air above the land, provided the rights have not been preempted by law, may be sold or leased independently. **Air rights** can be an important part of real estate, particularly in large cities, where air rights over railroads must be purchased to construct office buildings, such as the MetLife Building in New York City and the Prudential Building in Chicago. To construct such a building, the developer must purchase not only the air rights but also numerous small portions of the land's surface for the building's foundation supports.

Before air travel was common, a property's air rights were considered to be unlimited, extending upward into the farthest reaches of outer space. However, now that air travel is common, the courts and the U.S. Congress have put limits on air rights. Today, the courts permit reasonable interference with these rights, such as that necessary for aircraft (and presumably spacecraft), as long as the owner's right to use and occupy the land is not unduly lessened. Governments and airport authorities often purchase adjacent air rights to provide approach patterns for air traffic.

With the continuing development of solar power, air rights—and, more specifically, light or solar rights—are being closely examined by the courts. A new tall building that blocks sunlight from a smaller existing building may be held to be interfering with the smaller building's right to sunlight, particularly if systems in the smaller building are solar powered. Air and solar rights are established by laws and ordinances that vary widely from state to state and community to community.

Water rights are special common-law rights held by owners of land adjacent to rivers, lakes, or oceans and are restrictions on the rights of land ownership. Water rights are a particularly important issue in drier western states, where water is a scarce and valuable public commodity. Issues related to water rights are discussed in Chapter 7.

■ REAL PROPERTY AND PERSONAL PROPERTY

Personal property, sometimes called *personalty,* is *all property that does not fit the definition of real property;* that is, if it's not real property, it's personal property.

An important distinction between the two is that personal property is *movable.* Items of personal property, also referred to as **chattels,** include such tangibles as chairs, tables, clothing, money, bonds, and bank accounts. Trade fixtures, discussed below, are included in this category.

WWWeb.Link   www.mfghome.org

Manufactured Housing (Mobile Homes)

The distinction between real and personal property is not always obvious. Manufactured housing (or *mobile homes*), for example, is generally considered personal property even though its mobility may be limited to a single trip to a park or development to be hooked up to utilities. Manufactured housing may, however, be considered real property if it becomes permanently affixed to the land. The distinction is generally one of state law. Whether manufactured housing is characterized as real or personal property may have an effect on how it is taxed. Real estate licensees should be familiar with local laws before attempting to sell manufactured housing. Some states permit only specially licensed dealers to sell such housing; other states require no special licensing.

Plants

Trees and crops generally fall into one of two classes: (1) Trees, perennial shrubbery, and grasses that do not require annual cultivation, known as *fructus naturales,* are considered real estate; (2) annual plantings or crops of wheat, corn, vegetables, and fruit, known as **emblements** or *fructus industriales,* are generally considered personal property. As long as an annual crop is growing, it will be transferred as part of the real property unless other provisions are made in the sales contract. For example, a farmer won't have to dig up growing corn plants and haul them away unless the sales contract says so: The young corn remains on the land. The farmer may come back and harvest the corn when it's ready. The former owner or tenant is entitled to harvest the crops that result from his or her labor. Perennial crops, such as orchards or vineyards, are not personal property and so convey with the land.

The term used in the law for plants that do not require annual cultivation (such as trees and shrubbery) is *fructus naturales* (fruits of nature); **emblements** are known in the law as *fructus industriales* (fruits of industry).

An item of real property can become personal property by severance. For example, a growing tree is real estate until the owner cuts it down, literally severing it from the property. Similarly, an apple becomes personal property once it is picked from a tree.

It is also possible to change personal property into real property. If, for example, a landowner buys cement, stones, and sand, mixes them into concrete, and constructs a sidewalk across his or her land, the landowner has converted personal property (cement, stones, and sand) into real property (a sidewalk). This process is called annexation.

Licensees need to know whether property is real or personal for many reasons. An important distinction arises, for instance, when the property is transferred from one owner to another. Real property is conveyed by deed, while personal property is conveyed by a bill of sale. Transfers of property are discussed in Chapter 12.

Classifications of Fixtures

In considering the differences between real and personal property, it is necessary to distinguish between a *fixture* and personal property.

Fixtures. A fixture is *personal property that has been so affixed to land or a building that, by law, it becomes part of the real property.* Examples of fixtures are heating systems, elevator equipment in highrise buildings, radiators, kitchen cabinets, light fixtures, and plumbing. Almost any item that has been added as a permanent part of a building is considered a fixture.

During the course of time, the same materials may be both real and personal property, depending on their use and location.

Legal tests of a fixture. The overall test that is used in determining whether an item is a fixture (real property) or personal property is a question of *intent*. (See Figure 2.4.) Did the person who installed the item intend it to remain permanently on the property or to be removable in the future? In determining intent, courts use the following three basic tests:

1. *Method of annexation:* How *permanent* is the method of attachment? Can the item be removed without causing damage to the surrounding property?
2. *Adaptation to real estate:* Is the item being *used* as real property or personal property? For example, a refrigerator is usually considered personal property. However, if a refrigerator has been adapted to match the kitchen cabinetry, it becomes a fixture.
3. *Agreement:* Have the parties *agreed* on whether the item is real or personal property in an offer to purchase?

Although these tests may seem simple, court decisions have been complex and inconsistent. Property that appears to be permanently affixed has sometimes been ruled to be personal property, while property that seems removable has been ruled a fixture. It is important that an owner clarify what is to be sold with the real estate at the very beginning of the sales process.

IN PRACTICE

At the time a property is listed, the seller and listing agent should discuss which items to include in the sale. The written sales contract between the buyer and the seller should specifically list all articles that are being included in the sale, particularly if any doubt exists as to whether they are personal property or fixtures (for instance, built-in bookcases, chandeliers, ceiling fans, or exotic shrubbery). This will avoid a misunderstanding between the parties that could result in the collapse of the transaction and expensive lawsuits. The most common disputed items between buyers and sellers are draperies, light fixtures, and appliances.

FIGURE   2.4

Legal Tests of a Fixture

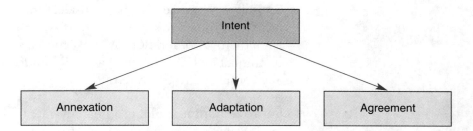

Trade fixtures. A special category of fixtures includes property used in the course of business. An article owned by a tenant and attached to a rented space or building or used in conducting a business is a **trade fixture**, or a *chattel fixture*. Some examples of trade fixtures would be bowling alleys, store shelves, and barroom and restaurant equipment. Agricultural fixtures, such as chicken coops and toolsheds, are also included in this category. Trade fixtures must be removed on or before the last day the property is rented. The tenant is responsible for any damage caused by the removal of a fixture. Trade fixtures that are not removed become the real property of the landlord. Acquiring the property in this way is known as **accession** (this is related to the legal principle of *constructive annexation*).

■ **FOR EXAMPLE** Paul's Pizza leases space in a small shopping center. Paul bolted a large iron oven to the floor of the unit. When Paul's Pizza goes out of business or relocates, Paul will be able to take his pizza oven with him if he can repair the bolt holes in the floor; the oven is a trade fixture. On the other hand, if the pizza oven was brought into the restaurant in pieces, welded together, and set in concrete, Paul might not be able to remove it without causing structural damage. In that case, the oven might become a fixture.

Trade fixtures differ from other fixtures in the following ways:

■ Fixtures belong to the owner of the real estate, but trade fixtures are usually owned and installed by a tenant for the tenant's use.

■ Fixtures are considered a permanent part of a building, but trade fixtures are removable. Trade fixtures may be attached to a building so they appear to be fixtures.

Legally, fixtures are real property, so they are included in any sale or mortgage. Trade fixtures, however, are considered personal property and are not included in the sale or mortgage of real estate, except by special agreement.

■ CHARACTERISTICS OF REAL PROPERTY

Real property possesses seven basic characteristics that define its nature and affect its use. These characteristics fall into two broad categories—*economic* characteristics and *physical* characteristics.

Economic Characteristics

The four economic characteristics of land that affect its value as a product in the marketplace are scarcity, improvements, permanence of investment, and area preference.

Scarcity. We usually do not consider land a rare commodity, but only about a quarter of the earth's surface is dry land; the rest is water. The total supply of land, then, is not limitless. While a considerable amount of land remains unused or uninhabited, the supply in a given location or of a particular quality is generally considered to be finite.

Improvements. Building an improvement on one parcel of land can affect the land's value and use as well as that of neighboring tracts and whole communities. For example, constructing a new shopping center or selecting a site for a nuclear power plant or toxic waste dump can dramatically change the value of land in a large area.

Permanence of investment. The capital and labor used to build an improvement represent a large fixed investment. Although even a well-built structure can be razed to make way for a newer building, improvements such as drainage, electricity, water, and sewerage remain. The return on such investments tends to be long term and relatively stable.

Four Economic Characteristics of Real Estate

1. Scarcity
2. Improvements
3. Permanence of Investment
4. Location or Area Preference

Location. Most people are familiar with the popular saying that the three most important characteristics of a property are location, location, and location. Sometimes referred to as **area preference** or **situs,** this economic characteristic does not refer only to geography. Rather, it refers to people's preferences for one area over another, based on a number of factors. Area preference is based on such factors as history, reputation, convenience, and scenic beauty—as well as simple geography. It is the unique quality of these preferences that result in the different values for similar properties. Whatever it's called, however, remember: *Location is the single most important economic characteristic of land.*

▨ **FOR EXAMPLE** A river runs through Bedford Falls, dividing the town more or less in half. On the north side of the river, known as North Town, houses sell for an average of $150,000. On the south side of the river, known as Southbank, identical houses sell for more than $200,000. The only difference is that homebuyers think that Southbank is a better neighborhood, even though no obvious difference exists between the two equally pleasant sides of town.

Physical Characteristics

Land has three certain physical characteristics: immobility, indestructibility, and uniqueness.

Immobility. It is true that some of the substances of land are removable and that topography can be changed, but *the geographic location of any given parcel of land can never be changed.* It is fixed, *immobile.*

Indestructibility. Land is also *indestructible.* This permanence of land, coupled with the long-term nature of improvements, tends to stabilize investments in real property.

The fact that land is indestructible does not, however, change the fact that the improvements on land depreciate and can become obsolete, which may dramatically reduce the land's value. This gradual depreciation should not be confused with the knowledge that the *economic desirability* of a given location can change.

<table>
<tr><td>

**Three Physical
Characteristics
of Real Estate**

1. Immobility
2. Indestructibility
3. Uniqueness

</td><td>

Uniqueness. No two parcels of land are ever exactly the same. Although they may be substantially similar, all parcels differ geographically because each parcel has its own location. The characteristics of each property, no matter how small, differ from those of every other. An individual parcel has no substitute because each is unique. The *uniqueness* of land is also referred to as its **heterogeneity or nonhomogeneity.**

</td></tr>
</table>

■ LAWS AFFECTING REAL ESTATE

The unique nature of real estate has given rise to an equally unique set of laws and rights. Even the simplest real estate transaction involves a body of complex laws. Licensees must have a clear and accurate understanding of the laws that affect real estate.

The specific areas important to the real estate practitioner include the *law of contracts,* the *general property law,* the *law of agency,* and his or her state's *real estate license law.* All of these will be discussed in this text. Federal regulations, such as environmental laws, as well as federal, state, and local tax laws, also play an important role in real estate transactions. State and local land-use and zoning laws have a significant effect on the practice of real estate, too.

**Laws Affecting
Real Estate**

■ Contract law
■ General property law
■ Agency law
■ Real estate license law
■ Federal regulations
■ Federal, state, and local tax laws
■ Zoning and land use laws
■ Federal, state, and local environmental regulations

Obviously, a real estate practitioner can't be an expert in all areas of real estate law. However, licensees should know and understand some basic principles. Perhaps most important is the ability to recognize problems that should be referred to a competent attorney. Only attorneys are trained and licensed to prepare documents defining or transferring rights in property and to give advice on matters of law. *Under no circumstances may a broker or salesperson act as an attorney unless he or she is also a licensed attorney representing a client in that capacity.*

All phases of a real estate transaction should be handled with extreme care. Carelessness in handling the negotiations and documents connected with a real estate sale can lead to disputes and expensive legal actions. The result can be a financial loss, a loss of goodwill in the community, a loss of business, or, in some cases, the loss or suspension of a real estate license.

Real estate license laws. Because brokers and salespersons are involved with other people's real estate and money, the need for regulation of their activities has long been recognized. The purpose of real estate license laws is to protect the public from fraud, dishonesty and incompetence in real estate transactions. All 50 states, the District of Columbia, and all Canadian provinces have passed laws that require real estate brokers and salespersons to be licensed. Although state license laws are similar in many respects, they differ in some details, such as the amount and type of prelicense education required.

In all states, applicants must meet specific personal and educational qualifications. In addition, they must pass an examination to ensure at least a minimum level of competency. To qualify for license renewal, licensees must follow certain standards of business conduct. Many states also require that licensees complete continuing education courses.

Alabama	www.arec.state.al.us	Missouri	www.ecodev.state.mo.us/pr/restate
Alaska	www.dced.state.ak.us/occ/prec.htm	Montana	www.com.state.mt.us
Arizona	www.re.state.az.us	Nebraska	www.state.ne.us/
Arkansas	www.state.ar.us/arec/frmain.htm	Nevada	www.red.state.nv.us
California	www.dre.ca.gov	New Hampshire	www.state.nh.us/nhrec
Colorado	www.dora.state.co.us/Real-Estate	New Jersey	www.state.nj.us/dobi remnu.shtml
Connecticut	www.state.ct.us/dcp	New Mexico	www.state.nm.us/nmrec
District of Columbia	www.dcra.org	New York	www.dos.state.ny.us/lcns/realest.html
Florida	www.state.fl.us/dbpr	North Carolina	www.ncrec.state.nc.us
Georgia	www.state.ga.us/Ga.Real_Estate	Ohio	www.com.state.oh.us/real
Hawaii	www.hawaii.gov	Oregon	www.rea.state.or.us
Idaho	www.state.id.us/irec	Pennsylvania	www.dos.state.pa.us/bpoa
Illinois	www.obre.state.il.us	South Carolina	www.llr.state.sc.us/pol.asp
Indiana	www.ai.org/pla/index.html	South Dakota	www.state.sd.us/SDREC
Iowa	www.state.ia.us/government/com/prof/realesta/realesta.htm	Texas	www.trec.state.tx.us
Kansas	www.accesskansas.org/krec	Utah	www.commerce.state.ut.us
Kentucky	www.krec.net	Vermont	www.vtprofessionals.org/opr1/real_estate
Louisiana	www.lrec.state.la.us	Virginia	www.state.va.us/dpor
Maine	www.state.me.us/pfr/olr	Washington	www.wa.gov/dol/bpd/recom.htm
Maryland	www.dllr.state.md.us/license/real_est/reintro.html	West Virginia	www.state.wv.us/wvrec
Massachusetts	www.state.ma.us/reg	Wisconsin	www.wra.org/Become_Realtor/Licensing/license.htm
Michigan	www.cis.state.mi.us	Wyoming	realestate.state.wy.us
Minnesota	www.commerce.state.mn.us		

It is extremely important that anyone planning to become a licensed real estate professional be fully aware of his or her state's specific license laws, licensure requirements, and rules and regulations governing the conduct of real estate agents in the state. When a licensee's practice is likely to extend into other states, he or she must be aware of these laws and regulations as well.

■ SUMMARY

Although most people think of land as the surface of the earth, land includes the earth's surface, the mineral deposits under the earth, and the air above it. The term real estate further expands this definition to include all natural and human-made improvements attached to the land. The term real property describes real estate plus the bundle of legal rights associated with its ownership.

The various rights to the same parcel of real estate may be owned and controlled by different parties, one owning the surface rights, one owning the air rights, and one owning the subsurface rights.

All property that does not fit the definition of real estate is classified as personal property, or chattel. When articles of personal property are affixed to land, they may become fixtures and, as such, are considered part of the real estate. However, personal property attached to real estate by a tenant for business purposes is classified as a trade, or chattel, fixture and remains personal property.

The special nature of land as an investment is apparent in both its economic and physical characteristics. The economic characteristics are scarcity, improvements, permanence of investment, and area preference. Physically, land is immobile, indestructible, and unique.

Even the simplest real estate transactions reflect a complex body of laws. A buyer of real estate actually purchases from the seller the legal rights to use the land in certain ways.

Every U.S. state and Canadian province has some type of licensing requirement for real estate brokers and salespersons. Students must become familiar with the real estate laws and licensing requirements not only of their own states but of those into which their practice may extend as well.

QUESTIONS

1. Real estate generally includes all the following *EXCEPT*
   a. trees.
   b. air rights.
   c. annual crops.
   d. mineral rights.

2. Harry owns a building in a commercial area of town. Tina rents space in the building and operates a bookstore. In Tina's bookstore, she has installed large reading tables fastened to the walls and bookshelves that create aisles from the front of the store to the back. These shelves are bolted to both the ceiling and the floor. Which of the following best characterizes the contents of Tina's bookstore?
   a. The shelves and tables are trade fixtures and will convey when Harry sells the building.
   b. The shelves and tables are trade fixtures and may properly be removed by Tina before her lease expires.
   c. Because Tina is a tenant, the shelves and tables are fixtures and may not be removed except with Harry's permission.
   d. Because the shelves and tables are attached to the building, they are treated the same as other fixtures.

3. The term *nonhomogeneity* refers to
   a. scarcity.
   b. immobility.
   c. uniqueness.
   d. indestructibility.

4. Bowling alleys, store shelves, and restaurant equipment installed by business tenants are examples of
   a. real property.
   b. real estate.
   c. trade fixtures.
   d. general fixtures.

5. When an owner of real estate sells the property to someone else, which of the "sticks" in the bundle of legal rights is he or she using?
   a. Exclusion
   b. Legal enjoyment
   c. Control
   d. Disposition

6. Sam inherited Rolling Hills from his uncle. The first thing he did with the vacant property was to remove all the topsoil, which he sold to a landscaping company. Sam then removed a thick layer of limestone and sold it to a construction company. Finally, he dug 40 feet into the bedrock and sold it for gravel. When Sam died, he left Rolling Hills to his daughter, Pat. Which of the following statements is true?
   a. Pat inherits nothing, because Rolling Hills no longer exists.
   b. Pat inherits a large hole in the ground, but it is still Rolling Hills, down to the center of the earth.
   c. Pat owns the gravel, limestone, and topsoil, no matter where it is.
   d. Sam's estate must restore Rolling Hills to its original condition.

7. The buyer and the seller of a home are debating whether a certain item is real or personal property. The buyer says it is real property and should convey with the house; the seller says it is personal property and would not convey without a separate bill of sale. In determining whether an item is real or personal property, a court would *not* consider which of the following?
   a. The cost of the item when it was purchased
   b. Whether its removal would cause severe damage to the real estate
   c. Whether the item is clearly adapted to the real estate
   d. Any relevant agreement of the parties in their contract of sale

8. Which of the following is a physical characteristic of land?
   a. Indestructibility
   b. Improvements
   c. Area preference
   d. Scarcity

9. Which of the following describes the act by which real property can be converted into personal property?
   a. Severance
   b. Accession
   c. Conversion
   d. Separation

10. When moving into a newly purchased home, the buyer discovered that the seller had taken the electric lighting fixtures that had been installed over the vanity in the bathroom at the time of purchase. The seller had not indicated that the fixtures would be removed, and the contract did not address this issue. Which of the following is true?

a. Lighting fixtures are normally considered to be real estate.

b. The lighting fixtures belong to the seller because he installed them.

c. These lighting fixtures are considered trade fixtures.

d. Original lighting fixtures are real property, but replacement fixtures would be personal property.

11. A buyer purchased a parcel of land and immediately sold the mineral rights to an oil company. The buyer gave up which of the following?

a. Air rights

b. Surface rights

c. Subsurface rights

d. Occupancy rights

12. Jerome is building a new enclosed front porch on his home. A truckload of lumber that he purchased has been left on his driveway for use in building the porch. At this point, the lumber is considered to be

a. real property, because it will be permanently affixed to the existing structure.

b. personal property.

c. a chattel that is real property.

d. a trade or chattel fixture.

13. Intent of the parties, method of annexation, adaptation to real estate, and agreement between the parties are the legal tests for determining whether an item is

a. a trade fixture or personal property.

b. real property or real estate.

c. a fixture or personal property.

d. an improvement.

14. Parking spaces in multiunit buildings, water rights, and similar things of value are classified as

a. covenants.   c. chattels.

b. emblements.   d. appurtenances.

15. A paint company purchases 100 acres of scenic forest land and builds several tin shacks there to store used turpentine, varnish, and similar chemical waste. Based on these facts alone, which of the following statements is true?

a. The company's action constitutes improvement of the property.

b. The chemicals are considered appurtenances.

c. If the company is in the business of storing toxic substances, the tin shacks are considered trade fixtures.

d. Altering the property in order to store waste is not included in the bundle of legal rights.

CHAPTER  THREE

CONCEPTS OF HOME OWNERSHIP

■ **LEARNING OBJECTIVES** *When you've finished reading this Chapter, you should be able to:*

■ **identify** the various types of housing choices available to home buyers.

■ **describe** the issues involved in making a home ownership decision.

■ **explain** the tax benefits of home ownership and the provisions of recent changes to the Tax Code.

■ **distinguish** the various types of homeowner's insurance policy coverage.

■ **define** the following *key terms:*

coinsurance clause	homeowner's insurance	liability coverage
equity	policy	replacement cost

■ WHY LEARN ABOUT...   HOME OWNERSHIP CONCEPTS?

In the past, most homes were single-family dwellings bought by married couples with small children. Today, social, demographic, and economic changes have altered the residential real estate market considerably. Many real estate buyers today are single men and women, childless professional couples, unmarried couples, and domestic partners. An aging Baby Boom generation has given rise to empty nesters—couples whose children have moved away from home. Still other buyers may be friends or relatives who plan to co-own a home together in the same way they might share an apartment lease. Today's homebuyers come from all economic classes, from all ethnic backgrounds, and from all over the world. ■

There are nearly as many different *kinds* of home ownership as there are people who own homes. As the real estate market changes and evolves over time, the successful real estate agent will understand the various (and sometimes conflicting) motivations that move people to buy property and the options and opportunities that are broadening their range of choices.

■ HOME OWNERSHIP

People buy their own homes for psychological as well as financial reasons. To many people, home ownership is a sign of financial stability. It is an investment that can appreciate in value and provide federal income tax deductions. Home ownership also offers benefits that may be less tangible but are no less valuable, such as pride, security, and a sense of belonging to the community.

Types of Housing

As U.S. society evolves, the needs of its homebuyers become more specialized. The following paragraphs describe the types of housing currently available to meet these needs. Some housing types are not only innovative uses of real estate, but they also incorporate a variety of ownership concepts. These different forms of housing respond to the demands of a diverse marketplace.

Apartment complexes are groups of apartment buildings with any number of units in each building. The buildings may be lowrise or highrise, and may include parking, security, clubhouses, swimming pools, tennis courts, and even golf courses.

The *condominium* is a popular form of residential ownership, particularly for people who want the security of owning property without the care and maintenance that a house demands. It is also a popular ownership option in areas where property values make single-unit ownership inaccessible for many people. Condominium owners own their units individually and share ownership of common facilities (called *common elements*) such as halls, elevators, swimming pools, clubhouses, tennis courts, and surrounding grounds. Management and maintenance of building exteriors and common facilities are provided by the governing association and outside contractors, with expenses paid out of monthly assessments charged to owners. While condos are often apartment-style homes, this ownership form includes single-family and even commercial properties. The condominium form of ownership is discussed in detail in Chapter 8.

A *cooperative* also has units that share common walls and facilities within a larger building. The owners, however, do not actually *own* the units. Instead, a corporation holds title to the real estate itself. The unit owners actually purchase shares of stock in the corporation, not their individual units. Owners receive *proprietary leases, not conventional deeds,* that entitle them to occupy particular units. Like condominium unit owners, cooperative unit owners pay their share of the building's expenses. Cooperatives are discussed further in Chapter 8.

> Condo = conventional ownership
>
> Co-op = proprietary lease

Planned unit developments (PUDs), sometimes called *master-planned communities,* merge such diverse land uses as housing, recreation, and commercial units in one self-contained development. PUDs are planned under special zoning ordinances. These ordinances permit maximum use of open space by reducing lot sizes and street areas. Owners do not have direct ownership interest in the common areas. A community association is formed to maintain these areas, with fees collected from the owners. A PUD may be a small development of just a few homes or an entirely planned city.

Retirement communities, many of them in temperate climates, are often structured as PUDs. They may provide shopping, recreational opportunities, and health care facilities in addition to residential units. Security and convenience are major advantages offered by retirement communities to older homeowners.

Highrise developments, sometimes called *mixed-use developments* (MUDs), combine office space, stores, theaters, and apartment units in a single vertical community. MUDs usually are self-contained and offer laundry facilities, restaurants, food stores, valet shops, beauty parlors, barbershops, swimming pools, and other attractive and convenient features.

Converted-use properties are factories, warehouses, office buildings, hotels, schools, barns, churches, and other structures that have been converted to residential use. Developers often find renovation of such properties more aesthetically and economically appealing than demolishing a perfectly sound structure to build something new. An abandoned warehouse may be transformed into luxury loft condominium units; a closed hotel may reopen as an apartment building; and an old factory may be recycled into a profitable shopping mall.

Manufactured housing (also known as *mobile homes*) were once considered useful only as temporary residences. Now, however, they are more often permanent principal residences or stationary vacation homes. Relatively low cost, coupled with the increased living space available in the newer models, has made such homes an attractive option for many people. Increased sales have resulted in growing numbers of "housing parks" in some communities. These parks offer complete residential environments with permanent community facilities as well as semipermanent foundations and hookups for gas, water, and electricity.

Modular homes (also referred to as *prefabricated homes*) are also gaining popularity as the price of newly constructed "stick-built" homes rises. Each room is preassembled at a factory, driven to the building site on a truck, then lowered onto its foundation by a crane. Later, workers finish the structure and connect plumbing and wiring. Entire developments can be built at a fraction of the time and cost of conventional construction.

Through *time-shares,* multiple purchasers share ownership of a single property, usually a vacation home. Each owner is entitled to use the property for a certain period of time each year, usually a specific week or month. In addition to the purchase price, each owner pays an annual maintenance fee.

■ HOUSING AFFORDABILITY

Congress, state legislatures, and local governments have been working to increase the affordability of housing for all people. As a result, according to the U.S. Bureau of the Census, by the end of year 2000, 67.5 percent of households were homeowners. However, real estate prices have risen, making it difficult for some buyers to save the down payment and closing costs needed for a conventional loan. Because more homeowners mean more business opportunities, real estate and related industry groups have a vital interest in ensuring affordable housing for all segments of the population.

Certainly, not everyone wants to own a home. Home ownership involves substantial commitment and responsibility. People whose work requires frequent moves or whose financial position is uncertain particularly benefit from renting. Renting also provides more leisure time by freeing tenants from management and maintenance.

Those who choose home ownership must evaluate many factors before they decide to purchase property. And the purchasing decision must be weighed carefully in light of each individual's financial circumstances. Renters can probably make a higher mortgage payment than their current rent payment, without requiring a pay increase, because of the tax savings realized by home ownership.

The decision of buying or renting property involves considering

- ■ how long a person wants to live in a particular area,
- ■ a person's financial situation,
- ■ housing affordability,
- ■ current mortgage interest rates,
- ■ tax consequences of owning versus renting property, and
- ■ what may happen to home prices and tax laws in the future.

WWWeb.Link
www.hud.gov   www.va.gov
www.hud.gov/offices/hsg/index.cfm

Mortgage Terms

Liberalized mortgage terms and payment plans offer many people the option of purchasing a home. Low down-payment mortgage loans are available under programs sponsored by the Federal Housing Administration (FHA) and the Department of Veterans Affairs (VA).

An increasing number of creative mortgage loan programs are being offered by various government agencies and private lenders. Adjustable-rate loans, whose lower initial interest rate makes it possible for many buyers to qualify for a mortgage loan, are now common. Specific programs may offer lower closing costs or deferred interest or principal payments for purchasers in targeted neighborhoods or for first-time buyers. Many innovative loans are tailored to suit the younger buyer, who may need a low interest rate to qualify but whose income is expected to increase in the coming years.

Ownership Expenses and Ability To Pay

Home ownership involves many expenses, including utilities, such as electricity, natural gas, and water, trash removal, sewer charges, and maintenance and repairs. Owners also must pay real estate taxes and buy property insurance, and they must repay the mortgage loan with interest.

To determine whether a prospective buyer can afford a certain purchase, lenders traditionally have used a "rule of thumb" formula for homebuyers who are able to provide at least 10 percent of the purchase price as a down payment: The monthly cost of buying and maintaining a home—mortgage payments, both principal and interest, plus taxes and insurance impounds—should not exceed 28 percent of gross, i.e., pretax, monthly income. The payments on all debts—normally including long-term debt such as car payments, student loans, or other mortgages—should not exceed 36 percent of monthly income. Expenses such as insurance premiums, utilities, and routine medical care are not included in the 36 percent figure but are considered to be covered by the remaining 64 percent of the buyer's monthly income. These formulas may vary, however, depending on the type of loan program and the borrower's earnings, credit history, number of dependents, and other factors. (Note that these financial qualification ratios are true for most FNMA and FHLMC conforming mortgages, but there are many loans available with ratios more liberal than these.)

Memory Tip

The basic costs of owning a home—mortgage **P**rincipal and **I**nterest, **T**axes, and **I**nsurance, can be remembered by the acronym ***PITI***.

■ **FOR EXAMPLE** A prospective homebuyer wants to know how much house he or she can afford to buy. The buyer has a gross monthly income of $3,000. The buyer's allowable housing expense may be calculated as follows:

$3,000 gross monthly income × 28% = $840 total housing expense allowed
$3,000 gross monthly income × 36% = $1,080 total housing and other debt expense allowed

These formulas allow for other debts of 8 percent of gross monthly income—the difference between the 36 percent and 28 percent figures. If actual debts exceed the amount allowed and the borrower is unable to reduce them, the monthly payment would have to be lowered proportionately because the debts and housing payment combined cannot exceed 36 percent of gross monthly income. However, lower debts would not result in a higher allowable housing payment; rather, it would be considered a factor for approval.

Investment Considerations

Purchasing a home offers several financial advantages to a buyer. First, if the property's value increases, a sale could bring in more money than the owner paid—a long-term gain. Second, as the total mortgage debt is reduced through monthly payments, the owner's actual ownership interest in the property increases. This increasing ownership interest is called **equity** and represents the paid-off share of the property, held free of any mortgage. A tenant accumulates nothing except a good credit rating by paying the rent on time; a homeowner's mortgage payments build equity and so increase his or her net worth. Equity builds even further when the property's value rises. The third financial advantage of home ownership is the tax deduction available to homeowners but not to renters.

Tax Benefits

To encourage home ownership, the federal government allows homeowners certain income tax advantages. Homeowners may deduct from their income some or all of the mortgage interest paid, as well as real estate taxes and certain other expenses. Tax considerations may be an important part of any decision to purchase a home.

> Current Market Value – Property Debt = **Equity**

In the late 1990s, the federal government enacted several federal tax reforms that significantly changed the importance of tax considerations for most home-sellers. For instance, $500,000 is now excluded from capital gains tax for profits on the sale of a principal residence by married taxpayers who file jointly. Taxpayers who file singly are entitled to a $250,000 exclusion. The exemption may be used repeatedly, as long as the homeowners have occupied the property as their residence for at least two of the past five years. On investment real estate, the required period for a noncorporate taxpayer was changed from 18 months to 12 months for long-term capital gain.

First-time homebuyers may make penalty-free withdrawals from their tax-deferred individual retirement funds (IRAs) for down payments on their homes. However, these withdrawals are still subject to income tax. The limit on such withdrawals is $10,000 and must be spent entirely within 120 days on a down payment to avoid the 10 percent penalty.

In short, the changes in tax laws have generally benefitted home ownership, which is good news for homeowners and real estate professionals.

Tax deductions. Homeowners may deduct from their gross income

- mortgage *interest* payments on first and second homes (for mortgage balances below $1 million or $500,000 if married filing separately),
- real estate taxes (but *not* interest paid on overdue taxes),
- certain loan origination fees,
- loan discount points (whether paid by the buyer or the seller), and
- loan prepayment penalties.

IN PRACTICE   Note that appraisal fees, notary fees, preparation costs, mortgage insurance premiums, and VA funding fees are not interest but are part of the cost of acquiring a home. When it is sold at a later date, these charges can be figured into the cost *basis*. Points are deductible in the year of a house purchase if certain criteria are met. Points are deducted over the life of the loan for a refinance. Note that real estate licensees should not provide tax advice and that homeowners should consult with accountants or attorneys about home ownership tax deductions. The rules are complicated and constantly changing.

■ HOMEOWNER'S INSURANCE

A home is frequently the biggest investment many people ever make. Most homeowners see the wisdom in protecting such an important investment by insuring it. Lenders usually require that a homeowner obtain insurance when the debt is secured by the property. While owners can purchase individual policies that insure against destruction of property by fire or windstorm, injury to others and theft of personal property, most buy a packaged homeowner's insurance policy to cover all these risks.

Coverage and Claims

The most common homeowner's policy is called a *basic form*. It provides property coverage against

- ■ fire and lightning,
- ■ glass breakage,
- ■ windstorm and hail,
- ■ explosion,
- ■ riot and civil commotion,
- ■ damage by aircraft,
- ■ damage from vehicles,
- ■ damage from smoke,
- ■ vandalism and malicious mischief,
- ■ theft, and
- ■ loss of property removed from the premises when it is endangered by fire or other perils.

A *broad-form* policy is also available. It covers

- ■ falling objects;
- ■ damage due to the weight of ice, snow, or sleet;
- ■ collapse of all or part of the building;
- ■ bursting, cracking, burning, or bulging of a steam or hot water heating system or of appliances used to heat water;
- ■ accidental discharge, leakage, or overflow of water or steam from within a plumbing, a heating, or an air-conditioning system;
- ■ freezing of plumbing, heating, and air-conditioning systems and domestic appliances; and
- ■ injury to electrical appliances, devices, fixtures, and wiring from short circuits or other accidentally generated currents.

Further insurance is available from policies that cover almost all possible perils. Special apartment and condominium policies generally provide fire and windstorm, theft, and public liability coverage for injuries or losses sustained within the unit. However, they do not usually cover losses or damages to the structure. The basic structure is insured by either the landlord or the condominium owners' association.

Most homeowner's insurance policies contain a ~~coinsurance clause~~. This provision usually requires that the owner maintain insurance equal to at least 80 percent of the *replacement cost* of the dwelling (not including the price of the land). An owner who has this type of policy may make a claim for the full cost of the repair or replacement of the damaged property without deduction for depreciation or annual wear and tear.

If the homeowner carries less than 80 percent of the full replacement cost, however, the claim will be handled in one of two ways. Either the loss will be settled for the *actual cash value* (replacement cost less depreciation) or it will be *prorated* by dividing the percentage of replacement cost actually covered by the policy by the minimum coverage requirement (usually 80 percent).

■ **FOR EXAMPLE** Tom's insurance policy is for 80 percent of the replacement cost of his home, or $80,000. His home is valued at $100,000, and the land is valued at $40,000. Tom sustains $30,000 in fire damage to his house. Tom can make a claim for the full cost of the repair or replacement of the damaged property, without deduction for depreciation. However, if Tom had insurance of only $70,000, his claim would be handled in one of two ways. He would receive either actual cash value (replacement cost of $30,000 less depreciation cost of say $3,000, or $27,000), or his claim would be prorated by dividing the percentage of replacement cost actually covered (.70) by the policy minimum coverage requirement (.80). So, .70 divided by .80 equals .875, and $30,000 multiplied by .875 equals $26,250.

IN PRACTICE

In the 1990s, problems with synthetic stucco exterior finishes on some residential properties began to emerge. This *exterior insulating finishing system* (EIFS) is a highly effective moisture barrier that also tends to "seal in" moisture—trapping water in the home's walls and resulting in massive wood rot. Frequently, the effects of the rotting cannot be seen until the damage is extensive and sometimes irreparable. If a homeowner suspects that EIFS was used on their home and is causing damage, the homeowner should have the property inspected. Some insurance companies refuse to cover homes with EIFS exteriors, and class action lawsuits have been brought against builders by distressed homeowners.

 **WWWeb.Link**

www.fema.gov

■ FEDERAL FLOOD INSURANCE PROGRAM

The National Flood Insurance Act of 1968 was enacted by Congress to help owners of property in flood-prone areas by subsidizing flood insurance and by taking land-use and land-control measures to improve future management for floodplain areas. The Federal Emergency Management Agency (FEMA) administers the flood program. The Army Corps of Engineers has prepared maps that identify specific flood-prone areas throughout the country. To finance property with federal or federally related mortgage loans, owners in flood-prone areas must obtain flood insurance. If they do not obtain the insurance, either they don't want it or they don't qualify because their communities have not properly entered the program, they are not eligible for this financial assistance.

In designated areas, flood insurance is required on all types of buildings—residential, commercial, industrial, and agricultural—for either the value of the property or the amount of the mortgage loan, subject to the maximum limits available. Policies are written annually and can be purchased from any licensed property insurance broker, the National Flood Insurance Program (NFIP), or the designated servicing companies in each state. However, if a borrower can produce a survey showing that the lowest part of the building is located above the 100-year flood mark, the borrower may be exempted from the flood insurance requirement, even if the property is in a flood-prone area.

IN PRACTICE

Massive losses in the Federal Flood Insurance Program due to the Mississippi floods in 1993 caused Congress to pass laws that greatly increase the number of properties that are required to be covered by the NFIP. This requirement not only results in higher expenses for the buyer but can also negatively affect property values. Agents should pay attention to what property is in a flood zone and communicate that to potential buyers.

■ SUMMARY

Current trends in home ownership include single-family homes, apartment complexes, condominiums, cooperatives, planned unit developments, retirement communities, highrise developments, converted-use properties, modular homes, manufactured housing, and time-shares.

Prospective buyers should be aware of both the advantages and disadvantages of home ownership. While a homeowner gains financial security and pride of ownership, the costs of ownership—the initial price and the continuing expenses—must be considered.

One of the income tax benefits available to homeowners is the ability to deduct mortgage interest payments (with certain limitations) and property taxes from their federal income tax returns. Changes in income tax exemptions mean that most homeowners will never need to pay capital gains taxes on the properties in which they reside.

To protect their investment in real estate, most homeowners purchase insurance. A standard homeowner's insurance policy covers fire, theft, and liability and can be extended to cover many types of less common risks. Another type of insurance, which covers personal property only, is available to people who live in apartments and condominiums.

Many homeowner's policies contain a coinsurance clause that requires that the policyholder maintain insurance in an amount equal to 80 percent of the replacement cost of the home. If this percentage is not met, the policyholder may not be reimbursed for the full repair costs if a loss occurs.

In addition to homeowner's insurance, the federal government requires flood insurance for people living in flood-prone areas who wish to obtain federally regulated or federally insured mortgage loans.

QUESTIONS

1. Which of the following are *not* costs or expenses of owning a home?
   a. Interest paid on borrowed capital
   b. Homeowner's insurance
   c. Maintenance and repairs
   d. Taxes on personal property

2. When a person buys a house using a mortgage loan, the difference between the amount owed on the property and its market value represents the homeowner's
   a. tax basis.
   b. equity.
   c. replacement cost.
   d. capital gain.

3. A building that is remodeled into residential units and is no longer used for the purpose for which it was originally built is an example of a(n)
   a. converted-use property.
   b. urban homesteading.
   c. planned unit development.
   d. modular home.

4. A highrise development that includes office space, stores, theaters, and apartment units is an example of which of the following?
   a. Planned unit development
   b. Mixed-use development
   c. Proprietary lease properties
   d. Special cluster zoning

5. Each room of Jan's house was preassembled at a factory, driven to the building site on a truck, then lowered onto its foundation by a crane. Later, workers finished the structure and connected plumbing and wiring before Jan moved in. Which of the following terms best describes what type of home Jan owns?
   a. Mobile
   b. Modular
   c. Manufactured
   d. Converted

6. Five years ago, Marcia bought a home for $250,000. Home values in her area have improved, and the current market value of Marcia's house has increased by 15 percent. If Marcia has $95,875 left to pay on her mortgage loan, what is her current equity in her home?
   a. $138,712
   b. $154,125
   c. $191,625
   d. $250,000

7. For which of the following risks would a homeowner have to purchase a special policy in addition to a typical basic or broad-form homeowner's insurance policy?
   a. The cost of medical expenses for a person injured in the policyholder's home
   b. Theft
   c. Vandalism
   d. Flood damage

8. Peter wants to buy his first home but doesn't know how much he can afford to pay. He has a gross monthly income of $3,000. According to the traditional lender's rule of thumb formula, what is the total housing expense (principal, interest, taxes, and insurance) Peter can bear?
   a. $1,080
   b. $840
   c. $648
   d. $1,152

9. Marcia and Bob are a married couple who bought their house ten years ago for $150,000. Last week, they sold their home for $225,500. Based on these facts, how much capital gains tax will Marcia and Bob have to pay this year?
   a. None
   b. $7,550
   c. $11,325
   d. $75,500

10. Which of the following best expresses the concept of equity?
    a. Current Market Value minus Capital Gain
    b. Current Market Value minus Property Debt
    c. Current Market Value minus Cost of Land
    d. Replacement Cost minus Depreciation

11. Carol and her husband bought their house in 1968 (when they were 21) for $25,000 and have lived in it ever since. Today, the neighborhood has become very fashionable, and they sell the house for $450,000. How much of the gain is taxable on the couple's joint return this year?

    a. $25,000   c. None
    b. All   d. $637,000

12. Sam and Alice are a married couple who file a joint income tax return and have lived in their home for 20 years. Greg is a single homeowner who has lived in his home for five years. Mike and Cindy are father and daughter and bought their home together last year. Based on these facts, which of the following statements is true if all three homes are sold today?

    a. All of these homeowners qualify for a $500,000 exclusion from capital gains taxation on the transactions.
    b. A $500,000 exclusion applies to Sam and Alice as well as to Mike and Cindy; a $250,000 exclusion applies to Greg.
    c. A $500,000 exclusion applies to Sam and Alice; a $250,000 exclusion applies to Greg; and no exclusion applies to Mike and Cindy.
    d. Only Sam and Alice qualify for any exclusion from capital gains taxation.

13. Theft, smoke damage, and damage from fire are covered under which type of homeowner's insurance policy?

    a. Basic form
    b. Broad form
    c. Coinsurance
    d. National Flood Insurance Program policies

14. A development that combines office space, stores, and residential units in a single vertical community is called a

    a. PUD.
    b. MUD.
    c. master-planned community.
    d. condominium.

15. All of the following would be covered by a basic-form homeowner's insurance policy, EXCEPT damage caused by

    a. glass breakage.
    b. riot.
    c. frozen pipes.
    d. vandalism.

AGENCY

■ **LEARNING OBJECTIVES** *When you've finished reading this Chapter, you should be able to:*

■ **identify** the various types of agency relationships common in the real estate profession and the characteristics of each.

■ **describe** the fiduciary duties involved in an agency relationship.

■ **explain** the process by which agency is created and terminated and the role of disclosure in agency relationships.

■ **distinguish** the duties owed by an agent to his or her client from those owed to customers.

■ **define** the following *key terms:*

agency	express agency	listing agreement
agency coupled with an interest	express agreement	negligent misrepresentation
	fiduciary relationship	
agent	fraud	principal
buyer's agents	general agent	puffing
client	implied agency	special agent
customer	implied agreement	subagent
designated agent	latent defect	universal agent
dual agency	law of agency	

■ WHY LEARN ABOUT... AGENCY?

The key for successful agents is to focus on the consumer. Consumers are increasingly knowledgeable and have access to most of the information they need that was formerly obtainable only through real estate professionals. In the absence of being information providers, real estate professionals must become information consultants, representatives, and advocates for their clients. They must provide a service that is valuable to their clients. ■

In addition to providing valuable service, there's an even more important reason to understand agency relationships. Agency is governed by state laws that establish the duties, responsibilities, and acceptable activities for agents in their relationships with clients, customers, and the general public. Adherence to these expectations is not just a matter of good business practice, which, of course, it is; you could lose your license if you don't. Further, agency is a legal relationship that creates duties—and liabilities—to the principal. This Chapter cannot provide details on each state's laws, but it will give you a solid grounding in the fundamental principles of modern real estate agency practice.

■ INTRODUCTION TO REAL ESTATE AGENCY

The relationship between a real estate licensee and the parties involved in a real estate transaction is not a simple one. In addition to the parties' assumptions and expectations, the licensee is subject to a wide range of legal and ethical requirements designed to protect the seller, the buyer, and the transaction itself. *Agency* is the word used to describe that special relationship between a real estate licensee and the person he or she represents. Agency is governed by two kinds of law: *common law*, the rules of a society established by tradition and court decisions, and *statutory law*, the laws, rules, and regulations enacted by legislatures and other governing bodies.

The History of Agency

The basic framework of the law that governs the legal responsibilities of the broker to the people he or she represents is known as the *common-law law of agency*. The fundamentals of agency law have remained largely unchanged for hundreds of years. However, the *application* of the law has changed dramatically, particularly in residential transactions and especially in recent years. As states enact legislation that defines and governs the broker-client relationship, brokers are reevaluating their services. They must determine whether they will represent the seller, the buyer, or both (if that is permitted by state law) in a transaction. Where state laws permit, an increasing number of brokers are choosing to represent buyers exclusively. They also must decide how they will cooperate with other brokers, depending on which party each broker represents. In short, the brokerage business is undergoing many changes as brokers focus on ways to enhance their services to buyers and sellers.

Even as the laws change, however, the underlying assumptions that govern the agency relationship remain intact. The principal-agent relationship evolved from the master-servant relationship under English common law. In that relationship, the servant owed absolute loyalty to the master. This loyalty replaced the servant's personal interests as well as any loyalty the servant might owe to others. In a modern-day agency relationship, the agent owes the principal similar loyalty. As masters used the services of servants to accomplish what they could not or did not want to do for themselves, principals use the services of agents. The agent is regarded as an expert on whom the principal can rely for specialized professional advice.

■ LAW OF AGENCY

The law of agency defines the rights and duties of the principal and the agent. It applies to a variety of business transactions. In real estate transactions, contract law and real estate licensing laws—in addition to the law of agency—interpret the relationship between licensees and their clients. The law of agency is a common-law concept; it is being widely replaced by state statute.

Creation of Agency

An agency relationship may be based on a formal agreement between the parties, an express agency, or it may result from the parties' behavior, an implied agency.

Express agency. The principal and agent may enter into a contract, or an express agreement, in which the parties formally express their intention to establish an agency and state its terms and conditions. The agreement may be either oral or written. An agency relationship between a seller and a broker is generally created by a written employment contract, commonly referred to as a listing agreement, which authorizes the broker to find a buyer or tenant for the owner's property. Although a written listing agreement is usually preferred, some states consider an oral agreement binding. An express agency relationship between a buyer and a broker is created by a *buyer agency agreement*. Similar to a listing agreement, it stipulates the activities and responsibilities the buyer expects from the broker in finding the appropriate property for purchase or rent.

Implied agency. An agency may also be created by implied agreement. This occurs when the actions of the parties indicate that they have mutually consented to an agency. A person acts on behalf of another as agent; the other person, as principal, delegates the authority to act. Even though the parties may not have consciously planned to create an agency relationship, nonetheless, they can create one *unintentionally*, *inadvertently*, or *accidentally* by their actions.

■ **FOR EXAMPLE** Nancy tells Betsy, a real estate broker, that she is thinking about selling her home. Betsy immediately contacts several prospective buyers. One of them makes an attractive offer without even seeing the property. Betsy goes to Nancy's house and presents the offer, which Nancy accepts. Although no formal agency agreement was entered into either orally or in writing, Betsy's actions *implied* to prospective buyers that Betsy was acting as Nancy's agent. If Betsy made any misrepresentations to the buyer, Nancy may be held liable.

Even though licensees may be required to disclose their agency status, it is often difficult for customers to understand the complexities of the law of agency. A buyer can easily assume that when he or she contacts a salesperson to show the buyer property, the salesperson becomes his or her agent, even though, under a listing contract, the salesperson may *legally* represent the seller. An implied agency with the buyer can result if the words and conduct of the salesperson do not dispel this assumption. Otherwise, one agency relationship is created in conflict with another. *Dual representation*, which will be discussed in greater detail later, may occur, even though it was not intended.

Compensation. The *source of compensation does not determine agency.* An agent does not necessarily represent the person who pays his or her commission. In fact, agency can exist even if no fee is involved (called a *gratuitous agency*). For instance, a seller could agree to pay a commission to the buyer's agent, even though the agent is representing the buyer. The written agency agreement should state how the agent is being compensated and explain all the alternatives available.

Definitions

Real estate brokers and salespersons are commonly called *agents*. Legally, however, the term refers to strictly defined legal relationships. In the case of real estate, it is a relationship with buyers and sellers or with landlords and tenants. In the law of agency, the body of law that governs these relationships, the following terms have specific definitions:

An **agent** is a person authorized to act on behalf of another.

- **Agent**—the individual who is authorized and consents to represent the interests of another person. In the real estate business, a firm's broker is the agent, and he or she shares this responsibility with the licensees who work for the firm.
- **Subagent**—the agent of an agent. If the original agency agreement permits it, an agent may delegate some of his or her authority or responsibility to a third party. The subagent is also an agent of the principal.
- **Principal**—the individual who hires the agent and delegates to him or her the responsibility of representing the principal's interests. In the real estate business, the principal is the buyer or seller, landlord or tenant.
- **Agency**—the fiduciary relationship between the principal and the agent.
- **Fiduciary**—the relationship in which the agent is held in a position of special trust and confidence by the principal.
- **Client**—the principal.
- **Customer**—the third party for whom some level of service is provided and who is entitled to fairness and honesty.
- **Nonagent**—(also referred to as a *facilitator, intermediary, transactional broker, transactional coordinator,* or *contract broker*) a middleman between a buyer and seller (or landlord and tenant) who assists both parties with the transaction without representing either party's interests. Nonagents are often subject to specific statutory responsibilities. Transactional brokers are discussed in Chapter 5.

IN PRACTICE   The general discussion in this Chapter is limited to the concepts and principles that govern traditional common-law agency relationships. In many states, agency reform legislation that includes language superseding the common-law of agency has been passed, drafted, or is under consideration.

An agent works *for* the *client* and *with* the *customer*.

It should be noted, however, that many agency statutes make the common-law duties a matter of statutory law rather than (or in addition to) creating totally new legal relationships. While this Chapter provides an overview of current agency legislation, a licensee should be familiar with the specific terms of any agency statute adopted by his or her state legislature.

There is a distinction between the level of services an agent provides to a *client* and those services that the agent provides to a *customer*. The *client* is the principal to whom the agent gives advice and counsel. The agent is entrusted with certain *confidential information* and has *fiduciary responsibilities* (discussed in greater detail later) to the principal. In contrast, the *customer* is entitled to factual information and fair and honest dealings as a consumer but does not receive advice and counsel or confidential information about the principal. The *agent works **for** the principal and **with** the customer*. Essentially, the agent supports and defends the principal's interests, not the customer's.

The relationship between the principal and agent must be *consensual;* that is, the principal *delegates* authority, and the agent *consents* to act. The parties must agree to form the relationship. An agent may be authorized by the principal to use the assistance of another, who may or may not, depending on local state law, become a **subagent** of the principal. The practice of subagency, while still legal in most states, is seldom practiced in most real estate markets due to the increased liability it entails for listing brokers.

Just as the agent owes certain duties to the principal, the principal has responsibilities toward the agent. The principal's primary duties are to comply with the agency agreement and cooperate with the agent, that is, the principal must not hinder the agent and must deal with the agent in good faith. The principal also must compensate the agent according to the terms of the agency agreement.

IN PRACTICE

Subagency is rapidly becoming the dinosaur of the real estate industry. In some areas, the multiple-listing service (MLS) or individual companies are refusing even to accept subagency. The general acceptance of buyer agency has led to much less use of subagency.

Fiduciary Responsibilities

The agency agreement usually authorizes the broker to act for the principal. The agent's **fiduciary relationship** of trust and confidence with the principal means that the broker owes the principal certain specific duties. These duties are not simply moral or ethical; they are the law—the common-law of agency or the statutory law governing real estate transactions. Under the common-law of agency, an agent owes the principal the five duties of *care, obedience, accounting, loyalty* (including confidentiality), and *disclosure.* Table 4.1 illustrates the differences between client and customer services provided to a buyer and seller.

Care. The agent must exercise a reasonable degree of care while transacting the business entrusted to him or her by the principal. The principal expects the agent's skill and expertise in real estate matters to be superior to that of the average person. The most fundamental way in which the agent exercises care is to use that skill and knowledge in the principal's behalf. The agent should know all facts pertinent to the principal's affairs, such as the physical characteristics of the property being transferred and the type of financing being used.

If the agent represents the seller, care and skill include helping the seller arrive at an appropriate and realistic listing price, discovering and disclosing facts that affect the seller, and properly presenting the contracts that the seller signs. It also means making reasonable efforts to market the property, such as advertising and holding open houses, and helping the seller evaluate the terms and conditions of offers to purchase.

An agent who represents the buyer is expected to help the buyer locate suitable property and evaluate property values, neighborhood and property conditions, financing alternatives, and offers and counteroffers with the buyer's interest in mind.

An agent who does not make a reasonable effort to properly represent the interests of the principal could be found by a court to have been negligent. The agent is liable to the principal for any loss resulting from the agent's negligence or carelessness. The standard of care will vary from market to market and depends on the expected behavior for a particular type of transaction in a particular locale.

IN PRACTICE Because real estate licensees have, under the law, enormous exposure to liability, some brokers purchase what is known as *errors and omissions* (E&O) *insurance* for their firms. Similar to malpractice insurance in the medical and legal fields, E&O policies cover liability for errors and negligence in the usual listing and selling activities of a real estate office. Individual salespersons might also be insured. Licensing laws in several states now require E&O insurance for brokers and, in some cases, for individual salespersons as well. However, no insurance policy will protect a licensee from a lawsuit or prosecution arising from criminal acts. Insurance companies normally exclude coverage for violation of civil rights and antitrust laws as well.

Obedience. The fiduciary relationship obligates the agent to act in good faith at all times, obeying the principal's instructions in accordance with the contract.

However, that obedience is not absolute. The agent may not obey instructions that are unlawful or unethical. Because illegal acts do not serve the principal's best interests, obeying such instructions violates the broker's duty of loyalty. On the other hand, an agent who exceeds the authority assigned in the contract will be liable for any losses that the principal suffers as a result.

FOR EXAMPLE A seller tells the listing agent, "I don't want you to show this house to any, you know, minorities." Because refusing to show a property to someone on the basis of race is illegal, the agent may not follow the seller's instructions and should withdraw from the agency.

Accounting. The agent must be able to report the status of all funds received from or on behalf of the principal. Most state real estate license laws require that a broker give accurate copies of all documents to all parties affected by them and keep copies on file for a specified period of time. Most license laws also require

T A B L E   4.1   **Customer-Level versus Client-Level Service**

THE SELLING BROKER	
Customer-Level Service as Seller's Agent or Subagent	**Client-Level Service as Buyer's Broker**

Responsibilities

Be honest with buyer but responsible to seller, including duty of skill and care to promote and safeguard seller's best interests.	Be fair with seller but responsible to buyer, including duty of skill and care to promote and safeguard buyer's best interests.

Earnest Money Deposit

Collect amount sufficient to protect seller.	Suggest minimum amount, perhaps a promissory note; put money in interest-bearing account if required by state law; suggest that forfeiture of earnest money be sole remedy if buyer defaults.

Seller Financing

Can discuss but should not encourage financing terms and contract provisions unfavorable to seller, such as (1) no due-on-sale clause, (2) no deficiency judgment (nonrecourse), (3) unsecured note. If a corporate buyer, suggest seller require personal guaranty.	Suggest terms in best interests of buyer, such as low down payment, deferred interest, long maturity dates, no due-on-sale clause, long grace period, nonrecourse.

Disclosure

Disclose to seller pertinent facts (which might not be able to disclose if a buyer's broker), such as (1) buyer's willingness to offer higher price or better terms, (2) buyer's urgency to buy, (3) buyer's plans to resell at profit or resubdivide to increase value, (4) buyer is related to broker.	Disclose to buyer pertinent facts (which might not be able to disclose if subagent of seller), such as (1) seller near bankruptcy or foreclosure, (2) property overpriced, (3) other properties available at better buys, (4) negative features such as poor traffic flow, (5) construction of chemical plant down the street that may affect property value.

Nondisclosure

Refrain from disclosing to buyer facts that may compromise seller's position (e.g., seller's pending divorce) unless under legal duty to disclose (e.g., zoning violation).	Refrain from disclosing to seller facts regarding buyer's position. No duty to disclose name of buyer.

Property Condition

Suggest use of "as is" clause, if appropriate to protect seller (still must specify hidden defects).	Require that seller sign property condition statement, and confirm representations of condition; require soil and termite inspections, if appropriate; look for negative features and use them to negotiate better price and terms.

Documents

Give buyer a copy of important documents, such as mortgage to be assumed, declaration of restrictions, title report, condominium bylaws, house rules.	Research and explain significant portions of important documents affecting transaction, such as prepayment penalties, subordination, right of first refusal; refer buyer to expert advisers when appropriate.

Negotiation

Use negotiating strategy and bargaining talents in seller's best interests.	Use negotiating strategy and bargaining talents in buyer's best interests.

Showing

Show buyer properties in which broker's commission is protected, such as in-house or MLS-listed properties. Pick best times to show properties. Emphasize attributes and amenities.	Search for best properties for buyer to inspect, widening marketplace to "for sale by owner" properties, lender-owned (REO) properties, probate sales, unlisted proper ties. View properties at different times to find negative features, such as evening noise, afternoon sun, traffic congestion.

THE SELLING BROKER	
Customer-Level Service as Seller's Agent or Subagent	**Client-Level Service as Buyer's Broker**

Property Goals

Find buyer the type of property buyer seeks; more concerned with *sale* of seller's property that fits buyer's stated objectives.	Counsel buyer as to developing accurate objectives; may find that buyer who wants apartment building might be better off with duplex at half the price or that buyer looking for vacant lot would benefit more from investment in improved property.

Offers

Can help prepare and transmit buyer's offer on behalf of seller; must reveal to seller that buyer has prepared two offers, in case first offer not accepted.	Help buyer prepare strongest offer; can suggest buyer prepare two offers and have broker submit lower offer first without revealing fact of second offer.

Possession Dates

Consider best date for seller in terms of moving out, notice to existing tenants, impact on insurance, risk of loss provision.	Consider best date for buyer in terms of moving in, storage, favorable risk of loss provision if fire destroys property before closing.

Default

Discuss remedies upon default by either party. Point out to seller any attempt by buyer to limit liability (nonrecourse, deposit money is sole liquidated damages).	Suggest seller's remedy be limited to retention of deposit money; consider having seller pay buyer's expenses and cancellation charges if seller defaults.

Bidding

Can bid for own account against buyer customer, but disclose this to buyer and seller.	Cannot bid for own account against buyer client.

Efficiency

Don't expend much time and effort, as in an open listing, because in competition with the listing broker, seller and other brokers to sell buyer a property before someone else does.	Broker's role is to assist buyer in locating and acquiring best property, not to sell buyer a particular property.

Appraisal

Unless asked, no duty to disclose low appraisal or fact broker sold similar unit yesterday for $10,000 less.	Suggest independent appraisal be used to negotiate lower price offer; review seller's comparables from buyer's perspective.

Bonus

Cannot agree to accept bonus from buyer for obtaining reduction in listed price.	Can receive incentive fee for negotiating reduction in listed price.

Termination

Easier to terminate subagency relationship (as when broker decides to bid on property).	Legal and ethical implications of agency relationship and certain duties may continue even after clearly documented termination.

Source: *Agency Relationships in Real Estate*, 2nd Edition, by John Reilly. © 1994 Dearborn Financial Publishing®. Used with permission.

the broker to deposit immediately, or within a statutory time frame, all funds entrusted to the broker (such as earnest money deposits) in a special trust, or escrow, account. Commingling such monies with the broker's personal or general business funds is strictly illegal. *Conversion* is the practice of using those commingled funds as the broker's own money. It is illegal as well.

Loyalty. The duty of loyalty requires that the agent place the principal's interests above those of all others, including the agent's own self-interest. The agent must be particularly sensitive to any possible conflicts of interest. *Confidentiality* about the principal's personal affairs is a key element of loyalty. An agent may not, for example, disclose the principal's financial condition. When the principal is the seller, the agent may not reveal such things as the principal's willingness to accept less than the listing price or his or her anxiousness to sell unless the principal has authorized the disclosure. If the principal is the buyer, the agent may not disclose, for instance, that the buyer will pay more than the offered price if necessary, or that the buyer is under a tight moving schedule, or any other fact that might harm the principal's bargaining position. Under the laws of most states, the agent *must* disclose material facts about the condition of the property itself. Some states, however, permit a seller *disclaimer*—essentially a statement that the property is sold "as is," with no promises regarding its quality.

Because the agent may not act out of self-interest, the negotiation of a sales contract must be conducted without regard to how much the agent will earn in commission. All states forbid agents to buy property listed with them for their own accounts or for accounts in which they have a personal interest without first disclosing that interest and receiving the principal's consent. Neither brokers nor salespersons may sell property in which they have a personal interest without informing the purchaser of that interest.

Remember: Anything an agent learns about a client must remain confidential *forever*.

Disclosure. It is the agent's duty to keep the principal informed of all facts or information that could affect a transaction. Duty of disclosure includes relevant information or *material facts* that the agent *knows* or *should have known*.

The agent is obligated to discover facts that a reasonable person would feel are important in choosing a course of action, regardless of whether those facts are favorable or unfavorable to the principal's position. The agent may be held liable for damages for failing to disclose such information. For example, an agent for the seller has a duty to disclose

- all offers;
- the identity of the prospective purchasers, including any relationship the agent has to them (such as when the licensee or a relative is a purchaser);
- the purchaser's ability to complete the sale or offer a higher price;
- any interest the agent has in the buyer (such as the broker's agreement to manage the property after it is purchased);
- the buyer's intention to resell the property for a profit; and
- the agent's best judgment of the fair market value of the property.

However, a seller's agent is also expected (and required under many states' laws) to disclose information about known material defects in the property to prospective buyers. While this seems a violation of the agent's duty of total allegiance to the seller, this requirement falls under the real estate professional's broader duty to serve the general public and is in the agent's long-term best interest.

An agent for the buyer must disclose deficiencies of a property as well as sales contract provisions and financing that do not suit the buyer's needs. The agent would suggest the lowest price the buyer should pay based on comparable values, regardless of the listing price. The agent also would disclose information—about how long a property has been listed or why the owner is selling—that would affect the buyer's ability to negotiate the lowest purchase price possible. If the agent represents the seller, of course, disclosure of any of this information would violate the agent's fiduciary duty to the seller.

IN   PRACTICE

Remember that saying the condition of property is "as is" does not preclude provisions already in the contract. "As is" sellers sometimes complain because they are still expected to have plumbing, electrical, and mechanical systems, plus all appliances, in working order as is often specified in the contract. If sellers truly mean "as is," they must cross out any printed provisions existing in the contract that relate to the condition of systems and appliances.

Termination of Agency

An agency may be terminated for any of the following reasons:

- *Death or incapacity* of either party (notice of death is not necessary)
- *Destruction or condemnation* of the property
- *Expiration* of the terms of the agency
- *Mutual agreement* by all parties to the contract
- *Breach* by one of the parties (in which case the breaching party might be liable for damages)
- By *operation of law*, as in bankruptcy of the principal (bankruptcy terminates the agency contract, and title to the property transfers to a court-appointed receiver)
- *Completion, performance,* or *fulfillment* of the purpose for which the agency was created

An **agency coupled with an interest** is an agency relationship in which the agent is given an interest in the subject of the agency, such as the property being sold. An agency coupled with an interest cannot be revoked by the principal or be terminated upon the principal's death.

■ **FOR EXAMPLE** A broker agrees to provide the financing for a condominium building being constructed by a developer in exchange for the exclusive right to sell the units once the building is completed. The developer may not revoke the listing agreement once the broker has provided the financing because this is an agency coupled with an interest.

■ TYPES OF AGENCY RELATIONSHIPS

What an agent may do as the principal's representative depends solely on what the principal authorizes the agent to do.

Limitations on an Agent's Authority

A **universal agent** is a person empowered to do anything the principal could do personally. The universal agent's authority to act on behalf of the principal is virtually unlimited. This type of agency can be created by a general power of attorney, which makes the agent an attorney-in-fact. A real estate broker typically does *not* have this scope of authority as an agent in a real estate transaction.

> A general agent represents the principal *generally*; a special agent represents the principal only for *special occasions*, such as the sale of a house.

A **general agent** may represent the principal in a broad range of matters related to a particular business or activity. The general agent may, for example, bind the principal to any contract within the scope of the agent's authority. A property manager typically is a general agent for the owner.

A **special agent** or *limited agent* is authorized to represent the principal in *one specific act or business transaction only, under detailed instructions*. A real estate broker is usually a special agent. If hired by a seller, the broker is limited to finding a ready, willing, and able buyer for the property. A special agent for a buyer would have the limited responsibility of finding a property that fits the buyer's criteria. As a special agent, the broker may not bind the principal to any contract. A *special power of attorney* is another means of authorizing an agent to carry out only a specified act or acts.

■ **FOR EXAMPLE** You are very busy with an important project, so you give your colleague $5 and ask him to buy your lunch. Your colleague is your *general agent:* You have limited his scope of activity to a particular business (buying your lunch) and established the amount that may be spent (up to $5). Still, he has broad discretion in selecting what you will eat and where he will buy it. However, if you had told your colleague, "Please buy me a Number 3 salad at Lettuce Eat Lettuce," you would have further limited his authority to a very specific task. Your colleague, therefore, would have been your *special agent.*

Finally, a **designated agent** (or *designated representative*) is a person authorized by the broker to act as the agent of a specific principal. A designated agent is the only agent in the company who has a fiduciary responsibility toward the principal. When one salesperson in the company is a designated agent, the others are free to act as agents for the other party in a transaction. Thus, two salespersons from the same real estate company may end up representing opposite sides in a property sale. In designated agency situations, the broker is often put in the position of being a dual agent, so disclosure of that status is required. Again, the availability of designated agency varies from state to state. Licensees should be sure to find out their states' positions on designated agency.

Single Agency

In single agency, the agent represents only one party in any single transaction. The agent owes either fiduciary or statutory duties exclusively to one principal, who may be *either* the buyer or the seller (or the landlord or tenant) in a transaction. Any third party is a customer. (See Figure 4.1.)

FIGURE   4.1

Single Agency

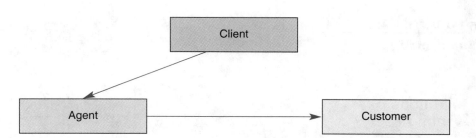

While a single agency broker may represent both sellers and buyers, he or she cannot represent both in the same transaction and remain a single agent. This avoids conflicts and results in client-based service and loyalty to only one client. On the other hand, it traditionally rules out the sale of in-house listings to represented buyers, although in designated agency states this may be permitted. The broker must establish policies for the firm that define for whom the client services are performed.

Seller as principal. If a seller contracts with a broker to market the seller's real estate, the broker becomes an *agent* of the seller; the seller is the *principal*, the broker's *client*. In single agency, a buyer who contacts the broker to review properties listed with the broker's firm is the broker's *customer*. Though obligated to deal fairly with all parties to a transaction and to comply with all aspects of the license law, the broker is strictly accountable only to the principal—in this case, the seller. The customer (in this case, the buyer) represents himself or herself.

The listing contract usually authorizes the broker to use licensees employed by the broker, as well as the services of other cooperating brokers in marketing the seller's real estate. These cooperating brokers may assist the broker (agent) as subagents, buyer's agents, or nonagents, or they may be the agents for other parties.

The relationship of a salesperson or an associate broker to an employing broker is also an agency. These licensees are thus agents of the broker and owe the same fiduciary duties as the broker to the principal.

IN   PRACTICE   Under the agency statutes of some states, real estate agents are specifically prohibited from making offers of subagency through an MLS. Licensees should be aware of their states' laws regarding subagency.

Subagency. A subagency is created when one broker, usually the seller's agent, appoints other brokers (with the seller's permission) to help perform client-based functions on the principal's behalf. These *cooperating brokers* have the same fiduciary obligation to the seller as does the listing broker, helping produce a ready, willing, and able buyer for the property. This arrangement may be created through an offer of cooperation and compensation made in an MLS.

FIGURE   4.2

Subagency

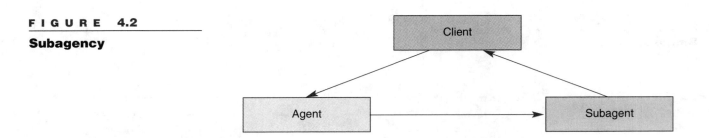

IN PRACTICE   Many broker transactions use cooperative agents. When a broker puts a seller's house in an MLS, the broker is basically inviting other agents from other companies to cooperate with the the broker in his or her representation of the seller. The broker is still the seller's agent, and the other agents are not the seller's agent. They represent the seller just as the broker does, under the broker's agency agreement. If a cooperative agent helps a broker sell a house, the broker pays the agent a co-op fee out of the broker's commission. The amount of the fee is noted in the MLS listing. For example, it might say, "CC:04," meaning the cooperative commission is 4 percent.

Participation in an MLS, by itself, does not necessarily create a subagency relationship. Because of widespread agency reforms, a cooperating broker cannot be presumed to be a subagent. The listing broker is liable for the conduct of all of the subagents and their salespersons. (See Figure 4.2.)

■ **FOR EXAMPLE**   If you give your colleague $5 and ask him to buy your lunch, your colleague is your *agent.* If your colleague is busy, he may hand your money to a friend, along with your instructions. The friend is a *subagent*—an agent of your agent. Your colleague's friend is still responsible for buying *your* lunch in accordance with *your* instructions. The subagent, like the agent, is ultimately responsible to you, the principal.

Buyer as principal. When a buyer contracts with a broker to locate property and represent his or her interests in a transaction, the buyer is the *principal*—the broker's client. The broker, as *agent,* is strictly accountable to the buyer. The seller is the customer.

In the past, it was simple: Brokers always represented sellers, and buyers were expected to look out for themselves. With the widespread use of MLSs and subagency, a buyer often had the mistaken impression that the subagent was the buyer's agent, although the reality was that both agent and subagent represented the seller's interests.

Today, however, most residential brokers and salespersons are discovering opportunities of buyer representation. Some brokers and salespersons have become specialists in the emerging field of buyer brokerage, representing buyers exclusively. Real estate commissions or boards across the country have developed rules and procedures to regulate such *buyer's brokers,* and local real estate associations develop agency representation forms and other materials for them to use. Professional organizations offer assistance, certification, training, and networking opportunities for **buyer's agents.**

A buyer agency relationship is established in the same way as any other agency relationship: by contract or agreement. The buyer's agent may receive a flat fee or a share of the commission or both, depending on the terms of the agency agreement. Buyer brokerage and buyer agency agreements are discussed in Chapter 6.

Owner as principal: property management. An owner may employ a broker to market, lease, maintain or manage the owner's property. Such an arrangement is known as *property management*. The broker is made the agent of the property owner through a property management agreement. As in any other agency relationship, the broker has a fiduciary or statutory responsibility to the client-owner. Sometimes, an owner may employ a broker for the sole purpose of marketing the property to prospective tenants. In this case, the broker's responsibility is limited to finding suitable tenants for the owner's property. Property management is discussed further in Chapter 17.

Dual Agency

In **dual agency** (sometimes called *limited agency*), the agent represents two principals in the same transaction. Dual agency requires equal loyalty to two separate principals at the same time. Because agency originates with the broker, dual agency arises when the broker is the agent of the buyer *and* either the agent or subagent of the seller. The salespersons, as agents of the broker, have fiduciary or statutory responsibilities to the same principals as well. The challenge is to fulfill the fiduciary or statutory obligations to one principal without compromising the interests of the other, especially when the parties' interests may not only be separate, but even opposite. While practical methods of ensuring fairness and equal representation may exist, it should be noted that a dual agent can never fully represent either party's interests. (See Figure 4.3.)

Because of the obvious risks inherent in dual agency—ranging from conflicts of interest to outright abuse of trust—the practice is illegal in some states. In those states where dual agency is permitted, however, all parties must consent to it, usually in writing.

▨ **FOR EXAMPLE** Mary, a real estate broker, is the agent for the owner of Roomy Manor, a large mansion. Jody, a prospective buyer, comes into Mary's office and asks Mary to represent her in her search for a modest home. After several weeks of activity, including two offers unsuccessfully negotiated by Mary, Jody spots the For Sale sign in front of Roomy Manor. She tells Mary she wants to make an offer and asks for Mary's advice on a likely price range. Mary is now in the difficult position of being a dual agent: Mary represents the seller (who naturally is interested in receiving the highest possible price) and the buyer (who is interested in making a successful low offer).

Disclosed dual agency. Real estate licensing laws may permit dual agency only if the buyer and seller are *informed* and *consent* to the broker's representation of both in the same transaction. Although the possibility of conflict of interest still exists, disclosure is intended to minimize the risk for the broker by ensuring that both principals are aware of the effect of dual agency on their respective interests. The disclosure alerts the principals that they may have to

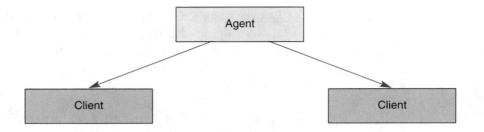

assume greater responsibility for protecting their interests than they would if they had independent representation. The broker must reconcile how, as agent, he or she will discharge the fiduciary duties on behalf of both principals, particularly providing loyalty and protecting confidential information. Because the duties of disclosure and confidentiality are limited by mutual agreement, they must be carefully explained to the parties in order to establish "informed consent."

Dual agency has existed in everyday real estate practice in every state for more than a century. In small, mostly rural market areas, there was often only one broker available. Because of the limited population of the market, the broker knew most of the local properties and residents (and possibly their parents and grandparents) very well. In situations like this, it was virtually impossible to avoid dual agency. Of course, in such circumstances, there is usually no problem because the parties all know and trust each other. Such situations are rare today, having been complicated by changes in society and in the license laws.

Designated agency is a process that accommodates an "in-house" sale where two different agents are involved. The broker designates one agent to represent the seller, and one agent to represent the buyer. Designated agency is currently legal in about half the states. However, designated agency does not apply to a single agent who represents both parties at the same in the same transaction.

Undisclosed dual agency. A broker may not intend to create a dual agency. However, like any other agency, it may occur *unintentionally* or *inadvertently*. Sometimes the cause is carelessness. Other times a salesperson does not fully understand his or her fiduciary responsibilities. Some salespersons lose sight of other responsibilities when they focus intensely on bringing buyers and sellers together. For instance, a salesperson representing the seller might suggest to a buyer that the seller will accept less than the listing price. Or that same salesperson might promise to persuade the seller to accept an offer that is in the buyer's best interests. *Giving a buyer any specific advice on how much to offer can lead him or her to believe that the salesperson represents the buyer's interests and is acting as the buyer's advocate.*

Any of these actions can create an *implied* agency with the buyer and violate the duties of loyalty and confidentiality to the principal-seller. Because neither party has been informed of the situation and been given the opportunity to seek separate representation, the interests of both are jeopardized. This undisclosed dual agency violates licensing laws. It can result in the rescission of the sales contract, forfeiture of a commission, a lawsuit for damages, and possible license problems.

■ **FOR EXAMPLE** Using the previous Roomy Manor example, if Mary doesn't tell Jody that Mary represents the seller of the property, Mary will be an undisclosed dual agent. Mary has two options. First, knowing Jody's comfortable financial situation and intense desire for the property, Mary might choose not to tell Jody about the dual agency situation. Instead, Mary could tell her that Roomy Manor's owner will accept nothing less than the full asking price. While this will ensure that Mary receives the maximum possible commission, it will also subject Mary to severe penalties for violating the state's licensing laws. Alternatively, Mary may disclose her relationship with the seller and work out a dual agency agreement with both parties in which Mary legally represents both parties' interests.

A more common example of dual agency would be if Mary employed two salespersons, Ryan and Sally. Ryan is the listing salesperson for Roomy Manor, and Sally meets and begins representing the buyer, Jody. Because both Ryan and Sally are associated with Mary's real estate brokerage, Mary may be construed as a dual agent and will have to enter into a disclosed dual agency agreement with the parties.

Disclosure of Agency

Licensees are required to reveal for whom they provide client-based services. Understanding the scope of the service a party can expect from the agent allows a customer to make an informed decision about whether to seek his or her own representation.

Mandatory agency disclosure laws now exist in every state. These laws stipulate when, how, and to whom disclosures must be made. They may, for instance, dictate that a particular type of written form be used. The laws might state what information an agent must provide to gain informed consent where disclosed dual agency is permitted. The laws might even go so far as to require that all agency alternatives be explained, including the brokerage firm's policies regarding its services. Frequently, printed brochures outlining agency alternatives are available to a firm's clients and customers.

Whether or not the law requires it, licensees should explain to both buyers and sellers what agency alternatives exist, how client and customer services differ, and how these services affect the interests of each party. Once a client-based relationship is established, it is critical that customers understand how this affects their interests. If the broker represents two principals in the same transaction, the impact on both parties must be explained. A general rule of thumb is to make the disclosure before any confidential information is disclosed about an individual's motivation or financial situation. (See Figure 4.4.)

Agency Statutes

A rapidly growing number of state legislatures are enacting agency reform legislation. Such laws are either in place or under consideration in most states. While each state's agency statute is different, many still incorporate the common-law fiduciary principles discussed here. For instance, most statutes contain language requiring agents to

- exercise reasonable *care* and skill in performing his or her duties,
- *obey* the client's specific directions,
- *account* for all money and property received,
- promote the client's best interests at all times (i.e., *loyalty*),

Agency Disclosure Form

DISCLOSURE OF BROKERAGE RELATIONSHIP

THIS IS NOT A CONTRACT; IT DOES NOT CREATE AN OBLIGATION

In connection with this transaction, whether purchase, sale, lease or option,
the client of the Broker/Firm is: *(check one)*

☐ Seller   ☐ Buyer

☐ Lessor (Landlord)   ☐ Lessee (Tenant)

☐ Optionor   ☐ Optionee

The duties of real estate licensees in Virginia are set forth in Section 54.1-2130 et seq. of the Code of Virginia and in the regulations of the Virginia Real Estate Board. You should be aware that in addition to the information contained in this disclosure pertaining to brokerage relationships, there may be other information relative to the transaction which may be obtained from other sources. Each party should carefully read all documents to assure that the terms accurately express his or her understanding and intent. Licensees can counsel on real estate matters, but if legal or tax advice is desired, you should consult an attorney or a financial professional.

_____   _____

Date   Name   Date   Name

_____   _____

Date   Name   Date   Name

_____   _____

Brokerage Firm   Sales Associate

NVAR - 1207 - 10/00

Source: Reprinted with permission from the Northern Virginia Associations of REALTORS®, Inc. (NVAR), for educational purposes only. Any other use of these forms without the express written consent of NVAR is strictly prohibited.

- *disclose* material facts concerning the transaction,
- perform according to the terms of the brokerage agreement,
- keep confidential all confidential information received from the client, and
- generally comply with the terms of the statute.

If a state's agency law does not specifically replace the common law of agency, a licensee will be subject to the requirements of both the statute and common law.

■ CUSTOMER-LEVEL SERVICES

Even though an agent's primary responsibility is to the principal, the agent also has duties to third parties. Any time a licensee works with a third party, or *customer*, the licensee is responsible for adhering to state and federal consumer protection laws as well as the ethical requirements imposed by professional associations and state regulators. In addition, the licensee's duties to the customer include

> An agent owes a *customer* the duties of *reasonable care and skill; honest and fair dealing;* and *disclosure of known facts.*

- reasonable care and skill in performance,
- honest and fair dealing; and
- disclosure of all facts that the licensee knows or should reasonably be expected to know that materially affect the value or desirability of the property.

As part of the recent trend toward public protection of purchasers, many states now have statutes requiring disclosure of property conditions to prospective buyers. Prepurchase structural inspections, termite infestation reports, or other protective documentation may also be used. The actual disclosures that sellers are required to make vary according to each state's law.

Environmental Hazards

Disclosure of environmental health hazards, which can render properties unusable for the buyer's intended purpose, may be required. For instance, federal law requires the disclosure of lead-based paint hazards. Frequently, the buyer or the buyer's mortgage lender requests inspections or tests to determine the presence or level of risk.

IN PRACTICE

Licensees are urged to obtain advice from state and local authorities responsible for environmental regulation whenever the following conditions may be present: toxic waste dumping; underground storage tanks; contaminated soil or water; nearby chemical or nuclear facilities; and health hazards such as radon, asbestos, and lead paint.

Opinion versus Fact

Brokers, salespersons, and other staff members must always be careful about the statements they make. They must be sure that the customer understands whether the statement is an opinion or a fact. Statements of opinion are permissible only as long as they are offered as opinions and without any intention to deceive.

Statements of fact, however, must be accurate. Exaggeration of a property's benefits is called **puffing.** While puffing is legal, licensees must ensure that none of their statements can be interpreted as fraudulent. **Fraud** is the *intentional misrepresentation* of a material fact in such a way as to harm or take advantage of another person. That includes not only making false statements about a property but also intentionally concealing or failing to disclose important facts.

The misrepresentation or omission does not have to be intentional to result in broker liability. A **negligent misrepresentation** occurs when the broker *should have known* that a statement about a material fact was false. The fact that the broker may actually be ignorant about the issue is no excuse. If the buyer relies on the broker's statement, the broker is liable for any damages that result. Similarly, if a broker accidentally fails to perform some act—for instance, if he or she forgets to deliver a counteroffer—the broker may be liable for damages that result from such a negligent omission.

■ **FOR EXAMPLE** While showing a potential buyer a very average-looking house, broker Dan described even its plainest features as "charming" and "beautiful." Because the statements were obviously Dan's personal opinions designed to encourage a positive feeling about the property (or puff it up), their truth or falsity is not an issue.

Broker Gil was asked by a potential buyer if a particular neighborhood was safe. Although Gil knew that the area was experiencing a skyrocketing rate of violent crime, Gil assured the buyer that no problem existed. Gil also neglected to inform the buyer that the lot next to the house the buyer was considering had been sold to a waste disposal company for use as a toxic dump. Both may be examples of fraudulent misrepresentation.

If a contract to purchase real estate is obtained as a result of fraudulent misstatements, the contract may be disaffirmed or renounced by the purchaser. In such a case, the broker not only loses a commission but can be liable for damages if either party suffers loss because of the misrepresentation. If the licensee's misstatements were based on the owner's own inaccurate statements and the licensee had no independent duty to investigate their accuracy, the broker may be entitled to a commission, even if the buyer rescinds the sales contract.

Latent Defects

The seller has a duty to discover and disclose any known latent defects that threaten structural soundness or personal safety. A **latent defect** is a *hidden structural defect that would not be discovered by ordinary inspection*. Buyers have been able to either rescind the sales contract or receive damages when a seller fails to reveal known latent defects. For instance, sellers were found liable where a house was built over a ditch covered with decaying timber; a buried drain tile caused water to accumulate; and a driveway was built partly on adjoining property. The courts also have decided in favor of the buyer when the seller neglected to reveal violations of zoning or building codes.

In addition to the seller's duty to disclose latent defects, in some states the agent has an independent duty to conduct a reasonably competent and diligent inspection of the property. It is the licensee's duty to discover any material facts that may affect the property's value or desirability, whether or not they are known to or disclosed by the seller. Any such material facts discovered by the licensee must be disclosed to prospective buyers. If the licensee should have known about a substantial defect that is detected later by the buyer, the agent may be liable to the buyer for any damages resulting from that defect.

■ **FOR EXAMPLE** Broker Kim knew that a house had been built on a landfill. A few days after the house was listed, one of Kim's salespersons noticed that the living room floor was uneven and sagging in places. Both Kim and the salesperson have a duty to conduct further investigations into the structural soundness of the property. They cannot simply ignore the problem or place throw rugs over particularly bad spots and hope buyers won't look underneath.

Stigmatized Properties

In recent years, questions have been raised about *stigmatized properties*—properties that society has branded undesirable because of events that occurred there or because of a sexual offender who currently lives in an area. While the specifics may vary from state to state, under Megan's Law, residents are notified when a sexual offender is released to and resides in an area. The residence of a known sexual offender can deem a property stigmatized because buyers may not want to live in that vicinity.

However, the more common stigma is a criminal event, such as homicide, illegal drug manufacturing, gang-related activity, or a tragedy, such as suicide. Properties have even been stigmatized by rumors that they are haunted. Because of the potential liability to a licensee for inadequately researching and disclosing material facts concerning a property's condition, licensees should seek competent counsel when dealing with a stigmatized property.

Some states have laws regarding the disclosure of information about such properties, designed to protect sellers and local property values against a baseless psychological reaction. In other states, the licensee's responsibility may be difficult to define because the issue is not a physical defect but merely a perception that a property is undesirable. The stigmatized property issue can be even more complicated: In some cultures, a house in which someone has died is considered uninhabitable. While licensees must not discriminate based on nationality, culture, or religious beliefs, state laws on stigmatized properties may put the agent in an awkward position. That's why getting competent legal counsel is important.

IN PRACTICE

A disclosure that a property's previous owner or occupant died of AIDS or was HIV-positive constitutes illegal discrimination against the handicapped under the federal Fair Housing Act, discussed in Chapter 20.

 **WWWeb.Link**

www.ired.com   www.law.cornell.edu/states/index.html

■ SUMMARY

The law of agency governs the principal-agent relationship. Agency relationships may be expressed either by the words of the parties or by written agreement or may be implied by the parties' actions. In single-agency relationships, the broker or agent represents one party, either the buyer or the seller, in the transaction. If the agent elicits the assistance of other brokers who cooperate in the transaction, the other brokers may become subagents of the principal. Many states have adopted statutes that replace the common-law of agency and that establish the responsibilities and duties of the parties.

Representing two opposing parties in the same transaction constitutes dual agency. Licensees must be careful not to create dual agency when none was intended. This unintentional or inadvertent dual agency can result in the sales contract being rescinded and the commission being forfeited or in a lawsuit. Disclosed dual agency requires that both principals be informed of and consent to the broker's multiple representation. In any case, the prospective parties in the transaction should be informed about the agency alternatives and how client-level versus customer-level services differ. Many states have mandatory agency disclosure laws. The source of compensation for the client services does not determine which party is represented.

Licensees have certain duties and obligations to their customers as well. Consumers are entitled to fair and honest dealings and to the information necessary for them to make informed decisions. This includes accurate information about the property. Some states have mandatory property disclosure laws.

QUESTIONS

1. In a real estate transaction, the term *fiduciary* typically refers to the
   a. sale of real property.
   b. person who gives someone else the legal power to act on his or her behalf.
   c. person who has legal power to act on behalf of another.
   d. agent's relationship to the principal.

2. The relationship between broker and seller is generally what type of agency?
   a. Special
   b. General
   c. Implied
   d. Universal

3. Which of the following statements is true of a real estate broker acting as the agent of the seller?
   a. The broker is obligated to render faithful service to the seller.
   b. The broker can disclose confidential information about the seller to a buyer if it increases the likelihood of a sale.
   c. The broker can agree to a change in price without the seller's approval.
   d. The broker can accept a commission from the buyer without the seller's approval.

4. Alan, a real estate broker, lists Miranda's home for $189,500. Later that same day, Claude comes into Alan's office and asks for general information about homes for sale in the $130,000 to $140,000 price range but refuses representation by Alan's company at this time. Based on these facts, which of the following statements is true?
   a. Both Miranda and Claude are Alan's customers.
   b. Miranda is Alan's client; Claude is a customer.
   c. Alan owes fiduciary duties to both Miranda and Claude.
   d. If Claude later asks for buyer representation by Alan's firm, he cannot have it because of the firm's earlier agreement with Miranda.

5. In a dual agency situation, a broker may collect a commission from both the seller and the buyer if
   a. the broker informs either the buyer or the seller that he or she will receive a commission from both parties.
   b. the buyer and the seller are related by blood or marriage.
   c. both parties give their informed consent, usually in writing, to the dual compensation.
   d. both parties are represented by attorneys.

6. Which of the following events will terminate an agency in a broker-seller relationship?
   a. The broker discovers that the market value of the property is such that he or she will not make an adequate commission.
   b. The owner declares personal bankruptcy.
   c. The owner abandons the property.
   d. The broker appoints other brokers to help sell the property.

7. Confidentiality is part of which of the following fiduciary duties?
   a. Care
   b. Obedience
   c. Disclosure
   d. Loyalty

8. A real estate broker hired by an owner to sell a parcel of real estate must comply with
   a. the common law of agency, even if a state agency statute exists.
   b. dual agency requirements.
   c. the concept of caveat emptor.
   d. all lawful instructions of the owner.

9. A licensee is hired as a buyer's agent by a first-time buyer to help the buyer purchase a home. The buyer confides that being approved for a mortgage loan may be complicated by the fact that the buyer filed for bankruptcy two years ago. A correct statement about the licensee's responsibility regarding this information during the presentation of an offer to purchase a property is that the licensee is

a. required to disclose it under the Fair Credit Registry Act.
b. required to disclose it because it is a material fact—information important to the seller's evaluation of the offer.
c. not required to disclose it because the seller might reject the offer.
d. not required to disclose it because the licensee has no agency relationship with the seller.

10. A licensee lists a residence. For various reasons, the owner must sell the house quickly and confides to the licensee that a lower price would probably be acceptable, although the asking price is reasonable. To expedite the sale, the licensee tells a prospective purchaser that the seller will accept up to $5,000 less than the asking price for the property. Based on these facts, which of the following statements is true?

a. The licensee has not violated any agency responsibilities to the seller.
b. The licensee should have disclosed this information, regardless of its accuracy.
c. The disclosure was improper—and possibly illegal—regardless of the licensee's motive.
d. The relationship between the licensee and the seller ends automatically if the purchaser submits an offer.

11. A buyer who is a client of the broker wants to purchase a house that the broker has listed for sale. Which of the following statements is true?

a. The broker may proceed to write an offer on the property and submit it.
b. The broker should refer the buyer to another broker to negotiate the sale.
c. The seller and buyer must be informed of the situation and agree, usually in writing, to the broker's representing both of them.
d. The buyer should not have been shown a house listed by the broker.

12. What does the phrase *the law of agency is a common-law doctrine* mean?

a. It is a legal doctrine that is not unusual.
b. It is one of the rules of society enacted by legislatures and other governing bodies.
c. It is part of a body of law established by tradition and court decisions.
d. It may not be superseded by statutory law.

13. A seller lists a home with a licensee for $98,000. Later that week, the licensee's neighbor comes into the broker's office, declines buyer representation, and asks for general information about homes for sale in the $90,000 to $100,000 price range. Based on these facts, which of the following statements is true?

a. Both the seller and the buyer are the broker's customers.
b. The seller is the broker's customer; the buyer is a client.
c. The buyer is the broker's customer; the seller is the broker's client.
d. If the buyer asks the broker to present an offer to the seller, the broker must ask both parties to sign a disclosed dual agency agreement.

14. A real estate licensee was representing a buyer. At their first meeting, the buyer explained that he planned to operate a dog-grooming business out of any house he bought. The licensee did not check the local zoning ordinances to determine in which parts of town such a business could be conducted. Which common-law duty did the licensee violate?

a. Care
b. Obedience
c. Loyalty
d. Disclosure

15. Broker Ben tells a prospective buyer, "This property has the most beautiful river view." In fact, the view includes the river and the back of a shopping center. In a separate transaction, Broker Betty fails to mention to some enthusiastic potential buyers that a six-lane highway is planned for construction within ten feet of a house the buyers think is perfect. Based on these facts, which of the following statements is true?

a. Broker Ben has committed fraud.
b. Broker Betty has committed puffing.
c. Both Broker Ben and Broker Betty are guilty of intentional misrepresentation.
d. Broker Ben is merely puffing; Broker Betty has misrepresented the property.

CHAPTER FIVE

5

REAL ESTATE BROKERAGE

■ **LEARNING OBJECTIVES** *When you've finished reading this Chapter, you should be able to:*

■ **identify** the role of technologies, personnel, and license laws in the operation of a real estate business.

■ **describe** the various types of antitrust violations common in the real estate industry and the penalties involved with each.

■ **explain** how a broker's compensation is usually determined.

■ **distinguish** employees from independent contractors and explain why the distinction is important.

■ **define** the following *key terms:*

antitrust laws	employee	ready, willing, and able
brokerage	independent contractor	buyer
commission	procuring cause	transactional broker

■ **WHY LEARN ABOUT...** REAL ESTATE BROKERAGE?

Real estate is an industry driven by small businesses. Most brokerages are not giant national companies, and even those that are members of large franchises are still small businesses at heart, run locally to serve what is essentially a local market. Like any small business, there are challenges and advantages. To be successful, a licensee has to know not only his or her product, real estate, but also how to run a business. There are financial challenges to running any operation, as well as personnel issues such as how many people to hire and in what capacity. What jobs need to be done, and what kinds of people are needed to do them best? Who are you competing with, and how can you successfully thrive in a marketplace with 5, 10, 20, or more different brokerages all competing for the same piece of the pie? The answers to these questions are not easy ones, but a successful licensee needs to think of himself or herself as a businessperson, not just as an agent. ■

■ THE HISTORY OF BROKERAGE

The nature of real estate brokerage services, particularly those provided in residential sales transactions, has changed significantly in recent years. Through the 1950s, real estate brokerage firms were primarily one-office, minimally-staffed, family-run operations. The broker listed an owner's property for sale and found a buyer without assistance from other brokerage companies. The sale was eventually negotiated and closed. It was relatively clear that the broker represented the seller's interests. The common-law doctrine of *caveat emptor* ("let the buyer beware") was the rule; buyers were pretty much on their own.

In the 1960s, however, the way buyers and sellers were brought together in real estate transactions began to change. Brokers started to share information about properties they listed, resulting in two brokers cooperating to sell a property. The brokers formalized this exchange of information by creating multiple-listing services (MLSs). The MLS expedited sales by increasing a single property's exposure to a greater number of potential buyers. Because it resulted in more sales, the MLS quickly became a widely used industry service. But one thing stayed the same: Both brokers still represented the seller's interest.

While this arrangement benefited sellers, buyers came to question whether their interests were being protected. They began to demand not only accurate, factual information but also objective advice, particularly in the face of increasingly complex real estate transactions. Buyers view the real estate licensee as the expert on whom they can rely for guidance. In short, buyers have begun to seek not only protection but representation as well. Almost all states recognize buyer agency today, and a large percentage of sales contracts are written by buyer agents.

■ REAL ESTATE LICENSE LAWS

All 50 states, the District of Columbia, and all Canadian provinces license and regulate the activities of real estate brokers and salespersons. While the laws share a common purpose, the details vary from state to state. Uniform policies and standards for administering and enforcing state license laws are promoted by an organization of state license law officials known as ARELLO, the Association of Real Estate License Law Officials.

Purpose of License Laws

Real estate license laws have been enacted to protect the public by ensuring a standard of competence and professionalism in the real estate industry. The laws achieve this goal by

- ■ establishing basic requirements for obtaining a real estate license and, in many cases, requiring continuing education to keep a license;
- ■ defining which activities require licensing;
- ■ describing the acceptable standards of conduct and practice for licensees; and
- ■ enforcing those standards through a disciplinary system.

The purpose of these laws is not merely to regulate the real estate industry. Their main objective is to make sure that the rights of purchasers, sellers, tenants, and owners are protected from unscrupulous or sloppy practices. *The laws are not intended to prevent licensees from conducting their businesses successfully or to interfere in legitimate transactions.* Laws cannot create an ethical or a moral marketplace. However, by establishing minimum levels of competency and the limits of permitted behavior, laws can make the marketplace safer and more honest.

Each state has a licensing authority—a commission, a department, a division, a board, or an agency—for real estate brokers and salespersons. This authority has the power to issue licenses, make real estate information available to licensees and the public, and enforce the statutory real estate law.

Each licensing authority has also adopted a set of administrative rules and regulations that further define the statutory law. The rules and regulations provide for administering the law and set operating guidelines for licensees. *The rules and regulations have the same force and effect as any law.* Both the law and the rules are usually enforced through fines and the denial, suspension, or revocation of licenses. Civil and criminal court actions can be brought against violators in some serious cases.

IN PRACTICE   Each state's real estate license laws and the rules and regulations of its real estate commission or board establish the framework for all of a licensee's activities. *It is vital that each licensee have a clear and comprehensive understanding of his or her state's laws and regulations, not only for purposes of the licensing examination, but to ensure that the licensee's practice of real estate is both legal and successful.*

■ REAL ESTATE BROKERAGE

Brokerage is simply the business of bringing parties together. Mortgage brokers match lenders with borrowers; stockbrokers bring together investors and corporations; customs brokers help importers navigate through complex customs procedures. A *real estate broker* is defined as a person licensed to buy, sell, exchange, or lease real property for others and to charge a fee for these services.

A brokerage business may take many forms. It may be a *sole proprietorship* (a single-owner company), a corporation, or a partnership with another broker. The office may be independent or part of a regional or national franchise. The business may consist of a single office or multiple branches. The broker's office may be located in a downtown highrise, a suburban shopping center, or the broker's home. A typical real estate brokerage may specialize in one kind of transaction or service or may offer an array of services.

No matter what form it takes, however, a real estate brokerage has the same demands, expenses, and rewards as any other small business. The real estate industry, after all, is made up of thousands of small businesses operating in defined local markets. A real estate broker faces the same challenges as an entrepreneur in any other industry. In addition to mastering the complexities of real estate transactions, the broker must be able to handle the day-to-day details of running a business. He or she must set effective policies for every aspect of the brokerage operation: maintaining space and equipment, hiring employees and salespersons, determining compensation, directing staff and sales activities, and implementing procedures to follow in carrying out agency duties. Each state's real estate license laws and regulations establish the business activities and methods of doing business that are permitted.

IN PRACTICE

At each step in a real estate transaction, the broker should advise the parties to secure legal counsel to protect their interests. *Although real estate brokers and salespersons may bring buyers and sellers together, and in most states may fill in preprinted blank purchase agreement forms, only an attorney may offer legal advice or prepare legal documents. Licensees who are not attorneys are prohibited from practicing law.*

Real Estate Assistants

A *real estate assistant* (also known as a *personal assistant* or *professional assistant*) is a combination office manager, marketer, organizer, and facilitator with a fundamental understanding of the real estate industry. An assistant may or may not have a real estate license, depending on state law. The extent to which the assistant can help the broker or salesperson with transactions is often determined by state license laws. Depending on state law, an assistant may perform duties ranging from clerical and secretarial functions to office management, telemarketing, market strategy development, and direct contact with clients and customers. A licensed assistant can set up and host open houses and assist in all aspects of a real estate transaction.

Technology

In addition to assistants, a wide range of technologies is available to help a real estate licensee do his or her job more efficiently and effectively. Computers are a necessary ingredient in any modern real estate brokerage.

Licensees can find community and mortgage information on the Internet via services such as America Online, Internet Explorer, and Prodigy. Multiple-listing and homefinder services are available to real estate professionals through their professional associations. Numerous software packages have been designed specifically for real estate professionals. Some of these programs help real estate brokers and salespersons with such office management tasks as billing, accounting, and timekeeping. Other software assists with marketing and advertising properties and services and with designing and producing flyers, business cards, pamphlets, and other promotional materials.

In some states, continuing education requirements can be met through the use of specially designed continuing education software. Real estate Web sites, home pages, and computer networks help licensees keep in touch, and some cable and satellite television channels are dedicated solely to real estate programming for both consumers and professionals.

The Internet has brought tremendous change to the real estate industry. Real estate practitioners and consumers rely heavily on Internet usage for a variety of services. Many real estate agencies have Web sites that provide extraordinary search databases for property and other searches.

The Internet is a powerful tool for consumers in finding information about properties, relocation services, and particular communities. Typically, real estate Web site information is updated daily. Many of the Web sites also have "disclaimers," indicating that the material on their site is solely for informational purposes and that no warranties or representations have been made.

E-mail is yet another powerful tool making communication between real estate agents and consumers much more efficient. Gone are the days of playing phone tag. Instead, sending a quick e-mail message saves both agents and consumers valuable time. A real estate agent should be prepared for consumers who primarily want to communicate through the use of e-mail.

Real estate brokers and salespersons can carry laptop computers with portable modems that link them with their offices or the Web, an MLS, or a mortgage company from virtually anywhere. Portable fax machines, pagers, and cellular phones make licensees available to their offices and clients 24 hours a day. Voice-mail systems can track caller response to advertisements and give callers information about specific properties when the broker or salesperson is unavailable. Yard signs are available that broadcast details about a property on an AM radio band, so drivers passing by can tune in for tempting information. And handheld PDAs (personal digital assistants) help licensees manage time much more effectively. In fact, PDAs can serve many functions, including use as a portable database of an MLS listing and as a place for storing information on prospective buyer's comments on a home, which then can be forwarded to the seller.

All this technology is a great boon to practitioners, but real estate brokers and salespersons must make careful decisions about which technologies best suit their needs. Furthermore, they must keep up with the rapidly changing world of high-tech real estate tools to remain competitive.

IN PRACTICE Home listings are available to the general public on the Internet, through real estate agency Web sites, and other sites such as CyberHomes (http://www.cyberhomes.com) and NAR (http://www.realtor.com). By accessing these services, potential buyers can preview photographs of properties and narrow their searches by price range, number of bedrooms, amenities, neighborhood, or school district.

Broker-Salesperson Relationship

Although brokerage firms vary widely in size, few brokers today perform their duties without the assistance of salespersons. Consequently, much of the business's success hinges on the broker-salesperson relationship.

A *real estate salesperson* is any person licensed to perform real estate activities on behalf of a licensed real estate broker. The broker is fully responsible for the actions performed in the course of the real estate business by all persons licensed under the broker. In turn, all of a salesperson's activities must be performed in the name of the supervising broker. The salesperson can carry out *only* those responsibilities assigned by the broker with whom he or she is affiliated and can receive compensation *only* from that broker. As an agent of the broker, the salesperson has no authority to make contracts with or receive compensation from any other party. The broker is liable for the acts of the salesperson within the scope of the employment agreement.

Independent contractor versus employee. The employment agreement between a broker and a salesperson should define the nature, obligations, and responsibilities of the relationship. Essentially, the salesperson may be either an *employee* or an *independent contractor*. State license laws generally treat the salesperson as the employee of the affiliate broker, regardless of whether the salesperson is considered to be an employee or an independent contractor for income tax purposes. Whether a salesperson is treated as an employee or an independent contractor affects the structure of the salesperson's responsibilities and the broker's liability to pay and withhold taxes from the salesperson's earnings.

A broker can exercise certain *controls* over salespersons who are employees. The broker may require an **employee** to follow rules governing such matters as working hours, office routine, attendance at sales meetings, assignment of sales quotas, and adherence to dress codes. As an employer, a broker is required by the federal government to withhold Social Security tax and income tax from wages paid to employees. The broker is also required to pay unemployment compensation tax on wages paid to one or more employees, as defined by state and federal laws. In addition, employees might receive benefits such as health insurance, profit-sharing plans, and worker's compensation.

A broker's relationship with a salesperson who is an **independent contractor** is very different. As the name implies, an independent contractor operates more independently than an employee, and a broker may not exercise the same degree of control over the salesperson's activities. While the broker may control *what* the independent contractor does, the broker cannot dictate how to do it. The broker cannot *require* the independent contractor to keep specific office hours or attend sales meetings. Independent contractors are responsible for paying their own income and Social Security taxes and receive nothing from brokers that could be construed as an employee benefit, such as health insurance or paid vacation time. As a rule, independent contractors use their own materials and equipment.

The Internal Revenue Service often investigates the independent contractor/employee situation in real estate offices. Under the *qualified real estate agent* category in the Internal Revenue Code, meeting the following three requirements can establish an independent contractor status:

1. The individual must have a current real estate license.
2. He or she must have a written contract with the broker that specifies that the salesperson will not be treated as an employee for federal tax purposes.
3. At least 90 percent of the individual's income as a licensee must be based on sales production and not on the number of hours worked.

IN PRACTICE

A broker should have a standardized employment agreement drafted and reviewed by an attorney to ensure its compliance with federal law. The broker should also be aware that written agreements carry little weight with an IRS auditor if the actions of the parties contradict the provisions of the contract. Specific legal and tax questions regarding independent contractors should be referred to a competent attorney or accountant.

WWWeb.Link

www.irs.gov

Broker's Compensation

The broker's compensation is specified in the contract with the principal. License laws may stipulate that a written agreement must establish the compensation to be paid. Compensation can be in the form of a **commission** or brokerage fee (computed as a percentage of the total sales price), a flat fee, or an hourly rate. *The amount of a broker's commission is negotiable in every case.* Attempting, however subtly, to impose uniform commission rates is a clear violation of state and federal antitrust laws (discussed later in this Chapter). *A broker may, however, set the minimum rate acceptable for that broker's firm.* The important point is for broker and client to agree on a rate before the agency relationship is established. A commission may be any percentage of the sales price that the market will bear. Brokers in different parts of the country and in different kinds of real estate charge commissions ranging from less than 5 percent to more than 8 percent.

A commission is usually considered *earned* when the work for which the broker was hired has been accomplished. Most sales commissions are payable when the sale is consummated by *delivery of the seller's deed.* This provision is generally included in the listing agreement. When the sales or listing agreement specifies no time for the payment of the broker's commission, the commission is usually earned when

■ a completed sales contract has been executed by a ready, willing, and able buyer;

- the contract has been accepted and executed by the seller; and
- copies of the contract are in the possession of all parties.

To be entitled to a sales commission, an individual must be

- a licensed broker,
- the procuring cause of the sale, and
- employed by the buyer or seller under a valid contract.

> To be a *procuring cause*, the broker must have started a chain of events that resulted in a sale.

To be considered the **procuring cause** of a sale, the broker must have started or caused a chain of events that resulted in the sale. A broker who causes or completes such an action without a contract or without having been promised payment is a volunteer and may not legally claim compensation. Many other factors affect a broker's status as procuring cause. For instance, if the agent abandons the transaction, he or she may not be able to return and claim to have been the procuring cause. In all cases, the key is determining *who really sold the property*. Procuring cause disputes between brokers are usually settled through an arbitration hearing conducted by the local board or association. Disputes between a broker and a client may go to court, however.

> A *ready, willing, and able buyer* is one prepared to buy on the seller's terms and ready to complete the transaction.

Once a seller accepts an offer from a ready, willing, and able buyer, the broker is entitled to a commission. A **ready, willing, and able buyer** is one *prepared to buy on the seller's terms and ready to take positive steps toward consummation of the transaction*. Courts may prevent the broker from receiving a commission if the broker knew the buyer was unable to perform. If the transaction is not consummated, the broker may still be entitled to a commission if the seller

- had a change of mind and refused to sell,
- has a spouse who refused to sign the deed,
- had a title with uncorrected defects,
- committed fraud with respect to the transaction,
- was unable to deliver possession within a reasonable time,
- insisted on terms not in the listing (for example, the right to restrict the use of the property), or
- had a mutual agreement with the buyer to cancel the transaction.

In general, then, a *broker is due a commission if a sale is not consummated because of the principal's default*.

In most states, it is illegal for a broker to pay a commission to anyone other than the salesperson licensed with the broker or to another broker. Fees, commissions, or other compensation cannot be paid to unlicensed persons for services that require a real estate license. "Other compensation" includes tangible gifts, such as a new television, or other premiums, such as a vacation. This is not to be confused with referral fees paid between brokers for leads. Referral fees are legal as long as both individuals are licensed.

Salesperson's Compensation

The amount of compensation a salesperson receives is set by mutual agreement between the broker and the salesperson. A broker may agree to pay a fixed salary or a share of the commissions from transactions originated by a salesperson. In some cases, a salesperson may draw from an account against earned shares of commissions. Some brokers require salespersons to pay all or part of the expenses of advertising listed properties.

Some firms have adopted a *100 percent commission plan*. Salespersons in these offices pay a monthly service charge to their brokers to cover the costs of office space, telephones, and supervision in return for keeping 100 percent of the commissions from the sales they negotiate. The 100 percent commission salesperson pays all of his or her own expenses.

Other companies have *graduated commission splits* based on a salesperson's achieving specified production goals. For instance, a broker might agree to split commissions 50/50 up to a $25,000 salesperson's share; 60/40 for shares from $25,000 to $30,000; and so on. Commission splits as generous as 80/20 or 90/10 are possible, however, particularly for high producers.

However the salesperson's compensation is structured, only the employing broker can pay it. In cooperating transactions, the commission must first be received by the employing broker and then paid to the salesperson, unless otherwise permitted by license laws and agreed to by the employing broker.

MATH CONCEPTS

% ÷
X +

SHARING COMMISSIONS

A commission might be shared by many people: The listing broker, the listing salesperson, the selling broker, and the selling salesperson. Drawing a diagram can help you determine which person is entitled to receive what amount of the total commission.

For example, salesperson Ed, while working for broker Harry, took a listing on a $73,000 house at a 6 percent commission rate. Salesperson Tom, while working for broker Matt, found the buyer for the property. If the property sold for the listed price, the listing broker and the selling broker shared the commission equally and the selling broker kept 45 percent of what he received, how much did salesperson Tom receive? (If the broker retained 45 percent of the total commission he received, his salesperson would receive the balance: 100% – 45% = 55%.)

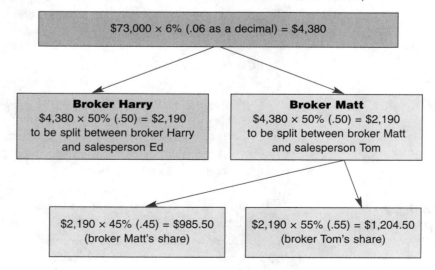

Transactional Brokerage

A **transactional broker** (also referred to as a *nonagent, facilitator, coordinator,* or *contract broker*) is not an agent of either party. A transactional broker's job is simply to help both the buyer and the seller with the necessary paperwork and formalities involved in transferring ownership of real property. The buyer and the seller negotiate the sale without representation.

The transactional broker is expected to treat all parties honestly and competently, to locate qualified buyers or suitable properties, to help the parties arrive at mutually acceptable terms, and to assist in the closing of the transaction. Transactional brokers are equally responsible to both parties and must disclose known defects in a property. However, they may not negotiate on behalf of either the buyer or the seller, and they must not disclose confidential information to either party. Transactional brokerage is legal only in a few states.

■ ANTITRUST LAWS

The real estate industry is subject to **antitrust laws.** At the federal level, the Sherman Antitrust Law provides specific penalties for a number of illegal business activities. Each state has its own antitrust laws as well. These laws prohibit monopolies and any contracts, combinations, and conspiracies that unreasonably restrain trade—that is, acts that interfere with the free flow of goods and services in a competitive marketplace. The most common antitrust violations are price-fixing, group boycotting, allocation of customers or markets, and tie-in agreements.

WWWeb.Link   www.us.doj.gov/atr

Price-Fixing

Price-fixing is the practice of setting prices for products or services rather than letting competition in the open market establish those prices. In real estate, price-fixing occurs when competing brokers agree to set sales commissions, fees, or management rates. *Price-fixing is illegal.* Brokers must independently determine commission rates or fees for their own firms only. These decisions must be based on a broker's business judgment and revenue requirements without input from other brokers.

Multiple-listing organizations, Boards of REALTORS®, and other professional organizations may not set fees or commission splits. Nor can they deny membership to brokers based on the fees the brokers charge. Either practice could lead the public to believe that the industry not only sanctions the unethical practice of withholding cooperation from certain brokers but also encourages the illegal practice of restricting open-market competition.

> **Antitrust violations include**
> - price-fixing,
> - group boycotting,
> - allocation of customers,
> - allocation of markets, and
> - tie-in agreements.

The broker's challenge is to avoid even the impression of price-fixing. Hinting to prospective clients that there is a "going rate" of commission or a "normal" fee implies that rates are, in fact, standardized. The broker must make it clear to clients that the rate stated is only what his or her firm charges.

Group Boycotting

Group boycotting occurs when two or more businesses conspire against another business or agree to withhold their patronage to reduce competition. Group boycotting is illegal under the antitrust laws.

■ **FOR EXAMPLE** Valerie and Nick, the only real estate brokers in Potterville, agree that there are too many apartment-finder services in town. They decide to refer all prospective tenants to the service operated by Valerie's niece rather than handing out a list of all providers, as they have done in the past. As a result, Valerie's niece runs the only apartment-finder service in Potterville by the end of the year.

Allocation of Customers or Markets

Allocation of customers or markets involves an agreement between brokers to divide their markets and refrain from competing for each other's business. Allocations may be made on a geographic basis, with brokers agreeing to specific territories within which they will operate exclusively. The division may also occur by markets, such as by price range or category of housing. These agreements result in reduced competition.

Tie-in Agreements

Finally, *tie-in agreements* (also known as *tying agreements*) are agreements to sell one product only if the buyer purchases another product as well. The sale of the first (desired) product is "tied" to the purchase of a second (less desirable) product.

■ **FOR EXAMPLE** Dan, a real estate broker, owns a vacant lot in a popular area of town. Bill, a builder, wants to buy the lot and build three new homes on it. Dan refuses to sell the lot to the builder unless Bill agrees to list the improved lot with Dan so that Dan can sell the homes. This sort of list-back arrangement violates antitrust laws.

Penalties

The penalties for violating antitrust laws are severe. For instance, under the Federal Sherman Antitrust Act, people who fix prices or allocate markets may be subject to a maximum $100,000 fine and three years in prison. For corporations, the penalty may be as high as $1 million. In a civil suit, a person who has suffered a loss because of the antitrust activities of a guilty party may recover triple the value of the actual damages plus attorney's fees and costs.

Fee-for-Services

The Internet has revolutionized the real estate profession in many ways. One of the more notable impacts of the Internet is that it has allowed buyers and sellers to have tremendous access to information about real estate, housing, financing, and legal issues. This has prompted a radical shift in the average consumer to be much more knowledgeable about real estate matters. With knowledge and information, a consumer is more innovative and independent. The advent of the Internet has also meant that the consumer is privy to information immediately. Consumers now want instant access to real estate information.

The successful licensee will understand and encourage consumers' innovation. In the process, it is critical for the licensee to identify what services he or she can provide and underscore the value of those services. While emphasizing the services that a licensee provides, it may be important for the licensee to think of him or herself as a *consultant*. While consumers are more independent, real estate expertise is almost always needed.

It may be important for licensees to be more flexible and open to seeing their occupation as a "bundle of services" that can be unbundled. Note that unbundling fee-for-services is different from discounted real estate services. Fee-for-services is the arrangement where the consumer decides which services he or she needs and works with and pays the licensee solely for those services. Discounted real estate services is the arrangement where a consumer receives all of the real estate services, but at a discounted price.

Communicating with consumers and identifying their real estate needs are key. Licensees provide an array of valuable services that consumers can pick and choose from. A knowledgeable and independent consumer public can seem threatening to a licensee; however, the licensee has the opportunity to emphasize the value and variety of real estate services offered, for varying fees.

■ **FOR EXAMPLE** Chris wants to buy a house without contracting with a licensee but needs help writing an offer. Chris asks Sally, a broker friend of hers, to write an offer to purchase. Sally consults with Chris, writes the offer to purchase, and charges Chris a set fee for her service.

■ SUMMARY

Real estate license laws and regulations govern the professional conduct of brokers and salespersons. The license laws are enacted to protect the public by ensuring a standard of competence and professionalism in the real estate industry.

Real estate brokerage is the act of bringing people together who wish to buy, sell, exchange, or lease real estate and charging a fee or commission for the service.

Technology has significantly changed the way that brokerage offices are managed and operated. The Internet, e-mail, cell phones, and PDAs play pivotal roles.

The broker's compensation in a real estate sale may take the form of a commission, a flat fee, or an hourly rate. The broker is considered to have earned a commission when he or she procures a ready, willing, and able buyer for a seller.

A broker may hire salespersons to assist in this work. The salesperson works on the broker's behalf as either an employee or an independent contractor.

Federal and state antitrust laws prohibit brokers from conspiring to fix prices, engaging in boycotts, allocating customers or markets, or establishing tie-in agreements.

Licensees need to emphasize the value and variety of services they provide and be open to different arrangements with customers, such as a fee-for-service arrangement.

QUESTIONS

1. Which of the following statements best explains the meaning of this sentence: "To recover a commission for brokerage services, a broker must *be employed* as the agent of the seller"?
   a. The broker must work in a real estate office.
   b. The seller must have made an express or implied agreement to pay a commission to the broker for selling the property.
   c. The broker must have asked the seller the price of the property and then found a ready, willing, and able buyer.
   d. The broker must have a salesperson employed in the office.

2. A licensee who is paid in a lump sum and who is personally responsible for paying his or her own taxes is probably a(n)
   a. transactional broker.
   b. buyer's agent.
   c. independent contractor.
   d. employee.

3. Margot is a licensed real estate salesperson. Her written contract with broker George specifies that she is not an employee. In the last year, just less than half of Margot's income from real estate activity came from sales commissions. The remainder was based on an hourly wage paid by George. Using these facts, it is likely that the IRS would classify Margot as which of the following for federal income tax purposes?
   a. Self-employed
   b. Employee
   c. Independent contractor
   d. Part-time real estate salesperson

4. When acting as an employee rather than an independent contractor, a salesperson is obligated to
   a. list properties in his or her own name.
   b. assume responsibilities assigned by the broker.
   c. accept a commission from another broker.
   d. advertise property on his or her own behalf.

5. A real estate broker learns that her neighbor wishes to sell his house. The broker knows the property well and is able to persuade a customer-buyer to make an offer for the property. The broker then asks the neighbor if she can present an offer from the prospective buyer, and the neighbor agrees. At this point, which of the following statements is true?
   a. The neighbor is not obligated to pay the broker a commission.
   b. The buyer is obligated to pay the broker for locating the property.
   c. The neighbor is obligated to pay the broker a commission for producing an offer to purchase.
   d. The broker may not be considered the procuring cause without a written contract.

6. A broker would have the right to dictate which of the following to an independent contractor?
   a. Number of hours the person would have to work
   b. Work schedule the person would have to follow
   c. Minimum acceptable dress code for the office
   d. Compensation the person would receive

7. Licensees Fred and Rick were found guilty of conspiring with each other to allocate real estate brokerage markets. Lucy suffered a $90,000 loss because of their activities. If Lucy brings a civil suit against Fred and Rick, what can she expect to recover?
   a. Nothing; a civil suit cannot be brought for damages resulting from antitrust activities
   b. Only $90,000—the amount of actual damages Lucy suffered
   c. Actual damages plus attorney's fees and costs
   d. $270,000 plus attorney's fees and costs

8. Jim and Ruth are both salespersons who work for NMN Realty. One afternoon, they agree to divide their town into a northern region and a southern region. Jim will handle listings in the northern region, and Ruth will handle listings in the southern region. Which of the following statements is true regarding this agreement?

   a. The agreement between Jim and Ruth does not violate antitrust laws.
   b. The agreement between Jim and Ruth constitutes illegal price-fixing.
   c. Jim and Ruth have violated the Sherman Antitrust Act and are liable for triple damages.
   d. Jim and Ruth are guilty of group boycotting with regard to other salespersons in their office.

9. A state has recently updated its *Rules and Regulations for the Real Estate Profession*. Assuming this state is like all other states and provinces, which of the following statements is true regarding this publication?

   a. The rules and regulations are state laws enacted by the legislature.
   b. The rules and regulations are a set of administrative rules adopted by the state Real Estate Commission and do not have the same force and effect as the statutory license law.
   c. The rules and regulations are a set of administrative rules adopted by the state Real Estate Commission that define the statutory license law and have the same force and effect as the license law itself.
   d. The rules and regulations create a suggested level of competence and behavior but are not enforceable against real estate licensees.

10. Louise is a skilled salesperson at Alpha Realty. After a particularly challenging transaction finally closes, the client gives her a check for $500 "for all your extra work." Which of the following statements is accurate?

    a. While such compensation is irregular, it is appropriate for Louise to accept the check.
    b. Louise may receive compensation only from her broker.
    c. Louise should accept the check and deposit it immediately in a special escrow account.
    d. Louise's broker is entitled to 80 percent of the check.

11. A broker has established the following office policy: "All listings taken by any salesperson associated with this real estate brokerage must include compensation based on a 7 percent commission. No lower commission rate is acceptable." If the broker attempts to impose this uniform commission requirement, which of the following statements is true?

    a. A homeowner may sue the broker for violating the antitrust law's prohibition against price-fixing.
    b. The salespersons associated with the brokerage will not be bound by the requirement and may negotiate any commission rate they choose.
    c. The broker must present the uniform commission policy to the local professional association for approval.
    d. The broker may, as a matter of office policy, legally set the minimum commission rate acceptable for the firm.

12. GHI Realty has adopted a 100 percent commission plan. The monthly desk rent required of sales associates is $900, payable on the last day of the month. In August, a sales associate closed an $89,500 sale with a 6 percent commission and a $125,000 sale with a 5.5 percent commission. The salesperson's additional expenses for the month were $1,265. How much of her total monthly income did the salesperson keep?

    a. $10,080   c. $11,345
    b. $10,980   d. $12,245

13. Diana, a salesperson, took a listing on a house that sold for $129,985. The commission rate was 8 percent. Carol, a salesperson employed by another broker, found the buyer. Diana's broker received 60 percent of the commission on the sale; Carol's broker received 40 percent. If Diana's broker kept 30 percent, and paid Diana the remainder, how much did she earn on this sale?

a. $1,247.86
b. $2,911.66
c. $4,367.50
d. $6,239.28

14. On the sale of any property, a salesperson's compensation is based on the total commission paid to the broker. The salesperson receives 30 percent of the first $2,500, 15 percent of any amount between $2,500 and $7,500, and 5 percent of any amount exceeding $7,500. If a property sells for $234,500 and the broker's commission rate is 6.5 percent, what is the salesperson's total compensation?

a. $1,887.13
b. $4,609.13
c. $6,626.67
d. $7,621.25

15. Two competing real estate brokers meet for lunch and decide that a local property developer is gaining too much influence in the market. The two brokers decide to try to drive the developer out of business. One of the brokers happens to own a parcel of farmland that is key to the success of the developer's planned new subdivision, Alphabet Acres. The other broker owns 17 acres of polluted swamp next to an oil refinery. When the developer offers to buy the farmland, the broker responds that the property is for sale only if the developer also buys the other broker's swamp at the same time. Without the farmland, Alphabet Acres will fail. Unfortunately, the developer doesn't have enough cash to pay the price demanded for the swamp. Rather than risk bankruptcy, the developer abandons the Alphabet Acres plan. This scenario is an example of which of the following violations of the antitrust laws?

a. Group boycotting and allocation of markets
b. Price-fixing and tie-in agreements
c. Tie-in agreements only
d. Allocation of customers and price-fixing

CHAPTER SIX

LISTING AGREEMENTS AND BUYER REPRESENTATION

■ **LEARNING OBJECTIVES** *When you've finished reading this Chapter, you should be able to:*

■ **identify** the different types of listing and buyer representation agreements and their terms.

■ **describe** the ways in which a listing may be terminated.

■ **explain** the listing process and the parts of the listing agreement.

■ **distinguish** among the characteristics of the various types of listing and buyer representation agreements.

■ **define** the following *key terms:*

competitive market analysis (CMA)	exclusive-right-to-sell listing	net listing
		open listing
exclusive-agency listing	market value	option listing
	multiple-listing service (MLS)	

■ **WHY LEARN ABOUT...**   LISTING AGREEMENTS AND BUYER REPRESENTATION?

A listing agreement is an employment contract that creates a special agency relationship between the property owner and the broker. The various types of listing agreements establish the basic relationship between the parties and provide different levels of rights and responsibilities for the listing broker. Perhaps most importantly, listings determine important questions such as how a property is marketed and how the agent will be compensated. A buyer agency agreement is an employment contract too. It establishes the rights and responsibilities of the broker as agent for the buyer. Various kinds of buyer agency agreements establish different levels of relationships between the agent and the buyer/principal.

In short, listing and buyer representation agreements are the fundamental, bedrock documents of the real estate profession. To understand who you are as a real estate professional, you must understand how these documents work, what they say, and what they mean to you. ■

■ LISTING AGREEMENTS

A listing agreement is an employment contract rather than a real estate contract. It is a contract for the personal professional services of the broker, not for the transfer of real estate. A listing agreement may be either written or oral. Most states, however, either by their statutes of frauds or by specific rule from their real estate licensing authorities, require that the listing be in writing to be enforceable in court.

As agent, the broker is authorized to represent the principal (and the principal's real estate) to third parties. That authorization includes obtaining and submitting offers for the property. The real estate salesperson's authority to provide brokerage services originates with his or her broker. Even though the real estate salesperson may perform most, if not all, of the listing services, the listing remains with the broker.

Under both the law of agency and most state license laws, only a broker can act as agent to list, sell, rent, or purchase another person's real estate and provide other services to a principal. A salesperson who performs these acts does so only in the name and under the supervision of the broker (a salesperson is a general agent of the broker). Throughout this Chapter, unless otherwise stated, the terms *broker, agent,* and *firm* are intended to include both the broker and a salesperson working for the broker. However, the parties to a listing contract are the seller and the broker.

FIGURE 6.1

**Who May Sell a Property and Receive a Commission
Under Three Types of Listing Agreements**

Open Listing

Exclusive-Agency Listing

Exclusive-Right-to-Sell Listing

Types of Listing Agreements

Exclusive right to sell: One authorized agent-broker receives a commission regardless of who sells the property.

Exclusive-agency listing:
- There is one authorized agent.
- Broker receives a commission only if he or she is the procuring cause.
- Seller retains the right to sell without obligation.

Open listing:
- There are multiple agents.
- Only selling agent is entitled to a commission.
- Seller retains the right to sell independently without obligation.

Several types of listing agreements exist. The type of contract determines the specific rights and obligations of the parties. (See Figure 6.1 and Table 6.1.)

Exclusive-right-to-sell listing. In an **exclusive-right-to-sell listing,** one broker is appointed as the seller's sole agent. The broker is given the exclusive right, or *authorization,* to market the seller's property. If the property is sold while the listing is in effect, the seller must pay the broker a commission *regardless of who sells the property.* In other words, if the seller finds a buyer without the broker's assistance, the seller *still* must pay the broker a commission. Sellers benefit from this form of agreement because the broker feels freer to spend time and money actively marketing the property, making a timely and profitable sale more likely. From the broker's perspective, an exclusive-right-to-sell listing offers the greatest opportunity to receive a commission.

Exclusive-agency listing. In an **exclusive-agency listing,** *one* broker is authorized to act as the exclusive agent of the principal. However, *the seller retains the right to sell the property without obligation to the broker.* The seller is obligated to pay a commission to the broker only if the broker (or an agent of the broker, including a buyer's agent) has been the procuring cause of a sale.

Open listing. In an **open listing** (also known in some areas as a *nonexclusive listing* or a *general listing*), the seller retains the right to employ any number of brokers as agents. The brokers can act simultaneously, and the seller is obligated to pay a commission to only that broker who successfully produces a ready, willing, and able buyer. If the seller personally sells the property *without the aid of any of the brokers,* the seller is not obligated to pay a commission. A listing contract that does not specifically provide for an exclusive-right-to-sell listing or an exclusive-agency listing ordinarily creates an open listing. An advertisement of property "for sale by owner" may indicate "brokers protected" or in some other way invite offers brought by brokers. Such an invitation does not by itself, however, create a listing agreement.

T A B L E   6.1

Types of Listing Agreements

Exclusive-Right-to-Sell	Exclusive-Agency	Open-Listing
One broker	One broker	Multiple brokers
Broker is paid regardless of who sells the house.	Broker is paid only if he or she is procuring cause.	Only selling broker is paid.
	Seller retains the right to sell without obligation.	Seller retains the right to sell without obligation.

The terms of even an open listing must be negotiated, however. These negotiated terms should be in writing to protect the agent's ability to collect an agreed-on fee from the seller. Written terms may be in the form of a listing agreement (if the agent represents the seller) or a fee agreement (if the agent represents the buyer or the seller does not wish to be represented).

Special Listing Provisions

Multiple listing. A *multiple-listing clause* may be included in an exclusive listing. It is used by brokers who are members of a **multiple-listing service (MLS).** As discussed earlier, an MLS is a marketing organization whose broker members make their own exclusive listings available through other brokers and gain access to other brokers' listed properties as well.

An MLS offers advantages to both brokers and sellers. Brokers develop a sizable inventory of properties to be sold and are assured a portion of the commission if they list property or participate in the sale of another broker's listing. Sellers gain because the property is exposed to a larger market.

The contractual obligations among the member brokers of an MLS vary widely. Most MLSs require that a broker turn over new listings to the service within a specific, fairly short period of time after the broker obtains the listing. The length of time during which the listing broker can offer a property exclusively without notifying the other member brokers varies. Some MLSs, however, permit a broker up to five days before he or she must submit the listing to the service.

Under the provisions of most MLSs, a participating broker makes a unilateral offer of cooperation and compensation to other member brokers. The broker must have the written consent of the seller to include the property in an MLS. *If a broker chooses to be an agent for the buyer of a property in the MLS, that broker must notify the listing broker before any communication with the seller takes place.* All brokers must determine the appropriate way to proceed to protect their clients.

IN   PRACTICE

Technology has enhanced the benefits of MLS membership. In addition to providing instant access to information about the status of listed properties, MLSs often offer a broad range of other useful information about mortgage loans, real estate taxes and assessments, and municipalities and school districts. They are equally helpful to the licensee who needs to make a competitive market analysis to determine the value of a particular property before suggesting an appropriate range of listing prices. Computer-assisted searches also help buyers select properties that best meet their needs.

Net listing. A net listing provision specifies that the seller will receive a net amount of money from any sale, with the excess going to the listing broker as

In a *net listing*, the broker is entitled to any amount exceeding the seller's stated net; in an *option listing*, the broker has the right to purchase the property.

commission. The broker is free to offer the property at any price greater than that net amount. Because a net listing can create a conflict of interest between the broker's fiduciary responsibility to the seller and the broker's profit motive, it is illegal in many states and is discouraged in others.

■ **FOR EXAMPLE** A seller explained her situation to her broker: "I want to sell my house, but I don't want to be bothered with percentages and bargaining and offers and counteroffers. I just need to walk out of this deal with $150,000 in my pocket. You sell the place for any price you want and keep anything over $150,000." The broker knows that comparable homes in the area are selling for more than $200,000. What should the broker do about this offer of a net listing?

Option listing.   An **option listing** provision gives the broker the right to purchase the listed property. Use of an option listing may open the broker to charges of fraud unless the broker is scrupulous in fulfilling all obligations to the property owner. In some states, a broker who chooses to exercise such an option must first inform the property owner of the broker's profit in the transaction and secure *in writing* the owner's agreement to it. An option listing differs from an option contract, which will be discussed in Chapter 11.

■ TERMINATION OF LISTINGS

A listing agreement is a personal service contract between a broker and a seller. Its success depends on the broker's personal, professional efforts. Because the broker's services are unique, he or she cannot turn over the listing to another broker without the principal's written consent. The property owner cannot force the broker to perform, but the broker's failure to work diligently toward fulfilling the contract's terms constitutes abandonment of the listing. In the event the listing is abandoned or revoked by the broker, the owner is entitled to sue the broker for damages.

Of course, the property owner might also fail to fulfill the terms of the agreement. A property owner who refuses to cooperate with the broker's reasonable requests, such as allowing the broker to show the property to prospective buyers, or who refuses to proceed with a complete sales contract could be liable for damages to the broker. If either party cancels the contract, he or she may be liable for damages to the other.

A listing agreement may be canceled for the following reasons:

- When the agreement's purpose is fulfilled, such as when a buyer or tenant is produced
- When the agreement's term expires without a successful transfer
- If the property is destroyed or its use is changed by some force outside the owner's control, such as a zoning change or condemnation by eminent domain (see Chapter 7)
- If title to the property is transferred by operation of law, as in the case of the owner's bankruptcy
- If the broker and seller mutually agree to end the listing or if one party ends it unilaterally (in which case he or she may be liable to the other party for damages)

- If either party dies or becomes incapacitated
- If either the broker or seller breaches the contract, the agreement is terminated and the breaching or canceling party may be liable to the other for damages

Expiration of Listing Period

All listings should specify a definite period of time during which the broker is to be employed. *In most states, failing to specify a definite termination date in a listing is grounds for the suspension or revocation of a real estate license.*

Courts have discouraged the use of *automatic extension clauses* in exclusive listings, such as a clause providing for a base period of 90 days that "continues thereafter until terminated by either party hereto by 30 days' notice in writing." Extension clauses are illegal in some states, and many listing contract forms specifically provide that there can be no automatic extensions of the agreement. Some courts have held that an extension clause actually creates an open listing rather than an exclusive-agency agreement.

Some listing contracts contain a *broker protection clause*. This clause provides that the property owner will pay the listing broker a commission if, within a specified number of days after the listing expires, the owner transfers the property to someone the broker originally introduced to the owner. This clause protects a broker who was the procuring cause from losing a commission because the transaction was completed after the listing expired. The time for such a clause usually parallels the terms of the listing agreement. A six-month listing may carry a broker protection clause of six months after the listing's expiration, for example. To protect the owner and prevent any liability of the owner for two separate commissions, most of these clauses stipulate that they cannot be enforced if the property is relisted under a new contract either with the original listing broker or with another broker.

■ THE LISTING PROCESS

Before signing a contract, the broker and seller must discuss a variety of issues. The seller's most critical concerns typically are the selling price of the property and the net amount the seller can expect to receive from the sale. The broker has several professional tools to provide information about a property's value and to calculate the proceeds from a sale.

Most sellers ask other questions as well: "How quickly will the property sell?" "What services will the broker provide during the listing period?" This is the broker's opportunity to explain the various types of listing agreements, the ramifications of different agency relationships, and the marketing services the broker provides. At the end of this process the seller should feel comfortable with his or her decision to list with the broker.

Similarly, before the listing agreement is finalized, the broker should be prepared to fulfill the fiduciary obligations the agreement imposes. The seller should have provided comprehensive information about both the property and his or her personal concerns. Based on this information, the broker can accept the listing with confidence that the seller's goals can be met in a profitable manner for both parties.

Pricing the Property

While it is the responsibility of the broker or salesperson to advise and assist, *it is the seller who must determine the listing price for the property*. Because the average seller does not have the resources needed to make an informed decision about a reasonable listing price, real estate agents must be prepared to offer their knowledge, information, and expertise.

> A *competitive market analysis* is an analysis of market activity among comparable properties; it is *not* the same as a formal appraisal.

A salesperson can help the seller determine a listing price for the property by using a **competitive market analysis (CMA).** This is a comparison of the prices of properties recently sold, properties currently on the market, and properties that did not sell. The comparisons must be made with properties similar in location, size, age, style, and amenities to the seller's property. Although a CMA is not a formal appraisal, the salesperson uses many of the same methods and techniques an appraiser uses in arriving at a reasonable value range. (See Chapter 18.) If no adequate comparisons can be made, or if the property is unique in some way, the seller may prefer that a professional appraiser conduct a detailed, formal estimate of the property's value.

Whether a CMA or a formal appraisal is used, the figure sought is the property's market value. **Market value,** discussed in Chapter 18, is *the most probable price property would bring in an arm's-length transaction under normal conditions on the open market*. A CMA estimates market value as likely to fall within a range of values (for instance, $135,000 to $140,000). A CMA, however, should not be confused with a formal appraisal, which will indicate a specific value rather than a range.

> **Market Value**
>
> The most probable price property would bring in an arm's-length transaction under normal conditions on the open market.

While it is the property owner's privilege to set whatever listing price he or she chooses, a broker should consider rejecting any listing in which the price is substantially exaggerated or severely out of line with the indications of the CMA or appraisal. These tools provide the best indications of what a buyer will likely pay for the property. An unrealistic listing price will make it difficult for the broker to properly market the seller's property within the agreed-upon listing period. Furthermore, a seller who is unreasonable about the property's value may prove uncooperative on other issues later on.

Seller's Return

The broker can easily calculate roughly how much the seller will net from a given sales price or what sales price will produce a desired net amount. The Math Concept on page 84 illustrates how the formulas are applied.

IN PRACTICE

When helping a seller determine an appropriate listing price, the broker must give an estimate of value that is reasonable, conservative, and as accurate as possible. Overpriced listings cost the broker time and money in wasted marketing and advertising and give sellers false hopes of riches to come. Ultimately, failing to move overpriced listings will cost the broker future business opportunities as well.

Information Needed for Listing Agreements

Once the real estate licensee and the owner agree on a listing price, the licensee must obtain specific, detailed information about the property. Obtaining as many facts as possible ensures that most contingencies can be

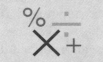

MATH CONCEPTS

CALCULATING SALES PRICES, COMMISSIONS, AND NETS TO SELLER

When a property sells, the sales price equals 100 percent of the money being transferred. Therefore, if a broker is to receive a 6 percent commission, 94 percent will remain for the seller's other expenses and equity. To calculate a commission using a sales price of $80,000 and a commission rate of 6 percent, multiply the sales price by the commission rate:

$$\$80,000 \times 6\% = \$80,000 \times .06 = \$4,800 \text{ commission}$$

To calculate a sales price using a commission of $4,550 and a commission rate of 7 percent, divide the commission by the commission rate:

$$\$4,550 \div 7\% = \$4,550 \div .07 = \$65,000 \text{ sales price}$$

To calculate a commission rate using a commission of $3,200 and a sales price of $64,000, divide the commission by the sales price:

$$\$3,200 \div \$64,000 = .05, \text{ or } 5\% \text{ commission rate}$$

To calculate the net to the seller using a sales price of $85,000 and a commission rate of 8 percent, multiply the sales price by 100 percent minus the commission rate:

$$\$85,000 \times (100\% - 8\%) = \$85,000 \times (1 - .08) = \$85,000 \times .92 = \$78,200$$

The same result could be achieved by calculating the commission ($85,000 × .08 = $6,800) and deducting it from the sales price ($85,000 − $6,800 = $78,200); however, this involves unnecessary extra calculations.

You may use this circle formula to help you with these calculations. In the circle, C is the commission amount, R is the rate, and P is the price of the property. If you know two of the figures, you can determine the third.

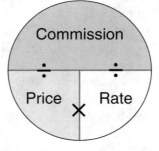

In Summary: Sales price × Commission rate = Commission
Commission ÷ Commission rate = Sales price
Commission ÷ Sales price = Commission rate
Sales price × (100% − Commission rate) = Net to seller

anticipated. This is particularly important when the listing will be shared with other brokers through an MLS and the other licensees must rely on the information taken by the lister.

The information needed for a listing agreement generally includes

- the names and relationship, if any, of the owners;
- the street address and legal description of the property;
- the size, type, age, and construction of improvements;
- the number of rooms and their sizes;
- the dimensions of the lot;
- existing loans, including such information as the name and address of each lender, the type of loan, the loan number, the loan balance, the interest rate, the monthly payment and what it includes (principal, interest, real estate tax impounds, hazard insurance impounds, mortgage insurance premiums), whether the loan may be assumed by the buyer and under what circumstances, and whether the loan may be prepaid without penalty;
- the possibility of seller financing;
- the amount of any outstanding special assessments and whether they will be paid by the seller or assumed by the buyer;
- the zoning classification of the property;
- the current (or most recent year's) property taxes;
- neighborhood amenities (for instance, schools, parks and recreational areas, churches, and public transportation);
- any real property to be removed from the premises by the seller and any personal property to be included in the sale for the buyer (both the listing contract and the subsequent purchase contract should be explicit on these points);
- any additional information that would make the property more appealing and marketable; and
- any required disclosures concerning agency representation and property conditions.

Disclosures

Disclosures of agency relationships and property conditions have become the focus of consumer safeguards in the 1990s. As discussed in Chapter 4, most states have enacted laws requiring that agents disclose whose interests they legally represent. This may be a particularly confusing issue when subagents are involved in a transaction. It is important that the seller be informed of the company's policies regarding single agency, dual agency, and buyer agency. In addition, the seller should be informed about potential cooperation with subagents and buyer's agents.

Chapter 4 also mentioned that seller disclosure of property conditions is required by law in many states. These disclosures normally cover a wide range of structural, mechanical, and other conditions that a prospective purchaser should know about to make an informed decision. Frequently, the laws require that the seller complete a standardized form. It is the licensee's responsibility to see that the seller complies with these disclosures. Agents should caution sellers to make truthful disclosures to avoid litigation arising from fraudulent or careless misrepresentations.

■ THE LISTING CONTRACT FORM

A wide variety of listing contract forms are available. Some brokers draft their own contracts, some use forms prepared by their multiple-listing services, and some use forms produced by their state real estate licensing authorities. Some brokers use a separate information sheet (also known as a *profile* or *data sheet*) for recording property features. That sheet is wed to a second form containing the contractual obligations between the seller and the broker: listing price, duration of the agreement, signatures of the parties, and so forth. Other brokers use a single form. A sample listing agreement appears in Figure 6.2.

Listing Agreement Issues

Regardless of which standard form of listing agreement is used, the same considerations arise in most real estate transactions. This means that all listing contracts tend to require similar information. However, licensees should review the specific forms used in their areas and refer to their states' laws for any specific requirements. Some of the considerations covered in a typical contract are discussed in the following paragraphs.

The type of listing agreement. The contract may be an exclusive-right-to-sell listing (the most common type), an exclusive-agency listing, or an open listing. The type of listing agreement determines the extent of a broker's authority to act on the principal's behalf. Most MLSs do not permit open listings to be posted in the MLS system.

The broker's authority and responsibilities. The contract should specify whether the broker may place a sign on the property and advertise and market the property. Another major consideration is whether the broker is permitted to authorize subagents or buyer's brokers through an MLS. Will the contract allow the broker to show the property at reasonable times and on reasonable notice to the seller? May the broker accept earnest money deposits on behalf of the seller, and what are the broker's responsibilities in holding the funds? Without the written consent of the seller, the broker cannot undertake any of these or other important activities.

The names of all parties to the contract. Anyone who has an ownership interest in the property must be identified and should sign the listing to validate it. If the property is owned under one of the forms of co-ownership discussed in Chapter 8, that fact should be clearly established. If one or more of the owners is married, it is wise to obtain the spouse's consent and signature on the contract to release any marital rights. If the property is in the possession of a tenant, that should be disclosed (along with the terms of the tenancy), and instructions should be included on how the property is to be shown to a prospective buyer.

The brokerage firm. The brokerage company name, the employing broker, and, if appropriate, the salesperson taking the listing must all be identified.

The listing price. This is the proposed gross sales price. The seller's proceeds will be reduced by unpaid real estate taxes, special assessments, mortgage and trust deed debts, and any other outstanding obligations.

Real property and personal property. Any personal property that will be left with the real estate when it is sold must be explicitly identified. Similarly, any items of real property that the seller expects to remove at the time of the sale must be specified as well. Some of these items may later become points of negotiation when a ready, willing, and able buyer is found for the property.

FIGURE 6.2

Sample Listing Agreement

VIRGINIA REGIONAL LISTING AGREEMENT - EXCLUSIVE RIGHT TO SELL

This Agreement is made on _____, _____, by and between _____ _____ ("Seller") and _____ ("Broker"). In consideration of providing the services and
(Firm Name)
facilities described herein, the Broker is hereby granted the exclusive right to sell the Property known as: _____, Virginia _____ ("Property").
Legal Description _____ Tax Map No./ ID#_____.

1. The Property is offered for sale at a selling price of $ _____, or such other price as later agreed upon, which price includes the Broker compensation. In the event of a sale, the Seller will sign a sales contract enforceable in the Commonwealth of Virginia.

The Sales Price includes the following personal property and fixtures which shall be transferred free of liens:
A. Any existing built-in heating and central air conditioning equipment, plumbing and lighting fixtures, storm windows, storm doors, screens, installed wall-to-wall carpeting, window shades, blinds, smoke and heat detectors, tv antennas, exterior trees and shrubs and B. The items marked YES below as currently installed or offered:

YES	NO	ITEM	YES	NO	ITEM	YES	NO	ITEM	YES	NO	ITEM
❑	❑	Stove or Range	❑	❑	Disposer	❑	❑	Ceiling Fan(s) #___	❑	❑	Alarm System
❑	❑	Cooktop	❑	❑	Freezer	❑	❑	Washer	❑	❑	Intercom
❑	❑	Wall Oven(s) # ___	❑	❑	Window Fan(s) # ___	❑	❑	Dryer	❑	❑	Storage Shed(s) # ___
❑	❑	Refrigerator(s) # ___	❑	❑	Window A/C Unit(s) # __	❑	❑	Furnace Humidifier	❑	❑	Garage Opener(s) #__
❑	❑	w/ ice maker	❑	❑	Pool, Equip. & Cover	❑	❑	Electronic Air Filter	❑	❑	w/ remote(s) #___
❑	❑	Dishwasher	❑	❑	Hot Tub, Equip. & Cover	❑	❑	Central Vacuum	❑	❑	Playground Equipment
❑	❑	Built-in Microwave	❑	❑	Satellite Dish and Equip.	❑	❑	Water Treatment Sys.	❑	❑	Wood Stove
❑	❑	Trash Compactor	❑	❑	Attic Fan(s)	❑	❑	Exhaust Fan(s)	❑	❑	Fireplace Screen/Doors
❑	❑	Sump Pump	❑	❑	Window Treatments						

Other inclusions or exclusions: _____
_____
_____

WATER, SEWAGE, HEATING, AND CENTRAL AIR CONDITIONING: (Check all that apply)
Water Supply: ❑ Public ❑ Well ❑ Other _____   Hot Water: ❑ Oil ❑ Gas ❑ Elec.
Sewage Disposal: ❑ Public ❑ Septic # BR ____   Air Conditioning: ❑ Gas ❑ Elec. ❑ Heat Pump
Heating: ❑ Oil ❑ Gas ❑ Elec. ❑ Heat Pump ❑ Other _____

The Seller will deliver the Property in substantially the same condition as on the Contract Date and in broom clean condition with all trash and debris removed. The Seller warrants that the existing appliances, heating, cooling, plumbing and electrical systems and equipment and smoke and heat detectors (as required) will be in normal working order as of the possession date.

2. **The Broker and the Sales Associate(s) shall promote the interests of the Seller by:**
A) performing the terms of this Agreement;
B) seeking a buyer at a price and terms agreed upon herein or otherwise acceptable to the Seller. However, the Broker and the Sales Associate(s) shall not be obligated to seek additional offers to purchase

the Property while the Property is subject to a contract of sale, unless stated herein or as the contract of sale so provides;

C) presenting in a timely manner all written offers or counteroffers to and from the Seller even when the Property is already subject to a contract of sale;

D) disclosing to the Seller all material facts related to the Property or concerning the transaction of which the Broker and Sales Associate(s) have actual knowledge;

E) accounting for in a timely manner all money and property received in which the Seller has or may have an interest.

Unless otherwise provided by law or the Seller consents in writing to the release of the information, the Broker and the Sales Associate(s) shall maintain the confidentiality of all personal and financial information and other matters identified as confidential by the Seller, if that information is received from the Seller during the brokerage relationship. In satisfying these duties, the Broker and the Sales Associate(s) shall exercise ordinary care, comply with all applicable laws and regulations and treat all prospective buyers honestly and not knowingly give them false information; and the Broker and Sales Associate(s) shall disclose to prospective buyers all material adverse facts pertaining to the physical condition of the Property which are actually known by them. In addition, the Broker and the Sales Associate(s) may provide assistance to a buyer or prospective buyer by performing ministerial acts that are not inconsistent with the Broker's and the Sales Associate's duties under this Agreement. The Seller acknowledges that the Broker and Sales Associate(s) and any cooperating brokers and sales associates may act on behalf of the Seller as the Seller's representatives.

Buyer representation occurs when buyers contract to use the services of their own broker (known as a buyer representative) to act on their behalf.

Designated representation occurs when a buyer and seller in one transaction are represented by different Sales Associate(s) affiliated with the same Broker. Each of these Sales Associates, known as a Designated Representative, represents fully the interests of a different client in the same transaction. Designated Representatives are not dual representatives if each represents only the buyer or only the seller in a specific real estate transaction. Except for disclosure of confidential information to the Broker, each Designated Representative is bound by the confidentiality requirements as above. The Broker remains a dual representative. ❑ The Seller consents to designated representation **OR** ❑ The Seller does not consent to designated representation which means the Seller does not allow the Property to be shown to a buyer represented by this Broker through another Designated Representative associated with the firm. The Broker will notify other associates within the firm via the MLS whether the Seller consents or does not consent.

Dual representation occurs when a buyer and seller in one transaction are represented by the same Broker and the same Sales Associate(s). When the parties agree to dual representation, the ability of the Broker and the Sales Associate(s) to represent either party fully and exclusively is limited. The confidentiality of all information of all clients shall be maintained as above.   ❑ The Seller consents to dual representation **OR** ❑ The Seller does not consent to dual representation which means the Seller does not allow the Property to be shown to a buyer represented by this Broker through the same Sales Associate(s).

3.   This Exclusive Right to Sell will expire at midnight on _____.

4.   This Property shall be shown and made available without regard to race, color, religion, sex, handicap, familial status or national origin as well as all classes protected by the laws of the United States, the Commonwealth of Virginia and applicable local jurisdictions.

5.   The Broker shall make a blanket unilateral offer of cooperation and compensation to other brokers in any Multiple Listing Service that the Broker deems appropriate. The Broker shall disseminate information regarding the Property, including the entry date, listing price(s), final price and all terms, and expired or withdrawn status, by printed form and/or electronic computer service during and after the expiration of this Agreement. The Broker shall enter the listing information into the MLS data base within 48 hours (unless otherwise instructed in writing by the Seller) after all Sellers' signatures have been obtained.

Sample Listing
Agreement (con't.)

6. A. The Seller shall pay the Broker compensation of _____ in cash if, during the term of this Agreement, anyone produces a buyer ready, willing and able to buy the Property. In addition to the Broker's compensation, an additional fee of _____ will be collected from the Seller payable to the Broker, at the time of settlement. The compensation is also earned if within _____ days after the expiration or termination of this Agreement, a contract is ratified with a ready, willing and able buyer to whom the Property has been shown during the term of this Agreement; provided, however, that the compensation need not be paid if a contract is ratified on the Property while the Property is listed with another real estate company.

    B. The Broker acknowledges receipt of a retainer fee in the amount of _____, which ❏ shall, **OR** ❏ shall not be subtracted from any compensation due the Broker under this Agreement. The retainer is non-refundable and is earned when paid. C. The Broker shall offer compensation to the selling broker as indicated: Subagency Compensation _____ Buyer Agency Compensation _____ Non Agency Compensation _____

    Note: Compensation shall be shown by a percentage of the gross selling price, a definite dollar amount or "N" for no compensation. No Multiple Listing Service or Association of REALTORS® is a party to this Agreement and no Multiple Listing Service or Association of REALTORS® sets, controls, recommends or suggests the amount of compensation for any brokerage service rendered pursuant to this Agreement.

7. The Seller is participating in any type of employee relocation program ❏ Yes **OR** ❏ No.

    If "Yes": A) the program is named: _____, Contact # _____ and B) terms of the program are: _____
    _____.

    If "No" or the Seller has failed to list a specific employee relocation program, then the Broker shall have no obligation to cooperate with or compensate any undisclosed program.

8. In consideration of the use of Broker's services and facilities and of the facilities of any REALTOR® Multiple Listing Service, the Seller and Seller's heirs and assigns hereby release the Broker, sales associates accompanying buyers or prospective buyers, any REALTORS® Multiple Listing Service and the directors, officers and employees thereof, including officials of any parent Association of REALTORS®, except for malfeasance on the part of such parties, from any liability to the Seller for vandalism, theft or damage of any nature whatsoever to the Property or its contents during the term of this Agreement, and that the Seller waives any and all rights, claims and causes of action against them and holds them harmless for any property damage or personal injury arising from the use or access to the Property by any person during the term of this Agreement.

9. The Seller retains full responsibility for the Property, including all utilities, maintenance, physical security and liability during the term of this Agreement and the sales contract period. Virginia licensed real estate salespersons and appraisers, inspectors and other persons shall be given access as needed to the Property to facilitate and/or consummate a sale. Authorization is granted to the Broker to show the Property during reasonable hours. Authority is granted to the Broker to:

    A.) Place a "For Sale" sign on the Property and to remove all other such signs
    B.) Place a common keysafe/lockbox on the Property containing keys and information necessary to obtain full access to the Property.

10. The Seller represents that the Property ❏ is, **OR** ❏ is not located within a development which is a Condominium or Cooperative. Condominiums or Cooperatives being offered for sale are subject to the receipt by buyers of the required Disclosures, and the Seller is responsible for payment of appropriate fees and for providing these disclosure documents to prospective buyers as prescribed in the Condominium Act, Section 55-79.39 <u>et seq.</u>, and the Cooperative Act, Section 55-424, <u>et seq.</u>, of the Code of Virginia.

F I G U R E   6.2

**Sample Listing
Agreement (con't.)**

11. The Seller represents that the Property ❑ is, **OR** ❑ is not located within a development(s) which is subject to the Virginia Property Owners' Association Act, Sections 55-508 through 55-516 of the Code of Virginia. If the Property is within such a development, the Seller is responsible for payment of the appropriate fees and for providing these disclosure documents to the buyers.

12. The Seller acknowledges that the Broker has informed the Seller of the Seller's rights and obligations under the Virginia Residential Property Disclosure Act. This Property ❑ is, **OR** ❑ is not exempt from the Act. If not exempt, the Seller has completed and provided to the Broker: ❑ a Residential Property Disclosure Statement where the Seller is making representations regarding the condition of the Property on which the buyer may rely, **OR** ❑ a Residential Property Disclaimer Statement where the Seller is making no representations regarding the condition of the Property and is selling the Property "as is", except as may be provided otherwise in the sales contract.

13. The Seller represents that the residential dwelling(s) at the Property ❑ were, **OR** ❑ were not constructed before 1978. If the dwelling(s) were constructed before 1978, the Seller is subject to Federal law concerning disclosure of the possible presence of lead-based paint at the Property, and the Seller acknowledges that the Broker has informed the Seller of the Seller's obligations under the law. If the dwelling(s) were constructed before 1978, unless exempt under 42 U.S.C. 4852d, the Seller has completed and provided to the Broker the form, "Sale: Disclosure And Acknowledgment Of Information On Lead-Based Paint And/Or Lead-Based Paint Hazards" or equivalent form.

14. The Property may be sold subject to existing Deed(s) of Trust, having a total unpaid balance of approximately $_____.

15. The Seller shall provide a _____ Deed of Trust Loan in the amount of $_____ with further terms to be negotiated.

16.   Other terms: _____
_____
_____

_____ Date _____ Seller _____   _____ Broker
                                                                                        (Firm)

_____ Date _____ Seller _____   _____
                                                                                        (Address)

The Seller ❑ is, **OR** ❑ is not a licensed (active/inactive) real estate agent/broker.

_____   _____, VA _____

_____
(Seller's Mailing Address)

_____   Date: _____ By: _____
(City, State, and Zip Code)   (Broker/Sales Manager)

                                                Sales Associate: _____
                                                                    (Designated Representative)

Phone (O) _____   Phone (O) _____

Phone (H) _____   Phone (H) _____

Fax #_____ Email _____   Fax #_____ Email _____

© 2002 Northern Virginia Association of REALTORS®, Inc.

Source: Reprinted with permission from the Northern Virginia Associations of REALTORS®, Inc. (NVAR), for educational purposes only. Any other use of these forms without the express written consent of NVAR is strictly prohibited.

Typical items to consider include major appliances, swimming pool and spa equipment, fireplace accessories, storage sheds, window treatments, stacked firewood, and stored heating oil.

Leased equipment. Will any leased equipment—security systems, cable television boxes, water softeners, special antennas—be left with the property? If so, the seller is responsible for notifying the equipment's lessor of the change of property ownership.

The description of the premises. In addition to the street address, the legal description, lot size, and tax parcel number may be required for future insertion into a purchase offer.

The proposed dates for the closing and the buyer's possession. These dates should be based on an anticipated sale date. The listing agreement should allow adequate time for the paperwork involved (including the buyer's qualification for any financing) and the physical moves to be arranged by the seller and the buyer.

The closing. Details of the closing—such as a closing attorney, title company, or escrow company—should be considered even at this early stage. Which designated party will complete the settlement statements, disburse the funds, and file the proper forms, such as documents to be recorded, documents to be sent to the Internal Revenue Service, and documents to be submitted for registering foreign owners? In some states, because the buyer designates the settlement agent, the seller must identify any special needs at the beginning of the process.

The evidence of ownership. The most commonly used proofs of title are a warranty deed and either a title insurance policy or an abstract and legal opinion.

Encumbrances. Which liens will be paid in full at the closing by the seller and which liens will be assumed by the buyer?

Home warranty program. In some situations, it may be advisable for a buyer or seller to purchase a home warranty with the property. Typically, a home warranty program covers such things as plumbing, electrical, and heating systems, hot water heaters, duct work, and major appliances. Some brokers offer this with every home they sell as a way of encouraging people to buy. In many states, a home warranty program can be provided in a listing contract or an offer to purchase. Coverages, deductibles, limitations, and exclusions in the contract should be read carefully.

The commission. The circumstances under which a commission will be paid must be specifically stated. Is payment earned only on the sale of the property or on any transfer of interest created by the broker? Will it be a percentage or a flat fee? When will it be paid? Will it be paid directly by the seller or by the party handling the closing?

The termination of the contract. A contract should provide some way for the parties to end it. Under what circumstances will the contract terminate? Can the seller arbitrarily refuse to sell or cooperate with the listing broker?

The broker protection clause. As previously discussed, brokers may be well advised to protect their interests against possible fraud or a reluctant buyer's change of heart. Under what circumstances will the broker be entitled to a commission after the agreement terminates? How long will the clause remain in effect?

Warranties by the owner. The owner is responsible for certain assurances and disclosures that are vital to the agent's ability to market the property successfully. Is the property suitable for its intended purpose? Does it comply with the appropriate zoning and building codes? Will it be transferred to the buyer in essentially the same condition as it was originally presented, considering repairs or alterations to be made as provided for in a purchase contract? Are there any known defects?

Indemnification (hold harmless) wording. The seller and the broker may agree to hold each other harmless (that is, not to sue one another) for any incorrect information supplied by one to the other. Indemnification may be offered regardless of whether the inaccuracies are intentional or unintentional.

Nondiscrimination (equal opportunity) wording. The seller must understand that the property will be shown and offered without regard to the race, color, creed or religious preference, national origin, family status, sex, sexual orientation, age, or handicap of the prospective buyer. Refer to federal, state, and local fair housing laws for protected classes. (See Chapter 20.)

Antitrust wording. The contract should indicate that all commissions have been negotiated between the seller and the broker. It is illegal for commissions to be set by any regulatory agency, trade association, or other industry organization.

The signatures of the parties. All parties identified in the contract must sign it, including all individuals who have a legal interest in the property.

The date the contract is signed. This date may differ from the date the contract actually becomes effective, particularly if a salesperson takes the listing, then must have his or her broker sign the contract to accept employment under its terms.

IN PRACTICE

Anyone who takes a listing should use *only* the appropriate documents provided by the broker. Most brokers are conscientious enough to use only documents that have been carefully drafted or reviewed by an attorney so that their construction and legal language comply with the appropriate federal, state, and local laws. Such contracts should also give consideration to local customs, such as closing dates and the proration of income and expenses, with which most real estate attorneys are familiar.

www.naeba.org

www.rebac.net/right.htm

■ BUYER AGENCY AGREEMENTS

Like a listing agreement, a **buyer agency agreement** is an employment contract. In this case, however, the broker is employed as the *buyer's* agent. The buyer, rather than the seller, is the principal. The purpose of the agreement is to find a suitable property. An agency agreement gives the buyer a degree of representation possible only in a fiduciary relationship. A buyer's broker must protect the buyer's interests at all points in the transaction. A typical buyer agency agreement appears in Figure 6.3.

Types of Buyer Agency Agreements

Three basic types of buyer agency agreements exist:

1. *Exclusive buyer agency agreement (or exclusive right to represent)*—This is a completely exclusive agency agreement. The buyer is legally bound to compensate the agent whenever the buyer purchases a property of the type described in the contract. The broker is entitled to payment regardless of whether he or she locates the property. Even if the buyer finds the property independently, the agent is entitled to payment.
2. *Exclusive-agency buyer agency agreement*—Like an exclusive buyer agency agreement, this is an exclusive contract between the buyer and the agent. However, this agreement limits the broker's right to payment. The broker is entitled to payment only if he or she locates the property the buyer ultimately purchases. The buyer is free to find a suitable property without obligation to pay the agent.
3. *Open buyer agency agreement*—This agreement is a nonexclusive agency contract between a broker and a buyer. It permits the buyer to enter into similar agreements with an unlimited number of brokers. The buyer is obligated to compensate only the broker who locates the property the buyer ultimately purchases.

Buyer Representation Issues

A number of issues must be discussed by a broker and a buyer before they sign a buyer agency agreement. For instance, the licensee should make the same disclosures to the buyer that the licensee would make to a seller in a listing agreement. The licensee should explain the forms of agency available and the parties' rights and responsibilities under each type. The specific services provided to a buyer-client should be clearly explained. Compensation issues need to be addressed as well. Buyer's agents may be compensated in the form of a flat fee for services, an hourly rate, or a percentage of the purchase price. The agent may require a *retainer fee* at the time the agreement is signed to cover initial expenses. The retainer may be applied as a credit toward any fees due at the closing. A buyer's agent also may be compensated by sharing the commission being paid by the seller.

F I G U R E   6.3

**Sample Buyer
Agency Agreement**

EXCLUSIVE RIGHT TO REPRESENT BUYER AGREEMENT

This Agreement is made on_____,_____ between _____
_____ ("Buyer") and _____("Broker").
(Name of brokerage firm)

In consideration of services and facilities, the Broker is hereby granted the right to represent the Buyer in the acquisition of real property. (As used in this Agreement, "acquisition of real property" shall include any purchase, option, exchange or lease of property or an agreement to do so.)

1. **BUYER'S REPRESENTATIONS**. The Buyer represents that as of the commencement date of this Agreement, the Buyer is not a party to a buyer representation agreement with any other brokerage firm. The Buyer further represents that the Buyer has disclosed to the Sales Associate information about any properties that the Buyer has previously visited at any new homes communities or resale "open houses", or that the Buyer has been shown by any other real estate sales associate(s) in any area where the Buyer seeks to acquire property under this Agreement.

2. **TERM**. This Agreement commences when signed and, subject to Paragraph 7, expires at_____ ☐ a.m. **OR** ☐ p.m. on _____,_____.

3. **RETAINER FEE**. The Broker,_____, acknowledges receipt
(Name of brokerage firm)
of a retainer fee in the amount of_____, which ☐ shall **OR** ☐ shall not be subtracted from any compensation due the Broker under this Agreement. The retainer is non-refundable and is earned when paid.

4. **BROKER'S DUTIES**. The Broker and the Sales Associate shall promote the interests of the Buyer by:
   A) performing the terms of this Agreement;
   B) seeking property at a price and terms acceptable to the Buyer;
   C) presenting in a timely manner all written offers or counteroffers to and from the Buyer;
   D) disclosing to the Buyer all material facts related to the property or concerning the transaction of which they have actual knowledge; E) accounting for in a timely manner all money and property received in which the Buyer has or may have an interest.

Unless otherwise provided by law or the Buyer consents in writing to the release of the information, the Broker shall maintain the confidentiality of all personal and financial information and other matters identified as confidential by the Buyer, if that information is received from the Buyer during the brokerage relationship. In satisfying these duties, the Broker shall exercise ordinary care, comply with all applicable laws and regulations, treat all prospective sellers honestly and not knowingly give them false information, and disclose whether or not the Buyer's intent is to occupy the property as a principal residence. In addition, the Broker may: show the same property to other buyers; represent other buyers on the same or different properties; represent Sellers relative to other properties; or provide assistance to a seller or prospective seller by performing ministerial acts that are not inconsistent with the Broker's duties under this Agreement.

5. **BUYER'S DUTIES**. The Buyer shall: (a) work exclusively with the Broker during the term of this Agreement; (b) pay the Broker, directly or indirectly, the compensation set forth below; (c) comply with the reasonable requests of the Broker to supply any pertinent financial or personal data needed to fulfill the terms of this Agreement; (d) be available during the Broker's regular working hours to view properties.

NVAR - 0009 - 06/02   Page 1 of 3   Initials: Buyer _____/ _____

Sample Buyer
Agreement (con't.)

6. **PURPOSE**. The Buyer is retaining the Broker to acquire the following type of property: _____
_____.

7. **COMPENSATION**. In consideration of the time and effort expended by the Broker on behalf of the Buyer, and in further consideration of the advice and counsel provided to the Buyer, the Buyer shall pay compensation ("Broker's Fee") to the Broker as described below. The Broker's Fee, less the retainer fee, if any, shall be earned, due and payable under any of these circumstances whether the transaction is consummated through the services of the Broker or otherwise:

    A) If the Buyer enters into a contract to acquire real property during the term of this Agreement and goes to settlement on that contract any time thereafter: **OR**

    B) If, within_____ days after expiration or termination of this Agreement, the Buyer enters into a contract to acquire real property that has been described to or shown to the Buyer by the Broker during the term of this Agreement, unless the Buyer has entered into a subsequent "Exclusive Right to Represent Buyer" agreement with another real estate broker; **OR**

    C) If, having entered into an enforceable contract to acquire real property during the term of this Agreement, the Buyer defaults under the terms of that contract.

    The Broker's Fee shall be _____. In addition to the Broker's compensation, an additional fee of _____ will be collected from the Buyer payable to the Broker, at the time of settlement. If the seller or the seller's representative offers compensation to the Broker, then the Buyer authorizes the Broker to receive such compensation and the amount of such compensation shall be credited against the Buyer's obligation to pay the Broker's Fee.

    Any obligation incurred under this Agreement on the part of the Buyer to pay the Broker's Fee shall survive the term of this Agreement.

8. The Buyer is participating in any type of employee relocation program ☐ Yes **OR** ☐ No.

If "Yes": (a) the program is named: _____, and
(b) terms of the program are: _____
_____.

If "No" or the Buyer has failed to list a specific employee relocation program, then the Broker shall have no obligation to cooperate with or compensate any undisclosed program.

9. **DISCLOSED DUAL REPRESENTATION.** The Buyer acknowledges that in the normal course of business the Broker may represent sellers of properties in which the Buyer is interested. If the Buyer wishes to acquire any property listed with the Broker, then the Buyer will be represented in one of the two ways that are permitted under Virginia law in this situation. The written consent required from the parties in each case will be accomplished via execution of the appropriate disclosure form at the time of the contract offer.

Dual representation occurs when a buyer and seller in one transaction are represented by the same Broker and the same Sales Associate. When the parties agree to dual representation, the ability of the Broker and the Sales Associate to represent either party fully and exclusively is limited. The confidentiality of all clients shall be maintained as in paragraph 4 above.

Designated representation occurs when a buyer and seller in one transaction are represented by different Sales Associates affiliated with the same Broker. Each of these Sales Associates, known as a Designated Representative, represents fully the interests of a different client in the same transaction. Designated Representatives are not dual representatives if each represents only the buyer or only the seller in a specific real estate transaction. Except for disclosure of confidential information to the Broker, each Designated Representative is bound by the confidentiality requirements in paragraph 4 above. The Broker remains a dual representative.

**Sample Buyer
Agency Agreement (con't.)**

CHECK ONE CHOICE IN EACH SECTION:
Dual representation: The Buyer ☐ does **OR** ☐ does not consent to be shown and to consider acquiring properties listed with the Broker through the Sales Associate.
Designated representation: The Buyer ☐ does **OR** ☐ does not consent to be shown and to consider acquiring properties listed with the Broker through another Designated Representative associated with the firm.

10. **DISCLAIMER.** The buyer acknowledges that the Broker is being retained solely as a real estate agent and not as an attorney, tax advisor, lender, appraiser, surveyor, structural engineer, mold or air quality expert, home inspector or other professional service provider. The Buyer is advised to seek professional advice concerning the condition of the property or concerning legal and tax matters. The Buyer should exercise whatever due diligence the Buyer deems necessary with respect to information on any sexual offenders registered under Chapter 23 (§19.2-387 et. seq.) of Title 19.2. Such information may be obtained by contacting your local police department or the Department of State Police, Central Criminal Records Exchange, at (804)674-2000 or www.vsp.state.va.us.

11. **EQUAL OPPORTUNITY.** Properties shall be shown and made available to the Buyer without regard to race, color, religion, sex, handicap, familial status or national origin as well as all classes protected by the laws of the United States, the Commonwealth of Virginia and applicable local jurisdictions.

12. **OTHER PROVISIONS.** _____
_____.

13. **MISCELLANEOUS.** This Agreement, any exhibits and any addenda signed by the parties constitute the entire agreement between the parties and supersedes any other written or oral agreements between the parties. This Agreement can only be modified in writing when signed by both parties. In any action or proceeding involving a dispute between the Buyer, the seller and/or the Broker, arising out of this Agreement, or to collect the Broker's Fee, the prevailing party shall be entitled to receive from the other party reasonable attorney's fees to be determined by the court or arbitrator(s).

(NOTE: The Buyer should consult with the Sales Associate before visiting any resale or new homes or contacting any other REALTORS® representing sellers, to avoid the possibility of confusion over the brokerage relationship and misunderstandings about liability for compensation.)

_____ _____(SEAL)   Brokerage Firm (Broker) _____
Date   Buyer's Signature   _____
                                                  Address
_____ _____(SEAL)   _____
Date   Buyer's Signature   City, State, Zip Code

The Buyer ☐ does **OR** ☐ does not hold an active or inactive Virginia real estate license.

_____   _____(SEAL)
Address   Date   Broker/Sales Manager's Signature

_____   _____
City, State, Zip Code   Sales Associate's/Designated Representative's Printed Name

Telephone: _____ _____   Telephone: _____ _____
              Work   Home   Work   Home
Fax_____ Email _____   Fax_____ Email _____

Source: Reprinted with permission from the Northern Virginia Associations of REALTORS®, Inc. (NVAR), for educational purposes only. Any other use of these forms without the express written consent of NVAR is strictly prohibited.

As in any agency agreement, the source of compensation is not the factor that determines the relationship. A buyer's agent may be compensated by either the buyer or the seller. Issues of compensation are *always* negotiable.

Because the agency contract employs the agent to represent the buyer and locate a suitable property, the licensee must obtain detailed financial information from the buyer. In addition, the buyer's agent needs information about the buyer's specific requirements for a suitable property.

IN PRACTICE   Buyer agency, like any other kind of real estate agency, is increasingly subject to detailed provisions of state law. If a state has adopted an agency statute, it is highly likely that the rights, duties, and obligations of buyer's agents are specifically established.

■ SUMMARY

To acquire an inventory of property to sell, brokers must obtain listings. Types of listings include exclusive-right-to-sell, exclusive-agency, and open listings.

With an exclusive-right-to-sell listing, the seller employs only one broker and must pay that broker a commission regardless of whether it is the broker or the seller who finds a buyer, provided the buyer is found within the listing period.

Under an exclusive-agency listing, the broker is given the exclusive right to represent the seller, but the seller can avoid paying the broker a commission by selling the property to someone not procured by the broker.

With an open listing, to obtain a commission the broker must find a ready, willing, and able buyer on the seller's terms before the property is sold by the seller or another broker.

A multiple-listing provision may appear in an exclusive-right-to-sell or an exclusive-agency listing. It gives the broker the additional authority and obligation to distribute the listing to other members of the broker's multiple-listing organization.

A net listing, which is illegal in some states and considered unethical in most areas, is based on the net price the seller will receive if the property is sold. The broker is free to offer the property for sale at the highest available price and will receive as commission any amount exceeding the seller's stipulated net.

An option listing, which also must be handled with caution, gives the broker the option to purchase the listed property.

A listing agreement may be terminated for the same reasons as any other agency relationship.

When listing a property for sale, the seller is concerned about the selling price and the net amount he or she will receive from the sale. A competitive market analysis (CMA) compares the prices of recently sold properties that are similar to the seller's property. The CMA or a formal appraisal report can be used to help the seller determine a reasonable listing price. The amount the seller will net from the sale is calculated by subtracting the broker's commission, along with any existing liens and any other expenses that the seller incurs, from the selling price.

A wide variety of listing contract forms may be used, depending on the customs and laws in an area. Typically, they are preprinted forms that include such information as the type of listing agreement, the broker's authority and responsibility under the listing, the listing price, the duration of the listing, information about the property, terms for the payment of commission (including antitrust concerns and encumbrances) and for the buyer's possession, and nondiscrimination laws. Detailed information about the property may be included in the listing contract or on a separate property data sheet. Disclosure of the broker's law of agency relationship and discussion of the broker's agency policies have become the focus of laws in many states. The seller may also be expected to comply with mandatory disclosure of property conditions.

A buyer agency agreement ensures a buyer that his or her interests will be represented. Different forms of buyer agency agreements exist. A buyer's broker is obligated to find a suitable property for the client, who is owed the traditional fiduciary duties. Buyer agency may be regulated by state agency laws.

QUESTIONS

1. A listing taken by a real estate salesperson is technically an employment agreement between the seller and the
   a. broker.
   b. local multiple-listing service.
   c. salesperson.
   d. salesperson and broker together.

2. Which of the following is a similarity between an exclusive-agency listing and an exclusive-right-to-sell listing?
   a. Under each, the seller retains the right to sell the real estate without the broker's help and without paying the broker a commission.
   b. Under each, the seller authorizes only one particular salesperson to show the property.
   c. Both types of listings give the responsibility of representing the seller to one broker only.
   d. Both types of listings are open listings.

3. The listing agreement on a residential property states that it expires on May 2. Which of the following events would *not* terminate the listing?
   a. The agreement is not renewed prior to May 2.
   b. The owner dies on April 29.
   c. On April 15, the owner tells the listing broker that the owner is dissatisfied with the broker's marketing efforts.
   d. The house is destroyed by fire on April 25.

4. A seller has listed a property under an exclusive-agency listing with a broker. If the seller sells the property personally during the term of the listing to someone who learns about the property through the seller, the seller will owe the broker
   a. no commission.
   b. the full commission.
   c. a partial commission.
   d. only reimbursement for the broker's costs.

5. A broker sold a residence for $85,000 and received $5,950 as her commission in accordance with the terms of the listing. What was the broker's commission rate?
   a. 6 percent   c. 7.25 percent
   b. 7 percent   d. 7.5 percent

6. Under a listing agreement, the broker is entitled to sell the property for any price, as long as the seller receives $85,000. The broker may keep any amount over $85,000 as a commission. This type of listing is called a(n)
   a. exclusive-right-to-sell listing.
   b. exclusive-agency listing.
   c. open listing.
   d. net listing.

7. Which of the following is a similarity between an open listing and an exclusive-agency listing?
   a. Under each, the seller avoids paying the broker a commission if the seller sells the property to someone the broker did not procure.
   b. Each grants a commission to any broker who procures a buyer for the seller's property.
   c. Under each, the broker earns a commission regardless of who sells the property, as long as it is sold within the listing period.
   d. Each grants the exclusive right to sell to whatever broker procures a buyer for the seller's property.

8. The final decision on a property's listed price should be made by
   a. the listing agent.
   b. the appraised value.
   c. the seller.
   d. the seller's attorney.

9. Which of the following statements is true of a listing contract?

a. It is an employment contract for the professional services of the broker.
b. It obligates the seller to convey the property if the broker procures a ready, willing, and able buyer.
c. It obligates the broker to work diligently for both the seller and the buyer.
d. It automatically binds the owner, broker, and MLS to its agreed-upon provisions.

10. A broker sold a property and received a 6.5 percent commission. The broker gave the listing salesperson $3,575, which was 30 percent of the firm's commission. What was the selling price of the property?

a. $55,000
b. $95,775
c. $152,580
d. $183,333

11. A seller hired Lana, a broker, under the terms of an open listing. While that listing was still in effect, the seller—without informing Lana—hired Frank under an exclusive-right-to-sell listing for the same property. If Lana produces a buyer for the property whose offer the seller accepts, then the seller must pay a

a. full commission only to Lana.
b. full commission only to Frank.
c. full commission to both Lana and Frank.
d. half commission to both Lana and Frank.

12. Gloria listed her residence with broker Dave. Dave brought an offer at full price and terms of the listing from buyers who are ready, willing, and able to pay cash for the property. However, Gloria changed her mind and rejected the buyers' offer. In this situation, Gloria

a. must sell her property.
b. owes a commission to Dave.
c. is liable to the buyers for specific performance.
d. is liable to the buyers for compensatory damages.

13. Which of the following is true of an open buyer agency listing?

a. The buyer may enter into agreements with multiple brokers and be obligated to pay only the broker who locates the property that the buyer ultimately purchases.
b. While the buyer may enter into agreements with multiple brokers, he or she is under no obligation to pay the broker; the seller bears all brokerage expenses.
c. Because multiple brokers may be involved, an open buyer agency agreement involves reduced fiduciary duties.
d. The buyer may not look for or make offers on properties on his or her own.

14. Nancy, a broker, and Jim enter into an exclusive-agency buyer agency agreement. What does this mean?

a. Jim is obligated to compensate Nancy, regardless of who locates the property ultimately purchased.
b. Nancy is entitled to payment only if she or any broker acting under her authority locates the property Jim ultimately purchases.
c. Jim may enter into similar agreements with any number of other brokers.
d. If Jim finds the property without any help from Nancy, Jim must pay Nancy a reduced compensation.

15. Which of the following statements is true of a competitive market analysis (CMA)?

a. A CMA is the same as an appraisal.
b. A CMA can help the seller price the property.
c. By law in most states, a CMA must be completed for each listing taken.
d. A CMA should not be retained in the property's listing file.

16. A property was listed with a broker who belonged to a multiple-listing service and was sold by another member broker for $53,500. The total commission was 6 percent of the sales price. The selling broker received 60 percent of the commission, and the listing broker received the balance. What was the listing broker's commission?

    a. $1,284
    b. $1,464
    c. $1,926
    d. $2,142

17. Sue signs a listing agreement with broker Ken to sell her home. The agreement states that Ken will receive a 7 percent commission. The home sells for $120,000. What is the net amount that Sue will receive from the sale?

    a. $8,400
    b. $102,877
    c. $111,600
    d. $120,000

18. A real estate broker and a seller enter into a listing agreement that contains the following language: "Seller will receive $100,000 from the sale of the subject property. Any amount greater than $100,000 will constitute Broker's sole and complete compensation." Which of the following statements is true regarding this agreement?

    a. This agreement is an example of an option listing.
    b. If the seller's home sells for exactly $100,000, the broker will still be entitled to receive the standard commission in the area.
    c. The broker may offer the property for any price over $100,000, but the listing agreement may be illegal.
    d. This type of listing is known as an *open listing,* because the selling price is left open.

19. All of the following would permit a listing agreement for residential property to be terminated *EXCEPT*

    a destruction of the listed property.
    b. seller dissatisfaction with the wording of a newspaper advertisement.
    c. seller's unreasonable refusal to permit showings of the property during any time other than 6:00 AM to 7:30 AM.
    d. a breach by the broker.

20. A written agreement between a broker and a client includes the following language: "In return for the compensation agreed upon, Broker will assist Client in locating and purchasing a suitable property. Broker will receive the agreed compensation regardless of whether Broker, Client, or some other party locates the property ultimately purchased by Client." What kind of agreement is this?

    a. Exclusive-agency listing
    b. Exclusive-agency buyer agency agreement
    c. Exclusive buyer agency agreement
    d. Open buyer agency agreement

CHAPTER

7

SEVEN

INTERESTS IN
REAL ESTATE

■ **LEARNING OBJECTIVES** *When you've finished reading this Chapter, you should be able to:*

■ **identify** the kinds of limitations on ownership rights that are imposed by government action and the form of conveyance of property.

■ **describe** the various estates in land and the rights and limitations they convey.

■ **explain** concepts related to encumbrances and water rights.

■ **distinguish** the various types of police powers and how they are exercised.

■ **define** the following *key terms:*

accretion	encroachment	license
appurtenant easement	encumbrance	lien
avulsion	erosion	life estate
condemnation	escheat	littoral rights
deed restrictions	estate in land	party wall
easement	fee simple	police power
easement by condemnation	fee simple absolute	prior appropriation
	fee simple defeasible	remainder interest
easement by necessity	fee simple determinable	reversionary interest
easement by prescription	freehold estate	riparian rights
	future interest	taxation
easement in gross	homestead	
eminent domain	leasehold estate	

■ WHY LEARN ABOUT... INTERESTS IN REAL ESTATE?

As discussed in Chapter 2, an extensive bundle of rights goes along with owning real estate. However, there are many different interests in real estate that can be acquired, and not all of them convey the entire bundle of legal rights to the owner. Licensees must take great care to ensure that prospective buyers understand exactly what interests a seller wishes to transfer. While only a lawyer can accurately (and legally) identify and interpret legal issues, a savvy licensee will be aware of any potential problems and address them in a timely manner. ■

■ LIMITATIONS ON THE RIGHTS OF OWNERSHIP

Ownership of real estate is not absolute, that is, a landowner's power to control his or her property is subject to other interests. Keep in mind that a landowner's power to control his or her property relates to the landowner having title of the property and the bundle of legal rights that accompanies the title. Even the most complete ownership the law allows is limited by public and private restrictions. These are intended to ensure that one owner's use or enjoyment of his or her property does not interfere with others' use or enjoyment of their property or with the welfare of the general public. Licensees should have a working knowledge of the restrictions that might limit current or future owners. A zoning ordinance that will not allow a doctor's office to coexist with a residence, a condo association bylaw prohibiting resale without board approval, or an easement allowing the neighbors to use the private beach may not only burden today's purchaser but also deter a future buyer.

This Chapter puts the various interests in real estate in perspective—what rights they confer and how use of the ownership may be limited.

■ GOVERNMENT POWERS

Individual ownership rights are subject to certain powers, or rights, held by federal, state, and local governments. These limitations on the ownership of real estate are imposed for the general welfare of the community and, therefore, supersede the rights or interests of the individual. Government powers include police power, eminent domain, taxation, and escheat.

Police Power

Every state has the power to enact legislation to preserve order, protect the public health and safety, and promote the general welfare of its citizens. That authority is known as a state's police power. The state's authority is passed on to municipalities and counties through legislation called *enabling acts*.

Of course, what is identified as being "in the public interest" varies widely from state to state and region to region. Generally, however, a police power is used to enact environmental protection laws, zoning ordinances, and building codes.

Memory Tip

The four government powers can be remembered as **PETE**: **P**olice, **E**minent domain, **T**axation, and **E**scheat.

Regulations that govern the use, occupancy, size, location, and construction of real estate also fall within the police powers.

Police powers may be used to achieve a community's needs or goals. A city that deems growth to be desirable, for instance, may exercise its police powers to enact laws encouraging the purchase and improvement of land. On the other hand, an area that wishes to retain its current character may enact laws that discourage development and population growth.

Like the rights of ownership, the state's power to regulate land use is not absolute. The laws must be uniform and nondiscriminatory; that is, they may not operate to the advantage or disadvantage of any one particular owner or owners. See Chapter 19 for more on police power.

WWWeb.Link   www.wld.com/conbus/weal/wemindom.htm

Eminent Domain

Eminent domain is the right of the government to acquire privately owned real estate for public use. **Condemnation** is the process by which the government exercises this right, by either judicial or administrative proceedings. The proposed use must be for the public good, just compensation must be paid to the owner, and the rights of the property owner must be protected by due process of law. *Public use* has been defined very broadly by the courts to include not only public facilities but also property that is no longer fit for use and must be closed or destroyed.

Eminent domain is the government's *right* to seize property; *condemnation* is the way the right is *exercised*.

Generally, the states delegate their power of eminent domain to quasi-public bodies and publicly held companies responsible for various facets of public service. For instance, a public housing authority might take privately owned land to build low-income housing; the state's land-clearance commission or redevelopment authority could use the power of eminent domain to make way for urban renewal. If there were no other feasible way to do so, a railway, utility company, or state highway department might acquire farmland to extend a railroad track, bring electricity to a remote new development, or build a highway. Again, all are allowable as long as the purpose contributes to the public good.

Ideally, the public agency and the owner of the property in question agree on compensation through direct negotiation, and the government purchases the property for a price considered fair by the owner. In some cases, the owner may simply dedicate the property to the government as a site for a school, park, library, or another beneficial use. Sometimes, however, the owner's consent cannot be obtained. In those cases, the government agency can initiate condemnation proceedings to acquire the property.

Taxation

Taxation is a charge on real estate to raise funds to meet the public needs of a government.

Although escheat is not actually a limitation on ownership, it is an avenue by which the state may acquire privately owned real or personal property. State laws provide for ownership to transfer, or *escheat,* to the state when an owner dies leaving no heirs (as defined by the law) and no will that directs how the real estate is to be distributed. In some states, real property escheats to the county where the land is located; in others, it becomes the property of the state. Escheat is intended to prevent property from being ownerless or abandoned.

■ ESTATES IN LAND

An **estate in land** defines the degree, quantity, nature, and extent of an owner's interest in real property. Many types of estates exist. However, not all *interests* in real estate are *estates.* To be an estate in land, an interest must allow possession (either now or in the future) and must be measurable by duration. Lesser interests such as easements (discussed later in this Chapter), which allow use but not possession, are not estates.

■ **FOR EXAMPLE** Bob owns a movie theater. Bob's ownership interest is an *estate* because Bob has the right to all the income from the theater, the right to change the theater into a restaurant, the right to tear down the theater and build something else on the land, and the right to sell the theater to someone else—in short, the theater belongs to Bob. When Matt buys a ticket and sits down to watch a movie in Bob's theater, Matt has an *interest* in the property, but it is *not* an estate. Matt's interest is limited to the temporary use of a limited part of the theater.

Historically, estates in land have been classified as freehold estates and leasehold estates. The two types of estates are distinguished primarily by their duration.

Freehold estates last for an *indeterminable length of time,* such as for a lifetime or forever. They include fee simple (also called an *indefeasible fee*), defeasible fee, and life estates. The first two of these estates continue for an indefinite period and may be passed along to the owner's heirs. A life estate is based on the lifetime of a person and ends when that individual dies. Freehold estates are illustrated in Figure 7.1.

Leasehold estates last for a *fixed period of time.* They include estates for years and estates from period to period. Estates at will and estates at sufferance are also leaseholds, though by their operation they are not generally viewed as being for fixed terms.

Fee Simple Estate

An estate in **fee simple** (or fee simple absolute) is the *highest interest in real estate recognized by law.* Fee simple ownership is absolute ownership: The holder is entitled to all rights to the property. It is limited only by public and private restrictions, such as zoning laws and restrictive covenants (discussed in Chapter 19). Because this estate is of unlimited duration, it is said to run forever. Upon the death of its owner, it passes to the owner's heirs or as provided by will. A fee simple estate is also referred to as an *estate of inheritance* or simply as *fee ownership.*

Freehold Estates

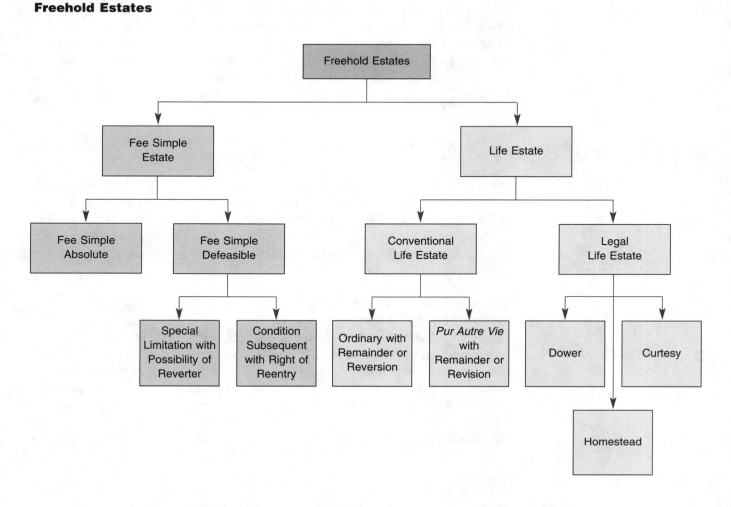

Fee simple defeasible. A fee simple defeasible (or *defeasible fee*) estate is a qualified estate—that is, it is subject to the occurrence or nonoccurrence of some specified event. Two types of defeasible estates exist: those subject to a condition subsequent and those qualified by a special limitation.

A fee simple estate may be qualified by a *condition subsequent*, which means that the new owner must *not* perform some action or activity. The former owner retains a *right of reentry* so that if the condition is broken, the former owner can retake possession of the property through legal action. Conditions in a deed are different from restrictions or covenants because of the grantor's right to reclaim ownership, a right that does not exist under private restrictions.

Fee simple *defeasible*:
"on the condition that"

Fee simple *determinable*:
"so long as"
"while"
"during"

■ **FOR EXAMPLE** A grant of land "on the condition that" there be no consumption of alcohol on the premises is a fee simple subject to a condition subsequent. If alcohol is consumed on the property, the former owner has the right to reacquire full ownership. It will be necessary for the grantor (or the grantor's heirs or successors) to go to court to assert that right, however.

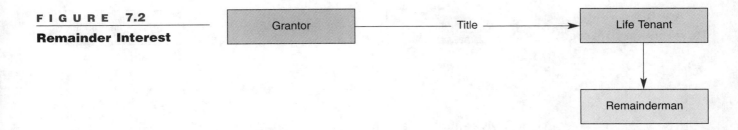

FIGURE 7.2
Remainder Interest

A fee simple estate also may be qualified by a *special limitation*. The estate ends *automatically* on the current owner's failure to comply with the limitation. The former owner retains a *possibility of reverter*. If the limitation is violated, the former owner (or his or her heirs or successors) reacquires full ownership, with no need to reenter the land or go to court. A fee simple with a special limitation is also called a **fee simple determinable** because it may end automatically. The language used to distinguish a special limitation— the words *so long as* or *while or during*—is the key to creating this estate.

The *right of entry* and *possibility of reverter* may never take effect. If they do, it will be only at some time in the future. Therefore, each of these rights is considered a **future interest.**

■ **FOR EXAMPLE** A grant of land from an owner to her church "so long as the land is used only for religious purposes" is a fee simple with a special limitation. The church has the full bundle of rights possessed by a property owner, but one of the "sticks" in the bundle—the "control" stick, in this case—has a string attached. If the church ever decides to use the land for a nonreligious purpose, the original owner will, in effect, "yank the string," causing title to revert to him or her (or to his or her heirs or successors).

Life Estate

A **life estate** is a freehold estate limited in *duration to the life of the owner or the life of some other designated person or persons*. Unlike other freehold estates, a life estate is not inheritable and cannot be devised. It passes to future owners according to the provisions of the life estate.

A life tenant is entitled to the rights of ownership, that is, the life tenant can enjoy both possession and the ordinary use and profits arising from ownership, just as if the individual were a fee owner. The ownership may be sold, mortgaged, or leased, but it is always subject to the limitation of the life estate.

A life tenant's ownership rights, however, are not absolute. The life tenant may not injure the property, such as by destroying a building or allowing it to deteriorate. In legal terms, this injury is known as *waste*. Those who will eventually own the property could seek an injunction against the life tenant or sue for damages.

Because the ownership will terminate on the death of the person against whose life the estate is measured, a purchaser, lessee, or lender can be affected. The life tenant can sell, lease, or mortgage only his or her interest— that is, ownership for a lifetime. Because the interest is obviously less desirable than a fee simple estate, the life tenant's rights are limited.

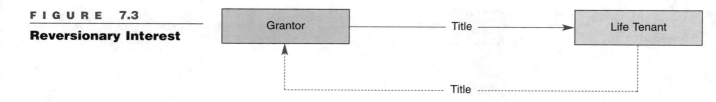

Conventional life estate. A *conventional life estate* is created intentionally by the owner. It may be established either by deed at the time the ownership is transferred during the owner's life or by a provision of the owner's will after his or her death. The estate is conveyed to an individual who is called the *life tenant*. The life tenant has full enjoyment of the ownership for the duration of his or her life. When the life tenant dies, the estate ends and its ownership passes to another designated individual or returns to the previous owner.

■ **FOR EXAMPLE** Alex, who has a fee simple estate in Blackacre, conveys a life estate to Peter for Peter's lifetime. Peter is the life tenant. On Peter's death, the life estate terminates, and Alex once again owns Blackacre. If Peter's life estate had been created by Alex's will, however, subsequent ownership of Blackacre would be determined by the provisions of the will.

Pur autre vie. A life estate also may be based on the lifetime of a person other than the life tenant. This is known as an *estate pur autre vie* ("for the life of another"). Although a life estate is not considered an estate of inheritance, a life estate pur autre vie provides for inheritance by the life tenant's heirs only until the death of the person against whose life the estate is measured. A life estate pur autre vie is often created for a physically or mentally incapacitated person in the hope of providing an incentive for someone to care for him or her.

■ **FOR EXAMPLE** Alex conveys a life estate in Blackacre to Peter as the life tenant for the duration of the life of Dale, Alex's elderly relative. Peter is still the life tenant, but the measuring life is Dale's. On Dale's death, the life estate ends. If Peter should die while Dale is still alive, Peter's heirs may inherit the life estate. However, when Dale dies, the heirs' estate ends.

Remainder and reversion. The fee simple owner who creates a conventional life estate must plan for its future ownership. When the life estate ends, it is replaced by a fee simple estate. The future owner of the fee simple estate may be designated in one of two ways:

1. Remainder interest: The creator of the life estate may name a *remainderman* as the person to whom the property will pass when the life estate ends. (*Remainderman* is the legal term; neither the term *remainderperson* nor the term *remainderwoman* is used.) (See Figure 7.2.)
2. Reversionary interest: The creator of the life estate may choose not to name a remainderman. In that case, the creator will recapture ownership when the life estate ends. The ownership is said to *revert* to the original owner. (See Figure 7.3.)

■ **FOR EXAMPLE** Alex conveys Blackacre to Peter for Peter's lifetime and designates Rick to be the remainderman. While Peter is still alive, Rick owns a *remainder* interest, which is a nonpossessory estate; that is, Rick does not possess the property but has an interest in it nonetheless. This is a *future interest* in the fee simple estate. When Peter dies, Rick automatically becomes the fee simple owner.

On the other hand, Alex may convey a life estate in Blackacre to Peter during Peter's life. On Peter's death, ownership of Blackacre reverts to Alex. Alex has retained a *reversionary* interest (also a nonpossessory estate). Alex has a *future interest* in the ownership and may reclaim the fee simple estate when Peter dies. If Alex dies before Peter, Alex's heirs (or other individuals specified in Alex's will) will assume ownership of Blackacre when Peter dies.

Legal life estate. A legal life estate is not created voluntarily by an owner. Rather, it is a form of life estate established by state law. It becomes effective automatically when certain events occur. *Dower, curtesy,* and *homestead* are the legal life estates currently used in some states.

Dower and curtesy provide the nonowning spouse with a means of support after the death of the owning spouse. *Dower* is the life estate that a wife has in the real estate of her deceased husband. *Curtesy* is an identical interest that a husband has in the real estate of his deceased wife. (In some states, dower and curtesy are referred to collectively as either dower or curtesy.)

Dower and curtesy provide that the nonowning spouse has a right to a one-half or one-third interest in the real estate for the rest of his or her life, even if the owning spouse wills the estate to others. Because a nonowning spouse might claim an interest in the future, both spouses may have to sign the proper documents when real estate is conveyed. The signature of the nonowning spouse would be needed to release any *potential* common-law interests in the property being transferred.

Most states have abolished the common-law concepts of dower and curtesy in favor of the Uniform Probate Code (UPC). The UPC gives the surviving spouse a right to an elective share on the death of the other spouse. Community property states never used dower and curtesy. (Community property is discussed in Chapter 8.)

A **homestead** is a legal life estate in real estate occupied as the family home. In effect, the home (or at least some part of it) is protected from creditors during the occupant's lifetime. In states that have homestead exemption laws, a portion of the area or value of the property occupied as the family home is exempt from certain judgments for debts such as charge accounts and personal loans. The homestead is not protected from real estate taxes levied against the property or a mortgage for the purchase or cost of improvements, that is, if the debt is secured by the property, the property cannot be exempt from a judgment on that debt.

In some states, all that is required to establish a homestead is for the head of a household (sometimes a single person) to own or lease the premises occupied by the family as a residence. In other states, the family is required by statute to file a notice. A family can have only one homestead at any given time.

How does the homestead exemption actually work? In most states, the homestead exemption merely reserves a certain amount of money for the family in the event of a court sale. In a few states, however, the entire homestead is protected from sale altogether. Once the sale occurs, any debts secured by the home (a mortgage, unpaid taxes, or mechanics' liens, for instance) will be paid from the proceeds. Then the family will receive the amount reserved by the homestead exemption. Finally, whatever remains will be applied to the family's unsecured debts.

■ **FOR EXAMPLE** Greenacre is Tim's homestead. In Tim's state, the homestead exemption is $25,000. At a court-ordered sale, the property is purchased for $60,000. First, Tim's remaining $15,000 mortgage balance is paid; then Tim receives $25,000. The remaining $20,000 is applied to Tim's unsecured debts.

Of course, no sale would be ordered if the court could determine that nothing would remain from the proceeds for the creditors. If Greenacre could not be expected to bring more than $40,000, the priority of the mortgage lien and homestead exemption would make a sale pointless.

■ ENCUMBRANCES

An **encumbrance** is a claim, charge, or liability that attaches to real estate. An encumbrance does not have a possessory interest in real property; it is not an estate. Simply put, an *encumbrance* is a right or an interest held by someone other than the fee owner of the property that affects title to real estate. An encumbrance may lessen the value or obstruct the use of the property, but it does not necessarily prevent a transfer of title.

Encumbrances may be divided into the following two general classifications:

1. *Liens* (usually monetary charges) and
2. *Encumbrances* such as restrictions, easements, and encroachments that affect the condition or use of the property.

Liens

A **lien** *is a charge against property that provides security for a debt or an obligation of the property owner.* If the obligation is not repaid, the lienholder is entitled to have the debt satisfied from the proceeds of a court-ordered or forced sale of the debtor's property. Real estate taxes, mortgages and trust deeds, judgments, and mechanics' liens all represent possible liens against an owner's real estate. Liens are discussed in detail in Chapter 10.

Deed Restrictions

Deed restrictions, also referred to as *covenants, conditions, and restrictions,* or CC&Rs, are private agreements that affect the use of land. They may be imposed by an owner of real estate and included in the seller's deed to the buyer. Typically, however, restrictive covenants are imposed by a developer or subdivider to maintain specific standards in a subdivision. Such restrictive covenants are listed in the original development plans for the subdivision filed in the public record. Deed restrictions are discussed further in Chapter 19.

FIGURE   7.4

Easement Appurtenant

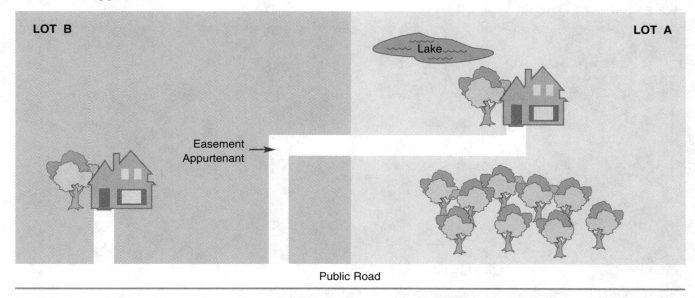

The owner of Lot A has an appurtenant easement across Lot B to gain access to his property from the paved road. Lot A is dominant. Lot B is servient.

Easements

An easement *is the right to use the land of another for a particular purpose.* An easement may exist in any portion of the real estate, including the airspace above or a right-of-way across the land.

An **appurtenant easement** is annexed to the ownership of one parcel and allows this owner the use of a neighbor's land. For an appurtenant easement to exist, two adjacent parcels of land must be owned by two different parties. The parcel over which the easement runs is known as the *servient tenement;* the neighboring parcel that benefits is known as the *dominant tenement.* (See Figure 7.4 and Figure 7.5.)

An appurtenant easement is part of the dominant tenement, and, if the dominant tenement is conveyed to another party, the easement transfers with the title. This type of easement is said to *run with the land.* It is an encumbrance on property and will transfer with the deed of the dominant tenement forever unless the holder of the dominant tenement somehow releases that right.

■ **FOR EXAMPLE** Kim and Larry own adjoining parcels of land near a lake. Kim's property borders the lake, and Larry's does not. Kim grants Larry an easement, established by a deed properly delivered, accepted, and recorded. The easement gives Larry the right to cross Kim's property to reach the lake. This is an easement appurtenant. When Kim sells the lakefront property to Mike, the easement is automatically included, even if Kim's deed fails to mention it. Larry's easement has become a limitation on the ownership rights of Kim's land.

An **easement in gross** is an *individual interest* in or right to use someone else's land. For instance, a railroad's right-of-way is an easement in gross. So is the right-of-way for a pipeline or high-tension power line (utility easements). Commercial easements in gross may be assigned, conveyed, and inherited.

FIGURE 7.5

**Easement Appurtenant
and Easement in Gross**

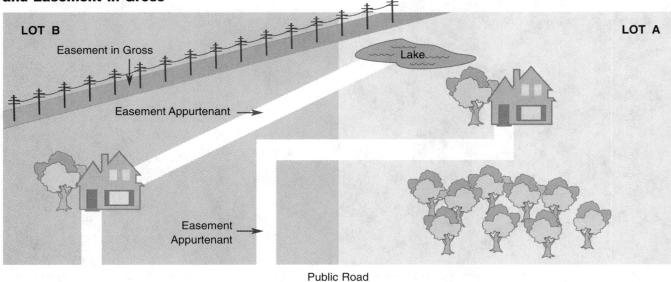

The owner of Lot B has an appurtenant easement across Lot A to gain access to the lake. Lot B is dominant and Lot A is servient. The utility company has an easement in gross across both parcels of land for its power lines. Note that Lot A also has an appurtenant easement across Lot B for its driveway. Lot A is dominant and Lot B is servient.

However, personal easements in gross usually are not assignable. Generally, a personal easement in gross terminates on the death of the easement owner. An easement in gross is often confused with the similar personal right of license, discussed later in this chapter.

Creating an easement. An easement is commonly created by a written agreement between the parties that establishes the easement right. It also may be created by the grantor in a deed of conveyance, where the grantor either *reserves* an easement over the sold land or *grants* the new owner an easement over the grantor's remaining land. An easement may be created by longtime *use,* as in an easement by prescription; by necessity; and by implication, that is, the situation or the parties' actions *imply* that they intend to create an easement.

The creation of an easement always involves two separate parties, one of whom is the owner of the land over which the easement runs. It is impossible for the owner of a parcel of property to have an easement over his or her own land.

Party wall easement. A party wall can be an exterior wall of a building that straddles the boundary line between two lots or it can be a commonly shared partition wall between two connected properties. Each lot owner owns the half of the wall on his or her lot, and each has an appurtenant easement in the other half of the wall. A written party wall agreement must be used to create the easement rights. Expenses to build and maintain the wall are usually shared. A fence built on the lot line is treated the same as a wall. A party driveway shared by and partly on the land of adjoining owners must also be created by written agreement, specifying responsibility for expenses.

Easement by necessity. An appurtenant easement that arises when an owner sells part of his or her land that has no access to a street or public way except over the seller's remaining land is an **easement by necessity**. An easement by necessity is created by court order based on the principle that owners have the right to enter and exit their land (the right of *ingress* and *egress*)—they should not be landlocked. Remember, this form of easement is called an *easement by necessity*; it is not merely for convenience and is not imposed simply to validate a shortcut.

Easement by prescription. When the claimant has made use of another's land for a certain period of time as defined by state law, an **easement by prescription,** or a *prescriptive easement*, may be acquired. The prescriptive period may be from 10 to 21 years. The claimant's use must have been continuous, exclusive, and without the owner's approval. The use must be visible, open, and notorious, that is, the owner must have been able to learn of it.

The concept of *tacking* provides that successive periods of continuous occupation by different parties may be combined (tacked) to reach the required total number of years necessary to establish a claim for a prescriptive easement. To tack on one person's possession to that of another, the parties must have been *successors in interest*, such as an ancestor and his or her heir, a landlord and a tenant, or seller and buyer.

■ **FOR EXAMPLE** Judy's property is located in a state with a prescriptive period of 20 years. For the past 22 years, Frank has driven his car across Judy's front yard several times a day to reach his garage from a more comfortable angle. Frank has an *easement by prescription*.

For 25 years, Lester has driven across Judy's front yard two or three times a year to reach his property when he's in a hurry. He does not have an easement by prescription because his use was not continuous.

For 15 years, Eric parked his car on Judy's property, next to Judy's garage. Six years ago, Eric sold his house to Nick, who continued to park his car next to Judy's garage. Last year, Nick acquired an *easement by prescription* through *tacking*.

Easement by condemnation. An **easement by condemnation** is acquired for a public purpose through the right of eminent domain. The owner of the servient tenement must be compensated for any loss in property value.

Terminating an easement. An easement may be ended

■ when the purpose for which the easement was created no longer exists;
■ when the owner of either the dominant or the servient tenement becomes the owner of both—the properties are merged under one legal description (also known as *termination by merger*);
■ by release of the right of easement to the owner of the servient tenement;
■ by abandonment of the easement (the intention of the parties is the determining factor);
■ by nonuse of a prescriptive easement;
■ by adverse possession by the owner of the servient tenement;

- by destruction of the servient tenement (for instance, the demolition of a party wall);
- by lawsuit (an *action to quiet title*) against someone claiming an easement; or
- by excessive use, as when a residential use is converted to a commercial purpose.

Note that an easement may not *automatically* terminate for these reasons. Certain legal steps may be required.

Licenses

A license is a personal privilege to enter the land of another for a specific purpose. A license differs from an easement in that *it can be terminated or canceled by the licensor* (the person who granted the license). If a right to use another's property is given orally or informally, it generally is considered to be a license rather than a personal easement in gross. A license ends on the death of either party or the sale of the land by the licensor.

■ **FOR EXAMPLE** Peter asks Harry for permission to park a boat in Harry's driveway. Harry says, "Sure, go ahead!" Peter has a *license,* but Harry may tell Peter to move the boat at any time. Similarly, a ticket to a theater or sporting event is a *license:* The holder is permitted to enter the facility and is entitled to a seat. But if the ticketholder becomes rowdy or abusive, he or she may be asked to leave.

Encroachments

Physical Encumbrances
- Restrictions
- Easements
- Licenses

An encroachment occurs when all or part of a structure, such as a building, fence, or driveway, *illegally extends beyond the land of its owner or beyond the legal building lines.* An encroachment usually is disclosed by either a physical inspection of the property or a spot survey. A *spot survey* shows the location of all improvements located on a property and whether they extend over the lot or building lines. As a rule, a spot survey is more accurate and reliable than a simple physical inspection. If a building encroaches on adjoining land, the neighbor may be able to either recover damages or secure removal of the portion of the building that encroaches. Encroachments that exceed a state's prescriptive period, however, may give rise to easements by prescription.

IN PRACTICE

Because an undisclosed encroachment could make a title unmarketable, an encroachment should be noted in a listing agreement and the sales contract. An encroachment is not disclosed by the usual title evidence provided in a real estate sale unless a survey is submitted while the title examination is being made.

■ WATER RIGHTS

Whether for agricultural, recreational, or other purposes, waterfront real estate has always been desirable. Each state has strict laws that govern the ownership and use of water as well as the adjacent land. The laws vary among the states, but all are closely linked to climactic and topographical conditions. Where water is plentiful, for instance, many states rely on the simple parameters set by the common-law doctrines of riparian and littoral rights. Where water is more scarce, a state may control all but limited domestic use of water according to the doctrine of prior appropriation.

Riparian Rights

Riparian rights are common-law rights granted to owners of land along the course of a river, stream, or similar body of water. Although riparian rights

FIGURE   7.6

Riparian Rights

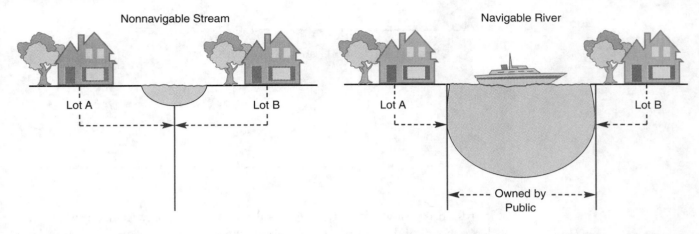

are governed by laws that vary from state to state, they generally include the unrestricted right to use the water. As a rule, the only limitation on the owner's use is that it cannot interrupt or alter the flow of the water or contaminate it in any way. In addition, an owner of land that borders a nonnavigable waterway, that is, a body of water unsuitable for commercial boat traffic, owns the land under the water to the exact center of the waterway. Land adjoining commercially navigable rivers, on the other hand, is usually owned to the water's edge, with the state holding title to the submerged land. (See Figure 7.6.) Navigable waters are considered public highways in which the public has an easement or right to travel.

Littoral Rights

Memory Tip

*R*iparian refers to rivers, streams, and similar waterways; *Littoral* refers to lakes, oceans, and similar bodies of water.

Closely related to riparian rights are the **littoral rights** of owners whose land borders commercially navigable lakes, seas, and oceans. Owners with littoral rights enjoy unrestricted use of available waters but own the land adjacent to the water only up to the mean (average) high-water mark. (See Figure 7.7.) All land below this point is owned by the government.

Riparian and littoral rights are appurtenant (attached) to the land and cannot be retained when the property is sold. The right to use the water belongs to whoever owns the bordering land and cannot be retained by a former owner after the land is sold.

Accretion, Erosion, and Avulsion

The amount of land an individual owns may be affected by the natural action of water. An owner is entitled to all land created through **accretion**—increases in the land resulting from the deposit of soil by the water's action. (Such deposits are called *alluvion* or *alluvium*.) If water recedes, new land is acquired by *reliction*.

On the other hand, an owner may lose land through **erosion.** Erosion is the gradual and imperceptible wearing away of the land by natural forces, such as wind, rain, and flowing water. Fortunately, erosion usually takes hundreds or even thousands of years to have any noticeable effect on a person's property. Flash floods or heavy winds, however, can increase the speed of erosion.

Littoral Rights

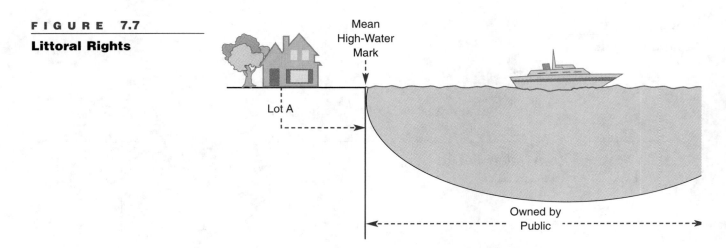

If erosion is a slow natural process, avulsion is its opposite. **Avulsion** is the sudden removal of soil by an act of nature. It is an event that causes the loss of land much less subtly than does erosion. An earthquake or a mudslide, for instance, can cause an individual's landholding to become much smaller very quickly.

Doctrine of Prior Appropriation

In states where water is scarce, ownership and use of water are often determined by the doctrine of **prior appropriation.** Under this doctrine, *the right to use any water, with the exception of limited domestic use, is controlled by the state rather than by the landowner adjacent to the water.*

To secure water rights in prior appropriation states, a landowner must demonstrate to a state agency that he or she plans a *beneficial* use for the water, such as crop irrigation. If the state's requirements are met, the landowner receives a permit to use a specified amount of water for the limited purpose of the beneficial use. Although statutes governing prior appropriation vary from state to state, the priority of water rights is usually determined by the oldest recorded permit date.

Once granted, water rights attach to the land of the permitholder. The permitholder may sell a water right to another party.

Issuance of a water permit does not grant access to the water source. All access rights-of-way over the land of another (easements) must be obtained from the property owner.

■ SUMMARY

An individual's ownership rights are subject to the powers held by government. These powers include police power, by which states can enact legislation such as environmental protection laws and zoning ordinances. The government may also acquire privately owned land for public use through the power of eminent domain. Real estate taxes are imposed to raise government funds. When a property becomes ownerless, ownership of the property may transfer, or escheat, to the state.

An estate is the degree, quantity, nature, and extent of interest a person holds in land. Freehold estates are estates of indeterminate length. Less-than-freehold estates are called leasehold estates, and they involve tenants.

A freehold estate may be a fee simple estate or a life estate. A fee simple estate can be absolute or defeasible upon the happening of some event. A conventional life estate is created by the owner of a fee estate; a legal life estate is created by law. Legal life estates include curtesy, dower, and homestead.

Encumbrances against real estate can be liens, deed restrictions, easements, licenses, or encroachments.

An easement is the right acquired by one person to use another's real estate. Easements are classified as interests in real estate but are not estates in land. There are two types of easements. Appurtenant easements involve two separately owned tracts. The tract benefited is known as the dominant tenement; the tract subject to the easement is called the servient tenement. An easement in gross is a personal right, such as that granted to utility companies to maintain poles, wires, and pipelines.

Easements may be created by agreement, express grant or reservation in a deed, necessity, prescription, or condemnation. An easement can be terminated when the purpose of the easement no longer exists, by merger of both interests, with an express intention to extinguish the easement by release, or by abandonment of the easement.

A license is permission to enter another's property for a specific purpose. A license is usually created orally; it is temporary and can be revoked.

An encroachment is an unauthorized use of another's real estate.

Ownership of land encompasses not only the land itself but also the right to use the water on or adjacent to it. Many states subscribe to the common-law doctrine of riparian rights, which gives the owner of land adjacent to a nonnavigable stream ownership of the stream to its midpoint. Littoral rights are held by owners of land bordering large lakes and oceans and include rights to the water and ownership of the land up to the mean high-water mark. In states where water is scarce, water use is often decided by the doctrine of prior appropriation. Under prior appropriation, water belongs to the state and is allocated to users who have obtained permits.

QUESTIONS

1. The right of a government body to take ownership of real estate for public use is called

   a. escheat.
   b. eminent domain.
   c. condemnation.
   d. police power.

2. A purchaser of real estate learns that his ownership rights could continue forever and that no other person claims to be the owner or has any ownership control over the property. This person owns a

   a. fee simple interest.
   b. life estate.
   c. determinable fee.
   d. fee simple on condition.

3. Joan owned the fee simple title to a vacant lot adjacent to a hospital and was persuaded to make a gift of the lot. She wanted to have some control over its use, so her attorney prepared her deed to convey ownership of the lot to the hospital "so long as it is used for hospital purposes." After completion of the gift the hospital will own a

   a. fee simple absolute estate.
   b. license.
   c. fee simple determinable.
   d leasehold estate.

4. After Dan had purchased his house and moved in, he discovered that his neighbor regularly used Dan's driveway to reach a garage located on the neighbor's property. Dan's attorney explained that ownership of the neighbor's real estate includes an easement over the driveway. Dan's property is properly called

   a. the dominant tenement.
   b. a freehold.
   c. a leasehold.
   d. the servient tenement.

5. A *license* is an example of a(n)

   a. appurtenant easement.
   b. encroachment.
   c. temporary use right.
   d. restriction.

6. Betsy is the owner of Blueacre. During her lifetime, Betsy conveys a life estate in Blueacre to Chuck. Under the terms of the grant, Chuck's life estate will terminate when Betsy's uncle dies and Betsy will regain the property. However, Chuck dies shortly after moving to Blueacre, while Betsy's uncle is still alive. Chuck's will states, "I leave everything to Donna." Which of the following best describes the interests that the parties now hold?

   a. Chuck possessed a life estate pur autre vie, measured by the life of Betsy's uncle. Donna has the same interest as Chuck had. Donna's interest in Blueacre will end when Betsy's uncle dies. Betsy has a reversionary interest in Blueacre.
   b. Chuck possessed a life estate pur autre vie, measured by the life of Betsy's uncle. Donna is the remainderman and holds a nonpossessory estate until Betsy's uncle dies. When Betsy's uncle dies, Blueacre will escheat to the state.
   c. Chuck possessed a determinable life estate in Blueacre. Betsy's uncle is the measuring life. When Chuck died, Chuck's interest passed directly to Donna. When Betsy's uncle dies, Betsy may regain ownership of Blueacre only by suing Donna.
   d. Betsy has a remainder interest in the conventional life estate granted to Chuck. Because the grant was to Chuck alone, the estate may not pass to Donna. When Chuck died before Betsy's uncle, the estate automatically ended and Betsy now owns Blueacre in fee simple.

7. Wally owns a home in a state that recognizes a limited homestead exemption. Which of the following statements is true if Wally is sued by his creditors?
   a. The creditors can have the court sell Wally's home and apply the full proceeds of sale to the debts.
   b. The creditors have no right to have Wally's home sold.
   c. The creditors can force Wally to sell the home to pay them.
   d. The creditors can request a court sale and apply the sale proceeds, in excess of the statutory exemption and secured debts, to Wally's unsecured debts.

8. If the owner of real estate does not take action against a trespasser before the statutory period has passed, the trespasser may acquire the legal authority to continue using the property through
   a. an easement by necessity.
   b. a license.
   c. title by eminent domain.
   d. an easement by prescription.

9. A property owner wants to use water from a river that runs through the property to irrigate a potato field. To do so, the owner is required by state law to submit an application to the Department of Water Resources describing in detail the beneficial use he plans for the water. If the department approves the owner's application, it will issue a permit allowing a limited amount of river water to be diverted onto the property. Based on these facts, it can be assumed that this property owner's state relies on which of the following rules of law?
   a. Common-law riparian rights
   b. Common-law littoral rights
   c. Doctrine of prior appropriation
   d. Doctrine of highest and best use

10. Which of the following is not an example of governmental power?
    a. dedication.   c. eminent domain.
    b. police power.   d. taxation.

11. Property deeded to a town "for recreational purposes only" conveys a
    a. fee simple absolute.
    b. conditional fee estate.
    c. leasehold interest.
    d. determinable fee.

12. A property owner who has the legal right to cross over a neighbor's land holds a(n):
    a. estate in land.   c. police power.
    b. easement.   d. encroachment.

13. Which of the following is not a legal life estate?
    a. Leasehold   c. Homestead
    b. Curtesy   d. Dower

14. A father conveys ownership of his residence to his daughter but reserves for himself a life estate in the residence. The interest the daughter owns during her father's lifetime is
    a. pur autre vie.   c. a reversion.
    b. a remainder.   d. a leasehold.

15. Kevin has fenced his property. By mistake, the fence extends one foot over Kevin's lot line onto a neighbor's property. The fence is an example of a(n)
    a. license.
    b. encroachment.
    c. easement by necessity.
    d. easement by prescription.

16. A homeowner may be allowed certain protection from judgments of creditors as a result of his state's
    a. littoral rights.
    b. curtesy rights.
    c. homestead rights.
    d. dower rights.

17. Katie has permission from Todd to hike on his property during the autumn months. Katie has
    a. an easement by necessity.
    b. an easement by condemnation.
    c. riparian rights.
    d. a license.

18. Which of the following statements about encumbrances on real estate is true?

a. Easements and encroachments are always encumbrances on the land that is subject to them.

b. The presence of an encumbrance makes it impossible to sell the encumbered property.

c. All encumbrances must be removed before the title can be transferred.

d. An encumbrance is of no monetary value to its owner.

19. A tenant who rents an apartment from the owner of the property holds a(n)

a. easement.

b. license.

c. freehold interest.

d. leasehold interest.

20. Because a homeowner failed to pay her real estate taxes on time, the taxing authority imposed a claim against her property. This claim is known as a(n)

a. deed restriction.

b. lien.

c. easement.

d. reversionary interest.

C H A P T E R EIGHT

FORMS OF REAL ESTATE OWNERSHIP

■ **LEARNING OBJECTIVES** *When you've finished reading this Chapter, you should be able to:*

■ **identify** the four basic forms of co-ownership.

■ **describe** the ways in which various business organizations may own property.

■ **explain** how a tenancy in common, joint tenancy, and tenancy by the entirety are created and how they may be terminated.

■ **distinguish** cooperative ownership from condominium ownership.

■ **define** the following *key terms:*

common elements	joint venture	severalty
community property	limited liability company	syndicate
condominium	(LLC)	tenancy by the entirety
cooperative	limited partnership	tenancy in common
co-ownership	partition	time-sharing
corporation	partnership	trust
general partnership	right of survivorship	
joint tenancy	separate property	

■ WHY LEARN ABOUT... FORMS OF REAL ESTATE OWNERSHIP?

As we've seen, many different interests in land exist—fee simple, life estates, and easements, for instance. Licensees also have to understand *how* these interests in real property may be held. Although questions about forms of ownership should always be referred to an attorney, successful brokers and salespersons must understand the fundamental types of ownership so they will know who must sign various documents. They also must know what form of ownership a purchaser wants and what options are possible when more than one individual will take title. Because the form of ownership determines how the property can be reconveyed later, it is very important for the licensee to get it right the first time. ■

■ FORMS OF OWNERSHIP

Although the forms of ownership available are controlled by state laws, a fee simple estate may be held in three basic ways:

1. In *severalty*, where title is held by one individual
2. In *co-ownership*, where title is held by two or more individuals
3. In *trust*, where a third individual holds title for the benefit of another

■ OWNERSHIP IN SEVERALTY

When real estate is owned by one individual, that individual is said to own the property in **severalty**. The term comes from the fact that this sole owner is "severed" or "cut off" from other owners. The severalty owner has sole rights to the ownership and sole discretion over the transfer of the ownership. When either a husband or wife owns property in severalty, state law may affect how ownership is held.

■ CO-OWNERSHIP

When title to one parcel of real estate is held by two or more individuals, those parties are called *co-owners* or *concurrent owners*. Most states commonly recognize various forms of **co-ownership.** Individuals may co-own property as tenants in common, joint tenants, or tenants by the entirety, or they may co-own it as community property. During the lifetime of the co-owners, however, there is no apparent difference among the various types of ownership. Only when the property is conveyed or one of the owners dies do the differences become apparent.

Tenancy in Common

A parcel of real estate may be owned by two or more people as tenants in common. In a **tenancy in common,** each tenant holds an *undivided fractional interest* in the property. A tenant in common may hold, say, a one-half or one-third interest in a property. The physical property, however, is not divided into a specific half or third. The co-owners have *unity of possession,* that

TABLE 8.1

Remembering Legal Terminology: "OR" versus "EE"

Throughout this Chapter and the rest of the book, we will be referring to people as *grantor* and *grantee, trustor* and *trustee, mortgagor* and *mortgagee,* and so on. Because the terminology can be confusing, we've included this table to help you remember who's who in a transaction. Refer back to this table when the terms come up in other Chapters, too.

Product	Person Giving the Product	Person Receiving the Product
Devise	Devisor	Devisee
Grant	Grantor	Grantee
Legacy	Legator	Legatee
Lease	Lessor	Lessee
Mortgage*	Mortgagor	Mortgagee
Offer	Offeror	Offeree
Option	Optionor	Optionee
Sublease	Sublessor	Sublessee
Trust	Trustor	Trustee

*Note that a mortgage is a written agreement that pledges real estate as security for the payment of a debt. The mortgagor is the borrower. This person (the mortgagor) gives the mortgagee (the lender) a mortgage or deed of trust (property interest) on the property used to secure the loan.

Forms of Co-Ownership

1. Tenancy in common
2. Joint tenancy
3. Tenancy by the entirety
4. Community property

is, they are entitled to possession of the whole property. It is the *ownership* interest, not the property, that is divided.

The deed creating a tenancy in common may or may not state the fractional interest held by each co-owner. If no fractions are stated, the tenants are presumed to hold equal shares. For example, if five people hold title, each would own an undivided one-fifth interest.

Because the co-owners own separate interests, each can sell, convey, mortgage, or transfer his or her interest without the consent of the other co-owners. However, no individual tenant may transfer the ownership of the entire property. When one co-owner dies, the tenant's undivided interest passes according to his or her will. (See Figure 8.1.)

When two or more people acquire title to real estate and the deed does not indicate the form of the tenancy, the new owners are usually determined to have acquired title as tenants in common. But if the deed is made to a husband and wife with no further explanation, this assumption may not apply. In some states, a deed made to a husband and wife creates a tenancy by the entirety; in others, community property; and in at least one state, a joint tenancy.

Joint Tenancy

Most states recognize some form of **joint tenancy** in property owned by two or more people.

The most distinguishing feature of joint tenancy is the **right of survivorship.** Upon the death of a joint tenant, his or her interest does not pass to heirs or according to a will. Rather, the entire ownership remains in the surviving joint tenant(s). Essentially, there is simply one less owner.

As each successive joint tenant dies, the surviving joint tenants acquire the deceased tenant's interest. The last survivor takes title in severalty and has all

FIGURE   8.1

Tenancy in Common

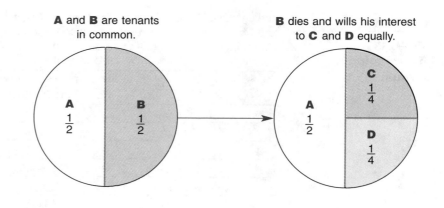

A and B are tenants in common.

B dies and wills his interest to C and D equally.

the rights of sole ownership, including the right to pass the property to his or her heirs. (See Figure 8.2.)

IN   PRACTICE

The form under which title is to be taken by individuals or married partners should always be discussed with an attorney. Licensees may not give legal advice or engage in the practice of law.

Creating joint tenancies. A joint tenancy can be created only by the intentional act of conveying a deed or giving the property by will. It cannot be implied or created by operation of law. The deed must specifically state the parties' intention to create a joint tenancy, and the parties must be explicitly identified as joint tenants. Some states, however, have abolished the right of survivorship as the distinguishing characteristic of joint tenancy. In these states, the deed must explicitly indicate the intention to create the right of survivorship for that right to exist.

> Special wording is required in a deed creating a joint tenancy, such as *"To A and B as joint tenants and not as tenants in common."*

The following four "unities" are required to create a joint tenancy:

1. Unity of *possession*—all joint tenants holding an undivided right to possession
2. Unity of *interest*—all joint tenants holding equal ownership interests
3. Unity of *time*—all joint tenants acquiring their interests at the same time
4. Unity of *title*—all joint tenants acquiring their interests by the same document

The four unities are present when the following requirements are met:

- Title is acquired by one deed.
- The deed is executed, signed, and delivered at one time.
- The deed conveys equal interests to all of the parties.
- The parties hold undivided possession of the property as joint tenants.

Because the unities must be satisfied, many states require the use of an intermediary when a sole owner wishes to create a joint tenancy between himself or herself and others. The owner conveys the property to a nominee, or *straw man*. Then the nominee conveys it back, naming all the parties as joint tenants in the deed. As a result, all the joint tenants acquire title at the same time by one deed.

**Joint Tenancy with
Right of Survivorship**

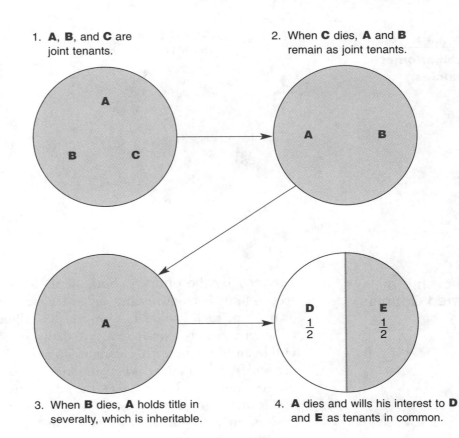

1. **A**, **B**, and **C** are joint tenants.

2. When **C** dies, **A** and **B** remain as joint tenants.

3. When **B** dies, **A** holds title in severalty, which is inheritable.

4. **A** dies and wills his interest to **D** and **E** as tenants in common.

Memory Tip

The four unities necessary to create a joint tenancy may be remembered by the acronym *PITT: P*ossession, *I*nterest, *T*ime, and *T*itle.

Some states have eliminated this "legal fiction" and allow the sole owner to execute a deed to himself or herself and others "as joint tenants and not as tenants in common," thereby creating a valid joint tenancy.

Terminating joint tenancies. A joint tenancy is destroyed when any one of the four unities of joint tenancy is terminated. A joint tenant is free to convey his or her interest in the jointly held property, but doing so destroys the unities of time and title. The new owner cannot become a joint tenant. Rights of other joint tenants, however, are unaffected.

■ **FOR EXAMPLE** Alva, Betty, and Cindy hold title to Blackacre as joint tenants. Alva conveys her interest to Doris. Doris now owns a fractional interest in Blackacre as a tenant in common with Betty and Cindy, who continue to own their undivided interest as joint tenants. (See Figure 8.3.) Doris is presumed to have a one-third interest, which may be reconveyed or left to Doris's heirs.

**Termination of
Co-Ownership by
Partition Suit**

Cotenants who wish to terminate their co-ownership may file an action in court to **partition** the property. Partition is a legal way to dissolve the relationship when the parties do not voluntarily agree to its termination. If the court determines that the land cannot be divided physically into separate parcels without destroying its value, the court will order the real estate sold. The proceeds of the sale will then be divided among the co-owners according to their fractional interests.

FIGURE 8.3

Combination of Tenancies

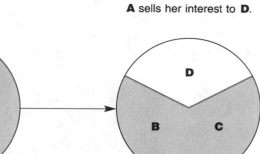

A, **B**, and **C** are joint tenants.

A sells her interest to **D**.

D becomes a tenant in common with **B** and **C** as joint tenants.

Ownership by Married Couples

Tenancy by the entirety. Some states allow husbands and wives to use a special form of co-ownership called **tenancy by the entirety.** In this form of ownership, each spouse has an equal, undivided interest in the property. (The term *entirety* refers to the fact that the owners are considered one indivisible unit because early common law viewed a married couple as one legal person.) A husband and wife who are tenants by the entirety have rights of survivorship. During their lives, they can convey title *only by a deed signed by both parties.* One party cannot convey a one-half interest, and generally they have no right to partition or divide. On the death of one spouse, the surviving spouse automatically becomes sole owner. Married couples often take title to property as tenants by the entirety so that the surviving spouse can enjoy the benefits of ownership without the delay of probate proceedings.

IN PRACTICE

An attorney should be consulted about the requirements to create a tenancy by the entirety. Under common law, a grant to a husband and wife automatically created a tenancy by the entirety, even when no form of ownership was specified in the deed. Some states, however, require that the intention to create a tenancy by the entirety be specifically stated. If it is not stated in the deed, a tenancy in common can result.

A tenancy by the entirety may be terminated in the following ways:

- By the death of either spouse (the surviving spouse becomes sole owner in severalty)
- By agreement between both parties (through the execution of a new deed)
- By divorce (which leaves the parties as tenants in common)
- By a court-ordered sale of the property to satisfy a judgment against the husband and wife as joint debtors (the tenancy is dissolved so that the property can be sold to pay the judgment)

Memory Tip

The methods of terminating a tenancy by the entirety may be remembered by the acronym J'S DAD: Judgment Sale, Death, Agreement, or Divorce.

Community property rights. Community property laws are based on the idea that a husband and wife, rather than merging into one entity, are equal partners in the marriage. Any property acquired during a marriage is considered to be obtained by mutual effort. The states' community property laws vary widely. Essentially, however, they all recognize two kinds of property: separate property and community property.

Separate property is real or personal property that was owned solely by either spouse before the marriage. It also includes property acquired by gift or inheritance during the marriage, as well as any property purchased with separate funds during the marriage. Any income earned from a person's separate property remains part of his or her separate property. Separate property can be mortgaged or conveyed by the owning spouse without the signature of the nonowning spouse.

Community property consists of all other property, both real and personal, acquired by either spouse during the marriage. Any conveyance or encumbrance of community property requires the signatures of *both* spouses. When one spouse dies, the survivor automatically owns one-half of the community property. The other half is distributed according to the deceased spouse's will. If the spouse dies without a will, the other half is inherited by the surviving spouse or by the decedent's other heirs, depending on state law. Community property does *not* provide an automatic right of survivorship as joint tenancy does.

■ TRUSTS

A **trust** is a device by which one person transfers ownership of property to someone else to hold or manage for the benefit of a third party. Perhaps a grandfather wishes to ensure the college education of his granddaughter, so he transfers his oil field to the grandchild's mother. He instructs the mother to use its income to pay for the grandchild's college tuition. In this case, the grandfather is the *trustor*—the person who creates the trust. The granddaughter is the *beneficiary*—the person who benefits from the trust. The mother is the *trustee*—the party who holds legal title to the property and is entrusted with carrying out the trustor's instructions regarding the purpose of the trust. The trustee is a *fiduciary*, who acts in confidence or trust and has a special legal relationship with the beneficiary. The trustee's power and authority are limited by the terms of the trust agreement, will or deed in trust.

IN PRACTICE   The legal and tax implications of setting up a trust are complex and vary widely from state to state. Attorneys and tax experts should always be consulted on the subject of trusts.

Most states allow real estate to be held in trust. Depending on the type of trust and its purpose, the trustor, trustee, and beneficiary can all be either people or legal entities, such as corporations. *Trust companies* are corporations set up for this specific purpose.

Real estate can be owned under living or testamentary trusts and land trusts. It can also be held by investors in a *real estate investment trust* (REIT), discussed in Appendix I.

Living and Testamentary Trusts

A property owner may provide for his or her own financial care or for that of the owner's family by establishing a trust. This trust may be created by agreement during the property owner's lifetime (a *living trust*) or established by will after the owner's death (a *testamentary trust*). (Note that neither of these are

	Property Held	Property Conveyed
Tenancy in Common	Each tenant holds a fractional undivided interest.	Each tenant can convey or devise his or her interest, but not entire interest.
Joint Tenancy	Unity of ownership. Created by intentional act; unities of possession, interest, time, title.	Right of survivorship; cannot be conveyed to heirs.
Tenants by the Entirety	Husband and wife have equal undivided interest in property.	Right of survivorship; convey by deed signed by both parties. One party can't convey one-half interest.
Community Property	Husband and wife are equal partners in marriage. Real or personal property acquired during marriage is community property.	Conveyance requires signature of both spouses. No right of survivorship; when spouse dies, survivor owns one-half of community property. Other one-half is distributed according to will or, if no will, according to state law.

related to the so-called living will, which deals with the right to refuse medical treatment.)

The person who creates the trust conveys real or personal property to a trustee (usually a corporate trustee), with the understanding that the trustee will assume certain duties. These duties may include the care and investment of the trust assets to produce an income. After paying the trust's operating expenses and trustee's fees, the income is paid to or used for the benefit of the beneficiary. The trust may continue for the beneficiary's lifetime, or the assets may be distributed when the beneficiary reaches a certain age or when other conditions are met.

Land Trusts

A few states permit the creation of *land trusts*, in which real estate is the only asset. As in all trusts, the title to the property is conveyed to a trustee, and the beneficial interest belongs to the beneficiary. In the case of land trusts, however, the beneficiary is usually also the trustor. While the beneficial interest is *personal property*, the beneficiary retains management and control of the real property and has the right of possession and the right to any income or proceeds from its sale.

One of the distinguishing characteristics of a land trust is that the *public records usually do not name the beneficiary*. A land trust may be used for secrecy when assembling separate parcels. There are other benefits as well. A beneficial interest can be transferred by assignment, making the formalities of a deed unnecessary. The beneficial interest in property can be pledged as security for a loan without having a mortgage recorded. Because the beneficiary's interest is personal, it passes at the beneficiary's death under the laws of the state in which the beneficiary lived. If the deceased owned property in several states, additional probate costs and inheritance taxes can be avoided.

A land trust ordinarily continues for a definite term, such as 20 years. If the beneficiary does not extend the trust term when it expires, the trustee is usually obligated to sell the real estate and return the net proceeds to the beneficiary.

IN PRACTICE   Licensees should exercise caution in using the term *trust deed.* It can mean both a *deed in trust* (which relates to the creation of a living, testamentary or land trust) and a *deed of trust* (a financing document similar to a mortgage). Because these documents are not interchangeable, using an inaccurate term can cause serious misunderstandings.

■ OWNERSHIP OF REAL ESTATE BY BUSINESS ORGANIZATIONS

A business organization is a legal entity that exists independently of its members. Ownership by a business organization makes it possible for many people to hold an interest in the same parcel of real estate. Investors may be organized to finance a real estate project in various ways. Some provide for the real estate to be owned by the entity; others provide for direct ownership by the investors.

Partnerships

A **partnership** is *an association of two or more persons who carry on a business for profit as co-owners.* In a general partnership, all the partners participate in the operation and management of the business and share full liability for business losses and obligations. A **limited partnership,** on the other hand, consists of one or more general partners as well as limited partners. The business is run by the general partner or partners. The limited partners are not legally permitted to participate, and each can be held liable for business losses only to the extent of his or her investment. The limited partnership is a popular method of organizing investors because it permits investors with small amounts of capital to participate in large real estate projects with a minimum of personal risk.

Most states have adopted the *Uniform Partnership Act* (UPA), which permits real estate to be held in the partnership name. The *Uniform Limited Partnership Act* (ULPA) also has been widely adopted. It establishes the legality of the limited partnership entity and provides that realty may be held in the limited partnership's name. Profits and losses are passed through the partnership to each partner, whose individual tax situation determines the tax consequences.

General partnerships are dissolved and must be reorganized if one partner dies, withdraws, or goes bankrupt. In a limited partnership, however, the partnership agreement may provide for the continuation of the organization following the death or withdrawal of one of the partners.

Corporations

A **corporation** is a legal entity—an artificial person—created under the authority of the laws of the state from which it receives its charter. A corporation is managed and operated by its *board of directors*. The charter sets forth the powers of the corporation, including its right to buy and sell real estate (based on a resolution by the board of directors). Because the corporation is a legal entity, it can own real estate in *severalty*. Some corporations are permitted by their charters to purchase real estate for any purpose; others are limited to purchasing only the land necessary to fulfill the entities' corporate purposes.

As a legal entity, a corporation continues to exist until it is formally dissolved. The death of one of the officers or directors does not affect title to property owned by the corporation.

Individuals participate, or invest, in a corporation by purchasing stock. Because stock is *personal property*, shareholders do not have direct ownership interest in the real estate owned by a corporation. Each shareholder's liability for the corporation's losses is usually limited to the amount of his or her investment.

One of the main disadvantages of corporate ownership of income property is that the profits are subject to *double taxation*. As a legal entity, a corporation must file an income tax return and pay tax on its profits. The portion of the remaining profits distributed to shareholders as dividends is taxed again as part of the shareholders' individual incomes.

An alternative form of business ownership that provides the benefit of a corporation as a legal entity but avoids double taxation is known as an *S corporation*. Profits of S corporations are taxed at the applicable rates of their shareholders, whether or not distributed to them as dividends. S corporations are generally small, closely-held corporations that are not taxed directly. S corporations are subject to strict requirements regulating their structure, membership, and operation. If the Internal Revenue Service (IRS) determines that an S corporation has failed to comply with these detailed rules, the entity will be redefined as some other form of business organization, and its favorable tax treatment will be lost.

Syndicates and Joint Ventures

Generally speaking, a **syndicate** is *two or more people or firms joined together to make and operate a real estate investment*. A syndicate is not in itself a legal entity; however, it may be organized into a number of ownership forms, including co-ownership (tenancy in common, joint tenancy), partnership, trust, or corporation. A **joint venture** is a form of partnership in which *two or more people or firms carry out a single business project*. The joint venture is characterized by a time limitation resulting from the fact that the joint venturers do not intend to establish a permanent relationship.

Limited Liability Companies

The **limited liability company (LLC)** is a relatively recent form of business organization. An LLC combines the most attractive features of limited partnerships and corporations. The members of an LLC enjoy the limited liability offered by a corporate form of ownership and the tax advantages of a partnership. In addition, the LLC offers flexible management structures without the complicated requirements of S corporations or the restrictions of limited partnerships. The structure and methods of establishing a new LLC, or of converting an existing entity to the LLC form, vary from state to state.

■ CONDOMINIUMS, COOPERATIVES, AND TIME-SHARES

"Home" does not refer only to a brick bungalow on a grassy lawn surrounded by a white picket fence. A growing urban population, diverse lifestyles, changing family structures, and heightened mobility have created a demand for new forms of ownership. Condominiums, cooperatives, and time-share arrangements are three types of property ownership that have arisen in residential, commercial, and industrial markets to address our society's changing real estate needs.

Condominium Ownership

The **condominium** form of ownership has become increasingly popular throughout the United States. Condominium laws, often called *horizontal property acts,* have been enacted in every state. Under these laws, the owner of each unit holds a *fee simple title* to the unit. The individual unit owners also own a specified share of the undivided interest in the remainder of the building and land, known as the **common elements.** Common elements typically include such items as land, courtyards, lobbies, the exterior structure, hallways, elevators, stairways, and the roof, as well as recreational facilities such as swimming pools, tennis courts, and golf courses. (See Figure 8.4.) The individual unit owners own these common elements as *tenants in common.* State law usually provides, however, that unit owners do not have the same right to partition that other tenants in common have. Condominium ownership is not restricted to highrise buildings; lowrises, town houses, and detached structures can all be condominiums.

WWWeb.Link   www.law.cornell.edu/uniform/vol7.html#condo

Creation of a condominium. Many states have adopted the *Uniform Condominium Act* (UCA). Under its provisions, a condominium is created and established when the owner of an existing building (or the developer of unimproved property) executes and records a *declaration of condominium.* The declaration includes

- a legal description of the condominium units and the common elements (including *limited* common elements—those that serve only one particular unit);
- a copy of the condominium's bylaws, drafted to govern the operation of the owners' association;
- a survey of the property;
- an architect's drawings, illustrating both the vertical and horizontal boundaries of each unit; and
- any restrictive covenants controlling the rights of ownership.

Owning a condominium. Once the property is established as a condominium, each unit becomes a separate parcel of real estate that is owned in fee simple and may be held by one or more persons in any type of ownership or tenancy recognized by state law. A condominium unit may be mortgaged like any other parcel of real estate. The unit can usually be sold or transferred to whomever the owner chooses, unless the condominium association provides for a *right of first refusal.* In this case, the owner is required to offer the unit at the same price to the other owners in the condominium or the association before accepting an outside purchase offer.

Real estate taxes are assessed and collected on each unit as an individual property. Default in the payment of taxes or a mortgage loan by one unit owner may

FIGURE 8.4

Condominium Ownership

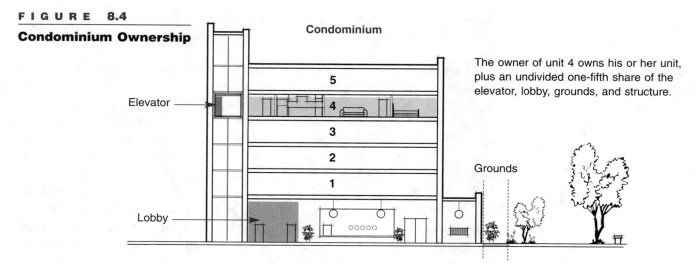

The owner of unit 4 owns his or her unit, plus an undivided one-fifth share of the elevator, lobby, grounds, and structure.

result in a foreclosure sale of that owner's unit. An owner's default, however, does not affect the other unit owners.

IN PRACTICE

When someone buys a condominium, he or she should do as much background research as possible. Examining and understanding association fees and rules are critical so the buyer is aware of his or her responsibilities and is not surprised by a particular fee or rule. Most states require the disclosure of condominium documents to buyers; it's important that the buyer examine them.

Operation and administration. The condominium property is administered by an association of unit owners. The association may be governed by a board of directors or another official entity, and it may manage the property on its own or hire a property manager.

The association must enforce any rules it adopts regarding the operation and use of the property. The association is responsible for the maintenance, repair, cleaning, and sanitation of the common elements and structural portions of the property. It must also maintain fire, extended-coverage, and liability insurance.

The expenses of maintaining and operating the building are paid by the unit owners in the form of fees and assessments. Both fees and assessments are imposed and collected by the owners' association. Recurring fees (referred to as *condo fees*) are paid by each unit owner. The fees may be due monthly, quarterly, semiannually, or annually, depending on the provisions of the bylaws. The size of an individual owner's fee is generally determined by the size of his or her unit. For instance, the owner of a three-bedroom unit pays a larger share of the total expense than the owner of a one-bedroom unit. If the fees are not paid, the association may seek a court-ordered judgment to have the delinquent owner's unit sold to cover the outstanding amount or place a lien on the property.

Assessments are special payments required of unit owners to address some specific expense, such as a new roof. Assessments are structured like condo fees: Owners of larger units pay proportionately higher assessments than owners of smaller units.

Cooperative Ownership

In a **cooperative,** a corporation holds title to the land and building. The corporation then offers *shares of stock* to prospective tenants. The price the corporation sets for each apartment becomes the price of the stock. The purchaser becomes a shareholder in the corporation by virtue of stock ownership and receives a *proprietary lease* to the apartment for the life of the corporation. Because stock is personal property, the cooperative tenant-owners do not own real estate, as is the case with condominiums. Instead, they own an interest in a corporation that has only one asset: the building.

Operation and management. The operation and management of a cooperative are determined by the corporation's bylaws. Through their control of the corporation, the shareholders of a cooperative control the property and its operation. They elect officers and directors who are responsible for operating the corporation and its real estate assets. Individual shareholders are obligated to abide by the corporation's bylaws.

An important issue in most cooperatives is the method by which shares in the corporation may be transferred to new owners. For instance, the bylaws may require that the board of directors approve any prospective shareholders. In some cooperatives, a tenant-owner must sell the stock back to the corporation at the original purchase price so that the corporation realizes any profits when the shares are resold.

■ **FOR EXAMPLE** In a highly publicized incident, former President Richard Nixon's attempt to move into a highly exclusive Manhattan cooperative apartment building was blocked by the cooperative's board. In refusing to allow the controversial ex-President to purchase shares, the board cited the unwanted publicity and media attention other celebrity tenants would suffer.

The corporation incurs costs in the operation and maintenance of the entire parcel, including both the common property and the individual apartments. These costs include real estate taxes and any mortgage payments the corporation may have. The corporation also budgets funds for such expenses as insurance, utilities, repairs and maintenance, janitorial and other services, replacement of equipment, and reserves for capital expenditures. Funds for the budget are assessed to individual shareholders, generally in the form of monthly fees similar to those charged by a homeowners' association in a condominium.

Unlike in a condominium association, which has the authority to impose a lien on the title owned by someone who defaults on maintenance payments, the burden of any defaulted payment in a cooperative falls on the remaining shareholders. Each shareholder is affected by the financial ability of the others. For this reason, approval of prospective tenants by the board of directors frequently involves financial evaluation. If the corporation is unable to make mortgage and tax payments because of shareholder defaults, the property might be sold by court order in a foreclosure suit. This would destroy the interests of all shareholders, including those who have paid their assessments.

Advantages. Cooperative ownership, despite its risks, has become more desirable in recent years for several reasons. Lending institutions view the shares of stock as acceptable collateral for financing. The availability of financing expands the transferability of shares beyond wealthy cash buyers. As a tenant-owner, rather than a tenant who pays rent to a landlord, the shareholder has some control over the property. Tenants in cooperatives also enjoy certain income tax advantages. The IRS treats cooperatives as it does fee simple interest in single homes or condominiums in regard to deductibility of loan interest, property taxes, and homesellers' tax exclusions. Finally, owners enjoy freedom from maintenance.

IN PRACTICE

The laws in some states may prohibit real estate licensees from listing or selling cooperative interests because the owners own only personal property. Individuals who participate in these transactions may need a securities license appropriate for the type of cooperative interest involved.

Time-Share Ownership

Time-sharing permits multiple purchasers to buy interests in real estate, usually a resort property. Each purchaser receives the right to use the facilities for a certain period of time. A *time-share estate* includes a real property interest in condominium ownership; a *time-share use* is a contract right under which the developer owns the real estate.

A time-share *estate* is a fee simple interest. The owner's occupancy and use of the property are limited to the contractual period purchased—for instance, the 17th complete week, Sunday through Saturday, of each calendar year. The owner is assessed for maintenance and common area expenses based on the ratio of the ownership period to the total number of ownership periods in the property. Time-share estates theoretically never end because they are real property interests. However, the physical life of the improvements is limited and must be looked at carefully when considering such a purchase.

■ **FOR EXAMPLE** Glengarry Estates offers 50 one-week time-shares in its six exclusive seaside residences. This totals 300 possible time-share estates. The maintenance and common-area expenses are $52,500 per year. If all the time-shares are taken by owners who buy only a single share, each owner must pay $175. If one owner buys a three-week share, he or she must pay $525. Finally, if Glengarry's developers manage to sell only six shares, those unfortunate owners might have to pay $8,750 each year to maintain their one-week vacation homes. (In practice, however, developers usually absorb the additional costs in such circumstances.)

The principal difference between a time-share *estate* and a time-share *use* lies in the interest transferred to an owner by the developer of the project. A time-share *use* consists of the right to occupy and use the facilities for a certain number of years. At the end of that time, the owner's rights in the property terminate. In effect, the developer has sold only a right of occupancy and use to the owner, not a fee simple interest.

Some time-sharing programs specify certain months or weeks of the year during which the owner can use the property. Others provide a rotation system under which the owner can occupy the unit during different times of the year in different years. Some include a swapping privilege for transferring the ownership period to another property to provide some variety for the owner. Time-shared properties typically are used 50 weeks each year, with the remaining two weeks reserved for maintenance of the improvements.

Membership camping is similar to time-share use. The owner purchases the right to use the developer's facilities, which usually consist of an open area with minimal improvements (such as camper and trailer hookups and restrooms). Normally, the owner is not limited to a specific time for using the property; use is limited only by weather and access.

<table>
<tr><td>

IN PRACTICE
</td><td>

The laws governing the development and sale of time-share units are complex and vary substantially from state to state. In addition, the sale of time-share properties may be subject to federal securities laws. In many states, time-share properties are now subject to subdivision requirements.
</td></tr>
</table>

■ SUMMARY

Sole ownership, or ownership in severalty, means that title is held by one natural person or legal entity. Under co-ownership, title can be held concurrently by more than one person in several ways. The differences among the various types of ownership only become apparent when the property is conveyed or when one of the owners dies.

Under tenancy in common, each party holds a separate title but shares possession with other tenants. Individual owners may sell their interests. On the death of a tenant in common, his or her interest passes to the tenant's heirs or according to a will. No special requirements for creating this interest exist. When two or more parties hold title to real estate, they do so as tenants in common unless they express another intention. Joint tenancy indicates two or more owners with the right of survivorship. The intention of the parties to establish a joint tenancy with right of survivorship must be stated clearly. The four unities of possession, interest, time, and title must be present.

Tenancy by the entirety, in those states where it is recognized, is actually a joint tenancy between husband and wife. It gives the couple the right of survivorship in all lands they acquired during marriage. During their lives, both must sign the deed for any title to pass to a purchaser. Community property rights exist only in certain states and pertain only to land owned by husband and wife. Usually, the property acquired by combined efforts during the marriage is community property, and each spouse owns one-half. Properties acquired by a spouse before the marriage and through inheritance or gifts during the marriage are considered separate property.

Real estate ownership may be held in trust. To create a trust, the trustor conveys title to the property to a trustee, who owns and manages the property.

Various types of business organizations may own real estate. A corporation is a legal entity and can hold title to real estate in severalty. While a partnership is technically not a legal entity, the Uniform Partnership Act and the Uniform Limited Partnership Act, adopted by most states, recognize a partnership as an entity that can own property in the partnership's name. A limited liability company (LLC) combines the limited liability offered by a corporate form and the tax advantages of a partnership without the complicated requirements of S corporations or the restrictions of limited partnerships. A syndicate is an association of two or more people or firms that invest in real estate. Many syndicates are joint ventures assembled for only a single project. A syndicate may be organized as a co-ownership trust, corporation, or partnership.

Cooperative ownership indicates title in one entity (a corporation or trust) that must pay taxes, mortgage interest and principal, and all operating expenses. Reimbursement comes from shareholders through monthly assessments. Shareholders have proprietary, long-term leases entitling them to occupy their apartments. Under condominium ownership, each owner-occupant holds fee simple title to a unit plus a share of the common elements. Each unit owner receives an individual tax bill and may mortgage the unit. Expenses for operating the building are collected by an owners' association through monthly assessments. Time-share ownership enables multiple purchasers to own estates or use interests in real estate, with the right to use the property for a part of each year.

QUESTIONS

1. The four unities of possession, interest, time, and title are associated with which of the following?
   a. Community property
   b. Severalty ownership
   c. Tenants in common
   d. Joint tenancy

2. A parcel of property was purchased by two friends, Kevin and Zelda. The deed they received from the seller at closing conveyed the property "to Kevin and Zelda" without further explanation. Kevin and Zelda took title as which of the following?
   a. Joint tenants
   b. Tenants in common
   c. Tenants by the entirety
   d. Community property owners

3. Mary, Nick, and Oliver are joint tenants with rights of survivorship in a tract of land. Oliver conveys his interest to Violet. Which of the following statements is true?
   a. Mary and Nick are still joint tenants.
   b. Mary, Nick, and Violet are joint tenants.
   c. Mary, Nick, and Violet are tenants in common.
   d. Violet now has severalty ownership.

4. Ann owns one of 20 townhouses in the Luxor Lakes development in fee simple, along with a 5 percent ownership share in the parking facilities, recreation center, and grounds. What kind of property does Ann own?
   a. Cooperative
   b. Condominium
   c. Time-share
   d. Land trust

5. Paul conveys a vineyard in trust to Ruth, with the instruction that any income derived from the vineyard be used for Tanya's medical care. Which of the following statements most accurately describes the relationship of these parties?
   a. Paul is the trustee, Ruth is the trustor, and Tanya is the beneficiary.
   b. Paul is the trustor, Ruth is the trustee, and Tanya is the beneficiary.
   c. Paul is the beneficiary, Ruth is the trustor, and Tanya is the trustee.
   d. Paul is the trustor, Ruth is the beneficiary, and Tanya is the trustee.

6. Under the laws of one state, any real property that either member of a married couple owns at the time of their marriage remains separate property. Further, any real property acquired by either party during the marriage (except by gift or inheritance) belongs to both of them equally. What is this form of ownership called?
   a. Partnership
   b. Joint tenancy
   c. Tenancy by the entirety
   d. Community property

7. Ed, Frank, and Gina were concurrent owners of a parcel of real estate. Frank died, and his interest passed according to his will to become part of his estate. Frank was a
   a. joint tenant.
   b. tenant in common.
   c. tenant by the entirety.
   d. severalty owner.

8. A legal arrangement under which the title to real property is held to protect the interests of a beneficiary is a
   a. trust.
   b. corporation.
   c. limited partnership.
   d. general partnership.

9. A condominium form of ownership—a condominium *regime*—is officially established when

   a. the construction of the improvements is completed.
   b. the owner files a declaration in the public record.
   c. the condominium owners' association is established.
   d. all the unit owners file their documents in the public record.

10. An owner purchased an interest in a house in Beachfront. The owner is entitled only to the right of possession between July 10 and August 4 of each year. Which of the following is most likely the type of ownership that has been purchased?

    a. Cooperative   c. Time-share
    b. Condominium   d. Trust

11. Because a corporation is a legal entity—a "person" in the eyes of the law—title to real estate owned by it is taken in

    a. trust.
    b. partnership.
    c. severalty.
    d. survivorship tenancy.

12. Which of the following refers to ownership by one person?

    a. Tenancy by the entirety
    b. Community property
    c. Tenancy in common
    d. Severalty

13. Tom and Rose are married and co-own Barrin Farm, with right of survivorship. Theirs is most likely

    a. severalty ownership.
    b. community property.
    c. a tenancy in common.
    d. an estate by the entirety.

14. All of the following can be classified as real property EXCEPT

    a. ownership in severalty.
    b. cooperative unit ownership.
    c. condominium unit ownership.
    d. a tenancy in common.

15. Bleak House is owned by Fred, George, and Harry as tenants in common. If George dies intestate, to whom will his interest pass?

    a. Fred and Harry equally
    b. George's heirs
    c. The state, by the law of escheat
    d. Fred and Harry in joint tenancy

16. Which of the following is most likely evidence of ownership in a cooperative?

    a. Tax bill for an individual unit
    b. Existence of a reverter clause
    c. Shareholder's stock certificate
    d. Right of first refusal

17. Sandra lives in the elegant Howell Tower. Sandra's possessory interest is evidenced by a proprietary lease. What does Sandra own?

    a. Condominium unit   c. Time-share
    b. Cooperative unit   d. Leasehold

18. Which of the following statements applies to both joint tenancy and tenancy by the entirety?

    a. There is no right to file a partition suit.
    b. The last survivor becomes a severalty owner.
    c. A deed signed by one owner will convey a fractional interest.
    d. A deed will not convey any interest unless signed by both spouses.

19. An owner has purchased a fee simple interest in a lakefront cottage along with 6 percent of the parking lot, laundry room, and boat house. What kind of ownership interest has been bought?

    a. Membership camping interest
    b. Time-share estate
    c. Cooperative unit
    d. Condominium unit

20. If property is held by two or more owners as survivorship tenants, the interest of a deceased cotenant will be passed to the

    a. surviving owner or owners.
    b. heirs of the deceased.
    c. state under the law of escheat.
    d. trust under which the property was owned.

CHAPTER NINE

LEGAL DESCRIPTIONS

■ **LEARNING OBJECTIVES** *When you've finished reading this Chapter, you should be able to:*

■ **identify** the three methods used to describe real estate.

■ **describe** how a survey is prepared.

■ **explain** how to read a rectangular survey description.

■ **distinguish** the various units of land measurement.

■ **define** the following *key terms:*

air lots	legal description	principal meridians
base lines	lot-and-block (recorded plat) system	ranges
benchmarks		rectangular (government) survey system
correction lines	metes-and-bounds description	
datum		sections
fractional sections	monuments	townships
government check	plat map	township lines
government lots	point of beginning (POB)	township tiers

■ WHY LEARN ABOUT... LEGAL DESCRIPTIONS?

Because your customers are paying a lot of money for their real estate, they expect to become the owners of every bit of land they're entitled to. Certainly the lawyers will review the plats and make sure the legal descriptions are accurate, but the licensee should be able to at least know what, in general, the lawyers are talking about. Knowing how land is described, and understanding the reasoning behind it, will help you gain a firmer comprehension of the product your profession deals in.

■ DESCRIBING LAND

People often refer to real estate by its street address, such as "1234 Main Street." While that is usually enough for the average person to find a particular building, it is not precise enough to be used on documents affecting the ownership of land. Further, addresses can change as streets are renamed or rural roads become absorbed into growing communities. Sales contracts, deeds, mortgages, and trust deeds, for instance, require a much more specific (or *legally sufficient*) description of property to be binding.

Courts have stated that a description is legally sufficient if it allows a competent surveyor to *locate* the parcel. In this context, however, "locate" means the surveyor must be able to define the exact boundaries of the property. The street address "1234 Main Street" would not tell a surveyor how large the property is or where it begins and ends. Several alternative systems of identification have been developed that express a **legal description** of real estate: one that is sufficiently specific that an independent surveyor could locate the exact dimensions of the property being described.

■ METHODS OF DESCRIBING REAL ESTATE

Three basic methods can be used to describe real estate:

1. Metes and bounds
2. Rectangular (or government) survey
3. Lot and block (recorded plat)

Although each method can be used independently, the methods may be combined in some situations. Some states use only one method; others use all three. (See Figure 9.1.)

Metes-and-Bounds Method

The **metes-and-bounds description** is the oldest type of legal description. *Metes* means distance, and *bounds* means compass directions or angles. The method relies on a property's physical features to determine the boundaries and measurements of the parcel. A metes-and-bounds description starts at a designated place on the parcel, called the **point of beginning (POB).** From there, the surveyor proceeds around the property's boundaries. The boundaries are recorded by referring to linear measurements, natural and artificial landmarks (called *monuments*), and directions. A metes-and-bounds description always ends back at the POB so that the tract being described is completely enclosed.

FIGURE 9.1

Map of U.S. and Land Description Systems

 These states generally use the metes and bounds legal description:

Maine
Massachusetts
Connecticut
Rhode Island
Vermont
New York
Pennsylvania
Delaware
New Jersey
Kentucky
Tennesee
New Hampshire
Georgia
North Carolina
South Carolina
Maryland
Virginia
West Virginia
Texas
Hawaii

The remaining 30 states use the rectangular or government survey legal description.

Source: www.outfitters.com/genealogy/land.

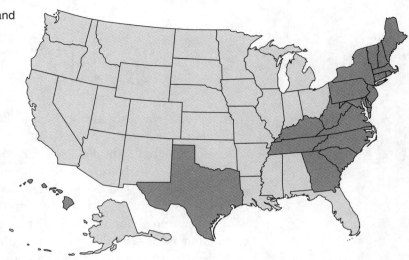

Monuments are fixed objects used to identify the POB, the ends of boundary segments, or the location of intersecting boundaries. A monument may be a natural object, such as a stone, large tree, lake, or stream. It also may be a human-made object, such as a street, highway, fence, canal, or markers (iron pins or concrete posts) placed by surveyors. Measurements often include the words *more or less* because the location of the monuments is more important than the distance stated in the wording. The actual distance between monuments takes precedence over any linear measurements in the description.

An example of a metes-and-bounds description of a parcel of land (pictured in Figure 9.2) follows:

A tract of land located in Red Skull, Boone County, Virginia, described as follows: Beginning at the intersection of the east line of Jones Road and the south line of Skull Drive; then east along the south line of Skull Drive 200 feet; then south 15° east 216.5 feet, more or less, to the center thread of Red Skull Creek then northwesterly along the center line of said creek to its intersection with the east line of Jones Road; then north 105 feet, more or less, along the east line of Jones Road to the point of beginning.

When used to describe property within a town or city, a metes-and-bounds description may begin as follows:

Beginning at a point on the southerly side of Kent Street, 100 feet easterly from the corner formed by the intersection of the southerly side of Kent Street and the easterly side of Broadway; then...

In this description, the POB is given by reference to the corner intersection. *Again, the description must close by returning to the POB.*

FIGURE 9.2

Metes-and-Bounds Tract

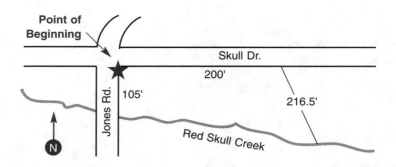

Metes-and-bounds descriptions can be complex. When they include detailed compass directions or concave and convex lines, they can be difficult to understand. Sometimes the lines are curved on an arc or radius that becomes part of the description. Natural deterioration or destruction of the monuments in a description can make boundaries difficult to identify. For instance, "Raney's Oak" may have died long ago, and "Hunter's Rock" may no longer exist. Computer programs are available that convert the data of the compass directions and dimensions to a drawing that verifies that the description closes to the POB. Professional surveyors should be consulted for definitive interpretations of any legal description.

Rectangular (Government) Survey System

The **rectangular survey system,** sometimes called the *government survey system,* was established by Congress in 1785 to standardize the description of land acquired by the newly formed federal government. By dividing the land into rectangles, the survey provided land descriptions by describing the rectangle(s) in which the land was located. The system is based on two sets of intersecting lines: principal meridians and base lines. The **principal meridians** run north and south, and the **base lines** run east and west. Both are located by reference to degrees of longitude and latitude. Each principal meridian has a name or number and is crossed by a base line. Each principal meridian and its corresponding base line are used to survey a definite area of land, indicated on the map by boundary lines. There are 35 principal meridians in the United States.

Each principal meridian describes only specific areas of land by boundaries. No parcel of land is described by reference to more than one principal meridian. The meridian used may not necessarily be the nearest one.

Further divisions are used in the same way as monuments in the metes-and-bounds method. They are

- townships,
- ranges,
- sections, and
- quarter-section lines.

Township tiers. Lines running east and west, *parallel to the base line* and six miles apart, are referred to as **township lines.** They form strips of land called **township tiers.** (See Figure 9.3.) These township tiers are designated by consecutive numbers north or south of the base line. For instance, the strip of land between 6 and 12 miles north of a base line is Township 2 North.

FIGURE 9.3

Township Lines

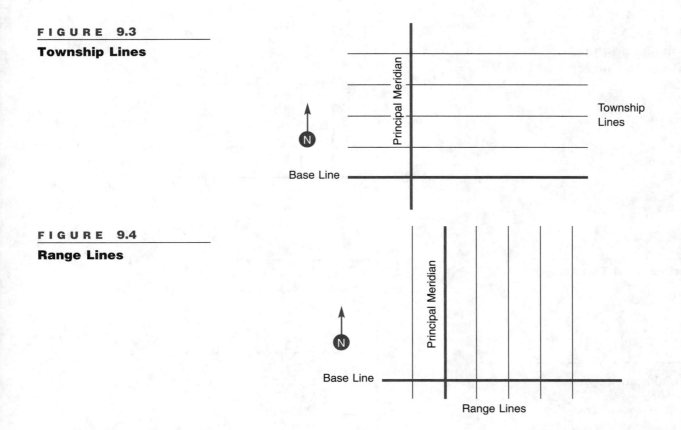

FIGURE 9.4

Range Lines

The directions of township lines and range lines may be easily remembered by thinking of the words this way:

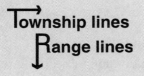

Ranges. The land on either side of a principal meridian is divided into six-mile-wide strips by lines that run north and south, *parallel to the meridian*. These north-south strips of land are called **ranges**. (See Figure 9.4.) They are designated by consecutive numbers east or west of the principal meridian. For example, Range 3 East would be a strip of land between 12 and 18 miles east of its principal meridian.

Township squares. When the horizontal township lines and the vertical range lines intersect, they form squares. These *township* squares are the basic units of the rectangular survey system. (See Figure 9.5.) **Townships** are 6 miles square and contain 36 square miles (23,040 acres).

Note that although a township square is *part* of a township tier, the two terms *do not* refer to the same thing. In this discussion, the word *township* used by itself refers only to the township square.

Each township is given a legal description. The township's description includes the following:

- Designation of the township tier in which the township is located
- Designation of the range strip
- Name or number of the principal meridian for that area

■ **FOR EXAMPLE** In Figure 9.5, the shaded township is described as Township 3 North, Range 4 East of the Principal Meridian. This township is the third strip, or tier, north of the base line, and it designates the township number and direction. The township is also located in the fourth range strip (those running north and

**Townships in the
Rectangular Survey
System**

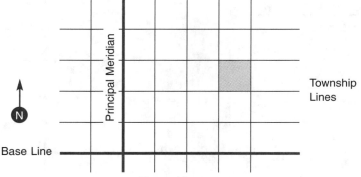

F I G U R E   9.6

Sections in a Township

6	5	4	3	2	1
7	8	9	10	11	12
18	17	**16**	15	14	13
19	20	21	22	23	24
30	29	28	27	26	25
31	32	33	34	35	36

Townships are numbered the same way a field is plowed. (The word for such a system is *boustrophedonic*—literally, "turning like oxen pulling a plow.") Remember: *right to left, left to right, right to left.*

Math Shortcut

To calculate acres in a survey system description, multiply all the denominators and divide that number into 640 acres. For instance, the SE¼ of SE¼ of SE¼ of Section 1 = 4 × 4 × 4 = 64; 640 ÷ 64 = 10 acres.

south) east of the principal meridian. Finally, reference is made to the principal meridian because the land being described is within the boundary of land surveyed from that meridian. This description is abbreviated as *T3N, R4E 4th Principal Meridian.*

Sections. Township squares are subdivided into sections and subsections called "halves" and "quarters" that can be further divided. Each township contains 36 **sections.** Each section is one square mile, or 640 acres. Sections are numbered 1 through 36, as shown in Figure 9.6. Section 1 is always in the northeast, or upper right-hand, corner. The numbering proceeds right to left to the upper left-hand corner. From there, the numbers drop down to the next tier and continue from left to right, then back from right to left. By law, each section number 16 is set aside for school purposes. The sale or rental proceeds from this land were originally available for township school use. The schoolhouse was usually located in this section so it would be centrally located for all of the students in the township. As a result, Section 16 is always referred to as a *school section.*

Sections are divided into *halves* (320 acres) and *quarters* (160 acres). (See Figure 9.7.) In turn, each of those parts is further divided into halves and quarters. The southeast quarter of a section, which is a 160-acre tract, is abbreviated SE¼. The SE¼ of SE¼ of SE¼ of Section 1 would be a ten-acre square in the lower right-hand corner of Section 1.

FIGURE 9.7

A Section

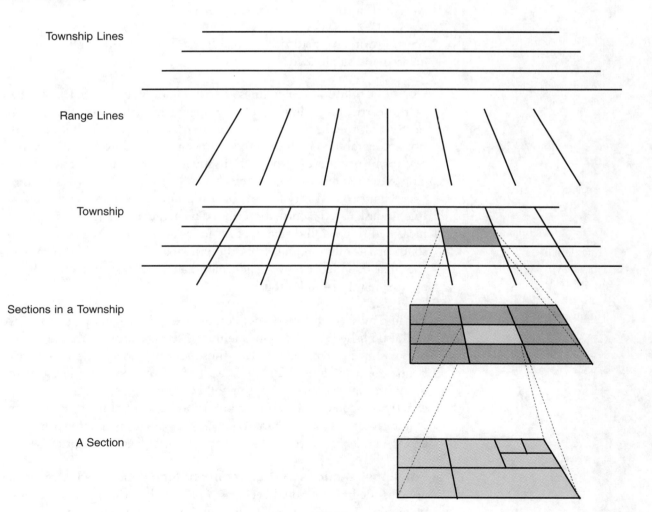

FIGURE 9.8

Parts of a Township

Township Lines

Range Lines

Township

Sections in a Township

A Section

**Correction Lines and
Guide Meridians**

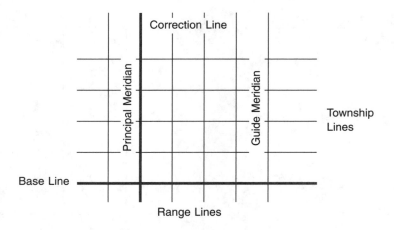

The rectangular survey system sometimes uses a shorthand method in its descriptions. For instance, a comma may be used in place of the word *of*: SE¼, SE¼, SE¼, Section 1. It is possible to combine portions of a section, such as NE¼ of SW¼ and N½ of NW¼ of SE¼ of Section 1, which could also be written NE¼, SW¼; N½, NW¼, SE¼ of Section 1. A semicolon means *and*. Because of the word *and* in this description, the area is 60 acres.

Starting with township and range lines, Figure 9.8 illustrates how sections are created and subdivided.

Correction lines. Range lines are parallel only in theory. Due to the curvature of the earth, range lines gradually approach each other. If they are extended northward, they eventually meet at the North Pole. The fact that the earth is not flat, combined with the crude instruments used in the early days, means that few townships are exactly six-mile squares or contain exactly 36 square miles. The system compensates for this "round earth problem" with **correction lines.** (See Figure 9.9.) Every fourth township line, both north and south of the base line, is designated a correction line. On each correction line, the range lines are measured to the full distance of six miles apart. Guide meridians run north and south at 24-mile intervals from the principal meridian. A government check is the area bounded by two guide meridians and two correction lines—an area approximately 24 miles square.

Because most townships do not contain exactly 36 square miles, surveyors follow well-established rules of adjustment. These rules provide that any irregularity in a township must be adjusted in those sections adjacent to its north and west boundaries (Sections 1, 2, 3, 4, 5, 6, 7, 18, 19, 30, and 31). These are called *fractional sections* (discussed in the following paragraph). All other sections are exactly one square mile and are known as *standard sections*. These provisions for making corrections explain some of the variations in township and section acreage under the rectangular survey system of legal description.

Fractional sections and government lots. Undersized or oversized sections are classified as **fractional sections.** Fractional sections may occur for a number of reasons. In some areas, for instance, the rectangular survey may have been made by separate crews, and gaps less than a section wide remained when the surveys met. Other errors may have resulted from the physical difficulties encountered in the actual survey. For example, part of a section may be submerged in water.

Areas smaller than full quarter-sections were numbered and designated as **government lots** by surveyors. These lots can be created by the curvature of the earth, by land bordering or surrounding large bodies of water, or by artificial state borders. An overage or a shortage was corrected whenever possible by placing the government lots in the north or west portions of the fractional sections. For example, a government lot might be described as Government Lot 2 in the northwest quarter of fractional Section 18, Township 2 North, Range 4 East of the Salt Lake Meridian.

Reading a rectangular survey description. To determine the location and size of a property described in the rectangular or government survey style, *start at the end* and work backward to the beginning, *reading from right to left*. For example, consider the following description:

> The S½ of the NW¼ of the SE¼ of Section 11, Township 8 North, Range 6 West of the Fourth Principal Meridian.

To locate this tract of land from the citation alone, first search for the fourth principal meridian on a map of the United States and note its base line. Then, on a regional map, find the township in which the property is located by counting six range strips west of the fourth principal meridian and eight townships north of its corresponding base line. After locating Section 11, divide the section into quarters. Then divide the SE¼ into quarters, and then the NW¼ of that into halves. The S½ of that NW¼ contains the property in question.

In computing the size of this tract of land, first determine that the SE¼ of the section contains 160 acres (640 acres divided by 4). The NW¼ of that quarter-section contains 40 acres (160 acres divided by 4), and the S½ of that quarter-section—the property in question—contains 20 acres (40 acres divided by 2).

In general, if a rectangular survey description does not use the conjunction *and* or a semicolon (indicating various parcels are combined), the *longer* the description, the *smaller* the tract of land it describes.

Legal descriptions should always include the name of the county and state in which the land is located because meridians often relate to more than one state and occasionally relate to two base lines. For example, the description "the southwest quarter of Section 10, Township 4 North, Range 1 West of the Fourth Principal Meridian" could refer to land in either Illinois or Wisconsin.

Metes-and-bounds descriptions within the rectangular survey system.
Land in states that use the rectangular survey system may also require a metes-and-bounds description. This usually occurs in one of three situations: (1) when describing an irregular tract; (2) when a tract is too small to be described by quarter-sections; or (3) when a tract does not follow the lot or block lines of a recorded subdivision or section, quarter-section lines, or other fractional section lines. The following is an example of a combined metes-and-bounds and rectangular survey system description. (See Figure 9.10.)

FIGURE 9.10

Combined Metes-and-Bounds and Rectangular Survey Description

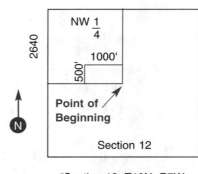

"Section 12, T10N, R7W,
Third Principal Meridian"

That part of the northwest quarter of Section 12, Township 10 North, Range 7 West of the Third Principal Meridian, bounded by a line described as follows: Commencing at the southeast corner of the northwest quarter of said Section 12 then north 500 feet; then west parallel with the south line of said section 1,000 feet; then south parallel with the east line of said section 500 feet to the south line of said northwest quarter; then east along said south line to the point of beginning.

Lot-and-Block System

The third method of legal description is the **lot-and-block** (or *recorded plat*) system. This system uses lot-and-block numbers referred to in a **plat map** filed in the public records of the county where the land is located. The lot-and-block system is often used to describe property in subdivisions.

A lot-and-block survey is performed in two steps. First, a large parcel of land is described either by the metes-and-bounds method or by rectangular survey. Once this large parcel is surveyed, it is broken into smaller parcels. As a result, a lot-and-block legal description always refers to a prior metes-and-bounds or rectangular survey description. For each parcel described under the lot-and-block system, the *lot* refers to the numerical designation of any particular parcel. The *block* refers to the name of the subdivision under which the map is recorded. The *block* reference is drawn from the early 1900s, when a city block was the most common type of subdivided property.

The lot-and-block system starts with the preparation of a *subdivision plat* by a licensed surveyor or an engineer. (See Figure 9.11.) On this plat, the land is divided into numbered or lettered lots and blocks, and streets or access roads for public use are indicated. Lot sizes and street details must be described completely and must comply with all local ordinances and requirements. When properly signed and approved, the subdivision plat is recorded in the county in which the land is located. The plat becomes part of the legal description. In describing a lot from a recorded subdivision plat, three identifiers are used:

1. Lot and block number
2. Name or number of the subdivision plat
3. Name of the county and state

FIGURE 9.11

Subdivision Plat Map

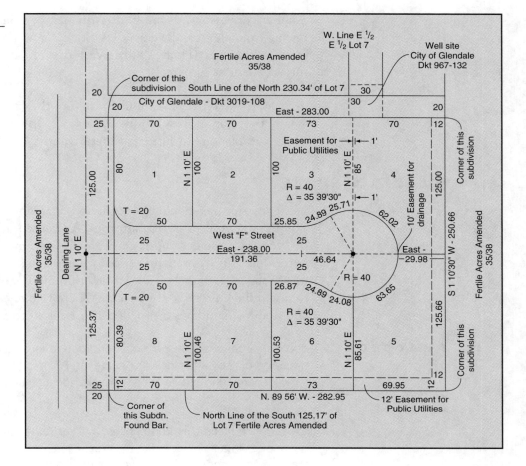

The following is an example of a lot-and-block description:

> Lot 71, Happy Valley Estates 2, located in a portion of the southeast quarter of Section 23, Township 7 North, Range 4 East of the Seward Principal Meridian in ____ County, ____ [state].

Anyone who wants to locate this parcel would start with the map of the Seward principal meridian to identify the township and range reference. Then he or she would consult the township map of Township 7 North, Range 4 East, and the section map of Section 23. From there, he or she would look at the quarter-section map of the southeast quarter. The quarter-section map would refer to the plat map for the subdivision known as the second unit (second parcel subdivided) under the name of Happy Valley Estates.

Some lot-and-block descriptions are not dependent on a government survey system and may refer to the plat recording in the land records of the county. An example might read:

> Being known and designated as Lot No. 15 on "Final Plat Section Two Waterford Subdivision" which plat is duly recorded among the land records of Baltimore County in Plat Book No. 27, Folio 59.

Some subdivided lands are further divided by a later resubdivision. In the following example, one developer (Western View) purchased a large parcel from a second developer (Homewood). Western View then resubdivided the property into different-sized parcels:

> Lot 4, Western View Resubdivision of the Homewood Subdivision, located in a portion of west half of Section 19, Township 10 North, Range 13 East of the Black Hills Principal Meridian in _____ County, _____ [state].

■ PREPARING A SURVEY

Legal descriptions should not be altered or combined without adequate information from a surveyor or title attorney. A licensed surveyor is trained and authorized to locate and determine the legal description of any parcel of land. The surveyor does this by preparing two documents: a survey and a survey sketch. The *survey* states the property's legal description. The *survey sketch* shows the location and dimensions of the parcel. When a survey also shows the location, size, and shape of buildings on the lot, it is referred to as a *spot survey*.

IN PRACTICE   Because legal descriptions, once recorded, affect title to real estate, they should be prepared only by a professional surveyor. Real estate licensees who attempt to draft legal descriptions create potential risks for themselves and their clients and customers.

Legal descriptions should be copied with extreme care. An incorrectly worded legal description in a sales contract may result in a conveyance of more or less land than the parties intended. Often, even punctuation is extremely critical. Title problems can arise for the buyer who seeks to convey the property at a future date. Even if the contract can be corrected before the sale is closed, the licensee risks losing a commission and may be held liable for damages suffered by an injured party because of an improperly worded legal description.

■ MEASURING ELEVATIONS

Just as surface rights must be identified, surveyed, and described, so must rights to the property above the earth's surface. Recall from Chapter 2 that *land* includes the space above the ground. In the same way land may be measured and divided into parcels, the air itself may be divided. An owner may subdivide the air above his or her land into air lots. Air lots are composed of the airspace within specific boundaries located over a parcel of land.

The *condominium laws* passed in all states (see Chapter 8) require that a registered land surveyor prepare a plat map that shows the elevations of floor and ceiling surfaces and the vertical boundaries of each unit with reference to an official *datum* (discussed later in this Chapter). A unit's floor, for instance, might be 60 feet above the datum and its ceiling, 69 feet. Typically, a separate plat is prepared for each floor in the condominium building.

The following is an example of the legal description of a condominium apartment unit that includes a fractional share of the common elements of the building and land:

> UNIT _____ as delineated on survey of the following described parcel of real estate (hereinafter referred to as Development Parcel): The north 99 feet of the west ½ of Block 4 (except that part, if any, taken and used for street), in Sutton's Division Number 5 in the east ½ of the southeast ¼ of Section 24, Township 3 South, Range 68 West of the Sixth Principal Meridian, in Denver County, Colorado, which survey is attached as Exhibit A to Declaration made by Colorado National Bank as Trustee under Trust No.1250, recorded in the Recorder's Office of Denver County, Colorado, as Document No. 475637; together with an undivided _____% interest in said Development Parcel (excepting from said Development Parcel all the property and space comprising all the units thereof as defined and set forth in said Declaration and Survey).

Subsurface rights can be legally described in the same manner as air rights. However, they are measured *below* the datum rather than above it. Subsurface rights are used not only for coal mining, petroleum drilling, and utility line location but also for multistory condominiums—both residential and commercial—that have several floors below ground level.

Datum

A **datum** *is a point, line, or surface from which elevations are measured or indicated.* For the purpose of the United States Geological Survey (USGS), *datum* is defined as the mean sea level at New York Harbor. A surveyor would use a datum in determining the height of a structure or establishing the grade of a street.

Benchmarks. Monuments are traditionally used to mark surface measurements between points. A monument could be a marker set in concrete, a piece of steel-reinforcing bar (rebar), a metal pipe driven into the soil, or simply a wooden stake stuck in the dirt. Because such items are subject to the whims of nature and vandals, their accuracy is sometimes suspect. As a result, surveyors rely most heavily on benchmarks to mark their work accurately and permanently.

Benchmarks are permanent reference points that have been established throughout the United States. They are usually embossed brass markers set into solid concrete or asphalt bases. While used to some degree for surface measurements, their principal reference use is for marking datums.

IN PRACTICE

All large cities have established a local official datum used in place of the USGS datum. For instance, the official datum for Chicago is known as the *Chicago City Datum.* It is a horizontal plane that corresponds to the low-water level of Lake Michigan in 1847 (the year in which the datum was established) and is considered to be at zero elevation. Although a surveyor's measurement of elevation based on the USGS datum will differ from one computed according to a local datum, it can be translated to an elevation based on the USGS.

MATH CONCEPTS

LAND ACQUISITION COSTS

To calculate the cost of purchasing land, use the same unit in which the cost is given. Costs quoted per square foot must be multiplied by the proper number of square feet; costs quoted per acre must be multiplied by the proper number of acres; and so on.

To calculate the cost of a parcel of land of three acres at $1.10 per square foot, convert the acreage to square feet before multiplying:

> 43,560 square feet per acre × 3 acres = 130,680 square feet
> 130,680 square feet × $1.10 per square foot = $143,748

To calculate the cost of a parcel of land of 17,500 square feet at $60,000 per acre, convert the cost per acre into the cost per square foot before multiplying by the number of square feet in the parcel:

> $60,000 per acre ÷ 43,560 square feet per acre = $1.38 (rounded) per square foot
> 17,500 square feet × $1.38 per square foot = $24,150

Cities with local datums also have designated official local benchmarks, which are assigned permanent identifying numbers. Local benchmarks simplify surveyors' work because the basic benchmarks may be miles away.

WWWeb.Link   www.usgs.gov

■ LAND UNITS AND MEASUREMENTS

It is important to understand land units and measurements because they are integral parts of legal descriptions. Some commonly used measurements are listed in Table 9.1.

■ SUMMARY

A legal description is a precise method of identifying a parcel of land. Three methods of legal description can be used: metes-and-bounds system, rectangular (government) survey system, and lot-and-block (plat map) system. A property's description should always be noted by the same method as the one used in previous documents.

A metes-and-bounds description uses direction and distance measurement to establish precise boundaries for a parcel. Monuments are fixed objects that establish these boundaries. Their actual location takes precedence over the written linear measurement in a document. When property is being described by metes

T A B L E   9.1

Units of Land Measurement

Unit	Measurement
mile	5,280 feet; 1,760 yards; 320 rods
rod	16.5 feet; 5.50 yards
square mile	640 acres (5,280 x 5,280 = 27,878,400 ÷ 43,560)
acre	43,560 square feet; 160 square rods
cubic yard	27 cubic feet
square yard	9 square feet
square foot	144 square inches
chain	66 feet; 4 rods; 100 links

and bounds, the description must always enclose a tract of land; that is, the boundary line must end at the point at which it started, the point of beginning.

The rectangular (government) survey system is used in 37 states. It involves surveys based on 35 principal meridians. Under this system, each principal meridian and its corresponding base line are specifically located. Any parcel of land is surveyed from only one principal meridian and its base line.

East and west lines parallel with the base line form six-mile-wide strips called *township tiers* or *strips*. North and south lines parallel with the principal meridian form range strips. The resulting squares are 36 square miles in area and are called *townships*. Townships are designated by their township and range numbers and their principal meridians—for example, Township 3 North, Range 4 East of the Meridian. Townships are divided into 36 sections of one square mile each.

When a tract is irregular or its boundaries do not coincide with a section, regular fractions of a section, or a boundary of a lot or block in a subdivision, a surveyor can prepare a combination rectangular survey and metes-and-bounds description.

Land in every state can be subdivided into lots and blocks by means of a plat map. An approved plat of survey showing the division into blocks, giving the size, location, and designation of lots, and specifying the location and size of streets to be dedicated for public use is filed for record in the recorder's office of the county in which the land is located. A subdivision plat gives the legal description of a building site in a town or city by lot, block, and subdivision in a section, township, and range of a principal meridian in a county and state.

Air lots, condominium descriptions, and other measurements of vertical elevations may be computed from the United States Geological Survey datum, which is the mean sea level in New York Harbor. Most large cities have established local survey datums for surveying within the areas. The elevations from these datums are further supplemented by reference points, called *benchmarks,* placed at fixed intervals from the datums.

QUESTIONS

1. What is the proper description of this shaded area of a section?

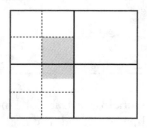

   a. SW¼ of the NE¼ and the N½ of the SE¼ of the SW¼
   b. N½ of the NE¼ of the SW¼ and the SE¼ of the NW¼
   c. SW¼ of the SE¼ of the NW¼ and the N½ of the NE¼ of the SW¼
   d. S½ of the SW¼ of the NE¼ and the NE¼ of the NW¼ of the SE¼

2. When surveying land, a surveyor refers to the principal meridian that is
   a. nearest the land being surveyed.
   b. in the same state as the land being surveyed.
   c. not more than 40 townships or 15 ranges distant from the land being surveyed.
   d. within the rectangular survey system area in which the land being surveyed is located.

3. The N½ of the SW¼ of a section contains how many acres?
   a. 20   c. 60
   b. 40   d. 80

4. In describing real estate, the system that may use a property's physical features to determine boundaries and measurements is
   a. rectangular survey.
   b. metes and bounds.
   c. government survey.
   d. lot and block.

Questions 5 through 8 refer to the following illustration of a whole township and parts of the adjacent townships.

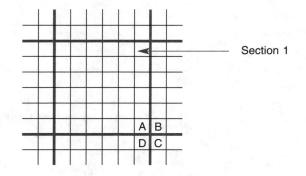

5. The section marked A is which of the following?
   a. School section
   b. Section 31
   c. Section 36
   d. Government lot

6. Which of the following is Section 6?
   a. A   c. C
   b. B   d. D

7. The section directly below C is
   a. Section 7.   c. Section 25.
   b. Section 12.   d. Section 30.

8. Which of the following is Section D?
   a. Section 1   c. Section 31
   b. Section 6   d. Section 36

9. Which of these shaded areas of a section depicts the NE¼ of the SE¼ of the SW¼?
   a. Area 1   c. Area 3
   b. Area 2   d. Area 4

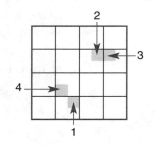

10. A buyer purchased a half-acre parcel for $2.15 per square foot. What was the selling price of the parcel?

a, $774
b. $46,827
c. $1,376
d. $93,654

11. How many acres are contained in the tract described as "beginning at the NW corner of the SW¼, then south along the west line to the SW corner of the section, then east along the south line of the section 2,640 feet, more or less, to the SE corner of the said SW¼, then in a straight line to the POB"?

a. 80 acres
b. 90 acres
c. 100 acres
d. 160 acres

12. In the diagram below, the bold N/S line represents the area's principal meridian and the bold E/W line represents its base line. The proper description of the shaded township area in this illustration is

a. T7N R7W.
b. T4W R7N.
c. T4N R2E.
d. T4N R7E.

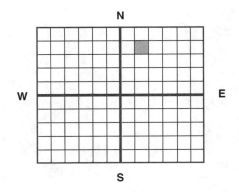

13. If a farm described as "the NW¼ of the SE¼ of Section 10, Township 2 North, Range 3 West of the 6th. P.M." sold for $1,500 an acre, what would the total sales price be?

a. $15,000
b. $30,000
c. $45,000
d. $60,000

14. As a legal description "the northwest ¼ of the southwest ¼ of Section 6, Township 4 North, Range 7 West" is defective because it contains no reference to

a. lot numbers.
b. boundary lines.
c. a principal meridian.
d. a record of survey.

15. Which of the following terms does not involve the elevation of real estate?

a. Benchmark
b. POB
c. Air lot
d. Datum

16. In the rectangular survey system, fractional sections along the northern or western border of a check that are less than a quarter-section in area are known as

a. fractional parcels.
b. government lots.
c. hiatus.
d. fractional townships.

17. Tom purchased 4.5 acres of land for $78,400. An adjoining owner wants to purchase a strip of Tom's land measuring 150 feet by 100 feet. What should this strip cost the adjoining owner if Tom sells it for the same price per square foot he originally paid for it?

a. $3,000
b. $6,000
c. $7,800
d. $9,400

18. Which of the following are not basic components of metes-and-bounds descriptions?

a. Tangible and intangible monuments
b. Base lines, principal meridians, and townships
c. Degrees, minutes, and seconds
d. Points of beginning

19. A property contains ten acres. How many lots of not less than 50 feet by 100 feet could be subdivided from the property if 26,000 square feet were dedicated for roads?

a. 80
b. 81
c. 82
d. 83

20. A parcel of land is 400 feet by 640 feet. The parcel is cut in half diagonally by a stream. How many acres are there in each half of the parcel?
    a. 2.75
    b. 2.94
    c. 5.51
    d. 5.88

21. What is the shortest distance between Section 1 and Section 36 in the same township?
    a. 3 miles
    b. 4 miles
    c. 5 miles
    d. 6 miles

22. Hattie owns the NW¼ and the SW¼ of Section 17, and Judith owns the NE¼ and the SE¼ of Section 18. If they agree that each will install one-half of a common fence, how many rods of fence will each install?
    a. 0
    b. 160
    c. 320
    d. 440

23. The section due west of Section 18, Township 5 North, Range 8 West, is Section
    a. 12, T5N, R7W.
    b. 13, T5N, R9W.
    c. 17, T5N, R8W.
    d. 19, T5N, R8W.

24. In any township, what is the number of the section designated as the school section?
    a. 1
    b. 16
    c. 25
    d. 36

25. The least specific method for identifying real property is
    a. rectangular survey.
    b. metes and bounds.
    c. street address.
    d. lot and block.

CHAPTER TEN

REAL ESTATE TAXES AND OTHER LIENS

■ **LEARNING OBJECTIVES** *When you've finished reading this Chapter, you should be able to:*

■ **identify** the various classifications of liens.

■ **describe** how real estate taxes are applied through assessments, tax liens, and the use of equalization ratios.

■ **explain** how nontax liens, such as mechanics' liens, mortgage liens, and judgment liens are applied and enforced.

■ **distinguish** the characteristics of voluntary, involuntary, statutory, and equitable liens.

■ **define** the following *key terms:*

ad valorem tax	inheritance taxes	special assessments
assessment	involuntary lien	specific lien
attachment	judgment	statutory lien
encumbrance	lien	subordination agree-
equalization factor	lis pendens	ments
equitable lien	mechanic's lien	tax liens
estate taxes	mill	tax sale
general liens	mortgage lien	vendor's lien
general real estate tax	redemption	voluntary lien

■ WHY LEARN ABOUT... REAL ESTATE TAXES AND OTHER LIENS?

There's an old saying that that there are only two things certain in life: Death and taxes. As a real estate professional, you'll have to know your share about death (for estate sales and property transfers by will or trust, for instance), but a more present issue on your client's mind will be taxes. What's more, properties may be subject to liens, which impose significant limits on both their marketability and, in some cases, their market value. Having some basic knowledge of taxes and liens will help you provide more valuable service to your clients as you guide them through some confusing property ownership issues. ■

■ LIENS

A **lien** is a charge or claim against a person's property, made to enforce the payment of money. Whenever someone borrows money, the lender generally requires some form of *security*. Security (also referred to as *collateral*) is something of value that the borrower promises to give the lender if the borrower fails to repay the debt. When the lender's security is in the form of real estate, the security is called a *lien*.

Liens are not limited to security for borrowed money (such as *mortgage liens*). Liens can be enforced against property by a government agency to recover taxes owed by the owner (**tax liens**). A lien can be used to compel the payment of an assessment or other special charge as well. A *mechanic's lien* represents an effort to recover payment for work performed. In all these ways, a person or an entity can use another's property to ensure payment for work performed, services rendered, or debts incurred.

> All liens are encumbrances, but not all encumbrances are liens.

A lien represents only an *interest* in ownership; it does not constitute actual ownership of the property. It is an encumbrance on the owner's title. An **encumbrance** is any charge or claim that attaches to real property and lessens its value or impairs its use. An encumbrance does not necessarily prevent the transfer or conveyance of the property, but because it is "attached" to the property, it transfers or conveys along with it. Liens differ from other encumbrances, however, because they are financial or monetary in nature and attach to the property because of a debt. Other encumbrances may be physical in nature (such as the easements and encroachments discussed in Chapter 7).

Generally, a lienholder must institute a legal action to force the sale of the property or acquire title. The debt is then paid out of the proceeds.

There are many different types of liens. (See Figure 10.1.) One way liens are classified is by *how* they are created. A **voluntary lien** is created *intentionally* by the property owner's action, such as when someone takes out a mortgage loan. An **involuntary lien**, on the other hand, is not a matter of choice: It is created

Types of Liens

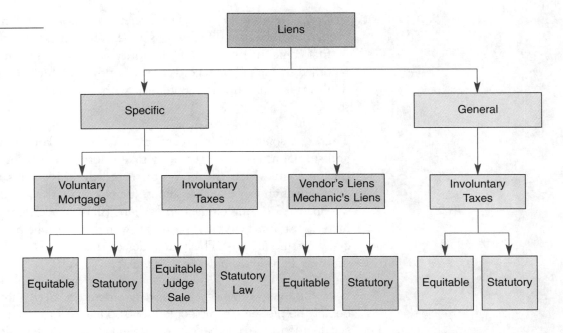

by law. It may be either statutory or equitable. A **statutory lien** is created by statute. A real estate tax lien, for example, is an involuntary, statutory lien. It is created by statute without any action by the property owner. An **equitable lien** arises out of common law. It is created by a court based on fairness. A court-ordered judgment that requires a debtor to pay the balance on a delinquent charge account, for instance, would be an involuntary, equitable lien on the debtor's real estate. A **vendor's lien** is a lien belonging to a vendor for the unpaid purchase price of land, where the vendor has not taken any other lien or security beyond the personal obligation of the purchaser.

Liens may also be classified according to the type of property involved. **General liens** affect all the property, both real and personal, of a debtor. This includes judgments, estate and inheritance taxes, decedent's debts, corporate franchise taxes, and Internal Revenue Service taxes. A lien on real estate differs from a lien on personal property, however. A lien attaches to real property *at the moment it is filed.* In contrast, the lien does not attach to personal property *until the personal property is seized.* **Specific liens** are secured by specific property and affect only that particular property. Specific liens on real estate include mechanics' liens, mortgage liens, real estate tax liens, and liens for special assessments and utilities. (Specific liens can also secure personal property, as when a lien is placed on a car to secure payment of a car loan.)

Effects of Liens on Title

The existence of a lien does not necessarily prevent a property owner from conveying title to someone else. The lien might reduce the value of the real estate, however, because few buyers will take on the risk of a property that has a lien on it. Because the lien attaches to the property, not the property owner, a new owner could lose the property if the creditors take court action to enforce payment. Once properly established, a lien *runs with the land* and will bind all successive owners until the lien is paid and cleared.

Priority of liens. *Priority of liens* refers to the order in which claims against the property will be paid off (that is, *satisfied*). In general, the rule for priority of liens is "first come, first served." The priority of payment is from the date the liens are recorded in the public records of the county in which the property is located. A lien's priority is also in accordance with state law, which varies from state to state.

There are some notable exceptions to this rule. For instance, real estate taxes and special assessments generally take priority over all other liens, regardless of the order in which the liens are recorded. This means that outstanding real estate taxes and special assessments are paid from the proceeds of a court-ordered sale *first*. For example, mechanics' liens (liens for performing labor or furnishing material in improving real property) would never take priority over tax and special assessment liens. The remainder of the proceeds is used to pay other outstanding liens *in the order of their priority*.

■ **FOR EXAMPLE** Mottley Mansion is ordered sold by the court to satisfy Bob's debts. The property is subject to a $50,000 judgment lien, incurred as a result of a suit to recover a mechanic's lien for installing a new addition to the mansion. $295,000 in interest and principal remain to be paid on Mottley Mansion's mortgage. This year's unpaid real estate taxes amount to $5,000. The judgment lien was entered in the public record on February 7, 2002, and the mortgage lien was recorded January 22, 1998. If Mottley Mansion is sold at the tax sale for $375,000, the proceeds of the sale will be distributed in the following order:

1. $5,000 to the taxing bodies for this year's real estate taxes
2. $295,000 to the mortgage lender (the entire amount of the mortgage loan outstanding as of the date of sale)
3. $50,000 to the creditor named in the judgment lien
4. $25,000 to Bob (the proceeds remaining after paying the first three items)

However, if Mottley Mansion sold for $325,000, the proceeds would be distributed as follows:

1. $5,000 to the taxing bodies for this year's real estate taxes
2. $295,000 to the mortgage lender (the entire amount of the mortgage loan outstanding as of the date of sale)
3. $25,000 to the creditor named in the judgment lien
4. $0 to Bob

Although the creditor is not repaid in full, this outcome is considered fair for two reasons:

1. The creditor's interest arose later than the others, so the others' interests took priority.
2. The creditor knew (or should have known) about the creditors ahead of it when it extended credit to Bob, so it was aware (or should have been aware) of the risk involved.

Subordination agreements are written agreements between lienholders to change the priority of mortgage, judgment, and other liens. Under a subordination agreement, the holder of a superior or prior lien agrees to permit a junior lienholder's interest to move ahead of his or her lien. Priority and recording of liens are discussed further in Chapter 14.

■ REAL ESTATE TAX LIENS

As discussed in Chapter 7, the ownership of real estate is subject to certain government powers. One of these is the right of state and local governments to impose (levy) taxes to pay for their functions. Because the location of real estate is permanently fixed, the government can levy taxes with a high degree of certainty that the taxes will be collected. The annual taxes levied on real estate usually have priority over previously recorded liens, so they may be enforced by a court-ordered sale.

There are two types of real estate taxes: general real estate taxes (also called *ad valorem taxes*) and special assessments or improvement taxes. Both are levied against specific parcels of property and automatically become liens on those properties.

WWWeb.Link   www.irs.ustreas.gov

General Tax (Ad Valorem Tax)

The general real estate tax, or ad valorem tax, is made up of the taxes levied on real estate by various government agencies and municipalities. These taxing bodies include

■ states;
■ counties;
■ cities, towns, and villages;
■ school districts (local elementary and high schools, publicly funded junior colleges, and community colleges);
■ drainage districts;
■ water districts;
■ sanitary districts; and
■ parks, forest preserves, and recreation districts.

Ad valorem is Latin for "according to value." Ad valorem taxes are based on the *value of the property being taxed*. They are specific, involuntary, statutory liens. General real estate taxes are levied to fund the operation of the government agency that imposes the taxes.

Exemptions from general taxes. Most state laws exempt certain real estate from taxation. Such property must be used for tax-exempt purposes, as defined in the statutes. The most common exempt properties are owned by

■ cities;
■ various municipal organizations (such as schools, parks, and playgrounds);
■ state and federal governments;
■ religious and charitable organizations;
■ hospitals; and
■ educational institutions.

Many state laws also allow special exemptions to reduce real estate tax bills for certain property owners or land uses. For instance, senior citizens and veterans are frequently granted reductions in the assessed values of their homes. Some state and local governments offer real estate tax reductions to attract industries and sports franchises. Many states also offer tax reductions for agricultural land.

Assessment. Real estate is valued for tax purposes by county or township assessors or appraisers. This official valuation process is called **assessment.** A property's *assessed value* is generally based on the sales prices of comparable properties, although practices may vary. Land values may be assessed separately from buildings or other improvements, and different valuation methods may be used for different types of property. State laws may provide for property to be reassessed periodically.

Sometimes, a property owner may feel that an error was made in determining the assessed value of his or her property—usually that the assessment is too high in comparison with the assessments of neighboring properties. Such owners may present their objections to a local board of appeal or board of review. Protests or appeals regarding tax assessments may ultimately be taken to court.

Equalization. In some jurisdictions, when it is necessary to correct inequalities in statewide tax assessments, an **equalization factor** is used to achieve uniformity. An equalization factor may be applied to raise or lower assessments in a particular district or county. The assessed value of each property in the area is multiplied by the equalization factor, and the tax rate is then applied to the *equalized assessment*.

■ **FOR EXAMPLE** The assessments in Laslo County are 20 percent lower than the average assessments throughout the rest of the state. This underassessment can be corrected by requiring the application of an equalization factor of 125 percent to each assessment in Laslo County. Therefore, a parcel of land assessed for tax purposes at $120,000 would be taxed on an equalized value of $150,000 ($120,000 × 1.25 = $150,000).

Tax rates. The process of arriving at a real estate tax rate begins with the *adoption of a budget* by each taxing district. Each budget covers the financial requirements of the taxing body for the coming fiscal year. The fiscal year may be the January through December calendar year or some other 12-month period designated by statute. The budget must include an estimate of all expenditures for the year. In addition, the budget must indicate the amount of income expected from all fees, revenue sharing, and other sources. The net amount remaining to be raised from real estate taxes is then determined by the difference between these figures.

The next step is *appropriation*. Appropriation is the way a taxing body authorizes the expenditure of funds and provides for the sources of the funding. Appropriation generally involves the adoption of an ordinance or the passage of a law that states the specific terms of the proposed taxation.

The amount to be raised from the general real estate tax is then imposed on property owners through a *tax levy*. A *tax levy* is the formal action taken to impose the tax, usually a vote of the taxing district's governing body.

The *tax rate* for each taxing body is computed separately. To arrive at a tax rate, the total monies needed for the coming fiscal year are divided by the total assessments of all real estate located within the taxing body's jurisdiction.

■ **FOR EXAMPLE** A taxing district's budget indicates that $800,000 must be raised from real estate tax revenues. The assessment roll (assessor's record) of all taxable real estate within the district equals $100 million. The tax rate is computed as follows:

$$\$800,000 \div \$100,000,000 = .008, \text{ or } .08\%$$

The *tax rate* may be stated in a number of ways. In many areas, it is expressed in mills. A mill is *1/1,000 of a dollar*, or *$.001*. The tax rate may be expressed as a mill-per-dollar ratio, for instance, in dollars per hundred or in dollars per thousand. A tax rate of .008 or .08 percent could be expressed as 8 mills or $.80 per $100 of assessed value or $8 per $1,000 of assessed value.

Tax bills. A property owner's tax bill is computed by applying the tax rate to the assessed valuation of the property.

Generally, one tax bill that incorporates all real estate taxes levied by the various taxing districts is prepared for each property. In some areas, however, separate bills are prepared by each taxing body. Sometimes, the real estate taxing bodies may operate on different budget years so that the taxpayer receives separate bills for various taxes at different times during the year.

■ **FOR EXAMPLE** If a property is assessed for tax purposes at $160,000, at a tax rate of 3 percent, or 30 mills, the tax will be $4,800: $160,000 × .03.

If an equalization factor is used, the computation with an equalization factor of 120 percent will be $5,760: $160,000 × 1.20 = $192,000, then $192,000 × .03 = $5,760.

The due dates for tax payments (also called the *penalty dates*) are usually set by statute. Taxes may be payable in 2 installments (semiannually), 4 installments (quarterly), or 12 installments (monthly). In some areas, taxes become due at the beginning of the current tax year and must be paid in advance (for example, the year 2002 taxes must be paid at the beginning of 2002). In other areas, taxes are payable during the year after the taxes are levied (2002 taxes are paid throughout 2002). And in still other areas, a partial payment is due in the year of the tax, with the balance due in the following year (2002 taxes are payable partly during 2002 and partly during 2003).

Some states offer discounts to encourage prompt payment of real estate taxes. Penalties, in the form of monthly interest charges, are added to all taxes that are not paid when due. (See Table 10.1.)

Enforcement of tax liens. Real estate taxes must be valid to be enforceable. That means they must be levied properly, must be used for a legal purpose, and must be applied equitably, that is, fairly, to all property. Real estate taxes that have remained delinquent for the statutory period can be collected through a tax

T A B L E   10.1

Calculating Real Estate Taxes

Shown here is a summary example of calculating taxes on a home with a market value of $200,000 with a rate of 3 mill (6 mill in the last two examples). Three different methods are used in calculating the taxes: (1) the rate per the assessed value; (2) an equalization factor to obtain assessments to fair market value; and (3) the tax rate or mill rate.

Calculating Tax Base	Tax Rate based on $100 increments, $3 per $100 (doubled in last row)	Tax Rate Based on $1,000 increment or mill rate of 3, $30 per $1,000 (doubled in last row)
100 percent market value in the assessment.	$200,000 ÷ $100 × $3 = $6,000	$200,000 ÷ $1,000 × $30 = $6,000
Assessment is 20 percent lower than market value with a 125 percent equalization.	$160,000 × 1.25 ÷ $100 × 3 = $6,000	$160,000 × 1.25 ÷ $1,000 × $30 = $6,000
Assessed value is 50 percent of the market value. No equalization is used, but tax rate is doubled in this row.	$100,000 ÷ $100 × $6 = $6,000	$100,000 ÷ $1,000 × $60 = $6,000

sale. While the methods and details of the various states' tax sale procedures differ substantially, the results are the same.

A tax sale is usually held according to a published notice after a court has rendered a judgment for the tax and penalties and has ordered that the property be sold. Because a specific amount of delinquent tax and penalty must be collected, the purchaser at a tax sale must pay at least that amount. A *certificate of sale* is usually given to the successful bidder when he or she pays the delinquent tax amount.

Generally, the delinquent taxpayer can redeem the property any time before the tax sale. The taxpayer exercises this *equitable right of redemption* by paying the delinquent taxes plus interest and charges (any court costs or attorney's fees). In those states that permit **redemption,** the bidding at a tax sale is based on the interest rate the defaulted taxpayer would have to pay to redeem the property, that is, the person who bids the lowest redemption interest rate (the one most beneficial for the taxpayer) becomes the successful bidder. That interest rate theoretically would be the easiest for the taxpayer to pay to redeem the property.

Some state laws also grant a period of redemption *after the tax sale*. In this case, the defaulted owner (or the defaulted owner's creditors) may redeem the property by paying the amount collected at the tax sale plus interest and charges (including any taxes levied since the sale). This is known as a *statutory right of redemption*. (The right of redemption is discussed further in Chapter 14.) If the property is not redeemed within the statutory period, the certificate holder can apply for a *tax deed*. The quality of the title conveyed by a tax deed varies from state to state.

In some states, tax-delinquent land is sold or conveyed to the state or a taxing authority. At the expiration of the redemption period, the state or other taxing authority sells the property at auction and issues a tax deed to the highest bidder. The deed issued to the purchaser conveys good title because it is considered a conveyance by the state of state-owned land. In some jurisdictions, tax-delinquent land that is not sold at a tax sale due to lack of buyers is forfeited to the state. The state may then either use the land for its own purposes or sell it later.

Special Assessments (Improvement Taxes)

Special assessments are taxes levied on real estate to fund public improvements to the property. Property owners in the area of the improvements are required to pay for them because their properties benefit directly from the improvements. For example, the installation of paved streets, curbs, gutters, sidewalks, storm sewers, or street lighting increases the values of the affected properties. The owners, in effect, reimburse the levying authority. However, dollar-for-dollar increases in value are rarely the result.

Special assessments are always specific and statutory, but they can be either involuntary or voluntary liens. Improvements initiated by a public agency create involuntary liens. However, when property owners petition the local government to install a public improvement for which the owners agree to pay, such as a sidewalk or paved alley, the assessment lien is voluntary.

Whether the lien is voluntary or involuntary, each property in the improvement district is charged a prorated share of the total amount of the assessment. The share is determined either on a fractional basis (four houses may equally share the cost of one streetlight) or on a cost-per-front-foot basis (wider lots incur a greater cost than narrower lots for street paving and curb and sidewalk installation).

Special assessments are generally paid in equal annual installments over a period of years. The first installment is usually due during the year following the public authority's approval of the assessment. The first bill includes one year's interest on the property owner's share of the entire assessment. Subsequent bills include one year's interest on the unpaid balance. Property owners have the right to prepay any or all installments to avoid future interest charges.

Strict subdivision regulations have almost eliminated special assessments in some parts of the country. Most items for which assessments have traditionally been levied are now required to be installed at the time of construction as a condition of a subdivision's approval.

■ OTHER LIENS ON REAL PROPERTY

In addition to real estate tax and special assessment liens, a variety of other liens may be charged against real property.

Mortgage Liens (Deed of Trust Liens)

A mortgage lien, or, as used in some states, a *deed of trust lien*, is a voluntary lien on real estate given to a lender by a borrower as security for a real estate loan. It becomes a lien on real property when the lender records the documents in the county where the property is located. Lenders generally require a preferred lien, referred to as a *first mortgage lien*. This means that no other liens against the property (aside from real estate taxes) would take priority over the mortgage lien. Subsequent liens are referred to as *junior liens*. (Mortgages and deeds of trust are discussed in detail in Chapter 14.)

Mechanics' Liens

A mechanic's lien is a specific, involuntary lien that gives security to persons or companies that perform labor or furnish material to improve real property. A mechanic's lien is available to contractors, subcontractors, architects, equipment lessors, surveyors, laborers, and other providers. This type of lien is filed when the owner has not fully paid for the work or when the general contractor has been compensated but has not paid the subcontractors or suppliers of materials. However, statutes in some states prohibit subcontractors from placing liens directly on certain types of property, such as owner-occupied residences.

To be entitled to a mechanic's lien, the person who did the work must have had a contract (express or implied) with the owner or the owner's authorized representative. If improvements that were not ordered by the property owner have commenced, the property owner should execute a document called a *notice of nonresponsibility* to relieve himself or herself from possible mechanics' liens. By posting this notice in some conspicuous place on the property and recording a verified copy of it in the public record, the owner gives notice that he or she is not responsible for the work done.

A person claiming a mechanic's lien must file a notice of lien in the public record of the county where the property is located within a certain period of time after the work has been completed. According to state law, priority of a mechanic's lien may be established as of the date the construction began or materials were first furnished; the date the work was completed; the date the individual subcontractor's work was either commenced or completed; the date the contract was signed or work was ordered; or the date a notice of the lien was recorded, filed, posted, or served. In some states, mechanics' liens may be given priority over previously recorded liens such as mortgages.

IN PRACTICE

In most states, a mechanic's lien takes priority from the time it attaches. Nonetheless, a claimant's notice of lien will not be filed in the public record until some time after that. A prospective purchaser of property that has been recently constructed, altered, or repaired should be cautious about possible unrecorded mechanics' liens against the property.

Judgments

A judgment is a decree issued by a court. When the decree establishes the amount a debtor owes and provides for money to be awarded, it is referred to as a *money judgment*.

A judgment is a general, involuntary, equitable lien on both real and personal property owned by the debtor. A judgment is not the same as a mortgage because no specific parcel of real estate was given as security at the time the debt was created. A lien usually covers only property located within the county in which the judgment is issued. As a result, a notice of the lien must be filed in any county to which a creditor wishes to extend the lien coverage.

To enforce a judgment, the creditor must obtain a *writ of execution* from the court. A writ of execution directs the sheriff to seize and sell as much of the debtor's property as is necessary to pay both the debt and the expenses of the sale. A judgment does not become a lien against the personal property of a debtor until the creditor orders the sheriff to levy on the property and the levy is actually made.

A judgment lien's priority is established by one or a combination of the following (as provided by state law):

- Date the judgment was entered by the court
- Date the judgment was filed in the recorder's office
- Date a writ of execution was issued

When real property is sold to satisfy a debt, the debtor should demand a legal document known as a *satisfaction of judgment* (or *satisfaction piece*), or, in those states using trust deeds, a deed of reconveyance, which must be filed with either the clerk of the court or, in some states, the recorder of deeds. Filing the satisfaction of judgment clears the record of the lien.

Lis pendens. There is often a considerable delay between the time a lawsuit is filed and the time final judgment is rendered. When any suit is filed that affects title to real estate, a special notice, known as a **lis pendens** (Latin for "litigation pending"), is recorded. A lis pendens is not itself a lien, but rather *notice of a possible future lien*. Recording a lis pendens notifies prospective purchasers and lenders that there is a potential claim against the property. It also establishes a priority for the later lien: The lien is backdated to the recording date of the lis pendens.

Attachments. Special rules apply to realty that is not mortgaged or similarly encumbered. To prevent a debtor from conveying title to such previously unsecured real estate while a court suit is being decided, a creditor may seek a writ of **attachment.** By this writ, the court retains custody of the property until the suit concludes. First, the creditor must post a surety bond or deposit with the court. The bond must be sufficient to cover any possible loss or damage the debtor may suffer while the court has custody of the property. In the event the judgment is not awarded to the creditor, the debtor will be reimbursed from the bond.

Estate and Inheritance Tax Liens

Federal **estate taxes** and state **inheritance taxes** (as well as the debts of decedents) are general, statutory, involuntary liens that encumber a deceased person's real and personal property. These are normally paid or cleared in probate court proceedings. Probate and issues of inheritance are discussed in Chapter 12.

Liens for Municipal Utilities

Municipalities often have the right to impose a specific, equitable, involuntary lien on the property of an owner who refuses to pay bills for municipal utility services.

Bail Bond Lien

A real estate owner who is charged with a crime for which he or she must face trial may post bail in the form of real estate rather than cash. The execution and recording of such a bail bond creates a specific, statutory, voluntary lien against the owner's real estate. If the accused fails to appear in court, the lien may be enforced by the sheriff or another court officer.

Corporation Franchise Tax Lien

State governments generally levy a corporation franchise tax on corporations as a condition of allowing them to do business in the state. Such a tax is a general, statutory, involuntary lien on all real and personal property owned by the corporation.

WWWeb.Link   www.irs.ustreas.gov

IRS Tax Lien

A federal tax lien, or *Internal Revenue Service (IRS) tax lien*, results from a person's failure to pay any portion of federal taxes, such as income and withholding taxes. A federal tax lien is a general, statutory, involuntary lien on all real and personal property held by the delinquent taxpayer. Its priority, however, is based on the date of filing or recording; it does not supersede previously recorded liens.

■ SUMMARY

Liens are claims of creditors or taxing authorities against the real and personal property of a debtor. A lien is a type of encumbrance. Liens are either general, covering all real and personal property of a debtor-owner, or specific, covering only identified property. They are also either voluntary, arising from an action of the debtor, or involuntary, created by statute (statutory) or based on the concept of fairness (equitable).

With the exception of real estate tax liens and mechanics' liens, the priority of liens is generally determined by the order in which they are placed in the public record of the county in which the property is located, and in accordance with state law.

Real estate taxes are levied annually by local taxing authorities and are generally given priority over other liens. Payments are required before stated dates, after which penalties accrue. An owner may lose title to property for nonpayment of taxes because such tax-delinquent property can be sold at a tax sale. Some states allow a time period during which a defaulted owner can redeem his or her real estate from a tax sale.

Special assessments are levied to allocate the cost of public improvements to the specific parcels of real estate that benefit from them. Assessments are usually payable annually over a five-year or ten-year period, together with interest due on the balance of the assessment.

Mortgage liens (deed of trust liens) are voluntary, specific liens given to lenders to secure payment for real estate loans.

Mechanics' liens protect general contractors, subcontractors, and material suppliers whose work enhances the value of real estate.

A judgment is a court decree obtained by a creditor, usually for a monetary award from a debtor. A judgment lien can be enforced by court issuance of a writ of execution and sale by the sheriff to pay the judgment amount and costs.

Attachment is a means of preventing a defendant from conveying property before completion of a suit in which a judgment is sought.

Lis pendens is a recorded notice of a lawsuit that is pending in court and that may result in a judgment affecting title to a parcel of real estate.

Federal estate taxes and state inheritance taxes are general liens against a deceased owner's property.

Liens for water charges or other municipal utilities and bail bond liens are specific liens, while corporation franchise tax liens are general liens against a corporation's assets.

IRS tax liens are general liens against the property of a person who is delinquent in paying IRS taxes.

QUESTIONS

1. Which of the following liens affects all real and personal property of a debtor?
   a. Specific
   b. Voluntary
   c. Involuntary
   d. General

2. Priority of liens refers to which of the following?
   a. Order in which a debtor assumes responsibility for payment of obligations
   b. Order in which liens will be paid if property is sold to satisfy a debt
   c. Dates liens are filed for record
   d. Fact that specific liens have greater priority than general liens

3. A lien on real estate made to secure payment for a specific municipal improvement project is which of the following?
   a. Mechanic's lien
   b. Special assessment
   c. Ad valorem
   d. Utility lien

4. Which of the following would be classified as a general lien?
   a. Mechanic's lien
   b. Bail bond lien
   c. Judgment
   d. Real estate taxes

5. Which of the following liens usually would be given highest priority in disbursing funds from a foreclosure sale?
   a. Mortgage dated last year
   b. Real estate taxes due
   c. Mechanic's lien for work started before the mortgage was made
   d. Judgment rendered the day before foreclosure

6. A specific parcel of real estate has a market value of $160,000 and is assessed for tax purposes at 75 percent of market value. The tax rate for the county in which the property is located is 40 mills. The tax bill will be
   a. $6,400.
   b. $5,000.
   c. $5,200.
   d. $4,800.

7. Which of the following taxes would target homeowners in particular?
   a. Personal property tax
   b. Sales tax
   c. Real property tax
   d. Luxury tax

8. A mechanic's lien claim arises when a contractor has performed work or provided material to improve a parcel of real estate on the owner's order and the work has not been paid for. Such a contractor has a right to
   a. tear out his or her work.
   b. record a notice of the lien.
   c. record a notice of the lien and file a court suit within the time required by state law.
   d. have personal property of the owner sold to satisfy the lien.

9. What is the annual real estate tax on a property valued at $135,000 and assessed for tax purposes at $47,250, with an equalization factor of 125 percent, when the tax rate is 25 mills?
   a. $945
   b. $1,181
   c. $1,418
   d. $1,477

10. Which of the following is a voluntary, specific lien?
    a. IRS tax lien
    b. Mechanic's lien
    c. Mortgage lien
    d. Seller's lien

11. A seller sold a buyer a parcel of real estate. Title has passed, but to date the buyer has not paid the purchase price in full, as originally agreed on. If the seller wants to force payment, which of the following remedies would the seller be entitled to seek?
    a. Attachment
    b. Mechanic's lien
    c. Lis pendens
    d. Judgment

12. A general contractor recently filed suit against a homeowner for nonpayment. The contractor now learns that the homeowner has listed the property for sale with a real estate broker. In this situation, which of the following will the contractor's attorney use to protect the contractor's interest?

a. Seller's lien
b. Buyer's lien
c. Assessment
d. Lis pendens

13. Which of the following statements most accurately describes special assessment liens?

a. They are general liens.
b. They are paid on a monthly basis.
c. They take priority over mechanics' liens.
d. They cannot be prepaid in full without penalty.

14. Which of the following creates a lien on real estate?

a. Easement running with the land
b. Unpaid mortgage loan
c. License
d. Encroachment

15. Which of the following statements is true of both a mortgage lien and a judgment lien?

a. They must be entered by the court.
b. They involve a debtor-creditor relationship.
c. They are general liens.
d. They are involuntary liens.

16. A mechanic's lien would be available to all of the following EXCEPT a

a. subcontractor.
b. contractor.
c. surveyor.
d. broker.

17. The right of a defaulted taxpayer to recover property before its sale for unpaid taxes is the

a. statutory right of reinstatement.
b. equitable right of appeal.
c. statutory right of assessment.
d. equitable right of redemption.

18. Which of the following is a specific, involuntary, statutory lien?

a. Real estate tax lien
b. Income tax lien
c. Estate tax lien
d. Judgment lien

19. General real estate taxes levied for the operation of the government are called

a. assessment taxes.
b. ad valorem taxes.
c. special taxes.
d. improvement taxes.

20. All of the following probably would be exempt from real estate taxes EXCEPT a(n)

a. public hospital.
b. golf course operated by the park district.
c. community church.
d. apartment building.

CHAPTER ELEVEN

REAL ESTATE CONTRACTS

■ **LEARNING OBJECTIVES** *When you've finished reading this Chapter, you should be able to:*

■ **identify** the requirements for a valid contract.

■ **describe** the various types of contracts used in the real estate business.

■ **explain** how contracts may be discharged.

■ **distinguish** among bilateral and unilateral, executed and executory, and valid, void, and voidable contracts.

■ **define** the following *key terms:*

assignment	executed contract	reality of consent
bilateral contract	executory contract	rescission
breach of contract	express contract	statute of frauds
consideration	implied contract	suit for specific per-
contingencies	installment contract	formance
contract	land contract	time is of the essence
counteroffer	lease	unenforceable contract
disclosure	liquidated damages	unilateral contract
earnest money	novation	valid
equitable title	offer and acceptance	void
escrow contract	option	voidable

■ **WHY LEARN ABOUT...** REAL ESTATE CONTRACTS?

The real estate market is driven by contracts. Both listing and buyer representation agreements are contracts. Options are contracts, and an offer is the first half of a sales contract. Leases and escrows are contracts. Wherever you go as a real estate professional, whatever aspect of the real estate business you find yourself in, you will be dealing with contracts. And like any other tool of your profession, it is important that you know how a contract is created, what it means, what is required of the parties, and what kinds of actions can end it. ■

WWWeb.Link　　　　www.findlaw.com/01topics/07contracts

■ CONTRACT LAW

A **contract** is a voluntary agreement or promise between legally competent parties, supported by legal consideration, to perform (or refrain from performing) some legal act. That definition may be easier to understand if we consider its various parts separately. A contract must be

> A **contract** is a voluntary, legally enforceable promise between two competent parties to perform (or *not perform*) some legal act in exchange for consideration.

- *voluntary*—no one may be forced into a contract;
- *an agreement or a promise*—a contract is essentially a legally enforceable promise;
- made by *legally competent parties*—the parties must be viewed by the law as capable of making a legally binding promise;
- supported by *legal consideration*—a contract must be supported by some valuable thing that induces a party to enter into the contract and that must be legally sufficient to support a contract; and
- about a *legal act*—no one may make a legal contract to do something illegal.

Essentially, a contract is an enforceable promise—a promise that someone may be compelled by a court to keep. Brokers and salespersons use many types of contracts and agreements to carry out their responsibilities to sellers, buyers, and the general public. The general body of law that governs such agreements is known as *contract law*.

Express and Implied Contracts

A contract may be *express* or *implied*, depending on how it is created. An **express contract** exists when the parties state the terms and show their intentions in *words*. An express contract may be either oral or written. The majority of real estate contracts are express contracts; they have been reduced to writing. Under the **statute of frauds,** certain types of contracts must be in writing to be enforceable in a court of law. (*Enforceable* means that the parties may be forced to comply with the contract's terms and conditions.) In an **implied contract,** the agreement of the parties is demonstrated by their *acts and conduct.*

■ **FOR EXAMPLE** Harold approaches his neighbor, Bill, and says, "I will paint your house today for $50." Bill replies, "If you paint my house today, I will pay you $50." Harold and Bill have entered into an express contract.

Karen goes into a restaurant and orders a meal. Karen has entered into an implied contract with the restaurant to pay for the meal, even though payment was not mentioned before the meal was ordered.

Bilateral and Unilateral Contracts

Contracts may be classified as either bilateral or unilateral. In a **bilateral contract,** both parties promise to do something; one promise is given in exchange for another. A listing agreement is a bilateral contract in which the broker promises to use his or her skills to produce a buyer and the seller promises to pay a commission or brokerage fee. A real estate sales contract is a bilateral contract because the seller promises to sell a parcel of real estate and convey title to the property to the buyer, who promises to pay a certain sum of money for the property. An exclusive right to sell listing contract is a bilateral contract.

> *Bi-* means "two"—a *bilateral contract* must have two promises. *Uni-* means "one"—a *unilateral contract* has only one promise.

A **unilateral contract,** on the other hand, is a one-sided agreement. One party makes a promise to induce a second party to do something. The second party is not legally obligated to act. However, if the second party does comply, the first party is obligated to keep the promise. For instance, a law enforcement agency might offer a monetary payment to anyone who can aid in the capture of a criminal. Only if someone *does* aid in the capture is the reward paid. An option contract, which will be discussed later, is another example of a unilateral contract.

■ **FOR EXAMPLE** Bill puts up a sign that says, "If you paint my house today, I will pay you $500." If Harold paints Bill's house, Bill will be legally obligated to pay Harold. Bill and Harold have a *unilateral contract.* On the other hand, if Harold says to Bill, "I will paint your house for $500," and Harold replies, "I will pay you $500 for painting my house," they have a *bilateral contract,* a promise exchanged for a promise.

Executed and Executory Contracts

A contract may be classified as either executed or executory, depending on whether the agreement is performed. An **executed contract** is one in which all parties have fulfilled their promises: The contract has been performed. This should not be confused with the word *execute,* which refers to the signing of a contract. An **executory contract** exists when one or both parties still have an act to perform. A sales contract is an executory contract from the time it is signed until closing: Ownership has not yet changed hands, and the seller has not received the sales price. At closing, the sales contract is executed.

Table 11.1 highlights the issues involved in the formation of a contract, issues talked about in detail in this Chapter.

Essential Elements of a Valid Contract

A contract must meet certain minimum requirements to be considered legally valid. The following are the basic essential elements of a contract.

T A B L E   11.1

Contract Formation Issues

There are preformation, formation, and postformation issues involved in a contract.

Preformation	Formation	Postformation
Essential Elements	**Classification**	**Discharge**
Offer, Acceptance, Consideration, Legal Purpose, Legal Capacity	Valid, Void, Voidable, Enforceable, Unenforceable, Express, Implied, Unilateral, Bilateral, Executory, Executed	Performance, Breach, Remedies (Damages, Specific Performance, Recision)

Elements of a contract:

■ Offer and acceptance

■ Consideration

■ Legally competent parties

■ Consent

■ Legal purpose

Offer and acceptance. There must be an offer by one party that is accepted by the other. The person who makes the offer is the *offeror*. The person who accepts the offer is the *offeree*. This requirement is also called *mutual assent*. It means that there must be a "meeting of the minds," that is, there must be complete agreement between the parties about the purpose and terms of the contract. Courts look to the *objective intent of the parties* to determine whether they intended to enter into a binding agreement. In cases where the statute of frauds applies, the **offer and acceptance** must be in writing. The wording of the contract must express all the agreed-on terms and must be clearly understood by the parties.

An *offer* is a promise made by one party, requesting something in exchange for that promise. The offer is made with the intention that the offeror will be bound to the terms if the offer is accepted. The terms of the offer must be definite and specific and must be communicated to the offeree.

An *acceptance* is a promise by the offeree to be bound by the *exact* terms proposed by the offeror. The acceptance must be communicated to the offeror. Proposing any deviation from the terms of the offer constitutes a rejection of the original offer and becomes a new offer. This is known as a **counteroffer.** The counteroffer must be accepted by the original offering party for a contract to exist.

Besides being terminated by a counteroffer, an offer may be terminated by the offeree's outright rejection of it. Alternatively, an offeree may fail to accept the offer before it expires. The offeror may revoke the offer at any time before receiving the acceptance. This *revocation* must be communicated to the offeree by the offeror, either directly or through the parties' agents. The offer is also revoked if the offeree learns of the revocation and observes the offeror acting in a manner that indicates that the offer no longer exists.

Consideration. The contract must be based on consideration. **Consideration** is something of legal value offered by one party and accepted by another as an inducement to perform or to refrain from some act. There must be a definite statement of consideration in a contract to show that something of value was given in exchange for the promise. Consideration is some interest or benefit accruing to one party, or some loss or responsibility by the other party.

Consideration must be "good and valuable" between the parties. The courts do not inquire into the adequacy of consideration. Adequate consideration ranges from as little as a promise of "love and affection" to a substantial sum of money. Anything that has been bargained for and exchanged is legally sufficient to satisfy the requirement for consideration. The only requirements are that the parties agree and that no undue influence or fraud has occurred.

Reality of consent. A contract that complies with all of the basic requirements may still be either void or voidable. This is because of the doctrine of **reality of consent**. A contract must be entered into as the free and voluntary act of each party. Each party must be able to make a prudent and knowledgeable decision without undue influence. A mistake, misrepresentation, fraud, undue influence, or duress would deprive a person of that ability. If any of these circumstances is present, the contract is voidable by the injured party. If the other party were to sue for breach, the injured party could use lack of voluntary assent as a defense.

Legal purpose. A contract must be for a legal purpose, that is, even with all the other elements (consent, competent parties, consideration, and offer and acceptance), if the contract is to do something illegal, it is not a valid contract. So when movie gangsters talk about "taking out a contract" to do something unpleasant to some unfortunate person, remember that it is *not* a valid, enforceable contract.

Legally competent parties. All parties to the contract must have *legal capacity,* that is, they must be of legal age and have enough mental capacity to understand the nature or consequences of their actions in the contract. In most states, 18 is the age of contractual capacity. Under state law, an imprisoned felon or certain mentally ill persons may be legally incompetent to enter into a contract.

Validity of Contracts. A contract can be described as valid, void, voidable, or unenforceable, depending on the circumstances.

A contract is **valid** when it meets all the essential elements that make it legally sufficient, or enforceable.

A contract is **void** when it has no legal force or effect because it lacks some or all of the essential elements of a contract. A contract that is void was never a contract in the eyes of the law.

A contract that is **voidable** appears on the surface to be valid but may be rescinded or disaffirmed by one or both parties based on some legal principle. A voidable contract is considered by the courts to be valid if the party who has the option to disaffirm the agreement does not do so within a period of time prescribed by state law. A contract with a minor, for instance, is usually voidable. This is because minors are generally permitted to *disaffirm* real estate contracts at any time while under age and for a certain period of time after reaching majority age. By the same token, a minor may *affirm* a contract entered into when he or she was underage, in effect validating the contract after the fact. A contract entered into by a mentally ill person is usually voidable during the mental illness and for a reasonable period after the person is cured. On the other hand, a contract made by a person who has been adjudicated insane (that is,

A contract may be

- **valid**—has all legal elements: Fully enforceable;
- **void**—lacks one or all elements: No legal force or effect;
- **voidable**—has all legal elements: May be rescinded or disaffirmed; or
- **unenforceable**—has all legal elements: Enforceable only between the parties.

found to be insane by a court) is void on the theory that the judgment is a matter of public record.

Mental capacity to enter into a contract is not the same as medical sanity. The test is whether the individual in question is capable of understanding what he or she is doing. A party may suffer from a mental illness but have a clear understanding of the significance of his or her actions. This is a thorny legal and psychological question that requires consultation with experts.

An **unenforceable contract** also seems on the surface to be valid; however, neither party can sue the other to force performance. For example, an oral agreement for the sale of a parcel of real estate would be unenforceable. Because the statute of frauds requires that real estate sales contracts be in writing, the defaulting party could not be taken to court and forced to perform. There is, however, a distinction between a suit to force performance and a suit for damages, which is permissible in an oral agreement. An unenforceable contract is said to be "valid as between the parties." This means that once the agreement is fully executed and both parties are satisfied, neither has reason to initiate a lawsuit to force performance.

■ DISCHARGE OF CONTRACTS

A contract is *discharged* when the agreement is terminated. Obviously, the most desirable case is when a contract terminates because it has been completely performed, with all its terms carried out. However, a contract may be terminated for other reasons, such as a party's breach or default.

Performance of a Contract

Each party has certain rights and duties to fulfill. The question of *when* a contract must be performed is an important factor. Many contracts call for a specific time by which the agreed-on acts must be completely performed. In addition, many contracts provide that "time is of the essence." This means that the contract must be performed within the time limit specified. A party who fails to perform on time is liable for breach of contract.

When a contract does not specify a date for performance, the acts it requires should be performed within a reasonable time. The interpretation of what constitutes a reasonable time depends on the situation. Generally, unless the parties agree otherwise, if the act can be done immediately, it should be performed immediately. Courts have sometimes declared contracts to be invalid because they did not contain a time or date for performance.

Assignment

Assignment is a transfer of rights or duties under a contract. Normally, rights may be assigned to a third party (called the *assignee*) unless the contract forbids it. Obligations may also be assigned (or *delegated*), but the original party remains primarily liable unless specifically released. An assignment may be made without the consent of the other party unless the contract includes a clause that permits or forbids assignment.

■ **FOR EXAMPLE** John enters into a contract to paint Tim's toolshed. Under the terms of the contract, John will be paid $1,000 when the job is finished. John owes

$1,000 to Rob, and so John assigns to Rob the right to receive the payment. When the job is done, Tim will pay $1,000 to Rob.

On the other hand, suppose that the day after John contracts to paint Tim's toolshed for $1,000, Ken offers John $3,000 to paint a gazebo. John wants to take the better-paying job but doesn't want to breach the contract with Tim. If the contract with Tim permits it, John may assign both the right to be paid and the duty to paint the toolshed to Peter, another painter. If Peter fails to paint the toolshed, however, John will be liable to Tim for breach of contract.

Novation

A contract may be performed by **novation,** that is, the substitution of a new contract in place of the original. The new agreement may be between the same parties, or a new party may be substituted for either (this is *novation of the parties*). The parties' intent must be to discharge the old obligation. For instance, when a real estate purchaser assumes the seller's existing mortgage loan, the lender may choose to release the seller and substitute the buyer as the party primarily liable for the mortgage debt. When a contract is performed by novation, both parties must consent to novation.

Breach of Contract

A contract may be terminated if it is breached by one of the parties. A **breach of contract** is a violation of any of the terms or conditions of a contract without legal excuse. For instance, a seller who fails to deliver title to the buyer breaches a sales contract. The breaching or defaulting party assumes certain burdens, and the nondefaulting party has certain remedies.

> *Assignment* = substitution of *parties*
>
> *Novation* = substitution of *contracts*

If the seller breaches a real estate sales contract, the buyer may sue for *specific performance* unless the contract specifically states otherwise. In a **suit for specific performance,** the buyer asks the court to force the seller to go through with the sale and convey the property as previously agreed. The buyer may choose to sue for *damages,* however, in which case he or she asks that the seller pay for any costs and hardships suffered by the buyer as a result of the seller's breach.

If the buyer defaults, the seller can sue for damages or sue for the purchase price. A suit for the purchase price is essentially a suit for specific performance: The seller tenders the deed and asks that the buyer be compelled to pay the agreed price.

The contract may limit the remedies available to the parties, however. A *liquidated damages* clause permits the seller to keep the earnest money deposit and any other payments received from the buyer as the seller's sole remedy. The clause may limit the buyer's remedy to a return of the earnest money and other payments should the seller default.

Statute of limitations. The law of every state limits the time within which parties to a contract may bring legal suit to enforce their rights. The *statute of limitations* varies for different legal actions, and any rights not enforced within the applicable time period are lost.

Other reasons for termination. Contracts may also be discharged or terminated when any of the following occurs:

■ *Partial performance* of the terms, along with a written acceptance by the other party. For instance, if the parties agree that the work performed is "close enough" to complete, they can agree that the contract is discharged even if some minor elements remain unperformed.

■ *Substantial performance*, in which one party has substantially performed on the contract but does not complete all the details exactly as the contract requires. (Such performance may be enough to force payment, with certain adjustments for any damages suffered by the other party.) For instance, where a newly constructed addition to a home is finished except for polishing the brass doorknobs, the contractor is entitled to the final payment.

■ *Impossibility of performance*, in which an act required by the contract cannot be legally accomplished.

■ *Mutual agreement* of the parties to cancel.

■ *Operation of law*—such as in the voiding of a contract by a minor—as a result of fraud, due to the expiration of the statute of limitations, or because a contract was altered without the written consent of all parties involved.

■ *Rescission*—one party may cancel or terminate the contract as if it had never been made. Cancellation terminates a contract without a return to the original position. Rescission, however, returns the parties to their original positions before the contract, so any monies that have been exchanged must be returned. Rescission is normally a contractual remedy for a breach, but a contract may also be rescinded by the mutual agreement of the parties.

■ CONTRACTS USED IN THE REAL ESTATE BUSINESS

The written agreements most commonly used by brokers and salespersons are

■ listing agreements and buyer agency agreements,
■ real estate sales contracts,
■ options,
■ land contracts or contracts for deed, and
■ leases and escrow agreements.

Many states have specific guidelines for when and how real estate licensees may prepare contracts for their clients and customers. These guidelines are created by state real estate officials, court decisions, or statutes. A *real estate licensee who is not a licensed attorney may not practice law*. The practice of law includes preparing legal documents, such as deeds and mortgages, and offering advice on legal matters. A broker or salesperson may, however, be permitted to fill in the blanks on certain approved preprinted documents, such as sales contracts and leases, as directed by the client. No separate fee may be charged for completing the forms.

Contract forms. Because so many real estate transactions are very similar in nature, preprinted forms are available for most kinds of contracts. The use of preprinted forms raises three problems: (1) what to write in the blanks, (2) what words and phrases should be ruled out by drawing lines through them because they don't apply, and (3) what additional clauses or agreements (called *riders* or *addenda*) should be added. All changes and additions are usually initialed in the margin or on the rider by both parties when a contract is signed.

IN PRACTICE

It is essential that both parties to a contract understand exactly what they are agreeing to. Poorly drafted documents, especially those containing extensive legal language, may be subject to various interpretations and lead to litigation. The parties to a real estate transaction should be advised to have sales contracts and other legal documents examined by their lawyers before they sign to ensure that the agreements accurately reflect their intentions. When preprinted forms do not sufficiently cover special provisions in a transaction, the parties should have an attorney draft an appropriate contract.

Listing and Buyer Agency Agreements

A *listing agreement* is an employment contract. It establishes the rights and obligations of the broker as agent and the seller as principal. A buyer agency contract establishes the relationship between a buyer and his or her agent. Refer to Chapter 6 for a complete discussion of the various types of listing agreements and buyer agency agreements and to Figure 6.2 and Figure 6.3 for sample contracts.

Some states suggest or require the use of specific forms of listing contracts. Oral listing contracts for a period of less than one year are recognized in some states, while in other states only written listing contracts are recognized.

IN PRACTICE

If a contract contains any ambiguity, the courts generally interpret the agreement against the party who prepared it.

Sales Contracts

A real estate sales contract contains the complete agreement between a buyer of a parcel of real estate and the seller. Depending on the area, this agreement may be known as an *offer to purchase*, a *contract of purchase and sale*, a *purchase agreement*, an *earnest money agreement*, or a *deposit receipt*.

Whatever the contract is called, it is an offer to purchase real estate as soon as it has been prepared and signed by the purchaser. If the document is accepted and signed by the seller, it becomes a contract of sale. This transformation is referred to as *ripening*.

The contract of sale is the most important document in the sale of real estate. It establishes the legal rights and obligations of the buyer and seller. In effect, it dictates the contents of the deed.

Several details frequently appear in a sales contract in addition to the essential elements of a contract. These include

- the sales price and terms;
- a legal description of the land;
- a statement of the kind and condition of the title, and the form of deed to be delivered by the seller;
- the kind of title evidence required, who will provide it, and how many defects in the title will be eliminated; and
- a statement of all the terms and conditions of the agreement between the parties, and any contingencies (discussed later in this Chapter).

The following paragraphs discuss some of the issues that often arise as an offer to purchase ripens into a contract of sale.

Offer. A broker lists an owner's real estate for sale at whatever price and conditions the owner sets. When a prospective buyer is found, the broker helps him or her prepare an offer to purchase. The offer is signed by the prospective buyer and presented by the licensee to the seller. This is an offer.

Counteroffer. As discussed earlier in this Chapter, any change to the terms proposed by the buyer creates a *counteroffer*. Note, however, that a counteroffer is not created when the offer's language is simply clarified in an amendment to an offer. The original offer ceases to exist because the seller has rejected it. The buyer may accept or reject the seller's counteroffer. If the buyer wishes, he or she may continue the process by making another counteroffer. Any change in the last offer may result in a counteroffer until either the parties reach agreement or one of them walks away.

> A *counteroffer* is a *new offer;* it voids the original offer.

An offer or counteroffer *may be revoked at any time before it has been accepted,* even if the person making the offer or counteroffer agreed to keep the offer open for a set period of time.

Acceptance. If the seller agrees to the original offer or a later counteroffer *exactly as it was made* and signs the document, the offer has been *accepted.* Acceptance of the offer means that a contract is *formed.* The licensee must advise the buyer of the seller's acceptance and obtain the approval of the parties' attorneys if the contract calls for it. A duplicate original of the contract must be provided to each party.

An offer is not considered accepted until the person making the offer has been *notified of the other party's acceptance.* When the parties communicate through an agent or at a distance, questions may arise regarding whether an acceptance, a rejection, or a counteroffer has occurred. Current technologies make communication faster; a signed agreement that is faxed, for instance, would constitute adequate communication. The licensee must transmit all offers, acceptances, or other responses as soon as possible to avoid questions of proper communication.

Binder. In some states, brokers may prepare a shorter document, known as a *binder,* instead of a complete sales contract. The binder states the essential terms of the offer and acknowledges that the broker has received the purchaser's deposit. The parties have a more formal and complete contract of sale drawn up by an attorney once the seller accepts and signs the binder. A binder might also be used where the details of the transaction are too complex for the standard sales contract form.

Earnest money deposits. It is customary (although not essential) for a purchaser to provide a deposit when making an offer to purchase real estate. This deposit, usually in the form of a check, is referred to as **earnest money.** The earnest money deposit is evidence of the buyer's intention to carry out the terms of the contract in good faith. The check is given to the broker, who usually holds it for the parties in a special account. In some areas, it is common practice for deposits to be held in escrow by the seller's attorney. If the offer is not accepted, the earnest money deposit is immediately returned to the would-be buyer.

The amount of the deposit is a matter to be agreed on by the parties. Under the terms of most listing agreements, a real estate broker is required to accept a "reasonable amount" as earnest money. As a rule, the deposit should be an amount sufficient to

- discourage the buyer from defaulting,
- compensate the seller for taking the property off the market, and
- cover any expenses the seller might incur if the buyer defaults.

Most contracts provide that the deposit becomes the seller's property as liquidated damages if the buyer defaults. The seller might also claim further damages, however, unless the contract limits recovery to the deposit alone.

Earnest money held by a broker must be held in a special *trust,* or *escrow,* account. This money cannot be mixed with a broker's own personal funds (called *commingling*). A broker may not use earnest money funds for his or her personal use (called *conversion*). A separate escrow account does not have to be opened for each earnest money deposit received; all deposits may be kept in one account. A broker must maintain full, complete, and accurate records of all earnest money deposits.

The special account may or may not pay interest, depending on state law. If the account bears interest, there must be some provision in the contract for how the interest earned will be distributed. The broker must provide the parties with an accounting of the amount and dates of interest payments. Often, a check for the interest amount is given to the buyer at closing. On the other hand, the contract may provide for the interest to be paid to the seller as part of the purchase price.

Equitable title. When a buyer signs a contract to purchase real estate, he or she does not receive title to the land. Title transfers only upon delivery and acceptance of a deed. However, after both buyer and seller have executed a sales contract, the buyer acquires an *interest* in the land. This interest is known as **equitable title.** A person who holds equitable title has rights that vary from state to state. Equitable title may give the buyer an insurable interest in the property. If the parties decide not to go through with the purchase and sale, the buyer may be required to give the seller a *quitclaim deed* to release the equitable interest in the land.

Destruction of premises. In many states, once the sales contract is signed by both parties, the buyer bears the risk of any damage to the property that may occur before closing. Of course, the contract may provide otherwise. Furthermore, the laws and court decisions of a growing number of states have placed the risk of loss on the seller. Many of these states have adopted the *Uniform Vendor and Purchaser Risk Act,* which specifically provides that the seller bear any loss that occurs before the title passes or the buyer takes possession.

Liquidated damages. To avoid a lawsuit if one party breaches the contract, the parties may agree on a certain amount of money that will compensate the nonbreaching party. That money is called **liquidated damages.** If a sales contract specifies that the earnest money deposit is to serve as liquidated damages in case the buyer defaults, the seller will be entitled to keep the deposit if the buyer refuses to perform without good reason. The seller who keeps the deposit as liquidated damages may not sue for any further damages if the contract provides that the deposit is the seller's sole remedy.

Parts of a sales contract. All real estate sales contracts can be divided into a number of separate parts. Although each form of contract contains these divisions, their location within a particular contract may vary. Most sales contracts include the following information:

- The purchaser's name and a statement of the purchaser's obligation to purchase the property, including how the purchaser intends to take title.
- An adequate description of the property, such as the street address. (Note that while a street address may be adequate for a sales contract, it is not legally sufficient as a description of the real property being conveyed, as discussed in Chapter 9.)
- The seller's name and a statement of the type of deed a seller agrees to give, including any covenants, conditions, and restrictions that apply to the deed.
- The purchase price and how the purchaser intends to pay for the property, including earnest money deposits, additional cash from the purchaser, and the conditions of any mortgage financing the purchaser intends to obtain or assume.
- The amount and form of the down payment or earnest money deposit and whether it will be in the form of a check or promissory note.
- A provision for the closing of the transaction and the transfer of possession of the property to the purchaser by a specific date.
- A provision for title evidence (abstract and legal opinion, certificate of title, Torrens certificate, or title insurance policy).
- The method by which real estate taxes, rents, fuel costs, and other expenses are to be prorated.
- A provision for the completion of the contract should the property be damaged or destroyed between the time of signing and the closing date.
- A liquidated damages clause, a right-to-sue provision, or another statement of remedies available in the event of default.
- Contingency clauses (such as the buyer's obtaining financing or selling a currently owned property or the seller's acquisition of another desired property or clearing of the title; attorney approval and home inspection are other commonly included contingencies).
- The dated signatures of all parties (the signature of a witness is not essential to a valid contract). In some states, the seller's nonowning spouse may be required to release potential marital or homestead rights. An agent may sign for a principal if the agent has been expressly authorized to do so. When sellers are co-owners, all must sign if the entire ownership is being transferred.
- In most states, an agency disclosure statement.

Additional provisions. Many sales contracts provide for the following:

- Any personal property to be left with the premises for the purchaser (such as major appliances or lawn and garden equipment)
- Any real property to be removed by the seller before the closing (such as a storage shed)

- The transfer of any applicable warranties on items such as heating and cooling systems or built-in appliances
- The identification of any leased equipment that must be transferred to the purchaser or returned to the lessor (such as security systems, cable television boxes, and water softeners)
- The appointment of a closing or settlement agent
- Closing or settlement instructions
- The transfer of any impound or escrow account funds
- The transfer or payment of any outstanding special assessments
- The purchaser's right to inspect the property shortly before the closing or settlement (often called the *walk-through*)
- The agreement as to what documents will be provided by each party and when and where they will be delivered

Contingencies. Additional conditions that must be satisfied before a sales contract is fully enforceable are called **contingencies.** A contingency includes the following three elements:

1. The actions necessary to satisfy the contingency
2. The time frame within which the actions must be performed
3. Who is responsible for paying any costs involved

The most common contingencies include the

- *mortgage contingency.* A mortgage contingency protects the buyer's earnest money until a lender commits the mortgage loan funds.
- *inspection contingency.* A sales contract may be contingent on the buyer's obtaining certain inspections of the property. Inspections may include those for wood-boring insects, lead-based paint, structural and mechanical systems, sewage facilities, and radon or other toxic materials.
- *property sale contingency.* A purchaser may make the sales contract contingent on the sale of his or her current home. This protects the buyer from owning two homes at the same time and also helps ensure the availability of cash for the purchase.

The seller may insist on an *escape clause*. An escape clause permits the seller to continue to market the property until all the buyer's contingencies have been satisfied or removed. The buyer may retain the right to eliminate the contingencies if the seller receives a more favorable offer. (Note that contingencies create a *voidable contract:* If the contingencies are rejected or not satisfied, the contract is void.)

Amendments and addendums. An *amendment* is a change to the existing content of a contract. Any time words or provisions are *added to or deleted from the body of the contract,* the contract has been amended. For instance, a form contract's provision requiring closing in 90 days might be crossed out and replaced with a 60-day period. Amendments must be initialed by all parties.

On the other hand, an *addendum* is any provision added to an existing contract *without altering the content of the original.* An addendum is essentially a new contract between the parties that includes the original contract's provisions "by reference," that is, the addendum mentions the original contract. An addendum must be signed by the parties. For example, an addendum might be an agreement to split the cost of repairing certain flaws discovered in a home inspection.

Disclosures. As discussed in previous Chapters, many states have enacted mandatory **disclosure** laws. The purpose of these laws is to help consumers make informed decisions. Many brokers have instituted procedures for making disclosures and recommending technical experts to ensure that purchasers have accurate information about real estate. Disclosure of property conditions may be included as part of a sales contract, or it may be a separate form. As discussed in Chapter 4, disclosure of the broker's agency relationship may also be required by state law.

Options

An **option** is a contract by which an *optionor* (generally an owner) gives an *optionee* (a prospective purchaser or lessee) the right to buy or lease the owner's property at a fixed price within a certain period of time. The optionee pays a fee (the agreed actual consideration) for this option right. The optionee has no other obligation until he or she decides to either exercise the option right or allow the option to expire. An option is enforceable by only one party—the optionee.

An option contract is not a sales contract. At the time the option is signed by the parties, the owner does not sell, and the optionee does not buy. The parties merely agree that the optionee has the right to buy and the owner is obligated to sell *if* the optionee decides to exercise his or her right of option. Options must contain all the terms and provisions required for a valid contract.

The option agreement (which is a unilateral contract) requires that the optionor act only after the optionee gives notice that he or she elects to execute the option. If the option is not exercised within the time specified in the contract, both the optionor's obligation and the optionee's right expire. An option contract may provide for renewal, which often requires additional consideration. The optionee cannot recover the consideration paid for the option right. The contract may state whether the money paid for the option is to be applied to the purchase price of the real estate if the option is exercised.

A common application of an option is a lease that includes an option for the tenant to purchase the property. Options on commercial real estate frequently depend on some specific conditions being fulfilled, such as obtaining a zoning change or a building permit. The optionee may be obligated to exercise the option if the conditions are met. Similar terms could also be included in a sales contract.

Land Contracts

A real estate sale can be made under a **land contract.** A land contract is sometimes called a *contract for deed,* a *bond for title,* an **installment contract,** a *land sales contract,* or *articles of agreement for warranty deed.* Under a typical land contract, the seller (also known as the *vendor*) retains legal title. The buyer (called the vendee) takes possession and gets equitable title to the property. The buyer agrees to give the seller a down payment and pay regular monthly installments of principal and interest over a number of years. The buyer also agrees to pay real estate taxes, insurance premiums, repairs, and upkeep on the property. Although the buyer obtains possession under the contract, *the seller is not obligated to execute and deliver a deed to the buyer until the terms of the contract have been satisfied.* This frequently occurs when the buyer has made enough payments to obtain a mortgage loan and pay off the balance due on the contract. Although a land contract is usually assumable by subsequent purchasers, it generally must be approved by the seller.

IN PRACTICE

Legislatures and courts have not looked favorably on the harsh provisions of some real estate installment contracts. A seller and buyer contemplating such a sale should first consult an attorney to make sure that the agreement meets all legal requirements. The individual concerns of the parties must be addressed.

Leases and Escrow Agreements.   A **lease** is any agreement which gives rise to the relationship of landlord and tenant or lessor and lessee. A lease is a contract for exclusive possession of land, for a term of time, at will, usually for a specified rent or compensation. An **escrow contract** is an agreement between a buyer, seller, and escrow holder setting forth rights and responsibilities of each. An escrow contract is entered into when earnest money is deposited in a broker's escrow account.

■ SUMMARY

A contract is a legally enforceable promise or set of promises that must be performed; if a breach occurs, the law provides a remedy.

Contracts may be classified according to whether the parties' intentions are express or merely implied by their actions. They may also be classified as bilateral (when both parties have obligated themselves to act) or unilateral (when one party is obligated to perform only if the other party acts). In addition, contracts may be classified according to their legal enforceability as valid, void, voidable, or unenforceable.

Many contracts specify a time for performance. In any case, all contracts must be performed within a reasonable time. An executed contract is one that has been fully performed. An executory contract is one in which some act remains to be performed.

The essentials of a valid contract are legally competent parties, offer and acceptance, legality of object, and consideration. A valid real estate contract must include a description of the property. It should be in writing and signed by all parties to be enforceable in court.

In many types of contracts, either of the parties may transfer his or her rights and obligations under the agreement by assignment or novation (substitution of a new contract).

Contracts usually provide that the seller has the right to declare a sale canceled if the buyer defaults. If either party suffers a loss because of the other's default, he or she may sue for damages to cover the loss. If one party insists on completing the transaction, he or she may sue the defaulter for specific performance of the terms of the contract; a court can order the other party to comply with the agreement.

Contracts frequently used in the real estate business include listing agreements, sales contracts, options, land contracts (installment contracts), and leases.

A real estate sales contract binds a buyer and a seller to a definite transaction as described in detail in the contract. The buyer is bound to purchase the property for the amount stated in the agreement. The seller is bound to deliver title, free from liens and encumbrances (except those identified in the contract).

Under an option agreement, the optionee purchases from the optionor, for a limited time period, the exclusive right to purchase or lease the optionor's property. A land contract, or installment contract, is a sales/financing agreement under which a buyer purchases a seller's real estate on time. The buyer takes possession of and responsibility for the property but does not receive the deed immediately.

QUESTIONS

1. A legally enforceable agreement under which two parties promise to do something for each other is known as a(n)

   a. escrow agreement.
   b. legal pledge.
   c. valid contract.
   d. option agreement.

2. Dave approaches Bob and says, "I'd like to buy your house." Bob says, "Sure," and they agree on a price. What kind of contract is this?

   a. Implied
   b. Unenforceable
   c. Void
   d. There is no contract.

3. A contract is said to be *bilateral* if

   a. one of the parties is a minor.
   b. the contract has yet to be fully performed.
   c. only one party to the agreement is bound to act.
   d. all parties to the contract exchange binding promises.

4. During the period of time after a real estate sales contract is signed, but before title actually passes, the status of the contract is

   a. voidable.   c. unilateral.
   b. executory.   d. implied.

5. A contract for the sale of real estate that does not state the consideration to be paid for the property and is not signed by the parties is considered to be

   a. voidable.   c. void.
   b. executory.   d. enforceable.

6. Nick and Kelly sign a contract under which Nick will convey Raptor Manor to Kelly. Nick changes his mind, and Kelly sues for specific performance. What is Kelly seeking in this lawsuit?

   a. Money damages
   b. New contract
   c. Deficiency judgment
   d. Conveyance of the property

7. In a standard sales contract, several words were crossed out or inserted by the parties. To eliminate future controversy as to whether the changes were made before or after the contract was signed, the usual procedure is to

   a. write a letter to each party listing the changes.
   b. have each party write a letter to the other approving the changes.
   c. redraw the entire contract.
   d. have both parties initial or sign in the margin near each change.

8. Mark makes an offer on Yolanda's house, and Yolanda accepts. Both parties sign the sales contract. At this point, Mark has what type of title to the property?

   a. Equitable   c. Escrow
   b. Voidable   d. Contract

9. The sales contract says the buyer will purchase only if an attorney approves the sale by the following Saturday. The attorney's approval is a

   a. contingency.
   b. reservation.
   c. warranty.
   d. consideration.

10. A prospective buyer places an advertisement in the local paper. The ad reads: "I will pay $50,000 for any house, anywhere in town!" What kind of contract is this?

    a. Unilateral
    b. Option
    c. Implied
    d. It is not a contract.

11. An option to purchase binds which of the following parties?

    a. Buyer only
    b. Seller only
    c. Neither buyer nor seller
    d. Both buyer and seller

12. Carl and Hannah enter into a real estate sales contract. Under the contract's terms, Carl will pay Hannah $500 a month for ten years. Hannah will continue to hold legal title to Mandalay Mansion. Carl will live in Mandalay Mansion and pay all real estate taxes, insurance premiums, and regular upkeep costs. What kind of contract do Carl and Hannah have?

a. Option contract
b. Contract for mortgage
c. Unilateral contract
d. Land or installment contract

13. The purchaser of real estate under an installment contract

a. generally pays no interest charge.
b. receives title immediately.
c. is not required to pay property taxes for the duration of the contract.
d. has only an equitable interest in the property's title.

14. Under the statute of frauds, all contracts for the sale of real estate must be

a. originated by a real estate broker.
b. on preprinted forms.
c. in writing to be enforceable.
d. accompanied by earnest money deposits.

15. The Fitzgeralds offer in writing to purchase a house for $120,000, including its draperies, with the offer to expire on Saturday at noon. The Wonderlies reply in writing on Thursday, accepting the $120,000 offer, but excluding the draperies. On Friday, while the Fitzgeralds consider this counteroffer, the Wonderlies decide to accept the original offer, draperies included, and state that in writing. At this point, the Fitzgeralds

a. are legally bound to buy the house although they have the right to insist that the draperies be included.
b. are not bound to buy.
c. must buy the house and are not entitled to the draperies.
d. must buy the house but may deduct the value of the draperies from the $120,000.

16. A buyer makes an offer to purchase certain property listed with a broker and leaves a deposit with the broker to show good faith. The broker should

a. immediately apply the deposit to the listing expenses.
b. put the deposit in an account, as provided by state law.
c. give the deposit to the seller when the offer is presented.
d. put the deposit in the broker's personal checking account.

17. From June 5 through October 15, Madeline suffered from a mental illness that caused delusions, hallucinations, and loss of memory. On July 1, Madeline signed a contract to purchase Brown's Farm, with the closing set for October 31. On September 24, Madeline began psychiatric treatment. Madeline was declared completely cured by October 15. Which of the following statements is true regarding Madeline's contract to purchase Brown's Farm?

a. The contract is voidable.
b. The contract is void.
c. The contract lacks reality of consent.
d. The contract is fully valid and enforceable.

18. A broker has found a buyer for a seller's home. The buyer has indicated in writing a willingness to buy the property for $1,000 less than the asking price and has deposited $5,000 in earnest money with the broker. The seller is out of town for the weekend, and the broker has been unable to inform the seller of the signed document. At this point, the buyer has signed a(n)

a. voidable contract.
b. offer.
c. executory agreement.
d. implied contract.

19. A buyer and seller agree to the purchase of a house for $200,000. The contract contains a clause stating that time is of the essence. Which of the following statements is true?

a. The closing must take place within a reasonable period before the stated date.

b. A time-is-of-the-essence clause is not binding on either party.

c. The closing date must be stated as a particular calendar date, and not simply as a formula, such as "two weeks after loan approval."

d. If the closing date passes and no closing takes place, the contract may be rescinded by the party who was ready to settle on the scheduled date.

20. Robert signs a contract under which he is given the right to purchase Yellow Acres for $30,000 any time in the next three months. Robert pays Yellow Acre's current owner $500 at the time that contract is signed. Which of the following best describes this agreement?

a. Contingency   c. Installment

b. Option   d. Sales

12

TRANSFER OF TITLE

■ **LEARNING OBJECTIVES** *When you've finished reading this Chapter, you should be able to:*

■ **identify** the basic requirements for a valid deed.

■ **describe** the seven fundamental types of deeds.

■ **explain** how property may be transferred through involuntary alienation.

■ **distinguish** transfers of title by will from transfers by intestacy.

■ **define** the following *key terms:*

acknowledgment	grantor	testate
adverse possession	habendum clause	testator
bargain and sale deed	heirs	title
deed	intestate	transfer tax
deed of trust	involuntary alienation	trustee's deed
devise	probate	voluntary alienation
general warranty deed	quitclaim deed	will
grantee	reconveyance deed	
granting clause	special warranty deed	

■ **WHY LEARN ABOUT...**   TRANSFER OF TITLE?

The material in this Chapter is one of those things that a good real estate agent will know about but will rarely deal with directly: This aspect of a real estate transaction is generally handled by attorneys and title companies. Nonetheless, as with other "legal" aspects of the transaction, an agent who is aware of the fundamentals of deeds and other title issues will know the kinds of questions to ask, and the kinds of warning signs to look for, in order to alert the title professionals to potential title issues. ■

■ TITLE

The term *title* has two meanings. **Title** to real estate means *the right to or ownership of the land;* it represents the owner's bundle of rights, discussed in Chapter 2. *Title* also serves as *evidence* of that ownership. A person who holds the title would, if challenged in court, be able to recover or retain ownership or possession of a parcel of real estate. "Title" is just a way of referring to ownership; it is *not* an actual printed document. The document by which the owner transfers his or her title to another is the *deed*. The deed must be recorded to give public notice of the holder's ownership.

Real estate may be transferred *voluntarily* by sale or gift. Alternatively, it may be transferred *involuntarily* by operation of law. Real estate may be transferred while the owner lives or by will or descent after the owner dies. In any case, it is the title that is transferred as a symbol of ownership.

■ VOLUNTARY ALIENATION

A **grantor** conveys property to a grantee.

A **grantee** receives property from a grantor.

A **deed** is the instrument that conveys property from a grantor to a grantee.

Voluntary alienation is the legal term for the voluntary transfer of title. The owner may voluntarily transfer title by either making a gift or selling the property. To transfer during one's lifetime, the owner must use some form of deed of conveyance.

A **deed** is the written instrument by which an owner of real estate intentionally conveys the right, title, or interest in the parcel of real estate to someone else. The statute of frauds requires that all deeds be in writing. The owner who transfers the title is referred to as the **grantor.** The person who acquires the title is called the **grantee.** A deed is executed (that is, signed) only by the grantor. To be able to execute a valid deed, the grantor must have legal capacity.

Requirements for a Valid Deed

Although the formal requirements vary, most states require that a valid deed contain the following elements:

■ Grantor who has the legal competency to execute (sign) the deed
■ Grantee named with reasonable certainty to be identified
■ Recital of consideration

- Granting clause (words of conveyance)
- Habendum clause (to define ownership taken by the grantee)
- Accurate legal description of the property conveyed
- Any relevant exceptions or reservations
- Signature of the grantor, which must be acknowledged
- Delivery of the deed and acceptance by the grantee to pass title

A deed also may include a description of any *limitations* on the conveyance of a full fee simple estate and a recital of any *exceptions and reservations* (also known as *"subject to" clauses*) that affect title to the property.

Grantor. A grantor must be of *lawful age*, usually at least 18 years old. A deed executed by a minor is generally voidable.

A grantor also must be of *sound mind*. Generally, any grantor who can understand the action is viewed as mentally capable of executing a valid deed. A deed executed by someone who was mentally impaired at the time is voidable, but it is not void. If, however, the grantor has been judged legally incompetent, the deed will be void. Real estate owned by someone who is legally incompetent can be conveyed only with a court's approval.

The grantor's name must be spelled correctly and consistently throughout the deed. If the grantor's name has been changed since the title was acquired, as when a person changes his or her name by marriage, both names should be shown—for example, "Mary Smith, formerly Mary Jones."

Grantee. To be valid, a deed must name a grantee. The grantee must be specifically named so that the person to whom the property is being conveyed can be readily identified from the deed itself.

FOR EXAMPLE Olive wanted to convey Whiteacre to her nephew, Jack Jackson. In the deed, Olive wrote the following words of conveyance: "I, Olive Burbank, hereby convey to Jack all my interest in Whiteacre." The only problem was that Olive also had a son named Jack, a cousin Jack, and a neighbor Jack. The grantee's identity could not be discerned from the deed itself. Olive should have conveyed Whiteacre "to my nephew, Jack Jackson."

If more than one grantee is involved, the granting clause should specify their rights in the property. The clause might state, for instance, that the grantees will take title as joint tenants or tenants in common. This is especially important when specific wording is necessary to create a joint tenancy.

Consideration. A valid deed must contain a clause acknowledging that the grantor has received consideration. Generally, the amount of consideration is stated in dollars. When a deed conveys real estate as a gift to a relative, love and affection may be sufficient consideration. In most states, however, it is customary to recite a *nominal* consideration, such as "$10 and other good and valuable consideration."

Granting clause (words of conveyance)

A deed must contain a **granting clause** that states the grantor's intention to convey the property. Depending on the type of deed and the obligations agreed to by the grantor, the wording would be similar to one of the following:

- "I, *JKL*, convey and warrant . . ."
- "I, *JKL*, remise, release, alienate, and convey . . ."
- "I, *JKL*, grant, bargain, and sell . . ."
- "I, *JKL*, remise, release, and quitclaim . . ."

A deed that conveys the grantor's entire fee simple interest usually contains wording such as "to *ABC* and to her heirs and assigns forever." If the grantor conveys less than his or her complete interest, such as a life estate, the wording must indicate this limitation—for example, "to *ABC* for the duration of her natural life."

Habendum clause. When it is necessary to define or explain the ownership to be enjoyed by the grantee, a **habendum clause** may follow the granting clause. The habendum clause begins with the words *to have and to hold*. Its provisions must agree with those stated in the granting clause. For example, if a grantor conveys a time-share interest or an interest less than fee simple absolute, the habendum clause would specify the owner's rights as well as how those rights are limited (a specific time frame or certain prohibited activities, for instance).

Legal description of real estate. To be valid, a deed must contain an accurate legal description of the real estate conveyed. Land is considered adequately described if a competent surveyor can locate the property using the description.

Exceptions and reservations. A valid deed must specifically note any encumbrances, reservations, or limitations that affect the title being conveyed. This might include such things as restrictions and easements that run with the land. In addition to citing existing encumbrances, a grantor may reserve some right in the land, such as an easement, for his or her own use. A grantor may also place certain restrictions on a grantee's use of the property. Developers often restrict the number of houses that may be built on each lot in a subdivision. Such private restrictions must be stated in the deed or contained in a previously recorded document, such as the subdivider's master deed, that is expressly referred to in the deed. Many of these deed restrictions have time limits and often include renewal clauses.

Signature of grantor. To be valid, a deed must be signed by all grantors named in the deed. Some states also require witnesses to the grantor's signature.

Most states permit an attorney-in-fact to sign for a grantor. (An attorney-in-fact is not necessarily an attorney-at-law.) The attorney-in-fact must act under a *power of attorney*—the specific written authority to execute and sign one or more legal instruments for another person. Usually, the power of attorney must be recorded in the county where the property is located. The power of attorney terminates when the person on whose behalf it is exercised dies. As a result, adequate evidence must be submitted that the grantor was alive at the time the attorney-in-fact signed the deed.

In some states, a grantor's spouse is required to sign any deed of conveyance to waive any marital or homestead rights. This requirement varies according to state law and depends on the manner in which title to real estate is held.

Many states still require a *seal* (or simply the word *seal*) to be written or printed after an individual grantor's signature. The corporate seal may be required of a corporate grantor.

Acknowledgment. An **acknowledgment** is a formal declaration that the person who signs a written document does so *voluntarily* and that his or her signature is genuine. The declaration is made before a *notary public* or an authorized public officer, such as a judge, a justice of the peace, or some other person as prescribed by state law. An acknowledgment usually states that the person signing the deed or other document is known to the officer or has produced sufficient identification to prevent a forgery. The form of acknowledgment required by the state where the property is located should be used even if the party signing is a resident of another ("foreign") state.

An acknowledgment (that is, a formal declaration before a notary public) is not essential to the *validity* of the deed unless it is required by state statute. However, a deed that is not acknowledged is not a completely satisfactory instrument. In most states, an unacknowledged deed is not eligible for recording.

Delivery and acceptance. A title is not considered transferred until the deed is actually *delivered* to and *accepted* by the grantee. The grantor may deliver the deed to the grantee either personally or through a third party. The third party, commonly known as an *escrow agent* (or *settlement agent*), will deliver the deed to the grantee as soon as certain requirements have been satisfied. *Title is said to "pass" only when a deed is delivered and accepted.* The effective date of the transfer of title from the grantor to the grantee is the date of delivery of the deed itself. When a deed is delivered in escrow, the date of delivery generally relates back to the date it was deposited with the escrow agent. (However, under the Torrens system, as discussed in Chapter 13, title does not pass until the deed has been examined and accepted for registration.)

> Transfer of title requires both delivery and acceptance of the deed.

Execution of Corporate Deeds

The laws governing a corporation's right to convey real estate vary from state to state. However, two basic rules must be followed:

1. A corporation can convey real estate only by authority granted in its *bylaws* or on a proper resolution passed by its *board of directors*. If all or a substantial portion of a corporation's real estate is being conveyed, usually a resolution authorizing the sale must be secured from the *shareholders*.
2. Deeds to real estate can be signed *only by an authorized officer*.

Rules pertaining to religious corporations and not-for-profit corporations vary even more widely. Because the legal requirements must be followed exactly, an attorney should be consulted for all corporate conveyances.

Types of Deeds

A deed can take several forms, depending on the extent of the grantor's pledges to the grantee. Regardless of any guarantees the deed offers, however, the grantee will want additional assurance that the grantor has the right to offer what the deed conveys. To obtain this protection, grantees commonly seek evidence of title, discussed in Chapter 13.

The most common deed forms are the

- general warranty deed,
- special warranty deed,
- bargain and sale deed,
- quitclaim deed,
- deed in trust,
- trustee's deed,
- reconveyance deed, and
- deed executed pursuant to a court order.

General warranty deed. A **general warranty deed** provides the greatest protection to the buyer. It is called a *general warranty deed* because the grantor is legally bound by certain covenants or warranties. In most states, the warranties are implied by the use of certain words specified by statute. In some states, the grantor's warranties are expressly written into the deed itself. Each state law should be examined, but some of the specific words include *convey and warrant* or *warrant generally*. The basic warranties are as follows:

- *Covenant of seisin:* The grantor warrants that he or she owns the property and has the right to convey title to it. (*Seisin* simply means "possession.") The grantee may recover damages up to the full purchase price if this covenant is broken.
- *Covenant against encumbrances:* The grantor warrants that the property is free from liens or encumbrances, except for any specifically stated in the deed. Encumbrances generally include mortgages, mechanics' liens, and easements. If this covenant is breached, the grantee may sue for the cost of removing the encumbrances.
- *Covenant of quiet enjoyment:* The grantor guarantees that the grantee's title will be good against third parties who might bring court actions to establish superior title to the property. If the grantee's title is found to be inferior, the grantor is liable for damages.
- *Covenant of further assurance:* The grantor promises to obtain and deliver any instrument needed to make the title good. For example, if the grantor's spouse has failed to sign away dower rights, the grantor must deliver a quitclaim deed (discussed later in this Chapter) to clear the title.
- *Covenant of warranty forever:* The grantor promises to compensate the grantee for the loss sustained if the title fails at any time in the future.

These covenants in a general warranty deed are not limited to matters that occurred during the time the grantor owned the property; they extend back to its origins. The grantor defends the title against both himself or herself and *all those who previously held title*.

General Warranty Deed

Five covenants:
1. Covenant of seisin
2. Covenant against encumbrances
3. Covenant of quiet enjoyment
4. Covenant of further assurance
5. Covenant of warranty forever

Special warranty deed. A special warranty deed contains two basic warranties:

1. That the grantor received title
2. That the property was not encumbered *during the time the grantor held title,* except as otherwise noted in the deed

In effect, the grantor defends the title against himself or herself. The granting clause generally contains the words: "Grantor remises, releases, alienates, and conveys." The grantor may include additional warranties, but they must be specifically stated in the deed. In areas where a special warranty deed is more commonly used, the purchase of title insurance is viewed as providing adequate protection to the grantee.

A special warranty deed may be used by fiduciaries such as trustees, executors, and corporations. A special warranty deed is appropriate for a fiduciary because he or she lacks the authority to warrant against acts of *predecessors in title* (the former owners). A fiduciary may hold title for a limited time without having a personal interest in the proceeds. Sometimes, a special warranty deed may be used by a grantor who has acquired title at a tax sale.

Bargain and sale deed. A bargain and sale deed contains no express warranties against encumbrances. It does, however, *imply* that the grantor holds title and possession of the property. The words in the granting clause are usually *HIJ grants and releases* or *XYZ grants, bargains, and sells.* Because the warranty is not specifically stated, the grantee has little legal recourse if title defects appear later. In some areas, this deed is used in foreclosures and tax sales. The buyer should purchase, or the seller provide, title insurance for protection.

A covenant against encumbrances initiated by the grantor may be added to a standard bargain and sale deed to create a *bargain and sale deed with covenant against the grantor's acts.* This deed is roughly equivalent to a special warranty deed. Warranties used in general warranty deeds may be inserted into a bargain and sale deed to give the grantee similar protection.

Quitclaim deed. A quitclaim deed provides the grantee with the least protection of any deed. It carries *no covenants or warranties* and generally conveys only whatever interest the grantor may have when the deed is delivered. If the grantor has no interest, the grantee will acquire nothing. Nor will the grantee acquire any right of warranty claim against the grantor. A quitclaim deed can convey title as effectively as a warranty deed if the grantor has good title when he or she delivers the deed, but it provides none of the guarantees that a warranty deed does. Through a quitclaim deed, the grantor only "remises, releases, and quitclaims" his or her interest in the property, if any.

Usually, a quitclaim deed is the only type of deed that may be used to convey less than a fee simple estate. This is because a quitclaim deed conveys only the grantor's right, title, or interest.

A quitclaim deed is frequently used to cure a defect, called a *cloud on the title.* For example, if the name of the grantee is misspelled on a warranty deed filed in

---

Special Warranty Deed

Two warranties:
1. Warranty that grantor received title
2. Warranty that property was unencumbered by grantor

Bargain and Sale Deed

No express warranties
■ Implication that grantor holds title and possession

Quitclaim Deed

No express or implied covenants or warranties
■ Used primarily to convey less than fee simple or to cure a title defect

the public record, a quitclaim deed with the correct spelling may be executed to the grantee to perfect the title.

A quitclaim deed is also used when a grantor allegedly *inherits* property but is not certain that the decedent's title was valid. A warranty deed in such an instance could carry with it obligations of warranty, while a quitclaim deed would convey only the grantor's interest, whatever it may be.

One of the most common uses of the quitclaim deed, however, is a simple *transfer* of property from one family member to another.

Deed of trust. A deed of trust (or *deed in trust* in some states) is the means by which a *trustor* conveys real estate to a *trustee* for the benefit of a *beneficiary*. The real estate is held by the trustee to fulfill the purpose of the trust. (See Figure 12.1.)

Reconveyance deed. A reconveyance deed is used by a trustee to return title to the trustor. For example, when a loan secured by a deed of trust has been fully paid, the beneficiary notifies the trustee. The trustee then reconveys the property to the trustor. As with any document of title, a reconveyance deed should be recorded to prevent title problems in the future.

Trustee's deed. A deed executed by a trustee is a **trustee's deed**. It is used when a trustee conveys real estate held in the trust to anyone *other than the trustor*. The trustee's deed must state that the trustee is executing the instrument in accordance with the powers and authority granted by the trust instrument.

Deed executed pursuant to court order. Executors' and administrators' deeds, masters' deeds, sheriffs' deeds, and many other types are all *deeds executed pursuant to a court order*. These deeds are established by state statute and are used to convey title to property that is transferred by court order or by will. The form of such a deed must conform to the laws of the state in which the property is located.

One common characteristic of deeds executed pursuant to court order is that the *full consideration* is usually stated in the deed. Instead of "$10 and other valuable consideration," for example, the deed would list the actual sales price.

Transfer Tax Stamps

Many states have enacted laws providing for a state **transfer tax** (also referred to in some states as a *grantor's tax*) on conveyances of real estate. In these states, the tax is usually payable when the deed is recorded. In some states, the taxpayer purchases *stamps* (sometimes called *documentary stamps*) from the recorder of the county in which the deed is recorded. The stamps must be affixed to deeds and conveyances before the documents can be recorded. In other states, the taxpayer simply pays the clerk of court or county recorder the appropriate transfer tax amount in accordance with state and local law.

The transfer tax may be paid by the seller, by the buyer, or split between them, depending on local custom or agreement in the sales contract. The actual *tax rate* varies and may be imposed at the state, county, or city level. The rate might

Deed of Trust
Conveyance from trustor to trustee

Reconveyance Deed
Conveyance from trustee back to trustor

Trustee's Deed
Conveyance from trustee to third party

FIGURE 12.1

Trust Deeds

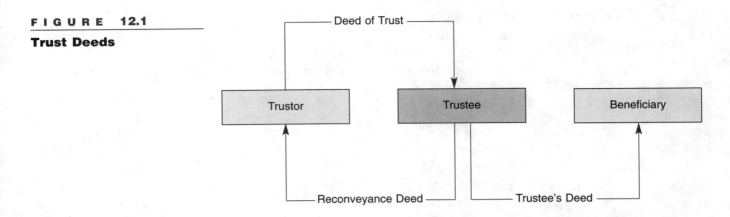

be calculated, for example, as $1.10 for every $1,000 of the sales price; as $.26 for every $500; or as a simple percentage.

MATH CONCEPTS

CALCULATING TRANSFER TAXES

In the state of New Columbia, the transfer tax is $1.50 for each $500 (or fraction of $500) of the sales price of any parcel of real estate. The transfer tax is paid by the seller. To calculate the transfer tax due in the sale of a $195,250 house, use the following formula:

(Value ÷ Unit) × Rate per Unit = Tax

In this example:

$195,250 ÷ $500 = 390.5, or 391 taxable units (390 "500s" + ½ of a "500")
391 × $1.50 = $586.50

The seller in this transaction must pay a transfer tax of $586.50 to the state.

In many states, a *transfer declaration form* (or a *transfer statement* or an *affidavit of real property value*) must be signed by both the buyer and the seller or their agents. The transfer declaration states

- the full sales price of the property;
- its legal description;
- the type of improvement;
- the address, date, and type of deed; and
- whether the transfer is between relatives or in accordance with a court order.

Certain deeds may be *exempted* from the tax, such as the following:

- Gifts of real estate
- Deeds not made in connection with a sale (such as a change in the form of co-ownership)
- Conveyances to, from, or between government bodies
- Deeds by charitable, religious, or educational institutions
- Deeds securing debts or releasing property as security for a debt

- Partitions
- Tax deeds
- Deeds pursuant to mergers of corporations
- Deeds from subsidiary to parent corporations for cancellations of stock

■ INVOLUNTARY ALIENATION

Title to property may be transferred without the owner's consent by **involuntary alienation.** (See Figure 12.2.) Involuntary transfers are usually carried out by operation of law—such as by condemnation or a sale to satisfy delinquent tax or mortgage liens. When a person dies intestate and leaves no heirs, the title to the real estate passes to the state by the state's power of escheat. As discussed in Chapter 7, land may be acquired through the process of accretion or actually lost through erosion.

Other acts of nature, such as earthquakes, hurricanes, sinkholes, and mudslides, may create or eliminate a landowner's holdings.

Transfer by Adverse Possession

Adverse possession is another means of involuntary transfer. An individual who makes a claim to certain property, takes possession of it, and, most important, uses it may take title away from an owner who fails to use or inspect the property for a period of years. The law recognizes that the use of land is an important function of its ownership. Usually, the possession by the claimant must be all of the following:

- *Open* (that is, obvious to anyone who looks)
- *Notorious* (that is, known by others)
- *Continuous* and uninterrupted
- *Hostile* (that is, without the true owner's consent)
- *Adverse* to the true owner's possession

The necessary period of uninterrupted possession is a matter of state law. The statutory periods range from as few as 5 years in some states to as many as 30 years in others. Through the principle of *tacking,* successive periods of different adverse possession by different adverse possessors can be combined, enabling a person who is not in possession for the entire required time to establish a claim.

In order to establish title by adverse possession, there must be proof of nonpermissive use that is actual, open, notorious, exclusive, and adverse for the statutorily prescribed period. To claim title, the adverse possessor normally files an action in court to receive undisputed title. A claimant who does not receive title may acquire an easement by prescription.

IN PRACTICE   The right of adverse possession is a statutory right. State requirements must be followed carefully to ensure the successful transfer of title. The parties to a transaction that might involve adverse possession should seek legal counsel.

■ TRANSFER OF A DECEASED PERSON'S PROPERTY

A person who dies **testate** has prepared a will indicating how his or her property will be disposed of. In contrast, when a person dies **intestate** (without a will), real estate and personal property pass to the decedent's heirs according to the

F I G U R E   12.2

Involuntary Alienation

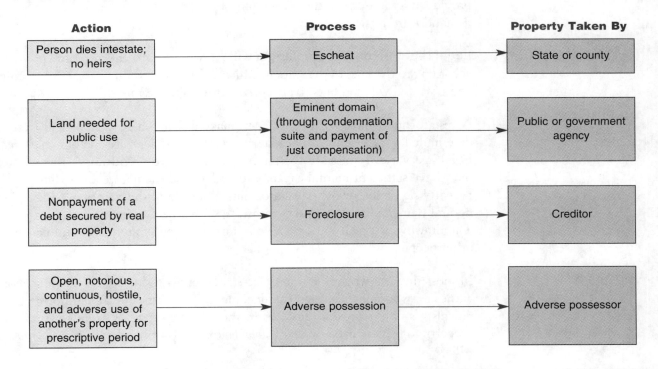

state's *statute of descent and distribution*. In effect, the state makes a will for an intestate decedent.

Legally, when a person dies, ownership of real estate immediately passes either to the heirs by descent or to the persons named in the will. Before these individuals can take full title and possession of the property, however, the estate must go through a judicial process called *probate*, and all claims against the estate must be satisfied.

Transfer of Title by Will

A will is an instrument made by an owner to convey title to real or personal property after the owner's death. A will is a testamentary instrument, that is, it takes effect only after death. This differs from a deed, which *must* be delivered during the lifetime of the grantor and which conveys a present interest in property. While the **testator,** the person who makes a will, is alive, any property included in the will still can be conveyed by the owner. The parties named in a will have no rights or interests as long as the party who made the will lives; they acquire interest or title only after the owner's death.

Only property owned by the testator at the time of his or her death may be transferred by will. The gift of real property by will is known as a **devise,** and a person who receives property by will is known as a *devisee*.

For title to pass to the devisees, state laws require that on the death of a testator, the will must be filed with the court and *probated*. Probate is a legal procedure for verifying the validity of a will and accounting for the decedent's assets. The process can take several months to complete.

A will cannot supersede the state laws of dower and curtesy, which were enacted to protect the inheritance rights of a surviving spouse. When a will does not provide a spouse with the minimum statutory inheritance, he or she may demand it from the estate.

Legal requirements for making a will. A will must be executed and prepared according to the laws of the state in which the real estate is located. Only a valid and probated will can effectively convey title to real estate.

A testator must have legal capacity to make a will. There are no rigid tests to determine legal capacity. Usually, a person must be of *legal age* and of *sound mind*. Legal age varies from state to state. To demonstrate sound mind, the testator must have sufficient mental capacity to understand the nature and extent of the property he or she owns. A testator must understand the identity of his or her natural heirs and that the property will go to those persons named in the will. The drawing of a will must be a voluntary act, free of any undue influence by other people.

In most states, a written will must be signed by its testator before two or more witnesses, who must also sign the document. The witnesses should not be individuals who are named as devisees in the will. Some states do not permit real property to be conveyed by oral (*nuncupative*) wills or handwritten (*holographic*) wills.

A testator may alter a will any time before his or her death. Any modification, amendment, or addition to a previously executed will is contained in a separate document called a *codicil*.

Transfer of Title by Descent

When a person dies intestate, title to his or her real estate and personal property passes to the decedent's heirs as determined by state law. Under a state's statute of descent and distribution, the primary **heirs** of the deceased are his or her spouse and close blood relatives (such as children, parents, brothers, sisters, aunts, uncles, and, in some cases, first and second cousins). The right to inherit under laws of descent varies from state to state, and intestate property is distributed according to the laws of the state in which the property is located. (See Table 12.1.)

Probate Proceedings

Probate is a formal judicial process that

- proves or confirms the validity of a will,
- determines the precise assets of the deceased person, and
- identifies the persons to whom the assets are to pass.

The purpose of probate is to see that the assets are distributed correctly. All assets must be accounted for, and the decedent's debts must be satisfied before any property is distributed to the heirs. In addition, estate taxes must be paid before any distribution. The laws of each state govern the probate proceedings and the functions of the individuals appointed to administer the decedent's affairs.

T A B L E   12.1

**Sample Statutory
Distributions**

This table illustrates how a state's statute of descent and distribution might provide for an intestate's estate. The specific persons entitled to property, and the various percentages involved, vary from state to state. Remember: *Licensees should never try to determine descent or ownership status without consulting with legal counsel.*

Decedent Status	Family Status	How Property Passes
Married, surviving spouse [1]	No children No other relatives	100% to surviving spouse
	Children	50% to surviving spouse 50% shared by children or descendants of deceased child
Married, no surviving spouse	Children	Children share equally, with descendants of a deceased child taking their parent's share
Unmarried, no children	Relatives	100% to father or mother, brothers or sisters, or other relatives (such as grandparents or great-grandparents; uncles or aunts; nieces or nephews; first or second cousins) in order of priority
	No relatives or heirs as defined by state law	100% to state by escheat

[1]Some states allow the decedent's spouse the right to elect a life estate of dower or curtesy (as discussed in Chapter 7) in place of the share provided for in the law of descent.

Assets that are distributed through probate are those that do not otherwise distribute themselves. For instance, property held in joint tenancy or tenancy by the entirety passes immediately. Probate proceedings take place in the county *in which the decedent resided.* If the decedent owned real estate in another county, probate would occur in that county as well.

The person who has possession of the will—normally the person designated in the will as *executor*—presents it for filing with the court. The court is responsible for determining that the will meets the statutory requirements for its form and execution. If a codicil or more than one will exists, the court will decide how these documents should be probated.

The court must rule on a challenge if a will is contested. Once the will is upheld, the assets can be distributed according to its provisions. Probate courts distribute assets according to statute only when no other reasonable alternative exists.

When a person dies *intestate*, the court determines who inherits the assets by reviewing proof from relatives of the decedent and their entitlement under the statute of descent and distribution. Once the heirs have been determined, the court appoints an *administrator* or a *personal representative* to administer the affairs of the estate—the role usually taken by an executor.

Whether or not a will is involved, the administrator or executor is responsible for having the estate's assets appraised and for ensuring that all the decedent's debts are satisfied. He or she is also responsible for paying federal estate taxes and state inheritance taxes out of the assets. Once all obligations have been satisfied, the representative distributes the remaining property according to the terms of the will or the state's law of descent.

IN PRACTICE

A broker entering into a listing agreement with the executor or administrator of an estate in probate should be aware that the amount of commission is fixed by the court and that the commission is payable only from the proceeds of the sale. The broker will not be able to collect a commission unless the court approves the sale.

■ SUMMARY

Title to real estate is the right to and evidence of ownership of the land. It may be transferred by voluntary alienation, involuntary alienation, will, and descent.

The voluntary transfer of an owner's title is made by a deed, executed (signed) by the owner as grantor to the purchaser or by donee as grantee.

Among the most common requirements for a valid deed are a grantor with legal capacity to contract, a readily identifiable grantee, a granting clause, a legal description of the property, a recital of consideration, exceptions and reservations on the title, and the signature of the grantor. In addition, the deed should be properly witnessed and acknowledged before a notary public or another officer to provide evidence that the signature is genuine and to allow recording. Title to the property passes when the grantor delivers a deed to the grantee and it is accepted. The obligation of a grantor is determined by the form of the deed. The words of conveyance in the granting clause are important in determining the form of deed.

A general warranty deed provides the greatest protection of any deed by binding the grantor to certain covenants or warranties. A special warranty deed warrants only that the real estate is not encumbered except as stated in the deed. A bargain and sale deed carries with it no warranties but implies that the grantor holds title to the property. A quitclaim deed carries with it no warranties whatsoever and conveys only the interest, if any, the grantor possesses in the property.

An owner's title may be transferred without his or her permission by a court action, such as a foreclosure or judgment sale, a tax sale, condemnation under the right of eminent domain, adverse possession, or escheat. Land may also be transferred by the natural forces of water and wind, which either increase property by accretion or decrease it through erosion or avulsion.

The real estate of an owner who makes a valid will (who dies testate) passes to the devisees through the probating of the will. The title of an owner who dies without a will (intestate) passes according to the provisions of the law of descent and distribution of the state in which the real estate is located.

QUESTIONS

1. The basic requirements for a valid conveyance are governed by
   a. state law.
   b. local custom.
   c. national law.
   d. the law of descent.

2. Every deed must be signed by the
   a. grantor.
   b. grantee.
   c. grantor and grantee.
   d. devisee.

3. Henry, age 15, recently inherited many parcels of real estate from his late father and has decided to sell one of them. If Henry entered into a deed conveying his interest in the property to a purchaser, such a conveyance would be
   a. valid.   c. invalid.
   b. void.   d. voidable.

4. An instrument authorizing one person to act for another is called a(n)
   a. power of attorney.
   b. release deed.
   c. quitclaim deed.
   d. attorney-in-fact.

5. The grantee receives greatest protection with what type of deed?
   a. Quitclaim
   b. General warranty
   c. Bargain and sale with covenant
   d. Executor's

6. Laura receives a deed from Greg. The granting clause of the deed states, "I, Greg, hereby remise, release, alienate, and convey to Laura the property known as Pearly Manor." What type of deed has Laura received?
   a. Special warranty
   b. Quitclaim
   c. General warranty
   d. Bargain and sale

7. Under the covenant of quiet enjoyment, the grantor
   a. promises to obtain and deliver any instrument needed to make the title good.
   b. guarantees that if the title fails in the future, he or she will compensate the grantee.
   c. warrants that he or she is the owner and has the right to convey title to the property.
   d. assures that the title will be good against the title claims of third parties.

8. A deed includes the following statement: "The full consideration for this conveyance is $125,480." Which type of deed is this most likely to be?
   a. Gift deed
   b. Trustee's deed
   c. Deed in trust
   d. Deed executed pursuant to court order

9. Which of the following types of deeds merely implies, but does not specifically warrant, that the grantor holds good title to the property?
   a. Special warranty
   b. Bargain and sale
   c. Quitclaim
   d. Trustee's

10. *Step 1:* Doris decided to convey Blue House to John. *Step 2:* Doris signed a deed transferring title to John. *Step 3:* Doris gave the signed deed to John, who accepted it. *Step 4:* John took the deed to the county recorder's office and had it recorded. At which step did title to Blue House actually transfer or pass to John?
    a. Step 1   c. Step 3
    b. Step 2   d. Step 4

11. Luis conveys property to Ken by deed. The deed contains the following: (1) Ken's name, spelled out in full; (2) a statement that Luis has received $10 and Ken's love and affection; and (3) a statement that the property is for Ken "to have and to hold." Which of the following correctly identifies, in order, these three elements of the deed?

    a. Grantee; consideration; granting clause
    b. Grantee; consideration; habendum clause
    c. Grantor; habendum clause; legal description
    d. Grantee; acknowledgment; habendum clause

12. Wally signed a deed transferring ownership of his house to Luke. To provide evidence that his signature was genuine, Wally executed a declaration before a notary. This declaration is known as an

    a. affidavit.
    b. acknowledgment.
    c. affirmation.
    d. estoppel.

13. Rachel executes a deed to Peter as grantee, has it acknowledged, and receives payment from the buyer. Rachel holds the deed, however, and arranges to meet Peter the next morning at the courthouse to give the deed to him. At this point

    a. Peter owns the property because he has paid for it.
    b. Legal title to the property will not officially pass until Peter has been given the deed the next morning.
    c. Legal title to the property will not pass until Peter has received the deed and records it the next morning.
    d. Peter will own the property when he signs the deed the next morning.

14. Title to real estate may be transferred during a person's lifetime by

    a. devise.
    b. descent.
    c. involuntary alienation.
    d. escheat.

15. Ben bought acreage in a distant county, never went to see the acreage, and did not use the ground. Hilda moved her mobile home onto the land, had a water well drilled, and lived there for 22 years. Hilda may become the owner of the land if she has complied with the state law regarding

    a. requirements for a valid conveyance.
    b. adverse possession.
    c. avulsion.
    d. voluntary alienation.

16. Condemnation and escheat are two examples of

    a. voluntary alienation.
    b. adverse possession.
    c. transfers of title by descent.
    d. involuntary alienation.

17. A deed contains a promise that the title conveyed is good and a promise to obtain and deliver any documents necessary to ensure good title. The second promise is an example of which covenant?

    a. Further assurance
    b. Seisin
    c. Quiet enjoyment
    d. Warranty forever

18. A deed contains a guarantee that the grantor will compensate the grantee for any loss resulting from the title's failure in the future. This is an example of which type of covenant?

    a. Warranty forever
    b. Further assurance
    c. Quiet enjoyment
    d. Seisin

19. A house sells for $155,000; the buyer pays $50,000 in cash and gives the seller a mortgage for the balance. If the state has a transfer tax rate of 1 percent, what is the amount of state transfer tax that must be paid?

    a. $1,550   c. $15,500
    b. $1,055   d. $105,000

20. A person who has died leaving a valid will is called a(n)

a. devisee.
b. testator.
c. legatee.
d. intestate.

21. Title to real estate can be transferred at death by which of the following documents?

a. Warranty deed
b. Special warranty deed
c. Trustee's deed
d. Will

22. Jacob, a bachelor, died owning real estate that he devised by his will to his niece, Koralee. When will full title *and* possession pass to his niece?

a. Immediately upon Jacob's death
b. After his will has been probated
c. After Koralee has paid all inheritance taxes
d. When Koralee executes a new deed to the property

23. An owner of real estate was declared legally incompetent and was committed to a state mental institution. While institutionalized, the owner wrote and executed a will. The owner later died and was survived by a spouse and three children. The real estate will pass

a. to the owner's spouse.
b. to the heirs mentioned in the owner's will.
c. according to the state laws of descent.
d. to the state.

24. When title to trust property is transferred back to the trustor by the trustee, which of the following deeds is used?

a. Trustee's deed
b. Trustor's deed
c. Deed of transfer
d. Deed of reconveyance.

25. Generally, where does a probate proceeding involving real property take place?

a. Only in the county in which the property is located
b. Only in the county in which the decedent resided
c. In both the county where the decedent resided and the county in which the property is located
d. In the county in which the executor or the beneficiary resides

13

TITLE RECORDS

■ **LEARNING OBJECTIVES** *When you've finished reading this Chapter, you should be able to:*

■ **identify** the various proofs of ownership.

■ **describe** recording, notice, and chain of title issues.

■ **explain** the process and purpose of a title search.

■ **distinguish** constructive and actual notice.

■ **define** the following *key terms:*

abstract of title	inquiry notice	title insurance
actual notice	marketable title	title search
attorney's opinion of title	priority	Torrens system
certificate of title	recording	Uniform Commercial
chain of title	security agreement	Code (UCC)
constructive notice	subrogation	
financing statement	suit to quiet title	

■ **WHY LEARN ABOUT...** TITLE RECORDS?

Public records are just that: records that are open to the public. This means that anyone interested in a particular property can review the records to learn about the documents, claims, and other issues that affect its ownership. A prospective purchaser, for example, needs to be sure that the seller can convey title to the property. If the property is subject to any liens or other encumbrances, a prospective buyer or lender needs to know that information. Typically, the attorney or title company performs a search of the public records to ensure that good title is being conveyed. Still, it is important for a professional in the real estate industry to understand what is in the public record and what the searchers are likely to find. Your clients will want to know about every step of the process, and you need to explain to them what is being done on their behalf. ■

■ **PUBLIC RECORDS**

Public records contain detailed information about each parcel of real estate in a city or county. These records are crucial in establishing ownership, giving notice of encumbrances, and establishing priority of liens. They protect the interests of real estate owners, taxing bodies, creditors, and the general public. The real estate recording system includes written documents that affect title, such as deeds and mortgages. Public records regarding taxes, judgments, probate, and marriage also may offer important information about the title to a particular property.

Public records are maintained by

■ recorders of deeds,
■ county clerks,
■ county treasurers,
■ city clerks,
■ collectors, and
■ clerks of court.

IN PRACTICE   Although we speak of prospective purchasers conducting title searches, the purchasers themselves rarely search the public records for evidence of title or encumbrances. Instead, *title companies* conduct searches before providing title insurance. An attorney also may search the title. A growing number of lending institutions require title insurance as part of the mortgage loan commitment.

Recording   Recording is the act of placing documents in the public record. The specific rules for recording documents are a matter of state law. However, although the details may vary, all recording acts essentially provide that any written document that affects any estate, right, title, or interest in land *must be recorded in the county where the land is located* to serve as public notice. That way, anyone interested

In most states, written documents that affect land *must be recorded in the county where the land is located.*

in the title to a parcel of property will know where to look to discover the various interests of all other parties. Recording acts also generally give legal priority to those interests recorded first (the "first in time, first in right" or "first come, first served" principle discussed in Chapter 10).

To be *eligible for recording,* a document must be drawn and executed according to the recording acts of the state in which the real estate is located. For instance, a state may require that the parties' names be typed below their signatures or that the document be acknowledged before a notary public. In some states, the document must be witnessed. Others require that the name of the person who prepared the document appear on it. States may have specific rules about the size of documents and the color and quality of paper they are printed on. Electronic recording—using computers or fax machines, for instance—is permitted in a growing number of localities. Some states require a certificate of real estate value and the payment of current property taxes due for recording.

Notice

Anyone who has an interest in a parcel of real estate can take certain steps, called *giving notice,* to ensure that the interest is available to the public. This lets others know about the individual's interest. There are three basic types of notice: constructive notice, actual notice, and inquiry notice.

Constructive notice is the legal presumption that information may be obtained by an individual through diligent inquiry. Properly recording documents in the public record serves as constructive notice to the world of an individual's rights or interest. So does the physical possession of a property. Because the information or evidence is readily available to the world, a prospective purchaser or lender is responsible for discovering the interest.

Actual notice means that not only is the information available but someone has been given the information and actually knows it. An individual who has searched the public records and inspected the property has actual notice. Actual notice is also known as *direct knowledge.* If an individual can be proved to have had actual notice of information, he or she cannot use a lack of constructive notice (such as an unrecorded deed) to justify a claim.

Inquiry notice is notice that the law presumes a reasonable person would obtain by making further inquiry into a property. For example, if a customer is considering buying a rural lot of land and, upon inspecting it, sees a dirt road cutting across the land that is not mentioned in the public records, the customer is expected to make further inquiry into the dirt road.

Priority

Priority refers to the order of rights in time. Many complicated situations can affect the priority of rights in a parcel of real estate—who recorded first; which party was in possession first; who had actual or constructive notice. How the courts rule in any situation depends, of course, on the specific facts of the case. These are strictly legal questions that should be referred to the parties' attorneys.

■ **FOR EXAMPLE** In May, Betsy purchased Grayacre from Andy and received a deed. Betsy never recorded the deed but began farming operations on the property in June. In November, Andy (who was forgetful) again sold Grayacre, this time to

Carrie. Carrie accepted the deed and promptly recorded it. However, because Carrie never inspected Grayacre to see whether someone was in possession, Betsy has the superior right to the property *even though Betsy never recorded the deed.* By taking possession, a purchaser gives constructive notice of his or her interest in the land.

Unrecorded Documents

Certain types of liens are not recorded. Real estate taxes and special assessments are liens on specific parcels of real estate and are not usually recorded until some time after the taxes or assessments are past due. Inheritance taxes and franchise taxes are statutory liens. They are placed against all real estate owned by a decedent at the time of death or by a corporation at the time the franchise taxes became a lien. Like real estate taxes, they are not recorded.

Notice of these liens must be gained from sources other than the recorder's office. Evidence of the payment of real estate taxes, special assessments, municipal utilities, and other taxes can be gathered from paid tax receipts and letters from municipalities. Creative measures are often required to get information about these "off the record" liens.

Chain of Title

Chain of title is the record of a property's ownership. Beginning with the earliest owner, title may pass to many individuals. Each owner is linked to the next so that a chain is formed. An unbroken chain of title can be traced through linking conveyances from the present owner back to the earliest recorded owner.

If ownership cannot be traced through an unbroken chain, it is said that there is a gap in the chain. In these cases, the cloud on the title makes it necessary to establish ownership by a court action called a **suit to quiet title.** A suit might be required, for instance, when a grantor acquired title under one name and conveyed it under another name. Or there may be a forged deed in the chain, after which no subsequent grantee acquired legal title. All possible claimants are allowed to present evidence during a court proceeding; then the court's judgment is filed. Often, the simple procedure of obtaining any relevant quitclaim deeds (discussed in Chapter 12) is used to establish ownership.

Title Search and Abstract of Title

A **title search** is an examination of all of the public records to determine whether any defects exist in the chain of title. The records of the conveyances of ownership are examined, beginning with the present owner. Then the title is traced backward to its origin (or 40 to 60 years, depending on local custom). The time beyond which the title must be searched is limited in states that have adopted the *Marketable Title Act.* This law extinguishes certain interests and cures certain defects arising before the *root of the title*—the conveyance that establishes the source of the chain of title. Normally, the root is considered to be 40 years or more. Under most circumstances, then, it is necessary to search only from the current owner to the root.

Other public records are examined to identify wills, judicial proceedings, and other encumbrances that may affect title. These include a variety of taxes, special assessments, and other recorded liens.

A title search usually is not ordered until after the major contingencies in a sales contract have been cleared—for instance, after a loan commitment has been secured. Before providing money for a loan, a lender generally orders a title search to ensure that no lien is superior to its mortgage lien. In most cases, the cost of the title search is paid by the buyer, although this is negotiable between the parties.

An **abstract of title** is a summary report of what the title search found in the public record. A person who prepares this report is called an *abstractor*. The abstractor searches all the public records, then summarizes the various events and proceedings that affected the title throughout its history. The report begins with the original grant (or root), then provides a chronological list of recorded instruments. All recorded liens and encumbrances are included, along with their current statuses. A list of all of the public records examined is also provided as evidence of the scope of the search.

IN PRACTICE   An abstract of title is a condensed history of those items that can be found in public records. It does not reveal such items as encroachments or forgeries or any interests or conveyances that have not been recorded.

Marketable Title

Under the terms of the typical real estate sales contract, the seller is required to deliver **marketable title** to the buyer at the closing. To be marketable, a title must

- disclose no serious defects and not depend on doubtful questions of law or fact to prove its validity;
- not expose a purchaser to the hazard of litigation or threaten the quiet enjoyment of the property; and
- convince a reasonably well-informed and prudent purchaser, acting on business principles and with knowledge of the facts and their legal significance, that he or she could sell or mortgage the property at a later time.

Although a title that does not meet these requirements still could be transferred, it contains certain defects that may limit or restrict its ownership. A buyer cannot be forced to accept a conveyance that is materially different from the one bargained for in the sales contract. However, questions of marketable title must be raised by a buyer *before acceptance of the deed*. Once a buyer has accepted a deed with unmarketable title, the only available legal recourse is to sue the seller under any covenants of warranty contained in the deed.

In some states, a preliminary title search is conducted as soon as an offer to purchase has been accepted. In fact, it may be customary to include a contingency in the sales contract that gives the buyer the right to review and approve the title report before proceeding with the purchase. A preliminary title report also benefits the seller by giving him or her an early opportunity to cure title defects.

■ PROOF OF OWNERSHIP

Proof of ownership is evidence that title is marketable. A deed by itself is not considered sufficient evidence of ownership. Even though a warranty deed conveys the grantor's interest, it contains no proof of the condition of the grantor's title at the time of the conveyance. The grantee needs some assurance that he or she is actually acquiring ownership and that the title is marketable. A certificate of title, title insurance, or a Torrens certificate (discussed below) are commonly used to prove ownership.

Certificate of Title

A **certificate of title** is a statement of opinion of the title's status on the date the certificate is issued. A *certificate of title is not a guarantee of ownership*. Rather, it certifies the condition of the title based on an examination of the public records—a title search. The certificate may be prepared by a title company, a licensed abstractor, or an attorney. An owner, a mortgage lender, or a buyer may request the certificate.

Although a certificate of title is used as evidence of ownership, it is not perfect. Unrecorded liens or rights of parties in possession cannot be discovered by a search of the public records. Hidden defects, such as transfers involving forged documents, incorrect marital information, incompetent parties, minors, or fraud, cannot be detected. A certificate offers no defense against these defects because they are unknown. The person who prepares the certificate is liable only for negligence in preparing the certificate.

IN PRACTICE

You may have heard the phrase *under color of title.* This refers to a situation in which title is conveyed in a transaction by a written instrument (such as a deed or will) that is actually inadequate to legally transfer ownership, whether because it was incorrectly executed or because it was executed by someone who did not, in fact, hold title in the first place.

An abstract and **attorney's opinion of title** are used in some areas of the country as evidence of title. It is an opinion of the status of the title based on a review of the abstract. Similar to a certificate of title, the opinion of title does not protect against defects that cannot be discovered from the public records. Many buyers purchase title insurance to defend the title from these defects.

Title Insurance

Title insurance is a contract under which the policyholder is protected from losses arising from defects in the title. A title insurance company determines whether the title is insurable, based on a review of the public records. If so, a policy is issued. Unlike other insurance policies that insure against *future losses,* title insurance protects the insured from an event that occurred *before* the policy was issued. Title insurance is considered the best defense of title: The title insurance company will defend any lawsuit based on an insurable defect and pay claims if the title proves to be defective.

After examining the public records, the title company usually issues what may be called a *preliminary report of title* or a *commitment* to issue a title policy. This describes the type of policy that will be issued and includes

- the name of the insured party;
- the legal description of the real estate;
- the estate or interest covered;
- conditions and stipulations under which the policy is issued; and
- a schedule of all exceptions, including encumbrances and defects found in the public records and any known unrecorded defects.

Standard Coverage	Extended Coverage	Not Covered by Either Policy
1. Defects found in public records 2. Forged documents 3. Incompetent grantors 4. Incorrect marital statements 5. Improperly delivered deeds	Standard coverage plus defects discoverable through the following: 1. Property inspection, including unrecorded rights of persons in possession 2. Examination of survey 3. Unrecorded liens not known of by policy holder	1. Defects and liens listed in policy 2. Defects known to buyer 3. Changes in land use brought about by zoning ordinances

The *premium* for the policy is paid once, at closing. The maximum loss for which the company may be liable cannot exceed the face amount of the policy (unless the amount of coverage has been extended by use of an *inflation rider*). When a title company makes a payment to settle a claim covered by a policy, the company generally acquires the right to any remedy or damages available to the insured. This right is called **subrogation.**

Coverage.   Exactly which defects the title company will defend depends on the type of policy. (See Table 13.1.) A *standard coverage policy* normally insures the title as it is known from the public records. In addition, the standard policy insures against such hidden defects as forged documents, conveyances by incompetent grantors, incorrect marital statements, and improperly delivered deeds.

Extended coverage, as provided by an *American Land Title Association* (ALTA) policy, includes the protections of a standard policy plus additional protections. An extended policy protects a homeowner against defects that may be discovered by inspection of the property: rights of parties in possession, examination of a survey, and certain unrecorded liens.

Title insurance does not offer guaranteed protection against all defects. A title company will not insure a bad title or offer protection against defects that clearly appear in a title search. The policy generally names certain uninsurable losses, called *exclusions*. These include zoning ordinances, restrictive covenants, easements, certain water rights, and current taxes and special assessments.

Types of policies.   The different types of policies depend on who is named as the insured. An *owner's policy* is issued for the benefit of the owner and his or her heirs or devisees. A *lender's policy* is issued for the benefit of the mortgage company. The amount of the coverage depends on the amount of the mortgage loan. As the loan balance is reduced, the coverage decreases. Because only the lender's interest is insured, it is advisable for the owner to obtain a policy as well.

A lessee's interest can be insured with a *leasehold* policy. *Certificate of sale* policies are available to insure the title to property purchased in a court sale.

The Torrens System

The Torrens system is a legal registration system used to verify ownership and encumbrances. Registration in the Torrens system provides evidence of title without the need for an additional search of the public records. Under the Torrens system, an owner of real property submits a written application to register his or her title. The application is submitted to the court clerk of the county in which the real estate is located. If the applicant proves that he or she is the owner, the court enters an order to register the real estate. The registrar of titles is directed to issue a certificate of title. The original Torrens certificate of title in the registrar's office reveals the owner of the land and all mortgages, judgments, and similar liens. It does not, however, reveal federal or state taxes and some other items. The Torrens system of registration relies on the physical title document itself; a person acquires title only when it is registered.

IN PRACTICE   The Torrens system is currently in use in fewer than ten states, and some of these states are in the process of phasing out Torrens registration altogether. Consult your state's law to determine whether the Torrens system is active in your area and whether new property transfers are subject to its procedures.

■ UNIFORM COMMERCIAL CODE

The **Uniform Commercial Code (UCC)** is a commercial law statute that has been adopted, to some extent, in all 50 states. The UCC is concerned with personal property transactions; it does not apply to real estate. The UCC governs the documents when personal property is used as security for a loan.

For a lender to create a security interest in personal property, including personal property that will become fixtures, the UCC requires the borrower to sign a **security agreement.** The agreement must contain a complete description of the items against which the lien applies. A short notice of this agreement (called a **financing statement** or a **UCC-1**) must be filed. It identifies any real estate involved when personal property is made part of the real estate. Once the financing statement is recorded, subsequent purchasers and lenders are put on notice of the security interest in personal property and fixtures. Many lenders require that a security agreement be signed and a financing statement filed when the real estate includes chattels or readily removable fixtures.

■ SUMMARY

The purpose of the recording acts is to give legal, public, and constructive notice to the world of parties' interests in real estate. The recording provisions have been adopted to create system and order in the transfer of real estate. Without them, it would be virtually impossible to transfer real estate from one party to another. The interests and rights of the various parties in a particular parcel of land must be recorded so that such rights are legally effective against third parties who do not have knowledge or notice of the rights.

Possession of real estate is generally interpreted as constructive notice of the rights of the person in possession. Actual notice is knowledge acquired directly and personally. Inquiry notice is notice presumed by the law that a person would further investigate property.

Title evidence shows whether a seller conveys marketable title. A deed of conveyance is evidence that a grantor has conveyed his or her interest in land, but it is not evidence of the title's kind or condition. Marketable title is generally one that is so free from significant defects that the purchaser can be ensured against having to defend the title.

Four forms of providing title evidence are commonly used throughout the United States: abstract and attorney's opinion of title, certificate of title, Torrens certificate, and title insurance policy. Each form reveals the history of a title. Each must be later dated, or continued, or reissued to cover a more recent date.

Under the Uniform Commercial Code (UCC), the filing of a financing statement gives notice to purchasers and mortgagees of the security interests in personal property and fixtures on the specific parcel of real estate.

QUESTIONS

1. A title search in the public records may be conducted by
   a. anyone.
   b. attorneys and abstractors only.
   c. attorneys, abstractors, and real estate licensees only.
   d. anyone who obtains a court order under the Freedom of Information Act.

2. Which of the following statements best explains why instruments affecting real estate are recorded?
   a. Recording gives constructive notice to the world of the rights and interests claimed by a party in a particular parcel of real estate.
   b. Failing to record will void the transfer.
   c. The instruments must be recorded to comply with the terms of the statute of frauds.
   d. Recording proves the execution of the instrument.

3. A purchaser went to the county building to check the recorder's records, which showed that the seller was the grantee in the last recorded deed and that no mortgage was on record against the property. The purchaser may assume which of the following?
   a. All taxes are paid, and no judgments are outstanding.
   b. The seller has good title.
   c. The seller did not mortgage the property.
   d. No one else is occupying the property.

4. The date and time a document was recorded help establish which of the following?
   a. Priority   c. Subrogation
   b. Abstract of title   d. Marketable title

5. Paul bought Linden's house, received a deed, and moved into the residence but neglected to record the document. One week later, Linden died, and his heirs in another city, unaware that the property had been sold, conveyed title to Mark, who recorded the deed. Who owns the property?
   a. Paul
   b. Mark
   c. Linden's heirs
   d. Both Paul and Mark

6. A property with encumbrances that will outlast the closing
   a. cannot be sold.
   b. can be sold only if title insurance is provided.
   c. cannot have a deed recorded without a survey.
   d. can be sold if a buyer agrees to take it subject to the encumbrances.

7. Which of the following would not be acceptable evidence of ownership?
   a. Attorney's opinion
   b. Title insurance policy
   c. Abstract
   d. Deed signed by the last seller

8. *Chain of title* is most accurately defined as a(n)
   a. summary or history of all documents and legal proceedings affecting a specific parcel of land.
   b. report of the contents of the public record regarding a particular property.
   c. instrument or document that protects the insured parties (subject to specific exceptions) against defects in the examination of the record and hidden risks such as forgeries, undisclosed heirs, errors in the public records, and so forth.
   d. record of a property's ownership.

9. A seller delivered title to a buyer at closing. A title search had disclosed no serious defects, and the title did not appear to be based on doubtful questions of law or fact or to expose the buyer to possible litigation. The seller's title did not appear to present a threat to the buyer's quiet enjoyment, and the title insurance policy provided was sufficient to convince a reasonably well-informed person that the property could be resold. The title conveyed would commonly be referred to as a(n)

   a. certificate of title.
   b. abstract of title.
   c. marketable title.
   d. attorney's opinion of title.

10. The person who prepares an abstract of title for a parcel of real estate

    a. searches the public records and then summarizes the events and proceedings that affect title.
    b. insures the condition of the title.
    c. inspects the property.
    d. issues a certificate of title.

11. Sally is frantic because she cannot find her deed and now wants to sell her property. She

    a. may need to sue for quiet title.
    b. must buy title insurance.
    c. does not need her original deed if it had been recorded.
    d. should execute a replacement deed to herself.

12. Mortgagee title policies protect which parties against loss?

    a. Buyers
    b. Sellers
    c. Lenders
    d. Buyers and lenders

13. Which of the following are traditionally covered by a standard title insurance policy?

    a. Unrecorded rights of persons in possession
    b. Improperly delivered deeds
    c. Changes in land use due to zoning ordinances
    d. Unrecorded liens not known to the policyholder

14. General Title Company settled a claim against its insured by making a substantial payment to the person who sued its client. General Title may now seek damages from the person who originally gave its insured a general warranty deed. Through what right can General Title recover the amount it paid out in the settlement?

    a. Escrow
    b. Encumbrance
    c. Subordination
    d. Subrogation

15. Which of the following is *not* covered by a standard title insurance policy?

    a. Forged documents
    b. Incorrect marital statements
    c. Unrecorded rights of parties in possession
    d. Incompetent grantors

16. Documents referred to as *title evidence* include

    a. policies of title insurance.
    b. general warranty deeds.
    c. security agreements.
    d. special warranty deeds.

17. Under the Uniform Commercial Code, a lender who wishes to give notice of its security interest in personal property used as security for a loan, must file a

    a. security agreement.
    b. financing statement.
    c. chattel agreement.
    d. quitclaim deed.

18. Kate sells a portion of her property to Lily. Lily promptly records the deed in the appropriate county office. If Kate tries to sell the same portion of her property to Mike, which of the following statements is true?

    a. Mike has been given constructive notice of the prior sale because Lily promptly recorded her deed.
    b. Mike has been given actual notice of the prior sale because Lily promptly recorded her deed.
    c. Because Mike's purchase of the portion of Kate's property is the more recent, it will have priority over Lily's interest, regardless of when Lily recorded the deed.
    d. Because Mike purchased the property from its rightful owner, Mike is presumed by law to be aware of Lily's prior interest.

19. David lives in Lake County, Wisconsin. While vacationing in Arlington County, Virginia, he finds a piece of property he likes very much. Its current owner lives in Orange County, California, and when David decides to buy the property the closing is held in Omaha County, Nebraska. Assuming that David will maintain his permanent residence in Wisconsin, where should title for the property be recorded?

    a. Lake County
    b. Arlington County
    c. Orange County
    c. Omaha County

20. Which of the following statements regarding the Uniform Commercial Code (UCC) is true?

    a. The UCC has been adopted in about half the states in the United States.
    b. The UCC governs all transactions involving personal or real property.
    c. The UCC is a legal registration system used to verify ownership and encumbrances.
    d. The UCC applies to credit transactions secured by personal property, not by real estate.

CHAPTER FOURTEEN

REAL ESTATE FINANCING: PRINCIPLES

■ **LEARNING OBJECTIVES** *When you've finished reading this Chapter, you should be able to:*

■ **identify** the basic provisions of security and debt instruments: promissory notes, mortgage documents, deeds of trust, and land contracts.

■ **describe** the effect of discount points on yield.

■ **explain** the procedures involved in a foreclosure.

■ **distinguish** between lien and title theories and among the three methods of foreclosure.

■ **define** the following *key terms:*

acceleration clause	foreclosure	prepayment penalty
alienation clause	hypothecation	promissory note
assume	interest	release deed
beneficiary	intermediate theory	satisfaction
deed in lieu of foreclo-	lien theory	statutory right of
sure	loan origination fee	redemption
deed of trust	mortgage	subject to
defeasance clause	mortgagee	title theory
deficiency judgment	mortgagor	trustor
discount points	negotiable instrument	usury
equitable right of	note	
redemption		

■ WHY LEARN ABOUT... REAL ESTATE FINANCING PRINCIPLES?

Perhaps the most important investment decision your clients will ever make is the one you help them with: buying a home. In the United States, relatively few homes are purchased for cash. Most homes are bought with borrowed money, and a huge lending industry has been built to service the financial requirements of homebuyers. In addition, by altering the terms of the basic mortgage or deed of trust and note, a borrower and a lender can tailor financing instruments to suit the type of transaction and the financial needs of both parties. In this Chapter and the next one, you will learn about the basic tools, concepts, and procedures involved in financing a real estate transaction. ■

These two Chapters will help you understand how to guide your customers through a process that enables them to buy (or sell) their property. You can be a marketing genius and an excellent agent, adhere to fair housing practices, and have the best listing agreements in the world, but if the buyer can't get the money to buy the property, none of your other skills will matter. To close the deal, a licensee has to be able to do the numbers.

IN PRACTICE

Although being knowledgeable about financing is important, licensees usually refer customers to lenders to get them preapproved for loans.

■ MORTGAGE LAW

A mortgage is a voluntary lien on real estate, that is, a person who borrows money to buy a piece of property voluntarily gives the lender the right to take that property if the borrower fails to repay the loan. The borrower, or **mortgagor,** pledges the property to the lender, or **mortgagee,** as *security* or *collateral* for the debt. Exactly what rights the mortgagor gives the mortgagee, however, varies from state to state.

> The *mortgagor* is the *borrower*.
>
> The *mortgagee* is the *lender*.

In **title theory** states, the mortgagor actually gives *legal title* to the mortgagee (or some other designated individual) and retains *equitable title*. Legal title is returned to the mortgagor only when the debt is paid in full (or some other obligation is performed). In theory, the lender actually owns the property until the debt is paid. The lender allows the borrower all the usual rights of ownership, such as possession and use. In effect, because the lender actually holds legal title, the lender has the right to immediate possession of the real estate and rents from the mortgaged property if the mortgagor defaults.

In **lien theory** states, the mortgagor retains both legal and equitable title. The mortgagee simply has a lien on the property as security for the mortgage debt. The mortgage, or deed of trust, is nothing more than collateral for the loan. If the mortgagor defaults, the mortgagee must go through a formal foreclosure proceeding to obtain legal title. The property is offered for sale at public auction, and the funds from the sale are used to pay the balance of the remaining debt. In some states, a defaulting mortgagor may *redeem* (buy back) the property during a certain period *after the sale*. A borrower who fails to redeem the property during that time loses the property irrevocably.

A number of states have adopted an **intermediate theory** that is based on the principles of title theory but requires that the mortgagee foreclose to obtain legal title.

IN PRACTICE

In reality, the differences between the parties' rights in a lien theory state and those in a title theory state are more technical than actual. Regardless of the theory practiced in any particular state, all borrowers and lenders observe the same general requirements to protect themselves in a loan transaction. Real estate loans are formal contracts that need to be in writing and include a description of the property pledged as collateral and a complete statement describing how the loan will be repaid. As with any contract, the parties must be legally competent, their signatures valid and attested, and adequate consideration exchanged.

■ SECURITY AND DEBT

A basic principle of property law is that no one can convey more than he or she actually owns. This principle also applies to mortgages. The owner of a fee simple estate can mortgage the fee. The owner of a leasehold or subleasehold can mortgage that leasehold interest. The owner of a condominium unit can mortgage the fee interest in the condominium. Even the owner of a cooperative interest may be able to offer that personal property interest as collateral for a loan.

Mortgage Loan Instruments

There are two parts to a mortgage loan: the debt itself and the security for the debt. When a property is to be mortgaged, the owner must *execute* (sign) two separate instruments:

1. The **promissory note,** also referred to simply as the *note* or *financing instrument*, is the borrower's personal promise to repay a debt according to agreed-upon terms. The note exposes all of the borrower's assets to claims by creditors. The mortgagor executes one or more promissory notes to total the amount of the debt.
2. The **mortgage** (or *deed of trust*, discussed below) also is known as the *security instrument*. The security instrument creates the lien on the property. The mortgage allows the lender to sue for foreclosure in the event the borrower defaults.

Hypothecation is the term used to describe the pledging of property as security for payment of a loan without actually surrendering possession of the property. A pledge of security—a mortgage or deed of trust—cannot be legally effective unless there is a debt to secure. Both a note and a mortgage are executed to create a secured loan.

Deeds of trust. In some situations, lenders may prefer to use a three-party instrument known as a **deed of trust,** or *trust deed*, rather than a mortgage. A trust deed conveys naked title or bare legal title, that is, title without the right

FIGURE   14.1

Mortgages

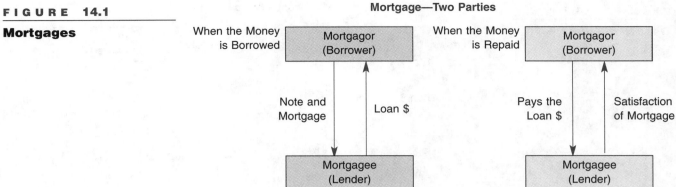

Mortgage—Two Parties

of possession. The deed is given as security for the loan to a third party, called the *trustee*. The trustee holds bare title on behalf of the lender, who is known as the **beneficiary.** The beneficiary is the holder of the note. The conveyance establishes the actions that the trustee may take if the borrower, the **trustor,** defaults under any of the deed of trust terms. (See Figure 14.1 and Figure 14.2 for a comparison of mortgages and deeds of trust.) In states where deeds of trust are generally preferred, foreclosure procedures for default are usually simpler and faster than for mortgage loans.

Usually, the lender chooses the trustee and reserves the right to substitute trustees in the event of death or dismissal. State law usually dictates who may serve as trustee. Although the deed of trust is particularly popular in certain states, it is used all over the country. For example, in the financing of a commercial or an industrial real estate venture that involves a large loan and several lenders, the borrower generally executes a single deed of trust to secure as many notes as necessary.

■ PROVISIONS OF THE NOTE

A promissory note executed by a borrower (known as the *maker* or *payor*) is a contract complete in itself. It generally states the amount of the debt, the time and method of payment, and the rate of interest. When signed by the borrowers and other necessary parties, the note becomes a legally enforceable and fully negotiable instrument of debt. When the terms of the note are satisfied, the debt is discharged. If the terms of the note are not met, the lender may choose to sue to collect on the note or to foreclose.

A note need not be tied to a mortgage or deed of trust. A note used as a debt instrument without any related collateral is called an unsecured note. Unsecured notes are used by banks and other lenders to extend short-term personal loans. However, a real estate loan is a secured loan and always includes security, i.e., a mortgage or deed of trust.

If a note is used with a mortgage, it names the lender (mortgagee) as the payee; if it is used with a deed of trust, the note may be made payable to the bearer. The note may also refer to or repeat several of the clauses that appear in the mortgage document or deed of trust. The note, like the mortgage or deed of trust, should be signed by all parties who have an interest in the property. In states

Deeds of Trust

Deed of Trust—Three Parties

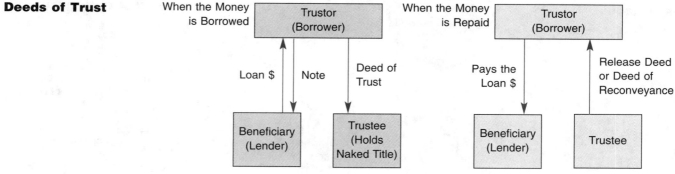

where dower and curtesy are in effect or where homestead or community property is involved, both spouses may have interests in the property, and both should sign the note and mortgage.

A **note** is a **negotiable instrument** like a check or bank draft. The lender who holds the note is referred to as the *payee,* and may transfer the right to receive payment to a third party in one of two ways:

1. By signing the instrument over (that is, by *assigning* it) to the third party
2. By delivering the instrument to the third party

IN PRACTICE

All notes should be clearly dated. Accurate dates are essential because "time is of the essence" in every real estate contract. Also, the dates of the notes may be necessary to determine the chronological order of priority rights.

Interest

A charge for using money is called **interest.** Interest may be due at either the end or the beginning of each payment period. When payments are made at the end of a period, it is known as payment *in arrears.* This is the general practice, and mortgages often call for end-of-period payments due on the first of the following month. Payments may also be made at the beginning of each period, however, when it is known as payment *in advance.* Whether interest is charged in arrears or in advance is specified in the note. This distinction is important if the property is sold before the debt is repaid in full.

Usury. To protect consumers from unscrupulous lenders, many states have enacted laws limiting the interest rate that may be charged on loans. In some states, the legal maximum rate is a fixed amount. In others, it is a floating interest rate, which is adjusted up or down at specific intervals based on a certain economic standard, such as the prime lending rate or the rate of return on government bonds.

Whichever approach is taken, charging interest in excess of the maximum rate is called **usury,** and lenders are penalized for making usurious loans. In some states, a lender that makes a usurious loan is permitted to collect the borrowed money, but only at the legal rate of interest. In others, a usurious lender may lose the right to collect any interest or may lose the entire amount of the loan in addition to the interest.

Loan origination fee. The processing of a mortgage application is known as *loan origination*. When a mortgage loan is originated, a **loan origination fee,** or transfer fee, is charged by most lenders to cover the expenses involved in generating the loan. These include the loan officer's salary, paperwork, and the lender's other costs of doing business. A loan origination fee is not prepaid interest; rather, it is a charge that must be paid to the lender. The typical loan origination fee is 1 percent of the loan amount, although origination fees may range from one to three points (a point equals 1 percent of the loan amount).

IN PRACTICE

Because many real estate loans are made by private loan companies that may not be covered by federal regulations, it is important that borrowers insist on receiving a statement in advance from their lender that clearly states the total amount of the loan closing costs and the effective interest rate to avoid unpleasant surprises at closing. This *good-faith estimate* is required by the Real Estate Settlement Procedures Act (RESPA). The good-faith estimate is discussed more fully in Chapter 22.

Discount points. A lender may sell a mortgage to investors (as discussed later in this Chapter). However, the interest rate that a lender charges for a loan might be less than the *yield* (true rate of return) an investor demands. To make up the difference, the lender charges the borrower **discount points.** The number of points charged depends on two factors:

1. The difference between the interest rate and the required yield
2. How long the lender expects it will take the borrower to pay off the loan

For the borrowers, one discount point equals 1 percent of the loan amount and is charged as prepaid interest at the closing. For instance, three discount points charged on a $100,000 loan would be $3,000 ($100,000 × 3%, or .03). If a house sells for $100,000 and the borrower seeks an $80,000 loan, each point would be $800, *not* $1,000. In some cases, however, the points in a new acquisition may be paid in cash at closing by the buyer (or, of course, by the seller on the buyer's behalf) rather than being financed as part of the total loan amount.

> A **point** is *not* 1 percent of the purchase price; a point is 1 percent of the *amount being borrowed.*

Most mortgage loans are paid in installments over a long period of time. As a result, the total interest paid by the borrower may add up to more than the principal amount of the loan. That does not come as a surprise to the lender; the total amount of accrued interest is carefully calculated during the origination phase to determine the profitability of each loan. If the borrower repays the loan before the end of the term, the lender collects less than the anticipated interest. For this reason, some mortgage notes contain a *prepayment clause*. This clause requires that the borrower pay a **prepayment penalty** against the unearned portion of the interest for any payments made ahead of schedule.

The penalty may be as little as 1 percent of the balance due at the time of prepayment or as much as all the interest due for the first ten years of the loan. Some lenders allow the borrower to pay off a certain percentage of the original loan without paying a penalty. However, if the loan is paid in full, the borrower may be charged a percentage of the principal paid in excess of that allowance. *Lenders may not charge prepayment penalties on mortgage loans insured or guaranteed by the federal government or on those loans which have been sold to Fannie Mae or Freddie Mac. Also, some states prohibit prepayment penalties* on all mortgage loans.

IN PRACTICE

Some states limit the amount of prepayment penalty lenders may impose, while others prohibit lenders from charging any penalty at all on prepaid residential mortgage or deed of trust loans. Some states allow lenders to charge a prepayment penalty *only* if the loan is paid off with funds borrowed from another source.

MATH CONCEPTS

$$\% \frac{\cdot}{\cdot}$$
$$\times \; +$$

DISCOUNT POINTS AND INVESTOR YIELD

Depending on the interest rate and loan term, it takes between six and ten discount points to change the interest rate 1 percent on a 30-year loan. For example, eight points will change a 25-year 8-percent loan to 9 percent. From the borrower's standpoint, one discount point equals 1 percent of the loan amount.

To calculate the net amount of a $75,000 loan after a three-point discount is taken, multiply the loan amount by 100 percent minus the discount:

$75,000 × (100% − 3%)
$75,000 × 97%
$75,000 × .97 = $72,750

Or deduct the dollar amount of the discount from the loan:

$75,000 − ($75,000 × 3%)
$75,000 − ($75,000 × .03)
$75,000 − $2,250 = $72,750

■ PROVISIONS OF THE MORTGAGE DOCUMENT OR DEED OF TRUST

The mortgage document or deed of trust clearly establishes that the property is security for a debt, identifies the lender and the borrower, and includes an accurate legal description of the property. Both the mortgage document and deed of trust incorporate the terms of the note by reference. They should be signed by all parties who have an interest in the real estate. Common provisions of both instruments are discussed below.

Duties of the Mortgagor or Trustor

The borrower is required to fulfill certain obligations. These usually include the following:

- Payment of the debt in accordance with the terms of the note
- Payment of all real estate taxes on the property given as security
- Maintenance of adequate insurance to protect the lender if the property is destroyed or damaged by fire, windstorm, or other hazard
- Maintenance of the property in good repair at all times
- Receipt of lender authorization before making any major alterations on the property

Failure to meet any of these obligations can result in a borrower's default. The loan documents may, however, provide for a grace period (such as 30 days) during which the borrower can meet the obligation and cure the default. If the borrower does not do so, the lender has the right to foreclose the mortgage or deed of trust and collect on the note.

**Provisions for
Default**

The mortgage or deed of trust typically includes an **acceleration clause** to assist the lender in foreclosure. If a borrower defaults, the lender has the right to accelerate the maturity of the debt. This means the lender may declare the *entire* debt due and payable *immediately*. Without an acceleration clause, the lender would have to sue the borrower every time a payment was overdue.

Other clauses in a mortgage or deed of trust enable the lender to take care of the property in the event of the borrower's negligence or default. If the borrower does not pay taxes or insurance premiums or fails to make necessary repairs on the property, the lender may step in and do so. The lender has the power to protect the security (the real estate). Any money advanced by the lender to cure a default may be either added to the unpaid debt or declared immediately due from the borrower.

**Assignment of the
Mortgage**

As mentioned previously, without changing the provisions of a contract, a note may be sold to a third party, such as an investor or another mortgage company. The original mortgagee endorses the note to the third party and executes an *assignment of mortgage*. The assignee becomes the new owner of the debt and security instrument. When the debt is paid in full (or satisfied), the assignee is required to execute the satisfaction (or release) of the security instrument.

**Release of the
Mortgage Lien or
Deed of Trust**

When all loan payments have been made and the note has been paid in full, the borrower will want the public record to show that the debt has been satisfied and that the lender is divested of all rights conveyed under the mortgage or deed of trust. By the provisions of the **defeasance clause** in the document, the lender is required to execute a **satisfaction** (also known as a *release* or *discharge*) when the note has been fully paid. This document returns to the borrower all interest in the real estate originally conveyed to the lender. Entering this release in the public record shows that the debt has been removed from the property.

If a mortgage or deed of trust has been assigned by a recorded assignment, the release must be executed by the assignee or mortgagee.

When a real estate loan secured by a deed of trust has been completely repaid, the beneficiary must make a written request that the trustee convey the property back to the grantor. The trustee executes and delivers a **release deed** (sometimes called a *deed of reconveyance*) to the trustor. The release deed conveys the same rights and powers that the trustee was given under the trust deed. The release deed should be acknowledged and recorded in the public records of the county in which the property is located.

**Tax and Insurance
Reserves**

Many lenders require that borrowers provide a reserve fund to meet future real estate taxes and property insurance premiums. This fund is called an *impound, a trust,* or an *escrow account*. When the mortgage or deed of trust loan is made, the borrower starts the reserve by depositing funds to cover the amount of unpaid real estate taxes. If a new insurance policy has just been purchased, the insurance premium reserve will be started with the deposit of one-twelfth of the insurance premium liability. The borrower's monthly loan payments will include principal, interest, tax, and insurance reserves, and sometimes other costs, such as flood insurance or homeowners' association dues. RESPA, the federal Real

> The basic recurring components of a borrower's monthly loan payment may be remembered as **PITI:** **P**rincipal, **I**nterest, **T**axes, and **I**nsurance.

Estate Settlement Procedures Act (discussed in Chapter 22), limits the total amount of reserves that a lender may require.

Flood insurance reserves. The *National Flood Insurance Reform Act of 1994* imposes certain mandatory obligations on lenders and loan servicers to set aside (*escrow*) funds for flood insurance on new loans for property in flood-prone areas. However, the act also applies to any loan still outstanding on October 1, 1996. This means that if a lender or servicer discovers that a secured property is in a flood hazard area, it must notify the borrower. The borrower then has 45 days to purchase flood insurance. If the borrower fails to procure flood insurance, the lender must purchase the insurance on the borrower's behalf. The cost of the insurance may be charged back to the borrower.

Assignment of Rents

If the property involved includes rental units, the borrower may provide for rents to be assigned to the lender in the event of the borrower's default. The assignment may be included in the mortgage or deed of trust, or it may be a separate document. In either case, the assignment should clearly indicate that the borrower intends to *assign* the rents, not merely pledge them as security for the loan. In title theory states, lenders are automatically entitled to any rents if the borrower defaults.

Buying Subject to or Assuming a Seller's Mortgage or Deed of Trust

When a person purchases real estate that has an outstanding mortgage or deed of trust, the buyer may take the property in one of two ways. The property may be purchased **subject to** the mortgage or deed of trust, or the buyer may **assume** the mortgage or deed of trust and agree to pay the debt. This technical distinction becomes important if the buyer defaults and the mortgage or deed of trust is foreclosed.

When the property is sold *subject to* the mortgage, the buyer is not personally obligated to pay the debt in full. The buyer takes title to the real estate knowing that he or she must make payments on the existing loan. Upon default, the lender forecloses and the property is sold by court order to pay the debt. If the sale does not pay off the entire debt, the purchaser is not liable for the difference. In some circumstances, however, the original seller might continue to be liable.

■ **FOR EXAMPLE** Robert owns an investment rental property that carries a mortgage. For health reasons, he wants to sell the property to Janet who has been managing the property and who also wants to use the rental property as an investment. Robert sells the property to Janet *subject to* the mortgage. In the sale, Janet takes title and assumes responsibilities for the loan, but after two months she can no longer make payments on the loan. There is a foreclosure sale and because Robert sold the property *subject to* the mortgage, Robert (not Janet) is personally liable if proceeds from the foreclosure sale do not meet the obligations.

In contrast, a buyer who purchases the property and *assumes* the seller's debt becomes *personally* obligated for the payment of the *entire debt*. If the debt is foreclosed and the court sale does not bring enough money to pay the debt in full, a *deficiency judgment* against the assumer and the original borrower may be obtained for the unpaid balance of the note. If the original borrower has been released by the assumer, only the assumer is liable.

■ **FOR EXAMPLE** When Judy bought her house a short time ago, interest rates were very low. Now, Judy has been unexpectedly transferred out of the country and needs to sell the house quickly. Because interest rates have risen dramatically since the time of Judy's loan, buyers may be attracted by the prospect of assuming Judy's mortgage. Clearly, if a buyer were to take out a mortgage now, the rate would be higher and the cost of home ownership would be increased. By assuming an existing loan with a more favorable interest rate, a buyer can save money.

The existence of a lien does not prevent the transfer of property; however, when a mortgage is assumed, the mortgagee must approve the release of liability of the original mortgagor. Because a loan may not be assumed without lender approval, the lending institution would require the assumer to qualify financially, and many lending institutions charge a transfer fee to cover the costs of changing the records. This charge usually is paid by the purchaser.

Alienation clause. The lender may want to prevent a future purchaser of the property from being able to assume the loan, particularly if the original interest rate is low. For this reason, most lenders include an **alienation clause** (also known as a *resale clause, due-on-sale clause,* or *call clause*) in the note. An alienation clause provides that when the property is sold, the lender may either declare the entire debt due immediately or permit the buyer to assume the loan at an interest rate acceptable to the lender. Land contracts that involve a due-on-sale clause also limit the assumption of the contract.

Recording a Mortgage or Deed of Trust

The mortgage document or deed of trust must be recorded in the recorder's office of the county in which the real estate is located. Recording gives constructive notice to the world of the borrower's obligations. Recording also establishes the lien's priority, as discussed in Chapter 10. If the property is registered in the Torrens system, notice of the lien must be entered on the original Torrens certificate.

Priority of a Mortgage or Deed of Trust

Priority of mortgages and other liens normally is determined by the order in which they were recorded. A mortgage or deed of trust on land that has no prior mortgage lien is a *first mortgage* or *deed of trust.* If the owner later executes another loan for additional funds, the new loan becomes a *second mortgage* or *deed of trust* (or a *junior lien*) when it is recorded. The second lien is subject to the first lien; the first has prior claim to the value of the land pledged as security. Because second loans represent greater risk to the lender, they are usually issued at higher interest rates.

The priority of mortgage or deed of trust liens may be changed by a *subordination agreement,* in which the first lender subordinates its lien to that of the second lender. To be valid, such an agreement must be signed by both lenders.

■ PROVISIONS OF LAND CONTRACTS

As discussed in Chapter 11, real estate can be purchased under a land contract, also known as a *contract for deed* or an *installment contract.* Real estate is usually sold on contract for specific financial reasons. For instance, mortgage financing may be unavailable to a borrower for some reason. High interest rates may make borrowing too expensive. Or the purchaser may not have a sufficient down payment to cover the difference between a mortgage loan and the selling price.

Under a land contract, the buyer (called the *vendee*) agrees to make a down payment and a monthly loan payment that includes interest and principal. The payment also may include real estate tax and insurance reserves. The seller (called the *vendor*) retains legal title to the property during the contract term, and the buyer is granted equitable title and possession. At the end of the loan term, the seller delivers clear title. The contract usually permits the seller to evict the buyer in the event of default. In that case, the seller may keep any money the buyer has already paid, which is construed as rent. Many states now offer some legal protection to a defaulting buyer under a land contract.

■ FORECLOSURE

When a borrower defaults on the payments or fails to fulfill any of the other obligations set forth in the mortgage or deed of trust, the lender's rights can be enforced through foreclosure. **Foreclosure** is a legal procedure in which property pledged as security is sold to satisfy the debt. The foreclosure procedure brings the rights of the parties and all junior lienholders to a conclusion. It passes title to either the person holding the mortgage document or deed of trust or to a third party who purchases the realty at a *foreclosure sale*. The purchaser could be the mortgagee. The property is sold *free of the foreclosing mortgage and all junior liens*.

Methods of Foreclosure

There are three general types of foreclosure proceedings—judicial, nonjudicial, and strict foreclosure. One, two, or all three may be available. The specific provisions and procedures for each vary from state to state.

Judicial foreclosure. Judicial foreclosure allows the property to be sold by court order after the mortgagee has given sufficient public notice. When a borrower defaults, the lender may *accelerate* the due date of all remaining monthly payments. The lender's attorney can then file a suit to foreclose the lien. After presentation of the facts in court, the property is ordered sold. A public sale is advertised and held, and the real estate is sold to the highest bidder.

Nonjudicial foreclosure. Some states allow nonjudicial foreclosure procedures to be used when the security instrument contains a *power-of-sale clause*. In nonjudicial foreclosure, no court action is required. In those states that recognize deed of trust loans, the trustee is generally given the power of sale. Some states allow a similar power of sale to be used with a mortgage loan.

To institute a nonjudicial foreclosure, the trustee or mortgagee may be required to record a notice of default at the county recorder's office. The default must be recorded within a designated time period to give notice to the public of the intended auction. The notice is generally provided by newspaper advertisements that state the total amount due and the date of the public sale. After selling the property, the trustee or mortgagee may be required to file a copy of a notice of sale or an affidavit of foreclosure.

Strict foreclosure. Although judicial foreclosure is the prevalent practice, it is still possible in some states for a lender to acquire mortgaged property through a *strict foreclosure* process. First, appropriate notice must be given to the delinquent borrower. Once the proper papers have been prepared and recorded, the court establishes a deadline by which time the balance of the defaulted debt must be paid in full. If the borrower does not pay off the loan by that date, the court simply awards full legal title to the lender. No sale takes place.

Deed in Lieu of Foreclosure

As an alternative to foreclosure, a lender may accept a **deed in lieu of foreclosure** from the borrower. This is sometimes known as a *friendly foreclosure* because it is carried out by mutual agreement rather than by lawsuit. The major disadvantage of the deed in lieu is that the mortgagee takes the real estate subject to all junior liens. In a foreclosure action, all junior liens are eliminated. Also, by accepting a deed in lieu of foreclosure, the lender usually loses any rights pertaining to FHA or private mortgage insurance or VA guarantees. Finally, it should be pointed out that a deed in lieu of foreclosure is still considered an adverse element in the borrower's credit history.

Redemption

Most states give defaulting borrowers a chance to redeem their property through the **equitable right of redemption.** (See Chapter 10.) If, after default *but before the foreclosure sale*, the borrower (or any other person who has an interest in the real estate, such as another creditor) pays the lender the amount in default, plus costs, the debt will be reinstated. In some cases, the person who redeems may be required to repay the accelerated loan in full. If some person other than the mortgagor or trustor redeems the real estate, the borrower becomes responsible to that person for the amount of the redemption.

Certain states also allow defaulted borrowers a period in which to redeem their real estate *after the sale*. During this period (which may be as long as one year), the borrower has a **statutory right of redemption.** The mortgagor who can raise the necessary funds to redeem the property within the statutory period pays the redemption money to the court. Because the debt was paid from the proceeds of the sale, the borrower can take possession free and clear of the former defaulted loan. The court may appoint a receiver to take charge of the property, collect rents, and pay operating expenses during the redemption period. Redemption is illustrated in Figure 14.3.

Deed to Purchaser at Sale

If redemption is not made or if state law does not provide for a redemption period, the successful bidder at the sale receives a deed to the real estate. A sheriff or master-in-chancery executes this deed to the purchaser to *convey whatever title the borrower had*. The deed contains no warranties. Title passes as is but is free of the former defaulted debt.

Deficiency Judgment

The foreclosure sale may not produce enough cash to pay the loan balance in full after deducting expenses and accrued unpaid interest. In this case, the mortgagee may be entitled to a *personal judgment* against the borrower for the unpaid balance. Such a judgment is a **deficiency judgment.** It may also be obtained against any endorsers or guarantors of the note and against any owners of the mortgaged property who assumed the debt by written agreement. However, if any money remains from the foreclosure sale after paying the debt and any other

FIGURE 14.3

Redemption

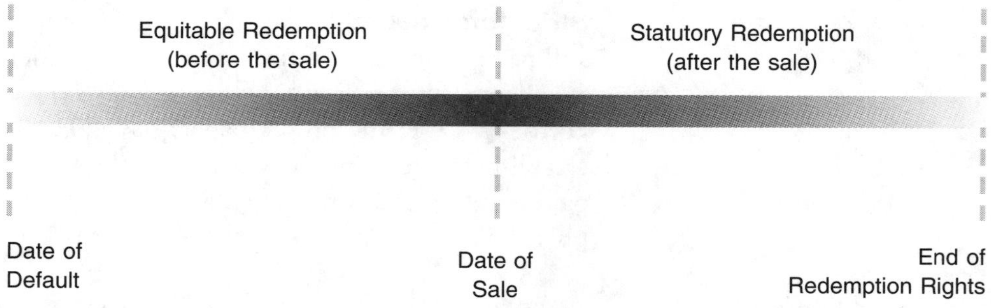

Equitable Redemption (before the sale)	Statutory Redemption (after the sale)

Date of
Default

Date of
Sale

End of
Redemption Rights

liens (such as a second mortgage or mechanic's lien), expenses, and interest, these proceeds are paid to the borrower.

■ SUMMARY

Some states, known as title theory states, recognize the lender as the owner of mortgaged property. Others, known as lien theory states, recognize the borrower as the owner of mortgaged property. A few intermediate states recognize modified versions of these theories.

Mortgage and deed of trust loans are the principal types of financing for real estate purchases. Mortgage loans involve a borrower (the mortgagor) and a lender (the mortgagee). Deed of trust loans involve a third party (the trustee) in addition to a borrower (the trustor) and a lender (the beneficiary).

After a lending institution has received, investigated, and approved a loan application, it issues a commitment to make the mortgage loan. The borrower is required to execute a note agreeing to repay the debt and a mortgage or deed of trust placing a lien on the real estate to secure the note. The security instrument is recorded to give notice to the world of the lender's interest.

The mortgage document or deed of trust secures the debt and sets forth the obligations of the borrower and the rights of the lender. Full payment of the note by its terms entitles the borrower to a satisfaction, or release, which is recorded to clear the lien from the public records. Default by the borrower may result in acceleration of payments, a foreclosure sale, and, after the redemption period (if provided by state law), loss of title.

QUESTIONS

1. A charge of three discount points on a $120,000 loan equals
   a. $450.
   b. $3,600.
   c. $4,500.
   d. $116,400.

2. A prospective buyer needs to borrow money to buy a house. The buyer applies for and obtains a real estate loan from the VGY Company. Then the buyer signs a note and a mortgage. In this example, the buyer is referred to as the
   a. mortgagor.
   b. beneficiary.
   c. mortgagee.
   d. vendor.

3. In the previous question, VGY Company is the
   a. mortgagor.
   b. beneficiary.
   c. mortgagee.
   d. vendor.

4. The borrower under a deed of trust is known as the
   a. trustor.
   b. trustee.
   c. beneficiary.
   d. vendee.

5. In a land contract the vendee
   a. is not responsible for the real estate taxes on the property.
   b. does not pay interest and principal.
   c. has possession during the term of the contract.
   d. obtains legal title at closing.

6. A state law provides that lenders cannot charge more than 24 percent interest on any loan. This kind of law is called
   a. a Truth-in-Lending Law.
   b. a usury law.
   c. the statute of frauds.
   d. RESPA.

7. After the foreclosure sale, a borrower who has defaulted on a loan may seek to pay off the debt plus any accrued interest and costs under what right?
   a. Equitable redemption
   b. Defeasance
   c. Usury
   d. Statutory redemption

8. Which of the following clauses would give a lender the right to have all future installments become due on default?
   a. Escalation
   b. Defeasance
   c. Alienation
   d. Acceleration

9. What document is available to the mortgagor when the mortgage debt is completely repaid?
   a. Satisfaction of mortgage
   b. Defeasance certificate
   c. Deed of trust
   d. Mortgage estoppel

10. Under a typical land contract, when does the vendor give the deed to the vendee?
    a. When the contract is fulfilled and all payments have been made
    b. At the closing
    c. When the contract for deed is approved by the parties
    d. After the first year's real estate taxes are paid

11. If a borrower must pay a discount fee of $4,500 for points on a $90,000 loan, how many points is the lender charging for this loan?
    a. 2
    b. 3
    c. 5
    d. 6

12. If a purchaser buys property in a transaction involving a land contract, the vendor would not do which of the following?
    a. Provide financing for the vendee
    b. Be liable for any senior financing
    c. Retain actual title
    d. Retain possession of the property.

13. Which of the following allows a mortgagee to proceed to a foreclosure sale without having to go to court first?

a. Waiver of redemption right
b. Power of sale
c. Alienation clause
d. Hypothecation

14. Pledging property for a loan without giving up possession is referred to as

a. hypothecation.   c. alienation.
b. defeasance.   d. novation.

15. Discount points on a mortgage are computed as a percentage of the

a. selling price.
b. amount borrowed.
c. closing costs.
d. down payment.

16. In the state of West Columbia, a mortgagee holds legal title to real property offered as collateral for a loan, and the mortgagor retains the rights of possession and use. If the borrower defaults, the lender is entitled to immediate possession and rents. West Columbia can be best characterized as what kind of state?

a. Lien theory
b. Mortgage theory
c. Intermediate theory
d. Title theory

17. In the state of North Superior, a mortgagee holds a lien on real property offered as collateral for a loan. The mortgagor retains both legal and equitable title to real property. If the borrower defaults on the loan, the lender must go through formal foreclosure proceedings to recover the debt. North Superior can be best characterized as what kind of state?

a. Lien theory
b. Mortgage theory
c. Intermediate theory
d. Title theory

18. With the help of a mortgage loan from Pleasant Lenders, Tom bought a house at 123 Charming Street. Pleasant Lenders promptly recorded the mortgage. Three years later, Tom needs additional cash, so he places a second mortgage with Best Bank. Based on these facts, which of the following statements is true?

a. Because it is older, the loan from Pleasant Lenders is subject to the loan from Best Bank, which assumes priority in time.
b. The loan from Best Bank is referred to as a *subordination loan*.
c. The loan from Pleasant Lenders has priority over the loan from Best Bank.
d. Best Bank cannot hold a security interest in the property already held as collateral by another lender.

19. A junior lien may become first in priority if the original lender agrees to execute a

a. deed of trust.
b. subordination agreement.
c. second mortgage agreement.
d. call clause.

20. A buyer purchased a home under an agreement that made the buyer personally obligated to continue making payments under the seller's existing mortgage. If the buyer defaults and the court sale of the property does not satisfy the debt, the buyer will be liable for making up the difference. The buyer has

a. purchased the home subject to the seller's mortgage.
b. assumed the seller's mortgage.
c. benefited from the alienation clause in the seller's mortgage.
d. benefited from the defeasance clause in the seller's mortgage.

REAL ESTATE
FINANCING: PRACTICE

■ **LEARNING OBJECTIVES** *When you've finished reading this Chapter, you should be able to:*

■ **identify** the types of institutions in the primary and secondary mortgage markets.

■ **describe** the various types of financing techniques available to real estate purchasers and the role of government financing regulations.

■ **explain** the requirements and qualifications for conventional, FHA, and VA loan programs.

■ **distinguish** among the different types of "creative" financing techniques that address borrowers' different needs.

■ **define** the following *key terms:*

adjustable-rate mortgage (ARM)	Farm Service Agency (FSA)	package loan
amortized loan	Farmer Mac	primary mortgage market
balloon payment	Freddie Mac	private mortgage insurance (PMI)
blanket loan	Federal Deposit Insurance Corporation (FDIC)	purchase-money mortgage (PMM)
buydown		
Community Reinvestment Act of 1977 (CRA)	Federal Reserve System	Regulation Z
	FHA loan	reverse-annuity mortgage (RAM)
computerized loan origination (CLO)	Ginnie Mae	sale-and-leaseback
construction loan	growing-equity mortgage (GEM)	secondary mortgage market
conventional loan	home equity loan	straight loan
Equal Credit Opportunity Act (ECOA)	loan-to-value ratios	trigger terms
	Office of Thrift Supervision (OTS)	Truth-in-Lending Act
Fannie Mae		VA loan
Farm Credit System (System)	open-end loan	wraparound loan

■ **WHY LEARN ABOUT...** REAL ESTATE FINANCING PRACTICE?

Like the previous Chapter, this one goes directly to the heart of your client's real estate transaction. Having an understanding of current financing techniques and sources of financing can help you direct buyers to the mortgage loans that will help the buyers reach their real estate goals. Most real estate transactions require some sort of financing. Few people have the cash in hand necessary to buy a house or another large property. Also, as economic conditions change, the forces of supply and demand reshape the real estate market. These factors have combined to create a complex and rapidly evolving mortgage market. One of the greatest challenges today's real estate licensees face is how to maintain a working knowledge of all the financing techniques available. If you understand financing techniques, the actors involved in the mortgage market, and the mortgage options available to your clients, you will be able to provide a valuable, attractive service to the public. ■

■ INTRODUCTION TO THE REAL ESTATE FINANCING MARKET

The real estate financing market has the following three basic components:

1. Government influences, primarily the Federal Reserve System, but also the Home Loan Bank System and the Office of Thrift Supervision
2. The primary mortgage market
3. The secondary mortgage market

Under the umbrella of the financial policies set by the Federal Reserve System, the primary mortgage market originates loans that are bought, sold, and traded in the secondary mortgage market. Before turning to the specific types of mortgage options available to consumers, it is important to have a clear understanding of the bigger picture: the market in which those mortgages exist.

The Federal Reserve System

The role of the **Federal Reserve System** (also known as the *Fed*) is to maintain sound credit conditions, help counteract inflationary and deflationary trends, and create a favorable economic climate. The Federal Reserve System divides the country into 12 federal reserve districts, each served by a federal reserve bank. All nationally chartered banks must join the Fed and purchase stock in its district reserve banks.

The Federal Reserve System regulates the flow of money and interest rates in the marketplace through its member banks by controlling their *reserve requirements* and *discount rates*. The Fed also can regulate the money supply through the *Federal Open Market Committee* (FOMC), which buys and sells U.S. government securities on the open market. When the FOMC sells securities, it effectively removes the money paid by buyers from circulation. When it buys them, it infuses its own reserves back into the general supply.

WWWeb.Link   www.federalreserve.gov

Reserve requirements. The Federal Reserve System requires that each member bank keep a certain amount of assets on hand as reserve funds. These reserves are unavailable for loans or any other use. This requirement not only protects customer deposits, but it also provides a means of manipulating the flow of cash in the money market.

By increasing its reserve requirements, the Federal Reserve in effect limits the amount of money that member banks can use to make loans. When the amount of money available for lending decreases, interest rates (the amount lenders charge for the use of their money) rise. By causing interest rates to rise, the government can slow down an overactive economy by limiting the number of loans that would have been directed toward major purchases of goods and services. The opposite is also true: By decreasing the reserve requirements, the Fed can encourage more lending. Increased lending causes the amount of money circulated in the marketplace to rise, while simultaneously causing interest rates to drop.

Discount rates. Federal Reserve member banks are permitted to borrow money from the district reserve banks to expand their lending operations. The discount rate is the rate charged by the Federal Reserve when it lends to its member banks. The Federal Funds rate is the rate recommended by the Federal Reserve for the member banks to charge each other on short-term loans. These rates form the basis on which the banks determine the percentage rate of interest they will charge their loan customers. The *prime rate*, the short-term interest rate charged to a bank's largest, most creditworthy customers, is strongly influenced by the Fed's discount rate. In turn, the prime rate is often the basis for determining a bank's interest rate on other loans, including mortgages. These rates are usually higher than the prime rate. In theory, when the Federal Reserve discount rate is high, bank interest rates are high. When bank interest rates are high, fewer loans are made and less money circulates in the marketplace. On the other hand, a lower discount rate results in lower overall interest rates, more bank loans, and more money in circulation.

The Primary Mortgage Market

The **primary mortgage market** is made up of the lenders that originate mortgage loans. These lenders make money available directly to borrowers. From a borrower's point of view, a loan is a means of financing an expenditure; from a lender's point of view, a loan is an investment. All investors look for profitable returns on their investments. For a lender, a loan must generate enough income to be attractive as an investment. Income on the loan is realized from the following two sources:

1. *Finance charges* collected at closing, such as loan origination fees and discount points
2. *Recurring income*, that is, the interest collected during the term of the loan

An increasing number of lenders look at the income generated from the fees charged in originating loans as their primary investment objective. Once the loans are made, they are sold to investors. By selling loans to investors in the secondary mortgage market, lenders generate funds with which to originate additional loans.

In addition to the income directly related to loans, some lenders derive income from servicing loans for other mortgage lenders or investors who have purchased the loans. Servicing involves such activities as

- collecting payments (including insurance and taxes),
- accounting,
- bookkeeping,
- preparing insurance and tax records,
- processing payments of taxes and insurance, and
- following up on loan payment and delinquency.

The terms of the servicing agreement stipulate the responsibilities and fees for the service.

Some of the major lenders in the primary market include the following:

- *Thrifts, savings associations, and commercial banks.* These institutions are known as *fiduciary lenders* because of their fiduciary obligations to protect and preserve their despositors' funds. "Thrifts" is a generic term for the savings associations. Mortgage loans are perceived as secure investments for generating income and enable these institutions to pay interest to their depositors. Fiduciary lenders are subject to standards and regulations established by government agencies such as the **Federal Deposit Insurance Corporation (FDIC)** and the **Office of Thrift Supervision (OTS).** These agencies govern the practices of fiduciary lenders. The various government regulations (which include reserve fund, reporting, and insurance requirements) are intended to protect depositors against the reckless lending that characterized the savings and loan industry in the 1980s.
- *Insurance companies.* Insurance companies accumulate large sums of money from the premiums paid by their policyholders. While part of this money is held in reserve to satisfy claims and cover operating expenses, much of it is free to be invested in profit-earning enterprises, such as long-term real estate loans. Although insurance companies are considered primary lenders, they tend to invest their money in large, long-term loans that finance commercial, industrial, and larger multifamily properties rather than single-family home mortgages.
- *Credit unions.* Credit unions are cooperative organizations whose members place money in savings accounts. In the past, credit unions made only short-term consumer and home improvement loans. Recently, however, they have branched out to originating longer-term first and second mortgage and deed of trust loans.
- *Pension funds.* Pension funds usually have large amounts of money available for investment. Because of the comparatively high yields and low risks offered by mortgages, pension funds have begun to participate actively in financing real estate projects. Most real estate activity for pension funds is handled through mortgage bankers and mortgage brokers.

Primary mortgage market

- Trusts
- Savings associations
- Commercial banks
- Insurance companies
- Credit unions
- Pension funds
- Endowment funds
- Investment group financing
- Mortgage banking companies
- Mortgage brokers

- *Endowment funds*. Many commercial banks and mortgage bankers handle investments for endowment funds. The endowments of hospitals, universities, colleges, charitable foundations, and other institutions provide a good source of financing for low-risk commercial and industrial properties.
- *Investment group financing*. Large real estate projects, such as highrise apartment buildings, office complexes, and shopping centers, are often financed as joint ventures through group financing arrangements like syndicates, limited partnerships, and real estate investment trusts. These complex investment agreements are discussed in Appendix 1.
- *Mortgage banking companies*. Mortgage banking companies originate mortgage loans with money belonging to insurance companies, pension funds, and individuals, and with funds of their own. They make real estate loans with the intention of selling them to investors and receiving a fee for servicing the loans. Mortgage banking companies are generally organized as stock companies. As a source of real estate financing, they are subject to fewer lending restrictions than are commercial banks or savings associations. Mortgage banking companies often are involved in all types of real estate loan activities and often serve as intermediaries between investors and borrowers. They are *not* mortgage brokers.
- *Mortgage brokers*. Mortgage brokers are not lenders. They are intermediaries who bring borrowers and lenders together. Mortgage brokers locate potential borrowers, process preliminary loan applications, and submit the applications to lenders for final approval. Frequently, they work with or for mortgage banking companies. They do not service loans once the loans are made. Mortgage brokers also may be real estate brokers who offer these financing services in addition to their regular real estate brokerage activities. Many state governments are establishing separate licensure requirements for mortgage brokers to regulate their activities.

IN PRACTICE

An exciting new trend for consumers is the prospect of applying for mortgage loans from their home computers via the Internet in the same way they can buy books or order airline tickets. Many major lenders have Web sites that offer substantial information to potential borrowers regarding their current programs and regulations. In addition, online brokerage or matchmaking organizations have emerged that link lenders with potential borrowers. Some borrowers prefer the speed of the Internet process as well as having access to a wide variety of loan programs. However, the loan approval process may not necessarily be faster than traditional application processing. Still, online "matchmakers," lenders, and brokers offer convenience and the ability to easily shop for the best rates and terms.

Information on the Internet regarding lenders and their programs is constantly changing. Consider using a search engine such as www.altavista.com, www.excite.com, www.google.com, www.lycos.com, or www.yahoo.com, to search for terms such as real estate, financing, lending programs, and/or home mortgages.

The Secondary Mortgage Market

In addition to the primary mortgage market, where loans are originated, there is a **secondary mortgage market**. Here, loans are bought and sold only after they have been funded. Lenders routinely sell loans to avoid interest rate risks and to realize profits on the sales. This secondary market activity helps lenders raise capital to continue making mortgage loans. Secondary market activity is especially desirable when money is in short supply; it stimulates both the housing construction market and the mortgage market by expanding the types of loans available. Growth in the use of secondary markets has greatly increased the standardization of loans.

When a loan is sold, the original lender may continue to collect the payments from the borrower. The lender then passes the payments along to the investor who purchased the loan. The investor is charged a fee for servicing of the loan.

In the secondary mortgage market, various agencies purchase a number of mortgage loans and assemble them into packages (called *pools*). These agencies purchase the mortgages from banks and savings associations. Securities that represent shares in these pooled mortgages are then sold to investors or other agencies. Loans are eligible for sale to the secondary market only when the collateral, borrower, and documentation meet certain requirements to provide a degree of safety for the investors. The major warehousing agencies are discussed in the following paragraphs. (See Table 15.1.)

Fannie Mae. Fannie Mae (formerly the *Federal National Mortgage Association* or *FNMA*) is a quasi-governmental agency. It is organized as a privately owned corporation that issues its own common stock and provides a secondary market for mortgage loans. Fannie Mae deals in conventional and FHA and VA loans. Fannie Mae buys a *block* or *pool* of mortgages from a lender in exchange for *mortgage-backed securities*, which the lender may keep or sell.

 www.fanniemae.com

Ginnie Mae. Unlike Fannie Mae, **Ginnie Mae** (formerly the *Government National Mortgage Association*, or *GNMA*) is entirely a governmental agency. Ginnie Mae is a division of the Department of Housing and Urban Development (HUD), organized as a corporation without capital stock. Ginnie Mae administers special-assistance programs and works with Fannie Mae in secondary market activities.

In times of tight money and high interest rates, Fannie Mae and Ginnie Mae can join forces through their tandem plan. The *tandem plan* provides that Fannie Mae can purchase high-risk, low-yield (usually FHA) loans at full market rates, with Ginnie Mae guaranteeing payment and absorbing the difference between the low yield and current market prices.

Ginnie Mae also guarantees investment securities issued by private offerors (such as banks, mortgage companies, and savings and loan associations) and backed by pools of FHA and VA mortgage loans. The *Ginnie Mae pass-through certificate* is a security interest in a pool of mortgages that provides for a monthly pass-through of principal and interest payments directly to the certificate holder. Such certificates are guaranteed by Ginnie Mae.

 www.ginniemae.gov

TABLE   15.1

Secondary Mortgage Market

Institution	Secondary Market Function	Entity
Fannie Mae	Conventional, VA, FHA Loans	Privately Owned Corporation
Ginnie Mae	Special Assistance Loans	Government Agency in HUD
Freddie Mac	Mostly Conventional Loans	Privately Owned Corporation

Freddie Mac. Freddie Mac (formerly the *Federal Home Loan Mortgage Corporation,* or *FHLMC*) provides a secondary market for mortgage loans, primarily conventional loans. Freddie Mac has the authority to purchase mortgages, pool them and sell bonds in the open market with the mortgages as security. However, Freddie Mac does not guarantee payment of Freddie Mac mortgages.

Many lenders use the standardized forms and follow the guidelines issued by Fannie Mae and Freddie Mac. In fact, the use of such forms is mandatory for lenders that wish to sell mortgages in the agencies' secondary mortgage market. The standardized documents include loan applications, credit reports, and appraisal forms.

WWWeb.Link   www.freddiemac.com

IN   PRACTICE   Because Fannie Mae's and Freddie Mac's involvement in the secondary market is so pervasive, many underwriting guidelines are written to comply with their regulations. Bank statements, tax returns, verifications of employment and child support—most of the paperwork a potential borrower must deal with—may be tied to Fannie Mae and Freddie Mac requirements.

■ FINANCING TECHNIQUES

Now that you understand *where* real estate financing comes from, we'll turn to the *what:* the types of financing available. Real estate financing comes in a wide variety of forms. While the payment plans described in the following sections are commonly referred to as *mortgages,* they are really *loans* secured by either a mortgage or a deed of trust.

Straight Loans

A **straight loan** (also known as a *term loan*) essentially divides the loan into two amounts, to be paid off separately. The borrower makes periodic payments of interest only, followed by the payment of the principal *in full at the end of the term.* Straight loans were once the only form of mortgage available. Today, they are generally used for home improvements and second mortgages rather than for residential first mortgage loans.

Balloon Payment Loan

When the periodic payments are not enough to fully amortize the loan by the time the final payment is due, the final payment is larger than the others. This is called a **balloon payment.** It is a *partially amortized loan* because principal is still owed at the end of the term. It is frequently assumed that if payments are made promptly, the lender will extend the balloon payment for another limited term. The lender, however, is not legally obligated to grant this extension and can require payment in full when the note is due.

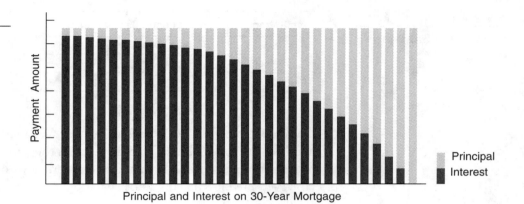

FIGURE   15.1

**Level-Payment
Amortized Loan**

Principal and Interest on 30-Year Mortgage

Amortized Loans

The word *amortize* literally means "to kill off slowly, over time." Most mortgage and deed of trust loans are amortized loans. That is, they are paid off slowly, over time, in equal payments. Regular periodic payments are made over a term of years. The most common periods are 15 years or 30 years, although 20-year mortgages are also available. Unlike a straight loan payment, the payment in an **amortized loan** partially pays off both principal and interest. Each payment is applied first to the interest owed; the balance of the payment is then applied to the principal amount.

At the end of the term, the full amount of the principal and all interest due is reduced to zero. Such loans are also called *direct reduction loans*. Most amortized mortgage and deed of trust loans are paid in monthly installments. However, some are payable quarterly (four times a year) or semiannually (twice a year).

Different payment plans tend alternately to gain and lose favor with lenders and borrowers as the cost and availability of mortgage money fluctuate. The most frequently used plan is the *fully amortized loan*, or *level-payment* loan. The mortgagor pays a *constant amount*, usually monthly. The lender credits each payment first to the interest due, then to the principal amount of the loan. As a result, while each payment remains the same, the portion applied to repayment of the principal grows and the interest due declines as the unpaid balance of the loan is reduced. (See Figure 15.1.) If the borrower pays additional amounts that are applied directly to the principal, the loan will amortize more quickly. This benefits the borrower because he or she will pay less interest if the loan is paid off before the end of its term. Of course, lenders are aware of this, too, and may guard against unprofitable loans by including penalties for early payment.

The amount of the constant payment of an amortizing loan is determined from a prepared mortgage payment book or a mortgage factor chart. (See Table 15.2.) The mortgage factor chart indicates the amount of monthly payment per $1,000 of loan, depending on the term and interest rate. This factor is multiplied by the number of thousands (and fractions of thousands) of the amount borrowed.

IN PRACTICE

Of course, there are relatively inexpensive calculators that will accurately perform most of the standard mortgage lending calculations. Most commercial lenders with a Web presence provide mortgage calculators on their Web sites. Nonetheless, it's valuable both to know what the calculator is doing and to be able to perform the calculations manually if the calculator breaks.

TABLE 15.2
Mortgage Factor Chart

Rate	Term 10 Years	Term 15 Years	Term 20 Years	Term 25 Years	Term 30 Years
6	11.10	8.44	7.16	6.44	6.00
6⅛	11.16	8.51	7.24	6.52	6.08
6¼	11.23	8.57	7.31	6.60	6.16
6⅜	11.29	8.64	7.38	6.67	6.24
6½	11.35	8.71	7.46	6.75	6.32
6⅝	11.42	8.78	7.53	6.83	6.40
6¾	11.48	8.85	7.60	6.91	6.49
6⅞	11.55	8.92	7.68	6.99	6.57
7	11.61	8.98	7.75	7.06	6.65
7⅛	11.68	9.06	7.83	7.15	6.74
7¼	11.74	9.12	7.90	7.22	6.82
7⅜	11.81	9.20	7.98	7.31	6.91
7½	11.87	9.27	8.05	7.38	6.99
7⅝	11.94	9.34	8.13	7.47	7.08
7¾	12.00	9.41	8.20	7.55	7.16
7⅞	12.07	9.48	8.29	7.64	7.25
8	12.14	9.56	8.37	7.72	7.34
8⅛	12.20	9.63	8.45	7.81	7.43
8¼	12.27	9.71	8.53	7.89	7.52
8⅜	12.34	9.78	8.60	7.97	7.61
8½	12.40	9.85	8.68	8.06	7.69
8⅝	12.47	9.93	8.76	8.14	7.78
8¾	12.54	10.00	8.84	8.23	7.87
8⅞	12.61	10.07	8.92	8.31	7.96
9	12.67	10.15	9.00	8.40	8.05

How To Use This Chart

To use this chart, start by finding the appropriate interest rate. Then follow that row over to the column for the appropriate loan term. This number is the *interest rate factor* required each month to amortize a $1,000 loan. To calculate the principal and interest (PI) payment, multiply the interest rate factor by the number of 1,000s in the total loan.

For example, if the interest rate is 8 percent for a term of 30 years, the interest rate factor is 7.34. If the total loan is $100,000, the loan contains 100 1,000s. Therefore, 100 × 7.34 = $734 PI only.

Adjustable-Rate Mortgages (ARMs)

An **adjustable-rate mortgage (ARM)** is generally originated at one rate of interest. That rate then fluctuates up or down during the loan term, based on some objective economic indicator. Because the interest rate may change, the mortgagor's loan repayments also may change. Details of how and when the interest rate will change are included in the note. Common components of an ARM include the following:

- The interest rate is tied to the movement of an objective economic indicator called an *index*. Most indexes are tied to U.S. Treasury securities.
- Usually, the interest rate is the index rate plus a premium, called the *margin*. The margin represents the lender's cost of doing business. For example, the loan rate may be 2 percent over the U.S. Treasury bill rate.
- *Rate caps* limit the amount the interest rate may change. Most ARMs have two types of rate caps—periodic and life-of-the-loan (or aggregate). A periodic rate cap limits the amount the rate may increase at any one time. An aggregate rate cap limits the amount the rate may increase over the entire life of the loan.
- The mortgagor is protected from unaffordable individual payments by the *payment cap*. The payment cap sets a maximum amount for payments. With a payment cap, a rate increase could result in negative amortization—that is, an increase in the loan balance.

MATH CONCEPTS

THE MORTGAGE AMORTIZATION TRIANGLE

If you know what the monthly payment and interest rate are, you can easily track how much of each month's payment is being applied toward principal and how much is applied toward interest.

Always begin at the shaded box and follow the direction of the arrows to perform the calculations described in each box for each month's calculation. Your result will show how much of a given month's mortgage payment goes to pay principal, and what portion pays interest on the loan to the lender. For instance, if you wanted to see how much the loan principal would be reduced after three months, you would "go around the triangle" three times.

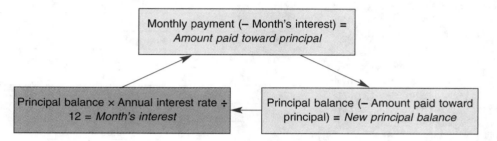

For example, assume a 30-year mortgage loan for $75,000 at a 7.75% annual interest rate and a monthly payment of $537.00 (75 × 7.16 = $537). You can see how the triangle can help you determine the amount of principal and interest in each payment for the first two months of the loan (shown in each box as "1" and "2").

The principal balance on the loan at the end of the second month (the beginning of the third month) is $74,894.42.

What is the principal balance on this loan at the end of the third month?

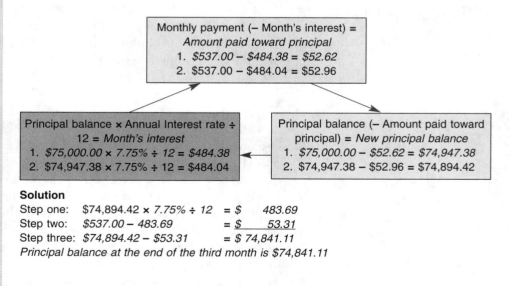

Solution

Step one: $74,894.42 × 7.75% ÷ 12   = $ 483.69
Step two: $537.00 − 483.69   = $ 53.31
Step three: $74,894.42 − $53.31   = $ 74,841.11
Principal balance at the end of the third month is $74,841.11

Principal balance at the end of the third month is $74,841.11

F I G U R E   15.2

**Adjustable-Rate
Mortgage**

Interest
Rates

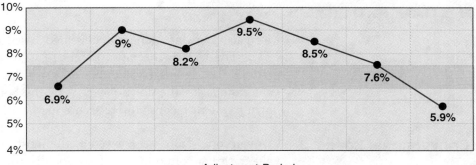

Adjustment Periods

- The *adjustment period* establishes how often the rate may be changed. For instance, the adjustment period may be monthly, quarterly, or annually.
- Lenders may offer a *conversion option,* which permits the mortgagor to convert from an adjustable-rate to a fixed-rate loan at certain intervals during the life of the mortgage. The option is subject to certain terms and conditions for the conversion.

Figure 15.2 illustrates the effect interest rate fluctuations and periodic caps have on an adjustable-rate mortgage. Obviously, without rate caps and payment caps, a single mortgage's interest rate could fluctuate wildly over several adjustment periods, depending on the behavior of the index to which it is tied. In Figure 15.2, the borrower's rate changes from a low of 5.9 percent to a high of 9.5 percent. Such unpredictability makes personal financial planning difficult. On the other hand, if the loan had a rate cap of 7.5 percent, the borrower's rate would never go above that level, regardless of the index's behavior. Similarly, a lender would want a floor to keep the rate from falling below a certain rate (here, 6.5 percent). The shaded area in the figure shows how caps and floors protect against dramatic changes in interest rates.

**Growing-Equity
Mortgage (GEM)**

A **growing-equity mortgage (GEM)** is also known as a *rapid-payoff mortgage.* The GEM uses a fixed interest rate, but payments of principal are increased according to an index or a schedule. Thus, the total payment increases, and the loan is paid off more quickly. A GEM is most frequently used when the borrower's income is expected to keep pace with the increasing loan payments.

**Reverse-Annuity
Mortgage (RAM)**

A **reverse-annuity mortgage (RAM)** is one in which payments are made by the lender *to the borrower.* The payments, which may be made as regular monthly payments, in one lump sum, or as a line of credit to be drawn against, are based on the equity the homeowner has invested in the property given as security for the loan. This loan allows senior citizens on fixed incomes to realize, or use, the equity they have built up in their homes without having to sell. The borrower is charged a fixed rate of interest, and the loan is eventually repaid from the sale of the property or from the borrower's estate on his or her death.

www.financialfreedom.com   www.reversemortgage.org

■ LOAN PROGRAMS

Mortgage loans are generally classified based on their loan-to-value ratios, or *LTVs*. The LTV is the ratio of debt to value of the property. Value is the sale price or the appraisal value, whichever is less. The *lower* the ratio of debt to value, the *higher* the down payment by the borrower. For the lender, the higher down payment means a more secure loan, which minimizes the lender's risk.

Conventional Loans

Conventional loans are viewed as the most secure loans because their loan-to-value ratios are often lowest. Traditionally, the ratio is 80 percent of the value of the property or less, because the borrower makes a down payment of at least 20 percent (although conventional loans with LTVs up to nearly 100 percent of the value of the property may be available). The security for the loan is provided solely by the mortgage; the payment of the debt rests on the ability of the borrower to pay. In making such a loan, the lender relies primarily on its appraisal of the security (the real estate). Information from credit reports that indicate the reliability of the prospective borrower is also important. Usually with a 20 percent down payment and a conventional loan, no additional insurance or guarantee on the loan is necessary to protect the lender's interest. A conventional loan is not government-insured or guaranteed, in contrast to the FHA-insured and VA-guaranteed loans described below.

Lenders can set criteria by which a borrower and the collateral are evaluated to qualify for a loan. However, in recent years the secondary mortgage market has had a significant impact on the borrower qualifications, standards for the collateral, and documentation procedures followed by lenders. Loans must meet strict criteria to be sold to Fannie Mae and Freddie Mac. Lenders still can be flexible in their lending decisions, but they may not be able to sell unusual loans in the secondary market.

To qualify for a conventional loan under Fannie Mae guidelines, for instance, the borrower's monthly housing expenses, including PITI, must not exceed 28 percent of total monthly gross income. Also, the borrower's total monthly obligations, including housing costs plus other regular monthly payments, must not exceed 36 percent of his or her total monthly gross income (33 percent in the case of 95 percent LTV loans). Loans that meet these criteria are called *conforming loans*, and are eligible to be sold in the secondary market. Loans that exceed the limits are referred to as *nonconforming loans* and are not marketable, but they must be held in the lender's investment portfolio.

Conforming loans with larger ratios may be available in certain situations. Both Fannie Mae and Freddie Mac currently have a variety of conforming affordable loan products with qualifying ratios of 33 percent for housing expense and up to 38 percent for total debt. These loans only require a 3 percent down payment but are subject to certain income limitations and may require the borrowers to attend home ownership classes.

■ **FOR EXAMPLE** Following is the qualifying math for a $100,000 loan at 7.5 percent interest for 30 years with payments of $699 per month in principal and interest:

Combined Monthly Gross Income	$5,000.00
Monthly Housing Expenses:	
Principal and Interest	699.00
Property Taxes	300.00
Hazard Insurance	30.00
PMI Insurance	62.50
Homeowner Association Dues	20.00
Total Housing Expense	$1,111.50

$$\$1,111.50 \div 5,000 = 22\%$$

Debt Expense:	
Installment Payments	$100.00
Revolving Charges	50.00
Auto Loan	175.00
Child Care	200.00
Other	100.00
Total Debt Expense	$625.00
Plus Housing	$1,111.50
Grand Total	$1,736.50

$$\$1,736.50 \div 5,000 = 35\%$$

Low LTV = *High* down payment

High down payment = *Low* lender risk

These borrowers will qualify for this loan under conventional loan guidelines of 28 percent and 36 percent.

Private Mortgage Insurance

One way a borrower can obtain a mortgage loan with a lower down payment is by obtaining **private mortgage insurance (PMI).** In a PMI program, the buyer purchases an insurance policy that provides the lender with funds in the event that the lendee defaults on the loan. This allows the lender to assume more risk so that the loan-to-value ratio is higher than for other conventional loans. The borrower purchases insurance from a private mortgage insurance company as additional security to insure the lender against borrower default. Currently, LTVs of up to 97 percent of the appraised value of the property are possible with mortgage insurance, although these percentages may change.

PMI protects the top portion of a loan, usually 25 to 30 percent, against borrower default. The borrower pays a monthly premium or fee while the insurance is in force. Other methods of payment are available, however: The premium may be financed. When a borrower has limited funds available for an initial investment, these alternative methods of reducing closing costs are very important. Because only a portion of the loan is insured, once the loan is repaid to a certain level, the lender may agree to allow the borrower to terminate the PMI coverage. Practices for termination vary from lender to lender.

IN PRACTICE

Effective on new loans originating after July, 1999, a federal law requires that PMI automatically terminates if a borrower
- has accumulated at least 22 percent equity in the home *and*
- is current on mortgage payments.

The 22 percent of equity is based on the purchase price of the home and no credit is given for appreciation of the property. However, there may be some easing of this requirement.

Under the law, a borrower with a good payment history may request that PMI be canceled when he or she has built up equity equal to 22 percent of the purchase price. Lenders are required by the law to inform borrowers of their right to cancel PMI. Before this law was enacted, lenders could (and often did) continue to require monthly PMI payments long after borrowers had built up substantial equity in their homes and the lender no longer risked a loss from the borrower's default. Fannie Mae and Freddie Mac have extended this option to all loans that are in good standing and that have no additional financing added to the original loan.

FHA-Insured Loans

The Federal Housing Administration (FHA), which operates under HUD, neither builds homes nor lends money itself. The common term **FHA loan** refers to a loan that is *insured* by the agency. These loans must be made by FHA-approved lending institutions. The FHA insurance provides security to the lender in addition to the real estate. As with private mortgage insurance, the FHA insures lenders against loss from borrower default.

MATH CONCEPTS

BALLOON PAYMENT LOAN

Consider a loan with the following terms: $80,000 at 8 percent interest, with only interest payable monthly and the loan fully repayable in 15 years. This is how to calculate the amount of the final balloon payment:

$80,000 × .08 = $6,400 annual interest
$6,400 annual interest ÷ 12 months = $533.33 monthly interest payment
$80,000 principal payment + $533.33 final month's interest
= $80,533.33 final balloon payment

The most popular FHA program is Title II, Section 203(b), fixed-interest rate loans for 10 years to 30 years on one-family to four-family residences. Rates are competitive with other types of loans, even though they are high-LTV loans. Certain technical requirements must be met before the FHA will insure the loans. These requirements include the following:

■ The borrower is charged a percentage of the loan as a premium for the FHA insurance. The *up-front premium* is paid at closing by the borrower or some other party. It also may be financed along with the total loan amount. The up-front premium is charged on all loans except those for the purchase of a condominium. All FHA loans will have the monthly premium charged. Insurance premiums vary for new loans, refinancing, and condominiums.

■ FHA regulations set standards for type and construction of buildings, quality of neighborhood, and credit requirements for borrowers.

■ The mortgaged real estate must be appraised by an *approved FHA appraiser*. The loan amount generally cannot exceed either of the following: (1) 98.75 percent for loans over $50,000 (for loans less than $50,000, the buyer must contribute 3 percent of the sales price to the down payment and closing cost) (1.25 percent down), or (2) 97.75 percent of the sales price or appraised value, for loans over $50,000 (2.25 percent down). If the purchase price exceeds the FHA-appraised value, the buyer may pay the difference in cash as part of the down payment. In addition, the FHA has set maximum loan amounts for various regions of the country. In all cases, the purchaser must contribute 3 percent of the sales price to the transaction, either in down payment or closing costs.

Other types of FHA loans are available, including one-year adjustable-rate mortgages, home improvement and rehabilitation loans, and loans for the purchase of condominiums. Specific standards for condominium complexes and the ratio of owner-occupants to renters must be met for a loan on a condominium unit to be financed through the FHA insurance programs.

Although lenders can charge interest until the next payment due date on an FHA payoff, lenders may not deny the assumption of the mortgage by a qualified buyer even if the interest rates have skyrocketed.

MATH CONCEPTS

DETERMINING LTV

If a property has an appraised value of $100,000, secured by a $90,000 loan, the LTV is 90 percent:

$90,000 ÷ $100,000 = 90%

IN PRACTICE

The FHA sets lending limits for single-unit and multiple-unit properties. The limits vary significantly, depending on the average cost of housing in different regions of the country. In addition, the FHA changes its regulations for various programs from time to time. Contact your local FHA office or mortgage lender for loan amounts in your area and for specific loan requirements, or visit www.hud.gov/offices/hsg/index.cfm.

WWWeb.Link

www.hud.gov/offices/hsg/index.cfm.

Prepayment privileges. A borrower may repay an FHA-insured loan on a one-family to four-family residence without penalty. For loans made *before* August 2, 1985, the borrower must give the lender written notice of intention to exercise the prepayment privilege at least 30 days before prepayment. If the borrower fails to provide the required notice, the lender has the option of charging up to 30 days' interest. For loans initiated *after* August 2, 1985, no written notice of prepayment is required.

Assumption rules. The assumption rules for FHA-insured loans vary, depending on the dates the loans were originated, as follows:

- FHA loans originating before December 1986, generally have no restrictions on their assumptions.
- For an FHA loan originating between December 1, 1986, and December 15, 1989, a creditworthiness review of the prospective assumer is required. If the original loan was for the purchase of a principal residence, this review is required during the first 12 months of the loan's existence. If the

original loan was for the purchase of an investment property, the review is required during the first 24 months of the loan.

■ For FHA loans originating on December 15, 1989, and later, no assumptions are permitted without complete buyer qualification.

WWWeb.Link

www.hud.gov/mortprog.html

Follow menu to Maximum Mortgage Limits.

Discount points. The lender of an FHA-insured loan may charge discount points in addition to a loan origination fee. The payment of points is a matter of negotiation between the seller and the buyer. However, if the seller pays more than 6 percent of the costs normally paid by the buyer (such as discount points, the loan origination fee, the mortgage insurance premium, buydown fees, prepaid items, and impound or escrow amounts), the lender will treat the payments as a reduction in sales price and recalculate the mortgage amount accordingly.

VA-Guaranteed Loans

The Department of Veterans Affairs (usually referred to simply as VA) is authorized to guarantee loans to purchase or construct homes for eligible veterans and their spouses (including unremarried spouses of veterans whose deaths were service-related). The VA also guarantees loans to purchase mobile homes and plots on which to place them. A veteran who meets any of the following time-in-service criteria is eligible for a VA loan:

■ 90 days of active service for veterans of World War II, the Korean War, the Vietnam conflict, and the Persian Gulf War

■ A minimum of 181 days of active service during interconflict periods between July 26, 1947, and September 6, 1980

■ Two full years of service during any peacetime period after September 7, 1980

■ Six or more years of continuous duty as a reservist in the Army, Navy, Air Force, Marine Corps, Coast Guard, or as a member of the Army or Air National Guard

The VA assists veterans in financing the purchase of homes with little or no down payments at market interest rates. The VA issues rules and regulations that set forth the qualifications, limitations and conditions under which a loan may be guaranteed.

Like the term *FHA loan*, *VA loan* is something of a misnomer. The VA does not normally lend money; it guarantees loans made by lending institutions approved by the agency. The term **VA loan** refers to a loan that is not made by the agency but is guaranteed by it.

There is no VA dollar limit on the amount of the loan a veteran can obtain; this is determined by the lender and qualification of the buyer. The VA limits the amount of the loan it will guarantee.

IN PRACTICE

The current VA loan guarantee maximum amount is $60,000. Typically, lenders will loan up to four times the veteran's available guarantee amount. The maximum loan now available to a qualified veteran, then, would be $240,000.

To determine what portion of a mortgage loan the VA will guarantee, the veteran must apply for a *certificate of eligibility*. This certificate does not mean that the veteran automatically receives a mortgage. It merely sets forth the maximum guarantee to which the veteran is entitled. For individuals with full eligibility, no down payment is required for a loan up to the maximum guarantee limit.

The VA also issues a *certificate of reasonable value* (CRV) for the property being purchased. The CRV states the property's current market value based on a VA-approved appraisal. The CRV places a ceiling on the amount of a VA loan allowed for the property. If the purchase price is greater than the amount cited in the CRV, the veteran may pay the difference in cash. The CRV is based on an appraisal. New VA regulations allow only one active VA loan at a time, and a veteran may own only two properties acquired using VA loan benefits. However, a veteran may use his or her VA benefits as many times as he or she chooses, as long as the previous benefit use has been paid.

The VA borrower pays a loan origination fee to the lender, as well as a funding fee (2 percent to 3 percent, depending on the down payment amount) to the Department of Veterans Affairs. The funding fee depends on whether it is first time use (2 percent) or a subsequent use (3 percent). Reservists and National Guard veterans pay higher funding fees. Reasonable discount points may be charged on a VA-guaranteed loan, and either the veteran or the seller may pay them.

Prepayment privileges. As with an FHA loan, the borrower under a VA loan can prepay the debt at any time without penalty.

Assumption rules. VA loans made before March 1, 1988, are freely assumable, although an assumption processing fee will be charged. The fee is usually $500. For loans made on or after March 1, 1988, the VA must approve the buyer and assumption agreement. The original veteran borrower remains personally liable for the repayment of the loan unless the VA approves a *release of liability*. The release of liability will be issued by the VA only if

■ the buyer assumes all of the veteran's liabilities on the loan and
■ the VA or the lender approves both the buyer and the assumption agreement.

A release also would be possible if another veteran used his or her own entitlement in assuming the loan.

IN PRACTICE

A release of liability issued by the VA does not release the veteran's liability to the lender. This must be obtained separately from the lender. Real estate licensees should contact their local mortgage lenders for specific requirements for obtaining or assuming VA-insured loans. The programs change from time to time.

WWWeb.Link

www.va.gov

Agricultural Loan Programs

The **Farm Service Agency (FSA),** formerly the *Farmers Home Administration*, is a federal agency of the Department of Agriculture. The FSA offers programs to help families purchase or operate family farms. Through the Rural Housing and Community Development Service (RHCDS), it also provides loans to help families purchase or improve single-family homes in rural areas (generally areas with populations of fewer than 10,000). Loans are made to low-income and moderate-income families, and the interest rate charged can be as low as 1 percent, depending on the borrower's income. The FSA provides assistance to rural and agricultural businesses and industry through the Rural Business and Cooperative Development Service (RBCDS).

FSA loan programs fall into two categories: guaranteed loans, made and serviced by private lenders and guaranteed for a specific percentage by the FSA, and loans made directly by the FSA.

The **Farm Credit System (System)** provides loans to more than a half million borrowers, including farmers, ranchers, rural homeowners, agricultural cooperatives, rural utility systems, and agribusinesses. Unlike commercial banks, system banks and associations do not take deposits. Instead, loanable funds are raised through the sale of Systemwide bonds and notes in the nation's capital markets.

 **WWWeb.Link**

www.fsa.usda.gov

Farmer Mac (formerly the *Federal Agricultural Mortgage Corporation*, or *FAMC*), is an agency that operates similarly to Fannie Mae and Freddie Mac in a context of agricultural loans. It provides a secondary market for farm loans by guaranteeing mortgage-backed securities based on pools of these loans. Farmer Mac pools or bundles agricultural loans from the original lenders and issues guaranteed mortgage-backed securities based on its own loan pools.

IN PRACTICE

In recent years, there have been many changes in all of the agricultural lending programs. Since 1994, the Farmer's Home Administration, the Rural Development Administration, the Rural Electrification Administration, and the Agricultural Cooperative Service have been combined into the USDA Rural Development Agency.

 **WWWeb.Link**

www.rurdev.usda.gov

■ OTHER FINANCING TECHNIQUES

Because borrowers often have different needs, a variety of other financing techniques have been created. Other techniques apply to various types of collateral.

The following pages consider some of the loans that do not fit into the categories previously discussed.

Purchase-Money Mortgages (PMMs)

A **purchase-money mortgage (PMM)** is a note and mortgage *created at the time of purchase*. Its purpose is to make the sale possible. The term is used in two ways. First, it may refer to any security instrument that originates at the time of sale. More often, it refers to the instrument given by the purchaser to a seller who takes back a note for part or all of the purchase price. The mortgage may be a first or a junior lien, depending on whether prior mortgage liens exist.

■ **FOR EXAMPLE** Ben wants to buy Brownacre for $200,000. Ben has a $40,000 down payment and agrees to assume an existing mortgage of $80,000. Because Ben might not qualify for a new mortgage under the circumstances, the owner agrees to take back a purchase-money second mortgage in the amount of $80,000. At the closing, Ben will execute a mortgage and note in favor of the owner, who will convey title to Ben.

Package Loans

A **package loan** includes not only the real estate, but also *all personal property and appliances installed on the premises*. In recent years, this kind of loan has been used extensively to finance furnished condominium units. Package loans usually include furniture, drapes, carpets, and the kitchen range, refrigerator, dishwasher, garbage disposal, washer, dryer, food freezer, and other appliances as part of the sales price of the home.

Blanket Loans

A **blanket loan** covers *more than one parcel or lot*. It is usually used to finance subdivision developments. However, it can finance the purchase of improved properties or consolidate loans as well. A blanket loan usually includes a provision known as a *partial release clause*. This clause permits the borrower to obtain the release of any one lot or parcel from the blanket lien by repaying a certain amount of the loan. The lender issues a partial release for each parcel released from the mortgage lien. The release form includes a provision that the lien will continue to cover all other unreleased lots.

Wraparound Loans

A **wraparound loan** enables a borrower with an existing mortgage or deed of trust loan to obtain additional financing from a second lender *without paying off the first loan*. The second lender gives the borrower a new, increased loan at a higher interest rate and assumes payment of the existing loan. The total amount of the new loan includes the existing loan as well as the additional funds needed by the borrower. The borrower makes payments to the new lender on the larger loan. The new lender makes payments on the original loan out of the borrower's payments.

A wraparound mortgage can be used to refinance real property or to finance the purchase of real property when an existing mortgage cannot be prepaid. The buyer executes a wraparound mortgage to the seller or lender, who collects payments on the new loan and continues to make payments on the old loan. It also can finance the sale of real estate when the buyer wishes to invest a minimum amount of initial cash. A wraparound loan is possible only if the original loan permits it. For instance, an acceleration and alienation or a due-on-sale clause in the original loan documents may prevent a sale under a wraparound loan.

IN PRACTICE
To protect themselves against a seller's default on a previous loan, buyers should require that protective clauses be included in any wraparound document to grant buyers the right to make payments directly to the original lender.

Open-End Loans

An **open-end loan** secures a *note* executed by the borrower to the lender. It also secures any future *advances* of funds made by the lender to the borrower. The interest rate on the initial amount borrowed is fixed, but interest on future advances may be charged at the market rate in effect. An open-end loan is often a less costly alternative to a home improvement loan. It allows the borrower to "open" the mortgage or deed of trust to increase the debt to its original amount, or the amount stated in the note, after the debt has been reduced by payments over a period of time. The mortgage usually states the maximum amount that can be secured, the terms and conditions under which the loan can be opened, and the provisions for repayment.

Construction Loans

A **construction loan** is made to *finance the construction of improvements* on real estate such as homes, apartments, and office buildings. The lender commits to the full amount of the loan but disburses the funds in payments during construction. These payments are also known as *draws*. Draws are made to the general contractor or the owner for that part of the construction work that has been completed since the previous payment. Before each payment, the lender inspects the work. The general contractor must provide the lender with adequate waivers that release all mechanic's lien rights for the work covered by the payment.

This kind of loan generally bears a higher-than-market interest rate because of the risks assumed by the lender. These risks include the inadequate releasing of mechanics' liens, possible delays in completing the construction, or the financial failure of the contractor or subcontractors. Construction loans are generally *short-term* or *interim financing*. The borrower pays interest only on the monies that have actually been disbursed. The borrower is expected to arrange for a permanent loan, also known as an *end loan* or *take-out loan*, that will repay or "take out" the construction financing lender when the work is completed. Some lenders now offer construction-to-permanent loans that become fixed mortgages upon completion. *Participation financing* is when a lender demands an equity position in the project as a requirement for the loan.

Sale-and-Leaseback

Sale-and-leaseback arrangements are used to finance large commercial or industrial properties. The land and building, usually used by the seller for business purposes, are sold to an investor. The real estate then is leased back by the investor to the seller, who continues to conduct business on the property as a tenant. The buyer becomes the lessor, and the original owner becomes the lessee. This enables a business to free money tied up in real estate to be used as working capital.

Sale-and-leaseback arrangements involve complicated legal procedures, and their success is usually related to the effects the transaction has on the firm's tax situation. Legal and tax experts should be involved in this type of transaction.

Buydowns

A **buydown** is a way to temporarily (or permanently) lower the interest rate on a mortgage or deed of trust loan. Perhaps a homebuilder wishes to stimulate sales by offering a lower-than-market rate. Or a first-time residential buyer may have trouble qualifying for a loan at the prevailing rates; relatives or the sellers might want to help the buyer qualify. In any case, a lump sum is paid in cash to the lender at the closing. The payment offsets (and so reduces) the interest rate and monthly payments during the mortgage's first few years. Typical buydown arrangements reduce the interest rate by 1 percent to 2 percent over the first one to two years of the loan term. After that, the rate rises. The assumption is that the borrower's income will also increase and that the borrower will be more able to absorb the increased monthly payments. In a permanent buydown, a larger upfront payment reduces the effective interest rate for the life of the loan.

Home Equity Loans

Using the equity buildup in a home to finance purchases is an alternative to refinancing. Home equity loans are a source of funds for homeowners to use for a variety of financial needs, including the following:

- To finance the purchase of expensive items
- To consolidate existing installment loans or credit card debt
- To pay medical, education, home improvement, or other expenses

The original mortgage loan remains in place; the home equity loan is junior to the original lien. If the homeowner completely refinances, the original mortgage loan and the home equity loan are paid off and replaced by a new loan. (This strategy is an alternative way to borrow the equity and is not really a home equity loan.)

A home equity loan can be taken out as a fixed loan amount or as an equity line of credit. With the home equity line of credit, the lender extends a line of credit that the borrower can use whenever he or she wants. The borrower receives the money by a check sent to him or her, by deposits made in a checking or savings account, or by a book of drafts the borrower can use up to his or her credit limit.

IN PRACTICE

The homeowner must consider a number of factors before deciding on a home equity loan, including

- the costs involved in obtaining a new mortgage loan or a home equity loan,
- current interest rates,
- total monthly payments, and
- income tax consequences.

Once the loan process has reached the point at which the borrowers' financial capability has been approved, the collateral's appraisal value is acceptable, and the legal title is clear, the loan is approved. At closing, a statement is prepared allocating credits and charges to the appropriate parties. Included in the prorations are loan interest, property taxes, insurance premiums, and rents and special assessments if applicable. Costs include points, placement fees, impound funds (escrows), mortgage insurance premium, credit report, appraisal fee, and escrow charges. After the final documents are signed and recorded, the monies are paid completing the process. (See Chapter 22.)

■ FINANCING LEGISLATION

The federal government regulates the lending practices of mortgage lenders through the Truth-in-Lending Act, the Equal Credit Opportunity Act, the Community Reinvestment Act of 1977, and the Real Estate Settlement Procedures Act.

Truth-in-Lending Act and Regulation Z

Regulation Z, which was promulgated pursuant to the **Truth-in-Lending** Act by the Federal Trade Commission (FTC), requires that credit institutions inform borrowers of the true cost of obtaining credit. Its purpose is to enable borrowers to compare the costs of various lenders and avoid the uninformed use of credit. Regulation Z applies when credit is extended to individuals for personal, familial or household uses. The amount of credit sought must be $25,000 or less. Regardless of the amount, however, *Regulation Z generally applies when a credit transaction is secured by a residence.* The regulation does *not* apply to business or commercial loans or to agricultural loans of more than $25,000. (So if an investor purchased a residential property for commercial purposes, Regulation Z would not apply.)

Under the Truth-in-Lending Act, a consumer must be fully informed of all finance charges and the true interest rate before a transaction is completed. The finance charge disclosure must include any loan fees, finder's fees, service charges and points, as well as interest. In the case of a mortgage loan made to finance the purchase of a dwelling, the lender must compute and disclose the *annual percentage rate* (APR). However, the lender does not have to indicate the total interest payable during the term of the loan. Also, the lender does not have to include actual costs such as title fees, legal fees, appraisal fees, credit reports, survey fees, and closing expenses as part of the finance charge. (See Chapter 22.)

Creditor. A *creditor,* for purposes of Regulation Z, is any person who extends consumer credit more than 25 times each year or more than 5 times each year if the transactions involve dwellings as security. The credit must be subject to a finance charge or payable in more than four installments by written agreement.

Three-day right of rescission. In the case of most consumer credit transactions covered by Regulation Z, the borrower has three days in which to rescind the transaction by merely notifying the lender. *This right of rescission does not apply to owner-occupied residential purchase-money or first mortgage or deed of trust loans.* It does, however, apply to refinancing a home mortgage or to a home equity loan. In an emergency, the right to rescind may be waived in writing to prevent a delay in funding.

Advertising. Regulation Z provides strict regulation of real estate advertisements (in all media, including newspapers, flyers, signs, billboards, Web sites, radio or television ads, and direct mailings) that refer to mortgage financing terms. General phrases like "liberal terms available" may be used, but if details are given, they must comply with the act. The annual percentage rate (APR)—which is calculated based on all charges rather than the interest rate alone—must be stated.

Advertisements for buydowns or reduced-interest rate mortgages must show both the limited term to which the interest rate applies and the annual percentage rate. If a variable-rate mortgage is advertised, the advertisement must include

- the number and timing of payments,
- the amount of the largest and smallest payments, and
- a statement of the fact that the actual payments will vary between these two extremes.

Specific credit terms, such as down payment, monthly payment, dollar amount of the finance charge, or term of the loan, are referred to as **trigger terms,** and may not be advertised unless the advertisement includes the following information:

- Cash price
- Required down payment
- Number, amounts, and due dates of all payments
- Annual percentage rate
- Total of all payments to be made over the term of the mortgage (unless the advertised credit refers to a first mortgage or deed of trust to finance the acquisition of a dwelling)

Penalties. Regulation Z provides penalties for noncompliance. The penalty for violation of an administrative order enforcing Regulation Z is $10,000 for each day the violation continues. A fine of up to $10,000 may be imposed for engaging in an unfair or a deceptive practice. In addition, a creditor may be liable to a consumer for twice the amount of the finance charge, for a minimum of $100 and a maximum of $1,000, plus court costs, attorney's fees, and any actual damages. Willful violation is a misdemeanor punishable by a fine of up to $5,000, one year's imprisonment, or both.

Equal Credit Opportunity Act

The federal **Equal Credit Opportunity Act (ECOA)** prohibits lenders and others who grant or arrange credit to consumers from discriminating against credit applicants on the basis of

- race,
- color,
- religion,
- national origin,
- sex,
- marital status,
- age (provided the applicant is of legal age), or
- dependence on public assistance.

In addition, lenders and other creditors must inform all rejected credit applicants of the principal reasons for the denial or termination of credit. The notice must be provided in writing, within 30 days. The federal ECOA also provides that a borrower is entitled to a copy of the appraisal report if the borrower paid for the appraisal.

Community Reinvestment Act of 1977 (CRA)

Community reinvestment refers to the responsibility of financial institutions to help meet their communities' needs for low-income and moderate-income housing. In 1977, Congress passed the **Community Reinvestment Act of 1977 (CRA).** Under the CRA, financial institutions are expected to meet the deposit and credit needs of their communities; participate and invest in local community development and rehabilitation projects; and participate in loan programs for housing, small businesses, and small farms.

The law requires any federally supervised financial institution to prepare a statement containing

- a definition of the geographic boundaries of its community;
- an identification of the types of community reinvestment credit offered, such as residential housing loans, housing rehabilitation loans, small-business loans, commercial loans, and consumer loans; and
- comments from the public about the institution's performance in meeting its community's needs.

Financial institutions are periodically reviewed by one of four federal financial supervisory agencies: the Comptroller of the Currency, the Federal Reserve's Board of Governors, the Federal Deposit Insurance Corporation, or the Office of Thrift Supervision. The institutions must post a public notice that their community reinvestment activities are subject to federal review, and they must make the results of these reviews public.

Real Estate Settlement Procedures Act

The federal Real Estate Settlement Procedures Act (RESPA) applies to any residential real estate transaction involving a new first mortgage loan. RESPA is designed to ensure that buyer and seller are both fully informed of all settlement costs. This important federal law is discussed in detail in Chapter 22.

■ COMPUTERIZED LOAN ORIGINATION AND AUTOMATED UNDERWRITING

A **computerized loan origination (CLO)** system is an electronic network for handling loan applications through remote computer terminals linked to several lenders' computers. With a CLO system, a real estate broker or salesperson can call up a menu of mortgage lenders, interest rates, and loan terms, then help a buyer select a lender and apply for a loan right from the brokerage office.

The licensee may assist the applicant in answering the on-screen questions and in understanding the services offered. The broker in whose office the terminal is located may earn fees of up to one half point of the loan amount. The *borrower,* not the mortgage broker or lender, *must pay the fee.* The fee amount may be financed, however. While multiple lenders may be represented on an office's CLO computer, consumers must be informed that other lenders are available. An applicant's ability to comparison shop for a loan may be enhanced by a CLO system; the range of options may not be limited. One-stop shopping real estate services and federal regulation pertaining to CLOs are discussed in Chapter 22.

On the lenders' side, new automated underwriting procedures can shorten loan approvals from weeks to minutes. Automated underwriting also tends to lower the cost of loan application and approval by reducing lenders' time spent on the approval process by as much as 60 percent. Freddie Mac uses a system called *Loan Prospector*. Fannie Mae has a system called *Desktop Underwriter* that reduces approval time to minutes, based on the borrower's credit report, a paycheck stub, and a drive-by appraisal of the property. Complex or difficult mortgages can be processed in less than 72 hours. Through automated underwriting, one of a borrower's biggest headaches in buying a home—waiting for loan approval—is eliminated. In addition, a prospective buyer can strengthen his or her purchase offer by including proof of loan approval.

Scoring and Automated Underwriting. Lenders have been using credit scoring systems to predict prospective borrowers' likelihood of default for many years. When used as a part of traditional "manual" evaluation of applicants, credit scoring provides a useful objective standard against which to balance the loan officer's more subjective professional judgment. When used in automated underwriting systems, however, the application of credit scores has become somewhat controversial. Critics of scoring are concerned that they may not be accurate or fair, and, in the absence of human discretion, could result in making it more difficult for low-income and minority borrowers to obtain mortgages.

Here's what Freddie Mac has to say:

> Whether using traditional or automated methods, underwriters must consider all three areas of underwriting—collateral, credit reputation, and capacity. When reviewing collateral, underwriters look at house value, down payment, and property type. Income, debt, cash reserves, and product type are considered when underwriters are looking at capacity. Credit scores are simply one consideration when underwriters are reviewing credit reputation. Even lenders who use an automated underwriting system such as *Loan Prospector*, still rely on human judgment when the scoring system indicates that the loan application is a higher risk.

IN PRACTICE   Recently, Fannie Mae and Freddie Mac have committed themselves to moving away from credit scoring in favor of their own underwriting criteria. Computerized origination systems have become more sophisticated and are making this possible.

■ SUMMARY

The federal government affects real estate financing money and interest rates through the Federal Reserve Board's discount rate and reserve requirements; it also participates in the secondary mortgage market. The secondary market is generally composed of the investors who ultimately purchase and hold the loans as investments. These include insurance companies, investment funds, and pension plans.

Types of loans include fully amortized and straight loans as well as adjustable-rate mortgages, growing-equity mortgages, balloon payment mortgages, and reverse-annuity mortgages.

Many mortgage and deed of trust loan programs exist, including conventional loans and those insured by the FHA or private mortgage insurance companies or guaranteed by the VA. FHA and VA loans must meet certain requirements for the borrower to obtain the benefits of government backing, which induces the lender to lend its funds. In certain market conditions the interest rates for these loans may be lower than those charged for conventional loans. Lenders may also charge points.

Other types of real estate financing include seller-financed purchase-money mortgages or deeds of trust, blanket mortgages, package mortgages, wraparound mortgages, open-end mortgages, construction loans, sale-and-leaseback agreements, and home equity loans.

Regulation Z, implementing the federal Truth-in-Lending Act, requires that lenders inform prospective borrowers who use their homes as security for credit of all finance charges involved in such loans. Severe penalties are provided for noncompliance. The federal Equal Credit Opportunity Act prohibits creditors from discriminating against credit applicants on the basis of race, color, religion, national origin, sex, marital status, age, or dependence on public assistance. The Real Estate Settlement Procedures Act requires that lenders inform both buyers and sellers in advance of all fees and charges required for the settlement or closing of residential real estate transactions.

QUESTIONS

1. The buyers purchased a residence for $95,000. They made a down payment of $15,000 and agreed to assume the seller's existing mortgage, which had a current balance of $23,000. The buyers financed the remaining $57,000 of the purchase price by executing a mortgage and note to the seller. This type of loan, by which the seller becomes the mortgagee, is called a

   a. wraparound mortgage.
   b. package mortgage.
   c. balloon note.
   d. purchase-money mortgage.

2. A buyer purchased a new residence for $175,000. The buyer made a down payment of $15,000 and obtained a $160,000 mortgage loan. The builder of the house paid the lender 3 percent of the loan balance for the first year and 2 percent for the second year. This represented a total savings for the buyer of $8,000. What type of mortgage arrangement is this?

   a. Wraparound
   b. Package
   c. Blanket
   d. Buydown

3. Which of the following is *not* a participant in the secondary market?

   a. Fannie Mae
   b. Ginnie Mae
   c. Lender Marc
   d. Freddie Mac

4. Fran purchased her home for cash 30 years ago. Today Fran receives monthly checks from a mortgage lender that supplement her retirement income. Fran most likely has obtained a(n)

   a. shared-appreciation mortgage.
   b. adjustable-rate mortgage.
   c. reverse-annuity mortgage.
   d. overriding deed of trust.

5. If buyers seek a mortgage on a single-family house, they would be least likely to obtain the mortgage from a

   a. mutual savings bank.
   b. life insurance company.
   c. credit union.
   d. commercial bank.

6. Which of the following characteristics is true of a fixed-rate home loan that is amortized according to the original payment schedule?

   a. The amount of interest to be paid is predetermined.
   b. The loan cannot be sold in the secondary market.
   c. The monthly payment amount will fluctuate each month.
   d. The interest rate change may be based on an index.

7. When the Federal Reserve Board raises its discount rate, all of the following are likely to happen *EXCEPT*

   a. buyer's points will increase.
   b. interest rates will fall.
   c. mortgage money will become scarce.
   d. the percentage of ARM's will increase.

8. In a loan that requires periodic payments that do not fully amortize the loan balance by the final payment, what term best describes the final payment?

   a. Adjustment   c. Balloon
   b. Acceleration   d. Variable

9. A developer received a loan that covers five parcels of real estate and provides for the release of the mortgage lien on each parcel when certain payments are made on the loan. This type of loan arrangement is called a

   a. purchase-money loan.
   b. blanket loan.
   c. package loan.
   d. wraparound loan.

10. Funds for Federal Housing Administration (FHA) loans are usually provided by

   a. the FHA.
   b. the Federal Reserve.
   c. qualified lenders.
   d. the seller.

11. The provisions of the Truth-in-Lending Act (Regulation Z) do not require which of the following to be disclosed to a residential buyer?

a. Discount points
b. The real estate brokerage commission
c. A loan origination fee
d. The loan interest rate

12. A home is purchased using a fixed-rate, fully amortized mortgage loan. Which of the following statements is true regarding this mortgage?

a. A balloon payment will be made at the end of the loan.
b. Each mortgage payment amount is the same.
c. Each mortgage payment reduces the principal by the same amount.
d. The principal amount in each payment is greater than the interest amount.

13. Which of the following *best* describes participants in the secondary market?

a. Lenders who deal exclusively in second mortgages
b. Institutional investors who buy and sell loans
c. The major lender of residential mortgages and deeds of trust
d. Institutional investors who supply money for FHA and VA loans

14. Which of the following is a correct statement about interest on a fully amortized mortgage or deed of trust loan?

a. Interest may be paid in arrears, that is, at the end of each period for which it is earned.
b. The interest portion of each payment increases throughout the term of the loan.
c. Only interest is paid each period.
d. The final interest payment will be determined after the last payment is made.

15. The primary activity of Freddie Mac is to

a. guarantee mortgages with the full faith and credit of the federal government.
b. buy and pool blocks of conventional mortgages and sell bonds that use them as security.
c. act in tandem with GNMA to provide special assistance in times of tight money.
d. buy and sell VA and FHA mortgages.

16. The federal Equal Credit Opportunity Act allows lenders to discriminate against potential borrowers on the basis of

a. race.
b. sex.
c. dependence on public assistance.
d. amount of income.

17. A borrower obtains a $100,000 mortgage loan for 30 years at 7 ½ percent interest. If the monthly payments of $699 are credited first to interest and then to principal, what will be the balance of the principal after the borrower makes the first payment?

a. $99,723.00   c. $99,097.32
b. $99,926.00   d. $100,000.00

18. Using Table 15.2 on page 243, what is the monthly interest rate factor required to amortize a loan at 8 ⅛ percent over a term of 25 years?

a. 7.72   c. 7.89
b. 7.81   d. 8.06

19. Using Table 15.2 on page 243, calculate the principal and interest payment necessary to amortize a loan of $135,000 at 7 ¾ percent interest over 15 years.

a. $1,111.85   c. $1,279.80
b. $1,270.35   d. $1,639.16

20. Hal borrowed $85,000, to be repaid in monthly installments of $823.76 at 11 ½ percent annual interest. How much of Hal's first month's payment was applied to reducing the principal amount of the loan?

a. $8.15   c. $91.80
b. $9.18   d. $814.58

21. If a lender agrees to make a loan based on an 80 percent LTV, what is the amount of the loan if the property appraises for $114,500 and the sales price is $116,900?

a. $83,200   c. $91,600
b. $91,300   d. $92,900

22. For a lender, income on the loan is realized from loan origination fees, discount points, and which of the following?

a. Recurring interest income
b. Investment groups
c. The discount rate
d. Amortization

23. In which of the following types of loans is the loan amount divided into two parts, to be paid off separately by periodic interest payments followed by payment of the principal in full at the end of the term?

a. Amortized
b. Straight
c. ARM
d. GEM

24. In an adjustable-rate mortgage, the interest rate is tied to an objective economic indicator called a(n)

a. mortgage factor.
b. discount rate.
c. index.
d. reserve requirement.

25. In determining the LTV ratio, the V (value) is

a. 80 percent of the sale price or less.
b. 95 percent of the appraised value.
c. appraised value or price, whichever is more.
d. price or appraised value, whichever is less.

CHAPTER SIXTEEN

16

LEASES

■ **LEARNING OBJECTIVES** *When you've finished reading this Chapter, you should be able to:*

- **identify** the four types of leasehold estates.

- **describe** the requirements and general conditions of a valid lease and how a lease may be discharged.

- **explain** the rights of landlords and tenants in an eviction proceeding and the effect of protenant legislation and civil rights laws on the landlord-tenant relationship.

- **distinguish** the various types of leases.

- **define** the following *key terms:*

actual eviction	gross lease	month-to-month tenancy
assignment	ground lease	net lease
cash rent	holdover tenancy	percentage lease
constructive eviction	lease	reversionary right
estate at sufferance	leasehold estate	security deposit
estate at will	lease purchase	sharecropping
estate for years	lessee	sublease
estate from period to period	lessor	

■ **WHY LEARN ABOUT...** LEASES?

According to the U.S. Bureau of the Census, 66 percent of Americans own their own homes. That means about a third of the population are renters. In the year 2000, there were more than 35 million renter-occupied housing units in the United States. In short, there are a lot of renters and a lot of rental housing, which together means there is a very large rental market. And many of those renters seek the advice of rental agents, who are required to be real estate licensees in most states. Even if you aren't a rental agent, a knowledge of the rental market and leases and landlord-tenant issues may prove valuable if your potential buyers turn out not to qualify for a home purchase and need help finding an apartment. ■

■ LEASING REAL ESTATE

A **lease** is a contract between an owner of real estate (the **lessor**) and a tenant (the **lessee**). It is a contract to transfer the lessor's rights to exclusive possession and use of the property to the tenant for a specified period of time. The lease establishes the length of time the contract is to run and the amount the lessee is to pay for use of the property. Other rights and obligations of the parties are set forth as well.

In effect, the lease agreement combines two contracts. It is a conveyance of an interest in the real estate and a contract to pay rent and assume other obligations. The lessor grants the lessee the right to occupy the real estate and use it for purposes stated in the lease. In return, the landlord receives payment for use of the premises and retains a **reversionary right** to possession after the lease term expires. The lessor's interest is called a *leased fee estate plus reversionary right*.

The statute of frauds in most states requires lease agreements for more than one year be in writing to be enforceable. If the lease cannot be performed within one year of being entered into, the statute of frauds also requires a written document. In general, oral leases for one year or less that can be performed within a year of their making are enforceable. Written leases should be signed by both the lessor and lessee.

IN PRACTICE   Even though an oral lease may be enforceable, such as a lease for one year commencing the day of agreement, it is always better practice to put lease agreements in writing. A written lease provides concrete evidence of the terms and conditions to which the parties have agreed. Any written agreement should be signed by both the landlord and tenant.

■ LEASEHOLD ESTATES

A tenant's right to possess real estate for the term of the lease is called a **leasehold (less-than-freehold) estate.** A leasehold is generally considered personal

FIGURE 16.1

Leasehold Estates

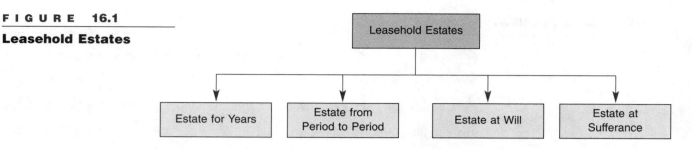

property. When the tenant assumes many of the landowner's obligations under a lease for life or for more than 99 years, certain states give the tenant some of the benefits and privileges of ownership.

Just as there are several types of freehold (ownership) estates, there are different kinds of leasehold estates. (See Figure 16.1.)

Estate for Years

An **estate** (tenancy) **for years** is a leasehold estate that continues for a *definite period of time*. That period may be years, months, weeks, or even days. An estate for years (sometimes referred to as an *estate for term*) always has specific starting and ending dates. When the estate expires, the lessee is required to vacate the premises and surrender possession to the lessor. *No notice is required to terminate the estate for years.* This is because the lease agreement states a specific expiration date. When the date comes, the lease expires, and the tenant's rights are extinguished.

> **Estate (or tenancy) for years** = *Any definite period*

If both parties agree, the lease for years may be terminated before the expiration date. Otherwise, neither party may terminate without showing that the lease agreement has been breached. Any extension of the tenancy requires that a new contract be negotiated.

As is characteristic of all leases, a tenancy for years gives the lessee the right to occupy and use the leased property according to the terms and covenants contained in the lease agreement. It must be remembered that a lessee has the right to use the premises for the entire lease term. That right is unaffected by the original lessor's death or sale of the property unless the lease states otherwise. If the original lease provides for an option to renew, no further negotiation is required; the tenant merely exercises his or her option.

Estate from Period to Period

An **estate from period to period,** or *periodic tenancy*, is created when the landlord and tenant enter into an agreement *for an indefinite time*, that is, the lease does not contain a specific expiration date. Such a tenancy is created initially to run for a definite amount of time—for instance, month to month, week to week, or year to year—but continues indefinitely until proper notice of termination is given. Rent is payable at definite intervals. A periodic tenancy is characterized by *continuity* because it is automatically renewable under the original terms of the agreement until one of the parties gives notice to terminate. In effect, the payment and acceptance of rent extend the lease for another period. A **month-to-month tenancy,** for example, is created when a tenant takes possession with no definite termination date and pays monthly rent. Periodic tenancy is commonly used in residential leases.

Estate from period to period (periodic tenancy) = *Indefinite term; automatically renewing*

If the original agreement provides for the conversion from an estate for years to a periodic tenancy, no negotiations are necessary; the tenant simply exercises his or her option.

An estate from period to period also might be created when a tenant with an estate for years remains in possession, or holds over, after the lease term expires. If no new lease agreement has been made, a **holdover tenancy** is created. The landlord may evict the tenant or treat the holdover tenant as one who holds a periodic tenancy. The landlord's acceptance of rent usually is considered conclusive proof of acceptance of the periodic tenancy. The courts customarily rule that a tenant who holds over can do so for a term equal to the term of the original lease, provided the period is for one year or less. For example, a tenant with a lease for six months would be entitled to a new six-month tenancy. However, if the original lease were for five years, the holdover tenancy could not exceed one year. Some leases stipulate that in the absence of a renewal agreement, a tenant who holds over does so as a month-to-month tenant. In some states, a holdover tenancy is considered a tenancy at will (discussed below).

To *terminate* a periodic estate, either the landlord or the tenant must *give proper notice*. The form and timing of the notice are usually established by state statute. Normally, the notice must be given *one period in advance*, that is, to terminate an estate from week to week, one week's notice is required; to terminate an estate from month to month, one month's notice is required. For an estate from year to year, however, the requirements vary from two months' to six months' notice.

Estate at Will

Estate (tenancy) at will = *Indefinite term; possession with landlord's consent*

An **estate** (tenancy) **at will** gives the tenant the right to possess property *with the landlord's consent* for an unspecified or uncertain term. An estate at will is a tenancy of indefinite duration. It continues until it is terminated by either party's giving proper notice. No definite initial period is specified, as is the case in a periodic tenancy. An estate at will is automatically terminated by the death of either the landlord or the tenant. It may be created by express agreement or by operation of law. During the existence of a tenancy at will, the tenant has all the rights and obligations of a lessor-lessee relationship, including the duty to pay rent at regular intervals.

As a practical matter, tenancy at will is rarely used in a written agreement and is viewed skeptically by the courts. It is usually interpreted as a periodic tenancy, with the period being defined by the interval of rental payments.

Estate at Sufferance

Estate (tenancy) at sufferance = *Tenant's previously lawful possession continued without landlord's consent*

An **estate** (tenancy) **at sufferance** arises when a tenant who lawfully possessed real property continues in possession of the premises *without the landlord's consent* after the rights expire. This estate can arise when a tenant for years fails to surrender possession at the lease's expiration. A tenancy at sufferance can also occur by operation of law when a borrower continues in possession after a foreclosure sale and beyond the redemption period's expiration.

When a tenant fails to surrender possession, or "holds over," one of two things happen. The first possibility is that the landlord accepts rent offered by the tenant and a periodic tenancy is created. The second possibility is that the landlord doesn't consent to the "holdover" and a tenancy in sufferance is created. In this latter situation, the tenant is evicted.

■ LEASE AGREEMENTS

Most states require no special wording to establish the landlord-tenant relationship. The lease may be written, oral, or implied, depending on the circumstances and the requirements of the statute of frauds. The law of the state where the real estate is located must be followed to ensure the validity of the lease. Figure 16.2 is an example of a typical residential lease.

Requirements of a Valid Lease

A lease is a form of contract. To be valid, a lease must meet essentially the same requirements as any other contract:

- *Capacity to contract.* The parties must have the legal capacity to contract.
- *Legal objectives.* The objectives of the lease must be legal.
- *Offer and acceptance.* The parties must reach a mutual agreement on all the terms of the contract.
- *Consideration.* The lease must be supported by valid consideration. Rent is the normal consideration given for the right to occupy the leased premises. However, the payment of rent is not essential as long as consideration was granted in creating the lease itself. Sometimes, for instance, this consideration is labor performed on the property. Because a lease is a contract, it is not subject to subsequent changes in the rent or other terms unless these changes are in writing and executed in the same manner as the original lease.

The elements of a **valid lease** can be remembered by the acronym **CLOAC:** Capacity, Legal objectives, Offer and Acceptance, and Consideration.

The leased premises should be clearly described. The legal description of the real estate should be used if the lease covers land, such as a ground lease. If the lease is for a part of a building, such as an apartment, the space itself or the apartment designation should be described specifically. If supplemental space is to be included, the lease should clearly identify it.

IN PRACTICE

Preprinted lease agreements are usually better suited to residential leases. Commercial leases are generally more complex, have different legal requirements, and may include complicated calculations of rent and maintenance costs. Drafting a commercial lease—or a complex residential lease, for that matter—may constitute the practice of law. Unless the real estate licensee is also an attorney, legal counsel should be sought.

Possession of Premises

The lessor, as the owner of the real estate, is usually bound by the implied *covenant of quiet enjoyment*. Quiet enjoyment does not have anything to do with barking dogs or late-night motorcycles. The covenant of quiet enjoyment is a presumed promise by the lessor that the lessee may take possession of the premises. The landlord further guarantees that he or she will not interfere in the tenant's possession or use of the property.

The lease may allow the landlord to enter the property to perform maintenance, to make repairs, or for other stated purposes. The tenant's permission is usually required and may be stipulated in the lease.

FIGURE 16.2

F I G U R E   16.2

**Sample Residential
Lease**

RESIDENTIAL LEASE

DATE OF LEASE	LEASE TERM		RENT PER MONTH	SECURITY DEPOSIT
	BEGINNING DATE	ENDING DATE		

THIS RESIDENTIAL LEASE AGREEMENT ("Lease") is made between the following parties:

NAME:_____   NAME:_____

ADDRESS OF   *BUSINESS*
PREMISES: *ADDRESS:*
                    "LESSEE"   **"LESSOR"**

SECTION ONE. RENT

1. Lessee will pay Lessor (or Lessor's authorized agent) the amount of _____Dollars ($_____) per month, in advance, as monthly rental for the Premises for the term of this Lease. Total rental for the initial term of this Lease shall be _____Dollars. Lessee's first monthly rental payment is due on or before _____, 19___, and each subsequent payment will be due on the _____ day of each month following for the term of this Lease. Payments will be made at the Lessor's address as stated in this Lease, or at any other address Lessor may specify in writing to Lessee.

2. Installments of rent that are not received by Lessor as required by this Lease are considered late. Late payment of rent constitutes default under the terms of this lease. If full payment is not received by the Lessor within _____ days of the date of default, Lessee agrees to pay to Lessor an administrative fee of _____Dollars ($_____). Lessee will pay Lessor a charge of _____Dollars ($_____) for any check returned to Lessor for insufficient funds. Lessor may require that any rent payment be made in the form of a certified check, money order or cashier's check.

3. Failure by Lessee to make any payment of rent, or any other fee or charge, under this Lease constitutes a default. In the event that Lessee fails to make any payment within _____ days after receiving written notice of Lessor's intention to terminate this Lease, Lessor may terminate this Lease and any and all unpaid rent for the full remaining term of this Lease shall then become due and payable. In the event of termination, Lessor shall be entitled to:
    A. Immediate possession of the Premises.
    B. Immediate payment of any unpaid rent or other charges.
    C. Recovery of any damages incurred due to Lessee's default, including but not limited
        to the cost of reletting the Premises, lost rental under this Lease and the cost of collections.
    D. Court costs and reasonable attorney's fees as permitted by law, arising due to Lessee's default.
    E. Any other remedy as provided by the law of the State of _____.

4. Lessor's rights and duties under the terms of this Lease are cumulative, and the exercise of any one or more of them does not prohibit Lessor from the exercise or use of any other right or remedy provided by this Lease or by law.

SECTION TWO. SECURITY DEPOSIT

1. Lessee has paid Lessor a Security Deposit in the amount of _____Dollars ($_____) as set forth above, to secure his or her performance of all the covenants, agreements and terms of this Lease. The Security Deposit is subject to the following conditions:

    A. Lessor may use, apply or retain any or all of the amount of the Security Deposit for the payment of any rent due from Lessee; for any administrative, maintenance or other charges set forth in this Lease; any damages or expenses incurred by Lessor arising from Lessee's failure to comply with any of the terms of this Lease (including but not limited to expenses incurred in reletting the Premises).

    B. If, during the term (or any extension of the term) of this Lease, Lessor is obligated to use all or any part of the Security Deposit in accordance with the terms and conditions of this Lease or any other law or agreement, Lessor shall notify Lessor of the expenditure, in writing, within _____ days of its being incurred, and provide along with such notice an itemized list of the charges and expenses, including the reasonable cost of Lessor's own time and labor. Lessee shall have _____ days in which to deposit with Lessor a sum equal to the amount used, to ensure that the full amount of the Security Deposit is maintained with the Lessor at all times during the term of this Lease.

    C. The use of all or any part of the Security Deposit by Lessor shall not be Lessor's sole remedy in the event of Lessee's default. If the costs of Lessor's expenses and/or damages incurred exceed the total amount of the Security Deposit, Lessee shall pay any excess. LESSEE MAY NOT APPLY THE SECURITY DEPOSIT AS RENT.

    E. During the term of this Lease, and during any extensions of this Lease agreement, the Security Deposit shall be held in a/an:☐ interest-bearing ☐ non-interest-bearing [*check one*] account. *Parties initial here:* _____ _____

    F. When Lessee has performed all obligations required under this Lease, has paid all rent and any other charges, and has surrendered the Premises, its keys, passes and any other documents or fixtures in the same condition as they were provided at the beginning of the term of this Lease, reasonable wear and tear excepted, Lessor shall return to Lessee any remaining amount of the Security Deposit, together with a fully itemized list of all charges deducted from it, with documentation, within _____ days of the termination of this Lease and the surrender of the Premises.

    G. In the event Lessor's interest in the Premises are sold, transferred or assigned, Lessor shall notify Lessee of the change in ownership and the name and business address of the new lessor. Lessor shall transfer the Security Deposit to the new lessor or owner and be released from all liability to Lessee.

**Sample Residential
Lease (cont'd)**

SECTION THREE. TERM OF LEASE AND EXTENSIONS

The term of this Lease shall be _____ year(s). This Lease will be automatically extended on a month to month basis, on the same terms and conditions as agreed to in this Lease, unless either party gives the other _____ days written notice of his or her intent not to extend the Lease at the end of the term. In the event that this Lease is extended, _____ days prior notice shall be required to terminate it. Such notice must be received by the non-terminating party no later than the _____ day of the month, and Lessee's tenancy shall terminate on the last day of that month.

SECTION FOUR. CONDITION OF PREMISES

Lessee has examined the condition of the Premises, and acknowledges that the Premises are received in good condition and repair except as otherwise specified in this Lease. Lessee is responsible for all day-to-day maintenance of the Premises as defined in the Rules and Regulations, including maintaining all devices and appliances in working order.

SECTION FIVE. USE OF PREMISES

1. The Premises are leased to Lessee exclusively, and shall be used strictly as a residence and for no other purpose. The Premises shall be occupied only by Lessee and any children born to, adopted by or placed under Lessee's legal care and/or guardianship. A violation of any condition of this lease by any guest of Lessee shall be construed as a violation by Lessee.

2. The Premises may not be assigned or sublet by Lessee without the prior written consent of Lessor. Lessee shall not undertake any modification or structural change to the Premises without the written consent of Lessor.

3. Lessee shall not use or allow the Premises to be used for any unlawful or disorderly purpose. The Premises may not be used in any way that represents a material detriment to the health or safety of others. Lessee shall comply with all applicable laws and any Rules and Regulations established by Lessor. Lessee shall be provided with a printed copy of the applicable Rules and Regulations at the time this Lease is signed. Lessor has the right to immediately terminate this lease based on any such violation.

SECTION SIX. ACCESS

Lessee shall permit Lessor, or Lessor's duly authorized agent or representatives, unrestricted access to the Premises at all reasonable times for any necessary purpose, including but not limited to inspection, maintenance and exhibition.

SECTION SEVEN. PETS

No pets of any kind may be kept in or around the Premises for any purpose. This provision does not apply to companion animals trained and certified to assist a person with a disability.

SECTION EIGHT. UTILITIES AND MAINTENANCE

1. Lessor will ensure that hot and cold running water are supplied to the Premises for Lessee's use at all times. Lessor will provide reasonable heating of the Premises at all times between the months of _____ and _____, as required by law. Lessor shall provide reasonable air conditioning to the Premises between the months of _____ and _____, or as provided by law. Lessor shall not be responsible to Lessee for any failure to provide water, heat or air conditioning due to causes beyond Lessor's control or for periods when any necessary systems are under repair.

2. Lessor covenants to maintain the Premises and all grounds and public areas appurtenant to the Premises, in good repair and tenantable condition. Lessor certifies that the Premises contains all smoke detectors and other devices required by law, and that all such detectors or other devices are in good working order. Lessee is responsible for maintaining such systems.

4. Should the Premises be damaged by fire or other casualty, Lessor may either (A) repair the damage within a reasonable time, not to exceed _____ days from the date Lessor is notified in writing of such damage, or (B) terminate this Lease by providing Lessee with written notice. Should such fire or other casualty impair Lessee's occupancy, Lessee may vacate the premises and provide Lessor with written notice, within _____ days of so vacating, of the intent to terminate this Lease. Such termination will be without penalty to Lessee. If such damage is caused by Lessee's own fault or negligence, or that of Lessee's agents, guests, visitors, servants or licensees, Lessee shall continue to be liable for all rent and charges during the remaining unexpired term of this Lease unless specifically released by Lessor.

SECTION NINE. SUBORDINATION, SEVERABILITY AND LAW

1. This Lease is subordinate to all mortgages, deeds of trust or other instruments now or later affecting the Premises.

2. If any provision of this Lease is or should become prohibited under any law, that provision shall be made ineffective, without invalidating any remaining provisions. The governing law of the jurisdiction in which the Premises are located is incorporated into and supersedes this Lease by reference, and the parties agree to be bound by such law.

SECTION TEN. MISCELLANEOUS

The words "Lessor" and "Lessee," as used in this Lease, are construed as including more than one lessor. All terms and conditions of this Lease are binding on and may be enforced by the parties, their heirs, assigns, executors, administrators and successors. This Lease represents the entire agreement between Lessor and Lessee. Neither party is bound by any representations made by any party that are not included in this Lease, except that the Rules and Regulations of the Premises and Lessee's Application are included by reference.

ADDITIONAL COVENANTS, TERMS, CONDITIONS AND AGREEMENTS: [*if none, write "NONE"*]

LESSEE:_____(SEAL)   LESSOR:_____(SEAL)

Date: _____   Date: _____

If the premises are occupied by a holdover tenant or an adverse claimant at the beginning of the new lease period, most states require the landlord to take whatever measures are necessary to recover actual possession. In a few states, however, the landlord is bound only to give the tenant the right of possession; it is the tenant who must bring a court action to secure actual possession.

Use of Premises

A lessor may restrict a lessee's use of the premises through provisions included in the lease. Use restrictions are particularly common in leases for stores or commercial space. For example, a lease may provide that the leased premises are to be used "only as a real estate office *and for no other purpose.*" In the absence of such clear limitations, a lessee may use the premises for any *lawful* purpose.

Term of Lease

The term of a lease is the period for which the lease will run. It should be stated precisely, including the beginning and ending dates, together with a statement of the total period of the lease. For instance, a lease might run "for a term of 30 years beginning June 1, 2000, and end May 31, 2030." A perpetual lease for an inordinate amount of time or an indefinite term usually will be ruled invalid. However, if the language of the lease and the surrounding circumstances clearly indicate that the parties intended such a term, the lease will be binding on the parties. Some states prohibit leases that run for 100 years or more.

Security Deposit

Most leases require that the tenant provide some form of **security deposit** to be held by the landlord during the lease term. If the tenant defaults on payment of rent or destroys the premises, the lessor may keep all or part of the deposit to compensate for the loss. Some state laws set maximum amounts for security deposits and specify how they must be handled. Some prohibit security deposits from being used for both nonpayment of rent and property damage. Some require that lessees receive annual interest on their security deposits.

Other safeguards against nonpayment of rent may include advancing the rental payment, contracting for a lien on the tenant's property, or requiring the tenant to have a third person guarantee payment.

IN PRACTICE

A lease should specify whether a payment is a security deposit or an advance rental. If it is a security deposit, the tenant is usually not entitled to apply it to the final month's rent. If it is an advance rental, the landlord must treat it as income for tax purposes.

Improvements

Neither the landlord nor the tenant is required to make any improvements to the leased property. The tenant may, however, make improvements with the landlord's permission. Any alterations generally become the landlord's property; that is, they become fixtures. However, the lease may give the tenant the right to install trade fixtures. Trade fixtures may be removed before the lease expires, provided the tenant restores the premises to their previous condition, with allowance for the wear and tear of normal use.

Accessibility. The federal Fair Housing Act (discussed in Chapter 20) makes it illegal to discriminate against prospective tenants on the basis of physical disability. Tenants with disabilities must be permitted to make reasonable modifications to a property at their own expense. However, if the modifications would interfere with a future tenant's use, the landlord may require that the premises be restored to their original condition at the end of the lease term.

The *Americans with Disabilities Act* (ADA) applies to commercial, nonresidential property in which public goods or services are provided. The ADA requires that such properties either be free of architectural barriers or provide reasonable accommodations for people with disabilities.

Maintenance of Premises

Many states now require a residential lessor to maintain dwelling units in a habitable condition. Landlords must make any necessary repairs to common areas, such as hallways, stairs, and elevators, and maintain safety features, such as fire sprinklers and smoke alarms. The tenant does not have to make any repairs but must return the premises in the same condition they were received, with allowances for ordinary wear and tear.

Destruction of Premises

In leases involving *agricultural land,* the courts have held that when improvements are damaged or destroyed, the tenant is obligated to pay rent to the end of the term. The tenant's liability does not depend on whether the damage was his or her fault. This ruling has been extended in most states to include *ground leases* for land on which the tenant has constructed a building. In many instances, it also includes leases that give possession of an entire building to the tenant. In this case, the tenant leases the land on which that building is located, as well as the structure itself. Insurance is available to cover such contingencies.

A tenant who leases only part of a building, such as office or commercial space or a residential apartment, however, is *not* required to continue to pay rent after the leased premises are destroyed. In some states, if the property was destroyed as a result of the landlord's negligence, the tenant can even recover damages.

Assignment and Subleasing

When a tenant transfers all of his or her leasehold interests to another person, the lease has been assigned. On the other hand, when a tenant transfers less than all the leasehold interests by *leasing* them to a new tenant, he or she has *subleased* (or sublet) the property. *Assignment* and subleasing are permitted whenever a lease does not prohibit them.

In most cases, the **sublease** or **assignment** of a lease does not relieve the original lessee of the obligation to pay rent. The landlord may, however, agree to waive the former tenant's liability. Most leases prohibit a lessee from assigning or subletting without the lessor's consent. This permits the lessor to retain control over the occupancy of the leased premises. As a rule, the lessor must not unreasonably withhold consent. The sublessor's (original lessee's) interest in the real estate is known as a *sandwich lease.*

Recording a Lease

Possession of leased premises is considered constructive notice to the world of the lessee's leasehold interests. Anyone who inspects the property receives actual notice. For these reasons, it is usually considered unnecessary to record a lease. However, most states do allow a lease to be recorded in the county in which the property is located. Furthermore, leases of three years or longer often are recorded as a matter of course. Some states *require* that long-term leases be recorded, especially when the lessees intend to mortgage the leasehold interests.

In some states, only a memorandum of lease is filed. A memorandum of lease gives notice of the interest, but does not disclose the terms of the lease. Only the names of the parties and a description of the property are included.

Options

A lease may contain a clause that grants the lessee the privilege of renewing the lease. The lessee must, however, give notice of his or her intention to exercise the option. Some leases grant the lessees the option to purchase the leased premises. This option normally allows the tenant the right to purchase the property at a predetermined price within a certain time period, possibly the lease term. Although it is not required, the owner may give the tenant credit toward the purchase price for some percentage of the rent paid. The lease agreement is a primary contract over the option to purchase.

IN PRACTICE

All of these general statements concerning provisions of a lease are controlled largely by the terms of the agreement and state law. Landlord-tenant laws also vary from state to state. Great care must be exercised in reading the entire lease document before signing it because every clause in the lease has an economic and a legal impact on either the landlord or the tenant. While preprinted lease forms are available, there is no such thing as a standard lease. When complicated lease situations arise, legal counsel should be sought.

■ TYPES OF LEASES

The manner in which rent is determined indicates the type of lease that exists. (See Table 16.1.)

Gross Lease

In a **gross lease,** the tenant pays a *fixed rental,* and the landlord pays all taxes, insurance, repairs, utilities, and the like connected with the property (usually called *property charges* or *operating expenses*). This is typically the type of rent structure involved in residential leasing.

Net Lease

In a **net lease,** the tenant pays *all or some of the property charges* in addition to the rent. The monthly rental is net income for the landlord after operating costs have been paid. Leases for entire commercial or industrial buildings and the land on which they are located, ground leases, and long-term leases are usually net leases.

In a *triple-net lease*, or *net-net-net lease*, the tenant pays all operating and other expenses in addition to a periodic rent. These expenses include taxes, insurance, assessments, maintenance, utilities, and other charges related to the premises.

Percentage Lease

Either a gross lease or a net lease may be a **percentage lease.** The rent is based on a minimum fixed rental fee plus a *percentage of the gross income* received by the tenant doing business on the leased property. This type of lease is usually used for retail businesses. The percentage charged is negotiable and varies depending on the nature of the business, the location of the property and general economic conditions.

TABLE 16.1

Types of Leases

Type of Lease	Lessee	Lessor
Gross lease	Pays basic rent	Pays property charges (taxes, repairs, insurance, etc.)
Net lease	Pays basic rent plus all or most property charges	May pay some property charges
Percentage lease (commercial and industrial)	Pays basic rent plus percent of gross sales (may pay property costs)	

Other Types of Leases

Variable lease. Several types of leases allow for increases in the rental charges during the lease periods. One of the more common is the *graduated lease*. A graduated lease provides for specified rent increases at set future dates. Another is the *index lease*, which allows rent to be increased or decreased periodically based on changes in the consumer price index or some other indicator.

Ground lease. When a landowner leases unimproved land to a tenant who agrees to erect a building on the land, the lease is usually referred to as a **ground lease**. Ground leases usually involve separate ownership of the land and buildings. These leases must be for a long enough term to make the transaction desirable to the tenant investing in the building. They often run for terms of 50 years up to 99 years. Ground leases are generally *net leases:* The lessee must pay rent on the ground as well as real estate taxes, insurance, upkeep, and repairs.

Oil and gas lease. When an oil company leases land to explore for oil and gas, a special lease agreement must be negotiated. Usually, the landowner receives a cash payment for executing the lease. If no well is drilled within the period stated in the lease, the lease expires. However, most oil and gas leases permit the oil company to continue its rights for another year by paying another flat rental fee. Such rentals may be paid annually until a well is produced. If oil or gas is found, the landowner usually receives a percentage of its value as a royalty. As long as oil or gas is obtained in significant quantities, the lease continues indefinitely.

A lease **purchase** is used when a tenant wants to purchase the property but is unable to do so. Perhaps the tenant cannot obtain favorable financing or clear title, or the tax consequences of a current purchase would be unfavorable. In this arrangement, the purchase agreement is the primary consideration, and the lease is secondary. Part of the periodic rent is applied toward the purchase price of the property until it is reduced to an amount for which the tenant can obtain financing or purchase the property outright, depending on the terms of the lease purchase agreement.

Agricultural landowners often lease their land to tenant farmers, who provide the labor to produce and bring in the crop. An owner can be paid by a tenant in one of two ways: as an agreed-on rental amount in cash in advance (**cash rent**) or as a percentage of the profits from the sale of the crop when it is sold (**sharecropping**).

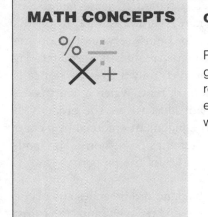

MATH CONCEPTS

CALCULATING PERCENTAGE LEASE RENTS

Percentage leases usually call for a minimum monthly rent plus a percentage of gross sales income exceeding a stated annual amount. For example, a lease might require minimum rent of $1,300 per month plus 5 percent of the business's sales exceeding $160,000. On an annual sales volume of $250,000, the annual rent would be calculated as follows:

$1,300 per month × 12 months = $15,600
$250,000 – $160,000 = $90,000
$90,000 × .05 (5%) = $4,500
$15,600 base rent + $4,500 percentage rent = $20,100 total rent

■ DISCHARGE OF LEASES

As with any contract, a lease is discharged when the contract terminates. Termination can occur when all parties have fully performed their obligations under the agreement. In addition, the parties may agree to cancel the lease. If the tenant, for instance, offers to surrender the leasehold interest, and if the landlord accepts the tenant's offer, the lease is terminated. A tenant who simply abandons leased property, however, remains liable for the terms of the lease—including the rent. The terms of the lease will usually indicate whether the landlord is obligated to try to rerent the space. If the landlord intends to sue for unpaid rent, however, most states require an attempt to mitigate damages by rerenting the premises to limit the amount owed.

The lease does not terminate if the parties die or if the property is sold. *There are two exceptions to this general rule*. A lease from the owner of a *life estate* ends when the measuring life ends. The death of either party terminates a tenancy at will. In all other cases, the heirs of a deceased landlord are bound by the terms of existing valid leases.

If leased real estate is sold or otherwise conveyed, the new landlord takes the property subject to the rights of the tenants. A lease agreement may, however, contain language that permits a new landlord to terminate existing leases. The clause, commonly known as a *sale clause*, requires that the tenants be given some period of notice before the termination. Because the new owner has taken title subject to the rights of the tenants, the sale clause enables the new landlord to claim possession and negotiate new leases under his or her own terms and conditions.

A tenancy may also be terminated by operation of law, as in a bankruptcy or condemnation proceeding.

Breach of Lease

When a tenant breaches any lease provision, the landlord may sue the tenant to obtain a judgment to cover past-due rent, damages to the premises, or other defaults. Likewise, when a landlord breaches any lease provision, the tenant is entitled to certain remedies. The rights and responsibilities of the landlord-tenant relationship are usually governed by state law.

Suit for possession—actual eviction. When a tenant breaches a lease or improperly retains leased premises, the landlord may regain possession through a legal process known as **actual eviction.** The landlord must serve notice on the tenant before commencing the lawsuit. Most lease terms require at least a ten-day notice in the case of default. In many states, however, only a five-day notice is necessary when the tenant defaults in the payment of rent. When a court issues a judgment for possession to a landlord, the tenant must vacate the property. If the tenant fails to leave, the landlord can have the judgment enforced by a court officer, who forcibly removes the tenant and the tenant's possessions. The landlord then has the right to reenter and regain possession of the property.

Tenants' remedies—constructive eviction. If a landlord breaches any clause of a lease agreement, the tenant has the right to sue and recover damages against the landlord. If the leased premises become unusable for the purpose stated in the lease, the tenant may have the right to abandon them. This action, called **constructive eviction,** terminates the lease agreement. The tenant must prove that the premises have become unusable *because of the conscious neglect of the landlord.* To claim constructive eviction, the tenant must leave the premises while the conditions that made the premises uninhabitable exist.

■ **FOR EXAMPLE** Tim's lease requires that the landlord furnish heat. The landlord fails to repair a defective furnace, and no heat is provided to Tim's apartment during the winter months. Tim is forced to abandon the apartment. Because the lack of heat was due to the landlord's negligence, Tim has been constructively evicted.

Fran's lease requires that the landlord furnish water. Although the landlord carefully maintains the building's plumbing system, the pipes develop a leak, and Fran's apartment is without water for several weeks while the problem is being repaired. Fran abandons the apartment. Because the lack of water was not due to the landlord's negligence, however, Fran has not been constructively evicted.

Harry owns a nightclub and a neighboring apartment building. Ben leased an apartment from Harry. The noise from the nightclub in the late evening and early morning was intense, and Ben complained about it to Harry. Harry posted a sign in the nightclub that said, "Shhh: We Have Neighbors!" but the noise continued. Finally, Ben abandoned the apartment, and Harry sued to recover rent. The court held that Ben had been constructively evicted because of the loud noise.

WWWeb.Link   www.law.cornell.edu/topics/landlord_tenant.html

Pro-Tenant Legislation

For the most part, leases are drawn up primarily for the benefit of the landlord. However, due to tenant's rights movements and increased consumer awareness, several states have adopted some variation of the *Uniform Residential Landlord and Tenant Act.* This model law addresses the need for both parties to a lease to fulfill certain basic obligations. The act address such issues as

- the landlord's right of entry,
- maintenance of the premises,
- the tenant's protection against retaliation by the landlord for complaints, and
- the disclosure of the property owners' names and addresses to the tenants.

The act further establishes the specific remedies available to both the landlord and the tenant if a breach of the lease agreement occurs.

■ FAIR HOUSING AND CIVIL RIGHTS LAWS

The fair housing laws affect landlords and tenants just as they do sellers and purchasers. All persons must have access to housing of their choice without any differentiation in the terms and conditions because of their race, color, religion, national origin, sex, handicap, or familial status. State and local municipalities may have their own fair housing laws that add protected classes such as age and sexual orientation. Withholding an apartment that is available for rent, segregating certain persons in separate sections of an apartment complex or parts of a building, and charging persons in the protected classes different amounts for rent or security deposits all constitute violations of the law. The fair housing laws are discussed in greater detail in Chapter 20.

It is important that landlords realize that changes in the laws stemming from the federal *Fair Housing Amendments Act of 1988* significantly alter past practices, particularly as they affect individuals with disabilities and families with children. The fair housing laws require that the same tenant criteria be applied to families with children that are applied to adults. A landlord cannot charge a different amount of rent or security deposit because one of the tenants is a child. While landlords have historically argued that children are noisy and destructive, the fact is that many adults are noisy and destructive as well.

■ SUMMARY

A lease is an agreement that grants one person the right to use the property of another in return for consideration.

A leasehold estate that runs for a specific length of time creates an estate for years; one that runs for an indefinite period creates an estate from period to period (year to year, month to month). An estate at will runs as long as the landlord permits; and an estate at sufferance is possession without the consent of the landlord. A leasehold estate is classified as personal property.

The requirements of a valid lease include capacity to contract, legal objectives, offer and acceptance, and consideration. In addition, state statutes of frauds generally require that any lease that will not be completed within one year of the date of its making must be in writing to be enforceable in court. Most leases also include clauses relating to rights and obligations of the landlord and tenant, such as the use of the premises, subletting, judgments, maintenance of the premises, and termination of the lease period.

There are several basic types of leases, including net leases, gross leases, and percentage leases. These leases are classified according to the method used in determining the rental rate of the property.

The Americans with Disabilities Act provides for access to goods and services by people with disabilities.

A lease may be terminated by the expiration of the lease period, the mutual agreement of the parties, or a breach of the lease by either the landlord or tenant. In most cases, neither the death of the tenant nor the landlord's sale of the rental property terminates a lease.

If a tenant defaults on any lease provision, the landlord may sue for a money judgment, actual eviction, or both. If the premises have become uninhabitable due to the landlord's negligence or failure to correct defects within a reasonable time, the tenant may have the remedy of constructive eviction, that is, the right to abandon the premises and refuse to pay rent until the premises are repaired.

The fair housing laws protect the rights of tenants. Besides prohibiting discrimination based on race, color, religion, familial status, national origin, and sex, the laws address the rights of individuals with disabilities and families with children.

QUESTIONS

1. Which of the following transactions would best be described as involving a ground lease?

   a. A landowner agrees to let a tenant drill for oil on a property for 75 years.

   b. A tenant agrees to pay proportionate, increased rental based on annual appraisals of the rented property.

   c. A landlord charges a commercial tenant separate amounts for the rented land and for the leased building.

   d. A tenant pays a base amount for the property plus a percentage of business-generated income.

2. A tenant enters into a commercial lease that requires a monthly rent of a minimum fixed amount, plus an additional amount determined by the tenant's gross receipts exceeding $5,000. This type of lease is called a

   a. standard lease.
   b. gross lease.
   c. percentage lease.
   d. net lease.

3. If a tenant moved out of a rented store building because access to the building was blocked as a result of the landlord's negligence,

   a. the tenant would have no legal recourse against the landlord.

   b. the landlord would be liable for the rent until the expiration date of the lease.

   c. the landlord would have to provide substitute space.

   d. the tenant would be entitled to recover damages from the landlord.

4. In June, Vivian signs a one-year lease and moves into Streetview Apartments. Vivian deposits the required security deposit with the landlord. Six months later, Vivian pays the January rent and mysteriously moves out. Vivian does not arrange for a sublease or an assignment and makes no further rent payments. The apartment is still in good condition. What is Vivian's liability to the landlord in these circumstances?

   a. Because half the rental amount has been paid and the apartment is in good condition, Vivian has no further liability.

   b. Vivian is liable for the balance of the rent, plus forfeiture of the security deposit.

   c. Vivian is liable for the balance of the rent, offset by the amount of the security deposit.

   d. Vivian is liable for the balance of the rent, plus the security deposit and any marketing costs the landlord incurred.

5. Kevin still has five months remaining on a one-year apartment lease. When Kevin moves to another city, he transfers possession of the apartment to Linda for the entire remaining term of the lease. Linda pays rent directly to Kevin. In this situation, Kevin has become a(n)

   a. assignor.   c. sublessee.
   b. sublessor.   d. lessor.

6. A tenant's lease has expired. The tenant has neither vacated nor negotiated a renewal lease, and the landlord has declared that the tenant is no longer welcome to remain in the building. This form of possession is called a(n)

   a. estate for years.
   b. periodic estate.
   c. estate at will.
   d. estate at sufferance.

7. A tenant's tenancy for years will expire in two weeks. The tenant plans to move to a larger apartment across town when the current tenancy expires. What must the tenant do to terminate this agreement?

   a. Give the landlord immediate notice or the lease will automatically renew.
   b. Give the landlord one week's prior notice or the lease will automatically renew.
   c. Nothing; the agreement will terminate automatically at the end of the current term.
   d. Sign a lease for the new apartment, which will automatically terminate the existing lease.

8. When a tenant holds possession of a landlord's property without a current lease agreement and without the landlord's approval,

   a. the tenant is maintaining a gross lease.
   b. the landlord can file suit for possession.
   c. the tenant has no obligation to pay rent.
   d. the landlord may be subject to a constructive eviction.

9. Under the negotiated terms of a certain residential lease, the landlord is required to maintain the water heater. If the tenant is unable to get hot water because of a faulty water heater that the landlord has failed to repair after repeated notification, the tenant could not

   a. sue the landlord for damages.
   b. sue the landlord for breach of the covenant of seisin.
   c. abandon the premises claiming constructive eviction.
   d. terminate the lease agreement.

10. Jody has a one-year leasehold interest in Harbor House. The interest automatically renews itself at the end of each year. Jody's interest is referred to as a tenancy

    a. for years.
    b. from period to period.
    c. at will.
    d. at sufferance.

11. Mary has assigned her apartment lease to Ben, and the landlord has agreed to the assignment. Who is liable for payment of the rent?

    a. Ben is liable to Mary; Mary is liable to the landlord.
    b. Both Ben and Mary are liable to the landlord.
    c. Only Mary is liable.
    d. Only Ben is liable.

12. Which of the following would automatically terminate a residential lease?

    a. Total destruction of the property
    b. Sale of the property
    c. Failure of the tenant to pay rent
    d. Death of the tenant

13. Which of the following describes a net lease?

    a. An agreement in which the tenant pays a fixed rent and the landlord pays all taxes, insurance, and expenses related to the property
    b. A lease in which the tenant pays rent, plus some—or all—of the operating expenses related to the property
    c. A lease in which the tenant pays the landlord a percentage of the monthly income derived from the property
    d. An agreement granting an individual a leasehold interest in fishing rights for shoreline properties

14. A tenancy in which the tenant continues in possession after the lease has expired, without the landlord's permission, is a

    a. tenancy for years.
    b. periodic tenancy.
    c. tenancy at will.
    d. tenancy at sufferance.

15. A commercial lease calls for a minimum rent of $1,200 per month plus additional annual rent of 4 percent of the year's gross business exceeding $150,000. If the total rent paid at the end of one year was $19,200, how much business did the tenant do during the year?

    a. $159,800   c. $270,000
    b. $250,200   d. $279,200

16. Which of the following describes a gross lease?

    a. An agreement in which the tenant pays a fixed rent and the landlord pays all taxes, insurance, and expenses related to the property
    b. A lease in which the tenant pays rent plus some of the operating expenses related to the property
    c. A lease in which the tenant pays the landlord a percentage of the monthly income derived from the property
    d. An agreement allowing the tenant to terminate the lease if certain conditions near the premises become unbearable.

17. A tenant signs a lease that includes a schedule of rent increases on specific dates over the course of the lease term. What kind of lease has this tenant signed?

    a. Percentage
    b. Net
    c. Graduated
    d. Index

18. A tenant signs a lease that includes the following clause: "The stated rent under this agreement will be increased or decreased every three months based on the percentage increase in the consumer price index (CPI) for that period." What kind of lease has this tenant signed?

    a. Percentage
    b. Net
    c. Graduated
    d. Index

19. The death of either the landlord or the tenant will terminate the lease and the parties' heirs will not be bound by its terms under which of the following tenancies?

    a. Tenancy for years
    b. Periodic tenancy
    c. Tenancy at will
    d. Tenancy at sufferance

20. Rickety Towers is a residential rental apartment building. The current landlord sells Rickety Towers to a new owner, who feels that the current leases are too generous. The purchaser wants to negotiate new leases with the tenants immediately, rather than wait for each lease to expire. Can a new owner do this?

    a. Yes. Leases terminate if the property is sold to a new owner.
    b. Yes, if the leases contain a sale clause.
    c. No. Leases are contracts, and the sale of the property cannot under any circumstances change the previously-negotiated rents.
    d. No, unless the leases contain a lease-purchase clause.

P A R T

II

PRACTICE

CHAPTER SEVENTEEN

PROPERTY MANAGEMENT

■ **LEARNING OBJECTIVES** *When you've finished reading this Chapter, you should be able to:*

■ **identify** the basic elements of a management agreement.

■ **describe** a property manager's functions.

■ **explain** the role of environmental regualtions and the Americans with Disabilities Act in the property manager's job.

■ **distinguish** the various types of insurance alternatives.

■ **define** the following *key terms:*

community association management	multiperil policies	routine maintenance
construction	preventive maintenance	surety bonds
corrective maintenance	property manager	tenant improvements
life cycle costing	repair	workers' compensation acts
management agreement	risk management	

■ **WHY LEARN ABOUT...** PROPERTY MANAGEMENT?

There are more than 6 billion square feet of commercial real estate in the United States. And each and every one of those square feet is managed by a property manager or by a property management company. That's a lot of responsibility. If you plan a career in property management, then the reason why you need to know the information in this Chapter is obvious: It's your job description. But even if you don't plan to become a property manager, you may find yourself managing properties on a temporary basis anyway. And even if you never manage a property, you may well have an office in a building that is managed by a property manager. Knowing what he or she is responsible for will help you protect your business interests. ■

■ THE PROPERTY MANAGER

Property management is a real estate specialization. It involves the leasing, managing, marketing, and overall maintenance of real estate owned by others, usually rental property. The **property manager** has three principal responsibilities:

Three Management Areas
1. Financial
2. Physical
3. Administrative

1. Financial management
2. Physical management (structure and grounds)
3. Administrative management (files and records)

The property manager is responsible for maintaining the owner's investment and making sure the property earns income. This can be done in several ways. The physical property must be maintained in good condition. Suitable tenants must be found, rent must be collected, and employees must be hired and supervised. The property manager is responsible for budgeting and controlling expenses, keeping proper accounts, and making periodic reports to the owner. In all of these activities, the manager's primary goal is to operate and maintain the physical property in such a way as to preserve and enhance the owner's capital investment.

A property manager
■ maintains the owner's investment and
■ ensures that the property produces income.

Some property managers work for property management companies. These firms manage properties for a number of owners under management agreements (discussed later in this Chapter). Other property managers are independent. The property manager has an agency relationship with the owner, which involves greater authority and discretion over management decisions than an employee would have. A property manager or an owner may employ building managers to supervise the daily operations of a building. In some cases, these individuals may be residents of the building.

IN PRACTICE

In most states, property managers who serve the public for a fee must be licensed real estate brokers. In other states, property managers must be licensed specifically as property managers.

Securing Management Business

Possible sources of property management business include

- community associations,
- corporate owners,
- apartment developers and landlords,
- condominium associations,
- homeowners' associations,
- investment syndicates,
- trusts,
- individual owners who want professional property management, and
- absentee owners.

When a property manager secures business from any of these sources, a good reputation is often the manager's best advertising. A manager who consistently demonstrates the ability to increase property income over previous levels should have little difficulty finding new business.

A growing trend for the management of associations and planned unit developments is for a **community association management** to provide a team of property managers, accounting staff, office staff, and property consultants for property management. The prevalence of homeowner and condominium associations combined with complex planning and development codes have placed new demands on property managers. Working as part of a team, property managers assist in providing a comprehensive array of services.

Before contracting to manage any property, however, the professional property manager should be certain that the building owner has realistic income expectations. Necessary maintenance, unexpected repairs, and effective marketing all take time and money. In addition, most states have landlord-tenant laws that require the landlord (owner) to keep the property repaired and make sure it complies with building codes. Through the agency relationship with the owner, the property manager becomes responsible for repairs and the building's condition.

The Management Agreement

The first step in taking over the management of any property is to enter into a management agreement with the owner. This **management agreement** creates an agency relationship between the owner and the property manager. The property manager usually is considered to be a *general agent*. As an agent, the property manager is charged with the fiduciary responsibilities of care, obedience, accounting, loyalty, and disclosure. After entering into an agreement with a property owner, a manager handles the property the same way the owner would. In all activities, the manager's first responsibility is to realize the highest return on the property in a manner consistent with the owner's instructions.

Like any other contract involving real estate, the management agreement should be in writing. It should include the following points:

- *Description* of the property.
- *Time period* the agreement covers and specific provisions for termination.
- *Definition of the management's responsibilities*. All the manager's duties should be specifically stated in the contract. Any limitations or restrictions on what the manager may do should be included.

- *Statement of the owner's purpose.* The owner should clearly state what he or she wants the manager to accomplish. One owner may want to maximize net income, while another will want to increase the capital value of the investment. What the manager does depends on the owner's long-term goals for the property.

- *Extent of the manager's authority.* This provision should state what authority the manager is to have in matters such as hiring, firing, and supervising employees; fixing rental rates for space; and making expenditures and authorizing repairs. Repairs that exceed a certain expense limit may require the owner's written approval.

- *Reporting.* The frequency and detail of the manager's periodic reports on operations and financial position should be agreed on. These reports serve as a means for the owner to monitor the manager's work. They also form a basis for both the owner and manager to spot trends that are important in shaping management policy. In general, state Real Estate Commissions have rules concerning reporting which must be followed.

- *Compensation.* The management fee or other form of compensation may be based on a percentage of gross or net income, a fixed fee, or some combination of these and other factors. The compensation provision of the agreement should state the base fee, as well as any leasing fees, supervision fees, or other commissions or compensations. Management fees are subject to the same antitrust considerations as sales commissions, that is, they cannot be standardized in the marketplace; standardization would be viewed as price-fixing. The fee *must* be negotiated between the agent and the principal. In addition, the property manager may be entitled to a commission on new rentals and renewed leases. Finally, the agreement should require that the manager be included as an "additional insured" on the property liability policy.

- *Allocation of costs.* The agreement should state which of the property manager's expenses—such as office rent, office help, telephone, advertising, and association fees—will be paid by the manager. Other costs will be paid by the owner.

MATH CONCEPTS

RENTAL COMMISSIONS

Residential property managers often earn commissions when they find tenants for a property. Rental commissions are usually based on the annual rent from a property. For example, if an apartment unit rents for $800 per month and the commission payable is 8 percent, the commission is calculated as follows:

$800 per month × 12 months = $9,600
$9,600 × .08 (8%) = $768

- *Equal opportunity statement.* Residential property management agreements should include a statement that the property will be shown, rented, and otherwise made available to all persons regardless of race, color, religion, sex, handicap, national origin, or family status, and to any class of person protected by state or federal law.

■ PROFESSIONAL ASSOCIATIONS

Most metropolitan areas have local associations of building and property owners and managers that are affiliates of regional and national associations. The *Institute of Real Estate Management* (IREM) is one of the affiliates of the National Association of REALTORS®. It awards the Certified Property Manager (CPM) designation. The *Building Owners and Managers Association International* (BOMA) is a federation of local associations of building owners and managers. The *Building Owners and Managers Institute International* (BOMI), an independent institute affiliated with BOMA, offers training courses leading to several designations: Real Property Administrator (RPA), Systems Maintenance Administrator (SMA), and Facilities Management Administrator (FMA). Other associations include the *National Apartment Association* (NAA) and the *National Association of Residential Property Managers* (NARPM). In addition, many specialized professional organizations provide information and contacts for condominium association managers, shopping center managers and others.

WWWeb.Link

www.amanet.org

www.boma.org

www.bomi-edu.org

www.irem.org/index2.html

www.naahq.org

www.nahb.com

www.narpm.org

■ MANAGEMENT FUNCTIONS

A property manager's specific responsibilities are determined by the management agreement. Certain duties, however, are found in most agreements. These include budgeting, capital expenditures, setting rental rates, selecting tenants, collecting rent, maintaining the property, and complying with legal requirements.

Budgeting Expenses

Before attempting to rent any property, the property manager should develop an *operating budget*. The budget should be based on anticipated revenues and expenses. In addition, it must reflect the owner's long-term goals. In preparing a budget, the manager should allocate money for *continuous, fixed expenses* such as employees' salaries, property taxes, and insurance premiums.

Next, the manager should establish a *cash reserve fund* for variable expenses such as repairs, decorating, and supplies. The amount allocated for the reserve fund can be computed from the previous yearly costs of the variable expenses.

Capital expenditures. The owner and the property manager may decide that modernization or renovation of a property will enhance its value. In this case, the manager should budget money to cover the costs of remodeling. The property manager should either be thoroughly familiar with the *principle of contribution* (discussed in Chapter 18) or seek expert advice when estimating any expected increase in value. In the case of large-scale construction, the expenses charged against the property's income should be spread over several years.

The cost of equipment to be installed in a modernization or renovation must be evaluated over its entire useful life. This is called **life cycle costing.** This term simply means that both the *initial* and the *operating* costs of equipment over its expected life must be measured to compare the total cost of one type of equipment with that of another.

Renting the Property

Effective rental of the property is essential. However, the role of the property manager in managing a property should not be confused with that of a broker who acts as a leasing agent. The manager must be concerned with the long-term financial health of the property; the broker is concerned solely with renting space. The property manager may use the services of a leasing agent, but that agent does not undertake the full responsibility of maintaining and managing the property.

Setting rental rates. Rental rates are influenced primarily by supply and demand. The property manager should conduct a detailed survey of the competitive space available in the neighborhood, emphasizing similar properties. In establishing rental rates, the property manager has the following four long-term considerations:

1. The rental income must be sufficient to cover the property's fixed charges and operating expenses.
2. The rental income must provide a fair return on the owner's investment.
3. The rental rate should be in line with prevailing rates in comparable buildings; it may be slightly higher or slightly lower, depending on the strength of the property.
4. The current vacancy rate in the property is a good indicator of how much of a rent increase is advisable. A building with a low vacancy rate (that is, few vacant units) is a better candidate for an increase than one with a high vacancy rate.

A rental rate for residential space is usually stated as the monthly rate *per unit.* Commercial leases—including office, retail and industrial space rentals—are usually stated according to either annual or monthly rates *per square foot.*

If the vacancy level is high, the manager should attempt to determine why. An elevated level of vacancy does not necessarily indicate that rents are too high. Instead, the problem may be poor management or a defective or an undesirable property. The manager should attempt to identify and correct the problems first rather than immediately lower rents. On the other hand, a high occupancy rate may mean that rental rates are too low. Whenever the occupancy level of an apartment house or office building exceeds 95 percent, serious consideration should be given to raising rents. First, however, the manager should investigate the rental market to determine whether a rent increase is warranted.

Selecting Tenants

A building manager's success depends on establishing and maintaining sound, long-term relationships with his or her tenants. The first and most important step is selection. The manager should be sure that the premises are suitable for a tenant in size, location, and amenities. Most important, the manager should be sure that the tenant is able to pay for the space.

MATH CONCEPTS

$$\% \quad \frac{\square}{\square}$$
$$\times \quad +$$

CALCULATING MONTHLY RENT PER SQUARE FOOT

1. Determine the total square footage of the rental premises (generally floorspace only.)

50 feet

30 feet   30 feet

50 feet

50 feet × 30 feet = 1,500 square feet

2. Find the total annual rent.
   $1,850 per month × 12 months = $22,200 per year

3. Divide the total annual rent by the total square feet to determine the annual rate per square foot.
   $22,200 ÷ 1,500 square feet = $14.80 per square foot

4. Convert the annual rate to a monthly rate.
   $14.80 ÷ 12 months = $1.23 per square foot

A commercial tenant's business should be compatible with the building *and the other tenants*. The manager must consider the business interests of his or her current tenants as well as the interests of the potential tenant. The types of businesses or services should be complementary, and the introduction of competitors into the same property should be undertaken with care. This not only pleases existing tenants but helps diversify the owner's investment and makes profitability more likely. Some commercial leases bar the introduction of similar businesses.

If a commercial tenant is likely to expand in the future, the manager should consider the property's potential for expansion.

The residential property manager must be sure to comply with all federal, state and local fair housing laws in selecting tenants (see Chapter 16 and Chapter 20). Although fair housing laws do not apply to commercial properties, commercial property managers need to be aware of federal, state, and local antidiscrimination and equal opportunity laws that may govern industrial or retail properties.

Collecting rents. A property manager should accept only those tenants who can be expected to meet their financial obligations. The manager should investigate financial references, check with local credit bureaus, and, when possible, interview a prospective tenant's former landlord.

The terms of rental payment should be spelled out in the lease agreement, including

- time and place of payment,
- provisions and penalties for late payment and bounced checks, and
- provisions for cancellation and damages in case of nonpayment.

The property manager should establish a firm and consistent *collection plan*. The plan should include a system of notices and records that complies with state and local law.

Every attempt must be made to collect rent without resorting to legal action. Legal action is costly and time-consuming and does not contribute to good tenant relations. In some cases, however, legal action is unavoidable. In these instances, a property manager must be prepared to initiate and follow through with the necessary legal steps. Obviously, legal action must be taken in cooperation with the property owner's or management firm's legal counsel.

Maintaining Good Relations with Tenants

The ultimate success of a property manager depends on the ability to maintain good relations with tenants. Dissatisfied tenants eventually vacate the property. A high tenant turnover rate results in greater expenses for advertising and redecorating. It also means less profit for the owner due to uncollected rents.

An effective property manager establishes a good communication system with tenants. Regular newsletters or posted memoranda help keep tenants informed and involved. Maintenance and service requests must be attended to promptly, and all lease terms and building rules must be enforced consistently and fairly. If a manager fails to treat all tenants the same in terms of rent collection and enforcement of lease terms or rule and regulations, the manager could be violating fair housing laws. A good manager is tactful and decisive and acts to the benefit of both owner and occupants.

The property manager must be able to handle residents who do not pay their rents on time or who break building regulations. When one tenant fails to follow the rules, the other tenants often become frustrated and dissatisfied. Careful record keeping shows whether rent is remitted promptly and in the proper amount. Records of all lease renewal dates should be kept so that the manager can anticipate expiration and retain good tenants who might otherwise move when their leases end.

Maintaining the Property

One of the most important functions of a property manager is the supervision of property maintenance. A manager must learn to balance the services provided with their costs, that is, to satisfy tenants' needs while minimizing operating expenses.

To maintain the property efficiently, the manager must be able to assess the building's needs and how best to meet them. Staffing and scheduling requirements vary with the type, size, and geographic location of the property, so the owner and manager usually agree in advance on maintenance objectives. In some cases, the best plan may be to operate a low-rental property, with minimal expenditures for services and maintenance. Another property may be more lucrative if kept in top condition and operated with all possible tenant services. A well-maintained, high-service property can command premium rental rates.

A primary maintenance objective is to *protect the physical integrity of the property over the long term*. For example, preserving the property by repainting the exterior or replacing the heating system helps decrease long-term maintenance costs. Keeping the property in good condition involves the following four types of maintenance:

1. Preventive
2. Repair or corrective
3. Routine
4. Construction

Preventive maintenance includes regularly scheduled activities such as painting and seasonal servicing of appliances and systems. Preventive maintenance preserves the long-range value and physical integrity of the building. This is both the most critical and the most neglected maintenance responsibility. Failure to perform preventive maintenance invariably leads to greater expense in other areas of maintenance.

Repair or **corrective maintenance** involves the actual repairs that keep the building's equipment, utilities, and amenities functioning. Repairing a boiler, fixing a leaky faucet, and mending a broken air-conditioning unit are acts of corrective maintenance.

A property manager also must supervise the **routine maintenance** of the building. Routine maintenance includes such day-to-day duties as cleaning common areas, performing minor carpentry and plumbing adjustments, and providing regularly scheduled upkeep of heating, air-conditioning, and landscaping. Good routine maintenance is similar to good preventive maintenance. Both head off problems before they become expensive.

Preventive maintenance helps prevent problems and expenses.
Corrective maintenance corrects problems after they've occurred.

Four Types of Maintenance
1. Preventive
2. Repair or Corrective
3. Routine
4. Construction

IN PRACTICE   One of the major decisions a property manager faces is whether to contract for maintenance services from an outside firm or hire on-site employees to perform such tasks. This decision should be based on a number of factors, including the

- size of the building,
- complexity of the tenants' requirements, and
- availability of suitable labor.

A commercial or an industrial property manager often is called on to make **tenant improvements.** These are alterations to the interior of the building to meet a tenant's particular space needs. Such **construction alterations** range from simply repainting or recarpeting to completely gutting the interior and redesigning the space by erecting new walls, partitions, and electrical systems. Tenant improvements are especially important when renting new buildings. In new construction, the interiors are usually left incomplete so that they can be adapted to the needs of individual tenants. One matter that must be clarified is which improvements will be considered trade fixtures (personal property belonging to the tenant) and which will belong to the owner of the real estate. Trade fixtures are discussed in Chapter 2.

Construction involves making a property meet a tenant's needs.

Modernization or renovation of buildings that have become functionally obsolete and thus unsuited to today's building needs is also important. (See Chapter

18 for a definition of *functional obsolescence*.) The renovation of a building often enhances the building's marketability and increases its potential income.

Handling Environmental Concerns

The environment is an increasingly important property management issue. A variety of environmental issues, from waste disposal to air quality, must be addressed by the property manager. Tenant concerns, as well as federal, state, and local regulations, determine the extent of the manager's environmental responsibilities. While property managers are not expected to be experts in all of the disciplines necessary to operate a modern building, they are expected to be knowledgeable in many diverse subjects, most of which are technical in nature. Environmental concerns are one such subject.

The property manager must be able to respond to a variety of environmental problems. He or she may manage structures containing asbestos or radon or be called on to arrange an environmental audit of a property. Managers must see that any hazardous wastes produced by their employers or tenants are properly disposed of. Even the normally nonhazardous waste of an office building must be controlled to avoid violation of laws requiring segregation and recycling of types of wastes. Of course, a property manager may want to provide recycling facilities for tenants even if he or she is not required by law to do so. On-site recycling creates an image of good citizenship that enhances the reputation (and value) of a commercial or residential property. Environmental issues, including lead-based paint abatement issues, are discussed in detail in Chapter 21.

The Americans with Disabilities Act

The *Americans with Disabilities Act* (ADA) has had a significant impact on the responsibilities of the property manager, both in building amenities and in employment issues.

Title I of the ADA provides for the employment of qualified job applicants regardless of their disability. Any employer with 15 or more employees must adopt nondiscriminatory employment procedures. In addition, employers must make reasonable accommodations to enable individuals with disabilities to perform essential job functions.

Property managers also must be familiar with Title III of the ADA, which prohibits discrimination in commercial properties and public accommodations. The ADA requires that managers ensure that people with disabilities have full and equal access to facilities and services.

■ **FOR EXAMPLE** A prospective tenant is visually impaired. The property manager should be prepared to provide a lease agreement that is enlarged or printed in Braille.

The property manager typically is responsible for determining whether a building meets the ADA's accessibility requirements. The property manager also must prepare a plan for retrofitting a building that is not in compliance when removal of existing barriers is "readily achievable"—that is, can be performed without much difficulty or expense. There are some tax advantages available to help offset the expense of complying with ADA. ADA experts may be consulted, as may architectural designers who specialize in accessibility issues.

To protect owners of existing structures from the massive expense of extensively remodeling, the ADA recommends *reasonably achievable accommodations* to provide access to the facilities and services. New construction and remodeling, however, must meet higher standards of accessibility and usability because it costs less to incorporate accessible features in the design than to retrofit. Though the law intends to provide for people with disabilities, many of the accessible design features and accommodations benefit everyone.

IN PRACTICE

The U.S. Department of Justice has ADA specialists available to answer general information questions about compliance issues. The ADA Information Line is at 1-800-514-0301 (TDD 1-800-514-0383).

 **WWWeb.Link**

www.usdoj.gov/crt/ada/adahom1.htm

Existing barriers must be removed when this can be accomplished in a *readily achievable* manner—that is, with little difficulty and at low cost. (See Figure 17.1.) The following are typical examples of readily achievable modifications:

■ Ramping or removing an obstacle from an otherwise accessible entrance
■ Lowering wall-mounted public telephones
■ Adding raised letters and braille markings on elevator buttons
■ Installing auditory signals in elevators
■ Reversing the direction in which doors open

Alternative methods can be used to provide reasonable accommodations if extensive restructuring is impractical or if retrofitting is unduly expensive. For instance, installing a cup dispenser at a water fountain that is too high for an individual in a wheelchair may be more practical than installing a lower unit.

IN PRACTICE

Federal, state, and local laws may provide additional requirements for accommodating people with disabilities. Licensees should be aware of the full range of laws to ensure that their practices are in compliance.

■ RISK MANAGEMENT

Enormous monetary losses can result from certain unexpected or catastrophic events. As a result, one of the most critical areas of responsibility for a property manager is **risk management**. Risk management involves answering the question, "What happens if something goes wrong?" The perils of any risk must be evaluated in terms of options. In considering the possibility of a loss, the property manager must decide whether it is better to

> The four alternative risk management techniques may be remembered by the acronym **ACTOR:** **A**void, **C**ontrol, **T**ransfer, *or* **R**etain.

■ *avoid it,* by removing the source of risk (for instance, a swimming pool may pose an unacceptable risk if a day-care center is located in the building);
■ *control it,* by preparing for an emergency before it happens (by installing sprinklers, fire doors, and security systems, for example);
■ *transfer it,* by shifting the risk onto another party (that is, by taking out an insurance policy); or
■ *retain it,* by deciding that the chances of the event occurring are too small to justify the expense of any other response (an alternative might be to

FIGURE 17.1

Reasonable Modifications to Public Facilities or Services

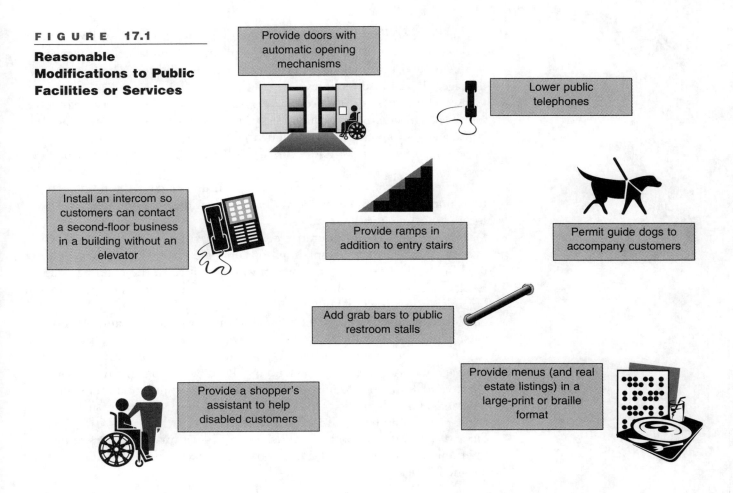

take out an insurance policy with a large *deductible*, which usually is considerably less expensive).

Security of Tenants

The physical safety of tenants of the leased premises is an important issue for property managers and owners. Recent court decisions in several parts of the country have held owners and their agents responsible for physical harm that was inflicted on tenants by intruders. These decisions have prompted property managers and owners to think about how to protect tenants and secure apartments from intruders. There is also the concern of wrongdoing or criminal behavior inflicted by tenants on other tenants in the building. Many leases now have a crime-free provision that makes criminal activity, such as drug use or assault, a ground for eviction.

Types of Insurance

Insurance is one way to protect against losses. Many types of insurance are available. An *insurance audit* should be performed by a competent, reliable insurance agent who is familiar with insurance issues for the type of property involved. The audit will indicate areas in which greater or lesser coverage is recommended and will highlight particular risks. The final decision, however, must be made by the property owner.

Some common types of coverage available to income property owners and managers follow:

- *Fire and hazard.* Fire insurance policies provide coverage against direct loss or damage to property from a fire on the premises. Standard fire coverage can be extended to include other hazards such as windstorm, hail, smoke damage, or civil insurrection.

- *Consequential loss, use, and occupancy.* Also known as *loss of rent* or *business interruption insurance,* consequential loss insurance covers the results, or consequences, of a disaster. Consequential loss can include the loss of rent or revenue to a business that occurs if the business's property cannot be used.

- *Contents and personal property.* This type of insurance covers building contents and personal property during periods when they are not actually located on the business premises.

- *Liability.* Public liability insurance covers the risks an owner assumes whenever the public enters the building. A claim paid under this coverage is used for medical expenses by a person who is injured in the building as a result of the owner's negligence. Claims for medical or hospital payments for injuries sustained by building employees hurt in the course of their employment are covered by state laws known as **workers' compensation acts.** These laws require that a building owner who is an employer obtain a workers' compensation policy from a private insurance company.

- *Casualty.* Casualty insurance policies include coverage against theft, burglary, vandalism, and machinery damage as well as health and accident insurance. Casualty policies are usually written on specific risks, such as theft, rather than being all-inclusive.

- *Surety bonds.* **Surety bonds** cover an owner against financial losses resulting from an employee's criminal acts or negligence while performing assigned duties.

Many insurance companies offer **multiperil policies** for apartment and commercial buildings. Such a policy offers the property manager an insurance package that includes standard types of commercial coverage, such as fire, hazard, public liability, and casualty. Special coverage for terrorism, earthquakes and floods is also available.

Claims

Two possible methods can be used to determine the amount of a claim under an insurance policy. One is the depreciated or actual cash value of the damaged property, that is, the property is not insured for what it would cost to replace it, but rather for what it was originally worth, less the depreciation in value that results from use and the passage of time. The other method is *current replacement cost.* In this sort of policy, the building or property is insured for what it would cost to rebuild or replace it today.

When purchasing insurance, a manager must decide whether a property should be insured at full replacement cost or at a depreciated cost. Full replacement cost coverage is generally more expensive than depreciated cost. As with the homeowner's policies discussed in Chapter 3, commercial policies include *coinsurance clauses* that require the insured to carry fire coverage, usually in an amount equal to 80 percent of a building's replacement value.

■ SUMMARY

Property management is a specialized service provided to owners of income-producing properties. The owner's managerial function may be delegated to an individual or a firm with particular expertise in the field. The manager, as agent of the owner, becomes the administrator of the project and assumes the executive functions required for the care and operation of the property.

A management agreement establishes the agency relationship between owner and manager. It must be prepared carefully to define and authorize the manager's duties and responsibilities.

This growing real estate specialty is supported by many regional and national organizations that help property managers maintain high professional standards.

Projected expenses, the manager's analysis of the building's condition, and local rent patterns form the basis for determining rental rates for the property. Once a rent schedule is established, the property manager is responsible for soliciting tenants whose needs are suited to the available space. The tenants must be financially capable of meeting the proposed rents. The manager collects rents, maintains the building, hires necessary employees, pays taxes for the building, and deals with tenant problems.

Maintenance includes safeguarding the physical integrity of the property and performing routine cleaning and repairs. It also includes making tenant improvements, such as adapting the interior space and overall design of the property to suit tenants' needs.

The manager is expected to secure adequate insurance coverage for the premises. Fire and hazard insurance covers the property and fixtures against catastrophes. Consequential loss, use, and occupancy insurance protects the owner against revenue losses. Casualty insurance provides coverage against losses such as theft, vandalism, and destruction of machinery. The manager should also secure public liability insurance to insure the owner against claims made by people injured on the premises. Workers' compensation policies cover the claims of employees injured on the job.

QUESTIONS

1. Which of the following types of insurance coverage insures an employer against most claims for job-related injuries?
   a. Consequential loss
   b. Workers' compensation
   c. Casualty
   d. Surety bond

2. Avoid, control, transfer, or retain are the four alternative techniques of
   a. tenant relations.
   b. acquiring insurance.
   c. risk management.
   d. property management.

3. From a management point of view, apartment building occupancy that reaches as high as 98 percent would tend to indicate that
   a. the building is poorly managed.
   b. the building has reached its maximum potential.
   c. building similar sites would not be profitable.
   d. rents could be raised.

4. A guest slips on an icy apartment building stair and is hospitalized. A claim against the building owner for medical expenses may be paid under which of the following policies held by the owner?
   a. Workers' compensation
   b. Casualty
   c. Liability
   d. Fire and hazard

5. Which of the following would a property manager not include in preparing an operating budget for a building?
   a. Heating oil
   b. Cleaning supplies
   c. Window replacement
   d. Management fees

6. A property manager is offered a choice of three insurance policies: One has a $500 deductible, one has a $1,000 deductible, and the third has a $5,000 deductible. If the property manager selects the policy with the highest deductible, which risk management technique is he or she using?
   a. Avoiding risk   c. Controlling risk
   b. Retaining risk   d. Transferring risk

7. Contaminated groundwater, toxic fumes from paint and carpeting, and lack of proper ventilation are all examples of
   a. issues beyond the scope of a property manager's job description.
   b. problems faced only by newly constructed properties.
   c. issues that arise under the ADA.
   d. environmental concerns that a property manager may have to address.

8. In the case of commercial or industrial properties, tenant improvements are
   a. tenant-owned fixtures.
   b. adaptations of space to suit tenants' needs.
   c. illegal unless authorized.
   d. landlord obligations.

9. In preparing a budget, a property manager should set up which of the following for variable expenses?
   a. Control account
   b. Floating allocation
   c. Cash reserve fund
   d. Asset account

10. In most market areas, rents are determined by
    a. supply and demand factors.
    b. the local apartment owners' association.
    c. HUD.
    d. a tenants' union.

11. Whittaker Towers, a highrise apartment building, burns to the ground. What type of insurance covers the landlord against the resulting loss of rent?

    a. Fire and hazard
    b. Liability
    c. Consequential loss, use, and occupancy
    d. Casualty

12. A property manager hires a full-time maintenance person. While repairing a faucet in one of the apartments, the maintenance person steals a television set, and the tenant sues the owner. The property manager could protect the owner against this type of loss by purchasing

    a. liability insurance.
    b. workers' compensation insurance.
    c. a surety bond.
    d. casualty insurance.

13. Commercial leases are usually expressed as a(n)

    a. monthly rate per unit.
    b. percentage of total space available.
    c. annual or monthly rate per square foot.
    d. annual rate per room.

14. A property manager repairs a malfunctioning boiler. This is classified as which type of maintenance?

    a. Preventive   c. Routine
    b. Corrective   d. Construction

15. A property manager who enters into a management agreement with an owner is usually a

    a. special agent.
    b. general agent.
    c. universal agent.
    d. designated agent.

16. The practice of measuring both the *initial* and the *operating costs* of equipment over its expected life so as to compare the total cost of one type of equipment with that of another is referred to as

    a. contribution.
    b. life cycle costing.
    c. allocation of costs.
    d. current replacement costing.

17. An insurance policy package that includes standard commercial property coverage such as fire, hazard, public liability, and casualty is referred to as what kind of policy?

    a. Coinsurance   c. Universal
    b. Multiperil   d. Surety

18. Title I of the Americans with Disabilities Act (ADA) applies to employers with how many employees?

    a. More than three   c. Fifteen or more
    b. Five or more   d. Fifty or more

19. Title III of the Americans with Disabilities Act (ADA) prohibits inadequate access to what type of property?

    a. Residential
    b. Commercial
    c. Commercial and public accommodations
    d. Public or private

20. A property manager submitted a claim to her insurer to cover damage to her building's garage door. The door was originally purchased for $1,500 and is subject to $475 depreciation due to age and use. A new door costs $2,150. If the building is covered by a current replacement cost policy, the insurance company will send the manager a check for which of the following amounts?

    a. $1,025   c. $1,975
    b. $1,500   d. $2,150

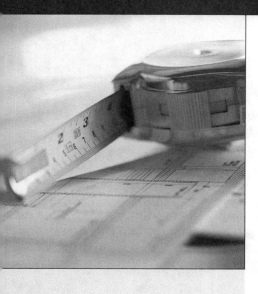

CHAPTER EIGHTEEN

REAL ESTATE APPRAISAL

■ **LEARNING OBJECTIVES** *When you've finished reading this Chapter, you should be able to:*

■ **identify** the different types and basic principles of value.

■ **describe** the three basic valuation approaches used by appraisers.

■ **explain** the steps in the appraisal process.

■ **distinguish** the four methods of determining reproduction or replacement cost.

■ **define** the following *key terms:*

anticipation	functional obsolescence	quantity-survey method
appraisal	gross income multiplier (GIM)	reconciliation
appraiser		regression
assemblage	gross rent multiplier (GRM)	replacement cost
capitalization rate		reproduction cost
change	highest and best use	sales comparison approach
competition	income approach	
conformity	increasing returns	square-foot method
contribution	index method	straight-line method
cost approach	market data approach	substitution
depreciation	market value	supply and demand
diminishing returns	physical deterioration	unit-in-place method
economic life	plottage	value
external obsolescence	progression	

■ WHY LEARN ABOUT... APPRAISAL?

Appraisal is a distinct area of specialization within the world of real estate professions. However, even real estate licensees who are not professional appraisers need to understand the fundamental principles of valuation to complete an accurate, effective, competitive market analysis (CMA) for their seller clients. Further, an understanding of the appraisal process will help you more clearly anticipate the likely outcome (and plan to avoid potential pitfalls) of a property's preclosing appraisal. ■

■ APPRAISING

An **appraisal** is an estimate or opinion of value based on supportable evidence and approved methods. An **appraiser** is an independent person trained to provide an *unbiased* estimate of value. Appraising is a professional service performed for a fee.

WWWeb.Link   www.appraisalfoundation.org   www.appraisalinstitute.org

Regulation of Appraisal Activities

Title XI of the Financial Institutions Reform, Recovery, and Enforcement Act of 1989 (FIRREA) requires that any appraisal used in connection with a federally related transaction must be performed by a competent individual whose professional conduct is subject to supervision and regulation. Appraisers must be licensed or certified according to state law. Each state adopts its own appraiser regulations. These laws must conform to the federal requirements, which in turn follow the criteria for certification established by the Appraiser Qualifications Board of the Appraisal Foundation. The Appraisal Foundation is a national body composed of representatives of the major appraisal and related organizations. Appraisers are also expected to follow the Uniform Standards of Professional Appraisal Practice established by the foundation's Appraisal Standards Board.

A *federally related transaction* is any real estate-related financial transaction in which a federal financial institution or regulatory agency engages. This includes transactions involving the sale, lease, purchase, investment, or exchange of real property. It also includes the financing, refinancing, or use of real property as security for a loan or an investment, including mortgage-backed securities. Appraisals of residential property valued at $250,000 or less and commercial property valued at $1 million or less in federally related transactions are exempt and need not be performed by licensed or certified appraisers.

Competitive Market Analysis

Not all estimates of *value* are made by professional appraisers. As discussed in Chapter 6, a salesperson often must help a seller arrive at a listing price or a buyer determine an offering price for property without the aid of a formal appraisal report. In such a case, the salesperson prepares a report compiled from research of the marketplace, primarily similar properties that have been sold, known as a *competitive market analysis* (CMA). The salesperson must be knowledgeable about the fundamentals of valuation to compile the *market data*. The competitive market analysis is not as comprehensive or technical as an appraisal and may be biased by a salesperson's anticipated agency relationship. A competitive market analysis should *not* be represented as an appraisal.

■ VALUE

> The four characteristics of value may be remembered by the acronym **DUST**: **D**emand, **U**tility, **S**carcity and **T**ransferability.

To have **value** in the real estate market—that is, to have monetary worth based on desirability—a property must have the following characteristics:

- *Demand*—the need or desire for possession or ownership backed by the financial means to satisfy that need
- *Utility*—the property's usefulness for its intended purposes
- *Scarcity*—a finite supply
- *Transferability*—the relative ease with which ownership rights are transferred from one person to another

Market Value

Generally, the goal of an appraiser is to estimate market value. The **market value** of real estate is *the most probable price that a property should bring in a fair sale*. This definition makes three assumptions. First, it presumes a competitive and open market. Second, the buyer and seller are both assumed to be acting prudently and knowledgeably. Third, market value depends on the price not being affected by unusual circumstances.

The following are essential to determining market value:

- The *most probable* price is not the average or highest price.
- The buyer and seller must be unrelated and acting without *undue pressure*.
- Both buyer and seller must be *well informed* about the property's use and potential, including both its defects and its advantages.
- A *reasonable time* must be allowed for exposure in the open market.
- Payment must be made in cash or its equivalent.
- The price must represent a normal consideration for the property sold, unaffected by special financing amounts or terms, services, fees, costs, or credits incurred in the market transaction.

> *Market value* is a reasonable *opinion* of a property's value; *market price* is the actual selling price of a property; *cost* may not equal either market value or market price.

Market value versus market price. *Market value* is an opinion of value based on an analysis of data. The data may include not only an analysis of comparable sales but also an analysis of potential income, expenses, and replacement costs (less any depreciation). *Market price*, on the other hand, is what a property *actually* sells for—its sales price. In theory, market price should be the same as market value. Market price can be taken as accurate evidence of current market value, however, *only* if the conditions essential to market value exist. Sometimes, property may be sold below market value—for instance, when the seller is forced to sell quickly or when a sale is arranged between relatives.

Market value versus cost. An important distinction can be made between market value and *cost*. One of the most common misconceptions about valuing property is that cost represents market value. Cost and market value *may* be the same. In fact, when the improvements on a property are new, cost and value are likely to be equal. But more often, cost does *not* equal market value. For example, a homeowner may install a swimming pool for $15,000; however, the cost of the improvement may not add $15,000 to the value of the property.

Basic Principles of Value

A number of economic principles can affect the value of real estate. The most important are defined in the text that follows.

Anticipation. According to the principle of **anticipation,** value is created by the *expectation* that certain events will occur. Value can increase or decrease in anticipation of some future benefit or detriment. For instance, the value of a house may be affected if rumors circulate that an adjacent property may be converted to commercial use in the near future. If the property has been a vacant *eyesore*, it is possible that the neighboring home's value will increase. On the other hand, if the vacant property had been perceived as a park or playlot that added to the neighborhood's quiet atmosphere, the news of its replacement might cause the house's value to decline.

Change. No physical or economic condition remains constant. This is the principle of **change.** Real estate is subject to natural phenomena such as tornadoes, fires, and routine wear and tear. The real estate business is subject to market demands, like any other business. An appraiser must be knowledgeable about both the past and, perhaps, the predictable future effects of natural phenomena and the behavior of the marketplace.

Competition. **Competition** is the *interaction* of supply and demand. Excess profits tend to attract competition. For example, the success of a retail store may cause investors to open similar stores in the area. This tends to mean less profit for all stores concerned unless the purchasing power in the area increases substantially.

Conformity. The principle of **conformity** says that value is created when a property is in harmony with its surroundings. Maximum value is realized if the use of land conforms to existing neighborhood standards. In single-family residential neighborhoods, for instance, buildings should be similar in design, construction, size, and age.

Contribution. Under the principle of **contribution,** the value of any part of a property is measured by its effect on the value of the whole. Installing a swimming pool, greenhouse, or private bowling alley may not add value to the property equal to the cost. On the other hand, remodeling an outdated kitchen or bathroom probably would.

Highest and best use. The most profitable single use to which a property may be put, or the use that is most likely to be in demand in the near future, is the property's **highest and best use.** The use must be

- legally permitted,
- financially feasible,
- physically possible, and
- maximally productive.

The highest and best use of a site can change with social, political, and economic forces. For instance, a parking lot in a busy downtown area may not maximize the land's profitability to the same extent an office building might. Highest and best use is noted in every appraisal.

Increasing and diminishing returns. The addition of improvements to land and structures increases value only to the assets' maximum value. Beyond that point, additional improvements no longer affect a property's value. As long as money spent on improvements produces an increase in income or value, the **law of increasing returns** applies. At the point where additional improvements do not increase income or value, the **law of diminishing returns** applies. No matter how much money is spent on the property, the property's value does not keep pace with the expenditures. For instance, a remodeled kitchen or bathroom might increase the value of a house; adding restaurant-quality appliances and gold faucets, however, would be an investment that the owner probably would not be able to recover.

Plottage. The principle of **plottage** holds that merging or consolidating adjacent lots into a single larger one produces a greater total land value than the sum of the two sites valued separately. For example, two adjacent lots valued at $35,000 each might have a combined value of $90,000 if consolidated. The *process* of merging two separately owned lots under one owner is known as **assemblage.** Plottage is the amount value is increased by successful assemblage.

> *Plottage:* The individual value of two adjacent properties may be greater if they are combined than if each is sold separately.

Regression and progression. In general, the worth of a better-quality property is adversely affected by the presence of a lesser-quality property. This is known as the principle of **regression.** Thus, in a neighborhood of modest homes, a structure that is larger, better maintained, or more luxurious would tend to be valued in the same range as the less lavish homes. Conversely, under the principle of **progression,** the value of a modest home would be higher if it were located among larger, fancier properties.

> *Regression:* the *lowering* of a property's value owing to its neighbors
>
> *Progression:* the *increasing* of a property's value owing to its neighbors

Substitution. The principle of **substitution** says that the maximum value of a property tends to be set by how much it would cost to purchase an equally desirable and valuable substitute property.

Supply and demand. The principle of **supply and demand** says that the value of a property depends on the number of properties available in the marketplace—the supply of the product. Other factors include the prices of other properties, the number of prospective purchasers, and the price buyers will pay.

■ THE THREE APPROACHES TO VALUE

To arrive at an accurate estimate of value, appraisers traditionally use three basic valuation techniques: the sales comparison approach, the cost approach, and the income approach. The three methods serve as checks against each other. Using them narrows the range within which the final estimate of value falls. Each method is generally considered most reliable for specific types of property.

The Sales Comparison Approach

In the **sales comparison approach** (also known as the **market data approach**), an estimate of value is obtained by comparing the property being appraised (the *subject property*) with recently sold *comparable properties* (properties similar to the subject). Because no two parcels of real estate are exactly alike, each comparable property must be analyzed for differences and similarities between it and the subject property. This approach is a good example of the principle of substitution, discussed above. The sales prices of the comparables must be adjusted for any dissimilarities. The principal factors for which adjustments must be made include the following:

- *Property rights.* An adjustment must be made when less than fee simple, the full legal bundle of rights, is involved. This includes land leases, ground rents, life estates, easements, deed restrictions, and encroachments.
- *Financing concessions.* The financing terms must be considered, including adjustments for differences such as mortgage loan terms and owner financing.
- *Conditions of sale.* Adjustments must be made for motivational factors that would affect the sale, such as foreclosure, a sale between family members, or some nonmonetary incentive.
- *Date of sale.* An adjustment must be made if economic changes occur between the date of sale of the comparable property and the date of the appraisal.
- *Location.* Similar properties might differ in price from neighborhood to neighborhood or even between locations within the same neighborhood.
- *Physical features and amenities.* Physical features, such as the structure's age, size, and condition, may require adjustments.

The sales comparison approach is considered the most reliable of the three approaches in appraising single-family homes, where the intangible benefits may be difficult to measure otherwise. Most appraisals include a minimum of three comparable sales reflective of the subject property. An example of the sales comparison approach is shown in Table 18.1.

The Cost Approach

The **cost approach** to value also is based on the principle of substitution. The cost approach consists of five steps:

1. Estimate the *value of the land* as if it were vacant and available to be put to its highest and best use. (Note that the value of the land is not subject to depreciation.)
2. Estimate the *current cost* of constructing buildings and improvements.
3. Estimate the *amount of accrued depreciation* resulting from the property's physical deterioration, functional obsolescence, and external depreciation.
4. *Deduct* the accrued depreciation (Step 3) from the construction cost (Step 2).
5. *Add* the estimated land value (Step 1) to the depreciated cost of the building and site improvements (Step 4) to arrive at the total property value.

■ **FOR EXAMPLE**   Value of the land   = $25,000

Current cost of construction = $85,000

Accrued depreciation   = $10,000

$85,000 - $10,000   = $75,000

$25,000 + $75,000   = $100,000

In this example, the *total property value* is $100,000.

There are two ways to look at the construction cost of a building for appraisal purposes: reproduction cost and replacement cost. **Reproduction** cost is the construction cost at current prices of an exact duplicate of the subject improvement, including both the benefits and the drawbacks of the property. **Replacement cost new** is the cost to construct an improvement similar to the subject property using current construction methods and materials, but not necessarily an exact duplicate. Replacement cost new is more frequently used in appraising older structures because it eliminates obsolete features and takes advantage of current construction materials and techniques.

An example of the cost approach to value, applied to the same property as in Table 18.1, is shown in Table 18.2.

Determining reproduction or replacement cost new. An appraiser using the cost approach computes the reproduction or replacement cost of a building using one of the following four methods:

1. **Square-foot method.** The cost per square foot of a recently built comparable structure is multiplied by the number of square feet (using exterior dimensions) in the subject building. The **square-foot method** is the most common and easiest method of cost estimation. Table 18.2 uses the square-foot method, which is also referred to as the *comparison method.* For some (usually nonresidential) properties, the cost per *cubic foot* of a recently built comparable structure is multiplied by the number of cubic feet in the subject structure.

2. **Unit-in-place method.** In the **unit-in-place method,** the replacement cost of a structure is estimated based on the construction cost per unit of measure of individual building components, including material, labor, overhead, and builder's profit. Most components are measured in square feet, although items such as plumbing fixtures are estimated by cost. The sum of the components is the cost of the new structure.

3. **Quantity-survey method.** The quantity and quality of all materials (such as lumber, brick, and plaster) and the labor are estimated on a unit cost basis. These factors are added to indirect costs (for example, building permit, survey, payroll, taxes, and builder's profit) to arrive at the total cost of the structure. Because it is so detailed and time-consuming, the **quantity-survey method** is usually used only in appraising historical properties. It is, however, the most accurate method of appraising new construction.

4. **Index method.** A factor representing the percentage increase of construction costs up to the present time is applied to the original cost of the subject property. Because it fails to take into account individual property vari-

T A B L E   18.1

Sales Comparison Approach to Value

	Subject Property: 155 Potter Drive	Comparables				
		A	B	C	D	E
Sales price		$118,000	$112,000	$121,000	$116,500	$110,000
Financing concessions	none	none	none	none	none	none
Date of sale		current	current	current	current	current
Location	good	same	poorer + 6,500	same	same	same
Age	6 years	same	same	same	same	same
Size of lot	60′ × 135′	same	same	larger −5,000	same	larger −5,000
Landscaping	good	same	same	same	same	same
Construction	brick	same	same	same	same	same
Style	ranch	same	same	same	same	same
No. of rooms	6	same	same	same	same	same
No. of bedrooms	3	same	same	same	same	same
No. of baths	1½	same	same	same	same	same
Sq. ft. of living space	1,500	same	same	same	same	same
Other space (basement)	full basement	same	same	same	same	same
Condition–exterior	average	better −1,500	poorer +1,000	better −1,500	same	poorer +2,000
Condition–interior	good	same	same	better −500	same	same
Garage	2-car attached	same	same	same	same	none +5,000
Other improvements	none	none	none	none	none	none
Net Adjustments		− 1,500	+7,500	−7,000	-0-	+2,000
Adjusted Value		$116,500	$119,500	$114,000	$116,500	$112,000

Note: The value of a feature that is present in the subject but not in the comparable property is *added* to the sales price of the comparable. Likewise, the value of a feature that is present in the comparable but not in the subject property is *subtracted*. The adjusted sales prices of the comparables represent the probable range of value of the subject property. From this range, a single market value estimate can be selected. Because the value range of the properties in the comparison chart (excluding comparables B and E) is close, and comparable D required no adjustment, an appraiser might conclude that the indicated market value of the subject is $116,500. However, appraisers use a complex process of evaluating adjustment percentages and may consider other objective factors or subjective judgments based on research.

TABLE 18.2

Cost Approach to Value

Subject Property: 155 Potter Drive

Land Valuation: Size 60′ × 135′ @ $450 per front foot	=	$ 27,000
Plus site improvements: driveway, walks, landscaping, etc.	=	8,000
Total		$ 35,000

Building Valuation: Replacement Cost
    1,500 sq. ft. @ $85 per sq. ft. = $127,500

Less Depreciation:
Physical depreciation
  Curable
    (items of deferred maintenance)

exterior painting	$4,000	
Incurable (structural deterioration)	9,750	
Functional obsolescence	2,000	
External depreciation	-0-	
Total Depreciation	$15,750	

Depreciated Value of Building	$111,750
Indicated Value by Cost Approach	$146,750

---

ables, the **index method** is useful only as a check of the estimate reached by one of the other methods.

Depreciation. In a real estate appraisal, **depreciation** is a loss in value due to any cause. It refers to a condition that adversely affects the value of an improvement to real property. Remember: Land does not depreciate—it retains its value indefinitely, except in such rare cases as downzoned urban parcels, improperly developed land, or misused farmland.

Depreciation is considered to be *curable* or *incurable*, depending on the contribution of the expenditure to the value of the property. For appraisal purposes (as opposed to depreciation for tax purposes, discussed in Appendix 1), depreciation is divided into three classes, according to its cause:

1. **Physical deterioration.** *Curable:* an item in need of repair, such as painting (deferred maintenance), that is economically feasible and would result in an increase in value equal to or exceeding the cost. *Incurable:* a defect caused by physical wear and tear if its correction would not be economically feasible or contribute a comparable value to the building. The cost of a major repair may not warrant the financial investment.

2. **Functional obsolescence.** *Curable:* outmoded or unacceptable physical or design features that are no longer considered desirable by purchasers. Such features, however, could be replaced or redesigned at a cost that would be offset by the anticipated increase in ultimate value. Outmoded plumbing, for instance, is usually easily replaced. Room function may be redefined at no cost if the basic room layout allows for it. A bedroom adjacent to a kitchen, for example, may be converted to a family room. *Incurable:* currently undesirable physical or design features that could not be easily reme-

died because the cost of cure would be greater than its resulting increase in value. An office building that cannot be economically air-conditioned, for example, suffers from incurable functional obsolescence if the cost of adding air-conditioning is greater than its contribution to the building's value.

3. **External obsolescence.** *Incurable:* caused by negative factors not on the subject property, such as environmental, social, or economic forces. This type of depreciation is always incurable. The loss in value cannot be reversed by spending money on the property. For example, proximity to a nuisance, such as a polluting factory or a deteriorating neighborhood, is one factor that could not be cured by the owner of the subject property.

The easiest but least precise way to determine depreciation is the **straight-line method,** also called the *economic age-life method.* Depreciation is assumed to occur at an even rate over a structure's **economic life,** the period during which it is expected to remain useful for its original intended purpose. The property's cost is divided by the number of years of its expected economic life to derive the amount of annual depreciation.

For instance, a $120,000 property may have a land value of $30,000 and an improvement value of $90,000. If the improvement is expected to last 60 years, the annual straight-line depreciation would be $1,500 ($90,000 divided by 60 years). Such depreciation can be calculated as an annual dollar amount or as a percentage of a property's improvements.

The cost approach is most helpful in the appraisal of newer or special-purpose buildings such as schools, churches, and public buildings. Such properties are difficult to appraise using other methods because there are seldom enough local sales to use as comparables and because the properties do not ordinarily generate income.

Much of the functional obsolescence and all of the external depreciation can be evaluated only by considering the actions of buyers in the marketplace.

The Income Approach

The **income approach** to value is based on the present value of the rights to future income. It assumes that the income generated by a property will determine the property's value. The income approach is used for valuation of income-producing properties such as apartment buildings, office buildings, and shopping centers. In estimating value using the income approach, an appraiser must take the following five steps, illustrated in Table 18.3.

1. Estimate annual *potential gross income.* An estimate of economic rental income must be made based on market studies. Current rental income may not reflect the current market rental rates, especially in the case of short-term leases or leases about to terminate. Potential income includes other income to the property from such sources as vending machines, parking fees and laundry machines.
2. Deduct an appropriate allowance for vacancy and rent loss, based on the appraiser's experience, and arrive at the *effective gross income.*

3. Deduct the annual *operating expenses,* enumerated in Table 18.3, from the effective gross income to arrive at the annual *net operating income* (NOI). Management costs are always included, even if the current owner manages the property. Mortgage payments (principal and interest) are *debt service* and are not considered operating expenses. Also, capital expenditures are not considered expenses; however, an allowance can be calculated representing the annual usage of each major capital item.

4. Estimate the price a typical investor would pay for the income produced by this particular type and class of property. This is done by estimating the rate of return (or yield) that an investor will demand for the investment of capital in this type of building. This rate of return is called the **capitalization (or "cap") rate** and is determined by comparing the relationship of net operating income with the sales prices of similar properties that have sold in the current market. For example, a comparable property that is producing an annual net income of $15,000 is sold for $187,500. The capitalization rate is $15,000 divided by $187,500, or 8 percent. If other comparable properties sold at prices that yielded substantially the same rate, it may be concluded that 8 percent is the rate that the appraiser should apply to the subject property.

5. Apply the capitalization rate to the property's annual net operating income to arrive at the estimate of the property's value.

With the appropriate capitalization rate and the projected annual net operating income, the appraiser can obtain an indication of value by the income approach.

This formula and its variations are important in dealing with income property:

Income ÷ Rate = Value
Income ÷ Value = Rate
Value × Rate = Income

These formulas may be illustrated graphically as

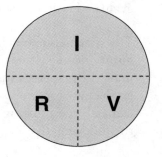

Net operating income ÷ Capitalization rate = Value
Example: $18,000 income ÷ 9% cap rate = $200,000 value or
$18,000 income ÷ 8% cap rate = $225,000 value

Note the relationship between the rate and value. As the rate goes down, the value increases.

A very simplified version of the computations used in applying the income approach is illustrated in Table 18.3.

Income Approach

The income approach uses five steps and may be remembered by the acronym **GIVEN: G**ross **I**ncome – **V**acancy and rent losses – operating **E**xpenses = **N**et operating income.

T A B L E 18.3

Income Capitalization Approach to Value

Potential Gross Annual Income		$60,000
Market rent (100% capacity)		
Income from other sources (vending machines and pay phones)	+ 600	
	$60,600	
Less vacancy and collection losses (estimated) @4%		–2,424
Effective Gross Income		$58,176
Expenses:		
Real estate taxes	$9,000	
Insurance	1,000	
Heat	2,500	
Maintenance	6,400	
Utilities, electricity, water, gas	800	
Repairs	1,200	
Decorating	1,400	
Replacement of equipment	800	
Legal and accounting	600	
Advertising	300	
Management	3,000	
Total		$27,000
Annual Net Operating Income		$31,176

Capitalization rate = 10% (overall rate)

Capitalization of annual net income: $31,176 ÷ .10 = $311,760

Indicated Value by Income Approach = $311,760

Gross rent or gross income multipliers. Certain properties, such as single-family homes and two-unit buildings, are not purchased primarily for income. As a substitute for a more elaborate income capitalization analysis, the **gross rent multiplier (GRM)** and **gross income multiplier (GIM)** are often used in the appraisal process. Each relates the sales price of a property to its rental income.

Because single-family residences usually produce only rental incomes, the gross rent multiplier is used. This relates a sales price to monthly rental income. However, commercial and industrial properties generate income from many other sources (rent, concessions, escalator clause income, and so forth), and they are valued using their annual income from all sources.

The formulas are as follows:

1. For five or more residential units, commercial or industrial property:
   Sales price ÷ Gross Income = Gross Income Multiplier (GIM)

   or

2. For one to four residential units:
   Sales price ÷ Gross Rent = Gross Rent Multiplier (GRM)

For example, if a home recently sold for $82,000 and its monthly rental income was $650, the GRM for the property would be computed

$82,000 ÷ $650 = 126.2 GRM

TABLE 18.4

Gross Rent Multiplier

Comparable No.	Sales Price	Monthly Rent	GRM
1	$93,600	$650	144
2	78,500	450	174
3	95,500	675	141
4	82,000	565	145
Subject	?	625	?

Note: Based on an analysis of these comparisons, a GRM of 145 seems reasonable for homes in this area. In the opinion of an appraiser, then, the estimated value of the subject property would be $625 × 145, or $90,625.

To establish an accurate GRM, an appraiser must have recent sales and rental data from at least four properties that are similar to the subject property. The resulting GRM can then be applied to the estimated fair market rental of the subject property to arrive at its market value. The formula would be

Rental income × GRM = Estimated market value

Table 18.4 shows some examples of GRM comparisons.

Reconciliation

When the three approaches to value are applied to the same property, they normally produce three separate indications of value. (For instance, compare Table 18.1 with Table 18.2.) **Reconciliation** is the art of analyzing and effectively weighing the findings from the three approaches.

The process of *reconciliation is not simply taking the average of the three estimates of value*. An average implies that the data and logic applied in each of the approaches are equally valid and reliable and should therefore be given equal weight. In fact, however, certain approaches are more valid and reliable with some kinds of properties than with others.

For example, in appraising a home, the income approach is rarely valid, and the cost approach is of limited value unless the home is relatively new. Therefore, the sales comparison approach is usually given greatest weight in valuing single-family residences. In the appraisal of income or investment property, the income approach normally is given the greatest weight. In the appraisal of churches, libraries, museums, schools, and other special-use properties, where little or no income or sales revenue is generated, the cost approach usually is assigned the greatest weight. From this analysis, or reconciliation, a single estimate of market value is produced.

■ THE APPRAISAL PROCESS

Although appraising is not an exact or a precise science, the key to an accurate appraisal lies in the methodical collection and analysis of data. The appraisal process is an orderly set of procedures used to collect and analyze data to arrive at an ultimate value conclusion. The data are divided into two basic classes:

FIGURE   18.1

The Appraisal Process

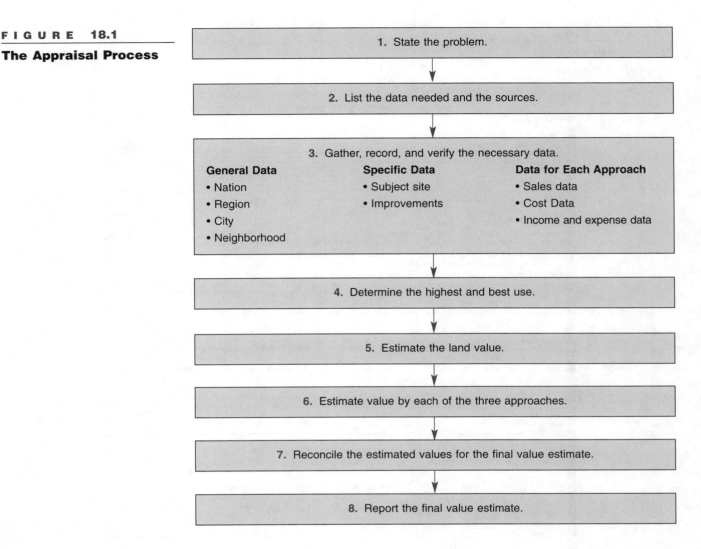

1. State the problem.

2. List the data needed and the sources.

3. Gather, record, and verify the necessary data.

General Data
- Nation
- Region
- City
- Neighborhood

Specific Data
- Subject site
- Improvements

Data for Each Approach
- Sales data
- Cost Data
- Income and expense data

4. Determine the highest and best use.

5. Estimate the land value.

6. Estimate value by each of the three approaches.

7. Reconcile the estimated values for the final value estimate.

8. Report the final value estimate.

1. *General data,* covering the nation, region, city, and neighborhood. Of particular importance is the neighborhood, where an appraiser finds the physical, economic, social, and political influences that directly affect the value and potential of the subject property.
2. *Specific data,* covering details of the subject property as well as comparative data relating to costs, sales, income, and expenses of properties similar to and competitive with the subject property.

Figure 18.1 outlines the steps an appraiser takes in carrying out an appraisal assignment.

Once the approaches have been reconciled and an opinion of value has been reached, the appraiser prepares a report for the client. The report should

- identify the real estate and real property interest being appraised;
- state the purpose and intended use of the appraisal;
- define the value to be estimated;
- state the effective date of the value and the date of the report;
- state the extent of the process of collecting, confirming, and reporting the data;

FIGURE   18.2

Uniform Residential Appraisal Report

Property Description

UNIFORM RESIDENTIAL APPRAISAL REPORT File No. _____

SUBJECT

Property Address		City	State Zip Code
Legal Description			County
Assessor's Parcel No.		Tax Year R.E. Taxes $	Special Assessments $
Borrower	Current Owner		Occupant: ☐ Owner ☐ Tenant ☐ Vacant
Property rights appraised ☐ Fee Simple ☐ Leasehold	Project Type ☐ PUD ☐ Condominium (HUD/VA only)	HOA$	/Mo.
Neighborhood or Project Name		Map Reference	Census Tract
Sale Price $	Date of Sale	Description and $ amount of loan charges/concessions to be paid by seller	
Lender/Client		Address	
Appraiser		Address	

NEIGHBORHOOD

Location	☐ Urban	☐ Suburban	☐ Rural	**Predominant occupancy**	**Single family housing** PRICE $(000) AGE (yrs)	**Present land use %**	**Land use change**
Built up	☐ Over 75%	☐ 25-75%	☐ Under 25%			One family ___	☐ Not likely ☐ Likely
Growth rate	☐ Rapid	☐ Stable	☐ Slow	☐ Owner	Low ___	2-4 family ___	☐ In process
Property values	☐ Increasing	☐ Stable	☐ Declining	☐ Tenant	High ___	Multi-family ___	To: ___
Demand/supply	☐ Shortage	☐ In balance	☐ Over supply	☐ Vacant (0-5%)	Predominant	Commercial ___	
Marketing time	☐ Under 3 mos.	☐ 3-6 mos.	☐ Over 6 mos.	☐ Vacant (over 5%)			

Note: Race and the racial composition of the neighborhood are not appraisal factors.

Neighborhood boundaries and characteristics: _____

Factors that affect the marketability of the properties in the neighborhood (proximity to employment and amenities, employment stability, appeal to market, etc.):
_____
_____
_____
_____

Market conditions in the subject neighborhood (including support for the above conclusions related to the trend of property values, demand/supply, and marketing time - - such as data on competitive properties for sale in the neighborhood, description of the prevalence of sales and financing concessions, etc.):
_____
_____
_____
_____

PUD

Project Information for PUDs (If applicable) - - Is the developer/builder in control of the Home Owners' Association (HOA)?   ☐ Yes   ☐ No

Approximate total number of units in the subject project_____   Approximate total number of units for sale in the subject project_____

Describe common elements and recreational facilities:

SITE

Dimensions _____			Topography _____
Site area _____	Corner Lot ☐ Yes ☐ No		Size _____
Specific zoning classification and description_____			Shape _____
Zoning compliance ☐ Legal ☐ Legal nonconforming (Grandfathered use) ☐ Illegal ☐ No zoning			Drainage _____
Highest & best use as improved: ☐ Present use ☐ Other use (explain)			View _____

Utilities	Public	Other	**Off-site Improvements**	Type	Public	Private	
Electricity	☐	___	Street	___	☐	☐	Landscaping _____
Gas	☐	___	Curb/gutter	___	☐	☐	Driveway Surface _____
Water	☐	___	Sidewalk	___	☐	☐	Apparent easements _____
Sanitary sewer	☐	___	Street lights	___	☐	☐	FEMA Special Flood Hazard Area ☐ Yes ☐ No
Storm sewer	☐	___	Alley	___	☐	☐	FEMA Zone ___ Map Date___
							FEMA Map No. _____

Comments (apparent adverse easements, encroachments, special assessments, slide areas, illegal or legal nonconforming zoning use, etc.): _____

DESCRIPTION OF IMPROVEMENTS

GENERAL DESCRIPTION	EXTERIOR DESCRIPTION	FOUNDATION	BASEMENT	INSULATION
No. of Units ___	Foundation ___	Slab ___	Area Sq. Ft. ___	Roof ___
No. of Stories ___	Exterior Walls ___	Crawl Space ___	% Finished ___	Ceiling ___
Type (Det./Att.) ___	Roof Surface ___	Basement ___	Ceiling ___	Walls ___
Design (Style) ___	Gutters & Dwnspts. ___	Sump Pump ___	Walls ___	Floor ___
Existing/Proposed ___	Window Type ___	Dampness ___	Floor ___	None ___
Age (Yrs.) ___	Storm/Screens ___	Settlement ___	Outside Entry ___	Unknown ___
Effective Age (Yrs.) ___	Manufactured House ___	Infestation ___		

ROOMS	Foyer	Living	Dining	Kitchen	Den	Family Rm.	Rec. Rm.	Bedrooms	# Baths	Laundry	Other	Area Sq. Ft.
Basement												
Level 1												
Level 2												

Finished area **above** grade contains: ___ Rooms; ___ Bedroom(s); ___ Bath(s); ___ Square Feet of Gross Living Area

INTERIOR	Materials/Condition	HEATING	KITCHEN EQUIP.	ATTIC	AMENITIES	CAR STORAGE:
Floors	___	Type ___	Refrigerator ☐	None ☐	Fireplace(s) # ___	None ☐
Walls	___	Fuel ___	Range/Oven ☐	Stairs ☐	Patio ___	Garage ___ # of cars
Trim/Finish	___	Condition ___	Disposal ☐	Drop Stair ☐	Deck ___	Attached ___
Bath Floor	___	COOLING	Dishwasher ☐	Scuttle ☐	Porch ___	Detached ___
Bath Wainscot	___	Central ___	Fan/Hood ☐	Floor ☐	Fence ___	Built-In ___
Doors	___	Other ___	Microwave ☐	Heated ☐	Pool ___	Carport ___
		Condition ___	Washer/Dryer ☐	Finished ☐		Driveway ___

COMMENTS

Additional features (special energy efficient items, etc.): _____

Condition of the improvements, depreciation (physical, functional, and external), repairs needed, quality of construction, remodeling/additions, etc.: _____

Adverse environmental conditions (such as, but not limited to, hazardous wastes, toxic substances, etc.) present in the improvements, on the site, or in the immediate vicinity of the subject property.: _____

F I G U R E   18.2

Uniform Residential Appraisal Report (cont'd)

Valuation Section   **UNIFORM RESIDENTIAL APPRAISAL REPORT**   **File No.**

COST APPROACH ESTIMATED SITE VALUE . . . . = $ _____ ESTIMATED REPRODUCTION COST-NEW-OF IMPROVEMENTS: Dwelling _____ Sq. Ft @ $ _____ = $ _____ _____ Sq. Ft @ $ _____ = $ _____ _____ = _____ Garage/Carport_____ Sq. Ft @ $ ____ = _____ Total Estimated Cost New . . . . = $ _____ Less Physical Functional External Depreciation _____ = $ _____ Depreciated Value of Improvements . . . . = $ _____ "As-is" Value of Site Improvements . . . . = $ _____ **INDICATED VALUE BY COST APPROACH** . . . . = $ _____	Comments on Cost Approach (such as, source of cost estimate, site value, square foot calculation and for HUD, VA and FmHA, the estimated remaining economic life of the property): _____ _____ _____ _____ _____ _____ _____ _____ _____

ITEM	SUBJECT	COMPARABLE NO. 1		COMPARABLE NO. 2		COMPARABLE NO. 3	
Address							
Proximity to Subject							
Sales Price	$		$		$		$
Price/Gross Liv. Area	$ ☑	$ ☑		$ ☑		$ ☑	
Data and/or Verification Source							
VALUE ADJUSTMENTS	DESCRIPTION	DESCRIPTION	+ (–) $ Adjustment	DESCRIPTION	+ (–) $ Adjustment	DESCRIPTION	+ (–) $ Adjustment
Sales or Financing Concessions							
Date of Sale/Time							
Location							
Leasehold/Fee Simple							
Site							
View							
Design and Appeal							
Quality of Construction							
Age							
Condition							
Above Grade	Total Bdrms Baths	Total Bdrms Baths		Total Bdrms Baths		Total Bdrms Baths	
Room Count							
Gross Living Area	Sq. Ft.	Sq. Ft.		Sq. Ft.		Sq. Ft.	
Basement & Finished Rooms Below Grade							
Functional Utility							
Heating/Cooling							
Energy Efficient Items							
Garage/Carport							
Porch, Patio, Deck, Fireplace(s), etc.							
Fence, Pool, etc.							
Net Adj. (total)		☐ + ☐ – $		☐ + ☐ – $		☐ + ☐ – $	
Adjusted Sales Price of Comparable		$		$		$	

Comments on Sales Comparison (including the subject property's compatibility to the neighborhood, etc.): _____
_____
_____
_____
_____

ITEM	SUBJECT	COMPARABLE NO. 1	COMPARABLE NO. 2	COMPARABLE NO. 3
Date, Price and Data Source, for prior sales within year of appraisal				

Analysis of any current agreement of sale, option, or listing of the subject property and analysis of any prior sales of subject and comparables within one year of the date of appraisal:
_____

INDICATED VALUE BY SALES COMPARISON APPROACH . . . . **$** _____
INDICATED VALUE BY INCOME APPROACH (If Applicable) Estimated Market Rent $ _____ /Mo. x Gross Rent Multiplier _____ = **$** ____
This appraisal is made ☐ "as is" ☐ subject to the repairs, alterations, inspections or conditions listed below ☐ subject to completion per plans and specifications.
Conditions of Appraisal: _____

Final Reconciliation: _____
_____

The purpose of this appraisal is to estimate the market value of the real property that is the subject of this report, based on the above conditions and the certification, contingent and limiting conditions, and market value definition that are stated in the attached Freddie Mac Form 439/Fannie Mae Form 1004B (Revised _____).
I (WE) ESTIMATE THE MARKET VALUE, AS DEFINED, OF THE REAL PROPERTY THAT IS THE SUBJECT OF THIS REPORT, AS OF _____
(WHICH IS THE DATE OF INSPECTION AND THE EFFECTIVE DATE OF THIS REPORT) TO BE $ _____

APPRAISER:	SUPERVISORY APPRAISER (ONLY IF REQUIRED):	
Signature	Signature	☐ Did ☐ Did Not
Name	Name	Inspect Property
Date Report Signed	Date Report Signed	
State Certification # State	State Certification # State	
Or State License # State	Or State License # State	

Freddie Mac Form 70 6-93   10 CH.   PAGE 2 OF 2   Fannie Mae Form 1004 6-93

- list all assumptions and limiting conditions that affect the analysis, opinion, and conclusions of value;
- describe the information considered, the appraisal procedures followed, and the reasoning that supports the report's conclusions (if an approach was excluded, the report should explain why);
- describe (if necessary or appropriate) the appraiser's opinion of the highest and best use of the real estate;
- describe any additional information that may be appropriate to show compliance with the specific guidelines established in the *Uniform Standards of Professional Appraisal Practice* (USPAP) or to clearly identify and explain any departures from these guidelines; and
- include a signed certification, as required by the Uniform Standards.

Figure 18.2 shows the *Uniform Residential Appraisal Report*, the form required by many government agencies. It illustrates the types of detailed information required of an appraisal of residential property.

IN PRACTICE

The role of an appraiser is not to determine value. Rather, an appraiser develops a supportable and objective report about the value of the subject property. The appraiser relies on experience and expertise in valuation theories to evaluate market data. The appraiser does not establish the property's worth; instead, he or she verifies what the market indicates. This is important to remember, particularly when dealing with a property owner who may lack objectivity about the realistic value of his or her property. The lack of objectivity also can complicate a salesperson's ability to list the property within the most probable range of market value. However, there are inherent conflicts between the appraiser's role and the real estate agent's and seller's roles. The agent and seller are seeking maximum value while looking ahead to the future. The appraiser, on the other hand, is seeking to justify the appraisal by looking at past events.

■ SUMMARY

To appraise real estate means to estimate its value. Although many types of value exist, the most common objective of an appraisal is to estimate market value—the most probable sales price of a property. Basic to appraising are certain underlying economic principles, such as highest and best use, substitution, supply and demand, conformity, anticipation, increasing and diminishing returns, regression, progression, plottage, contribution, competition, and change.

Appraisals are concerned with values, prices, and costs. It is vital to understand the distinctions among these terms. Value is an estimate of future benefits, cost represents a measure of past expenditures, and price reflects the actual amount of money paid for a property.

A professional appraiser analyzes a property through three approaches to value. In the sales comparison approach, the value of the subject property is compared with the values of others like it that have sold recently. Because no two properties are exactly alike, adjustments must be made to account for any differences. With the cost approach, an appraiser calculates the cost of building a similar structure on a similar site. The appraiser then subtracts depreciation (losses in value), which reflects the differences between new properties of this type and the present condition of the subject property. The income approach is an analysis based on the relationship between the rate of return that an investor requires and the net income that a property produces.

An informal version of the income approach, called the gross rent multiplier (GRM), may be used to estimate the value of single-family residential properties that are not usually rented, but could be. The GRM is computed by dividing the sales price of a property by its gross monthly rent. For commercial or industrial property, a gross income multiplier (GIM), based on annual income from all sources, may be used.

Normally, the application of the three approaches results in three different estimates of value. In the process of reconciliation, the validity and reliability of each approach are weighed objectively to arrive at the single best and most supportable estimate of value.

QUESTIONS

1. Which of the following appraisal methods uses a rate of investment return?
   a. Sales comparison approach
   b. Cost approach
   c. Income approach
   d. Gross income multiplier method

2. The elements of value include which of the following?
   a. Competition   c. Anticipation
   b. Scarcity   d. Balance

3. 457 and 459 Tarpepper Street are adjacent vacant lots, each worth approximately $50,000. If their owner sells them as a single lot, however, the combined parcel will be worth $120,000. What principle does this illustrate?
   a. Substitution   c. Regression
   b. Plottage   d. Progression

4. The amount of money a property commands in the marketplace is its
   a. intrinsic value.   c. subjective value.
   b. market value.   d. book value.

5. A homeowner constructs an eight-bedroom brick house with a tennis court, a greenhouse, and an indoor pool in a neighborhood of modest two-bedroom and three-bedroom frame houses on narrow lots. The value of this house is likely to be affected by what principle?
   a. Progression   c. Change
   b. Assemblage   d. Regression

6. In Question 5, the owners of the lesser-valued houses in the neighborhood may find that the values of their homes are affected by what principle?
   a. Progression   c. Competition
   b. Increasing returns   d. Regression

7. For appraisal purposes, accrued depreciation is not caused by
   a. functional obsolescence.
   b. physical deterioration.
   c. external obsolescence.
   d. accelerated depreciation.

8. *Reconciliation* refers to which of the following?
   a. Loss of value due to any cause
   b. Separating the value of the land from the total value of the property to compute depreciation
   c. Analyzing the results obtained by the different approaches to value to determine a final estimate of value
   d. Process by which an appraiser determines the highest and best use for a parcel of land

9. One method an appraiser can use to determine a building's cost as new construction involves the estimated cost of the materials needed to build the structure, plus labor and indirect costs. This is called the
   a. square-foot method.
   b. quantity-survey method.
   c. cubic-foot method.
   d. unit-in-place method.

10. If a property's annual net income is $24,000 and it is valued at $300,000, what is its capitalization rate?
    a. 8 percent   c. 12.5 percent
    b. 10.5 percent   d. 15 percent

11. Which of the following is not used by an appraiser using the income approach to value?
    a. Annual net operating income
    b. Capitalization rate
    c. Accrued depreciation
    d. Annual gross income

12. An appraiser asked to determine the value of an existing strip shopping center would probably give the most weight to which of the following approaches to value?
    a. Cost approach
    b. Sales comparison approach
    c. Income approach
    d. Index method

13. The market value of a parcel of real estate is
    a. an estimate of its future benefits.
    b. the amount of money paid for the property.
    c. an estimate of the most probable price it should bring.
    d. its value without improvements.

14. Capitalization is the process by which annual net operating income is used to
    a. determine cost.
    b. estimate value.
    c. establish depreciation.
    d. determine potential tax value.

15. From the reproduction or replacement cost of a building, the appraiser deducts depreciation, which represents
    a. the remaining economic life of the building.
    b. remodeling costs to increase rentals.
    c. loss of value due to any cause.
    d. costs to modernize the building.

16. The effective gross annual income from a property is $112,000. Total expenses for this year are $53,700. What capitalization rate was used to obtain a valuation of $542,325?
    a. 9.75 percent   c. 10.50 percent
    b. 10.25 percent   d. 10.75 percent

17. All of the following factors would be important in comparing properties under the sales comparison approach to value EXCEPT differences in
    a. dates of sale.
    b. financing terms.
    c. appearance and condition.
    d. original cost.

18. Trendsetter Terrace was purchased five years ago for $240,000. The building currently has an estimated remaining useful life of 55 years. What is the property's total depreciation to date?
    a. $14,364   c. $48,000
    b. $20,000   d. $54,000

19. In Question 18, what is the current value of Trendsetter Terrace?
    a. $235,636   c. $192,000
    b. $220,000   d. $186,000

20. The appraised value of a residence with four bedrooms and one bathroom would probably be reduced because of
    a. external obsolescence.
    b. functional obsolescence.
    c. curable physical deterioration.
    d. incurable physical deterioration.

21. An appraiser estimates that it would require 4,000 cubic feet of concrete, 10,000 feet of lumber, and $15,000 worth of copper pipe to replace a structure. The appraiser also estimates other factors, such as material, labor, overhead, and builder's profit. Which method of determining reproduction or replacement cost is this appraiser using?
    a. Square-foot method
    b. Quantity-survey method
    c. Index method
    d. Unit-in-place method

22. Which principle of value indicates that a developer's very profitable real estate project will attract others to engage in similar activity in the same area and thus drive down profits?
    a. Anticipation   c. Value
    b. Competition   d. Progression

23. Change, contribution, plottage, and substitution are some of the basic principles that affect what aspect of real estate?
    a. Demand   c. Value
    b. Depreciation   d. Supply

24. Gaslight fixtures in every unit of an apartment building would result in depreciation due to which of the following?
    a. Curable physical deterioration
    b. Curable functional obsolescence
    c. Incurable external obsolescence
    d. Incurable functional obsolescence

25. Which of the following methods of determining reproduction or replacement cost new is generally used primarily as a check on the result reached using another method?
    a. Square-foot method
    b. Quantity-survey method
    c. Index method
    d. Unit-in-place method

19

LAND-USE CONTROLS AND PROPERTY DEVELOPMENT

■ **LEARNING OBJECTIVES** *When you've finished reading this Chapter, you should be able to:*

■ **identify** the various types of public and private land-use controls.

■ **describe** how a comprehensive plan influences local real estate development.

■ **explain** the various issues involved in subdivision.

■ **distinguish** the function and characteristics of building codes and zoning ordinances.

■ **define** the following *key terms:*

buffer zone	density zoning	restrictive covenants
building code	developer	subdivider
certificate of occupancy	enabling acts	subdivision
clustering	gridiron	taking
comprehensive plan	Interstate Land Sales	variance
conditional-use permit	Full Disclosure Act	zoning ordinances
curvilinear	nonconforming use	
deed restriction	plat	

■ **WHY LEARN ABOUT...**   LAND-USE CONTROLS AND PROPERTY DEVELOPMENT?

A client comes to your office, wanting to buy a property for a specific commercial or residential development use. If you are familiar with land-use and property development issues, you will be able to show the client appropriate properties that can be lawfully developed according to the client's plans. If you aren't familiar with these concepts, it will be easy to erroneously assume that any development is legal anywhere or that because neighboring properties have been developed in a certain way, a vacant property can be developed the same way. Real estate agents have been successfully sued by buyers who discovered after a sale was closed that their intended use for their new property was prohibited by local law or private restriction. Understanding land-use controls and property development is important for your involvement in real estate. ■

■ LAND-USE CONTROLS

Land use is controlled and regulated through public and private restrictions and through the direct ownership of land by federal, state, and local governments. Over the years, the government's policy has been to encourage private ownership of land.

Home ownership is often referred to as the *American Dream*. It is necessary, however, for a certain amount of land to be owned by the government for such uses as municipal buildings, state legislative houses, schools, and military stations. Government ownership may also serve the public interest through urban renewal efforts, public housing, and streets and highways. Often, the only way to ensure that enough land is set aside for recreational and conservation purposes is through direct government ownership in the form of national and state parks and forest preserves. Beyond this sort of direct ownership of land, however, most government controls on property occur at the local level.

The states' *police power* is their inherent authority to create regulations needed to protect the public health, safety, and welfare. The states delegate to counties and local municipalities the authority to enact ordinances in keeping with general laws. The increasing demands placed on finite natural resources have made it necessary for cities, towns, and villages to increase their limitations on the private use of real estate. There are now controls over noise, air, and water pollution as well as population density.

■ THE COMPREHENSIVE PLAN

Local governments establish development goals by creating a **comprehensive plan.** This is also referred to as a *master plan*. Municipalities and counties develop plans to control growth and development. Each plan includes the municipality's (or other government body's) objectives for the future and the strategies and timing for those objectives to be implemented. For instance, a community may want to ensure that social and economic needs are balanced with environmental and aesthetic concerns. The comprehensive plan usually includes the following basic elements:

- *Land use,* that is, a determination of how much land may be proposed for residence, industry, business, agriculture, traffic and transit facilities, utilities, community facilities, parks and recreational facilities, floodplains, and areas of special hazards
- *Housing needs* of present and anticipated residents, including rehabilitation of declining neighborhoods as well as new residential developments
- *Movement of people and goods,* including highways and public transit, parking facilities, and pedestrian and bikeway systems
- *Community facilities and utilities* such as schools, libraries, hospitals, recreational facilities, fire and police stations, water resources, sewerage, waste treatment and disposal, storm drainage, and flood management
- *Energy conservation* to reduce energy consumption and promote the use of renewable energy sources

The preparation of a comprehensive plan involves surveys, studies, and analyses of housing, demographic, and economic characteristics and trends. The municipality's planning activities may be coordinated with other government bodies and private interests to achieve orderly growth and development.

■ **FOR EXAMPLE** After the Great Chicago Fire of 1871 reduced most of the city's downtown to rubble and ash, the city engaged planner Daniel Burnham to lay out a design for Chicago's future. The resulting Burnham Plan of orderly boulevards linking a park along Lake Michigan with other large parks and public spaces throughout the city established an ideal urban space. The plan is still being implemented today.

■ ZONING

Zoning ordinances are local laws that implement the comprehensive plan and regulate and control the use of land and structures within designated land-use districts. If the comprehensive plan is the big picture, zoning is the details. Zoning affects such things as

- permitted uses of each parcel of land,
- lot sizes,
- types of structures,
- building heights,
- setbacks (the minimum distance away from streets or sidewalks that structures may be built),
- style and appearance of structures,
- density (the ratio of land area to structure area), and
- protection of natural resources.

Zoning ordinances cannot be static; they must remain flexible to meet the changing needs of society.

■ **FOR EXAMPLE** In many large cities, factories and warehouses sit empty. Some cities have begun changing the zoning ordinances for such properties to permit new residential or commercial developments in areas once zoned strictly for heavy industrial use. Coupled with tax incentives, the changes lure developers back into the cities. The resulting housing is modern, conveniently located, and affordable. Simple zoning changes can help revitalize whole neighborhoods in big cities.

No nationwide or statewide zoning ordinances exist. Rather, zoning powers are conferred on municipal governments by state **enabling acts.** State and federal governments may, however, regulate land use through special legislation such as scenic easement, coastal management, and environmental laws.

Zoning Objectives

Zoning ordinances have traditionally classified land use into residential, commercial, industrial, and agricultural. These land-use areas are further divided into subclasses. For example, residential areas may be subdivided to provide for detached single-family dwellings, semidetached structures containing not more than four dwelling units, walkup apartments, highrise apartments, and so forth.

To meet both the growing demand for a variety of housing types and the need for innovative residential and nonresidential development, municipalities are adopting ordinances for subdivisions and planned residential developments. Some municipalities also use **buffer zones,** such as landscaped parks and playgrounds, to screen residential areas from nonresidential zones. Certain types of zoning that focus on special land-use objectives are used in some areas. These include

■ *bulk zoning* to control density and avoid overcrowding by imposing restrictions such as setbacks, building heights, and percentage of open area or by restricting new construction projects;
■ *aesthetic zoning* to specify certain types of architecture for new buildings; and
■ *incentive zoning* to ensure that certain uses are incorporated into developments, such as requiring the street floor of an office building to house retail establishments.

Constitutional issues and zoning ordinances. Zoning can be a highly controversial issue. Among other things, it often raises questions of constitutional law. The preamble of the U.S. Constitution provides for the promotion of the general welfare, but the Fourteenth Amendment prevents the states from depriving "any person of life, liberty, *or property,* without due process of law." How is a local government to enact zoning ordinances that protect public safety and welfare without violating the constitutional rights of property owners?

Any land-use legislation that is destructive, unreasonable, arbitrary, or confiscatory usually is considered void. Furthermore, zoning ordinances must not violate the various provisions of the constitution of the state in which the real estate is located. Tests commonly applied in determining the validity of ordinances require that the

■ power be exercised in a *reasonable manner;*
■ provisions be *clear and specific;*
■ ordinances be *nondiscriminatory;*

- ordinances promote *public health, safety, and general welfare* under the *police power* concept; and
- ordinances *apply to all property* in a *similar manner.*

Taking. The concept of **taking** comes from the *takings clause* of the Fifth Amendment to the U.S. Constitution. The clause reads, *"nor shall private property be taken for public use, without just compensation."* This means that when land is taken for public use through the government's power of eminent domain or condemnation, the owner must be compensated. In general, no land is exempt from government seizure. The rule, however, is that the government cannot seize land without paying for it. This payment is referred to as *just compensation*—compensation that is just, or fair.

Inverse condemnation is an action brought by a property owner seeking just compensation for land taken for a public use where it appears that the taker of the property does not intend to bring eminent domain proceedings. The property is condemned because its use and value have been diminished due to an adjacent property's public use, such as an airport or highway. For example, property along a newly constructed highway may be inversely condemned. While the property itself was not used in constructing the highway, the property's value may be significantly diminished due to the construction of the highway close to the property. The property owner may bring an inverse condemnation action to be compensated for the loss.

It is sometimes very difficult to determine what level of compensation is fair in any particular situation. The compensation may be negotiated between the owner and the government, or the owner may seek a court judgment setting the amount.

IN PRACTICE

One method used to determine just compensation is the *before-and-after method.* This method is used primarily where a portion of an owner's property is seized for public use. The value of the owner's remaining property after the taking is subtracted from the value of the whole parcel before the taking. The result is the total amount of compensation due to the owner.

Zoning Permits

Zoning laws are generally enforced through the use of permits. Compliance with zoning can be monitored by requiring that property owners obtain permits before they begin any development. A permit will not be issued unless a proposed development conforms to the permitted zoning, among other requirements. Zoning permits are usually required before building permits can be issued.

Zoning hearing board. Zoning hearing boards (or zoning boards of appeal) have been established in most communities to hear testimony (positive and negative) about the effects a zoning ordinance may have on specific parcels of property. Petitions for variances or exceptions to the zoning law may be presented to an appeal board.

Nonconforming use. Frequently, a lot or an improvement does not conform to the zoning use because it existed before the enactment or amendment of the zoning ordinance. Such a **nonconforming use** may be allowed to continue legally as long as it complies with the regulations governing nonconformities in the local ordinance, or until the improvement is destroyed or torn down, or until the current use is abandoned. If the nonconforming use is allowed to continue indefinitely, it is considered to be *grandfathered* into the new zoning.

■ **FOR EXAMPLE** Under Pleasantville's old zoning ordinances, the C&E Store was well within a commercial zone. When the zoning map was changed to accommodate an increased need for residential housing in Pleasantville, C&E was grandfathered into the new zoning; that is, it was allowed to continue its successful operations, even though it did not fit the new zoning rules.

Variances and conditional-use permits. Each time a plan or zoning ordinance is enacted, some property owners are inconvenienced and want to change the use of their property. Generally, these owners may appeal for either a **conditional-use permit** or a **variance** to allow a use that does not meet current zoning requirements.

A *conditional-use permit* (also known as a *special-use permit*) usually is granted to a property owner to allow a special use of property that is defined as an *allowable conditional use within that zone*, such as a house of worship or day-care center in a residential district. For a conditional-use permit to be appropriate, the intended use must meet certain standards set by the municipality.

Conditional-use permits allow nonconforming but related land uses.

Variances permit prohibited land uses to avoid undue hardship.

A *variance*, on the other hand, permits a landowner to use his or her property in a manner that is *strictly prohibited by the existing zoning*. Variances provide relief if zoning regulations deprive an owner of the reasonable use of his or her property. To qualify for a variance, the owner must demonstrate the unique circumstances that make the variance necessary. In addition, the owner must prove that he or she is harmed and burdened by the regulations. A variance might also be sought to provide relief if existing zoning regulations create a physical hardship for the development of a specific property. For example, if an owner's lot is level next to a road, but slopes steeply 30 feet away from the road, the zoning board may allow a variance so the owner can build closer to the road than the setback allows.

Both variances and conditional-use permits are issued by zoning boards only after public hearings. The neighbors of a proposed use must be given an opportunity to voice their opinions.

A property owner also can seek a change in the zoning classification of a parcel of real estate by obtaining an *amendment* to the district map or a zoning ordinance for that area, that is, the owner can attempt to have the zoning changed to accommodate his or her intended use of the property. The proposed amendment must be brought before a public hearing on the matter and approved by the governing body of the community.

■ BUILDING CODES AND CERTIFICATES OF OCCUPANCY

Most municipalities have enacted ordinances to specify construction standards that must be met when repairing or erecting buildings. These are called **building** codes, and they set the requirements for kinds of materials and standards of workmanship, sanitary equipment, electrical wiring, fire prevention, and the like.

A property owner who wants to build a structure or alter or repair an existing building usually must obtain a building permit. Through the permit requirement, municipal officials are made aware of new construction or alterations and can verify compliance with building codes and zoning ordinances. Inspectors will closely examine the plans and conduct periodic inspections of the work. Once the completed structure has been inspected and found satisfactory, the municipal inspector issues a **certificate of occupancy** or *occupancy permit*.

If the construction of a building or an alteration violates a *deed restriction* (discussed later in this Chapter), the issuance of a building permit will not cure this violation. A building permit is merely evidence of the applicant's compliance with municipal regulations.

Similarly, communities with historic districts, or those that are interested in maintaining a particular "look" or character, may have *aesthetic ordinances*. These laws require that all new construction or restorations be approved by a special board. The board ensures that the new structures will blend in with existing building styles. Owners of existing properties may need to obtain approval to have their homes painted or remodeled.

IN PRACTICE The subject of planning, zoning, and restricting the use of real estate is extremely technical, and the interpretation of the law is not always clear. Questions concerning any of these subjects in relation to real estate transactions should be referred to legal counsel. Furthermore, the landowner should be aware of the costs for various permits.

■ SUBDIVISION

Most communities have adopted **subdivision** and *land development ordinances* as part of their comprehensive plans. An ordinance includes provisions for submitting and processing subdivision plats. A major advantage of subdivision ordinances is that they encourage flexibility, economy, and ingenuity in the use of land. A **subdivider** is a person who buys undeveloped acreage and divides it into smaller lots for sale to individuals or developers or for the subdivider's own use. A **developer** (who may also be a subdivider) improves the land, constructs homes or other buildings on the lots, and sells them. Developing is generally a much more extensive activity than subdividing.

Regulation of Land Development

Just as no national zoning ordinance exists, no uniform planning and land development legislation affects the entire country. Laws governing subdividing and land planning are controlled by the state and local governing bodies where the land is located. Rules and regulations developed by government agencies have, however, provided certain minimum standards. Many local governments have established standards that are higher than the minimum standards.

Subdividers split up land into parcels.

Developers construct improvements on the subdivided parcels.

Land development plan. Before the actual subdividing can begin, the subdivider must go through the process of *land planning*. The resulting land development plan must comply with the municipality's comprehensive plan. Although comprehensive plans and zoning ordinances are not necessarily inflexible, a plan that requires them to be changed must undergo long, expensive, and frequently complicated hearings.

Plats. From the land development and subdivision plans, the subdivider draws plats. A **plat** is a detailed map that illustrates the geographic boundaries of individual lots. It also shows the blocks, sections, streets, public easements, and monuments in the prospective subdivision. A plat also may include engineering data and restrictive covenants. The plats must be approved by the municipality before they can be recorded. (See Figure 9.11 in Chapter 9 for an example of a subdivision plat map.) A developer is often required to submit an *environmental impact report* with the application for subdivision approval. This report explains what effect the proposed development will have on the surrounding area.

Subdivision Plans

In plotting out a subdivision according to local planning and zoning controls, a subdivider usually determines the size as well as the location of the individual lots. The maximum or minimum size of a lot is generally regulated by local ordinances and must be considered carefully.

The land itself must be studied, usually in cooperation with a surveyor, so that the subdivision takes advantage of natural drainage and land contours. A subdivider should provide for *utility easements* as well as easements for water and sewer mains.

Most subdivisions are laid out by use of *lots and blocks*. An area of land is designated as a block, and the area making up this block is divided into lots.

One negative aspect of subdivision development is the potential for increased tax burdens on all residents, both inside and outside the subdivision. To protect local taxpayers against the costs of a heightened demand for public services, many local governments strictly regulate nearly all aspects of subdivision development.

Subdivision Density

Zoning ordinances control land use. Such control often includes minimum lot sizes and population density requirements for subdivisions and land developments. For example, a typical zoning restriction may set the minimum lot area on which a subdivider can build a single-family housing unit at 10,000 square feet. This means that the subdivider can build four houses per acre. Many zoning authorities now establish special **density zoning** standards for certain subdivisions. Density zoning ordinances restrict the average *maximum number of houses per acre* that may be built within a particular subdivision. If the area is density zoned at an average maximum of four houses per acre, for instance, the subdivider may choose to *cluster* building lots to achieve an open effect. Regardless of lot size or number of units, the subdivider will be consistent with the ordinance as long as the average number of units in the development remains at or below the maximum density. This average is called *gross density*.

Gridiron   Curvilinear

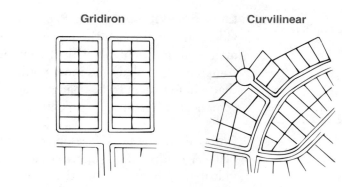

Street patterns. By varying street patterns and **clustering** housing units, a sub-divider can dramatically influence the amount of open or recreational space in a development. Two of these patterns are the **gridiron** and **curvilinear** patterns. (See Figure 19.1.)

The *gridiron* pattern evolved out of the government rectangular survey system. This pattern features large lots, wide streets, and limited-use service alleys. Sidewalks are usually adjacent to the streets or separated from them by narrow grassy areas. While the gridiron pattern provides for little open space and many lots may front on busy streets, it is an easy system to navigate.

The *curvilinear* system integrates major arteries of travel with smaller secondary and cul-de-sac streets carrying minor traffic. Curvilinear developments avoid the uniformity of the gridiron but often lack service alleys. The absence of straight-line travel and the lack of easy access tend to make curvilinear developments quieter and more secure. However, getting from place to place may be more challenging.

Clustering for open space. By slightly reducing lot sizes and clustering them around varying street patterns, a subdivider can house as many people in the same area as could be done using traditional subdividing plans but with substantially increased tracts of open space.

For example, compare the two subdivisions illustrated in Figure 19.2. Conventional Gardens is a conventionally designed subdivision containing 368 housing units. It uses 23,200 linear feet of street and leaves only 1.6 acres open for parkland. Contrast this with Cluster Estates. Both subdivisions are equal in size and terrain. But when lots are reduced in size and clustered around limited-access cul-de-sacs, the number of housing units remains nearly the same (366), with less street area (17,700 linear feet) and dramatically increased open space (23.5 acres). In addition, with modern building designs, this clustered plan could be modified to accommodate more than 1,000 town houses while retaining the attractive open spaces.

■ PRIVATE LAND-USE CONTROLS

Not all restrictions on the use of land are imposed by government bodies. Certain restrictions to control and to maintain the desirable quality and charac-

FIGURE   19.2

Subdivision Styles

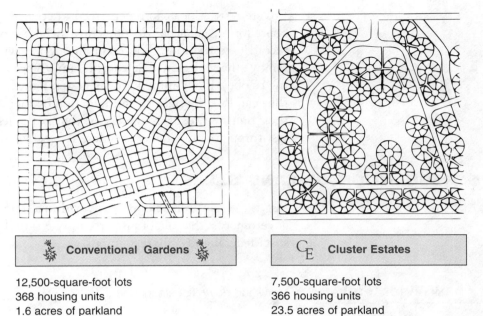

12,500-square-foot lots
368 housing units
1.6 acres of parkland

7,500-square-foot lots
366 housing units
23.5 acres of parkland

ter of a property or subdivision may be created by private entities, including the property owners themselves. These restrictions are separate from and in addition to the land-use controls exercised by the government. No private restriction can violate a local, state, or federal law.

Restrictive covenants. Restrictive covenants set standards for all the parcels within a defined subdivision. They usually govern the type, height, and size of buildings that individual owners can erect, as well as land use, architectural style, construction methods, setbacks, and square footage. The deed conveying a particular lot in the subdivision will refer to the plat or declaration of restrictions, thus limiting the title conveyed and binding all grantees. This is known as a **deed restriction.** Restrictions may have *time limitations*. A restriction might state that it is "effective for a period of 25 years from this date." After this time, it becomes inoperative. A time-limited covenant, however, may be extended by agreement.

Restrictive covenants are usually considered valid if they are reasonable restraints that benefit all property owners in the subdivision—for instance, to protect property values or safety. If, however, the terms of the restrictions are too broad, they will be construed as preventing the free transfer of property. If any restrictive covenant or condition is judged unenforceable by a court, the estate will stand free from the invalid covenant or condition. Restrictive covenants cannot be for illegal purposes, such as for the exclusion of members of certain races, nationalities, or religions.

Private land-use controls may be more restrictive of an owner's use than the local zoning ordinances. The rule is that the more restrictive of the two takes precedence.

Private restrictions can be enforced in court when one lot owner applies to the court for an *injunction* to prevent a neighboring lot owner from violating the recorded restrictions. The court injunction will direct the violator to stop or remove the violation. The court retains the power to punish the violator for failing to obey. If adjoining lot owners stand idly by while a violation is committed, they can lose the right to an injunction by their inaction. The court might claim their right was lost through *laches*, that is, the legal principle that a right may be lost through undue delay or failure to assert it.

■ REGULATION OF LAND SALES

Just as the sale and use of property within a state are controlled by state and local governments, the sale of property in one state to buyers in another is subject to strict federal and state regulations.

WWWeb.Link   www.hud.gov/offices/hsg/index.cfm

Interstate Land Sales Full Disclosure Act

The federal **Interstate Land Sales Full Disclosure Act** regulates the interstate sale of unimproved lots. The act is administered by the Secretary of Housing and Urban Development (HUD), through the office of Interstate Land Sales registration. It is designed to prevent fraudulent marketing schemes that may arise when land is sold without being seen by the purchasers. (You may be familiar with stories about gullible buyers whose land purchases were based on glossy brochures shown by smooth-talking salespersons. When the buyers finally went to visit the "little pieces of paradise" they'd bought, they frequently found worthless swampland or barren desert.)

The act requires that developers file statements of record with HUD before they can offer unimproved lots in interstate commerce by telephone or through the mail. The statements of record must contain numerous disclosures about the properties.

Developers are also required to provide each purchaser or lessee of property with a printed report before the purchaser or lessee signs a purchase contract or lease. The report must disclose specific information about the land, including

■ the type of title being transferred to the buyer,
■ the number of homes currently occupied on the site,
■ the availability of recreation facilities,
■ the distance to nearby communities,
■ utility services and charges, and
■ soil conditions and foundation or construction problems.

If the purchaser or lessee does not receive a copy of the report before signing the purchase contract or lease, he or she may have grounds to void the contract.

The act provides a number of exemptions. For instance, it does not apply to subdivisions consisting of fewer than 25 lots or to those in which the lots are of 20 acres or more. Lots offered for sale solely to developers also are exempt from the act's requirements, as are lots on which buildings exist or where a seller is obligated to construct a building within two years.

WWWeb.Link   www.hud.gov/complaints/landsales.cfm

State Subdivided-Land Sales Laws

Many state legislatures have enacted their own subdivided-land sales laws. Some affect only the sale of land located outside the state to state residents. Other states' laws regulate sales of land located both inside and outside the states. These state land sales laws tend to be stricter and more detailed than the federal law. Licensees should be aware of the laws in their states and how they compare with federal law.

■ SUMMARY

The control of land use is exercised through public controls, private (or nongovernment) controls, and direct public ownership of land.

Through power conferred by state enabling acts, local governments exercise public controls based on the states' police powers to protect the public health, safety, and welfare.

A comprehensive plan sets forth the development goals and objectives for the community. Zoning ordinances carrying out the provisions of the plan control the use of land and structures within designated land-use districts. Zoning enforcement problems involve zoning hearing boards, conditional-use permits, variances and exceptions, as well as nonconforming uses. Subdivision and land development regulations are adopted to maintain control of the development of expanding community areas so that growth is harmonious with community standards.

Building codes specify standards for construction, plumbing, sewers, electrical wiring, and equipment.

Public ownership is a means of land-use control that provides land for such public benefits as parks, highways, schools, and municipal buildings.

A subdivider buys undeveloped acreage, divides it into smaller parcels, and develops or sells it. A developer builds homes on the lots and sells them through the developer's own sales organization or through local real estate brokerage firms. City planners and land developers, working together, plan whole communities that are later incorporated into cities, towns, or villages.

Land development must comply with the master plans adopted by counties, cities, villages, or towns. This may entail approval of land-use plans by local planning committees or commissioners.

The process of subdivision includes dividing the tract of land into lots and blocks and providing for utility easements, as well as laying out street patterns and widths. A subdivider must generally record a completed plat of subdivision, with all necessary approvals of public officials, in the county where the land is located. Subdividers usually place restrictions on the use of all lots in a subdivision as a general plan for the benefit of all lot owners.

By varying street patterns and housing density and by clustering housing units, a subdivider can dramatically increase the amount of open and recreational space within a development.

Private land-use controls are exercised by owners through deed restrictions and restrictive covenants. These private restrictions may be enforced by obtaining a court injunction to stop a violator.

Subdivided land sales are regulated on the federal level by the Interstate Land Sales Full Disclosure Act. This law requires that developers engaged in certain interstate land sales or leases register the details of the land with HUD. Developers also must provide prospective purchasers or lessees with property reports containing all essential information about the property in any development that exceeds 25 lots.

QUESTIONS

1. A subdivision declaration reads, "No property within this subdivision may be further subdivided for sale or otherwise, and no property may be used for other than single-family housing." This is an example of

   a. a restrictive covenant.
   b. an illegal reverter clause.
   c. R-1 zoning.
   d. a conditional-use clause.

2. A landowner who wants to use property in a manner that is prohibited by a local zoning ordinance but that would benefit the community can apply for which of the following?

   a. Conditional-use permit
   b. Prescriptive easement
   c. Occupancy permit
   d. Property dedication

3. What is not included in public land-use controls?

   a. Subdivision regulations
   b. Restrictive covenants
   c. Environmental protection laws
   d. Comprehensive plan specifications

4. Under its police powers, a town may *not* legally regulate

   a. the number of buildings in a development.
   b. the size of buildings in a development.
   c. who may own buildings in a development.
   d. the special ages or income categories of people who may live in a development.

5. The purpose of a building permit is to

   a. assert a deed's restrictive covenant.
   b. maintain municipal control over the volume of building.
   c. provide evidence of compliance with municipal regulations.
   d. show compliance with restrictive covenants.

6. Zoning powers are conferred on municipal governments in which of the following ways?

   a. By state enabling acts
   b. Through the master plan
   c. By popular local vote
   d. Through city charters

7. The town of East Westchester enacts a new zoning code. Under the new code, commercial buildings are not permitted within 1,000 feet of Lake Westchester. A commercial building that is permitted to continue in its former use even though it is built on the lakeshore is an example of

   a. nonconforming use.
   b. variance.
   c. special use.
   d. adverse possession.

8. To determine whether a location can be put to future use as a retail store, one would examine the

   a. building code.
   b. list of permitted nonconforming uses.
   c. housing code.
   d. zoning ordinance.

9. Which of the following would not belong in a list of lawful deed restrictions?

   a. Types of buildings that may be constructed
   b. Allowable ethnic origins of purchasers
   c. Activities that are not to be conducted at the site
   d. Minimum size of buildings to be constructed

10. A restriction in a seller's deed may be enforced by which of the following?

    a. Court injunction
    b. Zoning board of appeal
    c. City building commission
    d. State legislature

11. Glenda owns a large tract of land. After an adequate study of all the relevant facts, Glenda legally divides the land into 30 lots suitable for the construction of residences. In this situation, Glenda is acting as a(n)

a. subdivider.
b. developer.
c. land planner.
d. urban planner.

12. A map illustrating the sizes and locations of streets and lots in a subdivision is called a

a. gridiron plan.
b. survey.
c. plat of subdivision.
d. property report.

13. In the city of Glendale, developers are limited by law to constructing no more than an average of three houses per acre in any subdivision. What does this restriction regulate?

a. Clustering
b. Gross density
c. Out-lots
d. Covenants

14. The city of Northbend is laid out in a pattern of intersecting streets and avenues. All streets run north and south; all avenues run east and west. Northbend is an example of which street pattern style?

a. Block plan
b. Gridiron system
c. Radial streets plan
d. Intersecting system

15. Permitted land uses and set-asides, housing projections, transportation issues, and objectives for implementing future controlled development would all be found in a community's

a. zoning ordinance.
b. comprehensive plan.
c. enabling act.
d. land-control law.

16. Which of the following items would usually not be shown on the plat for a new subdivision?

a. Easements for sewer and water mains
b. Land to be used for streets
c. Numbered lots and blocks
d. Prices of residential and commercial lots

17. Acorn Acres is a subdivision featuring spacious homes grouped on large cul-de-sac blocks connected to a central, winding road and surrounded by large, landscaped common areas. This is an example of which type of subdivision plan?

a. Cluster plan
b. Curvilinear system
c. Rectangular street system
d. Gridiron system

18. A subdivider can increase the amount of open or recreational space in a development by

a. varying street patterns.
b. meeting local housing standards.
c. scattering housing units.
d. eliminating multistory dwellings.

19. To protect the public from fraudulent interstate land sales, a developer involved in interstate land sales of 25 or more lots must

a. provide each purchaser with a printed report disclosing details of the property.
b. pay the prospective buyer's expenses to see the property involved.
c. provide preferential financing.
d. allow a 30-day cancellation period.

20. When is a certificate of occupancy issued?

a. When the owner of multifamily residential property wishes to limit the number of individuals who may live in a single unit
b. At the time a property owner applies for a building permit
c. After a newly-constructed building has been inspected and found satisfactory by the municipal inspector
d. When an application for a variance or conditional-use permit has been granted by the zoning board

CHAPTER TWENTY

20

FAIR HOUSING AND ETHICAL PRACTICES

■ **LEARNING OBJECTIVES** *When you've finished reading this Chapter, you should be able to:*

■ **identify** the classes of people who are protected against discrimination in housing by various federal laws.

■ **describe** how the Fair Housing Act is enforced.

■ **explain** how fair housing laws address a variety of discriminatory practices and regulate real estate advertising.

■ **distinguish** the protections offered by the Fair Housing Act, the Housing and Community Development Act, the Fair Housing Amendments Act, the Equal Credit Opportunity Act, and the Americans with Disabilities Act.

■ **define** the following *key terms:*

Americans with Disabilities Act (ADA)	Department of Housing and Urban Development (HUD)	ethics
blockbusting		Fair Housing Act
Civil Rights Act of 1866	Equal Credit Opportunity Act (ECOA)	redlining
code of ethics		steering
		Title VIII of the Civil Rights Act of 1968

■ **WHY LEARN ABOUT...** FAIR HOUSING AND ETHICAL PRACTICES?

The short answer is because if you don't follow the requirements of fair housing laws and ethical practices generally, you could very easily find yourself facing stiff fines, suspensions, and even the loss of your real estate license. But that's the negative side. On the positive side, understanding and following the fair housing laws and basic ethical practice will help create a more diverse, vibrant, and ultimately more profitable real estate market for everyone. Excluding customers on the basis of their skin color or religion, for instance, serves only to limit the number of potential customers. In the real estate market, it's just good business practice to treat everyone equally. ■

■ EQUAL OPPORTUNITY IN HOUSING

> "All citizens of the United States shall have the same right in every state and territory as is enjoyed by white citizens thereof to inherit, purchase, lease, sell, hold, and convey real and personal property."
>
> —*Civil Rights Act of 1866*

The purpose of civil rights laws that affect the real estate industry is to create a marketplace in which all persons of similar financial means have a similar range of housing choices. The goal is to ensure that everyone has the opportunity to live where he or she chooses. Owners, real estate licensees, apartment management companies, real estate organizations, lending agencies, builders, and developers must all take a part in creating this single housing market. Federal, state, and local fair housing or equal opportunity laws affect every phase of a real estate transaction, from listing to closing.

The U.S. Congress and the U.S. Supreme Court have created a legal framework that preserves the constitutional rights of all citizens. However, while the passage of laws may establish a code for public conduct, centuries of discriminatory practices and attitudes are not so easily changed. Real estate licensees cannot allow their own prejudices to interfere with the ethical and legal conduct of their profession. Similarly, the discriminatory attitudes of property owners or property seekers must not be allowed to affect compliance with the fair housing laws. This is not always easy, and the pressure to avoid offending the person who pays the real estate commission or flat fee can be intense. However, just remember: *Failure to comply with fair housing laws is both a civil and criminal violation and constitutes grounds for disciplinary action against a licensee.*

IN PRACTICE

Licensees must have a thorough knowledge of both state and federal fair housing laws. State laws may be stricter than the federal requirements and may provide protections for more classes of persons. State rules may provide for fines as well as the suspension or revocation of an offender's license.

The federal government's effort to guarantee equal housing opportunities to all U.S. citizens began with the passage of the **Civil Rights Act of 1866.** This law prohibits any type of discrimination based on race.

FIGURE 20.1

Federal Fair Housing Laws

Legislation	Race	Color	Religion	National Origin	Sex	Age	Marital Status	Disability	Discrimination	Familial Status	Public Assistance Income
Civil Rights Act of 1866	●										
Fair Housing Act of 1968 (Title VIII)	●	●	●	●					●		
Housing and Community Development Act of 1974					●			●			
Fair Housing Amendments Act of 1988								●	●	●	
Equal Credit Opportunity Act of 1974 (lending)	●	●	●	●	●	●	●		●		●

WWWeb.Link   www.fairhousing.com/legal_research/index.htm

The U.S. Supreme Court's 1896 decision in *Plessy v. Ferguson* established the "separate but equal" doctrine of legalized racial segregation. A series of court decisions and federal laws in the 20 years between 1948 and 1968 attempted to address the inequities in housing that were results of *Plessy*. Those efforts, however, tended to address only certain aspects of the housing market (such as federally funded housing programs). As a result, their impact was limited. Title VIII of the Civil Rights Act of 1968, however, prohibited specific discriminatory practices throughout the real estate industry.

■ FAIR HOUSING ACT

Title VIII of the Civil Rights Act of 1968 (called the *federal Fair Housing Act*) prohibited discrimination in housing based on race, color, religion, or national origin. In 1974, the *Housing and Community Development Act* added sex to the list of protected classes. In 1988, the *Fair Housing Amendments Act* included disability and familial status (that is, the presence of children). Today, these laws are known as the federal Fair Housing Act. (See Figure 20.1.) The **Fair Housing Act** prohibits discrimination on the basis of race, color, religion, sex, handicap, familial status, or national origin.

WWWeb.Link   www.hsh.com/pamphlets/fair_housing_act.html
www.hud.gov/fhe/fheact.html
www.hud.gov/groups/fairhousing.cfm

The act also prohibits discrimination against individuals because of their *association* with persons in the protected classes. This law is administered by the **Department of Housing and Urban Development (HUD).** HUD has established rules and regulations that further interpret the practices affected by the law. In addition, HUD distributes an *equal housing opportunity poster.* (See Figure

20.2.) The poster declares that the office in which it is displayed promises to adhere to the Fair Housing Act and pledges support for affirmative marketing and advertising programs.

IN PRACTICE

When HUD investigates a broker for discriminatory practices, it may consider failure to prominently display the equal housing opportunity poster in the broker's place of business as evidence of discrimination.

Table 20.1 describes the activities prohibited by the Fair Housing Act.

Definitions

HUD's regulations provide specific definitions that clarify the scope of the Fair Housing Act.

Housing. The regulations define *housing* as a "dwelling," which includes any building or part of a building designed for occupancy as a residence by one or more families. This includes a single-family house, condominium, cooperative, or manufactured housing, as well as vacant land on which any of these structures will be built.

> The *Fair Housing Act* prohibits discrimination based on
>
> - race,
> - color,
> - religion,
> - sex,
> - handicap,
> - familial status, and
> - national origin.

Familial status. *Familial status* refers to the presence of one or more individuals who have not reached the age of 18 and who live with either a parent or guardian. The term includes a woman who is pregnant. In effect, it means that the Fair Housing Act's protections extend to families with children. Unless a property qualifies as housing for older persons, all properties must be made available to families with children under the same terms and conditions as to anyone else. It is illegal to advertise properties as being for adults only or to indicate a preference for a certain number of children. The number of persons permitted to reside in a property (the occupancy standards) must be based on objective factors such as sanitation or safety. Landlords cannot restrict the number of occupants to eliminate families with children.

■ FOR EXAMPLE Gary owned an apartment building. One of his elderly tenants, Pam, was terminally ill. Pam requested that no children be allowed in the vacant apartment next door because the noise would be difficult for Pam to bear. Gary agreed and refused to rent to families with children. Even though Gary only wanted to make things easier for a dying tenant, Gary was nonetheless found to have violated the Fair Housing Act by discriminating on the basis of familial status.

Disability. A *disability* is a physical or mental impairment. The term includes having a history of, or being regarded as having, an impairment that substantially limits one or more of an individual's major life activities. Persons who have AIDS are protected by the fair housing laws under this classification.

IN PRACTICE

The federal fair housing law's protection of disabled persons does not include those who are current users of illegal or controlled substances. Nor are individuals who have been *convicted* of the illegal manufacture or distribution of a controlled substance protected under this law. However, the law does prohibit discrimination against those who are participating in addiction recovery programs. For instance, a landlord could lawfully discriminate against a cocaine addict, but not against a member of Alcoholics Anonymous.

It is unlawful to discriminate against prospective buyers or tenants on the basis of disability. Landlords must make reasonable accommodations to existing policies, practices, or services to permit persons with disabilities to have equal enjoyment of the premises. For instance, it would be reasonable for a landlord to permit support animals (such as guide dogs) in a normally no-pets building or to provide a designated handicapped parking space in a generally unreserved lot.

People with disabilities must be permitted to make reasonable modifications to the premises at their own expense. Such modifications might include lowering door handles or installing bath rails to accommodate a person in a wheelchair. Failure to permit reasonable modification constitutes discrimination.

However, the law recognizes that some reasonable modifications might make a rental property undesirable to the general population. In such a case, the landlord is allowed to require that the property be restored to its previous condition when the lease period ends, reasonable wear and tear excepted. Where it is necessary to ensure with reasonable certainty that funds will be available to pay for the restorations at the end of the tenancy, the landlord may negotiate as part of a restoration agreement a provision requiring the tenant pay into an interest bearing escrow account, over a reasonable period, a reasonable amount of money not to exceed the cost of the restorations. The interest in the account accrues to the benefit of the tenant. A landlord may not increase for handicapped persons any customarily required security deposit.

The law does not prohibit restricting occupancy exclusively to persons with handicaps in dwellings that are designed specifically for their accommodation.

For new construction of certain multifamily properties, a number of accessibility and usability requirements must be met under federal law. Access is specified for public and common-use portions of the buildings, and adaptive and accessible design must be implemented for the interior of the dwelling units. Some states have their own laws as well.

Racial Discrimination. Jones v. Mayer. In 1968, the Supreme Court heard the case of *Jones v. Alfred H. Mayer Company*, 392 U.S. 409 (1968). In its decision, the Court upheld the Civil Rights Act of 1866. This decision is important because although the federal Fair Housing Act exempts individual homeowners and certain groups, the 1866 law *prohibits all racial discrimination without exception. Where race is involved, no exceptions apply.* This decision is also important because it prohibited racial discrimination in the sale or rental of privately held property.

The U.S. Supreme Court has expanded the definition of the term *race* to include ancestral and ethnic characteristics, including certain physical, cultural, or linguistic characteristics that are shared by a group with a common national origin. These rulings are significant because discrimination on the basis of race, as it is now defined, affords due process of complaints under the provisions of the Civil Rights Act of 1866.

**Equal Opportunity
Housing Poster**

U.S. Department of Housing and Urban Development

**EQUAL HOUSING
OPPORTUNITY**

We Do Business in Accordance With the Federal Fair Housing Law

(The Fair Housing Amendments Act of 1988)

It is Illegal to Discriminate Against Any Person Because of Race, Color, Religion, Sex, Handicap, Familial Status, or National Origin

■ In the sale or rental of housing or residential lots

■ In advertising the sale or rental of housing

■ In the financing of housing

■ In the provision of real estate brokerage services

■ In the appraisal of housing

■ Blockbusting is also illegal

Anyone who feels he or she has been discriminated against may file a complaint of housing discrimination:
    1-800-669-9777 (Toll Free)
    1-800-927-9275 (TDD)

**U.S. Department of Housing and
Urban Development
Assistant Secretary for Fair Housing and
Equal Opportunity
Washington, D.C. 20410**

Previous editions are obsolete

form HUD-928.1A(8-93)

T A B L E   20.1

**Fair Housing Act
Restrictions**

Prohibited by Federal Fair Housing Act	Example
Refusing to sell, rent or negotiate the sale or rental of housing	K owns an apartment building with several vacant units. When an Asian family asks to see one of the units, K tells them to go away.
Changing terms, conditions, or services for different individuals as a means of discriminating	S, a Roman Catholic, calls on a duplex, and the landlord tells her the rent is $400 per month. When she talks to the other tenants, she learns that all the Lutherans in the complex pay only $325 per month.
Advertising any discriminatory preference or limitation in housing or making any inquiry or reference that is discriminatory in nature	A real estate agent places the following advertisement in a newspaper: "Just Listed! Perfect home for white family, near excellent parochial school!"
	A developer places this ad in an urban newspaper: "Sunset River Hollow-Dream Homes Just For You!" The ad is accompanied by a photo of several African-American families.
Representing that a property is not available for sale or rent when in fact it is	J, who uses a wheelchair, is told that the house J wants to rent is no longer available. The next day, however, the For Rent sign is still in the window.
Profiting by inducing property owners to sell or rent on the basis of the prospective entry into the neighborhood of persons of a protected class	N, a real estate agent, sends brochures to homeowners in the predominantly white Ridgewood neighborhood. The brochures, which feature N's past success selling homes, include photos of racial minorities, population statistics, and the caption, "The Changing Face of Ridgewood."
Altering the terms or conditions of a home loan, or denying a loan, as a means of discrimination	A lender requires M, a divorced mother of two young children, to pay for a credit report. In addition, her father must cosign her application. After talking to a single male friend, M learns that he was not required to do either of those things, despite his lower income and poor credit history.
Denying membership or participation in a multiple-listing service, a real estate organization, or another facility related to the sale or rental of housing as a means of discrimination	The Topper County Real Estate Practitioners' Association meets every week to discuss available properties and buyers. None of Topper County's black or female agents is allowed to be a member of the association.

342 Part 2 Practice

IN PRACTICE

A real estate agent or broker is not obligated to provide ethnic-diversity information to home buyers. In a 2001 case from Ohio, *Hannah v. Sibcy Cline Realtors,* the issues were whether an agent or broker had the fiduciary duty to 1) inform a client whether a neighborhood was ethnically diverse, or 2) direct the client to resources that provided such information. The court concluded that while an agent or broker might choose to provide such information to a client or direct a client to resources about the ethnic diversity of a particular area, the agent or broker does so at his or her own risk, and there is no fiduciary duty to do so.

Exemptions to the Fair Housing Act

The federal Fair Housing Act covers most housing. However, in some circumstances, the Act provides for certain exemptions. The Fair Housing Act exempts

- owner-occupied buildings with no more than four units,
- single-family housing sold or rented without the use of a broker, and
- housing operated by organizations and private clubs that limit occupancy to members.

The sale or rental of a single-family home is exempt when

- the home is owned by an individual who does not own more than three such homes at one time (and who does not sell more than one every two years);
- a real estate broker or salesperson is *not* involved in the transaction; and
- discriminatory advertising is not used.

The rental of rooms or units is exempted in an owner-occupied one-family to four-family dwelling.

Note that dwelling units owned by religious organizations may be restricted to people of the same religion if membership in the organization is not restricted on the basis of race, color, or national origin. A private club that is not open to the public may restrict the rental or occupancy of lodgings that it owns to its members as long as the lodgings are not operated commercially. Membership in a private club must be open to people of all races, colors, and national origins.

The Fair Housing Act does not require that housing be made available to any individual whose tenancy would constitute a direct threat to the health or safety of other individuals or that would result in substantial physical damage to the property of others.

Housing for older persons. While the Fair Housing Act protects families with children, certain properties can be restricted to occupancy by elderly persons. Housing intended for persons age 62 or older or housing occupied by at least one person 55 years of age or older per unit (where 80 percent of the units are occupied by individuals 55 or older) is exempt from the familial status protection.

Megan's Law. Federal legislation, known as Megan's Law, promotes the establishment of state registration systems to maintain residential information on every person who kidnaps children, commits sexual crimes against children, or commits sexually violent crimes. Upon release from prison, an offender must register his or her name with state authorities and indicate where he or she will be

> **The *Equal Credit Opportunity Act* prohibits discrimination in granting credit based on**
>
> ■ race,
> ■ color,
> ■ religion,
> ■ national origin,
> ■ sex,
> ■ marital status,
> ■ age, and
> ■ public assistance.

residing. Local law enforcement agencies may release relevant information about such an offender upon request if they deem it necessary for the protection of the public.

Megan's Law affects a licensee's duty of disclosure. In accordance with state law, a licensee may need to request that a customer sign a form indicating where the customer may obtain information about the sex offender registry. Typically, a licensee may be required to disclose information regarding a released offender if the licensee is aware that officals have informed individuals, groups, or the public that a sex offender resides in a particular area. (Megan's Law, in effect, creates another category of stigmatized property. See Chapter 4 for more information on stigmatized property.)

Equal Credit Opportunity Act

The federal **Equal Credit Opportunity Act (ECOA)** prohibits discrimination based on race, color, religion, national origin, sex, marital status, or age in the granting of credit. Note that the ECOA protects more classes of persons than the Fair Housing Act. The ECOA bars discrimination on the basis of marital status and age. It also prevents lenders from discriminating against recipients of public assistance programs such as food stamps and Social Security. The ECOA is the only federal law that grants protection on age, marital status, and receipt of public assistance. As in the Fair Housing Act, the ECOA requires that credit applications be considered only on the bases of income, net worth, job stability, and credit rating.

WWWeb.Link

www.usdoj.gov/crt/ada/adahom1.htm

Americans with Disabilities Act

Although **the Americans with Disabilities Act (ADA)** is not a housing or credit law, it still has a significant effect on the real estate industry. The ADA is important to licensees because it addresses the rights of individuals with disabilities in employment and public accommodations. Real estate brokers are often employers, and real estate brokerage offices are public spaces. The ADA's goal is to enable individuals with disabilities to become part of the economic and social mainstream of society. The ADA is discussed in detail in Chapter 17.

Title I of the ADA requires that employers (including real estate licensees) make *reasonable accommodations* that enable an individual with a disability to perform essential job functions. Reasonable accommodations include making the work site accessible, restructuring a job, providing part-time or flexible work schedules, and modifying equipment that is used on the job. The provisions of the ADA apply to any employer with 15 or more employees.

IN PRACTICE

In 1999, the U.S. Supreme Court strictly limited the definition of "persons with disabilities" protected by the ADA. The decision excludes individuals whose disability, such as nearsightedness, can be corrected. In 2002, the U.S. Supreme Court narrowed the definition even further by stating that in determining whether a person is disabled, you need to ask whether the impairment(s) prevented or restricted the person from performing tasks that are of central importance to most people's daily lives.

WWWeb.Link   www.law.cornell.edu   www.supremecourtus.gov

> The *Americans with Disabilities Act* requires **reasonable accommodations** in employment and access to goods, services, and public buildings.

Title III of the ADA provides for accessibility to goods and services for individuals with disabilities. While the federal civil rights laws have traditionally been viewed in the real estate industry as housing-related, the practices of licensees who deal with nonresidential property are significantly affected by the ADA. Because people with disabilities have the right to full and equal access to businesses and public services under the ADA, building owners and managers must ensure that any obstacle restricting this right is eliminated. The *Americans with Disabilities Act Accessibility Guidelines* (ADAAG) contain detailed specifications for designing parking spaces, curb ramps, elevators, drinking fountains, toilet facilities, and directional signs to ensure maximum accessibility. These requirements are discussed in detail in Chapter 17.

ADA and the Fair Housing Act. The ADA exempts the following two types of property from its requirements:

1. Property that is covered by the Fair Housing Act
2. Property that is exempt from coverage by the Fair Housing Act

Some properties, however, are subject to both laws. For example, in an apartment complex, the rental office is a "place of public accommodation." As such, it is covered by the ADA and must be accessible to persons with disabilities at the owner's expense. Individual rental units would be covered by the Fair Housing Act. If a tenant wished to modify the unit to make it accessible, he or she would be responsible for the cost.

Issues of housing and disability discrimination are often litigated in the courts. For example, in a 2001 case, *Dadian v. Village of Wilmette*, homeowners sued the village for discrimination under the ADA and the Fair Housing Act. The elderly homeowners wanted to rebuild their house with an attached garage in front, which required a curb cut to the street. They applied for a permit with the village. The village denied the permit because the new driveway would cause a safety hazard when backing out of it. The court found that the homeowners were disabled with osteoporosis and that the village must issue a permit to allow them to rebuild their house and driveway.

IN PRACTICE   Real estate agents need a general knowledge of the ADA's provisions. It is necessary for a broker's workplace and employment policies to comply with the law. Also, licensees who are building managers must ensure that the properties are legally accessible. However, ADA compliance questions may arise with regard to a client's property, too. Unless the agent is a qualified ADA expert, it is best to advise commercial clients to seek the services of an attorney, an architect, or a consultant who specializes in ADA issues. It is possible that an appraiser may be liable for failing to identify and account for a property's noncompliance.

■ FAIR HOUSING PRACTICES

For the civil rights laws to accomplish their goal of eliminating discrimination, licensees must apply them routinely. Of course, compliance also means that licensees avoid violating both the laws and the ethical standards of the profession. The following discussion examines the ethical and legal issues that confront real estate licensees.

Blockbusting

Blockbusting: Encouraging the sale or renting of property by claiming that the entry of a protected class of people into the neighborhood will negatively affect property values

Blockbusting is the act of encouraging people to sell or rent their homes by claiming that the entry of a protected class of people into the neighborhood will have some sort of negative impact on property values. Blockbusting was a common practice during the 1950s and 1960s, as unscrupulous real estate agents profited by fueling "white flight" from cities to suburbs. Any message, however subtle, that property should be sold or rented because the neighborhood is "undergoing changes" is considered blockbusting. It is illegal to assert that the presence of certain persons will cause property values to decline, crime or antisocial behavior to increase, and the quality of schools to suffer.

A critical element in blockbusting, according to HUD, is the profit motive. A property owner may be intimidated into selling his or her property at a depressed price to the blockbuster, who in turn sells the property to another person at a higher price. Another term for this activity is *panic selling*. To avoid accusations of blockbusting, licensees should use good judgment when choosing locations and methods for marketing their services and soliciting listings.

Steering

Steering: Channeling home seekers toward or away from particular neighborhoods based on race, religion, national origin, or some other consideration

Steering is the channeling of home seekers to particular neighborhoods. It also includes discouraging potential buyers from considering some areas. In either case, it is an illegal limitation of a purchaser's options.

Steering may be done either to preserve the character of a neighborhood or to change its character intentionally. Many cases of steering are subtle, motivated by assumptions or perceptions about a home seeker's preferences, based on some stereotype. Assumptions are not only dangerous—they are often *wrong*. The licensee cannot *assume* that a prospective home seeker expects to be directed to certain neighborhoods or properties. Steering anyone is illegal.

The number of immigrants in the United States continues to increase. After immigrants have lived in the United States for six years, about 67 percent of them buy property. Any person involved in the real estate profession should learn to work and communicate well with buyers and sellers of different nationalities and cultures.

Advertising

No advertisement of property for sale or rent may include language indicating a preference or limitation. No exception to this rule exists, regardless of how subtle the choice of words. HUD's regulations cite examples that are considered discriminatory. (See Figure 20.3.) Note, however, that an advertisement that is gender specific, such as "female roommate sought," is allowed as long as the advertiser seeks to share living quarters with someone of the same gender. The media used for promoting property or real estate services cannot target one population to the exclusion of others. The selective use of media, whether by lan-

FIGURE 20.3

HUD's Advertising Guidelines

CATEGORY	RULE	PERMITTED	NOT PERMITTED
Race Color National Origin	No discriminatory limitation/preference may be expressed	"master bedroom" "good neighborhood"	"white neighborhood" "no French"
Religion	No religious preference/limitation	"chapel on premises" "kosher meals available" "Merry Christmas"	"no Muslims" "nice Christian family" "near great Catholic school"
Sex	No explicit preference based on sex	"mother-in-law suite" "master bedroom" "female roommate sought"	"great house for a man" "wife's dream kitchen"
Handicap	No exclusions or limitations based on handicap	"wheelchair ramp" "walk to shopping"	"no wheelchairs" "able-bodied tenants only"
Familial Status	No preference or limitation based on family size or nature	"two-bedroom" "family room" "quiet neighborhood"	"married couple only" "no more than two children" "retiree's dream house"
Photographs or Illustrations of People	People should be clearly representative and nonexclusive	Illustrations showing ethnic races, family groups, singles, etc.	Illustrations showing only singles, African American families, elderly white adults, etc.

guage or geography, may have discriminatory impact. For instance, advertising property only in a Korean-language newspaper tends to discriminate against non-Koreans. Similarly, limiting advertising to a cable television channel available only to white suburbanites may be construed as a discriminatory act. However, if an advertisement appears in general-circulation media as well, it may be legal.

IN PRACTICE

A few years ago the Fair Housing Council of Oregon filed a complaint against a local multiple-listing service (MLS), charging that the phrase "adults only over 40" was included in the "Remarks" section of a condominium listing. While the condominium association's bylaws actually did contain the age restriction, the Fair Housing Council argued that including the phrase in the listing constituted discrimination against families with children in violation of the Fair Housing Act. The MLS paid $30,000 to settle with HUD, $20,000 of which went to support the antidiscrimination efforts of the Fair Housing Council of Oregon. The MLS also agreed to conduct regular computerized searches of its database for 67 different discriminatory words and phrases.

Appraising

Those who prepare appraisals or any statements of valuation, whether they are formal or informal, oral or written (including a competitive market analysis), may consider any factors that affect value. However, race, color, religion, national origin, sex, handicap, and familial status are not factors that may be considered.

Redlining

The practice of refusing to make mortgage loans or issue insurance policies in specific areas for reasons other than the economic qualifications of the applicants is known as **redlining.** Redlining refers to literally drawing a line around particular areas. This practice is often a major contributor to the deterioration of older neighborhoods. Redlining is frequently based on racial grounds rather than on any real objection to an applicant's creditworthiness, that is, the lender makes a policy decision that no property in a certain area is qualified for a loan, no matter who wants to buy it, because of the neighborhood's ethnic character. The federal Fair Housing Act prohibits discrimination in mortgage lending and covers not only the actions of primary lenders but also activities in the secondary mortgage market. A lending institution, however, can refuse a loan solely on *sound* economic grounds.

The *Home Mortgage Disclosure Act* requires all institutional mortgage lenders with assets in excess of $10 million and one or more offices in a given geographic area to make annual reports. The reports must detail all mortgage loans the institution has made or purchased, broken down by census tract. This law enables the government to detect patterns of lending behavior that might constitute redlining.

Intent and Effect

If an owner or real estate licensee *purposely* sets out to engage in blockbusting, steering, or other unfair activities, the intent to discriminate is *obvious*. However, owners and licensees must examine their activities and policies carefully to determine whether they have unintentional discriminatory *effects*. Whenever policies or practices result in unequal treatment of persons in the protected classes, they are considered discriminatory regardless of any innocent intent. This *effects test* is applied by regulatory agencies to determine whether an individual has been discriminated against.

■ ENFORCEMENT OF THE FAIR HOUSING ACT

WWWeb.Link   www.hud.gov/complaints/housediscrim.cfm
www.hud.gov/library/bookshelf09/index.cfm

The federal Fair Housing Act is administered by the Office of Fair Housing and Equal Opportunity (OFHEO) under the direction of the secretary of HUD. Any aggrieved person who believes illegal discrimination has occurred may file a complaint with HUD within one year of the alleged act. HUD also may initiate its own complaint. Complaints may be reported to the Office of Fair Housing and Equal Opportunity, Department of Housing and Urban Development, Washington, DC 20410, or to the Office of Fair Housing and Equal Opportunity in care of the nearest HUD regional office. Complaints may also be submitted directly to HUD using an online form available on the HUD Web site.

Upon receiving a complaint, HUD initiates an investigation. Within 100 days of the filing of the complaint, HUD either determines that reasonable cause exists to bring a charge of illegal discrimination or dismisses the complaint. During this investigation period, HUD can attempt to resolve the dispute informally through conciliation. *Conciliation* is the resolution of a complaint by obtaining assurance that the person against whom the complaint was filed (the respondent) will remedy any violation that may have occurred. The respondent further agrees to take steps to eliminate or prevent discriminatory practices in the future. If necessary, these agreements can be enforced through civil action.

The aggrieved person has the right to seek relief through administrative proceedings. Administrative proceedings are hearings held before *administrative law judges* (ALJs). An ALJ has the authority to award actual damages to the aggrieved person or persons and, if it is believed the public interest will be served, to impose monetary penalties. The penalties range from up to $10,000 for the first offense to $25,000 for a second violation within five years and $50,000 for further violations within seven years. The ALJ also has the authority to issue an injunction to order the offender to either do something (such as rent an apartment to the complaining party) or refrain from doing something (such as acting in a discriminatory manner).

The parties may elect civil action in federal court at any time within two years of the discriminatory act. For cases heard in federal court, unlimited punitive damages can be awarded in addition to actual damages. The court can also issue injunctions. As noted in Chapter 5, errors and omissions insurance carried by licensees normally does not pay for violations of the fair housing laws.

Whenever the attorney general has reasonable cause to believe that any person or group is engaged in a pattern or practice of resistance to the full enjoyment of any of the rights granted by the federal fair housing laws, he or she may file a civil action in any federal district court. Civil penalties may result in an amount not to exceed $50,000 for a first violation and an amount not to exceed $100,000 for second and subsequent violations.

Complaints brought under the Civil Rights Act of 1866 are taken directly to federal courts. The only time limit for action is a state's statute of limitations for *torts*—injuries one individual inflicts on another.

State and Local Enforcement Agencies

Many states and municipalities have their own fair housing laws. If a state or local law is *substantially equivalent* to the federal law, all complaints filed with HUD are referred to the local enforcement agencies. To be considered substantially equivalent, the local law and its related regulations must contain prohibitions comparable to those in the federal law. In addition, the state or locality must show that its local enforcement agency takes sufficient affirmative action in processing and investigating complaints and in finding remedies for discriminatory practices. It is important for all licensees to be aware of their states' fair housing laws, as well as applicable local ordinances.

Threats or Acts of Violence

Being a real estate agent is not generally considered a dangerous occupation. However, some licensees may find themselves the targets of threats or violence merely for complying with fair housing laws. The federal *Fair Housing Act of 1968* protects the rights of those who seek the benefits of the open housing law. It also protects owners, brokers, and salespersons who aid or encourage the enjoyment of open housing rights. Threats, coercion, and intimidation are punishable by criminal action. In such a case, the victim should report the incident immediately to the local police and to the nearest office of the Federal Bureau of Investigation.

■ IMPLICATIONS FOR BROKERS AND SALESPEOPLE

The real estate industry is largely responsible for creating and maintaining an open housing market. Brokers and salespersons are a community's real estate experts. Along with the privilege of profiting from real estate transactions comes the social and legal responsibilities to ensure that everyone's civil rights are protected. The reputation of the industry cannot afford *any* appearance that its licensees are not committed to the principles of fair housing. Licensees and the industry must be publicly conspicuous in their equal opportunity efforts. Establishing relationships with community and fair housing groups to discuss common concerns and develop solutions to problems is a constructive activity. What's more, a licensee who is active in helping to improve his or her community will earn a reputation for being a concerned citizen that may well translate into a larger client base.

Fair housing *is* the law. The consequences for anyone who violates the law are serious. In addition to the financial penalties, a real estate broker's or salesperson's livelihood will be in danger if his or her license is suspended or revoked. That the offense was unintentional is no defense. Licensees must scrutinize their practices and be particularly careful not to fall victim to clients or customers who expect to discriminate.

All parties deserve the same standard of service. Everyone has the right to expect equal treatment, within his or her property requirements, financial ability, and experience in the marketplace. A good test is to answer the question, "Are we doing this for everyone?" If an act is not performed consistently, or if an act affects some individuals differently from others, it could be construed as discriminatory. Standardized inventories of property listings, standardized criteria for financial qualification, and written documentation of all conversations are three effective means of self-protection for licensees.

HUD requires that its fair housing posters be displayed in any place of business where real estate is offered for sale or rent. Following HUD's advertising procedures and using the fair housing slogan and logo keep the public aware of the broker's commitment to equal opportunity.

Beyond being the law, fair housing is *good business*. It ensures the greatest number of properties available for sale and rent and the largest possible pool of potential purchasers and tenants.

■ PROFESSIONAL ETHICS

Professional conduct involves more than just complying with the law. In real estate, state licensing laws establish those activities that are illegal and therefore prohibited. However, merely complying with the letter of the law may not be enough: Licensees may perform *legally* yet not *ethically*. Ethics refers to a system of *moral* principles, rules, and standards of conduct. The ethical system of a profession establishes conduct that goes beyond merely complying with the law. These moral principles address the following two sides of a profession:

1. They establish standards for integrity and competence in dealing with consumers of an industry's services.
2. They define a code of conduct for relations within the industry, among its professionals.

Code of Ethics

One way that many organizations address ethics among their members or in their respective businesses is by adopting codes of professional conduct. A code of ethics is a written system of standards for ethical conduct. The code contains statements designed to advise, guide, and regulate job behavior. To be effective, a code of ethics must be specific by dictating rules that either prohibit or demand certain behavior. Lofty statements of positive goals are not especially helpful. By including sanctions for violators, a code of ethics becomes more effective.

The National Association of REALTORS® (NAR), the largest trade association in the country, adopted a Code of Ethics for its members in 1913. REALTORS® are expected to subscribe to this strict code of conduct. Not all licensees are REALTORS®—only those who are members of NAR. NAR has established procedures for professional standards committees at the local, state, and national levels of the organization to administer compliance. Practical applications of the Articles of the code are known as *Standards of Practice*. The Code of Ethics has proved helpful because it contains practical applications of business ethics. Many other professional organizations in the real estate industry have codes of ethics as well. In addition, many state real estate commissions are required by law to establish codes or canons of ethical behavior for the states' licensees.

■ SUMMARY

The federal regulations regarding equal opportunity in housing are contained principally in two laws. The Civil Rights Act of 1866 prohibits all racial discrimination, and the Fair Housing Act (Title VIII of the Civil Rights Act of 1968), as amended, prohibits discrimination on the basis of race, color, religion, sex, handicap, familial status, or national origin in the sale, rental, or financing of residential property. Discriminatory actions include refusing to deal with an individual or a specific group, changing any terms of a real estate or loan transaction, changing the services offered for any individual or group, creating statements or advertisements that indicate discriminatory restrictions, or otherwise attempting to make a dwelling unavailable to any person or group because of race, color, religion, sex, handicap, familial status, or national origin. The law also prohibits steering, blockbusting, and redlining.

Complaints under the Fair Housing Act may be reported to and investigated by the Department of Housing and Urban Development (HUD). Such complaints also may be taken directly to U.S. district courts. In states and localities that have enacted fair housing legislation that is substantially equivalent to the federal law, complaints are handled by state and local agencies and state courts. Complaints under the Civil Rights Act of 1866 must be taken to federal courts.

A real estate business is only as good as its reputation. Real estate licensees can maintain good reputations by demonstrating good business ability and adhering to ethical standards of business practices. Many licensees subscribe to a code of ethics as members of professional real estate organizations.

QUESTIONS

1. Which of the following actions is legally permitted?
   a. Advertising property for sale only to a special group
   b. Altering the terms of a loan for a member of a minority group
   c. Refusing to make a mortgage loan to a minority individual because of a poor credit history
   d. Telling an individual that an apartment has been rented when in fact it has not

2. Which of the following statements is true of complaints relating to the Civil Rights Act of 1866?
   a. They must be taken directly to federal courts.
   b. They are no longer reviewed in the courts.
   c. They are handled by HUD.
   d. They are handled by state enforcement agencies.

3. Why is the Civil Rights Act of 1866 unique?
   a. It has been broadened to protect the aged.
   b. It adds welfare recipients as a protected class.
   c. It contains "choose your neighbor" provisions.
   d. It provides no exceptions that would permit racial discrimination.

4. "I hear *they're* moving in. There goes the neighborhood! Better put your house on the market before values drop!" This is an example of what illegal practice?
   a. Steering
   b. Blockbusting
   c. Redlining
   d. Fraudulent advertising

5. The act of directing home seekers toward or away from particular areas either to maintain or to change the character of the neighborhood is
   a. blockbusting.
   b. redlining.
   c. steering.
   d. permitted under the Fair Housing Act of 1968.

6. A lender's refusal to lend money to potential homeowners attempting to purchase properties located in predominantly African American neighborhoods is known as
   a. redlining.   c. steering.
   b. blockbusting.   d. prequalifying.

7. Which of the following would *not* be permitted under the federal Fair Housing Act?
   a. An expensive club in New York rents rooms only to members who are graduates of a particular university.
   b. The owner of a 20-unit residential apartment building rents to men only.
   c. A Catholic convent refuses to furnish housing for a Jewish man.
   d. An owner refuses to rent the other side of her duplex to a family with children.

8. A real estate broker wants to end racial segregation. As an office policy, the broker requires that salespersons show prospective buyers from racial or ethnic minority groups only properties that are in certain areas of town where few members of their groups currently live. The broker has prepared a map illustrating the appropriate neighborhoods for each racial or ethnic group. Through this policy, the broker hopes to achieve racial balance in residential housing. Which of the following statements is true regarding this broker's policy?
   a. While the broker's policy may appear to constitute blockbusting, application of the effects test proves its legality.
   b. Because the effect of the broker's policy is discriminatory, it constitutes illegal steering regardless of the broker's intentions.
   c. The broker's policy clearly shows the intent to discriminate.
   d. While the broker's policy may appear to constitute steering, application of the intent test proves its legality.

9. If a mortgage lender discriminates against a loan applicant on the basis of marital status, it violates what law?

a. ADA
b. Civil Rights Act of 1866
c. ECOA
d. Fair Housing Act

10. A Lithuanian-American real estate broker offers a special discount to Lithuanian-American clients. This practice is

a. legal in certain circumstances.
b. illegal.
c. legal, but ill-advised.
d. an example of steering.

11. Which of the following statements describes the Supreme Court's decision in the case of *Jones v. Alfred H. Mayer Company?*

a. Racial discrimination is prohibited by any party in the sale or rental of real estate.
b. Sales by individual residential homeowners are exempted, provided the owners do not use brokers.
c. Laws against discrimination apply only to federally related transactions.
d. Persons with disabilities are a protected class.

12. After a broker takes a sale listing of a residence, the owner specifies that he will not sell his home to any Asian family. The broker should do which of the following?

a. Advertise the property exclusively in Asian-language newspapers
b. Explain to the owner that the instruction violates federal law and that the broker cannot comply with it
c. Abide by the principal's directions despite the fact that they conflict with the fair housing laws
d. Require that the owner sign a separate legal document stating the additional instruction as an amendment to the listing agreement

13. The fine for a first violation of the federal Fair Housing Act could be as much as

a. $500.   c. $5,000.
b. $1,000.   d. $10,000.

14. A single man with two small children has been told by a real estate salesperson that homes for sale in a condominium complex are available only to married couples with no children. Which of the following statements is true?

a. Because a single-parent family can be disruptive if the parent provides little supervision of the children, the condominium is permitted to discriminate against the family under the principal of rational basis.
b. Condominium complexes are exempt from the fair housing laws and can therefore restrict children.
c. The man may file a complaint alleging discrimination on the basis of familial status.
d. Restrictive covenants in a condominium take precedence over the fair housing laws.

15. The following ad appeared in the newspaper: "For sale: 4 BR brick home; Redwood School District; excellent Elm Street location; short walk to St. John's Church, and right on the bus line. Move-in condition; priced to sell." Which of the following statements is true?

a. The ad describes the property for sale and is very appropriate.
b. The fair housing laws do not apply to newspaper advertising.
c. The ad should state that the property is available to families with children.
d. The ad should not mention St. John's Church.

CHAPTER TWENTY-ONE

ENVIRONMENTAL ISSUES AND THE REAL ESTATE TRANSACTION

■ **LEARNING OBJECTIVES** *When you've finished reading this Chapter, you should be able to:*

■ **identify** the basic environmental hazards an agent should be aware of in order to protect his or her client's interests.

■ **describe** the warning signs, characteristics, causes, and solutions for the various environmental hazards most commonly found in real estate transactions.

■ **explain** the fundamental liability issues arising under environmental protection laws.

■ **distinguish** lead-based paint issues from other environmental issues.

■ **define** these following *key terms:*

asbestos	electromagnetic fields (EMFs)	radon
brownfields		retroactive liability
Brownfields Legislation	encapsulation	strict liability
capping	groundwater	underground storage tanks (USTs)
carbon monoxide	joint and several liability	
Comprehensive Environmental Response, Compensation, and Liability Act (CERCLA)	landfill	urea-formaldehyde foam insulation (UFFI)
	lead	water table
	mold	
	polychlorinated biphenyls (PCBs)	

■ WHY LEARN ABOUT... ENVIRONMENTAL ISSUES?

Environmental issues have become an important factor in the practice of real estate. Consumers are becoming more health-conscious and safety-concerned and are enforcing their rights to make informed decisions. Scientists are learning more about our environment, and consumers are reacting by demanding that their surroundings be free of environmental hazards. These developments affect not only sales trans-actions but also owners, buyers, sellers, contractors, appraisers, developers, lending institutions, and property managers. ■

WWWeb.Link

www.epa.gov
www.hud.gov/consumer/hhhchild.cfm

www.law.cornell.edu/topics/state_statutes.html#health

■ ENVIRONMENTAL ISSUES

Most states have recognized the need to balance the legitimate commercial use of land with the need to preserve vital resources and protect the quality of the states' air, water, and soil. A growing number of homebuyers base their decisions in part on the desire for fresh air, clean water, and outdoor recreational opportunities. Preservation of a state's environment both enhances the quality of life and helps strengthen property values. The prevention and cleanup of pollutants and toxic wastes not only revitalize the land but create greater opportunities for responsible development and are steps to ensure that the interests of all parties involved in real estate transactions are protected.

Environmental issues are health issues, and health issues based on environmental hazards have become real estate issues. For this reason, it is extremely important that licensees not only make property disclosures but also see that prospective purchasers get authoritative information about hazardous substances so that they can make informed decisions. Licensees should be familiar with state and federal environmental laws and the regulatory agencies that enforce them. Licensees are not expected to have the technical expertise necessary to determine whether a hazardous substance is present. However, they must *be aware* of environmental issues.

■ HAZARDOUS SUBSTANCES

Pollution and hazardous substances in the environment are of interest to real estate licensees because they affect the attractiveness, desirability, and market value of cities, neighborhoods, and backyards. A toxic environment is not a place where anyone would want to live. (See Figure 21.1.)

Asbestos

Asbestos is a mineral that was once used as insulation because it was resistant to fire and contained heat effectively. Before 1978, the year when the use of asbestos insulation was banned, asbestos was found in most residential construction. It was a component of more than 3,000 types of building materials. The Environmental Protection Agency (EPA) estimates that about 20 percent of the nation's commercial and public buildings contain asbestos.

Today, we know that inhaling microscopic asbestos fibers can result in a variety of respiratory diseases. The presence of asbestos insulation alone is not necessarily a health hazard. Asbestos is harmful only if it is disturbed or exposed, as often occurs during renovation or remodeling. Asbestos is highly friable. This means that as it ages, asbestos fibers break down easily into tiny filaments and particles. When these particles become airborne, they pose a risk to humans. Airborne asbestos contamination is most prevalent in public and commercial buildings, including schools, built before 1978. If the asbestos fibers in the indoor air of a building reach a dangerous level, the building becomes difficult to lease, finance, or insure.

Federal government regulations establish guidelines for owners of public and commercial buildings to test for asbestos-containing materials.

Asbestos contamination also can be found in residential properties. It was used to cover pipes, ducts, and heating and hot water units. Its fire-resistant properties made it a popular material for use in floor tile, exterior siding, roofing products, linoleum flooring materials, joint compounds, wallboard material, backing, and mastics. Though it may be easy to identify some asbestos-containing materials (for instance, insulation around heating and water pipes), identification may be more difficult when asbestos is behind walls or under floors.

Asbestos is costly to remove because the process requires state-licensed technicians and specially sealed environments. In addition, removal itself may be dangerous: Improper removal procedures may further contaminate the air within the structure. The waste generated should be disposed of at a licensed facility, which further adds to the cost of removal. **Encapsulation,** or the sealing off of disintegrating asbestos, is an alternate method of asbestos control that may be preferable to removal in certain circumstances. However, an owner must periodically monitor the condition of the encapsulated asbestos to make sure it is not disintegrating. Of course, encapsulated asbestos will still have to be dealt with during any renovation or demolition of a building, so it will be a future cost.

A certified asbestos inspector can perform an asbestos inspection of a structure to identify which building materials may contain asbestos. The inspector can also provide recommendations and costs associated with remediation. It is vital that a buyer knows where asbestos-containing materials are located so that they are not disturbed during any repair, remodeling, demolition, or even routine use. Appraisers also should be aware of the possible presence of asbestos.

More information on asbestos-related issues is available from the EPA at 202-554-1404 or on its Web site. In addition, the EPA has numerous publications that provide guidance, information, and assistance with asbestos issues.

FIGURE 21.1
Environmental Hazards

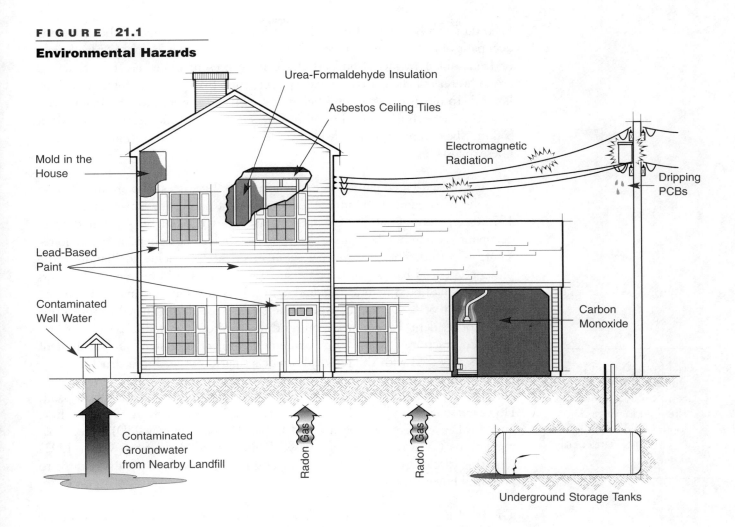

Urea-Formaldehyde Insulation

Asbestos Ceiling Tiles

Electromagnetic Radiation

Dripping PCBs

Mold in the House

Lead-Based Paint

Contaminated Well Water

Carbon Monoxide

Contaminated Groundwater from Nearby Landfill

Radon Gas

Radon Gas

Underground Storage Tanks

 www.epa.gov/oppt/asbestos

Lead-Based Paint and Other Lead Hazards

Lead was used as a pigment and drying agent in alkyd oil-based paint. Lead-based paint may be on any interior or exterior surface, but it is particularly common on doors, window, and other woodwork. The federal government estimates that lead is present in about 75 percent of all private housing built before 1978; that's approximately 57 million homes, ranging from low-income apartments to million-dollar mansions.

An elevated level of lead in the body can cause serious damage to the brain, kidneys, nervous system, and red blood cells. The degree of harm is related to the amount of exposure and the age at which a person is exposed. The federal government estimates that in the United States there are about 900,000 children ages one to five who have a blood-lead level above the level of concern. Even children who appear healthy can have dangerous levels of lead in their bodies.

Lead dust can be ingested from the hands by a crawling infant, inhaled by any occupant of a structure, or ingested from the water supply because of lead pipes or lead solder. In fact, lead particles can be present elsewhere too. Soil and groundwater may be contaminated by everything from lead plumbing in leaking landfills to discarded skeet and bullets from an old shooting range. High levels of lead have been found in the soil near waste-to-energy incinerators. The air or soil may be contaminated by leaded gasoline fumes from gas stations or automobile exhausts.

The use of lead-based paint was banned in 1978. Licensees who are involved in the sale, management, financing, or appraisal of properties constructed before 1978 face potential liability for any personal injury that might be suffered by an occupant. Numerous legislative efforts affect licensees, sellers, and landlords. There is considerable controversy about practical approaches for handling the presence of lead-based paint. Some suggest that it should be removed; others argue that it should be encapsulated; still others advocate testing to determine the amount of lead present, which then would be disclosed to a prospective owner or resident. Federal law requires that only licensed lead inspectors, abatement contractors, risk assessors, abatement project designers, and abatement workers may deal with the removal or encapsulation of lead in a structure.

No federal law requires that homeowners test for the presence of lead-based paint. However, *known* lead-based paint hazards must be disclosed. In 1996, the EPA and the Department of Housing and Urban Development (HUD) issued final regulations (known as the Lead-Based Paint Hazard Reduction Act of 1992) requiring disclosure of the presence of any known lead-based paint hazards to potential buyers or renters.

The Lead-Based Paint Hazard Reduction Act of 1992 requires the following:

- Landlords must disclose known information on lead-based paint and hazards before leases take effect. Leases must include a disclosure form regarding lead-based paint.
- Sellers have to disclose known information on lead-based paint and hazards before selling a house. Sales contracts must include a disclosure form about lead-based paint. (See Figure 21.2.) Buyers have up to ten days to check for lead hazards.
- Licensees provide buyers and lessees with the pamphlet created by the EPA, HUD, and the U.S. Consumer Product Safety Commission titled, "Protect Your Family From Lead in Your Home."
- Renovators must give homeowners the pamphlet, "Protect Your Family From Lead in Your Home," before starting any renovation work.
- Licensees must ensure that all parties comply with the law.

> *Lead* from paint or other sources can result in damage to the brain, nervous system, kidneys, and blood. Children under the age of six are particularly vulnerable.

F I G U R E   21.2

**Disclosure of Lead-
Based Paint and Lead-
Based Paint Hazards**

LEAD-BASED PAINT OR LEAD-BASED PAINT HAZARD ADDENDUM

It is a condition of this contract that, until midnight of _____ , Buyer shall have the right to obtain a risk assessment or inspection of the Property for the presence of lead-based paint and/or lead-based paint hazards* at Buyer's expense. This contingency will terminate at that time unless Buyer or Buyer's agent delivers to the Seller or Seller's agent a written inspection and/or risk assessment report listing the specific existing deficiencies and corrections needed, if any. If any corrections are necessary, Seller shall have the option of (i) completing them, (ii) providing for their completion, or (iii) refusing to complete them. If Seller elects not to complete or provide for completion of the corrections, then Buyer shall have the option of (iv) accepting the Property in its present condition, or (v) terminating this contract, in which case all earnest monies shall be refunded to Buyer. Buyer may waive the right to obtain a risk assessment or inspection of the Property for the presence of lead-based paint and/or lead based paint hazards at any time without cause.

*Intact lead-based paint that is in good condition is not necessarily a hazard. See EPA pamphlet "Protect Your Family From Lead in Your Home" for more information.

Disclosure of Information on Lead-Based Paint and Lead-Based Paint Hazards

Lead Warning Statement
Every Buyer of any interest in residential real property on which a residential dwelling was built prior to 1978 is notified that such property may present exposure to lead from lead-based paint that may place young children at risk of developing lead poisoning. Lead poisoning in young children may produce permanent neurological damage, including learning disabilities, reduced intelligence quotient, behavioral problems, and impaired memory. Lead poisoning also poses a particular risk to pregnant women. The Seller of any interest in residential real property is required to provide the Buyer with any information on lead-based paint hazards from risk assessments or inspections in the Seller's possession and notify the Buyer of any known lead-based paint hazards. A risk assessment or inspection for possible lead-based paint hazards is recommended prior to purchase.

Seller's Disclosure (initial)
_____ (a) Presence of lead-based paint and/or lead-based paint hazards (check one below):
   Known lead-based paint and/or lead-based paint hazards are present in the housing (explain).

   _____
   _____

   Seller has no knowledge of lead-based paint and/or lead-based paint hazards in the housing.
_____ (b) Records and reports available to the Seller (check one below):
   Seller has provided the Buyer with all available records and reports pertaining to lead-based paint and/or lead-based paint hazards in the housing (list documents below).

   _____
   _____

   Seller has no reports or records pertaining to lead-based paint and/or lead-based paint hazards in the housing.

Buyer's Acknowledgment (initial)
_____ (c) Buyer has received copies of all information listed above.
_____ (d) Buyer has received the pamphlet *Protect Your Family from Lead in Your Home.*
_____ (e) Buyer has (check one below):
   Received a 10-day opportunity (or mutually agreed upon period) to conduct a risk assessment or inspection for the presence of lead-based paint and/or lead-based paint hazards; or
   Waived the opportunity to conduct a risk assessment or inspection for the presence of lead-based paint and/or lead-based paint hazards.

Agent's Acknowledgment (initial)
_____ (f) Agent has informed the Seller of the Seller's obligations under 42 U.S.C. 4582(d) and is aware of his/her responsibility to ensure compliance.

Certification of Accuracy
The following parties have reviewed the information above and certify, to the best of their knowledge, that the information provided by the signatory is true and accurate.
Buyer: _____ (SEAL) Date _____
Buyer: _____ (SEAL) Date _____
Agent: _____   Date _____
Seller: _____ (SEAL) Date _____
Seller: _____ (SEAL) Date _____
Agent: _____   Date _____

IN PRACTICE

As part of a settlement, a realty company was fined $20,000 for failing to provide the lead-based paint pamphlet to home buyers. Licensees must remember to always provide buyers and lessees with the pamphlet, "Protect Your Family From Lead in Your Home." In another settlement, the EPA and HUD reached a landmark disclosure settlement with one of the nation's largest property management firms in January, 2002, where more than 130,000 apartments in 47 states will be tested, cleaned, and made lead-safe. In addition, the firm will pay a $129,580 penalty. The penalty and the number of units tested and cleaned are the largest ever in a lead disclosure settlement.

A home can be inspected for lead hazards in the following ways:

■ *Paint Inspection*—A paint inspection will provide the lead content of every different type of painted surface in a home. However, this inspection will not indicate whether the paint is a hazard or how the homeowner should deal with it.

■ *Risk Assessment*—A risk assessment indicates whether there are any sources of serious lead exposure, such as peeling paint or lead dust. It also describes what actions can be taken to address the hazards.

EPA guidance pamphlets, a list of professionals qualified to inspect or assess for lead-based paint, and other information about lead-based hazards are available from the National Lead Information Center at 1-800-424-5323 or www.epa.gov/lead/nlic.htm.

 **WWWeb.Link**

www.epa.gov/lead   www.hud.gov/offices/lead/leadhelp.cfm
www.nsc.org/ehc/lead.htm   www.hud.gov/offices/lead/disclosurerule.cfm

Radon

Radon is a radioactive gas produced by the natural decay of other radioactive substances. Although radon can occur anywhere, some areas are known to have abnormally high amounts of it. Radon is found in every state, with the highest concentrations in the plains states, the upper midwest, and northeastern United States. (See Figure 21.3.) If radon dissipates into the atmosphere, it is not likely to cause harm. However, when radon enters buildings and is trapped in high concentrations (often in basements with inadequate ventilation) it can cause health problems. Note that high radon levels can occur anywhere in a home, whether or not a basement even exists.

Opinions differ as to minimum safe levels. But growing evidence suggests that radon may be the most underestimated cause of lung cancer, particularly for children, individuals who smoke, and those who spend considerable time indoors.

Because radon is odorless and tasteless, it is impossible to detect without testing. Care should be exercised in the manner in which tests are conducted to ensure that the results are accurate. Radon levels vary, depending on the amount of fresh air that circulates through a house, the fissures or soil density beneath the house, the weather conditions, and the time of year. Because so many factors affect the presence of radon, two houses next door to each other may have very different levels. And because the risk of radon increases as it builds up in an

Radon is a naturally occurring gas that is a suspected cause of lung cancer.

enclosed space, testing vacant land for radon is not an accurate indicator of the risk once a building is constructed on the site. It is relatively easy to reduce levels of radon by installing ventilation systems or exhaust fans.

Interestingly, the modern practice of creating energy-efficient homes and buildings with practically airtight walls and windows may increase the potential for radon gas accumulation. Once radon accumulates in a basement, efficient heating and ventilation systems can rapidly spread the gas throughout the building.

Home radon-detection kits are available, although more accurate testing can be conducted by radon-detection professionals. The EPA's pamphlet "A Citizen's Guide to Radon" is available from your local EPA office or at the EPA's website. There is no federal requirement that properties be tested for radon. Local health departments, however, may maintain records of radon levels identified in particular areas.

WWWeb.Link

www.epa.gov/iedweb00/radon/pubs/citguide.html

www.epa.gov/iaq/radon

www.nsc.org/ehc/radon.htm

Urea-Formaldehyde

Urea-formaldehyde was first used in building materials, particularly insulation, in the 1970s. It was also used in some glues, resins, preservatives, bonding agents, pressed wood, and kitchen cabinets. Gases leak out of the **urea-formaldehyde foam insulation (UFFI)** as it hardens, and the gases become trapped in the interior of a building. In 1982, the Consumer Product Safety Commission banned the use of UFFI. The ban was reduced to a warning after courts determined that there was insufficient evidence to support a ban. Urea-formaldehyde is known to cause cancer in animals, though the evidence of its effect on humans is inconclusive.

UFFI is an insulating foam that can release harmful formaldehyde gases.

Formaldehyde does cause some individuals to suffer respiratory problems as well as eye and skin irritations. Consumers are becoming increasingly wary of the presence of formaldehyde, particularly if they are sensitive to it.

Because UFFI has received considerable adverse publicity, many buyers express concern about purchasing properties in which it was installed. Tests can be conducted to determine the level of formaldehyde gas in a house. Again, however, care should be exercised to ensure that the results of the tests are accurate and that the source of the gases is properly identified. Elevated levels could be due to a source other than the insulation.

Licensees should be careful that any conditions in an agreement of sale that require tests for formaldehyde are worded properly to identify the purpose for which the tests are being conducted, such as to determine the presence of the insulation or some other source. Appraisers should also be aware of the presence of UFFI.

FIGURE 21.3

Radon Concentrations in the United States

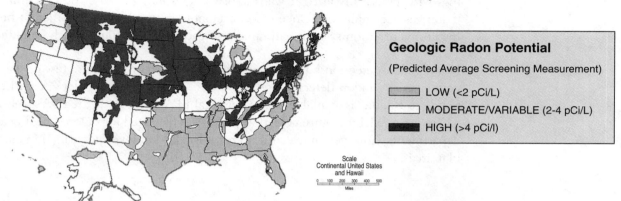

GENERALIZED GEOLOGIC RADON POTENTIAL OF THE UNITED STATES
by the U.S. Geological Survey

Geologic Radon Potential

(Predicted Average Screening Measurement)

LOW (<2 pCi/L)

MODERATE/VARIABLE (2-4 pCi/L)

HIGH (>4 pCi/l)

Scale
Continental United States
and Hawaii
0   100   200   300   400   500
Miles

Source: United States Geological Survey

WWWeb.Link　　www.epa.gov/iaq/formalde.html

Carbon Monoxide

Carbon monoxide is a by-product of fuel combustion that may result in death in poorly ventilated areas.

Carbon monoxide (CO) is a colorless, odorless gas that occurs as a by-product of burning such fuels as wood, oil, and natural gas owing to incomplete combustion. Furnaces, water heaters, space heaters, fireplaces, and wood stoves all produce CO as a natural result of their combustion of fuel. However, when these appliances function properly and are property ventilated, their CO emissions are not a problem. When improper ventilation or equipment malfunctions permit large quantities of CO to be released into a residence or commercial structure, it poses a significant health hazard. Its effects are compounded by the fact that CO is so difficult to detect. CO is quickly absorbed by the body. It inhibits the blood's ability to transport oxygen and results in dizziness and nausea. As the concentrations of CO increase, the symptoms become more severe. More than 200 deaths from carbon monoxide poisoning occur each year.

Carbon monoxide detectors are available, and their use is mandatory in some areas. Annual maintenance of heating systems helps avoid CO exposure.

WWWeb.Link　　www.epa.gov/iaq/co.html

Polychlorinated Biphenyls

Polychlorinated Biphenyls (PCBs) were often used as an insulating material in dielectric oil. PCBs may be present in electrical equipment, such as transformers, fluorescent light ballasts, and hydraulic oil in older equipment. PCBs are suspected of causing health problems and are known to linger in the environment for long periods of time. For example, in tests conducted on offspring of fish who were exposed to PCBs, the offspring also had elevated levels of PCBs.

In January, 1978, the manufacture, processing, commercial distribution, and use of PCB materials was prohibited, except when contained in a "totally enclosed manner." The Environmental Protection Agency, however, made case-by-case exceptions to these limitations if it determined that an unreasonable risk of injury to public health or the environment was not present. On January 1, 1979, the manufacture of PCBs was completely banned; commercial distribution of PCBs was banned on July 1, 1979.

PCBs linger in the environment for long periods of time and can cause health problems.

In general, PCBs should not cause problems on property unless they leak out of the containers they are stored in. For example, the presence of an electrical transformer or fluorescent light ballasts on a property does not in itself indicate a problem. However, if staining is observed on the outside of an electrical transformer or fluorescent light ballast, or if these items are observed to be disposed of on a property, it can pose a health hazard. Real estate licensees should be aware that PCBs may be a potential health risk and cause environmental problems if released to the environment.

Mold

Mold can be found almost anywhere and can grow on almost any organic substance, so long as moisture and oxygen are present. Moisture feeds mold growth. If a moisture problem is not discovered or addressed, mold growth can gradually destroy what it is growing on.

In addition, molds can cause serious health problems. They can trigger allergic reactions and asthma attacks. Molds are known to produce potent toxins and/or irritants.

Some moisture problems in homes and buildings have been directly linked to recent changes in construction practices. Some of these practices have resulted in buildings that are too tightly sealed, preventing adequate ventilation. Building materials, such as drywall, may not allow moisture to escape easily. Other moisture problems include roof leaks, unvented combustion appliances, and landscaping or gutters that direct water to the building.

The Environmental Protection Agency has published guidelines for the remediation and/or cleanup of mold and moisture problems in schools and commercial buildings. See the Web site below for these guidelines.

In the past ten years, there have been approximately 9,000 toxic mold and mildew-related claims filed in the United States and Canada. Awards and settlements in mold lawsuits have ranged in the millions of dollars. In the coming years, the number and size of toxic mold lawsuits is expected to increase substantially.

 **WWWeb.Link**   www.epa.gov/iaq/pubs/molds/index.html

Electromagnetic Fields

EMFs are produced by electrical currents and may be related to a variety of health complaints.

Electromagnetic fields (EMFs) are generated by the movement of electrical currents. The use of any electrical appliance creates a small field of electromagnetic radiation; clock radios, blow-driers, televisions, and computers all produce EMFs. A major concern regarding electromagnetic fields involves high-tension power lines. The EMFs produced by these high-voltage lines, as well as by secondary distribution lines and transformers, are suspected of causing cancer, hormonal changes, and behavioral abnormalities. There is considerable controversy (and much conflicting evidence) about whether EMFs pose a health hazard. Buyers who are aware of the controversy may, however, be unwilling to purchase property near power lines or transformers. As research into EMFs continues, real estate licensees should stay informed about current findings.

■ GROUNDWATER CONTAMINATION

Groundwater is the water that exists under the earth's surface within the tiny spaces or crevices in geological formations. Groundwater forms the **water table,** the natural level at which the ground is saturated. This may be near the surface (in areas where the water table is very high) or several hundred feet underground. Surface water can also be absorbed into the groundwater.

Any contamination of the underground water can threaten the supply of pure, clean water for private wells or public water systems. If groundwater is not protected from contamination, the earth's natural filtering systems may be inadequate to ensure the availability of pure water. Numerous state and federal laws have been enacted to preserve and protect the water supply.

Water can be contaminated from a number of sources. Runoff from waste disposal sites, leaking underground storage tanks, septic systems, drywells, and storm drains, as well as the illegal disposal of hazardous material and regular use of insecticides and herbicides, are some of the main culprits. Because water flows from one place to another, contamination can spread far from its source. Numerous regulations are designed to protect against water contamination. Once contamination has been identified, its source can be eliminated. The water may eventually become clean. However, the process can be time-consuming and extremely expensive.

IN PRACTICE

Real estate agents need to be aware of potential groundwater contamination sources both on and off a property. These include underground storage tanks, septic systems, holding ponds, drywells, buried materials, and surface spills. Remember, because groundwater flows over wide areas, the source of contamination may not be nearby.

■ UNDERGROUND STORAGE TANKS

Approximately 3 million to 5 million **underground storage tanks (USTs)** exist in the United States. According to the Environmental Protection Agency, approximately 40 percent of the tanks are leaking. Underground storage tanks are commonly found on sites where petroleum products are used or where gas stations and auto repair shops are located. They also may be found in a number of other commercial and industrial establishments—including printing and chemical plants, wood treatment plants, paper mills, paint manufacturers, dry cleaners, food processing plants, and chemical storage or process waste plants. Military bases and airports are also common sites for underground tanks. In residential areas, tanks are used to store heating oil.

Some tanks are currently in use, but many are long forgotten. It is an unfortunate fact that it was once common to dispose of toxic wastes by simple burial: out of sight, out of mind. Over time, however, neglected tanks may leak hazardous substances into the environment. This permits contaminants to pollute not only the soil around the tank but also adjacent parcels and groundwater. Licensees should be particularly alert to the presence of fill pipes, vent lines, stained soil, and fumes or odors, any of which may indicate the presence of a UST. Detection, removal, and cleanup of surrounding contaminated soil can be expensive.

■ **FOR EXAMPLE** In the 1940s, a gas station in a rural town went out of business. The building fell into disrepair and was torn down. The site was vacant for several years, and its former use was forgotten. A series of commercial ventures were built on the land: a grocery store, a drive-in restaurant, a convenience store. In the late 1980s, residents of the town began noticing strong gasoline fumes in their basements, particularly after a rainstorm. Government investigators concluded that the gasoline tanks buried beneath the former gas station had broken down with age and leaked their contents into the soil. Because the town was located over a large subsurface rock slab, the gasoline could not reach *down* into the soil but rather was forced to spread *out* under the entire town and surrounding farmland. Because the water table floated on the rock slab and the gasoline floated on the water, rains that raised the water table forced the gasoline into the soil near the residents' basements and crawlspaces, resulting in the unpleasant and potentially unhealthy fumes. When the gasoline fumes ignited and destroyed a local manufacturing plant, the residents learned that the problem was not only unpleasant but dangerous as well.

State and federal laws impose very strict requirements on landowners where underground storage tanks are located to detect and correct leaks in an effort to protect the groundwater. The federal UST program is regulated by the EPA. The regulations apply to tanks that contain hazardous substances or liquid petroleum products and that store at least 10 percent of their volume underground. UST owners are required to register their tanks and adhere to strict technical and administrative requirements that govern

- installation,
- maintenance,
- corrosion prevention,
- overspill prevention,
- monitoring, and
- record keeping.

Owners are also required to demonstrate that they have sufficient financial resources to cover any damage that might result from leaks.

The following types of tanks are among those that are exempt from the federal regulations:

- Tanks that hold less than 110 gallons
- Farm and residential tanks that hold 1,100 gallons or less of motor fuel used for noncommercial purposes
- Tanks that store heating oil burned on the premises
- Tanks on or above the floor of underground areas, such as basements or tunnels
- Septic tanks and systems for collecting stormwater and wastewater

Some states have adopted laws regulating underground storage tanks that are more stringent than the federal laws.

In addition to being aware of possible noncompliance with state and federal regulations, the parties to a real estate transaction should be aware that many older tanks have never been registered; exempt tanks are not required to be registered. There may be no visible sign of their presence.

■ WASTE DISPOSAL SITES

Americans produce vast quantities of garbage every day. Despite public and private recycling and composting efforts, huge piles of waste materials— from beer cans, junk mail, and diapers to food, paint, and toxic chemicals— must be disposed of. Landfill operations have become the main receptacles for garbage and refuse. Special hazardous waste disposal sites have been established to contain radioactive waste from nuclear power plants, toxic chemicals, and waste materials produced by medical, scientific, and industrial processes. Additional waste disposal sites used as on-site "garbage dumps" are located on rural property, such as farms, ranches, and residences. It is important for buyers to ask sellers about the potential existence of waste disposal sites on their property.

Perhaps the most prevalent method of common waste disposal is simply to bury it. A landfill is an enormous hole, either excavated for the purpose of waste disposal or left over from surface mining operations. The hole is lined with clay or a synthetic liner to prevent leakage of waste material into the water supply. A system of underground drainage pipes permits monitoring of leaks and leaching. Waste is laid on the liner at the bottom of the excavation, and a layer of topsoil is then compacted onto the waste. The layering procedure is repeated again and again until the landfill is full, the layers mounded up sometimes as high as several hundred feet over the surrounding landscape. Capping is the process of laying two to four feet of soil over the top of the site and then planting grass or some other vegetation on it to enhance the landfill's aesthetic value and to prevent erosion. A ventilation pipe runs from the landfill's base through the cap to vent off accumulated natural gases created by the decomposing waste.

IN PRACTICE

Environmental issues have a significant impact on the real estate industry. In 1995, a jury awarded $6.7 million to homeowners whose property values had been lowered because of the defendant tire company's negligent operation and maintenance of a hazardous waste dump site. The 1,713 plaintiffs relied on testimony from economists and a real estate appraiser to demonstrate how news stories about the site had lowered the market values of their homes. Nationwide, some landfill operators now offer price guarantees to purchasers of homes near waste disposal sites. A university study found that a home's value increases by more than $6,000 for each mile of its distance from a garbage incinerator.

Federal, state, and local regulations govern the location, construction, content, and maintenance of landfill sites. Test wells around landfill operations are installed to constantly monitor the groundwater in the surrounding area, and soil analyses can be used to test for contamination. Capped landfills have been used for such purposes as parks and golf courses. Rapid suburban growth has resulted in many housing developments and office campuses being built on landfill sites. Most newer sites are well documented, but the locations of many older landfill sites are no longer known.

■ **FOR EXAMPLE**   A suburban office building constructed on an old landfill site was very popular until its parking lot began to sink. While the building itself was supported by pylons driven deep into the ground, the parking lot was unsupported. As the landfill beneath it compacted, the wide concrete lot sank lower and lower around the building. Each year, the building's management had to relandscape to cover the exposed foundations. The sinking parking lot eventually severed underground phone and power lines and water mains, causing the tenants considerable inconvenience. Computers were offline for hours, and flooding was frequent on the ground floor. Finally, leaking gases from the landfill began causing unpleasant odors. The tenants moved out, and the building was left vacant, a victim of poorly conceived landfill design.

Hazardous and radioactive waste disposal sites are subject to strict state and federal regulation to prevent the escape of toxic substances into the surrounding environment. Some materials, such as radioactive waste, are sealed in containers and placed in "tombs" buried deep underground. The tombs are designed to last thousands of years, built according to strict federal and state regulations. These disposal sites are usually limited to extremely remote locations, well away from populated areas or farmland.

IN PRACTICE   In 2002, Congress approved the development of the nation's first long-term geologic repository (underground disposal facility) for high-level radioactive waste at Yucca Mountain in Nevada. The Congressional vote overrode the state's veto of the plan.

WWWeb.Link   http://es.epa.gov/oeca/ag/aglaws/super.html

■ OLD INDUSTRIAL SITES

For decades, old industrial sites have plagued communities as "eyesores" and as potentially dangerous and hazardous property. These old industrial sites are known as **brownfields** and are defined as defunct, derelict, or abandoned commercial or industrial sites. Many of the sites have toxic wastes. According to the U.S. General Accounting Office, there may be more than 500,000 brownfields across the country.

In 2002, the **Brownfields Legislation** became law. The law gives states and localities up to $250 million a year for five years to clean up polluted industrial sites. In the future, more funds may be allocated for the cleanup of brownfields.

The law is also important for property owners and developers because it shields innocent developers from liability for toxic wastes that existed at a site prior to the purchase of property. In effect, if a property owner neither caused nor contributed to the contamination, the property owner is not liable for the cleanup.

Significantly, the law will encourage the development of abandoned properties, some of which are located in prime real estate areas.

■ CERCLA AND ENVIRONMENTAL PROTECTION

The majority of legislation dealing with environmental problems has been instituted within the past two decades. Although the EPA was created at the federal level to oversee such problems, several other federal agencies' areas of concern generally overlap. The federal laws were created to encourage state and local governments to enact their own legislation.

Comprehensive Environmental Response, Compensation, and Liability Act

The **Comprehensive Environmental Response, Compensation, and Liability Act (CERCLA)** was created in 1980. It established a fund of $9 billion, called the *Superfund,* to clean up uncontrolled hazardous waste sites and to respond to spills. It created a process for identifying *potential responsible parties* (PRPs) and ordering them to take responsibility for the cleanup action. CERCLA is administered and enforced by the EPA.

Liability. A landowner is liable under CERCLA when a release or a threat of release of a hazardous substance has occurred on his or her property. Regardless of whether the contamination is the result of the landowner's actions or those of others, the owner can be held responsible for the cleanup. This liability includes the cleanup not only of the landowner's property but also of any neighboring property that has been contaminated. A landowner who is not responsible for the contamination can seek recovery reimbursement for the cleanup cost from previous landowners, any other responsible party or the Superfund. However, if other parties are not available, even a landowner who did not cause the problem could be solely responsible for the costs.

Once the EPA determines that hazardous material has been released into the environment, it is authorized to begin remedial action. First, it attempts to identify the PRPs. If the PRPs agree to cooperate in the cleanup, they must agree about how to divide the cost. If the PRPs do not voluntarily undertake the cleanup, the EPA may hire its own contractors to do the necessary work. The EPA then bills the PRPs for the cost. If the PRPs refuse to pay, the EPA can seek damages in court for up to three times the actual cost of the cleanup.

Liability under the Superfund is considered to be strict, joint and several, and retroactive. **Strict liability** means that the owner is responsible to the injured party without excuse. **Joint and several liability** means that each of the individual owners is personally responsible for the total damages. If only one of the owners is financially able to handle the total damages, that owner must pay the total and collect the proportionate shares from the other owners whenever possible. **Retroactive liability** means that the liability is not limited to the current owner but includes people who have owned the site in the past.

Superfund Amendments and Reauthorization Act

In 1986, the U.S. Congress reauthorized the Superfund. The amended statute contains stronger cleanup standards for contaminated sites and five times the funding of the original Superfund, which expired in September 1985.

The amended act also sought to clarify the obligations of lenders. As mentioned, liability under the Superfund extends to both the present and all previous owners of the contaminated site. Real estate lenders found themselves either as present owners or somewhere in the chain of ownership through foreclosure proceedings.

The amendments created a concept called *innocent landowner immunity*. It was recognized that in certain cases, a landowner in the chain of ownership was completely innocent of all wrongdoing and therefore should not be held liable. The innocent landowner immunity clause established the criteria by which to judge whether a person or business could be exempted from liability. The criteria included the following:

- The pollution was caused by a third party.
- The property was acquired after the fact.
- The landowner had no actual or constructive knowledge of the damage.
- Due care was exercised when the property was purchased (the landowner made a reasonable search, called an *environmental* or *Phase I site assessment*) to determine that no damage to the property existed.
- Reasonable precautions were taken in the exercise of ownership rights.

WWWeb.Link   www.epa.gov/superfund/action/law/cercla.htm

■ LIABILITY OF REAL ESTATE PROFESSIONALS

Environmental law is a relatively new phenomenon. Although federal and state laws have defined many of the liabilities involved, common law is being used for further interpretation. The real estate professional and all others involved in a real estate transaction must be aware of both actual and potential liability.

Sellers, as mentioned earlier, often carry the most exposure. Innocent landowners might be held responsible, even though they did not know about the presence of environmental hazards. Purchasers may be held liable, even if they didn't cause the contamination. Lenders may end up owning worthless assets if owners default on the loans rather than undertaking expensive cleanup efforts. Real estate licensees could be held liable for improper disclosure; therefore, it is necessary to be aware of the potential environmental risks from neighboring properties, such as gas stations, manufacturing plants, or even funeral homes.

Real estate licensees can avoid liability with environmental issues by

■ becoming familiar with common environmental problems in their area;

■ Looking for signs of environmental contamination;

■ Advising (and including as a contingency) an environmental audit if you suspect contamination; and

■ not giving advice on environmental issues.

Discovery of Environmental Hazards

Additional exposure is created for individuals involved in other aspects of real estate transactions. For example, real estate appraisers must identify and adjust for environmental problems. Adjustments to market value typically reflect the cleanup cost plus a factor of the degree of panic and suspicion that exist in the current market. Although the sales price can be affected dramatically, it is possible that the underlying market value would remain relatively equal to others in the neighborhood. The real estate appraiser's greatest responsibility is to the lender, which depends on the appraiser to identify environmental hazards. Although the lender may be protected under certain conditions through the 1986 amendments to the Superfund Act, the lender must be aware of any potential problems and may require additional environmental reports.

Insurance carriers also might be affected in the transactions. Mortgage insurance companies protect lenders' mortgage investments and might be required to carry part of the ultimate responsibility in cases of loss. More important, hazard insurance carriers might be directly responsible for damages if such coverage was included in the initial policy.

Real estate licensees are not expected to have the technical expertise necessary to discover the presence of environmental hazards. However, because they are presumed by the public to have special knowledge about real estate, licensees must be aware both of possible hazards and of where to seek professional help.

Obviously, the first step for a licensee is to ask the owner. He or she may already have conducted tests for carbon monoxide or radon. The owner may also be aware of a potential hazardous condition. An environmental hazard can actually be turned into a marketing plus if the owner has already done the detection and abatement work. Potential buyers can be assured that an older home is no longer a lead paint or an asbestos risk.

The most appropriate people on whom a licensee can rely for sound environmental information are scientific or technical experts. *Environmental auditors* (or *environmental assessors*) can provide the most comprehensive studies. Their services are usually relied on by developers and purchasers of commercial and industrial properties. An environmental assessment includes the property's history of use, a current use review, and an investigation into the existence of reported or known contamination sources in the subject area that may affect the property: testing of soil, water, air, and structures can be conducted, if warranted. Trained *inspectors* conduct air-sampling tests to detect radon, asbestos, or EMFs. They can test soil and water quality and can inspect for lead-based paints. Lead inspections covered by the Residential Lead-Based Paint Hazard Reduction Act must be conducted by *certified* inspectors. While an environmental auditor assessment may occur at any stage in a transaction, they are most frequently a condition of closing. Not only can environmental experts detect environmental problems, but they can usually offer guidance about how best to resolve the conditions.

IN PRACTICE

Environmental assessments and tests conducted by environmental consultants can take time. Licensees should be aware of the time involved and contact environmental consultants as soon as they know such tests are needed in order to prevent delays in closing a transaction.

Environmental Site Assessments

An *environmental site assessment* is often performed on a property to show that due care was exercised in determining if any environmental impairments exist. The assessment can help prevent parties from becoming involved in contaminated property and work as a defense to liability. It is often requested by a lending institution, developer, or a potential buyer. The assessment is commonly performed in phases, such as Phase 1 or Phase 2. A Phase 1 Environmental Report is requested first to determine if any potential environmental problems exist at or near the subject property that may cause impairment. Additional phases are performed, as warranted and requested.

There are no federal regulations that define what an environmental assessment must include. However, one of the most accepted industry standards is provided by the American Society for Testing Materials International. For standards and other information, visit www.astm.org.

Disclosure of Environmental Hazards

State laws address the issue of disclosure of known material facts regarding a property's condition. These same rules apply to the presence of environmental hazards. A real estate licensee may be liable if he or she should have known of a condition, even if the seller neglected to disclose it. Property condition disclosures are discussed in Chapter 4.

■ SUMMARY

Environmental issues are important to real estate licensees because they may affect real estate transactions by raising issues of health risk or cleanup costs. Some of the principal environmental hazards include asbestos, lead, radon, urea-formaldehyde foam insulation (UFFI), mold, underground storage tanks (heating oil, fuel), on-site waste disposal (dry wells, septic systems, dump areas), electromagnetic fields (EMFs), and off-site contamination problems (landfills, industrial areas, area releases of hazardous materials).

Licensees who are involved with the sale, management, financing, or appraisal of properties should be aware of specific federal regulations regarding potential environmental problems, such as the Residential Lead-Based Paint Hazard Reduction Act for homes constructed before 1978. Involved parties must also be aware that states may have specific regulations pertaining to environmental issues of a real estate transaction.

CERCLA established the Superfund to finance the cleanup of hazardous waste disposal sites. Under the Superfund, liability for those found to have created unlawful hazardous waste sites is strict, joint and several, and retroactive. However, purchasers of a property may have a defense to such liability if a due diligence (Phase 1 Environmental Site Assessment) is conducted prior to taking ownership.

QUESTIONS

1. Under the federal Lead-Based Paint Hazard Reduction Act, which of the following statements is true?

   a. All residential housing built prior to 1978 must be tested for the presence of lead-based paint before being listed for sale or rent.

   b. A disclosure statement must be attached to all sales contracts and leases involving properties built prior to 1978.

   c. A lead hazard pamphlet must be distributed to all prospective buyers, but not tenants.

   d. Purchasers of housing built before 1978 must be given five days to test the property for the presence of lead-based paint.

2. *Encapsulation* refers to the

   a. process of sealing a landfill with three to four feet of topsoil.

   b. way in which insulation is applied to pipes and wiring systems.

   c. method of sealing disintegrating asbestos.

   d. way in which lead-based paint particles becomes airborne.

3. John is a real estate salesman. He shows a pre-World War I house to Tina, a prospective buyer. Tina has two toddlers and is worried about potential health hazards. Which of the following is true?

   a. There is a risk that urea-foam insulation was used in the original construction.

   b. Because John is a licensed real estate salesperson, he can offer to personally inspect for lead and remove any lead risks.

   c. Because of the age of the house, there is a good likelihood of the presence of lead-based paint.

   d. Removal of lead-based paint and asbestos hazards is covered by standard title insurance policies.

4. Which of the following is true regarding asbestos?

   a. The removal of asbestos can cause further contamination of a building.

   b. Asbestos causes health problems only when it is eaten.

   c. The level of asbestos in a building is affected by weather conditions.

   d. HUD requires that all asbestos-containing materials be removed from all residential buildings.

5. Which of the following best describes the water table?

   a. Natural level at which the ground is saturated

   b. Level at which underground storage tanks may be safely buried

   c. Measuring device used by specialists to measure groundwater contamination

   d. Always underground

6. With reference to electromagnetic fields, it is *not* true that they are

   a. a suspected but unproven cause of a variety of health problems.

   b. generated by all electrical appliances.

   c. present only near high-tension wires or large electrical transformers.

   d. caused by the movement of electricity.

7. Which of the following describes the process of creating a landfill site?

   a. Waste is liquefied, treated, and pumped through pipes to "tombs" under the water table.

   b. Waste and topsoil are layered in a pit, mounded up, then covered with dirt and plants.

   c. Waste is compacted and sealed into a container, then placed in a "tomb" designed to last several thousand years.

   d. Waste is buried in an underground concrete vault.

8. Liability under the Superfund is
   a. limited to the owner of record.
   b. joint and several and retroactive, but not strict.
   c. voluntary.
   d. strict, joint and several, and retroactive.

9. Radon poses the greatest potential health risk to humans when it is
   a. contained in insulation material used in residential properties during the 1970s.
   b. found in high concentrations in unimproved land.
   c. trapped and concentrates in inadequately ventilated areas.
   d. emitted by malfunctioning or inadequately ventilated appliances.

10. What do UFFI, lead-based paint, and asbestos have in common?
   a. They all pose a risk to humans because they may emit harmful gases.
   b. They all were banned in 1978.
   c. All three were used in insulating materials.
   d. They were all used in residential housing built during the 1970s.

CLOSING THE REAL ESTATE TRANSACTION

■ **LEARNING OBJECTIVES** *When you've finished reading this Chapter, you should be able to:*

■ **identify** the issues of particular interest to the buyer and the seller as a real estate transaction closes.

■ **describe** the steps involved in preparing a closing statement.

■ **explain** the general rules for prorating.

■ **distinguish** the procedures involved in face-to-face closings from those in escrow closings.

■ **define** the following *key terms:*

accrued items	credit	survey
closing	debit	Uniform Settlement
closing statement	escrow	Statement
computerized loan origi-	prepaid item	
nation (CLO)	prorations	
controlled business	Real Estate Settlement	
arrangement (CBA)	Procedures Act	
	(RESPA)	

■ **WHY LEARN ABOUT...**   CLOSING THE REAL ESTATE TRANSACTION?

Everything a real estate licensee does in the course of a real estate transaction, from soliciting clients to presenting offers and coordinating inspections, leads to one final event: closing. Closing is the consummation of the real estate transaction. It is the time when the title to the real estate is transferred in exchange for payment of the purchase price. Closing marks the end of any real estate transaction; it is the goal toward which all the agent's efforts are driven. It's also a complicated time: Up until closing preparations begin, the agent's relationship has been primarily with the buyer or seller. During the closing period, new players come on the scene: appraisers, inspectors, loan officers, insurance agents, and lawyers. Negotiations continue, sometimes right up until the property is finally transferred, and the risk of a deal "cratering" or failing is high. For those reasons alone, it is vital that you understand how closings work—to ensure that they *do*. ■

■ PRECLOSING PROCEDURES

Closing actually involves two events: First, the promises made in the sales contract are fulfilled; second, the mortgage loan funds (if any) are distributed to the buyer. Before the property changes hands, however, important issues must be resolved, and both the buyer and the seller have specific issues to deal with.

Buyer's Issues

Closing is the point at which ownership of a property is transferred in exchange for the selling price.

The buyer will want to be sure that the seller delivers title. The buyer also should ensure that the property is in the promised condition. This involves inspecting

- ■ the title evidence;
- ■ the seller's deed;
- ■ any documents demonstrating the removal of undesired liens and encumbrances;
- ■ the survey;
- ■ the results of any required inspections, such as termite or structural inspections, or required repairs; and
- ■ any leases if tenants reside on the premises.

IN PRACTICE

One of the first efforts to put the NAR/HUD Homebuyer Protection Initiative into action is the Consumer Notice form that explains the difference between the appraisal and a home inspection and that emphasizes the importance of an inspection to protect buyers. The one-page notice must be signed on or before closing in all transactions in which an FHA-insured mortgage is involved.

Final property inspection. Shortly before the closing takes place, the buyer usually makes a *final inspection* of the property with the broker (often called the *walk-through*). The right to have a final property inspection is normally created in the real estate sales contract. Through this inspection, the buyer makes sure that necessary repairs have been made, that the property has been well maintained, that all fixtures are in place, and that there has been no unauthorized removal or alteration of any part of the improvements.

Survey. A **survey** gives information about the exact location and size of the property. The sales contract specifies who will pay for the survey. It is usual for the survey to "spot" the location of all buildings, driveways, fences, and other improvements located primarily on the premises being purchased. Any improvements located on adjoining property that may encroach on the premises being bought will also be noted. The survey should set out, in full, any existing easements and encroachments. Whether or not the sales contract calls for a survey, lenders frequently require one.

IN PRACTICE

A buyer should make sure that the survey is accurate so that property purchased is exactly what the buyer wanted. Relying on old surveys is not necessarily a good idea; the property should be resurveyed prior to closing by a competent surveyor, whether or not the title company or lender requires it.

Seller's Issues

Obviously, the seller's main interest is in receiving payment for the property. He or she will want to be sure that the buyer has obtained the necessary financing and has sufficient funds to complete the sale. The seller also will want to be certain that he or she has complied with all the buyer's requirements so the transaction will be completed.

Both parties will want to inspect the closing statement to make sure that all monies involved in the transaction have been accounted for properly. The parties may be accompanied by their attorneys or their real estate agents.

Title Procedures

Both the buyer and the buyer's lender will want assurance that the seller's title complies with the requirements of the real estate sales contract. Though the practice varies from state to state, the seller is usually required to produce a current *abstract of title* or *title commitment* from the title insurance company. When an abstract of title is used, the purchaser's attorney examines it and issues an opinion of title. This opinion, like the title commitment, is a statement of the status of the seller's title. It discloses all liens, encumbrances, easements, conditions, or restrictions that appear on the record and to which the seller's title is subject.

> The *Title* or *Opinion of Title* discloses all liens, encumbrances, easements, conditions, or restrictions on the property.

On the date when the sale is actually completed (the date of delivery of the deed), the buyer has a title commitment or an abstract that was issued several days or weeks before the closing. For this reason, there are sometimes two searches of the public records. The first shows the status of the seller's title on the date of the first search. Usually, the seller pays for this search. The second search, known as a *bring down*, is made after the closing and generally paid for by the purchaser. The abstract should be reviewed before closing to resolve any problems that might cause delays or threaten the transaction.

As part of this later search, the seller may be required to execute an *affidavit of title*. This is a sworn statement in which the seller assures the title insurance company (and the buyer) that there have been no judgments, bankruptcies, or divorces involving the seller since the date of the title examination. The affidavit promises that no unrecorded deeds or contracts have been made, no repairs or improvements have gone unpaid, and no defects in the title have arisen that the seller knows of. The seller also affirms that he or she is in possession of the premises. In some areas, this form is required before the title insurance company will issue an owner's policy to the buyer. The affidavit gives the title insurance company the right to sue the seller if his or her statements in the affidavit are incorrect.

When the purchaser pays cash or obtains a new loan to purchase the property, the seller's existing loan is paid in full and satisfied on record. The exact amount required to pay the existing loan is provided in a current *payoff statement* from the lender, effective on the date of closing. This payoff statement notes the unpaid amount of principal, the interest due through the date of payment, the fee for issuing the certificate of satisfaction or release deed, credits (if any) for tax and insurance reserves, and the amount of any prepayment penalties. The same procedure is followed for any other liens that must be released before the buyer takes title.

In a transaction in which the buyer assumes the seller's existing mortgage loan, the buyer will want to know the exact balance of the loan as of the closing date. In some areas, it is customary for the buyer to obtain a *mortgage reduction certificate* from the lender that certifies the amount owed on the mortgage loan, the interest rate and the last interest payment made.

In some areas, real estate sales transactions are customarily closed through an escrow (discussed below). In these areas, the escrow instructions usually provide for an extended coverage policy to be issued to the buyer as of the date of closing. The seller has no need to execute an affidavit of title.

IN PRACTICE   Licensees often assist in preclosing arrangements as part of their service to customers. In some states, licensees are required to advise the parties of the approximate expenses involved in closing when a real estate sales contract is signed. In other states, it is the licensees' statutory duty to coordinate and supervise closing activities.

■ CONDUCTING THE CLOSING

Closing is known by many names. For instance, in some areas closing is called *settlement and transfer*. In other parts of the country, the parties to the transaction sit around a single table and exchange copies of documents, a process known as *passing papers*. ("We passed papers on the new house Wednesday morning.") In still other regions, the buyer and seller may never meet at all; the paperwork is handled by an escrow agent. This process is known as *closing escrow*. ("We'll close escrow on our house next week.") Whether the closing occurs face to face or through escrow, the main concerns are that the buyer receives marketable title, the seller receives the purchase price, and certain other items are adjusted properly between the two.

Face-to-Face Closing

In a *face-to-face closing*, the parties meet face to face.

A face-to-face closing involves the resolution of two issues. First, the promises made in the real estate sales contract are fulfilled. Second, the buyer's loan is finalized, and the mortgage lender disburses the loan funds. The difference between a face-to-face closing and an escrow closing is that in a face-to-face closing, these two issues are resolved during a single meeting of all the parties and their attorneys. As discussed earlier, the parties in an escrow closing may never meet. The phrase *passing papers* vividly describes a face-to-face closing.

Face-to-face closings may be held at a number of locations, including the office of the title company, the lending institution, one of the parties' attorneys, the broker, the county recorder, or the escrow company. Those attending a closing *may* include

- the buyer;
- the seller;
- the real estate salespersons or brokers (both the buyer's and the seller's agents);
- the seller's and the buyer's attorneys;
- representatives of the lending institutions involved with the buyer's new mortgage loan, the buyer's assumption of the seller's existing loan, or the seller's payoff of an existing loan; and
- a representative of the title insurance company.

Closing agent or closing officer. One person usually conducts the proceedings at a closing and calculates the division of income and expenses between the parties (called *settlement*). In some areas, real estate brokers preside. In others, the closing agent is the buyer's or seller's attorney, a representative of the lender, or a representative of the title company. Some title companies and law firms employ paralegal assistants who conduct closings for their firms.

Preparation for closing involves ordering and reviewing an array of documents, such as the title insurance policy or title certificate, surveys, property insurance policies, and other items. Arrangements must be made with the parties for the time and place of closing. Closing statements and other documents must be prepared.

The exchange. When the parties are satisfied that everything is in order, the exchange is made. All pertinent documents are then recorded in the correct order to ensure continuity of title. For instance, if the seller pays off an existing loan and the buyer obtains a new loan, the seller's satisfaction of mortgage must be recorded before the seller's deed to the buyer. The buyer's new mortgage or deed of trust must then be recorded after the deed because the buyer cannot pledge the property as security for the loan until he or she owns it.

Closing in Escrow

An **escrow** is a method of closing in which a disinterested third party is authorized to act as escrow agent and to coordinate the closing activities. The escrow agent also may be called the *escrow holder*. The escrow agent may be an attorney, a title company, a trust company, an escrow company, or the escrow department of a lending institution. Many real estate firms offer escrow services. However, a broker cannot be a disinterested party in a transaction from which he or she expects to collect a commission. Because the escrow agent is placed in

In an *escrow closing,* a third party coordinates the closing activities on behalf of the buyer and seller.

a position of great trust, many states have laws regulating escrow agents and limiting who may serve in this capacity. Although a few states do not permit certain transactions to be closed in escrow, escrow closings are used to some extent in most states.

Escrow procedure. When a transaction will close in escrow, the buyer and seller execute escrow instructions to the escrow agent after the sales contract is signed. One of the parties selects an escrow agent. Which party selects the agent is determined either by negotiation or by state law. Once the contract is signed, the broker turns over the earnest money to the escrow agent, who deposits it in a special trust, or escrow, account.

Buyer and seller deposit all pertinent documents and other items with the escrow agent before the specified date of closing. The seller usually deposits

- the deed conveying the property to the buyer;
- title evidence (abstract and attorney's opinion, certificate of title, title insurance, or Torrens certificate);
- existing hazard insurance policies;
- a letter or mortgage reduction certificate from the lender stating the exact principal remaining (if the buyer assumes the seller's loan);
- affidavits of title (if required);
- a payoff statement (if the seller's loan is to be paid off); and
- other instruments or documents necessary to clear the title or to complete the transaction.

The buyer deposits

- the balance of the cash needed to complete the purchase, usually in the form of a certified check;
- loan documents (if the buyer secures a new loan);
- proof of hazard insurance, including (where required) flood insurance; and
- other necessary documents, such as inspection reports required by the lender.

The escrow agent has the authority to examine the title evidence. When marketable title is shown in the name of the buyer and all other conditions of the escrow agreement have been met, the agent is authorized to disburse the purchase price to the seller, minus all charges and expenses. The agent then records the deed and mortgage or deed of trust (if a new loan has been obtained by the purchaser).

If the escrow agent's examination of the title discloses liens, a portion of the purchase price can be withheld from the seller. The withheld portion is used to pay the liens to clear the title.

If the seller cannot clear the title, or if for any reason the sale cannot be consummated, the escrow instructions usually provide that the parties be returned to their former statuses, as if no sale occurred. The escrow agent reconveys title to the seller and returns the purchase money to the buyer.

Internal Revenue Service Reporting Requirements

Certain real estate closings must be reported to the Internal Revenue Service (IRS) on Form 1099-S. The affected properties include sales or exchanges of

- land (improved or unimproved), including air space;
- an inherently permanent structure, including any residential, commercial, or industrial building;
- a condominium unit and its appurtenant fixtures and common elements (including land); or
- stock in a cooperative housing corporation.

Information to be reported includes the sales price, the amount of property tax reimbursement credited to the seller, and the seller's Social Security number. If the closing agent does not notify the IRS, the responsibility for filing the form falls on the mortgage lender, although the brokers or the parties to the transaction ultimately could be held liable.

Broker's Role at Closing

Depending on local practice, the broker's role at closing can vary from simply collecting the commission to conducting the proceedings. Real estate brokers are not authorized to give legal advice or otherwise engage in the practice of law. This means that in some states, a broker's job is essentially finished as soon as the real estate sales contract is signed. After the contract is signed, the attorneys take over. Even so, a broker's service generally continues all the way through closing. The broker makes sure all the details are taken care of so that the closing can proceed smoothly. This means making arrangements for title evidence, surveys, appraisals, inspections or repairs for structural conditions, water supplies, sewerage facilities, or toxic substances.

Though real estate licensees do not always conduct closing proceedings, they usually attend. Often, the parties look to their agents for guidance, assistance, and information during what can be a stressful experience. Licensees need to be thoroughly familiar with the process and procedures involved in preparing a closing statement, which includes the expenses and prorations of costs to close the transaction. It is also in the brokers' best interests that the transactions they worked so hard to bring about move successfully and smoothly to a conclusion. Of course, a broker's (and a salesperson's) commission is generally paid out of the proceeds at closing.

IN PRACTICE

Licensees should avoid *recommending* sources for any inspection or testing services. If a buyer suffers any injury as a result of a provider's negligence, the licensee may also be liable. The better practice is to give clients the names of several professionals who offer high-quality services.

Lender's Interest in Closing

Whether a buyer obtains new financing or assumes the seller's existing loan, the lender wants to protect its security interest in the property. The lender has an interest in making sure the buyer gets good, marketable title and that tax and insurance payments are maintained. Lenders want their mortgage liens to have priority over other liens. They also want to ensure that insurance is kept up to date in case property is damaged or destroyed. For this reason, a lender generally requires a title insurance policy and a fire and hazard insurance policy (along with a receipt for the premium). In addition, a lender may require other information: a survey, a termite or another inspection report, or a certificate of occupancy (for a newly constructed building). A lender also may request that a reserve account be established for tax and insurance payments. Lenders sometimes even require representation by their own attorneys at closings.

■ RESPA REQUIREMENTS

The federal **Real Estate Settlement Procedures Act (RESPA)** was enacted to protect consumers from abusive lending practices. RESPA also aids consumers during the mortgage loan settlement process. It ensures that consumers are provided with important, accurate, and timely information about the actual costs of settling or closing a transaction. It also eliminates kickbacks and other referral fees that tend to inflate the costs of settlements unnecessarily. RESPA prohibits lenders from requiring excessive escrow account deposits.

RESPA requirements apply when a purchase is financed by a federally related mortgage loan. *Federally related loans* means loans made by banks, savings and loan associations, or other lenders whose deposits are insured by federal agencies. It also includes loans insured by the FHA and guaranteed by the VA; loans administered by HUD; and loans intended to be sold by the lenders to Fannie Mae, Ginnie Mae, or Freddie Mac. RESPA is administered by HUD.

RESPA regulations apply to first-lien residential mortgage loans made to finance the purchases of one-family to four-family homes, cooperatives, and condominiums, for either investment or occupancy. RESPA also governs second or subordinate liens for home equity loans. A transaction financed solely by a purchase-money mortgage taken back by the seller, an installment contract (contract for deed), and a buyer's assumption of a seller's existing loan are not covered by RESPA. However, if the terms of the assumed loan are modified, or if the lender charges more than $50 for the assumption, the transaction is subject to RESPA regulations.

IN PRACTICE

While RESPA's requirements are aimed primarily at lenders, some provisions of the Act affect real estate brokers and agents as well. Real estate licensees fall under RESPA when they refer buyers to particular lenders, title companies, attorneys, or other providers of settlement services. Licensees who offer computerized loan origination (CLO) services also are subject to regulation. Remember: Buyers have the right to select their own providers of settlement services.

WWWeb.Link

www.hud.gov/offices/hsg/sfh/res/respa_hm.cfm

Controlled Business Arrangements

A service that is increasing in popularity is one-stop shopping for consumers of real estate services. A real estate firm, title insurance company, mortgage broker, home inspection company, or even a moving company may agree to offer a package of services to consumers. RESPA permits such a **controlled business arrangement (CBA)** *as long as a consumer is clearly informed of the relationship among the service providers and that other providers are available.* Fees may not be exchanged among the affiliated companies simply for referring business to one another. This may be a particularly important issue for licensees who offer computerized loan origination (CLO) services to their clients and customers (discussed in Chapter 15). While a borrower's ability to comparison shop for a loan may be enhanced by a CLO system, his or her range of choices must not be limited. Consumers must be informed of the availability of other lenders.

Disclosure Requirements

Lenders and settlement agents have the following *disclosure* obligations at the time of loan application and loan closing:

- *Special information booklet.* Lenders must provide a copy of a special informational HUD booklet to every person from whom they receive or for whom they prepare a loan application (except for refinancing). The HUD booklet must be given at the time the application is received or within three days afterward. The booklet provides the borrower with general information about settlement (closing) costs. It also explains the various provisions of RESPA, including a line-by-line description of the Uniform Settlement Statement.
- *Good-faith estimate of settlement costs.* No later than three business days after receiving a loan application, the lender must provide to the borrower a good-faith estimate of the settlement costs the borrower is likely to incur. This estimate may be either a specific figure or a range of costs based on comparable past transactions in the area. In addition, if the lender requires use of a particular attorney or title company to conduct the closing, the lender must state whether it has any business relationship with that firm and must estimate the charges for this service.
- *Uniform Settlement Statement (HUD-1 Form).* RESPA requires that a special HUD form be completed to itemize all charges to be paid by a borrower and seller in connection with settlement. The **Uniform Settlement Statement** includes all charges that will be collected at closing, whether required by the lender or another party. Items paid by the borrower and seller outside closing and not required by the lender are not included on the HUD-1 form. Charges required by the lender that are paid for before closing are indicated as "paid outside of closing" (POC). RESPA prohibits lenders from requiring borrowers to deposit amounts in escrow accounts for taxes and insurance that exceed certain limits, thus preventing the lenders from taking advantage of the borrowers. *Sellers* are also prohibited from requiring, as a condition of a sale, that the buyer purchase title insurance from a particular company. A copy of the HUD-1 form is illustrated later in this Chapter. (See Figure 22.4.)

> **RESPA's Consumer Protections**
> - CLO regulation
> - CBA disclosure
> - Settlement cost booklet
> - Good-faith estimate of settlement costs
> - Uniform Settlement Statement
> - Prohibition of kickbacks and unearned fees

The settlement statement must be made available for inspection by the borrower *at or before* settlement. Borrowers have the right to inspect a completed HUD-1 form, to the extent that the figures are available, *one business day before the closing.* (Sellers are not entitled to this privilege.)

Lenders must retain these statements for two years after the dates of closing. In addition, state laws generally require that licensees retain all records of a transaction for a specific period. The Uniform Settlement Statement may be altered to allow for local custom, and certain lines may be deleted if they do not apply in an area.

Kickbacks and referral fees. RESPA prohibits the payment of kickbacks, or unearned fees, in any real estate settlement service. It prohibits referral fees *when no services are actually rendered.* The *payment* or *receipt* of a fee, a kickback, or anything of value for referrals for settlement services includes activities such as mortgage loans, title searches, title insurance, attorney services, surveys, credit reports, and appraisals.

■ PREPARATION OF CLOSING STATEMENTS

A typical real estate transaction involves, in addition to the purchase price, expenses for both parties. These include items prepaid by the seller for which he or she must be reimbursed (such as taxes) and items of expense the seller has incurred, but for which the buyer will be billed (such as mortgage interest paid in arrears when a loan is assumed).

The financial responsibility for these items must be prorated (or divided) between the buyer and the seller. All expenses and prorated items are accounted for on the settlement statement. This is how the exact amount of cash required from the buyer and the net proceeds to the seller are determined. (See Figure 22.1.)

How the Closing Statement Works

A *debit* is an amount *to be paid by* the buyer or seller; a *credit* is an amount *payable to* the buyer or seller.

The completion of a **closing statement** involves an accounting of the parties' debits and credits. A **debit** is a charge, that is, an amount that a party owes and must pay at closing. A **credit** is an amount entered in a person's favor—an amount that has already been paid, an amount being reimbursed, or an amount the buyer promises to pay in the form of a loan.

To determine the amount a buyer needs at closing, the buyer's debits are totaled. Any expenses and prorated amounts for items prepaid by the seller are added to the purchase price. Then the buyer's credits are totaled. These include the earnest money (already paid), the balance of the loan the buyer obtains or assumes, and the seller's share of any prorated items the buyer will pay in the future. (See Figure 22.2.) Finally, the total of the buyer's credits is subtracted from the total debits to arrive at the actual amount of cash the buyer must bring to closing. Usually, the buyer brings a cashier's or certified check.

A similar procedure is followed to determine how much money the seller will actually receive. The seller's debits and credits are each totaled. The credits include the purchase price plus the buyer's share of any prorated items that the seller has prepaid. The seller's debits include expenses, the seller's share of prorated items to be paid later by the buyer, and the balance of any mortgage loan or other lien that the seller pays off. Finally, the total of the seller's debits is subtracted from the total credits to arrive at the amount the seller will receive.

Broker's commission. The responsibility for paying the broker's commission will have been determined by previous agreement. If the broker is the agent for the seller, the seller is normally responsible for paying the commission. If an agency agreement exists between a broker and the buyer, or if two agents are involved, one for the seller and one for the buyer, the commission *may* be appor-

F I G U R E 22.1

Allocation of Expenses

Item	Paid by Seller	Paid by Buyer
Broker's commission	✗ by agreement	✗ by agreement
Attorney's fees	✗ by agreement	✗ by agreement
Recording expenses	✗ to clear title	✗ transfer charges
Transfer tax	✗	
Title expenses	✗ title search	✗ attorney inspection, title insurance
Loan fees	✗ prepayment penalty	✗ origination fee
Tax and insurance reserves (escrow or impound accounts)		✗
Appraisal fees	✗ by agreement	✗ by agreement
Survey fees	✗ if required to pay by sales contract	✗ new mortgage financing

* This chart is based on generally applicable practices. Please note that closing practice may be different in your state.

F I G U R E 22.2

Credits and Debits

Item	Credit to Buyer	Debit to Buyer	Credit to Seller	Debit to Seller	Prorated
Principal amount of new mortgage	✗				
Payoff of existing mortgage				✗	
Unpaid principal balance if assumed mortgage	✗			✗	
Accrued interest on existing assumed mortgage	✗			✗	✗
Tenants' security deposit	✗			✗	
Purchase-money mortgage	✗			✗	
Unpaid water and other utility bills	✗			✗	✗
Buyer's earnest money	✗				
Selling price of property		✗	✗		
Fuel oil on hand (valued at current market price)		✗	✗		✗
Prepaid insurance and tax reserve for mortgage assumed by buyer		✗	✗		✗
Refund to seller of prepaid water charges and similar utility expenses		✗	✗		✗
Prepaid general real estate taxes		✗	✗		✗

* This chart is based on generally applicable practices. Please note that closing practice may be different in your state.

tioned as an expense between both parties or according to some other arrangement.

Attorney's fees. If either of the parties' attorneys will be paid from the closing proceeds, that party will be charged with the expense in the closing statement. This expense may include fees for the preparation or review of documents or for representing the parties at settlement.

Recording expenses. The *seller* usually pays for recording charges (filing fees) necessary to clear all defects and furnish the purchaser with a marketable title. Items customarily charged to the seller include the recording of release deeds or satisfaction of mortgages, quitclaim deeds, affidavits, and satisfaction of mechanics' liens. The *purchaser* pays for recording charges that arise from the actual transfer of title. Usually, such items include recording the deed that conveys title to the purchaser and a mortgage or deed of trust executed by the purchaser.

Transfer tax. Most states require some form of transfer tax, conveyance fee, or tax stamps on real estate conveyances. This expense is most often borne by the seller, although customs vary. In addition, many cities and local municipalities charge transfer taxes. Responsibility for these charges varies according to local practice.

Title expenses. Responsibility for title expenses varies according to local custom. In most areas, the seller is required to furnish evidence of good title and pay for the title search. If the buyer's attorney inspects the evidence or if the buyer purchases title insurance policies, the buyer is charged for the expense.

Loan fees. When the buyer secures a new loan to finance the purchase, the lender ordinarily charges a loan origination fee of 1 percent to 2 percent of the loan. The fee is usually paid by the purchaser at the time the transaction closes. The lender may also charge discount points if the buyer has secured a loan with a below-market interest rate. If the buyer assumes the seller's existing financing, the buyer may pay an assumption fee. Also, under the terms of some mortgage loans, the seller may be required to pay a prepayment charge or penalty for paying off the mortgage loan before its due date.

Tax reserves and insurance reserves (escrow or impound accounts). Most mortgage lenders require that borrowers provide reserve funds or escrow accounts to pay future real estate taxes and insurance premiums. A borrower starts the account at closing by depositing funds to cover at least the amount of unpaid real estate taxes from the date of lien to the end of the current month. (The buyer receives a credit from the seller at closing for any unpaid taxes.) Afterward, an amount equal to one month's portion of the estimated taxes is included in the borrower's monthly mortgage payment.

The borrower is responsible for maintaining adequate fire or hazard insurance as a condition of the mortgage loan. Generally, the first year's premium is paid in full at closing. An amount equal to one month's premium is paid after that. The borrower's monthly loan payment includes the principal and interest on the loan, plus one-twelfth of the estimated taxes and insurance (PITI). The taxes and insurance are held by the lender in the escrow or impound account until the bills are due.

IN PRACTICE

RESPA permits lenders to maintain a "cushion" equal to one-sixth of the total amount of taxes and insurance paid out of the account, that is, approximately two months of escrow payments. However, if state law or mortgage documents allow for a smaller cushion, that lesser amount prevails.

WWWeb.Link   http://www.hud.gov/offices/hsg/sfh/res/respafaq.cfm

Appraisal fees. Either the seller or the purchaser pays the appraisal fees, depending on who orders the appraisal. When the buyer obtains a mortgage, it is customary for the lender to require an appraisal. In this case, the buyer usually bears the cost, although this is always a negotiable item. If the fee is paid at the time of the loan application, it is reflected on the closing statement as having already been paid.

Survey fees. The purchaser who obtains new mortgage financing customarily pays the survey fees. The sales contract may require that the seller furnish a survey.

Additional fees. An FHA borrower owes a lump sum for payment of the *mortgage insurance premium* (MIP) if it is not financed as part of the loan. A VA mortgagor pays a funding fee directly to the VA at closing. If a conventional loan carries *private mortgage insurance* (PMI), the buyer prepays one year's insurance premium at closing.

Accounting for Expenses

Expenses paid out of the closing proceeds are debited only to the party making the payment. Occasionally, an expense item, such as an escrow fee, a settlement fee, or a transfer tax, may be shared by the buyer and the seller. In this case, each party is debited for the share of the expense.

■ PRORATIONS

Most closings involve the division of financial responsibility between the buyer and seller for such items as loan interest, taxes, rents, fuel, and utility bills. These allowances are called **prorations.** Prorations are necessary to ensure that expenses are divided fairly between the seller and the buyer. For example, the seller may owe current taxes that have not been billed; the buyer would want this settled at the closing. Where taxes must be paid in advance, the seller is entitled to a rebate at the closing. If the buyer assumes the seller's existing mortgage or deed of trust, the seller usually owes the buyer an allowance for accrued interest through the date of closing.

Accrued items = buyer credits

Prepaid items = seller credits

Accrued items are expenses to be prorated (such as water bills and interest on an assumed mortgage) that are owed by the seller, but later will be paid by the buyer. The seller therefore pays for these items by giving the buyer credits for them at closing.

Prepaid items are expenses to be prorated, such as fuel oil in a tank, that have been prepaid by the seller but not fully used up. They are therefore credits to the seller.

The Arithmetic of Prorating

Accurate prorating involves the following four considerations:

1. Nature of the item being prorated
2. Whether it is an accrued item that requires the determination of an earned amount
3. Whether it is a prepaid item that requires the determination of an unearned amount (that is, a refund to the seller)
4. What arithmetic processes must be used

The computation of a proration involves identifying a yearly charge for the item to be prorated, then dividing by 12 to determine a monthly charge for the item. Usually, it also is necessary to identify a daily charge for the item by dividing the monthly charge by the number of days in the month. These smaller portions are then multiplied by the number of months or days in the prorated time period to determine the accrued or unearned amount that will be figured in the settlement.

Using this general principle, there are two methods of calculating prorations:

1. The yearly charge is divided by a *360-day year* (commonly called a *banking year*), or 12 months of 30 days each.
2. The yearly charge is divided by *365* (366 in a leap year) to determine the daily charge. Then the actual number of days in the proration period is determined, and this number is multiplied by the daily charge.

The final proration figure varies slightly, depending on which computation method is used. The final figure also varies according to the number of decimal places to which the division is carried. *All of the computations in this Chapter are computed by carrying the division to three decimal places*. The third decimal place is rounded off to cents only after the final proration figure is determined.

Accrued Items

When the real estate tax is levied for the calendar year and is payable during that year or in the following year, the accrued portion is for the period from January 1 to the date of closing (or to the day before the closing in states where the sale date is excluded). If the current tax bill has not yet been issued, the parties must agree on an estimated amount based on the previous year's bill and any known changes in assessment or tax levy for the current year.

Sample proration calculation. Assume a sale is to be closed on September 17. Current real estate taxes of $1,200 are to be prorated. A 360-day year is used. The accrued period, then, is 8 months and 17 days. First determine the prorated cost of the real estate tax per month and day:

$1,200 ÷ 12 months = $100 per month
$100 ÷ 30 days   = $3.333 per day

Next, multiply these figures by the accrued period, and add the totals to determine the prorated real estate tax:

$100 × 8 months   = $800
$3.333 × 17 days   = $56.661
$800.000 + 56.661 = $856.661

Thus, the accrued real estate tax for 8 months and 17 days is $856.66 (rounded off to two decimal places after the final computation). This amount represents the seller's accrued earned tax. It will be a *credit to the buyer* and *a debit to the seller on the closing statement.*

To compute this proration using the actual number of days in the accrued period, the following method is used: The accrued period from January 1 to September 17 runs 260 days (January's 31 days plus February's 28 days and so on, plus the 17 days of September).

$1,200 tax bill ÷ 365 days = $3.288 per day

$3.288 × 260 days   = $854.880, or $854.88

While these examples show proration as of the date of settlement, the agreement of sale may require otherwise. For instance, a buyer's possession date may not coincide with the settlement date. In this case, the parties could prorate according to the date of possession.

IN PRACTICE

On state licensing examinations, tax prorations are usually based on a 30-day month (360-day year) unless specified otherwise. This may differ with local customs regarding tax prorations. Many title insurance companies provide proration charts that detail tax factors for each day in the year. To determine a tax proration using one of these charts, multiply the factor given for the closing date by the annual real estate tax. (See Figure 22.3.)

Prepaid Items

A tax proration could be a prepaid item. Because real estate taxes may be paid in the early part of the year, a tax proration calculated for a closing taking place later in the year must reflect the fact that the seller has already paid the tax. For example, in the preceding problem, suppose that all taxes had been paid. The buyer, then, would have to reimburse the seller; the proration would be *credited to the seller* and *debited to the buyer.*

In figuring the tax proration, it is necessary to ascertain the number of future days, months, and years for which taxes have been paid. The formula commonly used for this purpose is as follows:

	Years	Months	Days
Taxes paid to (Dec. 31, end of tax year)	200–	12	30
Date of closing (Sept. 17, 200–)	200–	–9	–17
Period for which tax must be paid		3	13

With this formula, we can find the amount the buyer will reimburse the seller for the *unearned* portion of the real estate tax. The prepaid period, as determined using the formula for prepaid items, is 3 months and 13 days. Three months at $100 per month equals $300, and 13 days at $3.333 per day equals $43.33. Add this to determine that the proration is $343.33 *credited to the seller* and *debited to the buyer.*

FIGURE   22.3

**Calculating Real Estate
Taxes**

Real Estate Taxing Method	Closing Date	Proration or Accrual Calculation for Closing
Taxes for the property paid in advance (by December 31 for the coming year).	June 30th	Buyer will reimburse the seller at the closing for the taxes already paid for the half of the year from July 1 to December 31 when the buyer owned the property.
Taxes for the property paid in arrears (by December 31 for the previous year).	June 30th	Seller will pay the buyer at the closing for taxes not yet paid for the half of the year from January 1 to June 30 when the seller owned the property.
Blended or staggered system.	June 30th	Each tax due date is compared to the closing date, and if the taxes have been paid in advance, the buyer reimburses the seller for the taxes already paid. If the taxes are not yet paid for a portion of the time on which the property is being taxed, the seller pays the buyer for those yet unpaid taxes.

Sample prepaid item calculation. One example of a prepaid item is a water bill. Assume that the water is billed in advance by the city without using a meter. The six months' billing is $60 for the period ending October 31. The sale is to be closed on August 3. Because the water bill is paid to October 31, the prepaid time must be computed. Using a 30-day basis, the time period is the 27 days left in August plus two full months: $60 (6 = $10 per month. For one day, divide $10 by 30, which equals $0.333 per day. The prepaid period is 2 months and 27 days, so:

$$27 \times \$0.333 \text{ per day} = \$8.991$$
$$2 \text{ months} \times \$10 \quad = \underline{\$20.000}$$
$$\$28.991 \text{ or } \$28.99$$

This is a prepaid item; it is *credited to the seller* and *debited to the buyer* on the closing statement.

To figure this based on the actual days in the month of closing, the following process would be used:

$$\$10 \text{ per month} \div 31 \text{ days in August} = \$0.323 \text{ per day}$$
$$\text{August 4 through August 31} = 28 \text{ days}$$
$$28 \text{ days} \times \$0.323 = \$9.044$$
$$2 \text{ months} \times \$10 = \$20.000$$
$$\$9.044 + \$20 = \$29.044, \text{ or } \$29.04$$

**General Rules
for Prorating**

The rules or customs governing the computation of prorations for the closing of a real estate sale vary widely from state to state. The following are some general guidelines for preparing the closing statement:

■ In most states, the seller owns the property on the day of closing, and prorations or apportionments are usually made *to and including the day of clos-*

ing. In a few states, however, it is provided specifically that the buyer owns the property on the closing date. In that case, adjustments are made as of the day preceding the day on which title is closed.

■ Mortgage interest, general real estate taxes, water taxes, insurance premiums, and similar expenses are usually computed by using *360 days in a year and 30 days in a month.* However, the rules in some areas provide for computing prorations on the basis of the *actual number of days* in the calendar month of closing. The agreement of sale should specify which method will be used.

■ Accrued or prepaid *general real estate taxes* are usually prorated at the closing. When the amount of the current real estate tax cannot be determined definitely, the proration is usually based on the last obtainable tax bill.

■ *Special assessments* for municipal improvements such as sewers, water mains, or streets are usually paid in annual installments over several years, with annual interest charged on the outstanding balance of future installments. The seller normally pays the current installment, and the buyer assumes all future installments. *The special assessment installment generally is not prorated at the closing.* A buyer may insist that the seller allow the buyer a credit for the seller's share of the interest to the closing date. The agreement of sale may address the manner in which special assessments will be handled at settlement.

■ *Rents* are usually adjusted on the basis of the *actual number of days* in the month of closing. It is customary for the seller to receive the rents for the day of closing and to pay all expenses for that day. If any rents for the current month are uncollected when the sale is closed, the buyer often agrees by a separate letter to collect the rents if possible and remit the pro rata share to the seller.

■ *Security deposits* made by tenants to cover the last month's rent of the lease or to cover the cost of repairing damage caused by the tenant are generally transferred by the seller to the buyer.

Real estate taxes. Proration of real estate taxes varies widely depending on how the taxes are paid in the area where the real estate is located. In some states, real estate taxes are paid *in advance;* that is, if the tax year runs from January 1 to December 31, taxes for the coming year are due on January 1. In this case, the seller, who has prepaid a year's taxes, should be reimbursed for the portion of the year remaining after the buyer takes ownership of the property. In other areas, taxes are paid *in arrears,* on December 31 for the year just ended. In this case, the buyer should be credited by the seller for the time the seller occupied the property. Sometimes, taxes are due during the tax year, partly in arrears and partly in advance; sometimes they are payable in installments. It gets even more complicated: City, state, school, and other property taxes may start their tax years in different months. Whatever the case may be in a particular transaction, the licensee should understand how the taxes will be prorated.

Mortgage loan interest. On almost every mortgage loan the interest is paid *in arrears,* so the buyer and seller must understand that the mortgage payment due on June 1, for example, includes interest due for the month of May. Thus, the buyer who assumes a mortgage on May 31 and makes the June payment pays for the time the seller occupied the property and should be credited with a month's interest. On the other hand, the buyer who places a new mortgage loan on May

31 may be pleasantly surprised to hear that he or she will not need to make a mortgage payment until a month later.

■ SAMPLE CLOSING STATEMENT

Settlement computations take many possible formats. The remaining portion of this Chapter illustrates a sample transaction using the RESPA Uniform Settlement Statement in Figure 22.4. Because customs differ in various parts of the country, the way certain expenses are charged in some locations may be different from the illustration.

Basic Information of Offer and Sale

John and Joanne Iuro list their home at 3045 North Racine Avenue in Riverdale, East Dakota, with the Open Door Real Estate Company. The listing price is $118,500, and possession can be given within two weeks after all parties have signed the contract. Under the terms of the listing agreement, the sellers agree to pay the broker a commission of 6 percent of the sales price.

On May 18, the Open Door Real Estate Company submits a contract offer to the Iuros from Brook Redemann, a bachelor residing at 22 King Court, Riverdale. Redemann offers $115,000, with earnest money and down payment of $23,000 and the remaining $92,000 of the purchase price to be obtained through a new conventional loan. No private mortgage insurance is necessary because the loan-to-value ratio does not exceed 80 percent. The Iuros sign the contract on May 29. Closing is set for June 15 at the office of the Open Door Real Estate Company, 720 Main Street, Riverdale.

The unpaid balance of the Iuros' mortgage as of June 1, 200– will be $57,700. Payments are $680 per month, with interest at 11 percent per annum on the unpaid balance.

The sellers submit evidence of title in the form of a title insurance binder at a cost of $10. The title insurance policy, to be paid by the sellers at the time of closing, costs an additional $540, including $395 for lender's coverage and $145 for homeowner's coverage. Recording charges of $20 are paid for the recording of two instruments to clear defects in the sellers' title. State transfer tax stamps in the amount $115 ($.50 per $500 of the sales price or fraction thereof) are affixed to the deed. In addition, the sellers must pay an attorney's fee of $400 for preparing of the deed and for legal representation. This amount will be paid from the closing proceeds.

The buyer must pay an attorney's fee of $300 for examining the title evidence and for legal representation. He also must pay $20 to record the deed. These amounts also will be paid from the closing proceeds.

Real estate taxes in Riverdale are paid in arrears. Taxes for this year, estimated at last year's figure of $1,725, have not been paid. According to the contract, prorations will be made on the basis of 30 days in a month.

FIGURE 22.4

RESPA Uniform Settlement Statement

A. Settlement Statement

U.S. Department of Housing
and Urban Development

OMB Approval No. 2502-0265

B. Type of Loan

1. ☐ FHA 2. ☐ FmHA 3. ☒ Conv. Unins. 4. ☐ VA 5. ☐ Conv. Ins.	6. File Number: 7. Loan Number: 8. Mortgage Insurance Case Number:

C. Note: This form is furnished to give you a statement of actual settlement costs. Amounts paid to and by the settlement agent are shown. Items marked "(p.o.c.)" were paid outside the closing; they are shown here for informational purposes and are not included in the totals.

D. Name & Address of Borrower:	E. Name & Address of Seller:	F. Name & Address of Lender:
Brook Redemann 22 King Court Riverdale, ED 00000	John Iuro and Joanne Iuro 3045 North Racine Avenue Riverdale, ED 00000	Thrift Federal Savings 1100 Fountain Plaza Riverdale, ED 00000

G. Property Location:	H. Settlement Agent:	
3045 North Racine Avenue Riverdale, ED 00000	Open Door Real Estate Co. Place of Settlement: 720 Main Street Riverdale, ED 00000	I. Settlement Date: June 15, 200-

J. Summary of Borrower's Transaction		K. Summary of Seller's Transaction	
100. Gross Amount Due From Borrower		**400. Gross Amount Due To Seller**	
101. Contract sales price	$115,000.00	401. Contract sales price	$115,000.00
102. Personal property		402. Personal property	
103. Settlement charges to borrower (line 1400)	4,892.09	403.	
104.		404.	
105.		405.	
Adjustments for items paid by seller in advance		*Adjustments for items paid by seller in advance*	
106. City/town taxes to		406. City/town taxes to	
107. County taxes to		407. County taxes to	
108. Assessments to		408. Assessments to	
109.		409.	
110.		410.	
111.		411.	
112.		412.	
120. Gross Amount Due From Borrower	119,892.09	**420. Gross Amount Due To Seller**	$115,000.00
200. Amounts Paid By Or In Behalf Of Borrower		**500. Reductions In Amount Due To Seller**	
201. Deposit or earnest money	23,000.00	501. Excess deposit (see instructions)	
202. Principal amount of new loan(s)	92,000.00	502. Settlement charges to seller (line 1400)	8,285.00
203. Existing loan(s) taken subject to		503. Existing loan(s) taken subject to	
204.		504. Payoff of first mortgage loan	57,964.47
205.		505. Payoff of second mortgage loan	
206.		506.	
207.		507.	
208.		508.	
209.		509.	
Adjustments for items unpaid by seller		*Adjustments for items unpaid by seller*	
210. City/town taxes to		510. City/town taxes to	
211. County taxes 1/1 to 6/15	790.63	511. County taxes 1/1 to 6/15	790.63
212. Assessments to		512. Assessments to	
213.		513.	
214.		514.	
215.		515.	
216.		516.	
217.		517.	
218.		518.	
219.		519.	
220. Total Paid By/For Borrower	115,790.63	**520. Total Reduction Amount Due Seller**	67,040.10
300. Cash At Settlement From/To Borrower		**600. Cash At Settlement To/From Seller**	
301. Gross Amount due from borrower (line 120)	119,892.09	601. Gross amount due to seller (line 420)	115,000.00
302. Less amounts paid by/for borrower (line 220)	(115,790.63)	602. Less reductions in amt. due seller (line 520)	(67,040.10)
303. Cash ☒ From ☐ To Borrower	$ 4,101.46	**603. Cash** ☒ To ☐ From Seller	$ 47,959.90

Section 5 of the Real Estate Settlement Procedures Act (RESPA) requires the following: • HUD must develop a Special Information Booklet to help persons borrowing money to finance the purchase of residential real estate to better understand the nature and costs of real estate settlement services; • Each lender must provide the booklet to all applicants from whom it receives or for whom it prepares a written application to borrow money to finance the purchase of residential real estate; • Lenders must prepare and distribute with the Booklet a Good Faith Estimate of the settlement costs that the borrower is likely to incur in connection with the settlement. These disclosures are manadatory.

Section 4(a) of RESPA mandates that HUD develop and prescribe this standard form to be used at the time of loan settlement to provide full disclosure of all charges imposed upon the borrower and seller. These are third party disclosures that are designed to provide the borrower with pertinent information during the settlement process in order to be a better shopper.

The Public Reporting Burden for this collection of information is estimated to average one hour per response, including the time for reviewing instructions, searching existing data sources, gathering and maintaining the data needed, and completing and reviewing the collection of information.

This agency may not collect this information, and you are not required to complete this form, unless it displays a currently valid OMB control number.

The information requested does not lend itself to confidentiality.

F I G U R E   22.4

**RESPA Uniform
Settlement Statement
(cont'd)**

L. Settlement Charges

700. Total Sales/Broker's Commission based on price $ 115,000.00 @ 6 % = 6,900.00	Paid From Borrowers Funds at Settlement	Paid From Seller's Funds at Settlement
Division of Commission (line 700) as follows:		
701. $ to		
702. $ to		
703. Commission paid at Settlement		$ 6,900.00
704.		
800. Items Payable In Connection With Loan		
801. Loan Origination Fee %	$ 920.00	
802. Loan Discount %	1,840.00	
803. Appraisal Fee 250.00 to Swift Appraisal	POC	
804. Credit Report 60.00 to Amce Credit Bureau	POC	
805. Lender's Inspection Fee		
806. Mortgage Insurance Application Fee to		
807. Assumption Fee		
808.		
809.		
810.		
811.		
900. Items Required By Lender To Be Paid In Advance		
901. Interest from 6/16 to 6/30 @$25.556 /day	383.34	
902. Mortgage Insurance Premium for months to		
903. Hazard Insurance Premium for 1 years to Hite Insurance Co.	345.00	
904. years to		
905.		
1000. Reserves Deposited With Lender		
1001. Hazard insurance 2 months@$ 28.75 per month	57.50	
1002. Mortgage insurance months@$ per month		
1003. City property taxes months@$ per month		
1004. County property taxes 7 months@$ 143.75 per month	1,006.25	
1005. Annual assessments months@$ per month		
1006. months@$ per month		
1007. months@$ per month		
1008. months@$ per month		
1100. Title Charges		
1101. Settlement or closing fee to		
1102. Abstract or title search to		
1103. Title examination to		
1104. Title insurance binder to		10.00
1105. Document preparation to		
1106. Notary fees to		
1107. Attorney's fees to	300.00	400.00
(includes above items numbers:)		
1108. Title insurance to		540.00
(includes above items numbers:)		
1109. Lender's coverage $ 395.00		
1110. Owner's coverage $ 145.00		
1111.		
1112.		
1113.		
1200. Government Recording and Transfer Charges		
1201. Recording fees: Deed $ 20.00 ; Mortgage $ 20.00 ; Releases $ 20.00	40.00	20.00
1202. City/county tax/stamps: Deed $; Mortgage $		
1203. State tax/stamps: Deed $; Mortgage $		115.00
1204. Record 2 documents to clear title		40.00
1205.		
1300. Additional Settlement Charges		
1301. Survey to		175.00
1302. Pest inspection to		85.00
1303.		
1304.		
1305.		
1400. Total Settlement Charges (enter on lines 103, Section J and 502, Section K)	$ 4,892.09	$ 8,285.00

Computing the prorations and charges. The following list illustrates the various steps in computing the prorations and other amounts to be included in the settlement to this point:

- Closing date: June 15
- Commission: 6% (.06) × $115,000 sales price = $6,900
- Seller's mortgage interest: 11% (.11) × $57,700 principal due after June 1 payment = $6,347 interest per year; $6,347 ÷ 360 days = $17.631 interest per day; 15 days of accrued interest to be paid by the seller × $17.631 = $264.465 interest owed by the seller; $57,700 + $264.465 = $57,964.465, or $57,964.47 payoff of seller's mortgage
- Real estate taxes (estimated at $1,725): $1,725 ÷ 12 months = $143.75 per month; $143.75 ÷ 30 days = $ 4.792 per day
- The earned period, from January 1 to and including June 15, equals five months and 15 days: $143.75 × 5 months = $718.75; $4.792 × 15 days = $71.88; $718.75 + $71.88 = $790.63 seller owes buyer
- Transfer tax ($.50 per $500 of consideration or fraction thereof): $115,000 ÷ $500 = $230; $230 × $.50 = $115 transfer tax owed by seller

The sellers' loan payoff is $57,964.47. They must pay an additional $20 to record the mortgage release, as well as $85 for a pest inspection and $175 for a survey, as negotiated between the parties. The buyer's new loan is from Thrift Federal Savings, 1100 Fountain Plaza, Riverdale, in the amount of $92,000 at 10 percent interest. In connection with this loan, Redemann will be charged $250 to have the property appraised by Swift Appraisal. Acme Credit Bureau will charge $60 for a credit report. (Because appraisal and credit reports are performed before loan approval, they are paid at the time of loan application, whether or not the transaction eventually closes. These items are noted as POC—paid outside closing—on the settlement statement.) In addition, Redemann will pay for interest on his loan for the remainder of the month of closing: 15 days at $25.556 per day, or $383.34. His first full payment (including July's interest) will be due on August 1. He must deposit $1,006.25 into a tax reserve account. That's $^{7}/_{12}$ of the anticipated county real estate tax of $1,725. A one-year hazard insurance premium at $3 per $1,000 of appraised value ($115,000 ÷ 1,000 × 3 = $345) is paid in advance to Hite Insurance Company. An insurance reserve to cover the premium for two months is deposited with the lender. Redemann will have to pay an additional $20 to record the mortgage. He will also pay a loan origination fee of $920 and two discount points of $1,840.

The Uniform Settlement Statement

The Uniform Settlement Statement is divided into 12 sections. Sections J, K, and L contain particularly important information. The borrower's and seller's summaries (J and K) are very similar. In Section J, the buyer-borrower's debits are listed on lines 100 through 112. They are totaled on line 120 (gross amount due from borrower). The total of the settlement costs itemized in Section L of the statement is entered on line 103 as one of the buyer's charges. The buyer's credits are listed on lines 201 through 219 and totaled on line 220 (total paid by or for borrower). Then the buyer's credits are subtracted from the charges to arrive at the cash due from the borrower to close (line 303).

In Section K, the seller's credits are entered on lines 400 through 412 and totaled on line 420 (gross amount due to seller). The seller's debits are entered on lines 501 through 519 and totaled on line 520 (total reduction amount due seller). The total of the seller's settlement charges is on line 502. Then the debits are subtracted from the credits to arrive at the cash due to the seller to close (line 603).

Section L summarizes all the settlement charges for the transaction; the buyer's expenses are listed in one column and the seller's expenses in the other. If an attorney's fee is listed as a lump sum in line 1107, the settlement should list by line number the services that were included in that total fee.

■ SUMMARY

Closing a real estate sale involves both title procedures and financial matters. The real estate salesperson or broker is often present at the closing to see that the sale is actually concluded and to account for the earnest money deposit.

The federal Real Estate Settlement Procedures Act (RESPA) requires disclosure of all settlement costs when a residential real estate purchase is financed by a federally related mortgage loan. RESPA requires that lenders use a Uniform Settlement Statement to detail the financial particulars of a transaction.

The actual amount to be paid by a buyer at closing is computed on a closing, or settlement, statement. This lists the sales price, earnest money deposit and all adjustments and prorations due between buyer and seller. The purpose of this statement is to determine the net amount due the seller at closing. The buyer reimburses the seller for prepaid items such as unused taxes or fuel oil. The seller credits the buyer for bills the seller owes, but the buyer will have to pay accrued items such as unpaid water bills.

QUESTIONS

1. Which of the following statements is true of real estate closings in most states?
   a. Closings are generally conducted by real estate salespersons.
   b. The buyer usually receives the rents for the day of closing.
   c. The buyer must reimburse the seller for any title evidence provided by the seller.
   d. The seller usually pays the expenses for the day of closing.

2. All encumbrances and liens shown on the report of title other than those waived or agreed to by the purchaser and listed in the contract must be removed so that the title can be delivered free and clear. The removal of such encumbrances is typically the duty of the
   a. buyer.   c. broker.
   b. seller.   d. title company.

3. Legal title always passes from seller to buyer
   a. on the date of execution of the deed.
   b. when the closing statement has been signed.
   c. when the deed is placed in escrow.
   d. when the deed is delivered and accepted.

4. Which of the following would a lender generally require at the closing?
   a. Title insurance commitment
   b. Market value appraisal
   c. Application
   d. Credit report

5. Wilma is buying a house. In Wilma's area, closings are traditionally conducted in escrow. Which of the following items will Wilma deposit with the escrow agent before the closing date?
   a. Deed to the property
   b. Title evidence
   c. Estoppel certificate
   d. Cash needed to complete the purchase

6. The RESPA Uniform Settlement Statement must be used to illustrate all settlement charges for
   a. every real estate transaction.
   b. transactions financed by VA and FHA loans only.
   c. residential transactions financed by federally related mortgage loans.
   d. all transactions involving commercial property.

7. A mortgage reduction certificate is executed by a(n)
   a. abstract company.
   b. attorney.
   c. lending institution.
   d. grantor.

8. The principal amount of a purchaser's new mortgage loan is a
   a. credit to the seller.
   b. credit to the buyer.
   c. debit to the seller.
   d. debit to the buyer.

9. The earnest money left on deposit with the broker is a
   a. credit to the seller.
   b. credit to the buyer.
   c. balancing factor.
   d. debit to the buyer.

10. The annual real estate taxes on a property amount to $1,800. The seller has paid the taxes in advance for the calendar year. If closing is set for June 15, which of the following is true?
   a. Credit seller $825; debit buyer $975
   b. Credit seller $1,800; debit buyer $825
   c. Credit buyer $975; debit seller $975
   d. Credit seller $975; debit buyer $975

11. If a seller collected rent of $400, payable in advance, from an attic tenant on August 1, which of the following is true at the closing on August 15, if the closing date is an expense to the seller?

   a. Seller owes buyer $400
   b. Buyer owes seller $400
   c. Seller owes buyer $200
   d. Buyer owes seller $200

12. Security deposits should be listed on a closing statement as a credit to the

   a. buyer.   c. lender.
   b. seller.   d. broker.

13. A building was purchased for $85,000, with 10 percent down and a loan for the balance. If the lender charged the buyer two discount points, how much cash did the buyer need to come up with at closing if the buyer incurred no other costs?

   a. $1,700   c. $10,030
   b. $8,500   d. $10,200

14. A buyer of a $100,000 home has paid $2,000 as earnest money and has a loan commitment for 70 percent of the purchase price. How much more cash does the buyer need to bring to the closing, provided the buyer has no closing costs?

   a. $18,000   c. $58,000
   b. $28,000   d. $61,600

15. At closing, the listing broker's commission usually is shown as a

   a. credit to the seller.
   b. credit to the buyer.
   c. debit to the seller.
   d. debit to the buyer.

16. At the closing of a real estate transaction, the person performing settlement gave the buyer a credit for certain accrued items. These items were

   a. bills relating to the property that have already been paid by the seller.
   b. bills relating to the property that will have to be paid by the buyer.
   c. all of the seller's real estate bills.
   d. all of the buyer's real estate bills.

17. The Real Estate Settlement Procedures Act applies to the activities of

   a. brokers selling commercial and office buildings.
   b. security salespersons selling limited partnerships.
   c. Ginnie Mae or Fannie Mae when purchasing mortgages.
   d. lenders financing purchase of one-family to four-family residential properties.

18. The purpose of the Real Estate Settlement Procedures Act (RESPA) is to

   a. make sure buyers do not borrow more than they can repay.
   b. make real estate brokers more responsive to buyers' needs.
   c. help buyers know how much money is required.
   d. see that buyers know all settlement costs that will be charged to them.

19. The document that provides borrowers with general information about settlement costs, RESPA provisions and the Uniform Settlement Statement is the

   a. HUD-1 form.
   b. special information booklet.
   c. good-faith estimate of settlement costs.
   d. closing statement.

20. Which of the following statements is true of a computerized loan origination (CLO) system?

   a. The mortgage broker or lender may pay any fee charged by the real estate broker in whose office the CLO terminal is located.
   b. Consumers must be informed of the availability of other lenders—those not shown in the real estate broker's CLO.
   c. The real estate broker in whose office the CLO terminal is located may charge a fee of up to two points for the use of the system.
   d. The fee charged by the real estate broker for using the CLO terminal may not be financed as part of the loan.

INTRODUCTION TO REAL ESTATE INVESTMENT

■ KEY TERMS

adjusted basis	depreciation	liquidity
appreciation	equity buildup	pyramiding
basis	exchanges	real estate investment trust (REIT)
boot	income property	
capital gain	inflation	real estate mortgage investment conduit (REMIC)
cash flow	intrinsic value	
cost recovery	leverage	syndicate

■ INVESTING IN REAL ESTATE

Real estate is a popular investment. Even though changes in the economy have increased risk or lowered returns, the investment market continues to devise innovative and attractive investment strategies. These developments make it important for real estate licensees to have an elementary and up-to-date knowledge of real estate investment. Even the average homebuyer will want assurance that a residential purchase is a good investment. Of course, this does not mean that licensees should act as investment counselors. *They should always refer investors to competent tax accountants, attorneys, or investment specialists.* These are the professionals who can give expert advice on an investor's specific needs.

Advantages of Real Estate Investment

In recent years, real estate values have fluctuated widely in various regions of the country. This results in some investments failing to produce returns greater than the rate of inflation, that is, failing to serve as inflation hedges. Yet many real estate investments have shown above-average *rates of return,* generally greater than the prevailing interest rates charged by mortgage lenders. In theory, this means an investor can use the *leverage* of borrowed money to finance a real estate purchase and feel relatively sure that if held long enough, the asset will yield more money than it cost to finance the purchase.

Real estate offers investors greater control over their investments than do other options such as stocks, bonds, or other securities. Real estate investors also receive certain tax benefits. Both leveraging and taxes are discussed in full later in this Chapter.

Disadvantages of Real Estate Investment

Unlike stocks and bonds, real estate is not highly liquid over a short period of time. **Liquidity** refers to how quickly an asset may be converted into cash. For instance, an investor in listed stocks has only to call a stockbroker to sell stocks when funds are needed. The stockbroker sells the stock, and the investor receives the cash. In contrast, a real estate investor may have to sell the property at a substantially lower price than desired to ensure a quick sale. Of course, a real estate investor may be able to raise a limited amount of cash by refinancing the property.

Real estate investment is expensive. Large amounts of capital are usually required. It is difficult to invest in real estate without expert advice. Investment decisions must be based on careful studies of all the facts, reinforced by a thorough knowledge of real estate and the manner in which it is affected by the marketplace.

Real estate requires active management. A real estate investor can rarely sit idly by and watch his or her money grow. Management decisions must be made. How much rent should be charged? How should repairs and tenant grievances be handled? The investor may want to manage the property personally. On the other hand, it may be preferable to hire a professional property manager. *Sweat equity,* physical improvements accomplished by the investor personally, may be required to make the asset profitable. Many good investments fail because of poor management.

Finally, despite its popularity, real estate investment is far from a sure thing. In fact, it involves a high degree of risk. The possibility always exists that an investor's property will decrease in value during the period it is held or that it will not generate enough income to make it profitable.

The advantages and disadvantages of real estate investments are listed in Figure A-1.

■ THE INVESTMENT

Real estate investors hope to achieve various investment objectives. Their goals can be reached more effectively depending on the type of property and manner of ownership chosen. The most prevalent form of real estate investment is *direct ownership.* Both individuals and corporations may own real estate directly and manage it for appreciation or cash flow (income). Property held for appreciation is generally expected to increase in value while it's owned and to show a profit when it's sold. **Income property** is just that: property held for current income as well as a potential profit upon its sale.

Appreciation

Real estate is an avenue of investment open to those interested in holding property *primarily* for **appreciation.**

FIGURE A.1

Advantages and Disadvantages of Real Estate Investments

Advantages	Disadvantages
Generally, above-average rates of return	Investment is expensive
Use leverage of borrowed money to purchase real estate	Real estate is not highly liquid
Greater control over investment	Need expert advice for investment
Tax benefits	Must actively manage investment
	High degree of risk

Two main factors affect appreciation: inflation and intrinsic value. **Inflation** is the increase in the amount of money in circulation. When more money is available, its value declines. When the value of money declines, wholesale and retail prices rise. This is essentially an operation of supply and demand, as discussed in Chapter 1. The **intrinsic value** of real estate is the result of a person's individual choices and preferences for a given geographic area. For example, property located in a pleasant neighborhood near attractive business and shopping areas has a greater intrinsic value to most people than similar property in a more isolated location. As a rule, the greater the intrinsic value, the more money a property commands on its sale.

Unimproved land. Quite often, investors speculate in purchases of either agricultural land or undeveloped land located in what is expected to be a major path of growth. In these cases, however, the property's intrinsic value and potential for appreciation are not easy to determine. This type of investment carries with it many inherent risks. How fast will the area develop? Will it grow sufficiently for the investor to make a good profit? Will the expected growth occur? More important, will the profits eventually realized from the property be great enough to offset the costs of holding it, such as property taxes? Because these questions often cannot be answered with any degree of certainty, lending institutions may be reluctant to lend money for the purchase of raw land.

Income tax laws do not allow the depreciation (cost recovery) of land. Also, such land may not be liquid (salable) at certain times under certain circumstances because few people will purchase raw or agricultural land on short notice. Despite all the risks, however, land has historically been a good inflation hedge if held long term. It also can be a source of income to offset some of the holding costs. For example, agricultural land can be leased out for crops, timber production, or grazing.

Investment in land ultimately is best left to experts, and even they frequently make bad land investment decisions.

■ **FOR EXAMPLE** Mary, a real estate investor, learns from her friends in the state capital that the governor is about to announce that a major new international airport will be built at a rural site currently occupied by farm and pasture land. Mary immediately buys several large tracts near the proposed airport site. Once the airport is in place, Mary expects to sell the land to developers for the hotels, restaurants, and office buildings that are likely to be in demand. The governor announces the airport, and the value of Mary's investment soars. In an election before construction begins, however, the governor is defeated. The newly elected governor thinks the proposed airport would be a waste of taxpayer money, and the project dies. Mary's investment does not turn out to be profitable after all.

Income

The wisest initial investment for a person who wishes to buy and personally manage real estate may be the purchase of rental income property.

Cash flow. The object of directing funds into income property is to generate spendable income, usually called **cash flow.** Cash flow is the total amount of money remaining after all expenditures have been paid. These expenses include taxes, operating costs, and mortgage payments. The cash flow produced by any given parcel of real estate is determined by at least three factors: amount of rent received, operating expenses, and method of debt repayment.

Generally, the amount of *rent* (income) that a property may command depends on a number of factors, including the property's location, physical appearance, and amenities. If the cash flow from rents is not enough to cover all expenses, *negative cash flow* will result.

To keep cash flow high, an investor should attempt to *keep operating expenses reasonably low.* Such operating expenses include general maintenance of the building, repairs, utilities, taxes, and tenant services (switchboard facilities, security systems, and so forth).

IN PRACTICE

With many of the tax advantages of real estate investment being reduced or withdrawn by Congress, licensees should advise investors to analyze each proposed purchase carefully with an accountant. It is more important than ever to be sure an investment will cover its own expenses. Where negative cash flow is anticipated, the investor's tax bracket may be the deciding factor. (Income tax calculations are usually figured at the investor's marginal tax rate, that is, the rate at which his or her top dollar of income is taxed.)

An investor often stands to make more money by investing with borrowed money, usually obtained through a mortgage loan or deed of trust loan. Low mortgage payments spread over a long period of time result in a higher cash flow because they allow the investor to retain more income each month; conversely, high mortgage payments contribute to a lower cash flow.

Whether a property is tax-sheltered can have a significant impact on cash flow. The charts in Figure A-2 and Figure A-3 compare and contrast the cash flow of a taxable and tax-sheltered real estate investment.

You would probably not invest in Property A with a 2 percent to 3 percent annual return because the cash flow is not substantial, there are risks, and there is not much liquidity. But with a tax shelter situation on the same Property A, the cash flow improves a great deal, and the investment becomes more attractive.

Investment opportunities. Traditional income-producing properties include apartment and office buildings, hotels, motels, shopping centers, and industrial

FIGURE A.2

Cash Flow on Fully Taxed Property A

	Year 1	Year 2	Year 3
Beginning Equity	$20,000	$20,000	$20,500
Rental Income	6,000	6,300	6,600
Mortgage Payments	3,500	3,500	3,500
Upkeep	1,000	1,000	1,000
Taxes	2,000	1,900	1,800
Cash Flow	−500	−100	300
Equity + Cash Flow	19,500	19,900	20,800
Debt Retired	500	600	700
Final Equity	20,000	20,500	21,500
Straight Line Depreciation (deduction on which taxes are based)	500	500	500

FIGURE A.3

Cash Flow on Partially Tax-Sheltered Property A

	Year 1	Year 2	Year 3
Beginning Equity	$20,000	$21,500	$23,400
Rental Income	6,000	6,300	6,600
Mortgage Payments	3,500	3,500	3,500
Upkeep	1,000	1,000	1,000
Taxes	500	500	500
Cash Flow	1000	1,300	1,600
Equity + Cash Flow	21,000	22,800	25,000
Debt Retired	500	600	700
Final Equity	21,500	23,400	25,700

properties. Historically, investors have found well-located, one-family to four-family dwellings to be favorable investments. However, many communities have seen severe overbuilding of office space and shopping centers. The result has been high vacancy rates.

■ LEVERAGE

Leverage is the use of borrowed money to finance an investment. As a rule, an investor can receive a maximum return from the initial investment (the down payment and closing and other costs) by making a small down payment, paying a low interest rate, and spreading mortgage payments over as long a period as possible.

The effect of leveraging is to provide a return that reflects the result of market forces on the entire original purchase price, but that is measured against only the actual cash invested. For example, if an investor spends $100,000 for rental property, makes a $20,000 down payment, then sells the property five years later for $125,000, the return over five years is $25,000. Disregarding ownership expenses, the return is not 25 percent ($25,000 compared with $100,000), but 125 percent of the original amount invested ($25,000 compared with $20,000).

Risks *are directly proportionate to leverage*. A high degree of leverage translates into greater risk for the investor and lender because of the high ratio of borrowed money to the value of the real estate. Lower leverage results in less risk. When values drop in an area or vacancy rates rise, the highly leveraged investor may be unable to pay even the financing costs of the property.

Equity Buildup

Equity buildup is that portion of the loan payment directed toward the principal rather than the interest, plus any gain in property value due to appreciation. In a sense, equity buildup is like money in the investor's bank account. This accumulated equity is not realized as cash unless the property is sold or refinanced. However, the equity interest may be sold, exchanged, or mortgaged (refinanced) to be used as leverage for other investments.

Pyramiding

An effective method for a real estate investor to increase his or her holdings without investing additional capital is through *pyramiding*. **Pyramiding** is simply the process of using one property to drive the acquisition of additional properties. Two methods of pyramiding can be used: *pyramiding through sale* and *pyramiding through refinance*.

In pyramiding through selling, an investor first acquires a property. He or she then improves the property for resale at a substantially higher price. The profit from the sale of the first property is used to purchase additional properties. Thus, the proceeds from a single investment (the point of the pyramid) provide the means for acquiring other properties. These properties are also improved and sold, and the proceeds are reinvested, until the investor is satisfied with his or her return. Of course, the disadvantage is that the proceeds from each sale are subject to capital gains taxation, as discussed below.

■ **FOR EXAMPLE** Sally bought a house for $140,000. She put an addition on the house and a new roof. In three years, Sally sold the home at a selling price of $165,000. After deducting commission and selling expenses, she used the $15,000 profit to buy another property.

The goal of pyramiding through refinancing, on the other hand, is to use the value of the original property to drive the acquisition of additional properties while retaining all the properties acquired. The investor refinances the original property and uses the proceeds of the refinance to purchase additional properties. These properties are refinanced in turn to enable the investor to acquire further properties, and so on. By holding on to the properties, the investor increases his or her income-producing property holdings while simultaneously delaying the capital gains taxes that would result from a sale.

■ **FOR EXAMPLE** Tim had lived in his house for ten years and had plenty of equity in his house. Interest rates were good, and he decided to refinance his home which gave him $20,000 from his equity in proceeds. He used the proceeds to acquire an additional property.

■ TAX BENEFITS

Although tax laws change frequently and some tax advantages of owning investment real estate are altered periodically by Congress, an investor (with professional tax advice) can make a wise and profitable real estate purchase.

Capital Gains

Capital gain is defined as the difference between the adjusted basis of property and its net selling price. At various times, the tax law has excluded a portion of capital gains from income tax and taxed various types of gains differently.

Basis. A property's cost basis determines the amount of gain to be taxed. The **basis** of the property is the investor's initial cost of the real estate. The investor adds to the basis the cost of any physical improvements subsequently made to the property. The amount of any depreciation claimed as a tax deduction (explained later) is subtracted from the basis. The result is the property's **adjusted basis.** When the investor sells the property, the amount by which the sales price exceeds the property's adjusted basis is the capital gain.

■ **FOR EXAMPLE** Some time ago, an investor purchased a single-family home for use as a rental property. The purchase price was $45,000. The investor now sells the property for $100,000. Shortly before the sale date, the investor makes $3,000 worth of capital improvements to the home. Depreciation of $10,000 on the property improvements has been taken during the term of the investor's ownership. The investor will pay a broker's commission of 7 percent of the sales price. The investor's closing costs will be $600. The capital gain is computed as follows:

Selling price		$ 100,000
Less:		
7% commission	$ 7,000	
closing costs	+ 600	
	$ 7,600	– 7,600
Net sales price:		$ 92,400
Basis:		
original cost	$ 45,000	
improvements	+ 3,000	
	$ 48,000	
Less:		
depreciation	– 10,000	
Adjusted basis:	$ 38,000	– 38,000
Total capital gain:		$ 54,400

Current tax law specifies what percentage of capital gains is taxable as income. To determine the taxable amount, an investor multiplies the total capital gain by the current percentage (in decimal form).

Exchanges

Real estate investors can defer taxation of capital gains by making property **exchanges.** Even if property has appreciated greatly since its initial purchase, it may be exchanged for other property. A property owner will incur tax liability on a sale only if additional capital or property is also received. Note, however, that the tax is *deferred,* not *eliminated.* Whenever the investor sells the property, the capital gain will be taxed. In many states, state income taxes can also be deferred by using the exchange form of property transfer. Use of a qualified intermediary (also known as accommodator or facilitator) is considered a safe harbor by the IRS and is essential for a delayed exchange.

To qualify as a tax-deferred exchange, the properties involved must be of *like kind* under Section 1031 of the Internal Revenue Code, that is, real estate for real estate of equal value. Any additional capital or personal property included with the transaction to even out the value of the exchange is called **boot.** The IRS requires tax on the boot to be paid at the time of the exchange by the party who receives it. The value of the boot is added to the basis of the property for which it is given. Tax-deferred exchanges are governed by strict federal requirements, and competent guidance from a tax professional is essential.

■ **FOR EXAMPLE** Ann owns an apartment building with an adjusted basis of $225,000 and a market value of $375,000. Ann exchanges the building plus $75,000 in cash for another apartment building having a market value of $450,000. That building, owned by Bob, has an adjusted basis of $175,000. Ann's basis in the new building is $300,000 (the $225,000 basis of the building exchanged plus the $75,000 cash boot paid), and Ann has no tax liability on the exchange. Bob must pay tax on the $75,000 boot received and has a basis of $175,000 (the same as the previous building) in the building now owned.

Depreciation (Cost Recovery)

Depreciation, or cost recovery, allows an investor to recover the cost of an income-producing asset through tax deductions over the asset's useful life. While investors rarely purchase property without expecting it to appreciate over time, the tax laws maintain that all physical structures deteriorate (and lose value) over time. Cost recovery deductions may be taken only on personal property and improvements to land. Furthermore, they can be taken only if the property is used in a trade or business or for the production of income. Thus, a cost recovery deduction cannot be claimed on an individual's personal residence, and *land cannot be depreciated.* Technically, land never wears out or becomes obsolete.

Depreciation taken periodically in equal amounts over an asset's useful life is called *straight-line depreciation.* For certain property purchased before 1987 it was also possible to use an *accelerated cost recovery system* (ACRS) to claim greater deductions in the early years of ownership, gradually reducing the amount deducted in each year of useful life. *The Taxpayer Relief Act of 1997* established specific rules governing holding periods and taxability of depreciation for real property.

Deductions

In addition to tax deductions for depreciation, investors may be able to deduct losses from their real estate investments. The tax laws are very complex. The amount of loss that may be deducted depends on whether an investor actively participates in the day-to-day management of the rental property or makes management decisions. Other factors are the amount of the loss and the source of the income from which the loss is to be deducted. Investors who do not actively participate in the management or operation of the real estate are considered *passive investors*. Passive investors may not use losses to offset active income derived from active participation in real estate management, wages, or income from stocks, bonds, and the like. The tax code cites specific rules for active and passive income and losses and may be subject to changes.

Certain tax credits are allowed for renovation of older buildings, low-income housing projects, and historic property. A *tax credit* is a direct reduction in the tax due rather than a deduction from income before tax is computed. Tax credits encourage the revitalization of older properties and the creation of low-income housing. The tax laws governing these issues also are complex.

Real estate must be analyzed in conjunction with an investor's other investments and overall financial goals and objectives. Income tax consequences also have a significant bearing on an investor's decisions. *Competent tax advice should be sought to help an investor carefully evaluate the ramifications of an investment decision.*

Installment Sales

A taxpayer who sells real property and receives payment on an installment basis pays tax only on the profit portion of each payment received. Interest received is taxable as ordinary income. *Many complex laws apply to installment sales, and a competent tax adviser should be consulted.*

■ REAL ESTATE INVESTMENT SYNDICATES

A real estate investment **syndicate** is a business venture in which people pool their resources to own or develop a particular piece of property. This structure permits people with only modest capital to invest in large-scale operations. Typical syndicate projects include highrise apartment buildings and shopping centers. Syndicate members realize some profit from rents collected on the investment. The main return usually comes when the syndicate sells the property.

Syndicate participation can take many legal forms. For instance, syndicate members may hold property as tenants in common or joint tenants. Various kinds of partnership, corporate, and trust ownership options are possible.

Private syndication generally involves a small group of closely associated or experienced investors. Public syndication, on the other hand, involves a much larger group of investors who may or may not be knowledgeable about real estate as an investment. Any pooling of individuals' funds raises questions of securities registration under federal and state securities laws. These are commonly referred to as *blue-sky laws*.

To protect members of the public who are not sophisticated investors but who may still be solicited to participate in syndicates, securities laws govern the offer and sale of securities. Real estate securities that fall under the definition of a public offering must be registered with state officials and the federal Securities and Exchange Commission (SEC). Pertinent factors include the number of prospects solicited, the total number of investors, the financial background and sophistication of the investors, and the value or price per unit of investment. Salespersons of real estate securities may be required to obtain special licenses and state registration.

Forms of Syndicates

A *general partnership* is organized so that all members of the group share equally in the managerial decisions, profits, and losses involved with the investment. A certain member (or group of members) of the syndicate is designated to act as trustee for the whole group. The trustee holds title to the property and maintains it in the syndicate's name.

Under a *limited partnership* agreement, one party (or parties), usually a developer or real estate broker, organizes, operates, and holds responsibility for the entire syndicate. This person is called the *general partner*. The other members of the partnership are merely investors; they have no voice in the organization and direction of the operation. These passive investors are called *limited partners*.

The limited partners share in the profits, and the general partner is compensated out of the profits. The limited partners stand to lose only as much as they invest—nothing more. Like their level of participation, their risk of loss is limited. The general partner is totally responsible for any excess losses incurred by the investment.

The sale of a limited partnership interest involves the sale of an *investment security* as defined by the SEC. As a result, the sale is subject to state and federal laws concerning the sale of securities. Unless exempt, the securities must be registered with the SEC and the appropriate state authorities.

■ REAL ESTATE INVESTMENT TRUSTS

By directing their funds into a **real estate investment trust (REIT)**, real estate investors take advantage of the same tax benefits as do mutual fund investors. A real estate investment trust does not have to pay corporate income tax as long as 95 percent of its income is distributed to its shareholders. Certain other conditions also must be met. To qualify as a REIT, at least 75 percent of the trust's income must come from real estate. Investors purchase certificates in the trust, which in turn invests in real estate or mortgages (or both). Profits are distributed to investors.

REITs are subject to complex restrictions and regulations. A competent attorney should be involved at all stages of a REIT's development.

■ REAL ESTATE MORTGAGE INVESTMENT CONDUITS

A **real estate mortgage investment conduit (REMIC)** has complex qualification, transfer, and liquidation rules. For instance, the REMIC must satisfy the *asset test*. The asset test requires that after a start-up period, almost all assets must be qualified mortgages and permitted investments. Furthermore, investors' interests may consist of only one or more classes of *regular interests* and a single class of *residual interests*. Holders of regular interests receive interest or similar payments based on either a fixed rate or a variable rate. Holders of residual interests receive distributions (if any) on a pro rata basis.

■ SUMMARY

Traditionally, real estate investment has offered an above-average rate of return while acting as an effective hedge against inflation. It allows an investor to use other people's money through leverage. There may also be tax advantages to owning real estate. However, real estate is not a highly liquid investment and often carries a high degree of risk. Expert advice is often necessary.

Investment property held for appreciation purposes is generally expected to increase in value to a point at which its selling price covers holding costs and permits a profit. The two main factors that affect appreciation are inflation and the property's present and future intrinsic value. Real estate held for income purposes is generally expected to generate a steady flow of income, called cash flow, and to show a profit at the time of sale.

An investor who hopes to use maximum leverage in financing an investment should make a small down payment, pay low interest rates, and spread mortgage payments over as long a period as possible. By holding and refinancing properties, a practice known as *pyramiding,* an investor may substantially increase investment holdings without contributing additional capital. The highly leveraged investor has correspondingly high risk.

By exchanging one property for another with an equal or a greater selling value, an investor can defer paying tax on the gain realized until a sale is made. A total tax deferment is possible only if the investor receives no cash or other incentive to even out the exchange. If such cash or property is received, it is called boot, and it is taxed. In addition, there must also be no debt relief to defer paying taxes.

Depreciation (cost recovery) is a concept that allows an investor to recover in tax deductions the basis of an asset over its useful life. Only costs of improvements to land may be recovered, not costs for the land itself. The Tax Reform Act of 1986 greatly limited the potential for investment losses to shelter other income. But tax credits are still allowed for projects involving low-income housing and older buildings.

An investor may defer federal income taxes on a gain realized from the sale of an investment property through an installment sale of property.

Individuals may also invest in real estate through an investment syndicate. These usually consist of general and limited partnerships. Other forms of real estate investment include real estate investment trusts (REITs) and real estate mortgage investment conduits (REMICs).

Real estate brokers and salespersons should be familiar with the rudimentary tax implications of real property ownership but should refer clients to competent tax advisers for answers to specific questions.

QUESTIONS

1. A small multifamily property generates $50,000 in rental income, expenses of $10,000, and $35,000 in debt service. The property appreciates about $25,000 each year. What is the cash flow on this property?
   a. $5,000   c. $25,000
   b. $15,000   d. $30,000

2. *Cash flow* is
   a. equivalent to operating expense.
   b. the total amount of spendable income left after expenses.
   c. the use of borrowed money to finance an investment.
   d. selling costs plus depreciation.

3. The primary source of tax shelter in real estate investments comes from which of the following accounting concepts?
   a. Recapture
   b. Boot
   c. Net operating income
   d. Depreciation

4. Frank made an initial real estate investment of $45,000. He subsequently made $20,000 worth of improvements to the property. If Frank subtracts depreciation from the initial cost and adds the cost of improvements, what will be the result?
   a. Adjusted basis   c. Basis
   b. Capital gain   d. Salvage value

5. Phyllis, Quincy, and Rodney form an investment syndicate. All three members have equal managerial responsibility, and all three share equally in the profits and losses of the venture. What kind of business arrangement do the three investors have?
   a. Real estate investment trust
   b. Limited partnership
   c. Real estate mortgage trust
   d. General partnership

6. Sylvia, Teresa, and Victor form an investment syndicate. The parties agree as follows: Sylvia is given responsibility for managing and operating the venture; Teresa and Victor will compensate Sylvia out of their shares of the venture's profits; Teresa and Victor will be liable for losses only up to the amounts of their investment, while Sylvia will be responsible for any excess losses. What form of business partnership have Sylvia, Teresa, and Victor created?
   a. General   c. Passive
   b. Limited   d. Investment security

7. In an installment sale of Bret's home, when is taxable gain received and reportable as income by Bret?
   a. In the year in which the sale is initiated
   b. In the year in which the final installment payment is made by the buyer
   c. In each year in which Bret receives installment payments
   d. At any one time during the period in which Bret receives installment payments

8. A tax entity, created by the Tax Reform Act of 1986, that issues securities backed by a pool of mortgages is a
   a. REIT.
   b. REMIC.
   c. limited partnership.
   d. pyramid.

9. Yuri is selling an investment property. The original cost of the property was $80,000. The selling price is $125,000. Yuri paid an 8 percent commission and $1,000 in closing costs. Two years ago, Yuri made $10,000 worth of improvements to the property. Depreciation is $15,000. What is Yuri's adjusted basis in the property?
   a. $65,000   c. $80,000
   b. $75,000   d. $90,000

10. In Question 9, what is Yuri's total capital gain?
   a. $39,000   c. $80,000
   b. $45,000   d. $90,000

STATE STATUTES
WEB LINKS

If a state's Web site has changed from what is listed here, or if a state does not have a Web site with its statutes listed, try searching www.law.cornell.edu/statutes.html.

Alabama Legislature: www.legislature.state.al.us

Alaska Legislature: www.legis.state.ak.us

Arizona Legislature: www.azleg.state.az.us

Arkansas Legislature: www.arkleg.state.ar.us

California Legislative Counsel: www.leginfo.ca.gov

Colorado (State of):   www.state.co.us

Connecticut State Library: www.cslib.org/psaindex.htm

Florida Statutes: www.leg.state.fl.us/statutes

Georgia Code: www.state.ga.us/services/ocode/ocgsearch.htm

Hawaii State Legislature: www.capitol.hawaii.gov

Idaho Statutes: www3.state.id.us/idstat

Illinois Compiled Statutes: www.legis.state.il.us/ilcs/chapterlist.html

Indiana Code: www.state.in.us/legislative/ic/code

Iowa Law: www.legis.state.ia.us/ialaw.html

Kansas Laws and Legal Services: www.accesskansas.org/government/laws-legal.html

Kentucky Revised Statutes: www.lrc.state.ky.us/krs/titles.htm

Louisiana State Legislature: www.legis.state.la.us

Maine (State of):   www.state.me.us

Maryland General Assembly: http://mlis.state.md.us

Massachusetts (General Laws of):   www.state.ma.us/legis/laws/mgl

Michigan Legislature: www.michiganlegislature.org

Missouri Revised Statutes: www.moga.state.mo.us/homestat.htm

Montana Constitution and Laws: http://leg.state.mt.us/services/legal/laws.htm

Nebraska Statutes: http://statutes.unicam.state.ne.us

Nevada Law Library: www.leg.state.nv.us/law1.cfm

New Hampshire General Court: www.gencourt.state.nh.us

New Jersey Legislature: www.njleg.state.nj.us

New Mexico Supreme Court Law Library: http://fscll.org

New York Assembly: http://assembly.state.ny.us

North Carolina General Statutes: www.ncga.state.nc.us/statutes/statutes.html

Ohio Laws, Rules and Constitution: www.state.oh.us/ohio/ohiolaws.htm

Oregon Revised Statutes: www.leg.state.or.us/ors/home.html

South Carolina Code of Laws: www.lpitr.state.sc.us/code/statmast.htm

South Dakota Legislature: http://legis.state.sd.us/index.cfm

Texas Statutes: www.capitol.state.tx.us/statutes/statutes.html

Utah Code: www.le.state.ut.us/~code/code.htm

Virginia (Code of):   http://leg1.state.va.us/000/src.htm

Washington (Revised Code of):   www.leg.wa.gov/wsladm/rcw.htm

West Virginia Code: www.legis.state.wv.us/legishp.html

Wisconsin Statutes: www.legis.state.wi.us/rsb/statutes.html

Wyoming Statutes: http://legisweb.state.wy.us/titles/statutes.htm

3

WEB LINKS

■ WEB LINKS BY CHAPTER

■ CHAPTER 1

American Society of Home Inspectors: www.ashi.com

Building Owners and Managers Association International: www.boma.org

Commercial Investment Real Estate Institute: www.ccim.com

Counselors of Real Estate: www.cre.org

Fannie Mae: www.fanniemae.com

Federal Reserve Board: www.federalreserve.gov

Freddie Mac: www.freddiemac.com

Ginnie Mae: www.ginniemae.gov

Institute of Real Estate Management: www.irem.org/index2.html

National Association of Exclusive Buyer Agents: www.naeba.org

National Association of Independent Fee Appraisers: www.naifa.com

National Association of Real Estate Brokers: www.nareb.com

National Association of REALTORS®: www.realtor.com

Real Estate Buyer's Agent Council: www.rebac.net

Real Estate Educators Association: www.reea.org

U. S. Department of Housing and Urban Development: Office of Housing: www.hud.gov/fha/fhahome.html

■ CHAPTER 2

Arizona Department of Real Estate: www.re.state.az.us

Alabama Real Estate Commission: www.arec.state.al.us

Alaska Division of Occupational Licensing: www.dced.state.ak.us/occ/prec.htm

Arkansas Real Estate Commission: www.state.ar.us/arec/frmain.htm

California Department of Real Estate: www.dre.ca.gov

Colorado Department of Regulatory Agencies, Division of Real Estate: www.dora.state.co.us/real-estate

Connecticut Department of Consumer Protection: www.state.ct.us/dcp

District of Columbia Real Estate Commission: www.dcra.org

Florida Division of Real Estate: www.state.fl.us/dbpr

Georgia Real Estate Commission: www.state.ga.us/ga.real_estate

Hawaii State Government Home Page: www.hawaii.gov

Idaho Real Estate Commission: www.state.id.us/irec

Illinois Office of Banks and Real Estate: www.obre.state.il.us

Indiana Professional Licensing Agency: www.ai.org/pla/index.html

Iowa Real Estate Commission: www.state.ia.us/government/com/prof/realesta/realesta.htm

Kansas Real Estate Commission: www.accesskansas.org/krec

Kentucky Real Estate Commission: www.krec.net

Manufactured Housing Institute: www.mfghome.org

Maryland Real Estate Commission: www.dllr.state.md.us/license/real_est/reintro.html

Massachusetts Division of Registration: www.state.ma.us/reg

Michigan Department of Consumer & Industry Services: www.cis.state.mi.us

Minnesota Department of Commerce: www.commerce.state.mn.us

Missouri Real Estate Commission: www.ecodev.state.mo.us/pr/restate

Montana Department of Commerce: www.com.state.mt.us

Nevada Real Estate Division: www.red.state.nv.us

New Hampshire Real Estate Commission: www.state.nh.us/nhrec

New Jersey Real Estate Commission: www.state.nj.us/dobi/remna.shtml

New Mexico Real Estate Commission: www.state.nm.us/nmrec

New York Department of State, Division of Licensing Services: www.dos.state.ny.us/lcns/realest.html

North Carolina Real Estate Commission: www.ncrec.state.nc.us

Ohio Division of Real Estate and Professional Licensing: www.com.state.oh.us/real

Oregon Real Estate Agency: www.rea.state.or.us

Penn Central Transportation Co. v. City of New York: www2.law.cornell.edu

Pennsylvania Real Estate Commission: www.dos.state.pa.us/bpoa

South Carolina Real Estate Commission: www.llr.state.sc.us

South Dakota Real Estate Commission: www.state.sd.us/sdrec

State of Louisiana: www.lrec.state.la.us

State of Maine: www.state.me.us/pfr/olr

State of Nebraska: www.state.ne.us/

Texas Real Estate Commission: www.trec.state.tx.us

Utah Commerce Department, Real Estate Division: www.commerce.state.ut.us

Vermont Real Estate Commission: www.vtprofessionals.org/opr1/real_estate

Virginia Department of Professional and Occupational Regulation: www.state.va.us/dpor

Washington Real Estate Commission: www.wa.gov/dol/bpd/recom.htm

West Virginia Real Estate Commission (unofficial):   www.state.wv.us/wvrec

Wisconsin Department of Regulation and Licensing: www.drl.state.wi.us/
Wyoming Real Estate Commission: http://realestate.state.wy.us

■ CHAPTER 3

Federal Emergency Management Agency: www.fema.gov
Federal Housing Administration: www.hud.gov/offices/hsg/index.cfm
U.S. Department of Housing and Urban Development: www.hud.gov
U.S. Department of Veterans Affair: www.va.gov

■ CHAPTER 4

International Real Estate Digest: www.ired.com
Legal Information Institute: www.law.cornell.edu/states/index.html

■ CHAPTER 5

Cyberhomes MLS Listings: www.cyberhomes.com
National Association of REALTORS®:   www.Realtor.com
U.S. Department of Internal Revenue Service: www.irs.gov
U.S. Department of Justice, Antitrust Division: www.usdoj.gov/atr

■ CHAPTER 6

National Association of Exclusive Buyer Agents: www.naeba.org
Real Estate Buyer's Agent Council: www.rebac.net/right.htm

■ CHAPTER 7

West Legal Directory: Eminent Domain:
www.wld.com/conbus/weal/wemindom.htm

■ CHAPTER 8

Legal Information Institute: Uniform Condominium Act:
www.law.cornell.edu/uniform/vol7.html#condo

■ CHAPTER 9

Legal Descriptions in the USA: www.outfitters.com/genealogy/land
U.S. Geological Survey: www.usgs.gov

■ CHAPTER 10

U.S. Internal Revenue Service: Search for Real Estate Tax Information:
www.irs.ustreas.gov/

■ CHAPTER 11

FindLaw: Contract Law: www.findlaw.com/01topics/07contracts

■ CHAPTER 15

Altavista Search Engine: www.altavista.com
Excite Search Engine: www.excite.com
Fannie Mae: www.fanniemae.com

Freddie Mac: www.freddiemac.com

Ginnie Mae: www.ginniemae.gov

Google Search Engine: www.google.com

Lycos Search Engine: www.lycos.com

U.S. Department of Agriculture: Rural Development: www.rurdev.usda.gov

U.S. Department of Housing and Urban Development: www.hud.gov

U.S. Department of Veteran Affairs: www.va.gov

U.S. Farm Service Agency: www.fsa.usda.gov

U.S. Federal Reserve: www.federalreserve.gov

U.S. Hud: Federal Mortgage Programs: www.hud.gov/mortprog.html

Yahoo Search Engine: www.yahoo.com

■ CHAPTER 16

Legal Information Institute: Landlord-Tenant Law: www.law.cornell.edu/topics/landlord_tenant.html

■ CHAPTER 17

ADA Home Page: Information and Technical Assistance on the ADA: www.usdoj.gov/crt/ada/adahom1.htm

American Management Association: www.amanet.org

Building Owners and Managers Association International: www.boma.org

Building Owners and Managers Institute: www.bomi-edu.org

Institute of Real Estate Management: www.irem.org/index2.html

National Apartment Association: www.naahq.org

National Association of Home Builders: www.nahb.com

National Association of Residential Property Managers: www.narpm.org

■ CHAPTER 18

Appraisal Foundation: www.appraisalfoundation.org

Appraisal Institute: www.appraisalinstitute.org

■ CHAPTER 19

U.S. HUD Land Sales Complaints: www.hud.gov/complaints/landsales.cfm

U.S. HUD Office of Housing: www.hud.gov/offices/hsg/index.cfm

■ CHAPTER 20

HSH: Fair Housing Act Pamphlet: www.hsh.com/pamphlets/fair_housing_act.html

Legal Information Institute: www.law.cornell.edu

National Fair Housing Advocate Online: www.fairhousing.com/legal_research/index.htm

U.S. Department of Justice: ADA Home Page: www.usdoj.gov/crt/ada/ada hom1.htm

U.S. HUD: Fair Housing: www.hud.gov/groups/fairhousing.cfm

U.S. HUD: Fair Housing Act: www.hud.gov/groups/fairhousing.cfm

U.S. HUD: Fair Housing Library: www.hud.gov/library/bookshelf09/index.cfm

U.S. HUD: Housing Discrimination Complaints: www.hud.gov/complaints/housediscrim.cfm

U.S. Supreme Court: www.supremecourtus.gov

■ CHAPTER 21

A Citizen's Guide to Radon, 2d ed. (U.S. EPA): www.epa.gov/iedweb00/radon/pubs/citguide.html

Cercla/Superfund: www.epa.gov/superfund/action/law/cercla.htm

Legal Information Institute: State Statutes Topical Index: www.law.cornell.edu/topics/state_statutes.html#health

National Safety Council: Radon: www.nsc.org/ehc/radon.htm

National Safety Council's Environmental Health Center: www.nsc.org/ehc/lead.htm

U.S. Department of Housing and Urban Development: Healthy Homes for Healthy Children: www.hud.gov/consumer/hhchild.cfm

U.S. Environmental Protection Agency: www.epa.gov

U.S. Environmental Protection Agency: Asbestos: www.epa.gov/oppt/asbestos

U.S. EPA: CERCLA Overview: www.epa.gov/superfund/action/law/cercla.htm

U.S. EPA: Indoor Air Quality: Carbon Monoxide: www.epa.gov/iaq/co.html

U.S. EPA: Indoor Air Quality: Radon: www.epa.gov/ebtpages/airpolution.html

U.S. EPA: Mold Remediation in Schools and Commercial Buildings: www.epa.gov/iaq/molds/index.html

U.S. EPA: Office of Pollution Prevention and Toxics: www.epa.gov/lead

U.S. HUD: Office of Healthy Homes and Lead Hazard Control: www.hud.gov/offices/lead/disclosurerule.cfm

U.S. HUD: Office of Healthy Homes and Lead Hazard Control Pamphlet: www.hud.gov/offices/lead/leadhelp.cfm

■ CHAPTER 22

U.S. Department of Housing and Urban Development: FAQs About Escrows (RESPA): www.hud.gov/offices/hsg/sfh/res/reconsu.cfm

U.S. Department of Housing and Urban Development: RESPA: www.hud.gov/fha/sfh/res/respa_hm.html

■ WEB LINKS IN ALPHABETICAL ORDER

A Citizen's Guide to Radon, 2d ed. (U.S. EPA): www.epa.gov/iedweb00/radon/pubs/citguide.html

Alabama Legislature: www.legislature.state.al.us

Alabama Real Estate Commission: www.arec.state.al.us

Alaska Division of Occupational Licensing: www.dced.state.ak.us/occ/prec.htm

Alaska Legislature: www.legis.state.ak.us

Altavista Search Engine: www.altavista.com

American Management Association: www.amanet.org

American Society of Home Inspectors: www.ashi.com

Appraisal Foundation: www.appraisalfoundation.org

Appraisal Institute: www.appraisalinstitute.org

Arizona Department of Real Estate: www.re.state.az.us

Arizona Legislature: www.azleg.state.az.us

Arkansas Legislature: www.arkleg.state.ar.us

Arkansas Real Estate Commission: www.state.ar.us/arec/arecweb.html

Building Owners and Managers Association International: www.boma.org

Building Owners and Managers Institute: www.bomi-edu.org

California Department of Real Estate: www.dre.ca.gov

California Legislative Counsel: www.leginfo.ca.gov

CERCLA/Superfund: www.epa.gov/superfund/action/law/cercla.htm

Colorado Department of Regulatory Agencies, Division of Real Estate:
www.dora.state.co.us/real-estate

Colorado (State of):   www.state.co.us

Commercial Investment Real Estate Institute: www.ccim.com

Connecticut Department of Consumer Protection: www.state.ct.us/dcp

Connecticut State Library: www.cslib.org/psaindex.htm

Counselors of Real Estate: www.cre.org

Cyberhomes MLS Listings: www.cyberhomes.com

District of Columbia Real Estate Commission: www.dcra.org

Fannie Mae: www.fanniemae.com

EXCITE Search Engine: www.excite.com

Federal Emergency Management Agency: www.fema.gov

Federal Housing Administration: www.hud.gov/fha

Federal Reserve Board: www.federalreserve.gov

Findlaw: Contract Law: www.findlaw.com/01topics/07contracts

Florida Division of Real Estate: www.state.fl.us/dbpr

Florida Statutes: www.leg.state.fl.us/statutes

Freddie Mac: www.freddiemac.com

Georgia Code: www.state.ga.us/services/ocode/ocgsearch.htm

Georgia Real Estate Commission: www.state.ga.us/ga.real_estate

Ginnie Mae: www.ginniemae.gov

GOOGLE Search Engine: www.google.com

Hawaii State Government: www.hawaii.gov

Hawaii State Legislature: www.capitol.hawaii.gov

HSH: Fair Housing Act Pamphlet:
www.hsh.com/pamphlets/fair_housing_act.html

Idaho Real Estate Commission: www.state.id.us/irec

Idaho Statutes: www3.state.id.us/idstat

Illinois Compiled Statutes: www.legis.state.il.us/ilcs/chapterlist.html

Illinois Office of Banks and Real Estate: www.obre.state.il.us

Indiana Legislative: www.state.in.us/legislative/ic/code

Indiana Professional Licensing Agency: www.ai.org/pla/index.html

Institute of Real Estate Management: www.irem.org

International Real Estate Digest: www.ired.com

Iowa Law: www.legis.state.ia.us/ialaw.html

Iowa Real Estate Commission: www.state.ia.us/government/com/prof/realesta/realesta.htm

Kansas Laws and Legal Services: www.accesskansas.org/government/laws-legal.html

Kansas Real Estate Commission: www.accesskansas.org/krec

Kentucky Real Estate Commission: www.krec.net

Kentucky Revised Statutes: www.lrc.state.ky.us/krs/titles.htm

Legal Information Institute: www.law.cornell.edu/states/index.html

Legal Information Institute: Landlord-Tenant Law: www.law.cornell.edu/topics/landlord_tenant.html

Legal Information Institute: State Statutes Topical Index: www.law.cornell.edu/topics/state_statutes.html#health

Legal Information Institute: Uniform Condominium Act: www.law.cornell.edu/uniform/vol7.html#condo

Legal Land Descriptions in the USA: www.outfitters.com/genealogy/land

Louisiana State Legislature: www.legis.state.la.us

Lycos Search Engine: www.lycos.com

Maine (State of):   www.state.me.us

Manufactured Housing Institute: www.mfghome.org

Maryland General Assembly: www.mlis.state.md.us

Maryland Real Estate Commission: www.dllr.state.md.us/license/real_est/reintro.html

Massachusetts Division of Registration: www.state.ma.us/reg

Massachusetts (General Laws of):   www.state.ma.us/legis/laws/mgl

Michigan Department of Consumer & Industry Services: www.cis.state.mi.us

Michigan Legislature: www.michiganlegislature.org

Minnesota Department of Commerce: www.commerce.state.mn.us

Missouri Real Estate Commission: www.ecodev.state.mo.us/pr/restate

Missouri Revised Statutes: www.moga.state.mo.us/homestat.htm

Montana Constitution and Laws: http://leg.state.mt.us/services/legal/laws.htm

Montana Department of Commerce: www.com.state.mt.us

National Apartment Association: www/naahg.org

National Association of Exclusive Buyer Agents: www.naeba.org

National Association of Home Builders: www.nahb.com

National Association of Independent Fee Appraisers: www.naifa.com

National Association of Real Estate Brokers: www.nareb.com

National Association of REALTORS®:   www.realtor.com

National Association of Residential Property Managers: www.narpm.org

National Fair Housing Advocate Online:
www.fairhousing.com/legal_research/index.htm

National Safety Council's Environmental Health Center:
www.nsc.org/ehc/lead.htm

National Safety Council: Radon: www.nsc.org/ehc/radon.htm

Nebraska Statutes: http://statutes.unicam.state.ne.us

Nevada Law Library: www.leg.state.nv.us/law1.cfm

Nevada Real Estate Division: www.red.state.nv.us

New Hampshire General Court: www.gencourt.state.nh.us

New Hampshire Real Estate Commission: www.state.nh.us/nhrec

New Jersey Legislature: www.njleg.state.nj.us

New Jersey Real Estate Commission: www.state.nj.us/dobi/remnu.shtml

New Mexico Real Estate Commission: www.state.nm.us/nmrec

New Mexico Supreme Court Law Library: www.fscll.org

New York Assembly: http://assembly.state.ny.us

New York Department of State, Division of Licensing Service:
www.dos.state.ny.us/lcns/realest.html

North Carolina General Statutes: www.ncga.state.nc.us/statutes/statutes.html

North Carolina Real Estate Commission: www.ncrec.state.nc.us

Ohio Division of Real Estate and Professional Licensing:
www.com.state.oh.us/real

Ohio Laws, Rules and Constitution: www.state.oh.us/ohio/ohiolaws.htm

Oregon Real Estate Agency: www.rea.state.or.us

Oregon Revised Statutes: www.leg.state.or.us/ors/home.html

Penn Central Transportation Co. v. City of New York: www.law.cornell.edu

Pennsylvania Real Estate Commission: www.dos.state.pa.us/bpoa

Real Estate Buyer's Agent Council: www.rebac.net

Real Estate Buyer's Agent Council: www.rebac.net/right.htm

Real Estate Educators Association: www.reea.org

South Carolina Code of Laws: www.lpitr.state.sc.us/code/statmast.htm

South Carolina Real Estate Commission: www.llr.state.sc.us

South Dakota Real Estate Commission: www.state.sd.us/sdrec

South Dakota Legislature: http://legis.state.sd.us/index.cfm

State of Louisiana Real Estate Commission: www.lrec.state.la.us

State of Maine: www.state.me.us/pfr.olr

State of Nebraska Real Estate Commission: www.nrec.state.ne.us

Texas Real Estate Commission: www.trec.state.tx.us

Texas Statutes: www.capitol.state.tx.us/statutes/statutes.html

The Inside Story: A Guide to Indoor Air Quality (U.S. EPA):
www.epa.gov/region4/topics/air/indoorair.html

U.S. Department of Agriculture: Rural Development: www.rurdev.usda.gov

U.S. Department of Housing and Urban Development: www.hud.gov

U.S. Department of Housing and Urban Development: FAQs About Escrows (RESPA):   www.hud.gov/offices/hsg/sfh/res/reconsu.cfm

U.S. Department of Housing and Urban Development: Healthy Homes for Healthy Children: www.hud.gov/consumer.hhhchild.cfm

U.S. Department of Housing and Urban Development: Office of Housing: www.hud.gov/fha/fhahome.html

U.S. Department of Housing and Urban Development: RESPA: www.hud.gov/fha/sfh/res/respa_hm.html

U.S. Department of Internal Revenue Service: www.irs.gov

U.S. Department of Justice: ADA Home Page: www.usdoj.gov/crt/ada/adahom1.htm

U.S. Department of Justice, Antitrust Division: www.usdoj.gov/atr

U.S. Department of Veterans Affairs: www.va.gov

U. S. Environmental Protection Agency: www.epa.gov

U.S. EPA: Asbestos: www.epa.gov/oppt/asbestos

U.S. EPA: CERCLA Overview: www.epa.gov/superfund/action/law/cercla.htm

U.S. EPA: Indoor Air Quality: Carbon Monoxide: www.epa.gov/iaq/co.html

U.S. EPA: Indoor Air Quality: Radon: www.epa.gov/iaq/radon

U.S. EPA: Mold Remediation in Schools and Commercial Buildings: www.epa.gov/iaq/pubs/molds/index.html

U.S. EPA: Office of Pollution Prevention and Toxics: www.epa.gov/lead

U.S. Farm Service Agency: www.fsa.usda.gov

U.S. Geological Survey: www.usgs.gov

U.S. HUD: Fair Housing: www.hud.gov/groups/fairhousing.cfm

U.S. HUD: Fair Housing Act: www.hud.gov/fhe/fheact.html

U.S. HUD: Fair Housing Library: www.hud.gov/library/bookshelf09/index.cfm

U.S. HUD: Federal Mortgage Programs: www.hud.gov/mortprog.html

U.S. HUD: Housing Discrimination Complaints: www.hud.gov/complaints/housediscrim.cfm

U.S. HUD: Land Sales Complaints: www.hud.gov/complaints/landsales.cfm

U.S. HUD: Office of Healthy Homes and Lead Hazard Control: www.hud.gov/offices/lead/disclosurerule.cfm

U.S. HUD: Office of Healthy Homes and Lead Hazard Control Pamphlet: www.hud.gov/offices/lead/leadhelp.cfm

U.S. HUD: Office of Housing: www.hud.gov/offices/hsg/index.cfm

U.S. Internal Revenue Service: Search for Real Estate Tax Information: www.irs.ustreas.gov

U.S. Supreme Court: www.supremecourtus.gov

Utah Code: www.le.state.ut.us/~code/code.htm

Utah Commerce Department, Real Estate Division: www.commerce.state.ut.us

Vermont Real Estate Commission: www.vtprofessionals.org/opr1/real_estate

Virginia (Code of):   http://leg1.state.va.us/000/src.htm

Virginia Department of Professional and Occupational Regulation: www.state.va.us/dpor

Washington Real Estate Commission: www.dol.wa.gov/realestate/recom.htm

Washington (Revised Code of):   www.leg.wa.gov/wsladm/rcw.htm

West Legal Directory: eminent domain: http://directory.findlaw.com

West Virginia Code: www.legis.state.wv.us/code/toc.html

West Virginia Real Estate Commission: www.state.wv.us/wvrec

Wisconsin Department of Regulation and Licensing: www.drl.state.wi.us/

Wisconsin Statutes: www.legis.state.wi.us/rsb/statutes.html

Wyoming Real Estate Commission: http://realestate.state.wy.us

Wyoming Statutes: http://legisweb.state.wy.us/titles/statutes.htm

YAHOO Search Engine: www.yahoo.com

MATH FAQs

Answers to Your Most Frequently Asked Real Estate Math Questions

MATH FAQs CONTENTS

MATH FAQs INTRODUCTION

Math is a part of the real estate profession, as it is of most careers. The amount of math and the complexity of the math will vary, depending on the area of real estate chosen. Today, we have calculators and computers that are great time-savers, but we still need to have a good basic knowledge of math. It is a matter of taking the math concepts we were taught in school and adapting them to the real estate profession.

People react differently to the word *math*. Some people like math. Some people are comfortable with math. Some people, though, are uncomfortable with math and become very anxious and stressed when they encounter numbers. If you're that kind of person, you will find the approach taken here very comfortable and helpful. Even if you're someone who's comfortable working with numbers, this clear and simple review will reinforce what you know—and maybe teach you a few tricks and shortcuts, too.

This review covers the basics of real estate math to prepare you for those real-world situations you will encounter as well as the math problems you will be most likely to find on your real estate licensing examination.

Study, review, and practice will help you overcome stress and anxiety so you can become comfortable with math. Each time you review and practice your real estate math, you will find that your confidence and ability will increase.

■ USING THIS MATH REVIEW

This brief math review is designed to provide you with a quick check of your math knowledge and to help you reinforce what you already know. It's organized in a way that makes it easy for you to look up just the information you need, and the subject matter is presented in as straightforward a manner as we could think of, with a minimum of wordy explanations and a maximum of quick tips, examples, formulas, memory aids, and shortcuts to help you overcome any remaining "math phobias."

Divided into sections, this review is organized into the following five general subject areas:

1. Calculators
2. Fractions
3. Percentages
4. Measurement
5. Proration

Within each general subject heading are a series of **frequently asked questions (FAQs)** and brief, clear explanations. If you read Math FAQs through from start to finish, you'll get a good, general review of real estate math principles. You also can use Math FAQs for last-minute review of difficult issues or even as a memory-jogger in your daily real estate practice. Simply check Math FAQs Table of

Contents to see if your question is listed: if it is, go directly to that page. If your question is more complicated or fact-specific, you may have to look at several different items to find your answer. Either way, you'll probably find it here.

■ SPECIAL FEATURES

Throughout the text you will find **Math Tips** that offer insight into the trickier aspects of real estate math in general and the real estate exam's math content in particular. The **For Example . . .** feature applies formulas and concepts to practical situations to show how the concept works in the real world. A generous collection of **practice problems** at the end of the review gives you the opportunity to apply your understanding in an exam-style context, and the simple **T-Bar method** is offered as a shortcut that's both easy to understand and easy to apply.

We hope this math review helps you master real estate math. Good luck!

INTRODUCTION TO CALCULATORS

Calculators are permitted when taking most state licensing examinations. The rules usually state that the calculator must be silent, hand-held, battery-operated, and nonprinting. Many states will not allow a real estate or financial calculator to be used while taking the real estate exam. Check with your state in regard to the appropriate calculator for your exam.

■ WHAT KIND OF CALCULATOR DO I NEED?

A calculator that will add (+), subtract (–), multiply (×), and divide (÷) is all that is needed for licensing examinations. These calculators are available in many sizes, shapes, and colors. The keys and display may be small or large. Some are battery-powered, some are solar-powered, and others are solar-powered with a battery backup. A calculator with a battery only or solar power with a battery backup is recommended over solar-powered only. Choose a calculator that is most comfortable for you; allow yourself time to learn to use it correctly and to become comfortable with it before you take the licensing examination.

■ WHAT ARE THE SPECIFIC REAL ESTATE FUNCTIONS I SHOULD LOOK FOR?

There are many business or financial calculators available that have additional functions that are very beneficial to the real estate professional. Some of the keys you would want are "N" (number of interest compounding periods/number of payments), "I" (interest rate per period), "PV" (present value of money/loan), "PMT" (amount of payment), and "FV" (future value of money). Business or financial calculators vary according to brand and/or model; therefore, the user's manual should always be followed to use the calculator properly. For example, some have "TERM" instead of "N"; therefore, you enter the number of years of the term instead of the number of payments or compounding periods. Some have "LOAN" instead of "PV". Some instruct you to enter the interest rate as an annual rate instead of a monthly rate. You may wish to purchase a business or financial calculator that contains these extra functions. Check with your state real estate commission to see if you will be permitted to use them during the exam.

M A T H T I P

Be careful! Business or financial calculators are often set to round to two decimals at the factory. Follow the user's manual and set the decimal to float or to a minimum of five decimals. This will enable you to arrive at an answer with enough decimals to match multiple choice answers on exams. No matter which calculator you choose, *read the user's manual.*

F I G U R E   **1.1**

Calculator Functions to Look For

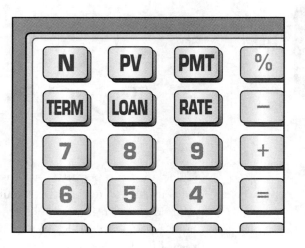

■ HOW DO I USE THE PERCENT KEY?

If you use the "%" key on calculators to solve percentage problems, read the user's manual for proper use of it. Some calculators require the use of the "%" key or the "=" key *but never both in the same calculation.* Other calculators require the use of *both* the "%" key and the "=" key to get a correct answer. No matter which calculator you choose, *read the user's manual.*

■ **FOR EXAMPLE** If a property sold for $100,000 and a 7% commission was paid to the broker, how much was the broker paid?

This question may be worked two ways, as illustrated below.

Convert 7% to the decimal .07. (How to convert percents to decimals is shown in Section 2 of this Math Unit.) Touch $100,000 into your calculator, then the × or multiplication key, then .07, then the = key to read $7,000.

or

Touch in $100,000, then the x or multiplication key, then 7, then the % key. If your calculator now reads $7,000, you've finished the question. If when you touch the % key, it reads 0.07, then you must touch the = key to complete the question.

The use of the percent key allows the calculator to convert to the proper decimal place, and there's no question about the placement of the decimal. The choice is yours: you can convert the percent to a decimal or use the percent key for the conversion.

FRACTIONS, DECIMALS, AND PERCENTAGES

■ WHAT ARE THE PARTS OF A FRACTION?

The **denominator** shows the number of equal parts in the whole or total. The **numerator** shows the number of those parts with which you are working. In the example below, the whole or total has been divided into eight equal parts, and you have seven of those equal parts.

$\dfrac{7}{8}$ $\dfrac{\text{Numerator}}{\text{Denominator}}$ $\dfrac{\text{(Top Number)}}{\text{(Bottom Number)}}$

■ WHAT IS MEANT BY A "PROPER FRACTION"?

$\frac{7}{8}$ is an example of a **proper fraction.** In a proper fraction the numerator is less than the whole or less than 1.

■ WHAT IS AN "IMPROPER FRACTION"?

$\dfrac{11}{8}$ $\dfrac{\text{Numerator}}{\text{Denominator}}$

This is an example of an **improper fraction.** In an improper fraction, the numerator is greater than the whole or greater than 1.

■ WHAT IS A MIXED NUMBER?

$11\frac{1}{2}$ is a **mixed number.** You have a whole number plus a fraction. A mixed number is greater than the whole or greater than 1.

■ HOW DO I MULTIPLY FRACTIONS?

When multiplying fractions, the numerator is multiplied by the numerator, and the denominator by the denominator. Let's start with an easy question. What is $\frac{1}{2} \times \frac{3}{4}$?

First multiply the numerators (top numbers) $1 \times 3 = 3$; then the denominators (bottom numbers) $2 \times 4 = 8$. Thus, $\frac{1}{2} \times \frac{3}{4} = \frac{3}{8}$.

What is $4\frac{2}{3} \times 10\frac{5}{8}$? The first step is to convert the whole number 4 into $\frac{1}{3}$s. This is done by multiplying $4 \times 3 = 12$. (Multiply the whole number 4, by the denominator of the fraction, 3.) Thus, the whole number 4 is equal to $\frac{12}{3}$.

431

$4\frac{2}{3}$ is equal to $\frac{12}{3} + \frac{2}{3} = \frac{14}{3}$.

The next step is to convert the whole number 10 into $\frac{1}{8}$s. This is done by multiplying $10 \times 8 = 80$. (Multiply the whole number 10, by the denominator of the fraction, 8.) Thus, the whole number 10 is equal to $\frac{80}{8}$. $\frac{80}{8} + \frac{5}{8} = \frac{85}{8}$.

So, what is $\frac{14}{3} \times \frac{85}{8}$? First multiply $14 \times 85 = 1{,}190$. Then, $3 \times 8 = 24$. $\frac{1{,}190}{24} = 49.58$. (That is $1{,}190 \div 24 = 49.58$.)

An easier way to work the question is to convert the fractions to decimals.

$\frac{2}{3}$ is equal to $2 \div 3$ or $.67$.

$\frac{5}{8}$ is equal to $5 \div 8$ or $.625$.

$4.67 \times 10.625 = 49.62$.

Whenever working with fractions or decimals equivalents, the answers will be close but not exact.

■ HOW DO I DIVIDE BY FRACTIONS?

Dividing by fractions is a two step process. What is $\frac{3}{4} \div \frac{1}{4}$?

First, invert the $\frac{1}{4}$ to $\frac{4}{1}$. Then, multiply $\frac{3}{4} \times \frac{4}{1} = \frac{12}{4}$. Finally, $12 \div 4 = 3$.

You may also convert $\frac{3}{4}$ to the decimal $.75$ and $\frac{1}{4}$ to the decimal $.25$.

$.75 \div .25 = 3$. (There are three $.25$ in $.75$.)

What is $100\frac{7}{8} \div \frac{3}{4}$?

$100 \times 8 = 800$.

$800 + 7 = \frac{807}{8}$.

$\frac{3}{4}$ is inverted to $\frac{4}{3}$.

$\frac{807}{8} \times \frac{4}{3} = 807 \times 4 = 3{,}228$; $8 \times 3 = 24$. $\frac{3{,}228}{24} = 3{,}228 \div 24 = 134.5$

Or $7 \div 8 = .875$ and $3 \div 4 = .75$.

$100.875 \div .75 = 134.50$.

■ HOW DO I CONVERT FRACTIONS TO DECIMALS?

Fractions will sometimes be used in real estate math problems. Since calculators may be used on most licensing examinations, it is best to convert fractions to decimals.

M A T H  T I P To convert a fraction to a decimal, the top number, called the numerator, is divided by the bottom number, the denominator.

For example:

$\frac{7}{8} = 7 \div 8 = \mathbf{0.875}$
$\frac{11}{8} = 11 \div 8 = \mathbf{1.375}$
$11\frac{1}{2} = 1 \div 2 = 0.5 + 11 = \mathbf{11.5}$

Once fractions have been converted to decimals, other calculations can be easily completed using the calculator. Note that many calculators automatically add the zero before the decimal point.

■ HOW DO I ADD OR SUBTRACT DECIMALS?

Line up the decimals, add or subtract, and bring the decimal down in the answer. You may add zeros if necessary as place holders. For example, 0.5 is the same as 0.50, or .5.

$$\begin{array}{r} 0.50 \\ +\ 3.25 \\ \hline =\ 3.75 \end{array} \qquad \begin{array}{r} 8.20 \\ -\ 0.75 \\ \hline =\ 7.45 \end{array}$$

M A T H T I P   When you use a calculator, the decimal will be in the correct place in the answer.
0.5 + 3.25 = 3.75, and 8.2 – 0.75 = 7.45

■ HOW DO I MULTIPLY DECIMALS?

Multiply the numbers, then count the number of decimal places in each number. Next, start with the last number on the right and move the decimal the total number of decimal places to the left in the answer.

Multiply as you normally would to get the 1,500, then count the four decimal places in the numbers (.20 and .75). In the 1,500, start at the last zero on the right, and count four decimal places to the left. The decimal is placed to the left of the **1.**

$$\begin{array}{r} 0.20 \\ \times\ 0.75 \\ \hline 100 \\ 140\ \ \\ \hline .1500\ \text{or}\ .15 \end{array}$$

Note: When you use a calculator, the decimal will be in the correct place in the answer ($0.2 \times 0.75 = \mathbf{0.15}$).

■ HOW DO I DIVIDE DECIMALS?

Divide the **dividend** (the number being divided) by the **divisor** (the number you are dividing by) and bring the decimal in the dividend straight up in the **quotient** (answer). If the divisor has a decimal, move the decimal to the right of the divisor and move the decimal the same number of places to the right in the dividend. Now divide as stated above.

$$
\begin{array}{r}
= 0.75 \\
2\overline{\smash{)}1.5} \\
\underline{1.4} \\
10 \\
\underline{10} \\
0
\end{array}
\qquad
0.5\,\overline{\smash{)}15.5} =
\begin{array}{r}
= 31. \\
5\overline{\smash{)}155.} \\
\underline{15} \\
05 \\
\underline{5} \\
0
\end{array}
$$

M A T H ✓ T I P

When you use a calculator, you can have a decimal in the divisor and the decimal will be in the correct place in the answer.

1.5 ÷ 2 = 0.75, and 15.5 ÷ 0.5 = 31

■ WHAT IS A PERCENTAGE?

Percent (%) means *per hundred* or *per hundred parts*. The whole or total always represents 100 percent.

$$
\begin{aligned}
5\% &= 5 \text{ parts of 100 parts, or } 5 \div 100 = 0.05 \text{ or } \tfrac{1}{20} \\
75\% &= 75 \text{ parts of 100 parts, or } 75 \div 100 = 0.75 \text{ or } \tfrac{3}{4} \\
120\% &= 120 \text{ parts of 100 parts, or } 120 \div 100 = 1.2 \text{ or } 1\tfrac{1}{5}
\end{aligned}
$$

■ HOW CAN I CONVERT A PERCENTAGE TO A DECIMAL?

Move the decimal *two places* to the *left* and *drop* the % sign.

$$
\begin{aligned}
20\% &= 2 \div 100 = 0.20 \text{ or } \mathbf{0.2} \\
1\% &= 1 \div 100 = \mathbf{0.01} \\
12\tfrac{1}{4}\% &= 12.25\%, \ 12.25 \div 100 = \mathbf{0.1225}
\end{aligned}
$$

See Figure 2.1.

■ HOW CAN I CONVERT A DECIMAL TO A PERCENTAGE?

Move the decimal *two places* to the *right* and *add* the % sign.

$$
\begin{aligned}
0.25 &= \mathbf{25\%} \\
0.9 &= \mathbf{90\%} \\
0.0875 &= \mathbf{8.75\%} \text{ or } \mathbf{8\tfrac{3}{4}\%}
\end{aligned}
$$

See Figure 2.1.

Decimal to Percentage   **Percentage to Decimal**

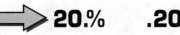 

.20 ⟹ 20.%   .20 ⟸ 20.%

2 places right   2 places left

■ HOW DO I MULTIPLY BY PERCENTAGES?

$$500 \times 25\% = 500 \times {}^{25}/_{100} = {}^{12,500}/_{100} = 125$$
or
$$500 \times 25\% = 125, \text{ or } 500 \times .25 = 125$$

■ HOW DO I DIVIDE BY PERCENTAGES?

$$100 \div 5\% = 100 \div {}^{5}/_{100} = 100 \times {}^{100}/_{5} = {}^{10,000}/_{5} = 2,000$$
or
$$100 \div 5\% = 2,000, \text{ or } 100 \div .05 = 2,000$$

■ IS THERE ANY EASY WAY TO REMEMBER HOW TO SOLVE PERCENTAGE PROBLEMS?

The following three formulas are important for solving all percentage problems:

$$\begin{array}{rcl}
\text{TOTAL} \times \text{RATE} & = & \text{PART} \\
\text{PART} \div \text{RATE} & = & \text{TOTAL} \\
\text{PART} \div \text{TOTAL} & = & \text{RATE}
\end{array}$$

There is a simple way to remember how to use these formulas:

- ■ *MULTIPLY* when PART is UNKNOWN.

- ■ *DIVIDE* when PART is KNOWN.

- ■ When you divide, always enter PART into the calculator first.

■ WHAT IS THE "T-BAR" METHOD?

The T-Bar is another tool to use to solve percentage problems. For some people, the "three-formula method" is more difficult to remember than the visual image of a *T*.

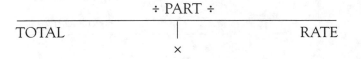

÷ PART ÷

TOTAL | RATE

×

■ HOW DO I USE THE T-BAR?

The procedure for using the T-Bar is as follows:

1. Enter the two *known* items in the correct places.
2. If the line between the two items is *vertical*, you *multiply* to equal the missing item.

FIGURE 2.2

Using the T-Bar

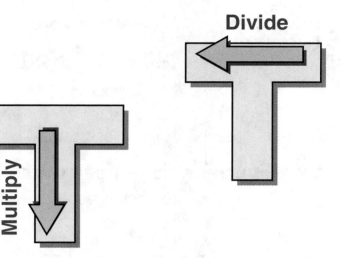

3. If the line between the two items is *horizontal*, you *divide* to equal the missing item. When you divide, the top (**Part**) always goes into the calculator first and is divided by the bottom (**Total** or **Rate**).

See Figure 2.2.

The following examples show how the T-Bar can be used to solve percentage problems. These examples deal with discounts because everyone can relate to buying an item that is on sale. Later we will see how the T-Bar can be used for many types of real estate problems.

■ **FOR EXAMPLE** John purchased a new suit that was marked $500. How much did John save if it was on sale for 20 percent off?

= ? ($100)		**$100 Saved**
$500	20%	
Total Price	0.2	
×		

$500 × 20% (.20) = $100

How much did John pay for the suit?

$500 Total Price – $100 Discount   **$400 Paid**
or
100% Total Price – 20% Discount = 80% Paid

= ? ($400)		**$400 Paid**
$500	80%	
Total Price	0.8	
×		

$500 × 80% (.80) = $400

■ **FOR EXAMPLE** Susie paid $112.50 for a dress that was reduced 25 percent. How much was it originally marked?

100% Original Price – 25% Discount = 75% Paid

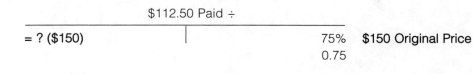

$112.50 Paid ÷

= ? ($150)   75%   **$150 Original Price**
                                         0.75

$112.50 ÷ 75% (.75) = $150

■ **FOR EXAMPLE** Chris paid $127.50 for a coat that was marked down from the original price of $150. What percent of discount did Chris receive?

$150 Original Price – $127.50 Discount Price = $22.50 Discount

÷ 22.50 Discount

$150   = ? (0.15 = 15%)   **15% Discount**
Original Price

$22.50 ÷ $150 = .15 or 15%

or

÷ $127.50 Paid

$150   = ? (0.85 = 85%)   85% of Original
                                                        Price Paid

$127.50 ÷ $150 = .85 or 85%

85% was the percent paid; therefore

100% Original Price – 85% Paid = **15% Discount**

■ WORD PROBLEMS CAN BE TRICKY. HOW SHOULD I DEAL WITH THEM?

There are five important steps that must be taken to solve word problems.

1. **Read** the problem carefully and completely. Never touch the calculator until you have read the entire problem.
2. **Analyze** the problem to determine what is being asked, what facts are given that *will* be needed to solve for the answer, and what facts are given that *will not* be needed to solve for the answer. Eliminate any information and/or numbers given that are not needed to solve the problem. Take the remaining information and/or numbers and determine which will be needed first, second, etc., depending on the number of steps it will take to solve the problem.
3. **Choose** the proper formula(s) and steps it will take to solve the problem.
4. **Insert** the known elements and calculate the answer.
5. **Check** your answer to be sure you keyed in the numbers and functions properly on your calculator. Be sure you finished the problem. For example, when the problem asks for the salesperson's share of the commission, do not stop at the broker's share of the commission and mark that answer just because it is one of the choices.

PERCENTAGE PROBLEMS

■ HOW DO I WORK COMMISSION PROBLEMS?

The full **commission** is a percentage of the sales price unless stated differently in the problem. Remember that full commission rates, commission splits between brokers, and commission splits between the broker and salespersons are always negotiable. Always read a problem carefully to determine the correct rate(s).

÷ Full Commission ÷	
Sales Price	Full Commission Rate

$\times$

Sales Price × Full Commission Rate = **Full Commission**
Full Commission ÷ Full Commission Rate = **Sales Price**
Full Commission ÷ Sales Price = **Full Commission Rate**

÷ Broker's Share of the Commission ÷	
Full Commission	% of Full Commission to the Broker

$\times$

Full Commission × % of Full Commission to the Broker = **Broker's Share of the Commission**

Broker's Share of the Commission ÷ % of Full Commission to the Broker = **Full Commission**

Broker's Share of the Commission ÷ Full Commission = **% of Full Commission to the Broker**

÷ Salesperson's Share of the Commission ÷	
Broker's Share of the Commission	Salesperson's % of the Broker's Share

$\times$

Broker's Share of the Commission	×	Salesperson's % of the Broker's Share	=	**Salesperson's Share of the Commission**

Salesperson's Share of the Commission	÷	Salesperson's % of the Broker's Share	=	**Broker's Share of the Commission**

Salesperson's Share of the Commission	÷	Broker's Share of the Commission	=	**Salesperson's % of the Broker's Share**

■ **FOR EXAMPLE** A seller listed a home for $200,000 and agreed to pay a full commission rate of 5 percent. The home sold 4 weeks later for 90 percent of the list price. The listing broker agreed to give the selling broker 50 percent of the commission. The listing broker paid the listing salesperson 50 percent of her share of the commission, and the selling broker paid the selling salesperson 60 percent of his share of the commission. How much commission did the selling salesperson receive?

$$= \$180,000 \text{ Sales Price}$$

$200,000		90%
List Price		or 0.9
	×	

$200,000 × 90% (.90) = $180,000

$$= \$9,000 \text{ Full Commission}$$

$180,000		5%
Sales Price		or 0.05
	×	

$180,000 × 5% (.05) = $9,000

$$= \$4,500 \text{ Broker's Share of the Commission}$$

$9,000		50%
Full Commission		or 0.5
	×	

$9,000 × 50% (.50) = $4,500

$$= \$2,700 \text{ Selling Salesperson's Commission}$$

$4,500		60%
Broker's Share of Comm.		or 0.6
	×	

$4,500 × 60% (.60) = $2,700

$2,700 Selling Salesperson's Commission is the answer.

■ WHAT IS MEANT BY "SELLER'S DOLLARS AFTER COMMISSION"?

The first deduction from the sales price is the real estate commission. For example, if a house sold for $100,000 and a 7% commission was paid, that means $7,000 was paid in commissions. The seller still has 93% or $93,000. The seller's dollars after commission will be used to pay the seller's other expenses and hopefully will leave some money for the seller.

÷ Seller's Dollars after Commission ÷

Sales Price	Percent after Commission

×

Remember, the sales price is 100%. Thus 100% – Commission % = Percent after Commission.

Sales Price × Percent after Commission = **Seller's Dollars after Commission**

Seller's Dollars after Commission ÷ Percent after Commission = **Sales Price**

Seller's Dollars after Commission ÷ Sales Price = **Percent after Commission**

■ **FOR EXAMPLE** After deducting $5,850 in closing costs and a 5 percent broker's commission, the sellers received their original cost of $175,000 plus a $4,400 profit. What was the sales price of the property?

$5,850 Closing Costs + $175,000 Original Cost + $4,400 Profit = $185,250 Seller's Dollars after Commission

100% Sales Price – 5% Commission = 95% Percent after Commission

$185,250 Seller's Dollars after Commission ÷

= $195,000 Sales Price	95% or 0.95

$185,250 ÷ 95% (.95) = $195,000

$195,000 Sales Price is the answer.

■ HOW DO I DETERMINE INTEREST?

Interest is the cost of using money. The amount of interest paid is determined by the agreed-on annual interest rate, the amount of money borrowed (loan amount) or amount of money still owed (loan balance), and the period of time the money is held. When a lender grants a loan for real estate, the loan-to-value (LTV) ratio is the percentage of the sales price or appraised value, whichever is less, that the lender is willing to lend.

$$\div \text{ Loan Amount } \div$$

Sales Price or Appraised Value (whichever is less)	Loan-to-Value Ratio (LTV)

$$\times$$

$$\text{Sales Price or Appraised Value (whichever is less)} \times \text{Loan-to-Value Ratio (LTV)} = \textbf{Loan Amount}$$

$$\text{Loan Amount} \div \text{Loan-to-Value Ratio (LTV)} = \textbf{Sales Price or Appraised Value (whichever is less)}$$

$$\text{Loan Amount} \div \text{Sales Price or Appraised Value (whichever is less)} = \textbf{Loan-to-Value Ratio (LTV)}$$

$$\div \text{ Annual Interest } \div$$

Loan Amount (Principal)	Annual Interest Rate

$$\times$$

$$\text{Loan Amount} \times \text{Annual Interest Rate} = \textbf{Annual Interest}$$

$$\text{Annual Interest} \div \text{Annual Interest Rate} = \textbf{Loan Amount}$$

$$\text{Annual Interest} \div \text{Loan Amount} = \textbf{Annual Interest Rate}$$

■ **FOR EXAMPLE** A parcel of real estate sold for $335,200. The lender granted a 90 percent loan at 7.5 percent for 30 years. The appraised value on this parcel was $335,500. How much interest is paid to the lender in the first monthly payment?

= $301,680 Loan Amount

$335,200 Sales Price	90% or 0.9

$$\times$$

$335,200 × 90% (.90) = $301,680 Loan

= $22,626 Annual Interest

$301,680 Loan Amount	7.5% or .075

$$\times$$

$301,680 × 7.5% (.075) = $22,626

$22,626 Annual Interest ÷ 12 Months = $1,885.50 Monthly Interest

$1,885.50 Interest in the First Monthly Payment is the answer.

■ HOW DO I DETERMINE MONTHLY PRINCIPAL AND INTEREST PAYMENTS?

A **loan payment factor** can be used to calculate the monthly principal and interest (PI) payment on a loan. The factor represents the monthly principal and interest payment to amortize a $1,000 loan and is based on the annual interest rate and the term of the loan.

See Table 15.2 for a loan factor chart.

Loan Amount ÷ $1,000 × Loan Payment Factor = **Monthly PI Payment**
Monthly PI Payment ÷ Loan Payment Factor = **Loan Amount**

▥ FOR EXAMPLE If the lender in the previous example uses a loan payment factor of $6.99 per $1,000 of loan amount, what will be the monthly PI (principal and interest) payment?

$301,680 Loan Amount ÷ $1,000 × $6.99 = $2,108.74 Monthly PI Payment

$2,108.74 Monthly PI Payment is the answer.

■ HOW DO I WORK PROBLEMS ABOUT POINTS?

One **point** equals 1 percent of the loan amount.

$$\frac{\div \text{ Amount for Points} \div}{\text{Loan Amount} \quad | \quad \text{Points Converted to a Percent}}$$

$$\times$$

$$\begin{array}{ccc} \text{Loan} \\ \text{Amount} \end{array} \times \begin{array}{c} \text{Points Converted} \\ \text{to a Percent} \end{array} = \begin{array}{c} \textbf{Amount for} \\ \textbf{Points} \end{array}$$

$$\begin{array}{c} \text{Amount of} \\ \text{Points} \end{array} \div \begin{array}{c} \text{Points Converted} \\ \text{to a Percent} \end{array} = \textbf{Loan Amount}$$

$$\begin{array}{c} \text{Amount of} \\ \text{Points} \end{array} \div \text{Loan Amount} = \begin{array}{c} \textbf{Points Converted} \\ \textbf{to a Percent} \end{array}$$

▥ FOR EXAMPLE The lender will charge 3½ loan discount points on an $80,000 loan? What will be the total amount due?

$$\frac{= \$2,800 \text{ for Points}}{\begin{array}{ccc} \$80,000 & | & 3.5\% \\ \text{Loan Amount} & & \text{or } 0.035 \end{array}}$$

$$\times$$

$80,000 × 3.5% (.035) = $2,800

$2,800 for Points is the answer.

■ HOW DO I DETERMINE PROFIT?

A **profit** is made when we sell something for more than we paid for it. If we sell something for less than we paid, we have suffered a **loss.**

Sales Price – Cost = Profit

÷ Profit ÷	
Cost	Percent of Profit

×

Cost	×	Percent of Profit	=	**Profit**
Profit	÷	Percent of Profit	=	**Cost**
Profit	÷	Cost	=	**Percent of Profit**
Cost	+	Profit	=	**Sales Price**

÷ Sales Price ÷	
Cost	Percent Sold of Cost

×

(100% Cost + % Profit = % Sales Price)

Cost	×	Percent Sold of Cost	=	**Sales Price**
Sales Price	÷	Percent Sold of Cost	=	**Cost**
Sales Price	÷	Cost	=	**Percent Sold of Cost**

■ **FOR EXAMPLE** Your home listed for $125,000 and sold for $123,200, which gave you a 10 percent profit over the original cost. What was the original cost?

100% Original Cost + 10% Profit = 110% Sales Price

$123,200 Sales Price	
= $112,000 Original Cost	110% or 1.1

×

$123,200 ÷ 110% (1.1) = $112,000

$112,000 Original Cost is the answer.

■ WHAT IS THE DIFFERENCE BETWEEN APPRECIATION AND DEPRECIATION?

Appreciation is increase in value. **Depreciation** is decrease in value. Both are based on the original cost. We only will cover the **straight-line method,** which is what should be used in math problems unless you are told differently. The straight-line method means that the value is increasing (appreciating) or decreasing (depreciating) the same amount each year. The amount of appreciation or depreciation is based on the original cost.

■ HOW DO I SOLVE APPRECIATION PROBLEMS?

$$\frac{\div \text{ Annual Appreciation } \div}{\text{Cost} \quad | \text{ Annual Appreciation Rate}}$$
$$\times$$

Cost	×	Annual Appreciation Rate	= **Annual Appreciation**
Annual Appreciation	÷	Annual Appreciation Rate	= **Cost**
Annual Appreciation	÷	Cost	= **Annual Appreciation Rate**

Annual Appreciation Rate × Number of Years = **Total Appreciation Rate**
100% Cost + Total Appreciation Rate = **Today's Value as a Percent**

$$\frac{\div \text{ Today's Value (Appreciated Value) } \div}{\text{Cost} \quad | \text{ Today's Value as a Percent}}$$
$$\times$$

Cost	×	Today's Value as a Percent	= **Today's Value (Appreciated Value)**
Today's Value (Appreciated Value)	÷	Today's Value as a Percent	= **Cost**
Today's Value (Appreciated Value)	÷	Cost	= **Today's Value as a Percent**

■ HOW DO I SOLVE DEPRECIATION PROBLEMS?

÷ Annual Depreciation ÷

| Cost | Annual Depreciation Rate |

×

Cost × Annual Depreciation Rate = **Annual Depreciation**

Annual Depreciation ÷ Annual Depreciation Rate = **Cost**

Annual Depreciation ÷ Cost = **Annual Depreciation Rate**

Annual Depreciation Rate × Number of Years = **Total Depreciation Rate**
100% Cost ÷ Total Depreciation Rate = **Today's Value as a Percent**

÷ Today's Value (Depreciated Value) ÷

| Cost | Today's Value as a Percent |

×

Cost × Today's Value as a Percent = **Today's Value (Depreciated Value)**

Today's Value (Depreciated Value) ÷ Today's Value as a Percent = **Cost**

Today's Value (Depreciated Value) ÷ Cost = **Today's Value as a Percent**

■ **FOR EXAMPLE** Seven years ago you purchased a piece of real estate for $93,700, including the original cost of the land, which was $6,700. What is the total value of the land today using an appreciation rate of 8 percent per year?

8% Appreciation per Year × 7 Years = 56% Total Appreciation Rate
100% cost + 56% Appreciation = 156% Today's Value

= **$10,452 Today's Value**

| $6,700 Original Cost | 156% or 1.56 |

×

$6,700 × 156% (1.56) = $10,452

$10,452 Today's Value is the answer.

■ **FOR EXAMPLE** The value of a house without the lot at the end of four years is $132,300. What was the original cost of the house if the yearly rate of depreciation was 2.5 percent?

2.5% depreciation per year × 4 years = 10% total depreciation rate

100% cost − 10% depreciation = 90% today's value

$132,300 Today's Value ÷	
= $147,000 Original Cost	90% or 0.9

$132,300 ÷ 90% (.90) = $147,000

$147,000 Original Cost is the answer.

■ HOW DO I DETERMINE VALUE FOR INCOME-PRODUCING PROPERTIES?

When appraising income-producing property, the value is determined by using the annual net operating income (NOI) and the current market rate of return or capitalization rate. Annual scheduled gross income is adjusted for vacancies and credit losses to arrive at the annual effective gross income. The annual operating expenses are deducted from the annual effective gross income to arrive at the annual NOI.

Annual Scheduled Gross Income − Vacancies and Credit Losses = **Annual Effective Gross Income**

Annual Effective Gross Income − Annual Operating Expenses = **Annual NOI**

÷ Annual NOI ÷	
Value	Annual Rate of Return or Annual Capitalization Rate

×

Annual NOI ÷ Annual Rate of Return = **Value**

Value × Annual Rate of Return = **Annual NOI**

Annual NOI ÷ Value = **Annual Rate of Return**

■ **FOR EXAMPLE** An office building produces $132,600 annual gross income. If the annual expenses are $30,600 and the appraiser estimates the value using an 8.5 percent rate of return, what is the estimated value?

$132,600 Annual Gross Income – $30,600 Annual Expenses = $102,000 Annual NOI

$102,000 Annual NOI ÷

| = $1,200,000 Value | | 8.5%
or 0.085 |

$102,000 ÷ 8.5% = $1,200,000

$1,200,000 Value is the answer.

The above formulas also can be used for investment problems. The total becomes *original cost* or *investment* instead of value.

■ **FOR EXAMPLE** You invest $335,000 in a property that should produce a 9 percent rate of return. What monthly NOI will you receive?

= $30,150 Annual NOI

| $335,000
Investment | | 9%
or 0.09 |

×

$335,000 × 9% (.09) = $30,150
$30,150 Annual NOI ÷ 12 Months = $2,512.50

$2,512.50 Monthly NOI is the answer.

■ HOW DO I SOLVE PROBLEMS INVOLVING PERCENTAGE LEASES?

When establishing the rent to be charged in a lease for retail space, the lease may be a **percentage lease** instead of a lease based on dollars per square foot. In the percentage lease, there is normally a base or minimum monthly rent plus a percentage of the gross sales in excess of an amount set in the lease. The percentage lease also can be set up as a percentage of the total gross sales or of the base/minimum rent, whichever is larger. We shall look at the minimum plus percentage lease only.

Gross Sales – Gross Sales Not
Subject to the
Percentage = **Gross Sales Subject
to the Percentage**

$$\frac{\div \text{ Percentage Rent} \div}{\begin{array}{c|c} \text{Gross Sales Subject} & \text{\% in the Lease} \\ \text{to the Percentage} & \end{array}}$$

$$\times$$

Gross Sales Subject to the Percentage	$\times$	% in the Lease	$=$	**Percentage Rent**
Percentage Rent	$\div$	% in the Lease	$=$	**Gross Sales Subject to the Percentage**
Percentage Rent	$\div$	Gross Sales Subject to the Percentage	$=$	**% in the Lease**
Percentage Rent	$+$	Base/ Minimum Rent	$=$	**Total Rent**

FOR EXAMPLE A lease calls for monthly minimum rent of $900 plus 3 percent of annual gross sales in excess of $270,000. What was the annual rent in a year when the annual gross sales were $350,600?

$900 Monthly Minimum Rent × 12 Months = $10,800 Annual Minimum Rent

$350,600 Annual Gross Sales − $270,000 Annual Gross Sales Not Subject to the Percentage = $80,600 Annual Gross Sales Subject to the Percentage

$$= \$2,418 \text{ Annual Percentage Rent}$$

$$\frac{\begin{array}{c|c} \text{\$80,600 Annual Gross} & \text{3\%} \\ \text{Subject to the Percentage} & \text{or } 0.03 \end{array}}{}$$

$$\times$$

$10,800 Annual Minimum Rent + $2,418 Annual Percentage Rent = $13,218

$13,218 Total Annual Rent is the answer.

MEASUREMENT PROBLEMS

■ **WHAT ARE LINEAR MEASUREMENTS?**

Linear measurement is line measurement. When the terms

- *per foot,*
- *per linear foot,*
- *per running foot, or*
- *per front foot*

are used, you are being asked to determine the *total length* of the object whether measured in a straight line, crooked line, or curved line. The abbreviation for feet is '. Thus, 12 feet could be written as 12'. The abbreviation for inches is ". Thus, 12 inches could be written as 12".

■ **WHAT DOES THE PHRASE "FRONT FOOT" REFER TO?**

When the term *per front foot* is used, you are dealing with the number of units on the **frontage** of a lot. The frontage is normally the street frontage, but it could be the water frontage if the lot is on a river, lake, or ocean. If two dimensions are given for a tract of land, the first dimension given is the frontage if the dimensions are not labeled.

■ **HOW DO I CONVERT ONE KIND OF LINEAR MEASUREMENT TO ANOTHER?**

12 inches = 1 foot

Inches ÷ 12 = Feet (144 inches ÷ 12 = 12 feet)
Feet × 12 = Inches (12 feet × 12 = 144 inches)

36 inches = 1 yard

Inches ÷ 36 = Yards (144 inches ÷ 36 = 4 yards)
Yards × 36 = Inches (4 yards × 36 = 144 Inches)

3 feet = 1 yard

Feet ÷ 3 = Yards (12 feet ÷ 3 = 4 yards)
Yards × 3 = Feet (4 yards × 3 = 12 feet)

5,280 feet = 1 mile

Feet ÷ 5,280 = Miles (10,560 feet ÷ 5,280 = 2 miles)
Miles × 5,280 = Feet (2 miles × 5,280 = 10,560 feet)

16½ feet = 1 rod

Feet ÷ 16.5 = Rods (82.5 feet ÷ 16.5 = 5 rods)
Rods × 16.5 = Feet (5 rods × 16.5 = 82.5 feet)

320 rods = 1 mile

Rods ÷ 320 = Miles (640 rods ÷ 320 = 2 miles)
Miles × 320 = Rods (2 miles × 320 = 640 rods)

■ **FOR EXAMPLE** A rectangular lot is 50 feet × 150 feet. The cost to fence this lot is priced per linear/running foot. How many linear/running feet will be used to calculate the price of the fence?

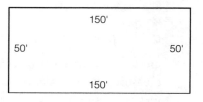

50 Feet + 150 Feet + 50 Feet + 150 Feet = 400 Linear/Running Feet

400 Linear/Running Feet is the answer.

■ **FOR EXAMPLE** A parcel of land that fronts on Interstate 45 in Houston, Texas, is for sale at $5,000 per front foot. What will it cost to purchase this parcel of land if the dimensions are 150' by 100'?

150 is the frontage because it is the first dimension given.
150 Front Feet × $5,000 = $750,000 Cost

$750,000 Cost is the answer.

■ HOW DO I SOLVE FOR AREA MEASUREMENT?

Area is the two-dimensional surface of an object. Area is quoted in *square units* or in *acres*. We will look at calculating the area of squares, rectangles, and triangles. Squares and rectangles are four-sided objects. All four sides of a square are the same. Opposite sides of a rectangle are the same. A triangle is a three-sided object. The three sides of a triangle can be the same dimension or three different dimensions.

When two dimensions are given, we assume it to be a rectangle unless told otherwise.

■ HOW DO I CONVERT ONE KIND OF AREA MEASUREMENT TO ANOTHER?

144 square inches = 1 square foot

Square Inches ÷ 144 = Square Feet (14,400 square inches ÷ 144 = 100 square feet)
Square Feet × 144 = Square Inches ÷ (100 square feet × 144 = 14,400 square inches)

1,296 square inches = 1 square yard

Square Inches ÷ 1,296 = Square Yards (12,960 ÷ 1,296 = 10 square yards)
Square Yards × 1,296 = Square Inches (10 square yards × 1,296 = 12,960 square yards)

9 square feet = 1 square yard

Square Feet ÷ 9 = Square Yards (90 square feet ÷ 9 = 10 square yards)
Square Yards × 9 = Square Feet (10 square yards × 9 = 90 square feet)

43,560 square feet = 1 acre

Square Feet ÷ 43,560 = Acres (87,120 ÷ 43,560 = 2 acres)
Acres × 43,560 = Square Feet (2 acres × 43,560 = 87,120 square feet)

640 acres = 1 section = 1 square mile

Acres ÷ 640 = Sections (Square Miles) (1,280 acres ÷ 640 = 2 sections)
Sections (Square Miles) × 640 = Acres (2 sections × 640 = 1,280 acres)

■ HOW DO I DETERMINE THE AREA OF A SQUARE OR RECTANGLE?

Length × Width = **Area of a Square or Rectangle**

■ **FOR EXAMPLE** How many square feet are in a room 15'6" × 30'9"?

Remember, we must use like dimensions, so the inches must be converted to feet.

6" ÷ 12 = 0.5' + 15' = 15.5' wide
9" ÷ 12 = 0.75' + 30' = 30.75' long
30.75' × 15.5' = 476.625 Square Feet

476.625 Square Feet is the answer.

■ **FOR EXAMPLE** If carpet costs $63 per square yard to install, what would it cost to carpet the room in the previous example?

476.625 Square Feet ÷ 9 = 52.958333 Square Yards × $63 per Square Yard = $3,336.375 or $3,336.38 rounded

$3,336.38 Carpet Cost is the answer.

■ **FOR EXAMPLE** How many acres are there in a parcel of land that measures 450' × 484'?

484' × 450' = 217,800 Square Feet ÷ 43,560 = 5 Acres

5 Acres of Land is the answer.

■ HOW DO I DETERMINE THE AREA OF A TRIANGLE?

½ Base × Height = **Area of a Triangle**

or

Base × Height ÷ 2 = **Area of a Triangle**

■ **FOR EXAMPLE** How many square feet are contained in a triangular parcel of land that is 400 feet on the base and 200 feet high?

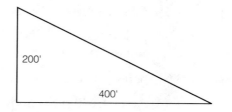

400' × 200' ÷ 2 = 40,000 Square Feet

40,000 Square Feet is the answer.

■ **FOR EXAMPLE** How many acres are in a three-sided tract of land that is 300' on the base and 400' high?

300' × 400' ÷ 2 = 60,000 Square Feet ÷ 43,560 = 1.377 Acres

1.377 Acres is the answer.

■ HOW DO I SOLVE FOR VOLUME?

Volume is the space inside a three-dimensional object. Volume is quoted in *cubic units*. We will look at calculating the volume of boxes and triangular prisms.

■ HOW DO I CONVERT FROM ONE KIND OF VOLUME MEASUREMENT TO ANOTHER?

1,728 cubic inches = 1 cubic foot

Cubic Inches ÷ 1,728 = Cubic Feet
(17,280 cubic inches ÷ 1,728 = 10 cubic feet)

Cubic Feet × 1,728 = Cubic Inches
(10 cubic feet × 1,728 = 17,280 cubic inches)

46,656 cubic inches = 1 cubic yard

Cubic ÷ Inches 46,656 = Cubic Yards
(93,312 cubic inches ÷ 46,656 = 2 cubic yards)

Cubic Yards × 46,656 = Cubic Inches
(2 cubic yards × 46,656 = 93,312 cubic inches)

27 cubic feet = 1 cubic yard

Cubic ÷ Feet 27 = Cubic Yards (270 cubic feet ÷ 27 = 10 cubic yards)
Cubic Yards × 27 = Cubic Feet (10 cubic yards × 27 = 270 cubic feet)

■ HOW DO I DETERMINE THE VOLUME OF A ROOM?

For purposes of determining volume, think of a room as if it were a box.

$$\text{Length} \times \text{Width} \times \text{Height} = \text{Volume of a Box}$$

■ **FOR EXAMPLE** A building is 500 feet long, 400 feet wide, and 25 feet high. How many cubic feet of space are in this building?

500' × 400' × 25' = 5,000,000 Cubic Feet

5,000,000 Cubic Feet is the answer.

■ **FOR EXAMPLE** How many cubic yards of concrete would it take to build a sidewalk measuring 120 feet long; 2 feet, 6 inches wide; and 3 inches thick?

6" ÷ 12' = .5' + 2' = 2.5' Wide
3" ÷ 12' = .25' Thick
120' × 2.5' × .25' = 75 Cubic Feet ÷ 27 = 2.778 Cubic Yards (rounded)

2.778 Cubic Yards is the answer.

■ HOW DO I DETERMINE THE VOLUME OF A TRIANGULAR PRISM?

The terms *A-frame, A-shaped* or *gable roof* on an exam describe a triangular prism.

$$\text{½ Base} \times \text{Height} \times \text{Width} = \text{Volume of a Triangular Prism}$$

or

$$\text{Base} \times \text{Height} \times \text{Width} \div 2 = \text{Volume of a Triangular Prism}$$

■ **FOR EXAMPLE** An A-frame cabin in the mountains is 50 feet long and 30 feet wide. The cabin is 25 feet high from the base to the highest point. How many cubic feet of space does this A-frame cabin contain?

50' × 30' × 25' ÷ 2 = 18,750 Cubic Feet

18,750 Cubic Feet is the answer.

■ **FOR EXAMPLE** A building is 40 feet by 25 feet with a 10-foot-high ceiling. The building has a gable roof that is 8 feet high at the tallest point. How many cubic feet are in this structure, including the roof?

40' × 25' × 10' = 10,000 Cubic Feet in the Building
40' × 25' × 8' ÷ 2 = 4,000 Cubic Feet in the Gable Roof
10,000 Cubic Feet + 4,000 Cubic Feet = 14,000 Total Cubic Feet

14,000 Cubic Feet is the answer.

PRORATION PROBLEMS

Prorate means to divide proportionately. Some expenses and income may be prorated for the closing of a real estate transaction. We will look at prorating interest on a loan, ad valorem taxes on a property, homeowner's insurance on a property, and rent on income-producing property.

■ WHAT ARE THE DIFFERENT CALENDARS USED FOR PRORATING?

When we prorate, we calculate the number of days owed for the expense or the rental income. The days may be calculated using a *banker's year*, *statutory year*, or *calendar year*. The **banker's year** and **statutory year** are the same because they both contain 12 months with 30 days in each month. The total number of days in both a banker's year and a statutory year is 360 days. The **calendar year** contains 12 months with 28 to 31 days in each month. The total number of days in a calendar year is 365 days. The total number of days in a calendar *leap* year is 366 days. The following shows the days in each month.

	Banker's or Statutory Year	Calendar Year	Calendar Leap Year
January	30	31	31
February	30	28	29
March	30	31	31
April	30	30	30
May	30	31	31
June	30	30	30
July	30	31	31
August	30	31	31
September	30	30	30
October	30	31	31
November	30	30	30
December	30	31	31
Total days in a year	360	365	366

■ WHAT IS THE DIFFERENCE BETWEEN PRORATING "THROUGH" AND PRORATING "TO" THE DAY OF CLOSING?

In a proration problem, we will be told whether to prorate *through* the day of closing or *to* the day of closing. **This is very important when calculating the days owed.** When we prorate *through* the day of closing, the *seller* is responsible for the day of closing. When we prorate *to* the day of closing, the *buyer* is responsible for the day of closing.

■ HOW DO I CALCULATE PRORATION PROBLEMS?

Once we know the number of days owed, we then need to know the amount of the expense or income per day. We take either the annual amount divided by the total days in the year to get the daily amount or the monthly amount divided by the total days in the month to get the daily amount.

M A T H ✓ T I P   Be sure you are using the correct type of year (banker's or statutory year, calendar year or calendar leap year) when computing the daily amount.

The final step is to multiply the amount per day by the number of days owed to get the prorated amount.

■ WHAT IS THE DIFFERENCE BETWEEN "DEBIT" AND "CREDIT" IN A PRORATION PROBLEM?

To calculate a proration problem, you need to know how expenses and income are posted on the closing statement. **Debit** takes money from a person. **Credit** gives money to a person. (See Figure 5.1.) When the prorated amount involves both the buyer and the seller, there will always be a double entry. If the seller owes the buyer, the prorated amount will be debited to the seller and credited to the buyer. If the buyer owes the seller, the prorated amount will be debited to the buyer and credited to the seller. When the prorated amount involves the buyer and someone other than the seller, there will be only a single entry. When the prorated amount involves the seller and someone other than the buyer, there will be only a single entry. We will discuss debits and credits as we learn to prorate each expense.

The five questions to ask when prorating are as follows:

1. What calendar do we use?
2. Is the expense paid in arrears or in advance?
3. Who has or will pay the expense?
4. Who has earned or received income?
5. When will the expense be paid?

■ HOW DO I CALCULATE INTEREST IN A PRORATION PROBLEM?

When a loan is assumed or paid off, the interest for the month of closing must be prorated. Interest is paid in arrears; therefore, the monthly payment made on the first day of the month pays interest for the entire previous month. The payment includes interest *up to but not including* the day of the payment unless spec-

F I G U R E   5.1

The Debit/Credit Flow

		Buyer	Seller
	Sales Price	DEBIT	CREDIT
	Tenants' Security Deposits	CREDIT	DEBIT
	Fuel Oil (in tank)	DEBIT	CREDIT
	Prorated Accrued Water Bill	CREDIT	DEBIT
	Unearned Rents	CREDIT	DEBIT
	Tax Reserve Account	DEBIT	CREDIT

Different items are treated differently as credits or debits to the buyer or seller on a closing statement.

ified otherwise. Not all payments are due on the first day of the month; therefore, pay attention when you are told what day the interest has been paid through. The sellers owe unpaid interest for the period of time they occupy the home. If the prorations are to be calculated *through* the day of closing, the seller will owe payments *including* the day of closing. If the prorations are to be calculated *to* the day of closing, the seller will *owe up to but not including* the day of closing. Remember to use the correct type of year. A banker's or statutory year has 360 days. A calendar year has 365 days. A calendar leap year has 366 days. On an assumption of the loan, the interest proration is a **debit** to the *seller* and a **credit** to the *buyer*. When a loan is paid off, unpaid interest is calculated and added to the outstanding loan balance and is a **debit** *to the seller only*.

■ **FOR EXAMPLE** A home was purchased on April 4, 2002, for $110,000, and the closing was set for May 8, 2002. The buyer assumed the balance of the seller's $93,600 loan with 11.5 percent interest and monthly payments of $990.29 due on the first day of each month. How much will the interest proration be, using a banker's year and prorating through the day of closing? Who will be debited and who will be credited?

Banker's Year/Statutory Year

Step 1. Find the exact number of days of earned or accrued interest.

Seller owes 8 days (May 1 *through* May 8).
Note: It would be 7 days (8 days minus 1 day) if the problem had said prorate *to* the day of closing.

Step 2. Find the daily interest charge. Outstanding Loan Balance × Annual Interest Rate = Annual Interest ÷ 360 Days per Year = Daily Interest.

$93,600 × 11.5% (.115) = $10,764 Annual Interest ÷ 360 Days = $29.90 Daily Interest

Step 3. Compute the total amount of accrued interest. Daily Interest × Days Owed = Interest Proration.

$29.90 Daily Interest × 8 Days = $239.20

$239.20 Debit Seller, Credit Buyer is the answer.

Calendar Year (if the problem had said to use a calendar year)

Step 1. Find the exact number of days of earned or accrued interest.

Seller owes 8 days (May 1 *through* May 8).

Note: It would be 7 days (8 days minus 1 day) if the problem had said pro-rate *to* the day of closing.

Step 2. Find the daily interest charge. Outstanding Loan Balance × Annual Interest Rate = Annual Interest ÷ 365 Days per Year = Daily Interest.

$93,600 × 11.5% (.115) $10,764 Annual Interest ÷ 365 Days = $29.49041096 Daily Interest

Step 3. Compute the total amount of accrued interest. Daily Interest × Days Owed = Interest Proration.

$29.49041096 Daily Interest × 8 Days = $235.92 Rounded

$235.92 Debit Seller, Credit Buyer is the answer.

■ HOW DO I PRORATE TAXES?

Real estate taxes are normally assessed from January 1 through December 31. The tax rate is *always* applied *to the assessed value of the property* instead of the market value. Taxes are usually paid in arrears; therefore, the seller will owe the buyer for accrued taxes from January 1 *through* the day of closing or *to* the day of closing. The most recent tax bill is used to compute the proration, and this is usually the past year's tax bill. Remember to use the correct type of year. A banker's or statutory year has 360 days. A calendar year has 365 days. A calendar leap year has 366 days.

If the taxes are paid in arrears, the tax proration will be a **debit** to the *seller* and a **credit** to the *buyer.* If the taxes are paid in advance, the tax proration will be a **debit** to the *buyer* and a **credit** to the *seller.*

■ **FOR EXAMPLE** The market value of a home is $115,000. For tax purposes, the home is assessed at 90 percent of the market value. The annual tax rate is $2.50 per $100 of assessed value. If the closing is on March 13, 1999, what is the prorated amount? Prorations are calculated through the day of closing and using a statutory year.

Bankers Year/Statutory Year

Step 1. Find the exact number of days of accrued taxes from the beginning of the tax period (January 1, 1999) up to and including the day of closing (March 13, 1999).

2 Months (January and February) × 30 Days per Month = 60 Days + 13 Days in March = 73 Days

Note: It would be 72 days (73 days minus 1 day) if the problem had said prorate *to* the day of closing.

Step 2. Calculate the annual taxes. Market Value × Assessment Ratio = Assessed Value ÷ $100 × Tax Rate per Hundred = Annual Taxes.

$115,000 × 90% = $103,500 ÷ $100 × $2.50 = $2,587.50 Annual Taxes

Step 3. Find the tax amount per day. Annual Taxes ÷ 360 days per Year = Daily Taxes.

$2,587.50 ÷ 360 Days = $7.1875 Daily Taxes

Step 4. Compute the prorated tax amount. Daily Taxes × Days Owed = Tax Proration.

$7.1875 per Day × 73 Days = $524.69 rounded

$524.69 Debit Seller, Credit Buyer is the answer.

Calendar Year (if the problem had said to use a calendar year)

Step 1. Find the exact number of days of accrued taxes from the beginning of the tax period (January 1, 1999) up to and including the day of closing (March 13, 1999).

31 Days in January + 28 Days in February + 13 Days in March = 72 Days

Note: It would be 71 days (72 days minus 1 day) if the problem had said prorate *to* the day of closing.

Step 2. Calculate the annual taxes. Market Value × Assessment Ratio = Assessed Value ÷ $100 × Tax Rate per Hundred = Annual Taxes.

$115,000 × 90% = $103,500 ÷ $100 × $2.50 = $2,587.50 Annual Taxes

Step 3. Find the tax amount per day. Annual Taxes ÷ 365 Days per Year = Daily Taxes.

$2,587.50 ÷ 365 Days = $7.089041096 Daily Taxes

Step 4. Compute the prorated tax amount. Daily Taxes × Days Owed = Tax Proration.

$7.089041096 per Day × 72 Days = $510.41 rounded

$510.41 Debit Seller, Credit Buyer is the answer.

■ IS INSURANCE ALWAYS PRORATED?

When buying a home, insurance coverage must be provided by the owners if they have a loan. The buyers normally purchase their own insurance policy. There will *not* be a proration if the buyers purchase a new policy because the sellers will cancel their existing policy effective as of the day of closing and the buyer's new policy will become effective as of the day of closing.

▪ IF INSURANCE IS PRORATED, HOW DO I CALCULATE IT?

If the insurance company will allow a policy to be assumed and the buyers choose to do so, there will be an insurance proration. Today insurance policies are written for one year. The premiums are payable in advance; therefore, the sellers have paid the entire yearly premium. If the policy is transferred to the buyers, the buyers owe the sellers for the unused portion of the policy. If you are to prorate *through* the day of closing, the buyers owe the sellers from the day after closing until the expiration of the policy. If you are to prorate *to* the day of closing, the buyers owe the sellers starting with the day of closing until the expiration of the policy. Insurance policies become effective at 12:01 A.M. and expire exactly one year later at 12:01 A.M.; therefore, no coverage is counted on the day of expiration of the insurance policy. Remember to use the correct type of year. A banker's or statutory year has 360 days. A calendar year has 365 days. A calendar leap year has 366 days. The insurance proration will be a **debit** to the *buyer* and a **credit** to the *seller*.

■ **FOR EXAMPLE** A one-year fire insurance policy expires on August 20, 2003. The total premium for this policy was $425 and was paid in full in 2002. The house was sold, and the closing date was set for January 25, 2003. The proration is to be calculated through the day of closing using a banker's year. What will be the total credit to the seller to transfer the insurance policy to the buyer?

Banker's Year/Statutory Year

Step 1. Compute the number of days of insurance coverage that the buyer assumed.

```
    30  days in January
  - 25  day of closing
     5  days left in January
+ 180  days (6 months × 30 days per month/February–July)
 + 19  days coverage in August
   204  days left on the policy
```

Note: It would be 205 days (204 days plus 1 day) if the problem had said prorate *to* the day of closing.

Step 2. Compute the amount of the policy cost per day. Annual Insurance Premium ÷ 360 Days per Year = Daily Insurance.

$425 Insurance Premium ÷ 360 Days = $1.1805556 Daily Insurance

Step 3. Calculate what the buyer owes. Daily Insurance × Days Left on the Policy = Insurance Proration.

$1.1805556 Daily Insurance × 204 Days = $240.83 rounded

$240.83 Credit Seller, Debit Buyer is the answer.

Calendar Year (if the problem had said to use a calendar year)

Step 1. Compute the number of days of insurance coverage that the buyer assumed.

```
 31  days in January
- 25  day of closing
  6  days left in January
+28  days in February
+31  days in March
+30  days in April
+31  days in May
+30  days in June
+31  days in July
+19  days coverage in August
206  days left on the policy
```

Note: It would be 207 days (206 days plus 1 day) if the problem had said prorate *to* the day of closing.

Step 2. Compute the amount of the policy cost per day. Annual Insurance Premium ÷ 365 Days per Year = Daily Insurance.

$425 Insurance Premium ÷ 365 Days = $1.1643836 Daily Insurance

Step 3. Calculate what the buyer owes. Daily Insurance × Days Left on the Policy = Insurance Proration.

$1.1643836 Daily Insurance × 206 Days = $239.86 rounded

$239.86 Credit Seller, Debit Buyer is the answer.

■ HOW DO I PRORATE RENT?

When prorating rents, the amount of rent collected for the month of closing is the only amount prorated. The seller owes the buyer for the unearned rent starting with the day after closing through the end of the month if you are prorating *through* the day of closing. The seller owes the buyer for the unearned rent starting with the day of closing through the end of the month if you are prorating *to* the day of closing. If security deposits are being held by the seller, they are not prorated; therefore, the entire amount of security deposits are transferred to the buyer. Always use the actual number of days in the month of closing for rent prorations unless you are told differently. Both the rent proration and the security deposit will be a **debit** to the *seller* and a **credit** to the *buyer*.

■ **FOR EXAMPLE** Bob is purchasing an apartment complex that contains 15 units that rent for $450 per month. A $450 security deposit is being held on each unit. The sale is to be closed on March 14, and the March rent has been received for all 15 units. Compute the rent proration by prorating through the day of closing. Compute the security deposit.

Calendar Days (remember to use actual days in the month unless specified differently)

Step 1. Compute the unearned days of rent for the month of closing.

          31 days in March
        – 14 day of closing
          17 days of unearned rent

Note: It would be 18 days (17 days plus 1 day) if the problem had said prorate *to* the day of closing.

Step 2. Compute the daily rent. Monthly Rent × Number of Units Paid = Total Rent Collected ÷ Number of Actual Days in the Month of Closing = Daily Rent.

$450 × 15 Units = $6,750 Monthly Rent Collected ÷ 31 Days in March = $217.7419355 Daily Rent

Step 3. Compute the prorated rent amount. Daily Rent × Days of Unearned Rent.

$217.7419355 Daily Rent × 17 Days = $3,701.61 rounded

Step 4. Compute the security deposit.

$450 per Unit × 15 Units = $6,750

$3,701.61 Rent Proration and **$6,750 Security Deposit** are the answers. They are both **Debit Seller** and **Credit Buyer**.

REAL ESTATE MATH PRACTICE PROBLEMS

1. The value of your house, not including the lot, is $91,000 today. What was the original cost if it has depreciated 5 percent per year for the past seven years?
   a. $67,407.41   c. $122,850.00
   b. $95,789.47   d. $140,000.00

2. What was the price per front foot for a 100' × 125' lot that sold for $125,000?
   a. $1,250   c. $556
   b. $1,000   d. $10

3. If the savings and loan gives you a 90 percent loan on a house valued at $88,500, how much additional cash must you produce as a down payment if you have already paid $4,500 in earnest money?
   a. $3,500   c. $4,350
   b. $4,000   d. $8,850

4. What did the owners originally pay for their home if they sold it for $98,672, which gave them a 12 percent profit over their original cost?
   a. $86,830   c. $89,700
   b. $88,100   d. $110,510

5. What would you pay for a building producing $11,250 annual net income and showing a minimum rate of return of 9 percent?
   a. $125,000   c. $101,250
   b. $123,626   d. $122,625

6. The sale of Mrs. Gates's home is to close on September 28. Included in the sale is a garage apartment that is rented to Sandy Dart for $350 per month. Sandy has paid the September rent. What is the rent proration, using actual days and prorating through the day of closing?
   a. $325.67   c. $350.00
   b. $23.33   d. $175.00

7. What is the total cost of a driveway 15' wide, 40' long and 4" thick if the concrete costs $60.00 per cubic yard and the labor costs $1.25 per square foot?
   a. $527.25   c. $1,194.00
   b. $693.75   d. $1,581.75

8. An owner agrees to list his property on the condition that he will receive at least $47,300 after paying a 5 percent broker's commission and paying $1,150 in closing costs. At what price must it sell?
   a. $48,450   c. $50,875
   b. $50,815   d. $51,000

9. The Loving Gift Shop pays rent of $600 per month plus 2.5 percent of gross annual sales in excess of $50,000. What was the average monthly rent last year if gross annual sales were $75,000?
   a. $1,125.00   c. $600.00
   b. $756.25   d. $652.08

10. If your monthly rent is $525, what percent would this be of an annual income of $21,000?
    a. 25%   c. 33%
    b. 30%   d. 40%

11. Two brokers split the 6 percent commission on a $73,000 home. The selling salesperson, Joe, was paid 70 percent of his broker's share. The listing salesperson, Janice, was paid 30 percent of her broker's share. How much did Janice receive?
    a. $657   c. $1,533
    b. $4,380   d. $1,314

12. Find the number of square feet in a lot with a frontage of 75 feet, 6 inches, and a depth of 140 feet, 9 inches.
    a. 10,626.63   c. 216.25
    b. 10,652.04   d. 25,510.81

13. You attempt to appraise a 28-unit apartment house, employing the income approach. You discover that each unit rents for $775 a month, an amount that seems consistent with like rental units in the vicinity. For the past five years the annual expenses of operation have averaged $82,460. The complex has maintained a consistent vacancy rate of 5%. A potential investor is only interested if the return is 9.5 percent. What value would you arrive at using these variables?
    a. $2,741,100   c. $1,736,000
    b. $868,000   d. $1,873,100

14. How much interest will the seller owe the buyer for a closing date of August 10 if the outstanding loan balance is $43,580? The interest rate on this assumable loan is 10.5 percent and the last payment was paid on August 1. Prorations are to be done through the day of closing and using a statutory year.
    a. $127.11   c. $125.37
    b. $254.22   d. $381.33

15. The buyer has agreed to pay $175,000 in sales price, 2.5 loan discount points and a 1 percent origination fee. If the buyer receives a 90 percent loan-to-value ratio, how much will the buyer owe at closing for points and the origination fee?
    a. $1,575.00   c. $5,512.50
    b. $3,937.50   d. $6,125.00

16. Calculate eight months' interest on a $5,000 interest-only loan at 9.5 percent.
    a. $475.00   c. $237.50
    b. $316.67   d. $39.58

17. A 100-acre farm is divided into lots for homes. The streets require ⅛ of the whole farm, and there are 140 lots. How many square feet are in each lot?
    a. 43,560   c. 31,114
    b. 35,004   d. 27,225

18. The 1999 tax bill on the Burnses' home was $1,282 and was paid in December 2000. The Burnses' have sold their home and will close on April 23, 2001. How much will the tax proration be, using a calendar year and prorating to the day of closing?
    a. $393.38   c. $396.89
    b. $402.41   d. $427.33

19. What is the monthly net income on an investment of $115,000 if the rate of return is 12.5 percent?
    a. $1,150.00   c. $7,666.67
    b. $1,197.92   d. $14,375.00

20. A salesperson sells a property for $58,500. The contract he has with his broker is 40 percent of the full commission earned. The commission due the broker is 6 percent. What is the salesperson's share of the commission?
    a. $2,106   c. $3,510
    b. $1,404   d. $2,340

21. Vicki buys 348,480 square feet of land at $0.75 per square foot. She divides the land into ½ acre lots. If she keeps three lots for herself and sells the others for $24,125 each, what percent of profit does she realize?
    a. 47.4%   c. 20%
    b. 32.2%   d. 16.7%

22. $437 was the insurance premium paid in full in 2001 for a one-year insurance policy that expires June 6, 2002. The house is sold and scheduled to close on February 16, 2002. The buyers are assuming the sellers' insurance policy. What is the amount of the insurance proration if a banker's year is used and all prorations are done through the day of closing?

    a. $132.31   c. $302.26
    b. $134.74   d. $304.69

23. What is the interest rate on a $10,000 loan with semiannual interest of $450?

    a. 7%   c. 11%
    b. 9%   d. 13.5%

24. A warehouse is 80' wide and 120' long with ceilings 14' high. If 1,200 square feet of floor surface has been partitioned off, floor to ceiling, for an office, how many cubic feet of space will be left in the warehouse?

    a. 151,200   c. 133,200
    b. 134,400   d. 117,600

25. An office building produces $68,580 annual net operating income. What price would you pay for this property to show a minimum return of 12 percent on your investment?

    a. $489,857   c. $685,800
    b. $571,500   d. $768,096

26. A buyer is assuming the balance of a seller's loan. The interest rate is 8 percent and the last monthly payment of $578.16 was paid on April 1, leaving an outstanding balance of $18,450. Using a banker's year, compute the interest to be paid by the seller if the sale is to be closed on April 19. Prorate through the day of closing.

    a. $110.83   c. $77.90
    b. $82.00   d. $123.00

27. The lot you purchased five years ago for $15,000 has appreciated 3.5 percent per year. What is it worth today?

    a. $12,375   c. $17,250
    b. $15,525   d. $17,625

28. A lot has a frontage of 100' and a depth of 150'. If the building line regulations call for a setback of 25' at the front and 6' on the two sides, how many square feet of usable space are left for the building?

    a. 10,350   c. 11,750
    b. 11,000   d. 15,000

29. A lease calls for $1,000 per month minimum plus 2 percent of annual sales in excess of $100,000. What is the annual rent if the annual sales were $150,000?

    a. $12,000   c. $14,000
    b. $13,000   d. $15,000

30. In the year 2000, taxes on Don Mark's home were paid in full and amounted to $1,468. Don sold his home to Chuck Harris and closed the sale on August 29, 2001. What was the prorated tax amount using a calendar year if the proration was calculated to the day of closing?

    a. $965.26   c. $970.51
    b. $502.74   d. $497.49

31. There is a tract of land that is 1.25 acres. The lot is 150 feet deep. How much will the lot sell for at $65 per front foot?

    a. $9,750   c. $23,595
    b. $8,125   d. $8,125

32. If the broker received a 6.5 percent commission that was $5,200, what was the sales price of the house?

    a. $80,400   c. $77,200
    b. $80,000   d. $86,600

33. Sue earns $20,000 per year and can qualify for a monthly PITI payment equal to 25 percent of her monthly salary. If the annual tax and insurance is $678.24, what is the loan amount she will qualify for if the monthly PI payment factor is $10.29 per $1,000 of loan amount?

    a. $66,000   c. $40,500

    b. $43,000   d. $35,000

34. Find the cost of building a house 29' × 34' × 17' with a gable roof 8' high at the highest point. The cost of construction is $2.25 per cubic foot.

    a. $55,462.50   c. $37,714.50

    b. $46,588.50   d. $27,731.25

35. You invest $50,000 at a rate of return of 12 percent. What is the net operating income?

    a. $6,000   c. $5,000

    b. $5,600   d. $4,167

36. You pay $65.53 monthly interest on a loan bearing 9.25 percent annual interest. What is the loan amount rounded to the nearest hundred dollars?

    a. $1,400   c. $6,300

    b. $2,800   d. $8,500

37. What percentage of profit would you make if you paid $10,500 for a lot, built a home on the lot that cost $93,000, and then sold the lot and house together for $134,550?

    a. 13%   c. 30%

    b. 23%   d. 45%

38. You are purchasing a fourplex and going to close on November 4. Each apartment rents for $575 per month. On November 1, one apartment is vacant and the others paid the November rent. Compute the rent proration through the day of closing.

    a. $230.00   c. $1,495.00

    b. $306.67   d. $1,993.33

39. An income-producing property has $62,500 annual gross income and monthly expenses of $1,530. What is the appraised value if the appraiser uses a 10 percent capitalization rate?

    a. $441,400   c. $183,600

    b. $625,000   d. $609,700

40. A new house and lot cost Mr. Jones $65,000. Of this total price, it was estimated that the lot was worth $13,000. Mr. Jones held the property for eight years. Using the straight-line method, assuming an annual depreciation of 1 percent on the house and an annual increase of 8 percent on the lot, what would be the total value of the property at the end of eight years?

    a. $47,840   c. $81,120

    b. $69,160   d. $101,400

41. The seller received a $121,600 check at closing after paying a 7 percent commission, $31,000 in other closing costs, and the $135,700 loan payoff. What was the total sales price?

    a. $288,300   c. $308,500

    b. $306,300   d. $310,000

42. A fence is being built to enclose a lot 125' by 350'. If there will be one 10' gate, how many running feet of fence will it take?

    a. 465   c. 940

    b. 600   d. 960

43. Alfred pays $2,500 each for four parcels of land. He subdivides them into six parcels and sells each of the six parcels for $1,950. What was Alfred's percentage of profit?

    a. 14.5%   c. 52%

    b. 17%   d. 78%

44. A property sells for $96,000. If it has appreciated 4 percent per year straight line for the past five years, what did the owner pay for the property five years ago?

    a. $76,800   c. $92,300

    b. $80,000   d. $115,200

45. Bill earns an annual income of $60,000, and Betty earns $2,400 per month. How much can Bill and Betty pay monthly for their mortgage payment if the lender uses a 28 percent qualifying ratio?
    a. $2,072
    b. $1,400
    c. $2,352
    d. $672

46. If Don borrows $4,400, agreeing to pay back principal and interest in 18 months, what annual interest rate is Don paying if the total payback is $5,588?
    a. 15%
    b. 18%
    c. 21.3%
    d. 27%

47. If you purchase a lot that is 125' ×150' for $6,468.75, what price did you pay per front foot?
    a. $23.52
    b. $43.13
    c. $51.75
    d. $64.69

48. Kelli has been granted a 90 percent loan for $340,500. How much will Kelli's monthly principal and interest payment be, using a loan payment factor of $7.16 per $1,000 of loan?
    a. $2,194.18
    b. $4,755.59
    c. $2,437.98
    d. $3,064.50

49. Calculate the amount of commission earned by a broker on a property selling for $61,000 if 6 percent is paid on the first $50,000 and 3 percent on the remaining balance.
    a. $3,330
    b. $3,830
    c. $3,600
    d. $3,930

50. A 50' × 100' lot has a 2,400-square-foot house on it that contains four bedrooms and three bathrooms. What percent of the lot is not taken up by the house?
    a. 21%
    b. 48%
    c. 50%
    d. 52%

ANSWER KEY FOR REAL ESTATE MATH PRACTICE PROBLEMS

1. d $140,000.00 Original Cost

5% Depreciation per Year × 7 Years = 35% Total Depreciation
100% Original Cost − 35% Total Depreciation = 65% Today's Value

$$\frac{\$91,000 \text{ Today's Value} \div}{\begin{array}{c|c} \textbf{= \$140,000} & 65\% \\ \textbf{Original Cost} & \text{or } 0.65 \end{array}}$$

$91,000 ÷ 65% (.65) = **$140,000 Original Cost**

2. a $1,250 Per Front Foot

$125,000 Sales Price ÷ 100 Front Feet = **$1,250 Per Front Foot**

3. c $4,350 Due at Closing

100% Value − 90% LTV = 10% Down Payment

$$\frac{\text{= \$8,850 Down Payment}}{\begin{array}{c|c} \$88,500 \text{ Value} & 10\% \\ \times & \text{or } 0.1 \end{array}}$$

$88,500 × 10% (.10) = $8,850
$8,850 Down Payment − $4,500 Earnest Money = **$4,350 Due at Closing**

4. b $88,100 Original Cost

100% Original Cost + 12% Profit = 112% Sales Price

$$\frac{\$98,672 \text{ Sales Price} \div}{\begin{array}{c|c} \textbf{= \$88,100} & 112\% \\ \textbf{Original Cost} & \text{or } 1.12 \end{array}}$$

$98,672 ÷ 112% (1.12) = **$88,100 Original Cost**

5. a $125,000 Price

$$\frac{\$11,250 \text{ Annual Net Income} \div}{\begin{array}{c|c} \textbf{= \$125,000} & 9\% \\ \textbf{Price} & \text{or } 0.09 \end{array}}$$

$11,250 ÷ 9% (.09) = **$125,000 Price**

6. b **$23.33 Rent Proration**

   30 Days in September – 28 Day of Closing = 2 Days Due
   $350 Monthly Rent ÷ 30 Days = $11.666667 per Day × 2 Days =
   $23.33 Rent Proration

7. c **$1,194.00 Total Cost**

   4" ÷ 12 = 0.333'
   Concrete: 40' × 15' × 0.333' = 199.8 Cubic Feet ÷ 27 = 7.4 Cubic Yards
   × $60 per Cubic Yard = $444
   Labor: 40' × 15' = 600 Square Feet × $1.25 per Square Foot = $750
   $444 Concrete + $750 Labor = **$1,194.00 Total Cost**

8. d **$51,000 Sales Price**

   $47,300 Net to Seller + $1,150 Closing Costs =
   $48,450 Seller's Dollars after Commission
   100% Sales Price – 5% Commission = 95% Seller's Percent after
   Commission

   $$\frac{\$48,450 \text{ Seller's Dollars after Commission} \div}{= \$51,000 \qquad\qquad\qquad\qquad\qquad 95\%}$$
   Sales Price   or 0.95

   $48,450 ÷ 95% (.95) = **$51,000 Sales Price**

9. d **$652.08 Average Monthly Rent**

   $75,000 Gross Annual Sales – $50,000 =
   $25,000 Gross Annual Sales Subject to 2.5%

   $$\frac{= \$625 \text{ Annual Percentage Rent}}{\$25,000 \qquad\qquad\qquad\qquad\qquad 2.5\%}$$
   Gross Annual Sales   ×   or .025

   $25,000 × 2.5% (.025) = $625

   $625 Annual Percentage Rent ÷ 12 Months =
   $52.08 Monthly Percentage Rent
   $600 Monthly Minimum Rent + $52.08 Monthly Percentage Rent =
   $652.08 Average Monthly Rent

10. b **30%**

   $525 Monthly Rent × 12 Months = $6,300 Annual Rent

   $$\frac{\div \$6,300 \text{ Annual Rent}}{\$21,000 \text{ Annual Income} \qquad\qquad = \textbf{0.3 or 30\%}}$$

   $6,300 ÷ $21,000 = .30 or **30%**

11. a **$657 Commission to Janice**

$$\frac{= \$4,380 \text{ Full Commission}}{\begin{array}{l}\text{\$73,000} \\ \text{Sales Price}\end{array} \quad \Big| \times \quad \begin{array}{l} 6\% \\ .06\end{array}}$$

$73,000 × 6% (.06) = $4,380
$4,380 Full Commission ÷ 2 Brokers =
$2,190 Broker's Share of the Commission

$$\frac{= \$657 \text{ Janice's Commission}}{\begin{array}{l}\text{\$2,190 Broker's Share} \\ \text{of the Commission}\end{array} \quad \Big| \times \quad \begin{array}{l} 30\% \\ .3\end{array}}$$

$2,190 × 30% (.30) = **$657 Commission**

12. a **10,626.63 Square Feet**

6" ÷ 12 = 0.5' + 75' = 75.5' Frontage
9" ÷ 12 = 0.75' + 140' = 140.75' Depth
140.75' × 75.5' = **10,626.63 Square Feet**

13. c **$1,736,000 Value**

$775 Monthly Rent × 28 Units × 12 Months =
$260,400 Annual Scheduled Gross Income
$260,400 Annual Scheduled Gross Income – 5% Vacancy Rate =
$247,380 Annual Effective Gross Income
$247,380 Annual Effective Gross Income – $82,460 Annual Expenses =
$164,920 Annual Net Operating Income

$$\frac{\$164,920 \text{ Annual Net Operating Income} \div}{\mathbf{= \$1,736,000 \text{ Value}} \quad \Big| \quad \begin{array}{l} 9.5\% \\ \text{or } 0.095\end{array}}$$

$164,920 ÷ 9.5% (.095) = **$1,736,000 Value**

14. a **$127.11 Interest Due**

Seller owes Buyer 10 Days (August 1 through August 10)

$$\frac{= \$4,575.90 \text{ Annual Interest}}{\text{\$43,580 Loan Balance} \quad \Big| \times \quad \begin{array}{l} 10.5\% \\ 0.105\end{array}}$$

$43,580 × 10.5% (.105) = $4,575.90
$4,575.90 Annual Interest ÷ 360 Days = $12.71083 per Day × 10 Days =
$127.11 Interest Due

15. c $5,512.50 for Points and the Origination Fee

2.5 Points Loan Discount + 1 Point Origination Fee = 3.5 Points

= $157,500 Loan	
$175,000 Sales Price	90%
×	or 0.9

$175,000 × 90% or (.90) = $157,500

= $5,512.50 for Points & Origination Fees	
$157,500 Loan	3.5%
×	or 0.035

$157,500 × 3.5% (.035) = **$5,512.50 for Points and Origination Fees**

16. b $316.67 Interest

= $475 Annual Interest	
$5,000 Loan	9.5%
×	or 0.095

$5,000 × 9.5% (.095) = $475
$475 Annual Interest ÷ 12 Months × 8 Months = **$316.67 Interest**

17. d   27,225 Square Feet per Lot

⅛ = 1 ÷ 8 = 0.125 for Streets
100 Acres × 0.125 = 12.5 Acres for Streets
100 Acres − 12.5 Acres for Streets = 87.5 Acres for Lots × 43,560 =
3,811,500 Square Feet ÷ 140 Lots = **27,225 Square Feet per Lot**

18. a $393.38 Tax Proration

Seller owes the Buyer January 1 to April 23

```
   31 January
+  28 February
+  31 March
+  22 April
  112 Days Due
```

$1,282 Annual Tax ÷ 365 Days = $3.51233 per Day × 112 Days =
$393.38 Tax Proration

19. b $1,197.92 Monthly Net Operating Income

$$\frac{= \$14{,}375 \text{ Annual Net Operating Income}}{\$115{,}000 \text{ Investment} \quad \Big| \quad \begin{array}{c} 12.5\% \\ \text{or } 0.125 \end{array}}$$

$115,000 × 12.5% (.125) = $14,375
$14,375 Annual Net Operating Income ÷ 12 Months =
$1,197.92 Monthly Net Operating Income

20. b $1,404 Salesperson's Commission

$$\frac{= \$3{,}510 \text{ Full Commission}}{\$58{,}500 \text{ Sales Price} \quad \Big| \quad \begin{array}{c} 6\% \\ \text{or } 0.06 \end{array}}$$

$58,500 × 6% (.06) = $3,510

$$\frac{= \$1{,}404 \text{ Salesperson's Commission}}{\$3{,}510 \text{ Full Commission} \quad \Big| \quad \begin{array}{c} 40\% \\ \text{or } 0.4 \end{array}}$$

$3,510 × 40% (.40) = **$1,404 Salesperson's Commission**

21. c   20% Profit

348,480 Square Feet × $.75 per Square Foot = $261,360 Cost
348,480 Square Feet ÷ 43,560 = 8 Acres × 2 Lots per Acre = 16 Lots –
3 Lots = 13 Lots Sold × $24,125 Each = $313,625 Total Sales Price
$313,625 Sales Price – $261,360 Cost = $52,265 Profit

$$\frac{\div \$52{,}265 \text{ Profit}}{\$261{,}360 \text{ Cost} \quad \Big| \quad \begin{array}{c} = 0.199973 \\ \textbf{or 20\% Profit} \end{array}}$$

$52,265 ÷ $261,360 = 0.199973 or **20% Profit**

22. a $132.31 Insurance Proration

```
 30  February
−16  Closing Date
 14  Days Left in February
+30  March
+30  April
+30  May
+ 5  June
109  Days Due
```

$437 Annual Premium ÷ 360 Days = $1.21389 per Day × 109 Days Due =
$132.31 Insurance Proration

23. b   9% Annual Interest Rate

$450 × 2 = $900 Annual Interest

$$\frac{÷\ \$900\ \text{Annual Interest}}{\$10,000\ \text{Loan}\ \Big|\ \quad = \textbf{0.9 or 9%}}$$

$900 ÷ $10,000 = **0.9 or 9% Interest Rate**

24. d   117,600 Cubic Feet

120' × 80' = 9,600 Square Feet in Building – 1,200 Square Feet for Office
= 8,400 Square Feet Left in Warehouse × 14' Ceiling =
117,600 Cubic Feet Left in Warehouse

25. b $571,500 Price

$$\frac{\$68,580\ \text{Annual Net Operating Income}\ ÷}{= \textbf{\$571,500 Price}\ \Big|\ \quad\quad \begin{array}{c}12\%\\ \text{or } 0.12\end{array}}$$

$68,580 ÷ 12% (.12) = **$571,500 Price**

26. c $77.90 Interest Proration

Seller owes Buyer 19 Days (April 1 *through* April 19)

$$\frac{= \$1,476\ \text{Annual Interest}}{\$18,450\ \text{Loan Balance}\ \Big|\ \begin{array}{c}\\ ×\end{array}\quad \begin{array}{c}8\%\\ \text{or } 0.08\end{array}}$$

$18,450 × 8% (.08) = $1,476
$1,476 Annual Interest ÷ 360 Days = $4.10 per Day × 19 Days =
$77.90 Interest Proration

27. d $17,625 Today's Value

3.5% Appreciation per Year × 5 Years = 17.5% Total Appreciation
100% Cost + 17.5% Total Appreciation = 117.5% Today's Value

$$\frac{= \$17,625\ \text{Today's Value}}{\$15,000\ \text{Original Cost}\ \Big|\ \begin{array}{c}\\ ×\end{array}\quad \begin{array}{c}117.5\%\\ \text{or } 1.175\end{array}}$$

$15,000 × 117.5% (1.175) = **$17,625 Today's Value**

28. b   11,000 Square Feet Left

150' Depth – 25' Setback = 125' Left
100' Frontage – 6' on One Side – 6' on One Side = 88' Left
125' × 88' = **11,000 Square Feet Left**

29. b $13,000 Annual Rent

$1,000 Monthly Minimum Rent × 12 Months =
$12,000 Annual Minimum Rent
$150,000 Annual Sales − $100,000 = $50,000 Annual Sales Subject to 2%

= $1,000 Annual Percentage Rent		
$50,000 Annual Sales		2%
Subject to 2%	×	or 0.02

$50,000 × 2% (.02) = $1,000

$12,000 Annual Minimum Rent + $1,000 Annual Percentage Rent =
$13,000 Annual Rent

30. a $965.26 Tax Proration

Seller owes Buyer January 1 *to* August 29

```
  31 January
 +28 February
 +31 March
 +30 April
 +31 May
 +30 June
 +31 July
 +28 August
 240 Days Due
```

$1,468 Annual Tax ÷ 365 Days = $4.02192 per Day × 240 Days =
$965.26 Tax Proration

31. c $23,595 Sales Price

1.25 Acres × 43,560 = 54,450 Square Feet ÷ 150' Deep = 363' Frontage ×
$65 per Front Foot = **$23,595 Sales Price**

32. b $80,000 Sales Price

$5,200 Full Commission ÷		
= $80,000		6.5%
		or 0.065

$5,200 ÷ 6.5% (.065) = $80,000 **Sale Price**

33. d **$35,000 Loan**

$20,000 Annual Salary ÷ 12 Months = $1,666.67 Monthly Salary

$$\frac{= \$416.67 \text{ Monthly PITI Payment}}{\$1,666.67 \text{ Monthly Salary} \mid \overset{\text{}}{\times} \quad \begin{array}{c} 25\% \\ \text{or } 0.25 \end{array}}$$

$1,666.67 × 25% = $416.67

$678.24 Annual Tax and Insurance ÷ 12 Months =
$56.52 Monthly Tax and Insurance
$416.67 Monthly PITI Payment – $56.52 Monthly TI =
$360.15 Monthly PI Payment
$360.15 Monthly PI Payment ÷ $10.29 × $1,000 = **$35,000 Loan**

34. b **$46,588.50 Cost**

29' × 34' × 17' = 16,762 Cubic Feet in House
29' × 34' × 8' ÷ 2 = 3,944 Cubic Feet in Roof
16,762 Cubic Feet + 3,944 Cubic Feet = 20,706 Cubic Feet Total ×
$2.25 per Cubic Foot **= $46,588.50 Cost**

35. a **$6,000 Annual Net Operating Income**

$$\frac{= \$6{,}000 \text{ Annual Net Operating Income}}{\$50{,}000 \text{ Investment} \mid \overset{\text{}}{\times} \quad \begin{array}{c} 12\% \\ \text{or } 0.12 \end{array}}$$

$50,000 × 12% (.12) = **$6,000 Annual Net Operating Income**

36. d **$8,500 Loan**

$65.53 Monthly Interest × 12 Months = $786.36 Annual Interest

$$\frac{\$786.36 \text{ Annual Interest} \div}{\begin{array}{c}= \$8{,}501.19 \\ \text{or } \textbf{\$8{,}500 Loan}\end{array} \mid \begin{array}{c} 9.25\% \\ \text{or } 0.0925 \end{array}}$$

$786.36 ÷ 9.25% (.0925) = **$8501.19 Loan**

37. c **30%**

$10,500 Cost of Lot + $93,000 Cost of Home = $103,500 Total Cost
$134,550 Sales Price – $103,500 Total Cost = $31,050 Profit

$$\frac{\div \$31{,}050 \text{ Profit}}{\$103{,}500 \text{ Total Cost} \mid \quad \textbf{= 0.3 or 30\%}}$$

$31,050 ÷ $103,500 = **0.3 or 30%**

38. c $1,495.00 Rent Proration

    30 November
  – 4 Day of Closing
    26 Days Due

$575 Monthly Rent × 3 Units = $1,725 Monthly Rent ÷ 30 Days =
$57.50 per Day × 26 Days = **$1,495 Rent Proration**

39. a $441,400 Value

$1,530 Monthly Expenses × 12 Months = $18,360 Annual Expenses
$62,500 Annual Gross Income – $18,360 Annual Expenses =
$44,140 Annual Net Operating Income

$$\frac{\$44{,}140 \text{ Annual Net Operating Income} \div}{= \mathbf{\$441{,}400 \text{ Value}}} \quad \Big| \quad \begin{array}{c} 10\% \\ \text{or } 0.1 \end{array}$$

$44,140 ÷ 10% (.10) = **$441,400 Value**

40. b $69,160 Property Value

$65,000 Cost of House and Lot – $13,000 Cost of Lot = $52,000 Cost of
House

Lot:
8% Annual Appreciation × 8 Years = 64% Total Appreciation
100% Cost + 64% Total Appreciation = 164% Today's Value

$$\frac{= \$21{,}320 \text{ Today's Value of Lot}}{\$13{,}000 \text{ Cost of Lot}} \quad \begin{array}{c} \\ \times \end{array} \quad \Big| \quad \begin{array}{c} 164\% \\ \text{or } 1.64 \end{array}$$

$13,000 × 164% (1.64) = $21,320

House:
1% Annual Depreciation × 8 Years = 8% Total Depreciation
100% Cost – 8% Total Depreciation = 92% Today's Value

$$\frac{= \$47{,}840 \text{ Today's Value of House}}{\$52{,}000 \text{ Cost of House}} \quad \begin{array}{c} \\ \times \end{array} \quad \Big| \quad \begin{array}{c} 92\% \\ \text{or } 0.92 \end{array}$$

$52,000 × 92% (.92) = $47,940

$21,320 Lot + $47,840 House = **$69,160 Property Value**

41. d $310,000 Sales Price

$121,600 Seller's Net + $31,000 Closing Costs + $135,700 Loan Payoff = $288,300 Sellers Dollars after Commission
100% Sales Price – 7% Commission = 93% Seller's Dollars after Commission

$$\frac{\$288{,}300 \text{ Seller's Dollars after Commission} \div}{= \$310{,}000 \text{ Sales Price} \quad | \quad \begin{array}{c} 93\% \\ \text{or } 0.93 \end{array}}$$

$288,300 ÷ 93% (.93) = **$310,000 Sales Price**

42. c   940 Running Feet

125' + 350' + 125' + 350' – 10' Gate = **940 Running Feet**

43. b   17% Profit

$2,500 Cost × 4 Parcels = $10,000 Total Cost
$1,950 Sales Price × 6 Parcels = $11,700 Sales Price
$11,700 Sales Price – $10,000 Cost = $1,700 Profit

$$\frac{\div \$1{,}700 \text{ Profit}}{\$10{,}000 \text{ Cost} \quad | \quad = \mathbf{0.17 \text{ or } 17\% \text{ Profit}}}$$

$1,700 ÷ $10,000 Cost = 0.17 or **17% Profit**

44. b $80,000 Original Cost

4% Annual Appreciation × 5 Years = 20% Total Appreciation
100% Cost + 20% Total Appreciation = 120% Today's Value

$$\frac{\$96{,}000 \text{ Today's Value} \div}{= \$80{,}000 \text{ Original Cost} \quad | \quad \begin{array}{c} 120\% \\ 1.2 \end{array}}$$

$96,000 ÷ 120% (1.20) = **$80,000 Original Cost**

45. a $2,072 Monthly Payment

$60,000 Annual Salary ÷ 12 Months = $5,000 Bill's Monthly Salary + $2,400 Betty's Monthly Salary = $7,400 Total Monthly Salary

$$\frac{= \$2{,}072 \text{ Monthly Payment}}{\begin{array}{l} \$7{,}400 \text{ Total 28\%} \\ \text{Monthly Salary} \quad \times \end{array} \quad | \quad \text{or } 0.28}$$

$7,400 × 28% (.28) = **$2,072 Monthly Payment**

46. b **18% Annual Interest Rate**

$5,588 Payback (Principal + Interest) – $4,400 Loan (Principal) = $1,188 Interest for 18 Months ÷ 18 Months = $66 Monthly Interest × 12 Months = $792 Annual Interest

$$\frac{÷\ \$792\ \text{Annual Interest}}{\$4,400\ \text{Loan}} \quad\Big|\quad = \textbf{0.18 or 18\% Annual Interest Rate}$$

$792 ÷ $4,400 = 0.18 or **18% Annual Interest Rate**

47. c **$51.75 per Front Foot**

$6,468.75 Price ÷ 125 Front Feet = **$51.75 per Front Foot**

48. c **$2,437.98 Monthly Principal and Interest Payment**

$340,500 Loan ÷ $1,000 × $7.16 = **$2,437.98 Monthly Principal and Interest Payment**

49. a **$3,330 Total Commission**

$$\frac{=\ \$3,000\ \text{Commission}}{\$50,000\ \text{Sales Price}} \quad\Big|\quad \begin{array}{l} 6\% \\ \text{or } 0.06 \end{array}$$
$$\times$$

$50,000 × 6% (.06) = $3,000

$61,000 Total Sales Price – $50,000 Sales Price at 6% = $11,000 Sales Price at 3%

$$\frac{=\ \$330\ \text{Commission}}{\$11,000\ \text{Sales Price}} \quad\Big|\quad \begin{array}{l} 3\% \\ \text{or } 0.03 \end{array}$$
$$\times$$

$11,000 × 3% (.03) = $330
$3,000 Commission + $330 Commission = **$3,330 Total Commission**

50. d **52% Not Taken Up by House**

50' × 100' = 5,000 Square Feet of Lot – 2,400 Square Feet of House = 2,600 Square Feet Not Taken up by House

$$\frac{÷\ 2,600\ \text{Square Feet}}{5,000\ \text{Square Feet Total}} \quad\Big|\quad \begin{array}{l} = \textbf{0.52 or 52\%} \\ \textbf{Not Taken up by House} \end{array}$$

2,600 ÷ 5,000 = **0.52 or 52% Not Taken Up by House**

SAMPLE EXAMINATIONS

■ PREVIEW: TESTING SERVICES

Several commercial organizations produce real estate licensing exams. Each state is free to choose its testing service. In some states, the Real Estate Commission itself writes and administers the examination. In others, the commercial testing service prepares a two-part examination that includes both state-specific license law questions and questions on broader national issues and general principles. Most states use the examinations produced by Applied Measurement Professional (AMP), Psychological System, Inc. (PSI), Promissor (formerly ASI), and Experior Assessments LLC (Experior). However, different states use many other testing services.

In this book, the Chapter Review Questions and the Sample Examinations that follow are generally based on the format and focus of questions of the two services most widely used: Promissor (ASI) and PSI. Your state, however, may use a different testing service. It's possible that the questions you encounter on your licensing examination may look slightly different from the practice questions you've been using here (an "a-b-c-d" format for answer choices rather than a "1-2-3-4" structure, for instance). Don't be flustered; just remember that it's still four choices, no matter what they're called.

The sample examinations included here are not intended to be a review of *Modern Real Estate Practice* or your real estate course. Rather, they are designed to imitate real estate exams, any one of which may emphasize some concepts and ignore others. The *Answer Key* for these sample examinations includes the relevant Chapter from which each question was drawn. Questions that involve mathematical calculations in addition to one or more real estate concepts will refer you to the math skills review in the Math FAQs review included here. If your answer is incorrect, it is advisable to restudy the suggested material. *Note that proration calculations here are based on a 30-day month unless otherwise stated.*

SAMPLE EXAM 1

1. Which of the following is a lien on real estate?
   a. Recorded easement
   b. Recorded mortgage
   c. Encroachment
   d. Deed restriction

2. A sales contract was signed under duress. Which of the following describes this contract?
   a. Voidable
   b. Breached
   c. Discharged
   d. Void

3. A broker receives a check for earnest money from a buyer and deposits the money in the broker's personal interest-bearing checking account over the weekend. This action exposes the broker to a charge of
   a. commingling.
   b. novation.
   c. subrogation.
   d. accretion.

4. A borrower takes out a mortgage loan that requires monthly payments of $875.70 for 20 years and a final payment of $24,095. This is what type of loan?
   a. Wraparound
   b. Accelerated
   c. Balloon
   d. Variable

5. If a borrower computed the interest charged for the previous month on a $60,000 loan balance as $412.50, what is the borrower's interest rate?
   a. 7.5%
   b. 7.75%
   c. 8.25%
   d. 8.5%

6. A broker signs a contract with a buyer. Under the contract, the broker agrees to help the buyer find a suitable property and to represent the buyer in negotiations with the seller. Although the buyer may not sign an agreement with any other broker, the buyer may look for and purchase a property without the broker's assistance. The broker is entitled to payment only if the broker locates the property that is purchased. What kind of agreement has this broker signed?
   a. Exclusive buyer agency agreement
   b. Exclusive-agency buyer agency agreement
   c. Open buyer agency agreement
   d. Option contract

7. A grantor conveys property by delivering a deed. The deed contains five covenants. This is most likely a
   a. general warranty deed.
   b. quitclaim deed.
   c. special warranty deed.
   d. deed in trust.

8. Pat, a real estate broker, does not show nonAsian clients any properties in several traditionally Asian neighborhoods. Pat bases this practice on the need to preserve the valuable cultural integrity of Asian immigrant communities. Which of the following statements is true regarding Pat's policy?
   a. Pat's policy is steering and violates the fair housing laws regardless of Pat's motivation.
   b. Because Pat is not attempting to restrict the rights of any single minority group, the practice does not constitute steering.
   c. Pat's policy is steering, but it does not violate the fair housing laws because Pat is motivated by cultural preservation, not by exclusion or discrimination.
   d. Pat's policy has the effect, but not the intent, of steering.

9. Helen grants a life estate to her son-in-law and stipulates that upon his death, the title to the property will pass to her grandson. This second estate is known as a(n)
   a. remainder.
   b. reversion.
   c. estate at sufferance.
   d. estate for years.

10. A primary feature of property held in joint tenancy is that
    a. a maximum of two people can own the real estate.
    b. the fractional interests of the owners can be different.
    c. additional owners may be added later.
    d. there is always right of survivorship.

11. Alan is a licensed real estate salesperson who has a written contract with his broker that specifies that he will not be treated as an employee. Alan's entire income is from sales commissions rather than an hourly wage. Based on these facts, Alan will be treated by the IRS as

a. a real estate assistant.
b. an employee.
c. a subagent.
d. self-employed.

12. The states in which the owner gives up legal title of mortgaged real estate are known as

a. title theory states.
b. lien theory states.
c. statutory title states.
d. strict title forfeiture states.

13. The form of tenancy that will expire on a specific date is a

a. joint tenancy.
b. tenancy for years.
c. tenancy in common.
d. tenancy by the entirety.

14. A suburban home that lacks sufficient indoor plumbing suffers from which of the following?

a. Functional obsolescence
b. Curable physical deterioration
c. Incurable physical deterioration
d. External obsolescence

15. A developer built a structure that has six stories. Several years later, an ordinance was passed in that area banning any building six stories or higher. This building is a

a. nonconforming use.
b. situation in which the structure would have to be demolished.
c. conditional use.
d. violation of the zoning laws.

16. Assuming that the listing broker and the selling broker in a transaction split their commission equally, what was the sales price of the property if the commission rate was 6.5 percent and the listing broker received $2,593.50?

a. $39,900   c. $79,800
b. $56,200   d. $88,400

17. Robert, a real estate broker, specializes in helping both buyers and sellers with the necessary paperwork involved in transferring property. While Robert is not an agent of either party, Robert may not disclose either party's confidential information to the other. Robert is best described as a(n)

a. buyer's agent.
b. independent contractor.
c. dual agent.
d. transactional broker.

18. Ellen, Mary, and Rhonda owned Bright House as joint tenants. In the year 2000, Ellen died. Last month, Mary died. Based on these facts, which of the following correctly describes Rhonda's remaining ownership interest in Bright House?

a. Joint tenancy with Ellen's and Mary's heirs
b. Tenancy in common with Ellen's and Mary's heirs
c. Severalty
d. Partitioned tenancy by the entirety

19. The listing and selling brokers agree to split a 7 percent commission 50-50 on a $95,900 sale. The listing broker gives the listing salesperson 30 percent of the listing broker's share, and the selling broker gives the selling salesperson 35 percent. How much does the selling salesperson earn from the sale after deducting expenses of $35?

a. $1,139.78   c. $1,183.95
b. $1,174.78   d. $1,971.95

20. Police powers include all of the following EXCEPT

a. zoning.
b. deed restrictions.
c. building codes.
d. subdivision regulations.

21. A seller wants to net $65,000 from the sale of a house after paying the broker's fee of 6 percent. The seller's gross sales price will be

a. $61,100.   c. $68,900
b. $64,752.   d. $69,149

22. Three acres equals how many square feet?
    - a. 43,560
    - b. 130,680
    - c. 156,840
    - d. 27,878,400

23. A buyer is purchasing a condominium unit in a subdivision and obtains financing from a local savings and loan association. In this situation, which of the following best describes this buyer?
    - a. Vendor
    - b. Mortgagor
    - c. Grantor
    - d. Lessor

24. The current value of a property is $40,000. The property is assessed at 40 percent of its current value for real estate tax purposes, with an equalization factor of 1.5 applied to the assessed value. If the tax rate is $4 per $100 of assessed valuation, what is the amount of tax due on the property?
    - a. $640
    - b. $960
    - c. $1,600
    - d. $2,400

25. A building was sold for $60,000, with the purchaser putting 10 percent down and obtaining a loan for the balance. The lending institution charged a 1 percent loan origination fee. What was the total cash used for the purchase?
    - a. $540
    - b. $6,000
    - c. $6,540
    - d. $6,600

26. A parcel of vacant land has an assessed valuation of $274,550. If the assessment is 85 percent of market value, what is the market value?
    - a. $315,732.50
    - b. $320,000.00
    - c. $323,000.00
    - d. $830,333.33

27. Which of the following best describes a capitalization rate?
    - a. Amount determined by the gross rent multiplier
    - b. Rate of return an income property will produce
    - c. Mathematical value determined by a sales price
    - d. Rate at which the amount of depreciation in a property is measured

28. A parcel of land described as "the NW¼ and the SW¼ of Section 6, T4N, R8W of the Third Principal Meridian" was sold for $875 per acre. The listing broker will receive a 5 percent commission on the total sales price. How much will the broker receive?
    - a. $1,750
    - b. $5,040
    - c. $14,000
    - d. $15,040

29. If a house was sold for $40,000 and the buyer obtained an FHA-insured mortgage loan for $38,500, how much money would the buyer pay in discount points if the lender charged four points?
    - a. $385
    - b. $1,500
    - c. $1,540
    - d. $1,600

30. The commission rate is 7¾ percent on a sale of $50,000. What is the dollar amount of the commission?
    - a. $3,500
    - b. $3,875
    - c. $4,085
    - d. $4,585

31. A prospective buyer signs an offer to purchase a residential property. Which of the following circumstances would *not* automatically terminate the offer?
    - a. The buyer signed a written offer to buy a house and then died.
    - b. The buyer revoked the offer between the presentation and a possible acceptance.
    - c. The seller made a counteroffer.
    - d. The seller received a better offer from another buyer.

32. A buyer purchased a home under a land contract. Until the contract is paid in full, the buyer
    - a. holds legal title to the premises.
    - b. has no legal interest in the property.
    - c. possesses a legal life estate in the premises.
    - d. has equitable title in the property.

33. A buyer and a seller sign a contract for the sale of real property. A few days later, they decide to change many of the terms of the contract, while retaining the basic intent to buy and sell. The process by which the new contract replaces the old one is called

a. assignment.
b. novation.
c. assemblage.
d. rescission.

34. Using the services of a mortgage broker, Glen borrowed $4,000 from a private lender. After deducting the loan costs, Glen received $3,747. What is the face amount of the note?

a. $3,747
b. $4,000
c. $4,253
d. $7,747

35. Whose signature is necessary for a signed offer to purchase real estate to become a contract?

a. Buyer's only
b. Buyer's and seller's
c. Seller's only
d. Seller's and seller's broker's

36. A borrower has just made the final payment on a mortgage loan. Regardless of this fact, the records will still show a lien on the mortgaged property until which of the following events occurs?

a. A mortgage satisfaction document is recorded.
b. A reconveyance of the mortgage document is delivered to the mortgage holder.
c. A novation of the mortgage document takes place.
d. An estoppel of the mortgage document is filed with the clerk of the county in which the mortgagee is located.

37. If the annual net income from a commercial property is $22,000 and the capitalization rate is 8 percent, what is the property worth if the income approach is used?

a. $176,000
b. $183,000
c. $200,000
d. $275,000

38. A broker enters into a listing agreement with a seller in which the seller will receive $120,000 from the sale of a vacant lot and the broker will receive any sale proceeds exceeding that amount. This is what type of listing?

a. Exclusive-agency
b. Net
c. Exclusive-right-to-sell
d. Multiple

39. Under a cooperative form of ownership, an owner

a. is a shareholder in the corporation.
b. owns his or her unit outright and a share of the common areas.
c. will have to take out a new mortgage loan on a newly acquired unit.
d. receives a fixed-term lease for the unit.

40. A known defect or a cloud on title to property may be cured by

a. obtaining quitclaim deeds from all appropriate parties.
b. recording the title after closing.
c. paying cash for the property at the settlement.
d. purchasing a title insurance policy at closing.

41. A buyer signed an exclusive-agency buyer agency agreement with a licensee. If the buyer finds a suitable property with no assistance, the licensee is entitled to

a. full compensation from the buyer.
b. full compensation from the seller.
c. partial compensation.
d. no compensation.

42. Under the terms of a net lease, a commercial tenant would usually be directly responsible for paying all of the following property expenses EXCEPT

a. maintenance expenses.
b. mortgage debt service.
c. fire and extended-coverage insurance.
d. real estate taxes.

43. The Civil Rights Act of 1866 prohibits discrimination based on

a. sex.
b. religion.
c. race.
d. familial status.

44. What would it cost to put new carpeting in a room measuring 15 feet by 20 feet if the carpet costs $6.95 per square yard, plus a $250 installation charge?

a. $232
b. $482
c. $610
d. $2,335

45. What is the difference between a general lien and a specific lien?

a. A general lien cannot be enforced in court, while a specific lien can.
b. A specific lien is held by only one person, while a general lien must be held by two or more.
c. A general lien is a lien against personal property, while a specific lien is a lien against real estate.
d. A specific lien is a lien against a certain parcel of real estate, while a general lien covers all of a debtor's property.

46. In an option to purchase real estate, which of the following statements is true of the optionee?

a. The optionee must purchase the property but may do so at any time within the option period.
b. The optionee is limited to a refund of the option consideration if the option is exercised.
c. The optionee cannot obtain third-party financing on the property until after the option has expired.
d. The optionee has no obligation to purchase the property during the option period.

47. The village board of Wright Park has decided that a parking lot would enhance the beauty, safety, and vitality of the community by keeping cars from parking on the streets. Unfortunately, Ann's house is located on land needed for the new parking lot. Based on these facts, which of the following statements is true?

a. Ann's constitutional right to own property cannot be infringed by the village under any circumstances.
b. The village may tear down Ann's house and build the parking lot without paying her any compensation, through the village's constitutional authority under the takings clause.
c. The village may tear down Ann's house, but must first pay her a fair amount for her home.
d. The village may not seize Ann's house because it has insufficient reason to do so.

48. How many acres are there in the N½ of the SW¼ and the NE¼ of the SE¼ of a section?

a. 20
b. 40
c. 80
d. 120

49. Betty's home is the smallest in a neighborhood of large, expensive houses. The effect of the other houses on the value of Betty's home is known as

a. regression.
b. progression.
c. substitution.
d. contribution.

50. A lien that arises as a result of a judgment, estate or inheritance taxes, a decedent's debts, or federal taxes is what sort of lien?

a. Specific
b. General
c. Voluntary
d. Equitable

51. Which of the following will *not* terminate an offer to purchase real estate?

a. Failure to accept the offer within a prescribed period
b. Revocation by the offeror communicated to the offeree after acceptance
c. A conditional acceptance of the offer by the offeree
d. The death of the offeror or offeree

52. Claude and Lucy are joint tenants. Lucy sells her interest to Juan. What is the relationship between Claude and Juan regarding the property?

a. Joint tenants
b. Tenants in common
c. Tenants by the entirety
d. No relationship exists because Lucy cannot sell her joint tenancy interest.

53. Steve and Win enter into a six-month oral lease. If Win defaults, Steve

a. may not bring a court action because leases must be in writing for a court to review them.
b. may not bring a court action because the statute of frauds governs six-month leases.
c. may bring a court action because six-month leases need not be in writing to be enforceable.
d. may bring a court action because the statute of limitations does not apply to oral leases, regardless of their term.

54. On Monday, the buyer offers to purchase a vacant lot for $10,500. On Tuesday, the owner counteroffers to sell the lot for $12,000. On Friday, the owner withdraws the counteroffer and accepts the buyer's original offer of $10,500. Under these circumstances

a. a valid agreement exists because the seller accepted the buyer's offer exactly as it was made, regardless of the fact that it was not accepted immediately.
b. a valid agreement exists because the seller accepted before the buyer provided notice that the offer was withdrawn.
c. no valid agreement exists because the buyer's offer was not accepted within 72 hours of its having been made.
d. no valid agreement exists because the seller's counteroffer was a rejection of the buyer's offer, and once rejected, it cannot be accepted later.

55. Yuri's neighbors use his driveway to reach their garage, which is on their property. Yuri's attorney explains that the neighbors have the right to use the driveway. Yuri's property is the

a. dominant tenement.
b. servient tenement.
c. fee simple defeasible estate.
d. fee simple determinable estate.

56. If the quarterly interest at 7.5 percent is $562.50, what is the principal amount of the loan?

a. $7,500
b. $15,000
c. $30,000
d. $75,000

57. A deed conveys ownership to the grantee "as long as the existing building is not torn down." What type of estate does this deed create?

a. Fee simple determinable estate
c. Homestead estate
b. Fee simple absolute estate
d. Life estate pur autre vie, with the measuring life being the building's expected structural lifetime

58. If the mortgage loan is 80 percent of the appraised value of a house and the interest rate of 8% amounts to $460 for the first month, what is the appraised value of the house?

a. $69,000
b. $71,875
c. $86,250
d. $92,875

59. Local zoning ordinances may regulate all of the following EXCEPT the

a. height of buildings in an area.
b. density of population.
c. appropriate use of buildings in an area.
d. market value of a property.

60. A broker took a listing and later discovered that the client had been declared incompetent by a court. What is the current status of the listing?

a. The listing is unaffected because the broker acted in good faith as the owner's agent.

b. The listing is of questionable value to the broker because the contract is voidable.

c. The listing entitles the broker to collect a commission from the client's guardian or trustee if the broker produces a buyer.

d. The listing must be renegotiated between the broker and the client, based on the new information.

61. After a borrower's default on home mortgage loan payments, the lender obtained a court order to foreclose on the property. At the foreclosure sale, the property sold for $64,000; the unpaid balance on the loan at the time of foreclosure was $78,000. What must the lender do to recover the $14,000 that the borrower still owes?

a. Sue for specific performance
b. Sue for damages
c. Seek a deficiency judgment
d. Seek a judgment by default

62. Which of the following is forbidden by the federal Fair Housing Act of 1968?

a. Limitation by religion and nationality in the sale of a single-family home where the property is not advertised by the listing broker

b. Limitation to members only in noncommercial lodgings of a private club

c. Limitations against familial status and disability in the rental of a unit in an owner-occupied three-family dwelling when no discriminatory advertising is used

d. Limitation by religion and sex in noncommercial housing in a convent or monastery

63. A buyer purchases a $37,000 property, depositing $3,000 as earnest money. If the buyer obtains a 75 percent loan-to-value loan on the property, no additional items are prorated, and there are no closing costs to the buyer, how much more cash will the buyer need at the settlement?

a. $3,250   c. $5,250
b. $3,500   d. $6,250

64. Broker Kay arrives to present a purchase offer to Dora, who is seriously ill, and finds Dora's son and daughter-in-law also present. The son and daughter-in-law angrily urge Dora to accept the offer, even though it is much less than the asking price for the property. If Dora accepts the offer, she may not be bound by it because

a. Kay improperly presented an offer that was less than the asking price.

b. Kay's failure to protect Dora from the son and daughter-in-law constituted a violation of Kay's fiduciary duties.

c. Dora's rights under the ADA have been violated by the son and daughter-in-law.

d. Dora was under undue influence from the son and daughter-in-law, so the contract is voidable.

65. Maria sold a property to Wally. The deed of conveyance contained only the following guarantee: "This property was not encumbered during the time Maria owned it except as noted in this deed." What type of deed makes such a covenant?

a. General warranty
b. Special warranty
c. Bargain and sale
d. Quitclaim

66. Stuart and Charlotte, who are not married, own a parcel of real estate. Each owns an undivided interest, with Stuart owning one-third and Charlotte owning two-thirds. The form of ownership under which Stuart and Charlotte own their property is

a. severalty.
b. joint tenancy.
c. tenancy at will.
d. tenancy in common.

67. Todd agrees to purchase a house for $84,500. Todd pays $2,000 as earnest money and obtains a new mortgage loan for $67,600. The purchase contract provides for a March 15 settlement. Todd and the sellers prorate the previous year's real estate taxes of $1,880.96, which have been prepaid. Todd has additional closing costs of $1,250, and the sellers have other closing costs of $850. How much cash must Todd bring to the settlement?

a. $16,389   c. $17,839
b. $17,639   d. $19,639

68. A broker listed a house for $47,900. A member of a racial minority group saw the house and was interested in it. When the prospective buyer asked the broker the price of the house, the broker said it was listed for $53,000 and that the seller was very firm on the price. Under the federal Fair Housing Act of 1968, such a statement is

a. legal because the law requires only that the buyer be given the opportunity to buy the house.
b. legal because the representation was made by the broker and not directly by the owner.
c. illegal because the difference in the offering price and the quoted price was greater than 10%.
d. illegal because the terms of the potential sale were changed for the prospective buyer.

69. Lu placed a property in a trust. When Lu died, her will directed the trustee to sell the property and distribute the proceeds of the sale to Lu's heirs. The trustee sold property in accordance with the will. What type of deed was delivered at settlement?

a. Trustee's deed
b. Trustor's deed
c. Deed of trust
d. Reconveyance deed

70. An appraiser has been hired to prepare an appraisal report of a property for loan purposes. The property is an elegant old mansion that is now used as a restaurant. To which approach to value should the appraiser probably give the greatest weight when making this appraisal?

a. Income
b. Sales comparison
c. Replacement cost
d. Reproduction cost

71. A borrower applies for a mortgage, and the loan officer suggests that the borrower consider a term mortgage loan. Which of the following statements best explains what the loan officer means?

a. All of the interest is paid at the end of the term.
b. The debt is partially amortized over the life of the loan.
c. The length of the term is limited by state law.
d. The entire principal amount is due at the end of the term.

72. Valley Place is a condominium community with a swimming pool, tennis courts, and biking trail. These facilities are most likely owned by the

a. Valley Place condominium board.
b. corporation in which the unit owners hold stock.
c. unit owners in the form of proportional divided interests.
d. unit owners in the form of percentage undivided interests.

In questions 73 and 74, identify how each item would be entered on a closing statement in a typical real estate transaction.

73. The buyer's earnest money deposit is a

a. credit to buyer only.
b. credit to seller, debit to buyer.
c. credit to buyer and seller.
d. debit to buyer only.

74. Prepaid insurance and tax reserves, where the buyer assumes the mortgage, is a

a. credit to buyer, debit to seller.
b. credit to seller only.
c. debit to seller only.
d. debit to buyer, credit to seller.

75. Real property can become personal property by the process known as

a. annexation.   c. hypothecation.
b. severance.   d. accretion.

76. Julie and Steve are next-door neighbors. Steve gives Julie permission to park a camper in Steve's yard for a few weeks. Steve does not charge Julie rent for the use of the yard. Steve has given Julie a(n)

a. revocable trust.
b. estate for years.
c. license.
d. permissive encroachment.

77. What is the cost of constructing a fence 6 feet, 6 inches high, around a lot measuring 90 feet by 175 feet, if the cost of erecting the fence is $1.25 per linear foot and the cost of materials is $.825 per square foot of fence?

a. $1,752   c. $2,084
b. $2,054   d. $3,505

78. Sally signs a listing agreement with broker Eric. Broker Nancy obtains a buyer for the house, and Eric does not receive a commission. Eric does not sue Sally, even though Sally compensated Nancy. The listing agreement between Sally and Eric was probably which of the following?

a. Exclusive-right-to-sell
b. Open
c. Exclusive-agency
d. Dual-agency

79. Antitrust laws do not prohibit

a. real estate companies agreeing on fees charged to sellers.
b. real estate brokers allocating markets based on the value of homes.
c. real estate companies allocating markets based on the location of commercial buildings.
d. real estate salespersons within the same office agreeing on a standard commission rate.

80. Tony leased an apartment from Laverne. Because Laverne failed to perform routine maintenance, the apartment building's central heating plant broke down in the fall. Laverne neglected to have the heating system repaired, and Tony had no heat for the first six weeks of winter. Tony had reported this problem repeatedly to Laverne. Although eight months remained on Tony's lease, Tony moved out of the apartment and refused to pay any rent. If Laverne sues to recover the outstanding rent, which of the following would be Tony's best defense?

a. Because Tony lived in the apartment for more than 25 percent of the lease term, he was entitled to move out at any time without penalty.
b. Tony was entitled to vacate the premises because the landlord's failure to repair the heating system constituted abandonment.
c. Because the apartment was made uninhabitable, the landlord's actions constituted actual eviction.
d. The landlord's actions constituted constructive eviction.

SAMPLE EXAM 2

1. A tenant's landlord plans to sell the building in which the tenant lives to the state so that a freeway can be built. The tenant's lease has expired, but the landlord permits the tenant to stay in the apartment until the building is torn down. The tenant continues to pay the rent as prescribed in the lease. What kind of tenancy does this tenant have?
   a. Holdover tenancy
   b. Month-to-month tenancy
   c. Tenancy at sufferance
   d. Tenancy at will

2. The owner of a house wants to fence the yard for the family pet. When the fence is erected, the fencing materials become real estate through
   a. severance.   c. annexation.
   b. subrogation.   d. attachment.

3. Glen is interested in selling his house as quickly as possible and believes that the best way to do this is to have several brokers compete against each other for the commission. Glen's listing agreements with four different brokers specifically promise that if one of them finds a buyer for Glen's property, Glen will be obligated to pay a commission to that broker only. What type of agreement has Glen entered into?
   a. Executed   c. Unilateral
   b. Discharged   d. Bilateral

4. In some states, by paying the debt after a foreclosure sale, the delinquent borrower has the right to regain the property under which of the following?
   a. Novation   c. Reversion
   b. Redemption   d. Recovery

5. Wally, owner of the Circle M ranch, enters into a sale-and-leaseback agreement with Glenda. Which of the following statements is true of this arrangement?
   a. Wally retains title to the ranch.
   b. Glenda receives possession of the property.
   c. Glenda is the lessor.
   d. Wally is the lessor.

6. Todd is a real estate broker employed by buyer Maria. When Todd finds a property that Maria might be interested in buying, he is careful to find out as much as possible about the property's owners and why their property is on the market. Todd's efforts to keep Maria informed of all facts that could affect a transaction is the duty of
   a. accounting.   c. confidentiality.
   b. loyalty.   d. disclosure.

7. A parcel of vacant land 80 feet wide and 200 feet deep was sold for $200 per front foot. How much money would a salesperson receive as a 60 percent share in the 10 percent commission?
   a. $640   c. $1,600
   b. $960   d. $2,400

8. Which of the following situations does not violate the federal Fair Housing Act of 1968?
   a. The refusal of a property manager to rent an apartment to a Catholic couple who are otherwise qualified
   b. The general policy of a loan company to avoid granting home improvement loans to individuals living in transitional neighborhoods
   c. The intentional neglect of a broker to show an Asian family any property listings in all-white neighborhoods
   d. A widowed woman's insistence on renting her spare bedroom only to another widowed woman

9. If a storage tank that measures 12 feet by 9 feet by 8 feet is designed to store a gas that costs $1.82 per cubic foot, what does it cost to fill the tank to one-half of its capacity?
   a. $685   c. $864
   b. $786   d. $1,572

10. A buyer bought a house for $125,000. The house, which had originally sold for $118,250, appraised for $122,500. Based on these facts, if the buyer applies for an 80 percent mortgage, what will be the amount of the loan?
    a. $94,600   c. $100,000
    b. $98,000   d. $106,750

11. A purchaser offers to buy a seller's property by signing a purchase contract. The seller accepts the offer. What kind of title interest does the buyer have in the property at this point?

    a. Legal
    b. Equitable
    c. Defeasible
    d. The buyer has no title interest at this point.

12. Which of the following federal laws requires that finance charges be stated as an annual percentage rate?

    a. Truth-in-Lending Act
    b. Real Estate Settlement Procedures Act (RESPA)
    c. Equal Credit Opportunity Act (ECOA)
    d. Federal Fair Housing Act

13. Frank signed a 90-day listing agreement with a broker. Two weeks later, Frank was killed in an accident. What is the present status of the listing?

    a. The listing agreement is binding on Frank's estate for the remainder of the 90 days.
    b. Because Frank's intention to sell was clearly defined, the listing agreement is still in effect and the broker may proceed to market the property on behalf of Frank's estate.
    c. The listing agreement is binding on Frank's estate only if the broker can produce an offer to purchase the property within the remainder of the listing period.
    d. The listing agreement was terminated automatically when Frank died.

14. Marge conveys the ownership of an office building to a nursing home. The nursing home agrees that the rental income will pay for the expenses of caring for Marge's parents. When Marge's parents die, ownership of the office building will revert to Marge. The estate held by the nursing home is a

    a. remainder life estate.
    b. legal life estate.
    c. life estate pur autre vie.
    d. temporary leasehold estate.

15. Henry is a real estate broker. Betty signs a buyer's brokerage agreement under which Henry will help Betty find a three-bedroom house in the $85,000 to $100,000 price range. Sue comes into Henry's office and signs a listing agreement to sell Sue's two-bedroom condominium for $70,000. Based on these facts, which of the following statements is true?

    a. Betty is Henry's client; Sue is Henry's customer.
    b. Betty is Henry's customer; Sue is Henry's client.
    c. While both Betty and Sue are clients, Henry owes the fiduciary duties of an agent only to Sue.
    d. Because both Betty and Sue are Henry's clients; Henry owes the fiduciary duties of an agent to both.

16. In a township of 36 sections, which of the following statements is true?

    a. Section 31 lies to the east of Section 32.
    b. Section 18 is by law set aside for school purposes.
    c. Section 6 lies in the northeast corner of the township.
    d. Section 16 lies to the north of Section 21.

17. A licensee who is representing a seller is asked by the client to make sure that the deed does not reveal the actual sales price. In this case, the licensee

    a. must inform the client that only the actual price of the real estate may appear on the deed.
    b. may ask that a deed be prepared that shows only nominal consideration of $10.
    c. should inform the seller that either the full price should be stated in the deed or all references to consideration should be removed from it.
    d. may show a price on the deed other than the actual price, provided that the variance is not greater than 10 percent of the purchase price.

18. A broker obtained a listing agreement to act as the agent in the sale of a house. A buyer has been found for the property, and all agreements have been signed. As an agent for the seller, the broker is responsible for which of the following?

a. Completing the buyer's loan application
b. Making sure that the buyer receives copies of all documents the seller is required to deliver to the buyer
c. Ensuring that the buyer is qualified for the new mortgage loan
d. Scheduling the buyer's inspection of the property

19. A broker's office policy is that the salesperson's share of a commission is 65 percent. What is the salesperson's compensation if the sales price of a property is $195,000 and the broker is entitled to a 7½ percent commission?

a. $950.63   c. $9,506.25
b. $8,872.50   d. $95,062.50

20. Which of the following is one of the components an appraiser would use in preparing a cost-approach appraisal?

a. Estimate the replacement cost of the improvements
b. Deduct for the depreciation of the land and buildings
c. Determine the original cost and adjust for depreciation
d. Review the sales prices of comparable properties

21. When a mortgage lender provides the buyer with statements of all fees and charges the seller will incur, the lender is complying with which of the following federal laws?

a. Equal Credit Opportunity Act (ECOA)
b. Truth-in-Lending Act (Regulation Z)
c. Real Estate Settlement Procedures Act (RESPA)
d. Fair Housing Act

22. The landlord of an apartment building neglected to repair the building's plumbing system. As a result, the apartments did not receive water, as provided by the leases. If a tenant's unit becomes uninhabitable, which of the following would most likely result?

a. Suit for possession
b. Claim of constructive eviction
c. Tenancy at sufferance
d. Suit for negligence

23. Paul conveys a life estate to Murray. Under the terms of Paul's conveyance, the property will pass to Teri on Murray's death. Which of the following best describes Teri's interest in the property during Murray's lifetime?

a. Remainder
b. Reversion
c. Life estate pur autre vie
d. Redemption

24. On a settlement statement, prorations for unpaid real estate taxes are shown as a

a. credit to the seller and a debit to the buyer.
b. debit to the seller and a credit to the buyer.
c. credit to both the seller and the buyer.
d. debit to both the seller and the buyer.

25. What type of lease establishes a rental payment and requires the lessor to pay for the taxes, insurance, and maintenance on the property?

a. Percentage   c. Expense-only
b. Net   d. Gross

26. A conventional loan was closed on July 1 for $57,200 at 13.5 percent interest amortized over 25 years at $666.75 per month. Using a 360-day year, what would the principal amount be after the monthly payment was made August 1?

a. $56,533.25   c. $57,065.35
b. $56,556.50   d. $57,176.75

27. In the preceding question, what would the interest portion of the payment be?

a. $610.65   c. $643.50
b. $620.25   d. $666.75

28. A seller listed her home with a licensee for $90,000 but tells the licensee, who is acting as a seller's agent, "I've got to sell quickly because of a job transfer. If necessary, I can accept a price as low as $75,000." The licensee tells a prospective buyer to offer $80,000 "because the seller is desperate to sell." The seller accepts the buyer's offer. In this situation, which of the following statements is true?

   a. The licensee's action did not violate any agency relationship with the seller because the licensee did not actually reveal the seller's lowest acceptable price.
   b. The licensee violated an established agency relationship with the seller.
   c. The licensee acted properly to obtain a quick offer on the seller's property, in accordance with the seller's instructions.
   d. The licensee violated established fiduciary duties toward the buyer by failing to disclose that the seller would accept a lower price than the buyer offered.

29. Which of the following best describes the capitalization rate under the income approach to estimating the value of real estate?

   a. Rate at which a property increases in value
   b. Rate of return a property earns as an investment
   c. Rate of capital required to keep a property operating most efficiently
   d. Maximum rate of return allowed by law on an investment

30. On a settlement statement, the cost of the lender's title insurance policy required for a new loan is usually shown as which of the following?

   a. Credit to the seller
   b. Credit to the buyer
   c. Debit to the seller
   d. Debit to the buyer

31. An FHA-insured loan in the amount of $57,500 at 8½ percent for 30 years was closed on July 17. The first monthly payment is due on September 1. Using a 360-day year and assuming that interest is being paid for the day of closing, what was the amount of the interest adjustment the buyer had to make at the settlement?

   a. $0
   b. $190.07
   c. $230.80
   d. $407.29

32. If a home that cost $142,500 three years ago is now valued at 127 percent of its original cost, what is its current market value?

   a. $164,025
   b. $172,205
   c. $174,310
   d. $180,975

33. A buyer makes an offer on a property and the seller accepts. Three weeks later, the buyer announces that "the deal's off" and refuses to go through with the sale. If the seller is entitled to keep the buyer's earnest money deposit, it is most likely because there is what kind of clause in the sales contract?

   a. Liquidated damages clause
   b. Contingent damages clause
   c. Actual damages clause
   d. Revocation clause

34. A search of the public record regarding title to a property is most likely to provide information about which of the following?

   a. Encroachments
   b. Rights of parties in possession
   c. Inaccurate survey
   d. Mechanics' liens

35. A rectangular lot is worth $193,600. This value is the equivalent of $4.40 per square foot. If one lot dimension is 200 feet, what is the other dimension?

   a. 110 feet
   b. 220 feet
   c. 400 feet
   d. 880 feet

36. A broker listed a property at an 8 percent commission rate. After the property was sold and the settlement had taken place, the seller discovered that the broker had been listing similar properties at 6 percent commission rates. Based on this information, which of the following statements is true?
    a. The broker has done nothing wrong because a commission rate is always negotiable between the parties.
    b. If the broker inflated the usual commission rate for the area, the broker may be subject to discipline by the state real estate commission.
    c. The seller is entitled to rescind the transaction based on the principle of lack of reality of consent.
    d. The seller is entitled to a refund from the broker of 2 percent of the commission.

37. Marge has six months remaining on her apartment lease. Marge's monthly rent is $875. Marge moves out of the apartment, and Terry moves in. Terry pays Marge a monthly rental of $700, and Marge continues paying the full rental amount under her lease to the landlord. When Marge's lease term expires, Terry will either move out or sign a new lease with the landlord. This is an example of
    a. assignment.
    b. subletting.
    c. rescission and renewal.
    d. surrender.

38. One broker asked another, "Will I have to prove that I was the procuring cause in order to collect a commission if my seller sells the property without my help?" The other broker answered, "No, not if you have an
    a. option listing."
    b. open listing."
    c. exclusive-agency listing."
    d. exclusive-right-to-sell listing."

39. The capitalization rate on a property reflects (among other things) which of the following factors?
    a. Risk of the investment
    b. Replacement cost of the improvements
    c. Real estate taxes
    d. Debt service

40. An investment property now worth $180,000 was purchased seven years ago for $142,000. At the time of the purchase, the land was valued at $18,000. Assuming a 31½-year life for straight-line depreciation purposes, what is the present book value of the property?
    a. $95,071   c. $114,444
    b. $113,071   d. $126,000

41. After Nell purchased a property from Erika, they both decided to rescind the recorded transfer. To do this, which of the following must happen?
    a. Nell must return the deed to Erika.
    b. The parties must record a notice of rescission.
    c. The parties must simply destroy the original deed in the presence of witnesses.
    d. Nell must make a new deed to Erika.

42. A farmer owns the W½ of the NW¼ of the NW¼ of a section. The adjoining property can be purchased for $300 per acre. Owning all of the NW¼ of the section would cost the farmer
    a. $6,000.   c. $42,000.
    b. $12,000.   d. $48,000.

43. A broker received a deposit, along with a written offer from a buyer. The offer stated: "The offeror will leave this offer open for the seller's acceptance for a period of ten days." On the fifth day, and before acceptance by the seller, the offeror notified the broker that the offer was withdrawn and demanded the return of the deposit. Which of the following statements is true in this situation?

   a. The offeror cannot withdraw the offer; it must be held open for the full ten-day period, as promised.

   b. The offeror has the right to withdraw the offer and secure the return of the deposit any time before being notified of the seller's acceptance.

   c. The offeror can withdraw the offer, and the seller and the broker will each retain one-half of the forfeited deposit.

   d. While the offeror can withdraw the offer, the broker is legally entitled to declare the deposit forfeited and retain all of it in lieu of the lost commission.

44. For each new tenant that the property manager signs, a building's owner pays an 8½ percent commission, based on the unit's annualized rent. Last year, the manager signed five new tenants. Three of the apartments rented for $795 per month; one rented for $1,200 per month; and one rented for $900 per month. What was the total amount of the manager's new-tenant commissions for that year?

   a. $381.23   c. $3,685.47

   b. $2,952.90   d. $4,574.70

45. The monthly rent on a warehouse was $1 per cubic yard. Assuming the warehouse was 36 feet by 200 feet by 12 feet high, what would the annual rent be?

   a. $3,200   c. $38,400

   b. $9,600   d. $115,200

46. If a veteran wishes to refinance a home by changing to a VA-guaranteed loan and the lender insists on 3½ discount points, which of the following options is available to the veteran?

   a. Refinance with a VA loan, provided the lender charges no discount points

   b. Refinance with a VA loan, provided the lender charges no more than two discount points

   c. Be required to pay a maximum of 1% of the loan as an origination fee

   d. Proceed with the refinance loan and pay the discount points

47. Gloria owns two properties: Redacre and Brownacre. Gloria conveys Redacre to Sue with no restrictions; Sue holds all rights to Redacre forever. Gloria then conveys Brownacre to Tom "so long as no real estate broker or salesperson ever sets foot on the property." If a broker or salesperson visits Brownacre, ownership will revert to Gloria. Based on these two conveyances, which of the following statements is true?

   a. Sue holds Redacre in fee simple; Tom holds Brownacre in fee simple determinable.

   b. Sue holds Redacre in fee simple absolute; Tom holds Brownacre in fee simple defeasible, subject to a condition subsequent.

   c. Tom may not transfer ownership of Brownacre without Gloria's permission.

   d. Gloria has retained a right of reentry with regard to Brownacre.

48. A real estate transaction had a closing date of November 15. The seller, who was responsible for costs up to and including the date of settlement, had already paid the property taxes of $1,116 for the calendar year. On the closing statement, the buyer would be

   a. debited $139.50.

   b. debited $976.50.

   c. credited $139.50.

   d. credited $976.50.

49. An agreement that names a new tenant who agrees to take on the obligations of the prior tenant and that ends the obligations of the prior tenant—all with the landlords formal approval is known as a(n)

    a. assumption.   c. surrender.

    b. novation.   d. breach.

50. A purchaser buys a house for $234,500 by making a $25,000 cash down payment and taking out a $209,500 mortgage for 30 years. The lot value is $80,000. If the purchaser wants to depreciate the property over a period of 31½ years, how much will be the annual depreciation amount using the straight-line method?

    a. $3,818.18   c. $4,904.76

    b. $4,709.09   d. $7,444.44

51. A property manager leased a store for three years. The first year, the store's rent was $1,000 per month, and the rent was to increase 10 percent per year thereafter. The manager received a 7 percent commission for the first year, 5 percent for the second year, and 3 percent for the balance of the lease. The total commission earned by the property manager was

    a. $840.   c. $1,936.

    b. $1,613.   d. $2,785.

52. Against a recorded deed from the owner of record, the party with the weakest position is a

    a. person with a prior unrecorded deed and who is not in possession.

    b. person in possession with a prior unrecorded deed.

    c. tenant in possession with nine months remaining on the lease.

    d. painter who is half-finished painting the house at the time of the sale and who has not yet been paid.

53. Alan and Betsy are a married couple who file their income taxes jointly. Last year they sold their home for $340,000. Seven years ago when they were first married they bought the house for $250,000 and have lived in it ever since. Based on these facts, which of the following statements is true?

    a. Under current tax law, Alan and Betsy will owe a capital gains tax this year on their $90,000 gain.

    b. Current tax law permits Alan and Betsy to exclude up to $250,000 in capital gain from their income tax.

    c. Because their gain is less than $500,000, Alan and Betsy will owe no capital gains tax this year.

    d. Under current tax law, Alan and Betsy are entitled to a penalty-free withdrawal of up to $10,000 from a 401(k) retirement account to use as a down-payment.

54. A squatter moved into an abandoned home and lived there for some years. Ultimately the squatter was granted title to the property by a court. Which of the following elements is *not* basic to acquiring title in this manner?

    a. Permission of the true owner

    b. Open and notorious use

    c. Occupancy for a period of time prescribed by state law

    d. Occupancy hostile to the best interests of the true owner

55. Wilma, Frank, and Judy are joint tenants. Judy sells her interest to Laura, and then Frank dies. As a result, which of the following statements is true?

    a. Frank's heirs are joint tenants with Laura and Wilma.

    b. Frank's heirs and Wilma are joint tenants, but Laura is a tenant in common.

    c. Wilma is a tenant in common with Laura and Frank's heirs.

    d. Wilma and Laura are tenants in common.

56. In a settlement statement, the selling price *always* is

a. a debit to the buyer.
b. a debit to the seller.
c. a credit to the buyer.
d. greater than the loan amount.

57. The state wants to acquire a strip of farmland to build a highway. Does the state have the right to acquire this land for public use?

a. Yes; the state's right is called *condemnation*.
b. Yes; the state's right is called *eminent domain*.
c. Yes; the state's right is called *escheat*.
d. No; under the U.S. Constitution, private property never may be taken by state governments or by the federal government.

58. Robert died, and his estate was distributed according to his will as follows: 54 percent to his spouse; 18 percent to his children; 16 percent to his grandchildren; and the remainder to his college. The college received $79,000. How much did Robert's children receive?

a. $105,333   c. $355,500
b. $118,500   d. $658,333

59. Which of the following is an example of external obsolescence?

a. Numerous pillars supporting the ceiling in a store
b. Leaks in the roof of a warehouse, making the premises unusable and therefore unrentable
c. Coal cellar in a house with central heating
d. Vacant, abandoned, and run-down buildings in an area

60. Which of the following phrases, when placed in a print advertisement, would most nearly comply with the requirements of the Truth-in-Lending Act (Regulation Z)?

a. "12 percent interest"
b. "12 percent rate"
c. "12 percent annual interest"
d. "12 percent annual percentage rate"

61. Which of the following statements is *false* regarding a capitalization rate?

a. The rate increases when the risk increases.
b. An increase in rate. while other elements remain the same, means a decrease in value.
c. The net income is divided by the rate to estimate value.
d. A decrease in rate, while other elements remain the same, results in a decrease in value.

62. The Equal Credit Opportunity Act (ECOA) makes it illegal for lenders to refuse credit to or otherwise discriminate against which of the following applicants?

a. Parent of twins who receives public assistance and who cannot afford the monthly mortgage payments
b. New homebuyer who does not have a credit history
c. Single person who receives public assistance
d. Unemployed person with no job prospects and no identifiable source of income

63. When Paul died, a deed was found in his desk drawer. While the deed had never been recorded, it was signed, dated, and acknowledged. The deed gave Paul's house to a local charity. Paul's will, however, provided as follows: "I leave all of the real and personal property that I own to my beloved nephew, Rupert." In this situation, the house most likely will go to the

a. charity because acknowledgment creates a presumption of delivery.
b. charity because Paul's intent was clear from the deed.
c. nephew because Paul still owned the house when he died.
d. nephew because the deed had not been recorded.

64. If a borrower takes out a $90,000 loan at 7½ percent interest to be repaid at the end of 15 years with interest paid annually, what is the total interest that the borrower will pay over the life of the loan?

a. $10,125   c. $101,250
b. $80,000   d. $180,000

65. After an offer is accepted, the seller finds that the broker was the undisclosed agent for the buyer as well as the agent for the seller. The seller may
    a. withdraw without obligation to broker or buyer.
    b. withdraw, but would be subject to liquidated damages.
    c. withdraw, but only with the concurrence of the buyer.
    d. refuse to sell, but would be subject to a suit for specific performance.

66. To net the owner $90,000 after a 6 percent commission is paid, the list price would have to be
    a. $95,400.   c. $95,906.
    b. $95,745.   d. $96,000.

67. Which of the following would most likely be legal under the provisions of the Civil Rights Act of 1968?
    a. A lender refuses to make loans in areas where more than 25 percent of the population is Hispanic.
    b. A private social club that discriminates against no protected group in granting membership, refuses to rent a suite in its members-only vacation facility to a Nigerian family who are not members of the club.
    c. A church excludes African Americans from membership and rents its nonprofit housing to church members only.
    d. A licensee directs prospective buyers away from areas where they are likely to feel uncomfortable because of their race.

68. It is discovered after a sale that the land parcel is 10 percent smaller than the seller represented it to be. The licensee who passed this information on to the buyer is
    a. not liable as long as the licensee only repeated the seller's data.
    b. not liable if the misrepresentation was unintentional.
    c. not liable if the buyer actually inspected the parcel.
    d. liable if the licensee knew or should have known of the discrepancy.

69. On a residential lot 70 feet square, the side yard building setbacks are 10 feet, the front yard setback is 25 feet, and the rear yard setback is 20 feet. The maximum possible size for a single-story structure would be how many square feet?
    a. 1,000   c. 1,250
    b. 1,200   d. 4,900

70. Which of the following is not a violation of the Real Estate Settlement Procedures Act (RESPA)?
    a. Providing a HUD-1 Uniform Settlement Statement to a borrower one day before the closing
    b. Accepting a kickback on a loan subject to RESPA requirements
    c. Requiring the buyer to use a particular title insurance company
    d. Accepting a fee or charging for services that were not performed

71. The rescission provisions of the Truth-in-Lending Act (Regulation Z) apply to which of the following transactions?
    a. Home purchase loans
    b. Construction lending
    c. Business financing
    d. Consumer credit

72. A property has a net income of $30,000. An appraiser decides to use a 12 percent capitalization rate rather than a 10 percent rate on this property. The use of the higher rate results in
    a. a 2% increase in the appraised value.
    b. a $50,000 increase in the appraised value.
    c. a $50,000 decrease in the appraised value.
    d. no change in the appraised value.

73. The section in a purchase contract that would provide for the buyer to forfeit any earnest money if the buyer fails to complete the purchase is known as a provision for
    a. liquidated damages.
    b. punitive damages.
    c. hypothecation.
    d. subordination.

74. In one commercial building, the tenant intends to start a small health food shop. In an identical adjacent building is a showroom leased to a major national retailing chain. Both tenants have long-term leases with identical rents. If the appraiser uses a capitalization rate for the store leased to the national retailing chain higher than the rate for the other building

a. the indicated value of the chain store property will be lower than the indicated value of the food shop property.

b. the indicated value of the chain store property will be higher than the indicated value of the food shop property.

c. the appraiser would then be compelled to make use of the sales comparison approach to value.

d. it would indicate the appraiser believes a building occupied by a chain store tenant is more valuable than an identical one occupied by a health food shop.

75. An insurance company agreed to provide a developer with financing for a shopping center at 11 percent interest plus an equity position. What type of loan is this?

a. Package   c. Open-end
b. Participation   d. Blanket

76. A $100,000 loan at 12 percent could be amortized with monthly payments of $1,200.22 on a 15-year basis or payments of $1,028.63 on a 30-year basis. The 30-year loan results in total payments of what percent of the 15-year total payments?

a. 146%   c. 171%
b. 158%   d. 228%

77. According to a broker's CMA, a property is worth $125,000. The homeowner bought the property for $90,000 and added $50,000 in improvements, for a total of $140,000. The property sold for $122,500. Which of these amounts represents the property's market value?

a. $90,000   c. $125,500
b. $122,500   d. $140,000

78. What will be the amount of tax payable where the property's assessed value is $85,000 and the tax rate is 40 mills in a community in which an equalization factor of 110 percent is used?

a. $2,337.50   c. $3,700.40
b. $3,090.91   d. $3,740.00

79. In a settlement statement, how will a proration of prepaid water, gas and electric charges be reflected?

a. Debit to the seller, credit to the buyer
b. Debit to the buyer, credit to the seller
c. Debit to the buyer only
d. Credit to the seller only

80. An apartment manager decides not to purchase flood insurance. Instead, the manager installs raised platforms in the basement storage areas and has the furnace placed on eight-inch legs. This form of risk management is known as

a. avoiding the risk.
b. controlling the risk.
c. retaining the risk.
d. transferring the risk.

GLOSSARY

abstract of title   The condensed history of a title to a particular parcel of real estate, consisting of a summary of the original grant and all subsequent conveyances and encumbrances affecting the property and a certification by the abstractor that the history is complete and accurate.

acceleration clause   The clause in a mortgage or deed of trust that can be enforced to make the entire debt due immediately if the borrower defaults on an installment payment or other covenant.

accession   Acquiring title to additions or improvements to real property as a result of the annexation of fixtures or the accretion of alluvial deposits along the banks of streams.

accretion   The increase or addition of land by the deposit of sand or soil washed up naturally from a river, lake, or sea.

accrued items   On a closing statement, items of expense that are incurred but not yet payable, such as interest on a mortgage loan or taxes on real property.

acknowledgment   A formal declaration made before a duly authorized officer, usually a notary public, by a person who has signed a document.

acre   A measure of land equal to 43,560 square feet, 4,840 square yards, 4,047 square meters, 160 square rods, or 0.4047 hectares.

actual eviction   The legal process that results in the tenant's being physically removed from the leased premises.

actual notice   Express information or fact; that which is known; direct knowledge.

adjustable-rate mortgage (ARM)   A loan characterized by a fluctuating interest rate, usually one tied to a bank or savings and loan association cost-of-funds index.

adjusted basis   *See* basis.

ad valorem tax   A tax levied according to value, generally used to refer to real estate tax. Also called the *general tax*.

adverse possession   The actual, open, notorious, hostile, and continuous possession of another's land under a claim of title. Possession for a statutory period may be a means of acquiring title.

affidavit of title   A written statement, made under oath by a seller or grantor of real property and acknowledged by a notary public, in which the grantor (1) identifies himself or herself and indicates marital status, (2) certifies that since the examination of the title, on the date of the contracts no defects have occurred in the

title and (3) certifies that he or she is in possession of the property (if applicable).

agency   The relationship between a principal and an agent wherein the agent is authorized to represent the principal in certain transactions.

agency coupled with an interest   An agency relationship in which the agent is given an estate or interest in the subject of the agency (the property).

agent   One who acts or has the power to act for another. A fiduciary relationship is created under the *law of agency* when a property owner, as the principal, executes a listing agreement or management contract authorizing a licensed real estate broker to be his or her agent.

air lot   A designated airspace over a piece of land. An air lot, like surface property, may be transferred.

air rights   The right to use the open space above a property, usually allowing the surface to be used for another purpose.

alienation   The act of transferring property to another. Alienation may be voluntary, such as by gift or sale, or involuntary, as through eminent domain or adverse possession.

alienation clause   The clause in a mortgage or deed of trust that states that the balance of the secured debt becomes immediately due and payable at the lender's option if the property is sold by the borrower. In effect this clause prevents the borrower from assigning the debt without the lender's approval.

allodial system   A system of land ownership in which land is held free and clear of any rent or service due to the government; commonly contrasted to the feudal system. Land is held under the allodial system in the United States.

American Land Title Association (ALTA) policy   A title insurance policy that protects the interest in a collateral property of a mortgage lender who originates a new real estate loan.

Americans with Disabilities Act   Act addresses rights of individuals with disabilities in employment and public accommodations.

amortized loan   A loan in which the principal as well as the interest is payable in monthly or other periodic installments over the term of the loan.

annexation   Process of converting personal property into real property.

annual percentage rate (APR)   The relationship of the total finance charges associated with a loan. This must be disclosed to borrowers by lenders under the Truth-in-Lending Act.

anticipation   The appraisal principle that holds that value can increase or decrease based on the expectation of some future benefit or detriment produced by the property.

antitrust laws   Laws designed to preserve the free enterprise of the open marketplace by making illegal certain private conspiracies and combinations formed to minimize competition. Most violations of antitrust laws in the real estate business involve either *price-fixing* (brokers conspiring to set fixed compensation rates) or *allocation of customers or markets* (brokers agreeing to limit their areas of trade or dealing to certain areas or properties).

appraisal   An estimate of the quantity, quality, or value of something. The process through which conclusions of property value are obtained; also refers to the report that sets forth the process of estimation and conclusion of value.

appraiser   An independent person trained to provide an unbiased estimate of value.

appreciation   An increase in the worth or value of a property due to economic or related causes, which may prove to be either temporary or permanent; opposite of depreciation.

appurtenance   A right, privilege, or improvement belonging to, and passing with, the land.

appurtenant easement   An easement that is annexed to the ownership of one parcel and allows the owner the use of the neighbor's land.

asbestos   A mineral once used in insulation and other materials that can cause respiratory diseases.

assemblage   The combining of two or more adjoining lots into one larger tract to increase their total value.

assessment   The imposition of a tax, charge, or levy, usually according to established rates.

assignment   The transfer in writing of interest in a bond, mortgage, lease, or other instrument.

assumption of mortgage   Acquiring title to property on which there is an existing mortgage and agreeing to be personally liable for the terms and conditions of the mortgage, including payments.

attachment   The act of taking a person's property into legal custody by writ or other judicial order to hold it available for application to that person's debt to a creditor.

attorney's opinion of title   An abstract of title that an attorney has examined and has certified to be, in his or her opinion, an accurate statement of the facts concerning the property ownership.

automated underwriting   Computer systems that permit lenders to expedite the loan approval process and reduce lending costs.

automatic extension   A clause in a listing agreement that states that the agreement will continue automatically for a certain period of time after its expiration date. In many states, use of this clause is discouraged or prohibited.

avulsion   The sudden tearing away of land, as by earthquake, flood, volcanic action, or the sudden change in the course of a stream.

balance   The appraisal principle that states that the greatest value in a property will occur when the type and size of the improvements are proportional to each other as well as the land.

balloon payment   A final payment of a mortgage loan that is considerably larger than the required periodic payments because the loan amount was not fully amortized.

bargain and sale deed   A deed that carries with it no warranties against liens or other encumbrances but that does imply that the grantor has the right to convey title. The grantor may add warranties to the deed at his or her discretion.

base line   The main imaginary line running east and west and crossing a principal meridian at a definite point, used by surveyors for reference in locating and describing land under the rectangular (government) survey system of legal description.

basis   The financial interest that the Internal Revenue Service attributes to an owner of an investment property for the purpose of determining annual depreciation and gain or loss on the sale of the asset. If a property was acquired by purchase, the owner's basis is the cost of the property plus the value of any capital expenditures for improvements to the property, minus any depreciation allowable or actually taken. This new basis is called the *adjusted basis*.

benchmark   A permanent reference mark or point established for use by surveyors in measuring differences in elevation.

beneficiary   (1) The person for whom a trust operates or in whose behalf the income from a trust estate is drawn. (2) A lender in a deed of trust loan transaction.

bilateral contract   *See* contract.

binder   An agreement that may accompany an earnest money deposit for the purchase of real property as evidence of the purchaser's good faith and intent to complete the transaction.

blanket loan   A mortgage covering more than one parcel of real estate, providing for each parcel's partial release from the mortgage lien upon repayment of a definite portion of the debt.

blockbusting   The illegal practice of inducing homeowners to sell their properties by making representations regarding the entry or prospective entry of persons of a particular race or national origin into the neighborhood.

blue-sky laws   Common name for those state and federal laws that regulate the registration and sale of investment securities.

boot   Money or property given to make up any difference in value or equity between two properties in an *exchange*.

branch office   A secondary place of business apart from the principal or main office from which real estate business is conducted. A branch office usually must be run by a licensed real estate broker working on behalf of the broker.

breach of contract   Violation of any terms or conditions in a contract without legal excuse; for example, failure to make a payment when it is due.

broker   One who acts as an intermediary on behalf of others for a fee or commission.

brokerage   The bringing together of parties interested in making a real estate transaction.

brownfields   Defunct, derelict, or abandoned commercial or industrial sites; many have toxic wastes.

Brownfields Legislation   Provides federal funding to states and localities to clean up brownfields sites.

buffer zone   A strip of land, usually used as a park or designated for a similar use, separating land dedicated to one use from land dedicated to another use (e.g., residential from commercial).

building code   An ordinance that specifies minimum standards of construction for buildings to protect public safety and health.

building permit   Written governmental permission for the construction, alteration, or demolition of an improvement, showing compliance with building codes and zoning ordinances.

bulk transfer   *See* Uniform Commercial Code.

bundle of legal rights   The concept of land ownership that includes ownership of all legal rights to the land—for example, possession, control within the law, and enjoyment.

buydown   A financing technique used to reduce the monthly payments for the first few years of a loan. Funds in the form of discount points are given to the lender by the builder or seller to buy down or lower the effective interest rate paid by the buyer, thus reducing the monthly payments for a set time.

buyer-agency agreement   A principal-agent relationship in which the broker is the agent for the buyer, with fiduciary responsibilities to the buyer. The broker represents the buyer under the law of agency.

buyer's agent   A residential real estate broker or salesperson who represents the prospective purchaser in a transaction. The buyer's agent owes the buyer/principal the common-law or statutory agency duties.

buyer's broker   A residential real estate broker who represents prospective buyers exclusively. As the *buyer's agent,* the broker owes the buyer/principal the common-law or statutory agency duties.

capital gain   Profit earned from the sale of an asset.

capitalization   A mathematical process for estimating the value of a property using a proper rate of return on the investment and the annual net operating income expected to be produced by the property. The formula is expressed as: Income ÷ Rate = Value.

capitalization rate   The rate of return a property will produce on the owner's investment.

cash flow   The net spendable income from an investment, determined by deducting all operating and fixed expenses from the gross income. When expenses exceed income, a *negative cash flow* results.

cash rent   In an agricultural lease, the amount of money given as rent to the landowner at the outset of the lease, as opposed to sharecropping.

caveat emptor   A Latin phrase meaning "Let the buyer beware."

certificate of reasonable value (CRV)   A form indicating the appraised value of a property being financed with a VA loan.

certificate of sale   The document generally given to the purchaser at a tax foreclosure sale. A certificate of sale does not convey title; normally it is an instrument certifying that the holder received title to the property after the redemption period passed and that the holder paid the property taxes for that interim period.

certificate of title   A statement of opinion on the status of the title to a parcel of real property based on an examination of specified public records.

chain of title   The succession of conveyances, from some accepted starting point, whereby the present holder of real property derives title.

change   The appraisal principle that holds that no physical or economic condition remains constant.

chattel   *See* personal property.

Civil Rights Act of 1866   An act that prohibits racial discrimination in the sale and rental of housing.

client   The principal.

closing   An event where promises made in a sales contract are fulfilled and mortgage loan funds (if any) are distributed to the buyer.

closing statement   A detailed cash accounting of a real estate transaction showing all cash received, all charges and credits made, and all cash paid out in the transaction.

cloud on title   Any document, claim, unreleased lien, or encumbrance that may impair the title to real property or make the title doubtful; usually revealed by a title search and removed by either a quitclaim deed or suit to quiet title.

clustering   The grouping of homesites within a subdivision on smaller lots than normal, with the remaining land used as common areas.

code of ethics   A written system of standards for ethical conduct.

codicil   A supplement or an addition to a will, executed with the same formalities as a will, that normally does not revoke the entire will.

coinsurance clause   A clause in insurance policies covering real property that requires the policyholder to maintain fire insurance coverage generally equal to at least 80 percent of the property's actual replacement cost.

commingling   The illegal act by a real estate broker of placing client or customer funds with personal funds. By law brokers are required to maintain a separate *trust* or *escrow account* for other parties' funds held temporarily by the broker.

commission   Payment to a broker for services rendered, such as in the sale or purchase of real property; usually a percentage of the selling price of the property.

common elements   Parts of a property that are necessary or convenient to the existence, maintenance, and safety of a condominium or are normally in common use by all of the condominium residents. Each condominium owner has an undivided ownership interest in the common elements.

common law   The body of law based on custom, usage, and court decisions.

community association management   Provides a team of property managers, accounting staff, office staff, and property consultants to manage property.

community property   A system of property ownership based on the theory that each spouse has an equal interest in the property acquired by the efforts of either spouse during marriage. A holdover of Spanish law found predominantly in western states; the system was unknown under English common law.

Community Reinvestment Act of 1977 (CRA)   Under the Act, financial institutions are expected to meet the deposit and credit needs of their communities; participate and invest in local community development and rehabilitation projects; and participate in loan programs for housing, small businesses, and small forms.

comparables   Properties used in an appraisal report that are substantially equivalent to the subject property.

competition   The appraisal principle that states that excess profits generate competition.

competitive market analysis (CMA)   A comparison of the prices of recently sold homes that are similar to a listing seller's home in terms of location, style, and amenities.

Comprehensive Environmental Response, Compensation, and Liability Act (CERCLA)   A federal law administered by the Environmental Protection Agency that establishes a process for identifying parties responsible for creating hazardous waste sites, forcing liable parties to clean up toxic sites, bringing legal action against responsible parties, and funding the abatement of toxic sites. *See* Superfund.

comprehensive plan   *See* master plan.

computerized loan origination (CLO) system   An electronic network for handling loan applications through remote computer terminals linked to various lenders' computers.

condemnation   A judicial or administrative proceeding to exercise the power of eminent domain, through which a government agency takes private property for public use and compensates the owner.

conditional-use permit   Written governmental permission allowing a use inconsistent with zoning but necessary for the common good, such as locating an emergency medical facility in a predominantly residential area.

condominium   The absolute ownership of a unit in a multiunit building based on a legal description of the airspace the unit actually occupies, plus an undivided interest in the ownership of the common elements, which are owned jointly with the other condominium unit owners.

confession of judgment clause   Permits judgment to be entered against a debtor without the creditor's having to institute legal proceedings.

conformity   The appraisal principle that holds that the greater the similarity among properties in an area, the better they will hold their value.

consideration   (1) That received by the grantor in exchange for his or her deed. (2) Something of value that induces a person to enter into a contract.

construction loan *See* interim financing.

constructive eviction Actions of a landlord that so materially disturb or impair a tenant's enjoyment of the leased premises that the tenant is effectively forced to move out and terminate the lease without liability for any further rent.

constructive notice Notice given to the world by recorded documents. All people are charged with knowledge of such documents and their contents, whether or not they have actually examined them. Possession of property is also considered constructive notice that the person in possession has an interest in the property.

contingency A provision in a contract that requires a certain act to be done or a certain event to occur before the contract becomes binding.

contract A legally enforceable promise or set of promises that must be performed and for which, if a breach of the promise occurs, the law provides a remedy. A contract may be either *unilateral*, by which only one party is bound to act, or *bilateral*, by which all parties to the instrument are legally bound to act as prescribed.

contribution The appraisal principle that states that the value of any component of a property is what it gives to the value of the whole or what its absence detracts from that value.

controlled business arrangement An arrangement where a package of services (such as a real estate firm, title insurance company, mortgage broker and home inspection company) is offered to consumers.

conventional loan A loan that requires no insurance or guarantee.

conveyance A term used to refer to any document that transfers title to real property. The term is also used in describing the act of transferring.

cooperating broker *See* listing broker.

cooperative A residential multiunit building whose title is held by a trust or corporation that is owned by and operated for the benefit of persons living within the building, who are the beneficial owners of the trust or stockholders of the corporation, each possessing a proprietary lease.

co-ownership Title ownership held by two or more persons.

corporation An entity or organization, created by operation of law, whose rights of doing business are essentially the same as those of an individual. The entity has continuous existence until it is dissolved according to legal procedures.

correction lines Provisions in the rectangular survey (government survey) system made to compensate for the curvature of the earth's surface. Every fourth township line (at 24-mile intervals) is used as a correction line on which the intervals between the north and south range lines are remeasured and corrected to a full six miles.

cost approach The process of estimating the value of a property by adding to the estimated land value the appraiser's estimate of the reproduction or replacement cost of the building, less depreciation.

cost recovery An Internal Revenue Service term for *depreciation.*

counteroffer A new offer made in response to an offer received. It has the effect of rejecting the original offer, which cannot be accepted thereafter unless revived by the offeror.

covenant A written agreement between two or more parties in which a party or parties pledge to perform or not perform specified acts with regard to property; usually found in such real estate documents as deeds, mortgages, leases, and contracts for deed.

covenant of quiet enjoyment The covenant implied by law by which a landlord guarantees that a tenant may take possession of leased premises and that the landlord will not interfere in the tenant's possession or use of the property.

credit On a closing statement, an amount entered in a person's favor—either an amount the party has paid or an amount for which the party must be reimbursed.

curtesy A life estate, usually a fractional interest, given by some states to the surviving husband in real estate owned by his deceased wife. Most states have abolished curtesy.

customer The third party for whom some level of service is provided.

datum A horizontal plane from which heights and depths are measured.

debit On a closing statement, an amount charged; that is, an amount that the debited party must pay.

decedent A person who has died.

dedication The voluntary transfer of private property by its owner to the public for some public use, such as for streets or schools.

deed A written instrument that, when executed and delivered, conveys title to or an interest in real estate.

deed in lieu of foreclosure A deed given by the mortgagor to the mortgagee when the mortgagor is in default under the terms of the mortgage. This is a way for the mortgagor to avoid foreclosure.

deed in trust An instrument that grants a trustee under a land trust full power to sell, mortgage, and subdivide a parcel of real estate. The beneficiary controls the trustee's use of these powers under the provisions of the trust agreement.

deed of trust *See* trust deed.

deed of trust lien *See* trust deed lien.

deed restrictions Clauses in a deed limiting the future uses of the property. Deed restrictions may impose a vast variety of limitations and conditions—for example, they may limit the density of buildings, dictate the types of structures that can be erected, or prevent buildings from being used for specific purposes or even from being used at all.

default The nonperformance of a duty, whether arising under a contract or otherwise; failure to meet an obligation when due.

defeasance clause A clause used in leases and mortgages that cancels a specified right upon the occurrence of a certain condition, such as cancellation of a mortgage upon repayment of the mortgage loan.

defeasible fee estate An estate in which the holder has a fee simple title that may be divested upon the occurrence or nonoccurrence of a specified event. There are two categories of defeasible fee estates: fee simple on condition precedent (fee simple determinable) and fee simple on condition subsequent.

deficiency judgment A personal judgment levied against the borrower when a foreclosure sale does not produce sufficient funds to pay the mortgage debt in full.

demand The amount of goods people are willing and able to buy at a given price; often coupled with *supply*.

density zoning Zoning ordinances that restrict the maximum average number of houses per acre that may be built within a particular area, generally a subdivision.

depreciation (1) In appraisal, a loss of value in property due to any cause, including *physical deterioration, functional obsolescence,* and *external obsolescence.* (2) In real estate investment, an expense deduction for tax purposes taken over the period of ownership of income property.

descent Acquisition of an estate by inheritance in which an heir succeeds to the property by operation of law.

designated agent A licensee authorized by a broker to act as the agent for a specific principal in a particular transaction.

developer One who attempts to put land to its most profitable use through the construction of improvements.

devise A gift of real property by will. The donor is the devisor, and the recipient is the devisee.

discount point A unit of measurement used for various loan charges; one point equals 1 percent of the amount of the loan.

dominant tenement A property that includes in its ownership the appurtenant right to use an easement over another person's property for a specific purpose.

dower The legal right or interest, recognized in some states, that a wife acquires in the property her husband held or acquired during their marriage. During the husband's lifetime the right is only a possibility of an interest; upon his death it can become an interest in land.

dual agency Representing both parties to a transaction. This is unethical unless both parties agree to it, and it is illegal in many states.

due-on-sale clause A provision in the mortgage that states that the entire balance of the note is immediately due and payable if the mortgagor transfers (sells) the property.

duress Unlawful constraint or action exercised upon a person whereby the person is forced to perform an act against his or her will. A contract entered into under duress is voidable.

earnest money Money deposited by a buyer under the terms of a contract, to be forfeited if the buyer defaults but applied to the purchase price if the sale is closed.

easement A right to use the land of another for a specific purpose, such as for a right-of-way or utilities; an incorporeal interest in land.

easement by condemnation An easement created by the government or government agency that has exercised its right under eminent domain.

easement by necessity An easement allowed by law as necessary for the full enjoyment of a parcel of real estate; for example, a right of ingress and egress over a grantor's land.

easement by prescription An easement acquired by continuous, open, and hostile use of the property for the period of time prescribed by state law.

easement in gross An easement that is not created for the benefit of any land owned by the owner of the easement but that attaches *personally to the easement owner.* For example, a right granted by Eleanor Franks to Joe Fish to use a portion of her property for the rest of his life would be an easement in gross.

economic life The number of years during which an improvement will add value to the land.

emblements Growing crops, such as grapes and corn, that are produced annually through labor and industry; also called *fructus industriales.*

eminent domain The right of a government or municipal quasi-public body to acquire property for public use through a court action called *condemnation*, in which the court decides that the use is a public use and determines the compensation to be paid to the owner.

employee Someone who works as a direct employee of an employer and has employee status. The employer is obligated to withhold income taxes and Social Security taxes from the compensation of employees. *See also* independent contractor.

employment contract A document evidencing formal employment between employer and employee or between principal and agent. In the real estate business this generally takes the form of a listing agreement or management agreement.

enabling acts State legislation that confers zoning powers on municipal governments.

encapsulation A method of controlling environmental contamination by sealing off a dangerous substance.

encroachment A building or some portion of it—a wall or fence for instance—that extends beyond the land of the owner and illegally intrudes on some land of an adjoining owner or a street or alley.

encumbrance Anything—such as a mortgage, tax, or judgment lien, an easement, a restriction on the use of the land or an outstanding dower right—that may diminish the value or use and enjoyment of a property.

Equal Credit Opportunity Act (ECOA) The federal law that prohibits discrimination in the extension of credit because of race, color, religion, national origin, sex, age, or marital status.

equalization The raising or lowering of assessed values for tax purposes in a particular county or taxing district to make them equal to assessments in other counties or districts.

equalization factor A factor (number) by which the assessed value of a property is multiplied to arrive at a value for the property that is in line with statewide tax assessments. The *ad valorem tax* would be based on this adjusted value.

equitable lien *See* statutory lien.

equitable right of redemption The right of a defaulted property owner to recover the property prior to its sale by paying the appropriate fees and charges.

equitable title The interest held by a vendee under a contract for deed or an installment contract; the equitable right to obtain absolute ownership to property when legal title is held in another's name.

equity The interest or value that an owner has in property over and above any indebtedness.

erosion The gradual wearing away of land by water, wind, and general weather conditions; the diminishing of property by the elements.

escheat The reversion of property to the state or county, as provided by state law, in cases where a decedent dies intestate without heirs capable of inheriting, or when the property is abandoned.

escrow The closing of a transaction through a third party called an *escrow agent*, or *escrowee*, who receives certain funds and documents to be delivered upon the performance of certain conditions outlined in the escrow instructions.

escrow account The trust account established by a broker under the provisions of the license law for the purpose of holding funds on behalf of the broker's principal or some other person until the consummation or termination of a transaction.

escrow contract An agreement between a buyer, seller, and escrow holder setting forth rights and responsibilities of each. An escrow contract is entered into when earnest money is deposited in a broker's escrow account.

escrow instructions A document that sets forth the duties of the escrow agent, as well as the requirements and obligations of the parties, when a transaction is closed through an escrow.

estate (tenancy) at sufferance The tenancy of a lessee who lawfully comes into possession of a landlord's real estate but who continues to occupy the premises improperly after his or her lease rights have expired.

estate (tenancy) at will An estate that gives the lessee the right to possession until the estate is terminated by either party; the term of this estate is indefinite.

estate (tenancy) for years An interest for a certain, exact period of time in property leased for a specified consideration.

estate (tenancy) from period to period An interest in leased property that continues from period to period—week to week, month to month, or year to year.

estate in land The degree, quantity, nature, and extent of interest a person has in real property.

estate taxes Federal taxes on a decedent's real and personal property.

estoppel Method of creating an agency relationship in which someone states incorrectly that another person is his or her agent and a third person relies on that representation.

estoppel certificate A document in which a borrower certifies the amount owed on a mortgage loan and the rate of interest.

ethics The system of moral principles and rules that becomes standards for professional conduct.

eviction A legal process to oust a person from possession of real estate.

evidence of title Proof of ownership of property; commonly a certificate of title, an abstract of title with lawyer's opinion, title insurance, or a Torrens registration certificate.

exchange A transaction in which all or part of the consideration is the transfer of *like-kind* property (such as real estate for real estate).

exclusive-agency listing A listing contract under which the owner appoints a real estate broker as his or her exclusive agent for a designated period of time to sell the property, on the owner's stated terms, for a commission. The owner reserves the right to sell without paying anyone a commission if he or she sells to a prospect who has not been introduced or claimed by the broker.

exclusive-right-to-sell listing A listing contract under which the owner appoints a real estate broker as his or her exclusive agent for a designated period of time, to sell the property on the owner's stated terms, and agrees to pay the broker a commission when the property is sold, whether by the broker, the owner, or another broker.

executed contract A contract in which all parties have fulfilled their promises and thus performed the contract.

execution The signing and delivery of an instrument. Also, a legal order directing an official to enforce a judgment against the property of a debtor.

executory contract A contract under which something remains to be done by one or more of the parties.

express agency An agency relationship based on a formal agreement between the parties.

express agreement An oral or written contract in which the parties state the contract's terms and express their intentions in words.

express contract *See* express agreement.

external depreciation Reduction in a property's value caused by outside factors (those that are off the property).

external obsolescence Incurable depreciation caused by factors not on subject property, such as environmental, social, or economic factors.

facilitator *See* nonagent.

Fair Housing Act The federal law that prohibits discrimination in housing based on race, color, religion, sex, handicap, familial status, and national origin.

Fannie Mae A quasi-government agency established to purchase any kind of mortgage loans in the secondary mortgage market from the primary lenders.

Farm Credit System A federal agency of the Department of Agricultural that offers programs to help families purchase or operate family farms.

Farmer Mac An agency that operates similarly to Fannie Mae and Freddie Mac, but for agricultural loans.

Farmer's Home Administration (FmHA) An agency of the federal government that provides credit assistance to farmers and other individuals who live in rural areas.

Federal Deposit Insurance Corporation (FDIC) An independent federal agency that insures the deposits in commercial banks.

Federal Home Loan Mortgage Corporation (FHLMC) *See* Freddie Mac.

Federal National Mortgage Association (FNMA) *See* Fannie Mae.

Federal Reserve System The country's central banking system, which is responsible for the nation's monetary policy by regulating the supply of money and interest rates.

fee-for-service Arrangement where a consumer asks a licensee to perform specific real estate services for a set fee.

fee simple The highest interest in real estate recognized by the law; the holder is entitled to all rights to the property.

fee simple absolute The maximum possible estate or right of ownership of real property, continuing forever.

fee simple defeasible *See* defeasible fee estate.

fee simple determinable A fee simple estate qualified by a special limitation. Language used to describe limitation includes the words, "so long as" or "while" or "during."

feudal system A system of ownership usually associated with precolonial England, in which the king or other sovereign is the source of all rights. The right to possess real property was granted by the sovereign to an individual as a life estate only. Upon the death of the individual, title passed back to the sovereign, not to the decedent's heirs.

FHA loan A loan insured by the Federal Housing Administration and made by an approved lender in accordance with the FHA's regulations.

fiduciary One in whom trust and confidence is placed; a reference to a broker employed under the terms of a listing contract or buyer agency agreement.

fiduciary relationship A relationship of trust and confidence, as between trustee and beneficiary, attorney and client, or principal and agent.

Financial Institutions Reform, Recovery, and Enforcement Act (FIRREA) This act restructured the savings and loan association regulatory system; enacted in response to the savings and loan crisis of the 1980s.

financing statement *See* Uniform Commercial Code.

fiscal policy The government's policy in regard to taxation and spending programs. The balance between these two areas determines the amount of money the government will withdraw from or feed into the economy, which can counter economic peaks and slumps.

fixture An item of personal property that has been converted to real property by being permanently affixed to the realty.

foreclosure A legal procedure whereby property used as security for a debt is sold to satisfy the debt in the event of default in payment of the mortgage note or default of other terms in the mortgage document. The foreclosure procedure brings the rights of all parties to a conclusion and passes the title in the mortgaged property to either the holder of the mortgage or a third party who may purchase the realty at the foreclosure sale, free of all encumbrances affecting the property subsequent to the mortgage.

fractional section A parcel of land less than 160 acres, usually found at the edge of a rectangular survey.

fraud Deception intended to cause a person to give up property or a lawful right.

Freddie Mac A corporation established to purchase primarily conventional mortgage loans in the secondary mortgage market.

freehold estate An estate in land in which ownership is for an indeterminate length of time, in contrast to a *leasehold estate*.

front footage The measurement of a parcel of land by the number of feet of street or road frontage.

functional obsolescence A loss of value to an improvement to real estate arising from functional problems, often caused by age or poor design.

future interest A person's present right to an interest in real property that will not result in possession or enjoyment until some time in the future, such as a reversion or right of reentry.

gap A defect in the chain of title of a particular parcel of real estate; a missing document or conveyance that raises doubt as to the present ownership of the land.

general agent One who is authorized by a principal to represent the principal in a specific range of matters.

general lien The right of a creditor to have all of a debtor's property—both real and personal— sold to satisfy a debt.

general partnership *See* partnership.

general real estate tax A tax which is made up of the taxes levied on the real estate by government agencies and municipalities.

general warranty deed A deed in which the grantor fully warrants good clear title to the premises. Used in most real estate deed transfers, a general warranty deed offers the greatest protection of any deed.

Ginnie Mae A government agency that plays an important role in the secondary mortgage market. It sells mortgage-backed securities that are backed by pools of FHA and VA loans.

government check The 24-mile-square parcels composed of 16 townships in the rectangular (government) survey system of legal description.

government lot Fractional sections in the rectangular (government) survey system that are less than one quarter-section in area.

Government National Mortgage Association (GNMA) *See* Ginnie Mae.

government survey system *See* rectangular (government) survey system.

graduated-payment mortgage (GPM) A loan in which the monthly principal and interest payments increase by a certain percentage each year for a certain number of years and then level off for the remaining loan term.

grantee A person who receives a conveyance of real property from a grantor.

granting clause Words in a deed of conveyance that state the grantor's intention to convey the property at the present time. This clause is generally worded as "convey and warrant"; "grant"; "grant, bargain, and sell"; or the like.

grantor The person transferring title to or an interest in real property to a grantee.

gross income multiplier A figure used as a multiplier of the gross annual income of a property to produce an estimate of the property's value.

gross lease A lease of property according to which a landlord pays all property charges regularly incurred through ownership, such as repairs, taxes, insurance, and operating expenses. Most residential leases are gross leases.

gross rent multiplier (GRM) The figure used as a multiplier of the gross monthly income of a property to produce an estimate of the property's value.

ground lease   A lease of land only, on which the tenant usually owns a building or is required to build as specified in the lease. Such leases are usually long-term net leases; the tenant's rights and obligations continue until the lease expires or is terminated through default.

growing-equity mortgage (GEM)   A loan in which the monthly payments increase annually, with the increased amount being used to reduce directly the principal balance outstanding and thus shorten the overall term of the loan.

habendum clause   That part of a deed beginning with the words "to have and to hold," following the granting clause and defining the extent of ownership the grantor is conveying.

heir   One who might inherit or succeed to an interest in land under the state law of descent when the owner dies without leaving a valid will.

highest and best use   The possible use of a property that would produce the greatest net income and thereby develop the highest value.

holdover tenancy   A tenancy whereby a lessee retains possession of leased property after the lease has expired and the landlord, by continuing to accept rent, agrees to the tenant's continued occupancy as defined by state law.

holographic will   A will that is written, dated, and signed in the testator's handwriting.

home equity loan   A loan (sometimes called a *line of credit*) under which a property owner uses his or her residence as collateral and can then draw funds up to a prearranged amount against the property.

homeowner's insurance policy   A standardized package insurance policy that covers a residential real estate owner against financial loss from fire, theft, public liability, and other common risks.

homestead   Land that is owned and occupied as the family home. In many states a portion of the area or value of this land is protected or exempt from judgments for debts.

hypothecate   To pledge property as security for an obligation or loan without giving up possession of it.

implied agency   Based on the actions of the parties which imply that they have mutually consented to an agency relationship, an implied agency relationship is formed.

implied agreement   A contract under which the agreement of the parties is demonstrated by their acts and conduct.

implied contract   *See* implied agreement.

implied warranty of habitability   A theory in landlord/tenant law in which the landlord renting residential property implies that the property is habitable and fit for its intended use.

improvement   (1) Any structure, usually privately owned, erected on a site to enhance the value of the property—for example, building a fence or a driveway. (2) A publicly owned structure added to or benefiting land, such as a curb, sidewalk, street, or sewer.

income approach   The process of estimating the value of an income-producing property through capitalization of the annual net income expected to be produced by the property during its remaining useful life.

incorporeal right   A nonpossessory right in real estate; for example, an easement or a right-of-way.

independent contractor   Someone who is retained to perform a certain act but who is subject to the control and direction of another only as to the end result and not as to the way in which the act is performed. Unlike an employee, an independent contractor pays for all expenses and Social Security and income taxes and receives no employee benefits. Most real estate salespeople are independent contractors.

index method   The appraisal method of estimating building costs by multiplying the original cost of the property by a percentage factor to adjust for current construction costs.

inflation   The gradual reduction of the purchasing power of the dollar, usually related directly to the increases in the money supply by the federal government.

inheritance taxes   State-imposed taxes on a decedent's real and personal property.

inquiry notice   Notice the law presumes a reasonable person would obtain by inquiring into a property.

installment contract   A contract for the sale of real estate whereby the purchase price is paid in periodic installments by the purchaser, who is in possession of the property even though title is retained by the seller until a future date, which may be not until final payment. Also called a *contract for deed* or *articles of agreement for warranty deed*.

installment sale   A transaction in which the sales price is paid in two or more installments over two or more years. If the sale meets certain requirements, a taxpayer can postpone reporting such income until future years by paying tax each year only on the proceeds received that year.

interest   A charge made by a lender for the use of money.

interim financing   A short-term loan usually made during the construction phase of a building project (in this case often referred to as a *construction loan*).

intermediate theory Adopted by a number of states, a theory based on the principles of title theory but requires the mortgagee foreclose to obtain legal title.

Interstate Land Sales Full Disclosure Act A federal law that regulates the sale of certain real estate in interstate commerce.

intestate The condition of a property owner who dies without leaving a valid will. Title to the property will pass to the decedent's heirs as provided in the state law of descent.

intrinsic value An appraisal term referring to the value created by a person's personal preferences for a particular type of property.

inverse condemnation An action brought by a property owner seeking just compensation for land taken for public use when the taker of the property does not intend to bring eminent domain proceedings. Property is condemned because its use and value have been diminished due to an adjacent property's public use.

investment Money directed toward the purchase, improvement, and development of an asset in expectation of income or profits.

involuntary alienation *See* alienation.

involuntary lien A lien placed on property without the consent of the property owner.

joint and several liability Each of the individual owners is personally responsible for the total damages.

joint tenancy Ownership of real estate between two or more parties who have been named in one conveyance as joint tenants. Upon the death of a joint tenant, the decedent's interest passes to the surviving joint tenant or tenants by the *right of survivorship*.

joint venture The joining of two or more people to conduct a specific business enterprise. A joint venture is similar to a partnership in that it must be created by agreement between the parties to share in the losses and profits of the venture. It is unlike a partnership in that the venture is for one specific project only, rather than for a continuing business relationship.

judgment The formal decision of a court upon the respective rights and claims of the parties to an action or suit. After a judgment has been entered and recorded with the county recorder, it usually becomes a general lien on the property of the defendant.

judicial precedent In law, the requirements established by prior court decisions.

junior lien An obligation, such as a second mortgage, that is subordinate in right or lien priority to an existing lien on the same realty.

laches An equitable doctrine used by courts to bar a legal claim or prevent the assertion of a right because of undue delay or failure to assert the claim or right.

land The earth's surface, extending downward to the center of the earth and upward infinitely into space, including things permanently attached by nature, such as trees and water.

land contract *See* installment contract.

latent defect A hidden structural defect that could not be discovered by ordinary inspection and that threatens the property's soundness or the safety of its inhabitants. Some states impose on sellers and licensees a duty to inspect for and disclose latent defects.

law of agency *See* agency.

lease A written or oral contract between a landlord (the lessor) and a tenant (the lessee) that transfers the right to exclusive possession and use of the landlord's real property to the lessee for a specified period of time and for a stated consideration (rent). By state law leases for longer than a certain period of time (generally one year) must be in writing to be enforceable.

leasehold estate A tenant's right to occupy real estate during the term of a lease, generally considered to be a personal property interest.

lease option A lease under which the tenant has the right to purchase the property either during the lease term or at its end.

lease purchase The purchase of real property, the consummation of which is preceded by a lease, usually long-term. Typically done for tax or financing purposes.

legacy A disposition of money or personal property by will.

legal description A description of a specific parcel of real estate complete enough for an independent surveyor to locate and identify it.

legally competent parties People who are recognized by law as being able to contract with others; those of legal age and sound mind.

lessee *See* lease.

lessor *See* lease.

leverage The use of borrowed money to finance an investment.

levy To assess; to seize or collect. To levy a tax is to assess a property and set the rate of taxation. To levy an execution is to officially seize the property of a person in order to satisfy an obligation.

license (1) A privilege or right granted to a person by a state to operate as a real estate broker or salesperson. (2) The revocable permission for a temporary use of land—a personal right that cannot be sold.

lien   A right given by law to certain creditors to have their debts paid out of the property of a defaulting debtor, usually by means of a court sale.

lien theory   Some states interpret a mortgage as being purely a lien on real property. The mortgagee thus has no right of possession but must foreclose the lien and sell the property if the mortgagor defaults.

life cycle costing   In property management, comparing one type of equipment with another based on both purchase cost and operating cost over its expected useful lifetime.

life estate   An interest in real or personal property that is limited in duration to the lifetime of its owner or some other designated person or persons.

life tenant   A person in possession of a life estate.

limited partnership   *See* partnership.

liquidated damages   An amount predetermined by the parties to a contract as the total compensation to an injured party should the other party breach the contract.

liquidity   The ability to sell an asset and convert it into cash, at a price close to its true value, in a short period of time.

lis pendens   A recorded legal document giving constructive notice that an action affecting a particular property has been filed in either a state or a federal court.

listing agreement   A contract between an owner (as principal) and a real estate broker (as agent) by which the broker is employed as agent to find a buyer for the owner's real estate on the owner's terms, for which service the owner agrees to pay a commission.

listing broker   The broker in a multiple-listing situation from whose office a listing agreement is initiated, as opposed to the *cooperating broker,* from whose office negotiations leading up to a sale are initiated. The listing broker and the cooperating broker may be the same person.

littoral rights   (1) A landowner's claim to use water in large navigable lakes and oceans adjacent to his or her property. (2) The ownership rights to land bordering these bodies of water up to the high-water mark.

loan origination fee   A fee charged to the borrower by the lender for making a mortgage loan. The fee is usually computed as a percentage of the loan amount.

loan-to-value ratio   The relationship between the amount of the mortgage loan and the value of the real estate being pledged as collateral.

lot-and-block (recorded plat) system   A method of describing real property that identifies a parcel of land by reference to lot and block numbers within a subdivision, as specified on a recorded subdivision plat.

management agreement   A contract between the owner of income property and a management firm or individual property manager that outlines the scope of the manager's authority.

market   A place where goods can be bought and sold and a price established.

marketable title   Good or clear title, reasonably free from the risk of litigation over possible defects.

market data approach (also known as the sales comparison approach)   An estimate of value obtained by comparing property being appraised with recently sold comparable properties.

market value   The most probable price property would bring in an arm's-length transaction under normal conditions on the open market.

master plan   A comprehensive plan to guide the long-term physical development of a particular area.

mechanic's lien   A statutory lien created in favor of contractors, laborers, and materialmen who have performed work or furnished materials in the erection or repair of a building.

Megan's Law   Federal legislation that promotes the establishment of state registration systems to maintain residential information on every person who kidnaps children, commits sexual crimes against children, or commits sexually violent crimes.

meridian   One of a set of imaginary lines running north and south and crossing a base line at a definite point, used in the rectangular (government) survey system of property description.

metes-and-bounds description   A legal description of a parcel of land that begins at a well-marked point and follows the boundaries, using directions and distances around the tract, back to the place of beginning.

mill   One-tenth of one cent. Some states use a mill rate to compute real estate taxes; for example, a rate of 52 mills would be $0.052 tax for each dollar of assessed valuation of a property.

minor   Someone who has not reached the age of majority and therefore does not have legal capacity to transfer title to real property.

monetary policy   Governmental regulation of the amount of money in circulation through such institutions as the Federal Reserve Board.

month-to-month tenancy   A periodic tenancy under which the tenant rents for one month at a time. In the absence of a rental agreement (oral or written) a tenancy is generally considered to be month to month.

monument   A fixed natural or artificial object used to establish real estate boundaries for a metes-and-bounds description.

mortgage A conditional transfer or pledge of real estate as security for the payment of a debt. Also, the document creating a mortgage lien.

mortgage banker Mortgage loan companies that originate, service, and sell loans to investors.

mortgage broker An agent of a lender who brings the lender and borrower together. The broker receives a fee for this service.

mortgagee A lender in a mortgage loan transaction.

mortgage lien A lien or charge on the property of a mortgagor that secures the underlying debt obligations.

mortgagor A borrower in a mortgage loan transaction.

multiperil policies Insurance policies that offer protection from a range of potential perils, such as those of a fire, hazard, public liability, and casualty.

multiple-listing clause A provision in an exclusive listing for the authority and obligation on the part of the listing broker to distribute the listing to other brokers in the multiple-listing organization.

multiple-listing service (MLS) A marketing organization composed of member brokers who agree to share their listing agreements with one another in the hope of procuring ready, willing, and able buyers for their properties more quickly than they could on their own. Most multiple-listing services accept exclusive-right-to-sell or exclusive-agency listings from their member brokers.

negotiable instrument A written promise or order to pay a specific sum of money that may be transferred by endorsement or delivery. The transferee then has the original payee's right to payment.

net lease A lease requiring the tenant to pay not only rent but also costs incurred in maintaining the property, including taxes, insurance, utilities, and repairs.

net listing A listing based on the net price the seller will receive if the property is sold. Under a net listing the broker can offer the property for sale at the highest price obtainable to increase the commission. This type of listing is illegal in many states.

net operating income (NOI) The income projected for an income-producing property after deducting losses for vacancy and collection and operating expenses.

nonagent An intermediary between a buyer and seller, or landlord and tenant, who assists both parties with a transaction without representing either. Also known as a *facilitator, transaction broker, transaction coordinator,* and *contract broker.*

nonconforming use A use of property that is permitted to continue after a zoning ordinance prohibiting it has been established for the area.

nonhomogeneity A lack of uniformity; dissimilarity. Because no two parcels of land are exactly alike, real estate is said to be nonhomogeneous.

note *See* promissory note.

novation Substituting a new obligation for an old one or substituting new parties to an existing obligation.

nuncupative will An oral will declared by the testator in his or her final illness, made before witnesses and afterward reduced to writing.

obsolescence The loss of value due to factors that are outmoded or less useful. Obsolescence may be functional or economic.

occupancy permit A permit issued by the appropriate local governing body to establish that the property is suitable for habitation by meeting certain safety and health standards.

offer and acceptance Two essential components of a valid contract; a "meeting of the minds."

offeror/offeree The person who makes the offer is the offeror. The person to whom the offer is made is the offeree.

Office of Thrift Supervision (OTS) A government agency which governs the practices of fiduciary lenders. OTS was created by the Financial Institutions Reform, Recovery, and Enforcement Act (FIRREA).

open-end loan A mortgage loan that is expandable by increments up to a maximum dollar amount, the full loan being secured by the same original mortgage.

open listing A listing contract under which the broker's commission is contingent on the broker's producing a ready, willing, and able buyer before the property is sold by the seller or another broker.

option An agreement to keep open for a set period an offer to sell or purchase property.

option listing Listing with a provision that gives the listing broker the right to purchase the listed property.

ostensible agency A form of implied agency relationship created by the actions of the parties involved rather than by written agreement or document.

package loan A real estate loan used to finance the purchase of both real property and personal property, such as in the purchase of a new home that includes carpeting, window coverings, and major appliances.

parol evidence Oral or verbal evidence.

parol evidence rule A rule of evidence providing that a written agreement is the final expression of the agreement of the parties, not to be varied or contradicted by prior or contemporaneous oral or written negotiations.

participation mortgage   A mortgage loan wherein the lender has a partial equity interest in the property or receives a portion of the income from the property.

partition   The division of cotenants' interests in real property when the parties do not all voluntarily agree to terminate the co-ownership; takes place through court procedures.

partnership   An association of two or more individuals who carry on a continuing business for profit as co-owners. Under the law, a partnership is regarded as a group of individuals rather than as a single entity. A *general partnership* is a typical form of joint venture in which each general partner shares in the administration, profits, and losses of the operation. A *limited partnership* is a business arrangement whereby the operation is administered by one or more general partners and funded, by and large, by limited or silent partners, who are by law responsible for losses only to the extent of their investments.

party wall   A wall that is located on or at a boundary line between two adjoining parcels of land and is used or is intended to be used by the owners of both properties.

patent   A grant or franchise of land from the United States government.

payment cap   The limit on the amount the monthly payment can be increased on an adjustable-rate mortgage when the interest rate is adjusted.

payoff statement   *See* reduction certificate.

percentage lease   A lease, commonly used for commercial property, whose rental is based on the tenant's gross sales at the premises; it usually stipulates a base monthly rental plus a percentage of any gross sales above a certain amount.

percolation test   A test of the soil to determine if it will absorb and drain water adequately to use a septic system for sewage disposal.

periodic estate (tenancy)   *See* estate from period to period.

personal property   Items, called *chattels,* that do not fit into the definition of real property; movable objects.

physical deterioration   A reduction in a property's value resulting from a decline in physical condition; can be caused by action of the elements or by ordinary wear and tear.

planned unit development (PUD)   A planned combination of diverse land uses, such as housing, recreation, and shopping, in one contained development or subdivision.

plat   A detailed map that illustrates the geographic boundaries of individual lots.

plat map   A map of a town, section, or subdivision indicating the location and boundaries of individual properties.

plottage   The increase in value or utility resulting from the consolidation (*assemblage*) of two or more adjacent lots into one larger lot.

point of beginning (POB)   In a metes-and-bounds legal description, the starting point of the survey, situated in one corner of the parcel; all metes-and-bounds descriptions must follow the boundaries of the parcel back to the point of beginning.

police power   The government's right to impose laws, statutes, and ordinances, including zoning ordinances and building codes, to protect the public health, safety, and welfare.

power of attorney   A written instrument authorizing a person, the *attorney-in-fact,* to act as agent for another person to the extent indicated in the instrument.

prepaid items   On a closing statement, items that have been paid in advance by the seller, such as insurance premiums and some real estate taxes, for which he or she must be reimbursed by the buyer.

prepayment penalty   A charge imposed on a borrower who pays off the loan principal early. This penalty compensates the lender for interest and other charges that would otherwise be lost.

price-fixing   *See* antitrust laws.

primary mortgage market   The mortgage market in which loans are originated and consisting of lenders such as commercial banks, savings and loan associations, and mutual savings banks.

principal   (1) A sum loaned or employed as a fund or an investment, as distinguished from its income or profits. (2) The original amount (as in a loan) of the total due and payable at a certain date. (3) A main party to a transaction—the person for whom the agent works.

principal meridian   The main imaginary line running north and south and crossing a base line at a definite point, used by surveyors for reference in locating and describing land under the rectangular (government) survey system of legal description.

prior appropriation   A concept of water ownership in which the landowner's right to use available water is based on a government-administered permit system.

priority   The order of position or time. The priority of liens is generally determined by the chronological order in which the lien documents are recorded; tax liens, however, have priority even over previously recorded liens.

private mortgage insurance (PMI) Insurance provided by private carrier that protects a lender against a loss in the event of a foreclosure and deficiency.

probate A legal process by which a court determines who will inherit a decedent's property and what the estate's assets are.

procuring cause The effort that brings about the desired result. Under an open listing the broker who is the procuring cause of the sale receives the commission.

progression An appraisal principle that states that, between dissimilar properties, the value of the lesser-quality property is favorably affected by the presence of the better-quality property.

promissory note A financing instrument that states the terms of the underlying obligation, is signed by its maker, and is negotiable (transferable to a third party).

property manager Someone who manages real estate for another person for compensation. Duties include collecting rents, maintaining the property, and keeping up all accounting.

property reports The mandatory federal and state documents compiled by subdividers and developers to provide potential purchasers with facts about a property, prior to their purchase.

proprietary lease A lease given by the corporation that owns a cooperative apartment building to the shareholder for the shareholder's right as a tenant to an individual apartment.

prorations Expenses, either prepaid or paid in arrears, that are divided or distributed between buyer and seller at the closing.

protected class Any group of people designated as such by the Department of Housing and Urban Development (HUD) in consideration of federal and state civil rights legislation. Currently includes ethnic minorities, women, religious groups, the handicapped, and others.

puffing Exaggerated or superlative comments or opinions.

pur autre vie "For the life of another." A life estate pur autre vie is a life estate that is measured by the life of a person other than the grantee.

purchase-money mortgage (PMM) A note secured by a mortgage or deed of trust given by a buyer, as borrower, to a seller, as lender, as part of the purchase price of the real estate.

pyramiding The process of acquiring additional properties by refinancing properties already owned and investing the loan proceeds in additional properties.

quantity-survey method The appraisal method of estimating building costs by calculating the cost of all of the physical components in the improvements, adding the cost to assemble them, and then including the indirect costs associated with such construction.

quiet title A court action to remove a cloud on the title.

quitclaim deed A conveyance by which the grantor transfers whatever interest he or she has in the real estate, without warranties or obligations.

radon A naturally occurring gas that is suspected of causing lung cancer.

range A strip of land six miles wide, extending north and south and numbered east and west according to its distance from the principal meridian in the rectangular (government) survey system of legal description.

rate cap The limit on the amount the interest rate can be increased at each adjustment period in an adjustable-rate loan. The cap may also set the maximum interest rate that can be charged during the life of the loan.

ratification Method of creating an agency relationship in which the principal accepts the conduct of someone who acted without prior authorization as the principal's agent.

ready, willing, and able buyer One who is prepared to buy property on the seller's terms and is ready to take positive steps to consummate the transaction.

real estate Land; a portion of the earth's surface extending downward to the center of the earth and upward infinitely into space, including all things permanently attached to it, whether naturally or artificially.

real estate investment syndicate *See* syndicate.

real estate investment trust (REIT) Trust ownership of real estate by a group of individuals who purchase certificates of ownership in the trust, which in turn invests the money in real property and distributes the profits back to the investors free of corporate income tax.

real estate license law State law enacted to protect the public from fraud, dishonesty, and incompetence in the purchase and sale of real estate.

real estate mortgage investment conduit (REMIC) A tax entity that issues multiple classes of investor interests (securities) backed by a pool of mortgages.

real estate recovery fund A fund established in some states from real estate license revenues to cover claims of aggrieved parties who have suffered monetary damage through the actions of a real estate licensee.

Real Estate Settlement Procedures Act (RESPA) The federal law that requires certain disclosures to consumers about mortgage loan settlements. The law also prohibits the payment or receipt of kickbacks and certain kinds of referral fees.

real property The interests, benefits, and rights inherent in real estate ownership.

REALTOR® A registered trademark term reserved for the sole use of active members of local REALTOR® boards affiliated with the National Association of REALTORS®.

reconciliation The final step in the appraisal process, in which the appraiser combines the estimates of value received from the sales comparison, cost, and income approaches to arrive at a final estimate of market value for the subject property.

reconveyance deed A deed used by a trustee under a deed of trust to return title to the trustor.

recording The act of entering or recording documents affecting or conveying interests in real estate in the recorder's office established in each county. Until it is recorded, a deed or mortgage ordinarily is not effective against subsequent purchasers or mortgagees.

rectangular (government) survey system A system established in 1785 by the federal government, providing for surveying and describing land by reference to principal meridians and base lines.

redemption The right of a defaulted property owner to recover his or her property by curing the default.

redemption period A period of time established by state law during which a property owner has the right to redeem his or her real estate from a foreclosure or tax sale by paying the sales price, interest, and costs. Many states do not have mortgage redemption laws.

redlining The illegal practice of a lending institution denying loans or restricting their number for certain areas of a community.

reduction certificate (payoff statement) The document signed by a lender indicating the amount required to pay a loan balance in full and satisfy the debt; used in the settlement process to protect both the seller's and the buyer's interests.

regression An appraisal principle that states that, between dissimilar properties, the value of the better-quality property is affected adversely by the presence of the lesser-quality property.

Regulation Z Implements the Truth-in-Lending Act requiring credit institutions to inform borrowers of the true cost of obtaining credit.

release deed A document, also known as a *deed of reconveyance*, that transfers all rights given a trustee under a deed of trust loan back to the grantor after the loan has been fully repaid.

remainder interest The remnant of an estate that has been conveyed to take effect and be enjoyed after the termination of a prior estate, such as when an owner conveys a life estate to one party and the remainder to another.

rent A fixed, periodic payment made by a tenant of a property to the owner for possession and use, usually by prior agreement of the parties.

rent schedule A statement of proposed rental rates, determined by the owner or the property manager or both, based on a building's estimated expenses, market supply and demand, and the owner's long-range goals for the property.

replacement cost The construction cost at current prices of a property that is not necessarily an exact duplicate of the subject property but serves the same purpose or function as the original.

reproduction cost The construction cost at current prices of an exact duplicate of the subject property.

rescission The practice of one party canceling or terminating a contract, which has the effect of returning the parties to their original positions before the contract was made.

Resolution Trust Corporation The organization created by the Financial Institutions Reform, Recovery, and Enforcement Act (FIRREA) to liquidate the assets of failed savings and loan associations.

restrictive covenants A clause in a deed that limits the way the real estate ownership may be used.

retroactive liability Liability is not limited to the current owner, but includes people who have owned the site in the past.

reverse-annuity mortgage (RAM) A loan under which the homeowner receives monthly payments based on his or her accumulated equity rather than a lump sum. The loan must be repaid at a prearranged date, or upon the death of the owner, or upon the sale of the property.

reversionary interest The remnant of an estate that the grantor holds after granting a life estate to another person.

reversionary right The return of the rights of possession and quiet enjoyment to the lessor at the expiration of a lease.

right of survivorship *See* joint tenancy.

right-of-way The right given by one landowner to another to pass over the land, construct a roadway, or use as a pathway, without actually transferring ownership.

riparian rights An owner's rights in land that borders on or includes a stream, river, or lake. These rights include access to and use of the water.

risk management Evaluation and selection of appropriate property and other insurance.

rules and regulations Real estate licensing authority orders that govern licensees' activities; they usually have the same force and effect as statutory law.

sale-and-leaseback A transaction in which an owner sells his or her improved property and, as part of the same transaction, signs a long-term lease to remain in possession of the premises.

sales comparison approach The process of estimating the value of a property by examining and comparing actual sales of comparable properties.

salesperson A person who performs real estate activities while employed by or associated with a licensed real estate broker.

satisfaction of mortgage A document acknowledging the payment of a mortgage debt.

secondary mortgage market A market for the purchase and sale of existing mortgages, designed to provide greater liquidity for mortgages; also called the *secondary money market*. Mortgages are first originated in the *primary mortgage market*.

section A portion of township under the rectangular (government) survey system. A township is divided into 36 sections, numbered 1 through 36. A section is a square with mile-long sides and an area of one square mile, or 640 acres.

security agreement *See* Uniform Commercial Code.

security deposit A payment by a tenant, held by the landlord during the lease term, and kept (wholly or partially) on default, or on destruction of the premises by the tenant.

separate property Under community property law, property owned solely by either spouse before the marriage, acquired by gift or inheritance after the marriage, or purchased with separate funds after the marriage.

servient tenement Land on which an easement exists in favor of an adjacent property (called a *dominant estate*); also called a *servient estate*.

setback The amount of space local zoning regulations require between a lot line and a building line.

severalty Ownership of real property by one person only, also called *sole ownership*.

severance Changing an item of real estate to personal property by detaching it from the land; for example, cutting down a tree.

sharecropping In an agricultural lease, the agreement between the landowner and the tenant farmer to split the crop or the profit from its sale, actually sharing the crop.

shared-appreciation mortgage (SAM) A mortgage loan in which the lender, in exchange for a loan with a favorable interest rate, participates in the profits (if any)

the borrower receives when the property is eventually sold.

situs The personal preference of people for one area over another, not necessarily based on objective facts and knowledge.

special agent One who is authorized by a principal to perform a single act or transaction; a real estate broker is usually a special agent authorized to find a ready, willing, and able buyer for a particular property.

special assessment A tax or levy customarily imposed against only those specific parcels of real estate that will benefit from a proposed public improvement like a street or sewer.

special warranty deed A deed in which the grantor warrants, or guarantees, the title only against defects arising during the period of his or her tenure and ownership of the property and not against defects existing before that time, generally using the language, "by, through, or under the grantor but not otherwise."

specific lien A lien affecting or attaching only to a certain, specific parcel of land or piece of property.

specific performance A legal action to compel a party to carry out the terms of a contract.

square-foot method The appraisal method of estimating building costs by multiplying the number of square feet in the improvements being appraised by the cost per square foot for recently constructed similar improvements.

statute of frauds That part of a state law that requires certain instruments, such as deeds, real estate sales contracts, and certain leases, to be in writing to be legally enforceable.

statute of limitations That law pertaining to the period of time within which certain actions must be brought to court.

statutory lien A lien imposed on property by statute—a tax lien, for example—in contrast to an *equitable lien*, which arises out of common law.

statutory right of redemption The right of a defaulted property owner to recover the property after its sale by paying the appropriate fees and charges.

steering The illegal practice of channeling home seekers to particular areas, either to maintain the homogeneity of an area or to change the character of an area, which limits their choices of where they can live.

stigmatized property A property that has acquired an undesirable reputation due to an event that occurred on or near it, such as violent crime, gang-related activity, illness, or personal tragedy. Some states restrict the disclosure of information about stigmatized properties.

straight-line method A method of calculating depreciation for tax purposes, computed by dividing the adjusted basis of a property by the estimated number of years of remaining useful life.

straight (term) loan A loan in which only interest is paid during the term of the loan, with the entire principal amount due with the final interest payment.

strict liability The owner is responsible to the injured party without excuse.

subagent One who is employed by a person already acting as an agent. Typically a reference to a salesperson licensed under a broker (agent) who is employed under the terms of a listing agreement.

subdivider One who buys undeveloped land, divides it into smaller, usable lots, and sells the lots to potential users.

subdivision A tract of land divided by the owner, known as the *subdivider,* into blocks, building lots, and streets according to a recorded subdivision plat, which must comply with local ordinances and regulations.

subdivision and development ordinances Municipal ordinances that establish requirements for subdivisions and development.

subdivision plat *See* plat map.

sublease *See* subletting.

subletting The leasing of premises by a lessee to a third party for part of the lessee's remaining term. *See also* assignment.

subordination Relegation to a lesser position, usually in respect to a right or security.

subordination agreement A written agreement between holders of liens on a property that changes the priority of mortgage, judgment, and other liens under certain circumstances.

subrogation The substitution of one creditor for another, with the substituted person succeeding to the legal rights and claims of the original claimant. Subrogation is used by title insurers to acquire from the injured party rights to sue in order to recover any claims they have paid.

substitution An appraisal principle that states that the maximum value of a property tends to be set by the cost of purchasing an equally desirable and valuable substitute property, assuming that no costly delay is encountered in making the substitution.

subsurface rights Ownership rights in a parcel of real estate to the water, minerals, gas, oil, and so forth that lie beneath the surface of the property.

suit for possession A court suit initiated by a landlord to evict a tenant from leased premises after the tenant

has breached one of the terms of the lease or has held possession of the property after the lease's expiration.

suit to quiet title A court action intended to establish or settle the title to a particular property, especially when there is a cloud on the title.

Superfund Popular name of the hazardous-waste cleanup fund established by the Comprehensive Environmental Response, Compensation, and Liability Act (CERCLA).

Superfund Amendments and Reauthorization Act (SARA) An amendatory statute that contains stronger cleanup standards for contaminated sites, increased funding for Superfund, and clarifications of lender liability and innocent landowner immunity. *See* Comprehensive Environmental Response, Compensation, and Liability Act (CERCLA).

supply The amount of goods available in the market to be sold at a given price. The term is often coupled with *demand.*

supply and demand The appraisal principle that follows the interrelationship of the supply of and demand for real estate. As appraising is based on economic concepts, this principle recognizes that real property is subject to the influences of the marketplace just as is any other commodity.

surety bond An agreement by an insurance or bonding company to be responsible for certain possible defaults, debts, or obligations contracted for by an insured party; in essence, a policy insuring one's personal and/or financial integrity. In the real estate business a surety bond is generally used to ensure that a particular project will be completed at a certain date or that a contract will be performed as stated.

surface rights Ownership rights in a parcel of real estate that are limited to the surface of the property and do not include the air above it (*air rights*) or the minerals below the surface (*subsurface rights*).

survey The process by which boundaries are measured and land areas are determined; the on-site measurement of lot lines, dimensions, and position of a house on a lot, including the determination of any existing encroachments or easements.

syndicate A combination of people or firms formed to accomplish a business venture of mutual interest by pooling resources. In a *real estate investment syndicate,* the parties own and/or develop property, with the main profit generally arising from the sale of the property.

tacking Adding or combining successive periods of continuous occupation of real property by adverse possessors. This concept enables someone who has not been in possession for the entire statutory period to establish a claim of adverse possession.

taking A concept which comes from the takings clause of the Fifth Amendment to the U.S. Constitution and means that when land is taken for public use through the government's power of eminent domain or condemnation, the owner must be compensated.

taxation The process by which a government or municipal quasi-public body raises monies to fund its operation.

tax credit An amount by which tax owed is reduced directly.

tax deed An instrument, similar to a certificate of sale, given to a purchaser at a tax sale. *See also* certificate of sale.

tax lien A charge against property, created by operation of law. Tax liens and assessments take priority over all other liens.

tax sale A court-ordered sale of real property to raise money to cover delinquent taxes.

tenancy by the entirety The joint ownership, recognized in some states, of property acquired by husband and wife during marriage. Upon the death of one spouse the survivor becomes the owner of the property.

tenancy in common A form of co-ownership by which each owner holds an undivided interest in real property as if he or she were sole owner. Each individual owner has the right to partition. Unlike joint tenants, tenants in common have right of inheritance.

tenant One who holds or possesses lands or tenements by any kind of right or title.

tenant improvements Alterations to the interior of a building to meet the functional demands of the tenant.

testate Having made and left a valid will.

testator A person who has made a valid will. A woman often is referred to as a *testatrix*, although testator can be used for either gender.

tier (township strip) A strip of land six miles wide, extending east and west and numbered north and south according to its distance from the base line in the rectangular (government) survey system of legal description.

time is of the essence A phrase in a contract that requires the performance of a certain act within a stated period of time.

time-share A form of ownership interest that may include an estate interest in property and that allows use of the property for a fixed or variable time period.

title (1) The right to or ownership of land. (2) The evidence of ownership of land.

title insurance A policy insuring the owner or mortgagee against loss by reason of defects in the title to a parcel of real estate, other than encumbrances, defects, and matters specifically excluded by the policy.

title search The examination of public records relating to real estate to determine the current state of the ownership.

title theory Some states interpret a mortgage to mean that the lender is the owner of mortgaged land. Upon full payment of the mortgage debt, the borrower becomes the landowner.

Title VIII of Civil Rights Act of 1968 (called the federal Fair Housing Act) Prohibits discrimination in housing based on race, color, religion, or national origin.

Torrens system A method of evidencing title by registration with the proper public authority, generally called the *registrar*, named for its founder, Sir Robert Torrens.

township The principal unit of the rectangular (government) survey system. A township is a square with six-mile sides and an area of 36 square miles.

township lines All the lines in a rectangular survey system that run east and west, parallel to the base line six miles apart.

township strips *See* tier.

township tiers Township lines that form strips of land and are designated by consecutive numbers north or south of the base line.

trade fixture An article installed by a tenant under the terms of a lease and removable by the tenant before the lease expires.

transactional broker Helps both the buyer and seller with paperwork and formalities in transferring ownership of real property, but is not an agent of either party.

transfer tax Tax stamps required to be affixed to a deed by state and/or local law.

trigger terms Specific credit terms, such as down payment, monthly payment, and amount of finance charge or term of loan.

trust A fiduciary arrangement whereby property is conveyed to a person or institution, called a *trustee*, to be held and administered on behalf of another person, called a *beneficiary*. The one who conveys the trust is called the *trustor*.

trust deed An instrument used to create a mortgage lien by which the borrower conveys title to a trustee, who holds it as security for the benefit of the note holder (the lender); also called a *deed of trust*.

trust deed lien A lien on the property of a trustor that secures a deed of trust loan.

trustee   The holder of bare legal title in a deed of trust loan transaction.

trustee's deed   A deed executed by a trustee conveying land held in a trust.

trustor   A borrower in a deed of trust loan transaction.

Truth-in-Lending Act   Federal government regulates the lending practices of mortgage lenders through this Act.

undivided interest   *See* tenancy in common.

unenforceable contract   A contract that has all the elements of a valid contract, yet neither party can sue the other to force performance of it. For example, an unsigned contract is generally unenforceable.

Uniform Commercial Code (UCC)   A codification of commercial law, adopted in most states, that attempts to make uniform all laws relating to commercial transactions, including chattel mortgages and bulk transfers. Security interests in chattels are created by an instrument known as a *security agreement*. To give notice of the security interest, a *financing statement* must be recorded. Article 6 of the code regulates *bulk transfers*— the sale of a business as a whole, including all fixtures, chattels, and merchandise.

uniform settlement statement   A special HUD form that itemizes all charges to be paid by a borrower and seller in connection with the settlement.

unilateral contract   A one-sided contract wherein one party makes a promise so as to induce a second party to do something. The second party is not legally bound to perform; however, if the second party does comply, the first party is obligated to keep the promise.

unit-in-place method   The appraisal method of estimating building costs by calculating the costs of all of the physical components in the structure, with the cost of each item including its proper installation, connection, etc.; also called the *segregated cost method*.

unity of ownership   The four unities that are traditionally needed to create a joint tenancy—unity of title, time, interest, and possession.

universal agent   A person empowered to do anything the principal could do personally.

usury   Charging interest at a higher rate than the maximum rate established by state law.

valid contract   A contract that complies with all the essentials of a contract and is binding and enforceable on all parties to it.

VA loan   A mortgage loan on approved property made to a qualified veteran by an authorized lender and guaranteed by the Department of Veterans Affairs in order to limit the lender's possible loss.

value   The power of a good or service to command other goods in exchange for the present worth of future rights to its income or amenities.

variance   Permission obtained from zoning authorities to build a structure or conduct a use that is expressly prohibited by the current zoning laws; an exception from the zoning ordinances.

vendee   A buyer, usually under the terms of a land contract.

vendor   A seller, usually under the terms of a land contract.

vendor's lien   A lien that belongs to a vendor for the unpaid purchase price of land, where the vendor has not taken any other lien or security beyond the personal obligation of the purchaser.

voidable contract   A contract that seems to be valid on the surface but may be rejected or disaffirmed by one or both of the parties.

void contract   A contract that has no legal force or effect because it does not meet the essential elements of a contract.

voluntary alienation   *See* alienation.

voluntary lien   A lien placed on property with the knowledge and consent of the property owner.

waste   An improper use or an abuse of a property by a possessor who holds less than fee ownership, such as a tenant, life tenant, mortgagor, or vendee. Such waste ordinarily impairs the value of the land or the interest of the person holding the title or the reversionary rights.

water rights   Common Law rights held by owners of land adjacent to rivers, lakes, or oceans, and includes restrictions on those rights and land ownership.

will   A written document, properly witnessed, providing for the transfer of title to property owned by the deceased, called the *testator*.

workers' compensation acts   Laws that require an employer to obtain insurance coverage to protect his or her employees who are injured in the course of their employment.

wraparound loan   A method of refinancing in which the new mortgage is placed in a secondary, or subordinate, position; the new mortgage includes both the unpaid principal balance of the first mortgage and whatever additional sums are advanced by the lender. In essence it is an additional mortgage in which another lender refinances a borrower by lending an amount over the existing first mortgage amount without disturbing the existence of the first mortgage.

zoning ordinance   An exercise of police power by a municipality to regulate and control the character and use of property.

ANSWER KEY

Following are the correct answers to the review questions included in each Chapter of the text. In parentheses following the correct answers are references to the pages where the question topics are discussed or explained. The references for the Sample Examinations are to Chapter numbers. If you have answered a question incorrectly, be sure to go back to the page or pages noted and restudy the material until you understand the correct answer.

CHAPTER 1
Introduction to the Real
Estate Business

1. b(3)
2. b(6)
3. d(7)
4. c(8)
5. b(2)
6. d(4)
7. b(6)
8. a(4)
9. d(3)
10. a(6)

CHAPTER 2
Real Property and the Law

1. c(17)
2. b(20)
3. c(21)
4. c(20)
5. d(14)
6. b(20)
7. a(18)
8. a(20)
9. a(17)
10. a(18)
11. c(15)
12. b(18)
13. c(18)
14. d(15)
15. a(13)

CHAPTER 3
Concepts of Home Ownership

1. d(30)
2. b(31)
3. a(28)
4. b(28)
5. b(29)
6. c(31)

7. d(32)
8. b(30)
9. a(31)
10. b(31)
11. c(31)
12. c(31)
13. a(32)
14. b(28)
15. c(32)

CHAPTER 4
Agency

1. d(41)
2. a(48)
3. a(46)
4. b(48)
5. c(51)
6. b(47)
7. d(46)
8. d(43)
9. b(55)
10. c(52)
11. c(51)
12. c(39)
13. c(49)
14. a(42)
15. d(55)

CHAPTER 5
Real Estate Brokerage

1. b(69)
2. c(67)
3. b(68)
4. b(67)
5. a(68)
6. d(68)
7. d(72)
8. a(72)
9. c(64)
10. b(70)

11. d(68)
12. a(69)
13. c(70)
14. a(71)
15. c(72)

CHAPTER 6
Listing Agreements and Buyer
Representation

1. a(78)
2. c(79)
3. c(81)
4. a(79)
5. b(84)
6. d(80)
7. a(79)
8. c(83)
9. a(78)
10. d(84)
11. c(79)
12. b(91)
13. a(91)
14. b(91)
15. b(83)
16. a(84)
17. c(84)
18. c(80)
19. b(81)
20. c(93)

CHAPTER 7
Interests in Real Estate

1. b(104)
2. a(105)
3. c(107)
4. d(111)
5. c(114)
6. a(108)
7. d(109)
8. d(113)

9. c(116)
10. a(103)
11. b(106)
12. b(111)
13. a(105)
14. b(108)
15. b(114)
16. c(109)
17. d(114)
18. a(110)
19. d(105)
20. b(110)

CHAPTER 8
Forms of Real Estate Ownership

1. d(124)
2. b(122)
3. a(124)
4. b(131)
5. b(127)
6. d(126)
7. b(122)
8. a(127)
9. b(131)
10. c(134)
11. c(129)
12. d(122)
13. d(126)
14. b(133)
15. b(123)
16. c(133)
17. b(133)
18. b(124)
19. d(131)
20. a(123)

CHAPTER 9
Legal Descriptions

1. b(144)
2. d(142)
3. d(144)
4. b(140)
5. c(144)
6. c(144)
7. a(144)
8. a(144)
9. a(144)

10. b(152)
11. a(142)
12. c(144)
13. d(152)
14. c(142)
15. b(150)
16. b(146)
17. b(152)
18. b(147)
19. b(152)
20. b(140)
21. b(144)
22. b(144)
23. b(144)
24. b(144)
25. c(140)

CHAPTER 10
Real Estate Taxes and Other Liens

1. d(159)
2. b(160)
3. b(165)
4. c(159)
5. b(160)
6. d(163)
7. c(161)
8. c(166)
9. d(163)
10. c(158)
11. d(159)
12. d(167)
13. c(159)
14. b(165)
15. b(166)
16. d(166)
17. d(164)
18. a(161)
19. b(161)
20. d(161)

CHAPTER 11
Real Estate Contracts

1. c(173)
2. b(177)
3. d(174)
4. b(174)
5. c(176)

6. d(178)
7. d(184)
8. a(182)
9. a(184)
10. d(175)
11. b(185)
12. d(185)
13. d(185)
14. c(173)
15. b(181)
16. b(182)
17. a(176)
18. b(175)
19. d(177)
20. b(185)

CHAPTER 12
Transfer of Title

1. a(192)
2. a(192)
3. d(193)
4. a(194)
5. b(196)
6. a(197)
7. d(196)
8. d(198)
9. b(197)
10. c(195)
11. b(194)
12. b(195)
13. b(195)
14. c(200)
15. b(200)
16. d(200)
17. a(196)
18. a(196)
19. a(199)
20. b(201)
21. d(201)
22. b(201)
23. c(202)
24. d(198)
25. c(203)

CHAPTER 13
Title Records

1. a(209)
2. a(209)
3. c(210)
4. a(210)
5. a(210)
6. d(212)
7. d(212)
8. d(211)
9. c(212)
10. a(212)
11. c(209)
12. c(213)
13. b(214)
14. d(214)
15. c(214)
16. a(213)
17. b(215)
18. a(210)
19. b(209)
20. d(215)

CHAPTER 14
Real Estate Financing:
Principles

1. b(225)
2. a(221)
3. c(221)
4. a(223)
5. c(230)
6. b(224)
7. d(231)
8. d(227)
9. a(227)
10. a(230)
11. c(225)
12. d(230)
13. b(230)
14. a(222)
15. b(225)
16. d(221)
17. a(221)
18. c(229)
19. b(229)
20. b(228)

CHAPTER 15
Real Estate Financing:
Practice

1. d(253)
2. d(255)
3. c(242)
4. c(245)
5. b(238)
6. a(240)
7. b(237)
8. c(241)
9. b(253)
10. c(248)
11. b(256)
12. b(242)
13. b(239)
14. a(242)
15. b(241)
16. d(257)
17. b(244)
18. b(243)
19. b(243)
20. b(244)
21. c(246)
22. a(237)
23. b(241)
24. c(243)
25. d(246)

CHAPTER 16
Leases

1. c(274)
2. c(273)
3. d(276)
4. c(275)
5. b(272)
6. d(267)
7. c(266)
8. b(276)
9. b(276)
10. b(266)
11. b(272)
12. a(272)
13. b(273)
14. d(267)
15. c(275)
16. a(273)
17. c(274)

18. d(274)
19. c(267)
20. b(275)

CHAPTER 17
Property Management

1. b(296)
2. c(294)
3. d(289)
4. c(296)
5. c(288)
6. b(294)
7. d(293)
8. b(292)
9. c(288)
10. a(289)
11. c(296)
12. c(296)
13. c(289)
14. b(292)
15. b(286)
16. b(289)
17. b(296)
18. c(293)
19. c(293)
20. d(296)

CHAPTER 18
Real Estate Appraisal

1. c(309)
2. b(302)
3. b(304)
4. b(302)
5. d(304)
6. a(304)
7. d(308)
8. c(312)
9. b(306)
10. a(310)
11. c(309)
12. c(309)
13. c(302)
14. b(309)
15. c(308)
16. d(310)
17. d(305)
18. b(309)
19. b(309)

20. b(308)
21. d(306)
22. b(303)
23. c(303)
24. b(308)
25. c(306)

CHAPTER 19
Land-Use Controls and Property Development

1. a(329)
2. a(325)
3. b(329)
4. c(323)
5. c(326)
6. a(323)
7. a(324)
8. d(322)
9. b(329)
10. a(330)
11. a(326)
12. c(327)
13. b(327)
14. b(328)
15. b(322)
16. d(327)
17. a(328)
18. a(328)
19. a(330)
20. c(326)

CHAPTER 20
Fair Housing and Ethical Practices

1. c(347)
2. a(348)
3. d(339)
4. b(345)
5. c(345)
6. a(347)
7. b(337)
8. b(345)
9. c(343)
10. b(341)
11. a(339)
12. b(336)
13. d(347)

14. c(338)
15. d(341)

CHAPTER 21
Environmental Issues and the Real Estate Transaction

1. b(358)
2. c(356)
3. c(357)
4. a(356)
5. a(364)
6. c(364)
7. b(366)
8. d(369)
9. c(360)
10. d(361, 357, 356)

CHAPTER 22
Closing the Real Estate Transaction

1. d(389)
2. b(379)
3. d(376)
4. a(376)
5. d(379)
6. c(381)
7. c(377)
8. b(384)
9. b(384)
10. d(388)
11. c(390)
12. a(384)
13. c(385)
14. b(384)
15. c(383)
16. b(386)
17. d(381)
18. d(381)
19. b(382)
20. b(382)

APPENDIX I:
Introduction to Real Estate Investment

1. a(401)
2. b(401)
3. d(405)

4. a(404)
5. d(406)
6. b(407)
7. c(406)
8. b(407)
9. b(404)
10. a(404)

Sample Examination One

1. b(10)
2. a(11)
3. a(11)
4. c(15)
5. c(15, Math FAQs)
6. b(6)
7. a(12)
8. a(20)
9. a(7)
10. d(8)
11. d(5)
12. a(14)
13. b(16)
14. a(18)
15. a(19)
16. c(5, Math FAQs)
17. d(5)
18. c(8)
19. a(5, Math FAQs)
20. b(7)
21. d(6)
22. b(9)
23. b(14)
24. b(10)
25. c(Math FAQs)
26. c(Math FAQs)
27. b(18)
28. c(9, Math FAQs)
29. c(14)
30. b(5)
31. d(11)
32. d(11)
33. b(11)
34. b(14,15)
35. b(11)
36. a(14)
37. d(18)
38. b(6)
39. a(8)

40. a(12,13)
41. d(6)
42. b(16)
43. c(20)
44. b(Math FAQs)
45. d(10)
46. d(11)
47. c(7)
48. d(9)
49. b(18)
50. b(10)
51. b(11)
52. b(8)
53. c(16)
54. d(11)
55. b(7)
56. c(15, Math FAQs)
57. a(7)
58. c(Math FAQs)
59. d(19)
60. b(11)
61. c(14)
62. a(20)
63. d(22)
64. d(11)
65. b(12)
66. d(8)
67. b(22)
68. d(20)
69. a(12)
70. a(18)
71. d(15)
72. d(8)
73. a(22)
74. d(22)
75. b(2)
76. c(7)
77. d(Math FAQs)
78. b(6)
79. d(5)
80. d(16)

Sample Examination Two

1. d(16)
2. c(2)
3. c(11)
4. b(14)
5. c(16)
6. d(4)
7. b(Math FAQs)
8. d(20)
9. b(Math FAQs)
10. b(15)
11. b(11)
12. a(15)
13. d(6)
14. c(7)
15. d(4)
16. d(9)
17. b(12)
18. b(22)
19. c(6)
20. a(18)
21. c(22)
22. b(16)
23. a(7)
24. b(22)
25. d(16)
26. d(15)
27. c(15)
28. b(4)
29. b(18)
30. d(22)
31. b(22)
32. d(18)
33. a(11)
34. d(13)
35. b(Math FAQs)
36. a(6)
37. a(16)
38. d(6)
39. a(18)
40. c(18)
41. d(12)
42. c(9)
43. b(11)
44. d(17)
45. c(Math FAQs)
46. d(15)
47. a(7)

48. a(22)
49. b(16)
50. c(18)
51. c(17)
52. a(13)
53. c(3)
54. a(12)
55. d(8)
56. a(22)
57. b(7)
58. b(12)
59. d(18)
60. d(15)
61. d(18)
62. c(20)
63. c(12)
64. c(15)
65. a(4)
66. b(6)
67. b(20)
68. d(4)
69. c(Math FAQs)
70. a(22)
71. d(15)
72. c(18)
73. a(11)
74. a(18)
75. b(15)
76. c(15)
77. b(6,18)
78. d(10)
79. b(22)
80. b(17)

INDEX

United States Geological Survey, 151
Unities, 124-25
Universal agent, 48
Unrecorded documents, 211
Up-front premium, 248
Urea-formaldehyde, 361-62
Usury, 224
Utility, 302

V
VA-guaranteed loans, 250-52
Valid contract, 176
Value, 302-304
    approaches to, 304-12
    principles of, 303
Variable lease, 274
Variances, 325
Vendee, 185, 230
Vendor, 185, 230
Vendor's lien, 159
Violence, 348-49
Voice mail, 66
Voidable contract, 176-77
Void contract, 176
Volume, 450
Volume measurement conversions, 450
Voluntary alienation, 192-200
Voluntary lien, 158

W
Wage levels, 8
Walk-through, 375-76
Warranty deed, 91
Waste disposal sites, 366-67
Water rights, 15, 16-17, 114-16
Web links, 410-21
Will, 201-2, 203
Workers' compensation, 296
Wraparound loans, 253-54
Writ of execution, 166-67

Z
Zoning, 21, 322-25, 326, 327
    hearing board, 324
    ordinances, 8
Zoning permits, 324

INSTALLATION INSTRUCTIONS FOR TEST-BUILDING CD-ROM

Insert CD into the CD-ROM drive. The InstallShield Wizard will help you install the program. When you reach the completion screen, verify that "Run MREP Custom Review Builder now?" is checked and click Finish. The program will automatically start. If already installed, the program will automatically run when you insert the CD-ROM into the drive.

Note: This CD-ROM requires several Microsoft components to be on your system, including ODBC, Internet Explorer 5, and DCOM98. If these are not already installed, the installation software will install them and prompt you to reboot at the end of the installation process. This is normal.

1. You will be prompted to choose a Name and User ID (1 to 25 characters). Important: Remember your Name and User ID. You must enter them on subsequent start ups.
2. Click OK.
3. Click on Exam Practice to build a practice exam.
4. Select a topic in the Exam Topics window and click on the right arrow to transfer it to the Selected Exam Topics window. Repeat until you have transferred all the topics you wish to review.
5. Choose the number of questions.
6. Click Build Exam.

When you finish an exam, click Turn in For Grading to generate Exam Practice Results, which indicate the percentage of correct answers as a fraction, e.g., 7/10 indicates seven correct answers out of ten. You may review incorrect answers and print exam results.

Completed practice exams are saved and can be accessed from the Main Menu. Select History and choose an exam from the pull-down list.

UNINSTALLATION INSTRUCTIONS

1. Click on Start and choose Settings from the menu.
2. Click on Control Panel.
3. Double-click on Add/Remove Programs.
4. Using the scroll bar, scroll down and choose MREP Custom Review Builder and click the Add/Remove... button.
5. You will be asked if you want to completely remove the selected application and all of its components. Click OK.
6. Click Finish.
7. Once uninstallation is complete, close the Control Panel window.

MINIMUM SYSTEM REQUIREMENTS

- Windows 95, Windows 98, Windows NT4, Service Pack 3, Windows ME, Windows 2000, and Windows XP
- 30 MB of hard disk space (installation requires 100 MB)
- 133 MHz Pentium processor
- 16 MB of RAM
- 4x CD-ROM drive
- 800 x 600 screen resolution
- 256 color resolution

Technical Support: 1-888-213-5124